MW01097496

Church Publishing Incorporated
19 East 34th Street
New York, NY 10016

Cover design by: Joseph Piliero
Typeset by: Nord Compo

A record of this book is available from the Library of Congress.

ISBN-13: 978-1-64065-639-0 (hardcover)
ISBN-13: 978-1-640656-40-6 (ebook)

Planning for Rites and Rituals

A Resource for Episcopal Worship,
Year B

Edited by Andrew R. Wright

Table of Contents

The calendar, from the Last Sunday after the Epiphany until the Second Sunday after Pentecost, has variable dates, depending on Easter Day.

Lent

Holy Week

Easter

Season after Pentecost: Summer and Autumn

Welcome and Introduction

Welcome to the newly revised and integrated permanent Year B edition of *Planning for Rites and Rituals*. This volume is intended to be used on a 3-year basis, rather than issuing a new volume tied to a specific calendar year, as has been produced for the last few years. This volume incorporates material from the two previous iterations of Year B (2017–2018 and 2020–2021), organizes some material differently, and adds new material.

While not everything from previous years could be used in this new edition, much has been retained. This volume still provides a wide range of thought-provoking, cresative options for Sundays and holy days throughout the liturgical year. Looking for ways to engage a range of ages? It's here. Looking for help "seeing" the images in each week's scripture? We've got that. Want hymns keyed to the lectionary or brief introductions to the scriptures? It's all here, in a single resource.

You will find that this resource offers two areas for engaging in planning, grouped by liturgical season and date. Each season begins with a "Preparing for . . ." section designed to get you thinking and your creative juices flowing. "Major Feasts, Seasonal Rites, and other Commemorations" follows, offering expansive ideas for worship within or outside the primary Sunday service and an overview of feast days and other important days to consider for the season or time of year. Since this is designed to be used for Year B for the foreseeable future, tying feasts to particular lectionary weeks was more challenging – since the liturgical calendar is based in part on movable feasts. Following these overview sections, each Sunday's set of resources offers all you need for putting together a Sunday (or holy day) service as well as other ideas for formation and community engagement within and beyond your church doors. Additional attention has been given to how to shape planning for a service, grounded in the propers (the readings, collect, preface) for the day.

As in previous volumes, dozens of individuals were part of the creation of the material used here. Parish clergy, educators, musicians, members of Altar Guilds, and many others are featured within these pages. Representation includes those working in small parishes and those in larger ones, those in rural locales and those in cities, clergy and lay.

New material has been prepared for this edition and revisions made as necessary to prior contributions. New material and contributors whose material may reappear in this volume include the following, related to these sections of the text:

» *Planning the Service of Holy Eucharist* (as well as the brief appendices on planning Morning Prayer and planning Ante-Communion) provides an overview to the planning process that the resources in this volume are here to support. Editor **Andrew Wright** offers an approach to planning that will help to create liturgies that are meaningful, coherent, integrative, and faithful.

» *Preaching the Gospel for Year B* was written by **Cynthia Briggs Kittredge**, dean and president of Seminary of the Southwest. The *Preparing for* seasonal overviews were originally adapted from *Planning the Church Year* by the late **Leonel Mitchell** and have been revised and updated by editor **Andrew Wright** of the Diocese of Newark. *Major Feasts Seasonal Rites, and Other Commemorations* include material previously provided by **Martha Baker**, writer, editor, and educator in St. Louis, Missouri.

» The *scriptural overviews* that open each Sunday or holy day come from *Preparing for Sunday* (www.preparingforsunday.com).

» *Reading Between the Lines*, by New Testament scholar Deirdre Good, identifies and describes aspects of the language in the day's readings, in addition to historical and theological features.

» *Central Themes* has incorporated material from previous sections *Ideas for the Day* and *Making Connections*. This section offers thoughts for approaching the day and its text in preaching and worship, including contemporary issues, movies, technology and social media, literature, historical events, and figures related to the Sunday lections and season. It also offers insights into connecting our Episcopal tradition to each Sunday. This may take the form of referencing other areas of the *Book of Common Prayer*, our Baptismal Covenant, or faith in daily life. Contributors from previous editions that may be reprinted here include: **Helen Svoboda Barber**, rector of St. Luke's Episcopal Church, Durham, North Carolina; **Jennifer Holt Enriquez**, Children and Youth Formation Director, St. Christopher's Episcopal Church, Oak Park, Illinois; United Methodist pastor **Robert W. Lee IV; Patrick Kangrga**, the Associate for Youth Ministries at Trinity Church, Menlo Park, California; **Hillary Raining**, rector of St. Christopher's Episcopal Church, Gladwyne, Pennsylvania; **Will Mebane**, of Saint Barnabas' Episcopal Church in Falmouth, Massachusetts; **Anna V. Ostenso Moore**, Associate for Family Ministry at Saint Mark's Episcopal Cathedral, Minneapolis, Minnesota; **Lelanda Lee,** a writer, poet, and church and community leader in Longmont, Colorado; **William (Billy) Daniel**, Saint Michael's Episcopal Church, Geneseo, New York; **Heidi J. A. Carter**, lay minister associate at St. Paul's Episcopal Church, Kansas City, Missouri; and **Victoria Garvey**, biblical scholar and educator based in Chicago, Illinois. New material has also been prepared here in some places by the editor.

» *Engaging all Ages* offers ideas for deepening all ages in their engagement with worship (children, youth, and adults). They include thoughts for the congregation to take home and discuss, things to notice or highlight during worship (colors, senses, symbols, gestures), and ideas for action. Contributors for these portions from prior years include: **Sharon Ely Pearson,** an educator from Norwalk, Connecticut; **Marisa Tabizon Thompson**, rector of All Saints Episcopal Church, Omaha, Nebraska; **Sarah Bentley Allred**, Director of Children and Family Ministries, St. John's Episcopal Church in Wake Forest, North Carolina; **Roger Hutchison**, Director of Christian Formation and Parish Life at Palmer Memorial Episcopal Church in Houston; **Wendy Claire Barrie**, Canon for Intergenerational Ministries at St. Mark's Episcopal Cathedral, Seattle, Washington; and **Elizabeth Hammond**, retired Christian educator of St. Paul's Episcopal Church in Greenville, South Carolina. Though not used in this volume, appreciation continues for those who contributed to this section in 2017–2018: **Linda Nichols**, a Christian educator in Gadsen, Alabama; **Jake Owensby** is the fourth bishop of the Episcopal Diocese of Western Louisiana; **Valerie Bailey Fischer,** adjunct lecturer at Bexley Hall Seabury Western Theological Federation, Chicago, Illinois; **Miguelina Espinal-Howell**, dean of Christ Church Cathedral, Hartford, Connecticut; **Emily Slichter Given**, director of parish participation at Saint Thomas Church, Whitemarsh, Pennsylvania; **Ernesto Medina**, rector of St. Martha's Episcopal Church, Papillion, Nebraska; **Mike Angell**, rector of the Episcopal Church of the Holy Communion in St. Louis; **Jay Fluellen**, composer, organist, and choir director of the African Episcopal Church of St. Thomas, Philadelphia; **Sharon Ely Pearson**, Christian educator from Norwalk, Connecticut; **Mark Bozzuti-Jones**, priest for pastoral care at Trinity Wall Street; **Demi Prentiss**, small congregation lay leader and ministry developer from Fort Worth; and **Megan Castellan**, associate rector and day school chaplain at St. Paul's Episcopal Church, Kansas City, Missouri.

» *Prayers of the People* draw from the work in 2017–2018 of **Lowell Grisham**, priest at St. Paul's Episcopal Church in Fayetteville, Arkansas, as well as the 2020–2021 contributions of **Lyn Zill Briggs**, vicar of Episcopal Church of the Resurrection in the Diocese of Utah. They are specifically designed to follow the child-friendly pattern of her lectionary volume, *God's Word, My Voice*. Additional prayers of the people have been provided from editor **Andrew Wright**, composed over the years with parishioners in Trinity Episcopal Church, Fort Worth, Texas, Grace Episcopal Church, Monroe, New York; and with seminarians at the Chapel of the Good Shepherd of the General Theological Seminary, New York. Some intercessions provided here rely on the work of late **Ormonde Plater**[1] and are adaptations of his extensive archives, hosted now by the Association for Episcopal Deacons.

» *Hymn suggestions* are drawn from **Carl Daw Jr.** and **Thomas Pavlechko**'s *Liturgical Music for the Revised Common Lectionary, Year B*, 2nd Edition (Church Publishing Incorporated, 2023). These complement the theme and readings of the day and come from *The Hymnal 1982, Lift Every Voice and Sing II*, and *Wonder, Love, and Praise.*

Thank you for the trust you put in Church Publishing Incorporated to provide liturgical planning tools for your parish use. We value our partnership on the journey and are grateful for the many ways in which you care for the church's worship.

1 Plater, Ormonde. "Deacon Ormonde Plater Archived Documents" Association for Episcopal Deacons, https://www.episcopaldeacons.org/ormonde-plater-archive.html, accessed February 27, 2023.

Planning the Service of Holy Eucharist

These guidelines are written with the Sunday service of Holy Eucharist in mind. They can be easily adapted for midweek services or other occasions as well.

Liturgical worship creates an opportunity to receive and be shaped by an encounter of the presence of God in community, as we worship. That is not the primary purpose of worship, however – the primary purpose is to respond to God in love, praise, and adoration. Nor does the liturgy, even if impeccably planned and enacted, have anything to do with "making" that encounter with the divine happen. We encounter God all the time. In all times and all places, God is already there. Human beings are often not able to see that right away or may be distracted. A secondary function of liturgical worship is that it frames this encounter with God and helps develop the congregation's spiritual sensibilities so that we can take notice that God is already with us and so that we can allow that experience to shape us more deeply into the People of God that we are called to be.

Naturally, we have no control whatsoever over God's presence and action in our midst during worship (or any other time). Nor should we seek to have control over the experience of the congregation gathered, of course, since that can become manipulative and exploitative. What we do have the opportunity to do is create worship that expresses the tradition and culture of a particular church or assembly and do so in such a way to give the best possibility of the congregation taking notice of the presence and work of God in their midst. Planning liturgy is about framing the service in ways that highlight the implicit themes and provide entry points for congregational participation and reflection. Good liturgy, then, is meaningful, coherent, integrative, and faithful. To accomplish those hallmarks involves careful planning to know where to be flexible and where to uphold tradition; to know when to add or expand what we do and to know how to show restraint.

Planning for the Season

Before discussing planning a particular Sunday service, some choices are typically made for an entire season or may be ongoing congregational practice year round. Among these might be the following:

» Liturgical Color – While most Episcopal congregations follow a similar custom there is not an official approved color scheme in The Episcopal Church. The following pattern or something similar is used in most Episcopal churches:
  - Advent – Violet/Blue;
  - Christmas and Epiphany – White, Gold, or Festive;
  - Season after Epiphany – Green;
  - Lent – Violet/Lenten Array;
  - Holy Week – Violet/Red;
  - Easter Day and Season – White, Gold, or Festive;
  - Day of Pentecost – Red;
  - Season after Pentecost – Green;
  - Other Feasts – White, Gold, or Festive (or Red, if a martyr's feast day).

» Language of the Rite – Rite I, Rite II, or elements from *Enriching Our Worship 1*?

» Collect for Purity? Yes or no (required in Rite I)

» Nicene Creed – Always required on Sundays and Major Feasts; which version? Rite I, Rite II, EOW1? Renewal of Baptismal Vows (BCP 292) is encouraged to be used on Baptismal Feasts

» Confession of Sin – Usually included; may be omitted on occasion

» Eucharistic Prayer – Multiple options with different emphases, described below

Planning for the Day

The planning process for a particular service of Holy Eucharist always begins with the lessons, the readings from Scripture. This is the heart not only of preaching for the day and, often formation for the day, but also for liturgy. Read the lessons through, including the psalm, a few times before making liturgical choices. The second layer to consider for planning is the nature of the day or season. What liturgical season is it and are there themes for that season that should be incorporated? This is especially important from Advent I through the Day of Pentecost, since those seasons have very particular emphases. Reading the collect of the day is part of this layer as well. The collects in *the Book of Common Prayer* are not always clearly related to or connected to the particular readings for that lectionary year (or any lectionary year in some cases), but may express other elements of seasonal themes or provide additional focal points to work with. Once you have the propers in mind (the appointed lessons and the collect for the day) and the season, it is time to make some choices. The propers are the anchor points for planning the rest of the service.

The first part of the service, called The Word of God in *the Book of Common Prayer* (often also called The Liturgy or Ministry of the Word), focuses on the reading of scripture and how we respond to it. As sacramental Christians, this portion of the service points to encountering the Word of God, Jesus, in the Scriptures, just as the second part of the service, is focused on encountering Christ in the meal. In this first portion of the rite, we will need to determine the Entrance Rite and the responses to Scripture.

Entrance Rite: Option 1

The first option for the Entrance Rite, and probably the most common choice in Episcopal Churches on a given Sunday, could include an opening hymn followed by the opening acclamation, collect for purity, and the Song of Praise.[1] A procession to the Altar area, if desired, could accompany the opening hymn (we'll talk about music selection below) or could take place during the Song of Praise. Opening acclamations are designated by season, with additional options found in *Enriching Our Worship 1*. The collect for purity is required in Rite I, but optional in Rite II. The Song of Praise is often the Gloria in excelsis (except in Advent and Lent, of course), but could be any canticle (found in Morning and Evening Prayer). If other hymns are considered in place of a canticle, it is important that the hymn be focused on praise to God, since that is the purpose of this element of the liturgy. The Kyrie eleison or Trisagion may be used instead of the Song of Praise in Rite II. The Kyrie or Trisagion is generally required in Rite I, but may be supplemented by or replaced by the Song of Praise. *Each of these choices, which opening hymn, if any, which acclamation, whether or not to use the collect for purity, which song of praise, should be chosen in light of the question "Which of these options best expresses and connects to the readings and themes of the day?"*

Entrance Rite: Option 2

The second option for the Entrance Rite is to begin with the Penitential Order.[2] The primary difference in this option is that it places the Confession of Sin and Absolution at the beginning of the Rite. (If you are planning a liturgy of "Ante-Communion" or using the liturgy of the word that includes the Confession of Sin, the Penitential Order is required. See Appendix 2 for more information on that service variation). If the Penitential Order is used, it also may begin with an opening hymn and it includes an opening acclamation for whichever season it may be (suggesting that it does not have to be used only in penitential seasons). This Entrance Rite also has the option of including the Decalogue, or Ten Commandments, and a sentence of scripture prior to the Confession and absolution. The Confession of Sin and Absolution are required in this form. The service then continues with either the Gloria in excelsis, the Kyrie eleison, or the Trisagion. *So, in light of the lessons of the day and the season, which opening acclamation is best? Should the Decalogue be used on this occasion? Which of the three sentences of scripture (or none) is best? And, finally, does the entrance rite conclude with the Gloria, the Kyrie, or the Trisagion?*

Entrance Rite: Option 3

The third Entrance Rite option is to begin with the Great Litany.[3] When the Great Litany is used, no opening hymn is needed and it concludes with the Kyrie eleison. There is a contemporary form for the Great Litany in *Enriching Our Worship 1*, which allows for that form to be used in its entirety or in smaller sections. If the Great Litany is used, the Prayers of the People may be omitted. *Is the Great Litany the best option for these readings or for this season/occasion?*

There are a few other options that are uncommon, such as "Order of Worship for the Evening," or special

1 Rite I, p. 323–325; Rite II, p. 355–356 in *The Book of Common Prayer 1979* (New York, NY: Church Publishing, 2007). All references in this volume to the prayer book are to *The Book of Common Prayer* 1979 (hereafter BCP) unless otherwise noted.

2 BCP: Rite I, p. 319; Rite II, p. 353.

3 BCP, 148.

services such as Holy Baptism or Confirmation. These will not make up the vast majority of Sunday Eucharist services that one is planning, however.

Ministry of the Word

Once an Entrance Rite is determined, the Word of God, the first part of the liturgy, may be planned. The salutation for the Collect of the Day can be drawn from *the Book of Common Prayer* or *Enriching Our Worship 1.* The collect is appointed, as are the readings. In most cases the appointed psalm will follow the first reading, though the manner in which the psalm is to be read must be determined (see BCP 582 for more details on these options). Typically, a hymn will follow the second reading.

The remainder of this part of the service is focused on responding to the readings – the Sermon, the Creed, the Prayers, the Confession, the Peace. The Nicene Creed is used on Sundays and Major Feasts, though there are three versions that are authorized: the version in Rite I that uses "I" statements,[4] the version in both Rite I and Rite II that uses "We" statements,[5] and the version in *Enriching Our Worship 1.*[6] On a baptismal feast day, if there are no baptisms, the Renewal of Baptismal Vows is encouraged to be used instead.[7] Prayers of the People may be written by the congregation, conforming to the instructions on page 383 of *the Book of Common Prayer*, or one of the seven prepared examples (one in Rite I and six in Rite II) may be used. Forms drawn from other sources or authors may be used as well (such as those found in this volume). If you choose to write your own intercessions or use a form written by others, the content should be shaped by and connected to the imagery of the lessons for the day. The Confession of Sin and Absolution may be omitted on occasion, but are intended to be routinely in use. In Rite I, the Absolution is followed by optional Sentences of Scripture ("the Comfortable Words") of which one, some, all, or none may be used. There are alternative forms for the Confession and Absolution in *Enriching Our Worship 1.* The Peace is given here, recalling the Gospel of Matthew's admonition that we come to the Altar after having resolved our differences and conflicts.[8] It may also take place after the Breaking of the Bread, but that is an uncommon choice in the Episcopal Church. The Peace, for which there is an alternative in *Enriching Our Worship 1*, concludes the Word of God.

4 BCP, 327.

5 BCP: Rite I, p. 326, 327; Rite II, p. 358.

6 *Enriching Our Worship 1* (New York, NY: Church Publishing 1998), 53. Hereafter, referred to as EOW1.

7 Baptismal Feast days are listed in the BCP on page 312; the Renewal of Baptismal Vows is on page 292.

8 Matthew 5:22–24.

The Holy Communion

The second major section of the liturgy is The Holy Communion (sometimes called The Liturgy of the Table). This part of the rite may begin with a sentence of scripture. While there are examples provided in *the Book of Common Prayer* (pages 343–344 for Rite I and pages 376–377 for Rite II), any sentence of Scripture may be used. Rather than using the same sentence throughout the year, this is an opportunity to emphasize the themes of the day and carry them forward into Holy Communion. Whenever possible, selecting a sentence from the readings of the day may help reinforce the themes of the day and help tie the liturgy together more strongly. The psalm is often a good source for Offertory Sentences. Suggested Offertory Sentences from the readings are among the resources provided for most Sundays in this volume. After the Offertory Sentence, a hymn, psalm, or anthem may be sung.

The primary planning choice for this section of the liturgy involves which Eucharistic Prayer to use. There are 8 options in *the Book of Common Prayer* and 3 in *Enriching Our Worship 1.*[9] Which Eucharistic Prayer seems most apt with these readings, for this season, on this day? Some churches do prefer to choose a Eucharistic Prayer for a season, to emphasize the themes of the season that the Prayer reinforces. Suggestions for this choice will be included in the Sunday pages below.

Generally speaking, in Rite I, both prayers offer the use of a proper preface,[10] that would permit the use of thematic language for the season. These two prayers are quite similar to each other, Prayer II being an adaptation of Prayer I. As such, Prayer I is more traditional, preserving more of the language that goes back to Cranmer's 1549 prayer (though influenced along the way by Scottish prayers and others). Prayer I has language that emphasizes the atonement and may come across as more penitential to some ears than Prayer II.

9 Additionally, there are authorized expansive language versions of the Rite II Eucharistic Prayers available from General Convention. Thematically, these latter prayers are not different from their Book of Common Prayer counterpart, but may be more suitable in congregations using inclusive and expansive language on a regular basis. These may be found at https://www.episcopalcommonprayer.org/existing-liturgies1.html, accessed March 19, 2023.

10 The preface is the paragraph that introduces the Sanctus ("Holy, holy, holy"). In many prayers, it is a "fixed preface," which is the same for every Sunday or Feast Day. Some prayers, however, have a changeable preface that can be inserted into the prayer. These are called "Proper Prefaces" because they convey the themes of the propers of the day. The appointed proper preface is listed with the Collect of the Day in the BCP and the proper prefaces themselves are on pages 344–349 for Rite I and 377–382 for Rite II.

In Rite II, Prayer A and B both permit proper prefaces and so can be adapted to any season or day. Generally speaking, Prayer A, which is a contemporized, shorter version of Rite I: Prayer I, has more language focused on the cross and atonement than many of the other prayers. Prayer B emphasizes incarnational imagery and is often selected for Advent and/or Christmas.[11] Prayer C is unique in its extensive dialogue between the celebrant and congregation and was written for the 1979 BCP. It inspires a variety of opinions from those who use it across the church. If your parish is open to using it, it has sections that emphasize seeing God at work in the world, so may be suitable to use in the Season after Epiphany, but also has significant penitential themes, so may be suitable for Lent. In a given year, one would use Prayer C for one or the other of those seasons (or some other time, during part of the Season After Pentecost, perhaps), but not back to back for both seasons. Prayer D is drawn from the Liturgy of St. Basil, originating in the fourth century. It has very powerful language of praise and glory for God as well as a section allowing additional intercessions to be included. It may be useful for significant feast days or more solemn celebrations.

Enriching Our Worship 1 has three prayers. Prayer 1 has a proper preface that may be used or the appointed proper preface for the day may be used, to provide a seasonal thematic connection. Prayer 1 also contains some intentional language about the need for repentance and narrates salvation history in a way that may be helpful during Lent in particular. Eucharistic Prayer 2 in EOW1 uses expansive language of creation and includes feminine imagery for God. This prayer could be suitable at any time, but perhaps most useful during the Season after Epiphany and the Season after Pentecost. EOW1 Prayer 3 employs Wisdom language, a reference to Jesus as a light to the nations, and also incorporates feminine imagery. Perhaps Advent, Christmas, or the Season after Epiphany would be the most fruitful times of year to use this prayer, thematically.

In addition to determining the eucharistic prayer, the form of the Lord's Prayer needs to be chosen (often a congregation will have a consistent practice as to which form is used) and which sentence to use at the Breaking of the Bread (usually called a "Fraction Anthem" – whether said or sung). There are multiple options between *the Book of Common Prayer*, *Enriching Our Worship 1*, and in *The Hymnal 1982* (S 151 through S 172; just the text can be used, if singing is not an option).

11 Marion Hatchett notes that Rite II: Prayer B merges an early prayer, attributed to Hippolytus, and a draft written for this prayer book by the late Frank T. Griswold, III, while he was a parish priest, prior to becoming Bishop of Chicago and, eventually, Presiding Bishop of The Episcopal Church (*Commentary on the American Prayer Book*, 375).

Postcommunion and Conclusion

After Communion, there is a single postcommunion prayer in Rite I, two options in Rite II, and two others provided in *Enriching Our Worship 1* as alternates. While these prayers are all similar, it is worth asking which best responds to the themes for the day that are being emphasized. The blessing may use one of the forms in Rite I, *The Book of Occasional Services* (Seasonal Blessings) or *Enriching Our Worship 1*, or the priest may devise their own, in Rite II. The Blessing is optional in Rite II but is required (and prescribed) in Rite I. The Dismissal is required in Rite II, but optional in Rite I. Consider which Blessing text and which Dismissal best ties in with and connects with the themes of the day.

Regarding Music

There are about six places for music in the service of Holy Eucharist: Opening Hymn, Song of Praise, Sequence/ Gradual Hymn, Offertory Hymn, Communion Hymns, and Postcommunion Hymn. Music sometimes is offered as Prelude and Postlude to the service, of course, and several parts of the service may be sung or chanted, such as the Sanctus.

Opening Hymn – usually you would want something that is strong and either familiar or easy for the congregation to pick up. This is the first opportunity for people to be involved in the service and contribute directly to the worship experience, so you want a hymn that is accessible. Often this hymn ties in with seasonal or general themes for the day. On some special feast days/seasons, there are hymns that are directly intended for that season or day and should be considered.

Song of Praise – Intended as an opportunity to use the canticles, if the Gloria in excelsis is not used. There are many good settings for Canticles in the Service Music section of *The Hymnal 1982* that could be used here and could underscore seasonal themes, especially from Advent through the Day of Pentecost. Please also note that *Enriching Our Worship 1* has added a large number of new canticles that may also be used. As noted, a song or hymn may be used here, but should be focused on praise.

Sequence or Gradual Hymn – This hymn is typically sung following the second reading, prior to the Gospel reading. It accompanies a Gospel procession, in many churches. For this hymn, it is helpful to consider hymns that are closely tied to the readings in particular, since it is sung in the midst of the readings.

Offertory – In churches with choirs (large or small), the offertory is often a choral anthem. However, a hymn may also be used here. Themes from the readings and season should be considered, but also the location in the service should be considered. This hymn is an opportunity to express preparing oneself for Communion, whether focused on forgiveness or the giving of oneself in service or ministry.

Communion Hymns – Usually these hymns are thematically tied to the action of the rite while this hymn is being sung, the administration of Holy Communion. The section in *The Hymnal 1982* that focuses on Holy Communion is often useful for this selection.

Postcommunion Hymn – If this is used for an exit procession, it is helpful to choose something strong and familiar to the congregation. This is the last opportunity to emphasize themes of the day in music.

Note: While choir anthems are often sung at the Offertory, they can be sung anywhere in the service and there may be occasions where it is more desirable for the choir to sing an anthem as a sequence or during communion – or for the opening or postcommunion. Additionally, instrumental music may be used in any of these six location instead of a sung hymn or anthem, if that is preferred.

Summary

To recap these guidelines for planning, briefly:

1. Review Lessons, Season, Collect; Ask the Preacher if they know their focal theme(s)
2. Are there additional concerns/events to consider?
3. Determine Entrance Rite
4. Determine Response to the Readings, particularly the Intercessions
5. Determine Offertory Sentence
6. Determine Eucharistic Prayer and Fraction Anthem
7. Choose Postcommunion Prayer
8. Choose music: Opening, Song of Praise, Sequence, Offertory, Communion, Postcommunion

It is helpful to select music after the other choices are made, since the intended emphasis will be clearer prior to selecting hymns. Hymns are among the most powerful, memorable choices one can make in the liturgy. As one liturgical scholar, of blessed memory, opined, "They won't be whistling the sermon in the parking lot."[12] The more intentionality that we bring to service planning, the more likely that the experience in worship is going to be formative for the people who assemble, allowing more and more opportunities to be aware of the encounter with God not only in liturgy, but in life.

12 Marion Hatchett in a lecture, probably more than once, in the late 1990s at the School of Theology in Sewanee.

Year B: The Year of Mark and John

The design of the Revised Common Lectionary Year B follows Mark's gospel and is supplemented by readings from the Gospel of John in Advent, Christmas, Epiphany, Lent, and Easter; and in the time after Pentecost, five Sundays of readings from John 6.

The Gospel of Mark

Not only is Mark the earliest of the four canonical gospels, but it is the first piece of literature to which we have given the name *gospel*, a word that describes both the book's genre and its subject: the gospel, *evangelion*, "good news." The first line of Mark announces itself as "The beginning of the good news of Jesus Christ, the Son of God." The "beginning" speaks of both the beginning of the book and the origin of the good news that the narrative itself proclaims. The Gospel of Mark tells the story of Jesus without reference to its author (cf. John 19:35; 21:24) or the circumstances of its writing (cf. Luke 1:1–2). The omniscient narrator tells the story with absolute authority from the citation of the prophet Isaiah in 1:2–3 to the silent flight from the tomb in 16:8. The narrator relates the story of Jesus in the language and imagery of the scriptures of Israel, creating a rich texture of allusions to exodus, exile, prophets, law, and covenant. The style is fast-paced, lacking smooth transitions between episodes. Its spare narrative casts specific details in high relief.

The World Behind the Text

Written around 70 CE during the violence of the Jewish war with Rome or after the destruction of the temple, the gospel presents traditions about Jesus's teaching and healing ministry, words and deeds, and an extended narrative of the events of his passion and death. Scholars have placed the gospel in Rome, Syria, or another part of the Roman Empire. The social setting of Mark's community is one of suffering and marginalization in Roman-occupied Palestine. In its depiction of the scribes and Pharisees as opponents of Jesus and in details of the trial, it reflects early stages in the mutual self-definition between the early Christian assembly and the Jewish community from which it came. The gospel shows Jesus reinforcing the teaching of Torah and emphasizing its true intention (Mark 7:9–23; 10:1–12; 12:28–34). Mark is the primary literary source for the composition of the Gospels of Matthew and Luke and a strong influence on John. The depiction of women as exemplars of faith and of the values taught by Jesus (1:30–31; 5:25–34; 7:24–30; 12:41–44; 14:1–9; 15:40–41; 16:1–8) may indicate the prominence of women as leaders in the ministry of Jesus and in the community of Mark's gospel.

The World in Front of the Text

Church historian Eusebius cites Papias's testimony that the gospel was written by Mark, who interpreted Peter's experience. Christian leaders in the second century thought it important to link the inherited gospels to apostles who knew Jesus. Sometime in the process of transmission, the shorter ending (16:8b) and the longer ending (16:9–20) were added to the original gospel, perhaps to resolve the mysterious ending and to make it resemble the pattern of the other gospels that report appearances of the risen Jesus.

How the Gospel "Works"

Literary critical scholarship on Mark has explored Mark as story, and studies of orality in the early Christian context have given renewed attention to how the story of Mark would have been heard. Contemporary performance of Mark displays how the drama plays out, creating suspense, surprise, irony, and paradox. Individual episodes refer backward and forward with repeated key words, summoning the entire good news. To preach one episode of healing or teaching in Mark, reading it in the larger context of the whole story, is most powerful.

As a rhetorical work, the Gospel of Mark does something to those who hear it. The good news provokes emotion and motivates to action. Older scholarship spoke of the outline or structure of Mark as a passion narrative with an extended introduction, noting that Mark 1–8 showed Jesus as a divine man doing deeds of power, then seeming to reverse or correct that picture with a narrative of arrest, humiliation, and death. Literary criticism explicated the plot of Mark in which the identity of Jesus as Messiah was both revealed and concealed as the story progressed. Understanding Mark as rhetorical performance highlights how the reader/hearer experiences the story: you know the end, and it is still a shock; you experience the shift from power to powerlessness; you are propelled from the tomb to speak or not and to meet Jesus in Galilee "just as he told you" (16:7). Some interpreters have read Mark's gospel as itself an ordeal or baptism into death as a kind of literary-liturgical journey.

The World of the Text: Narrative Arc and Peak Events

The citation of the prophet Isaiah in Mark 1:2–3 (actually, Malachi *and* Isaiah), followed by John baptizing in the wilderness, summons up the setting of the Exile and prophetic vision of redemption. Readers are propelled into Galilee, where God and Satan are at war for control of the cosmos, the society, and the human individual. Jesus's exorcisms demonstrate that he casts evil spirits from unwilling human hosts as he casts out a legion of demons into the countryside (5:1–20); the strong man is bound in order to plunder his house (3:23–27). Controversy ensues as conflict with the religious authorities escalates, and the disciples, despite being given the secret of the kingdom of God (4:11), misunderstand and misinterpret Jesus's teaching and the significance of his deeds of power. Jesus's family attempts to restrain him (3:21). At the same time, many without privilege exhibit confidence in Jesus's power to heal, those who are in desperate need of healing for themselves or someone close to them: a leper (1:40), friends of the paralyzed man (2:3–4), Jairus (5:22–23), a bleeding woman (5:25), and a Syrophoenician woman (7:25). Readers/hearers of Mark are caught up in the ironic dynamic that those on the inside misunderstand while those on the outside or at the edge respond with faith: "your faith has made you well" ("saved you") (5:34; 10:52).

Readers, like the characters in Mark, are confronted with how to comprehend Jesus's teaching that the Son of Man must be killed and rise again, announced three times with intensifying detail (8:31; 9:31; 10:33–34). Will they seek positions of glory as James and John and the Gentiles (10:42) or be those who lose their lives for "my sake, and for the sake of the gospel" (8:35)? Jesus's teaching in Mark 8:27 – 10:45 is bracketed by two stories of Jesus healing a blind man, one at Bethsaida, where Jesus gives sight in two stages (8:22–26), and another outside of Jericho, where Bartimaeus asks for and receives his sight, then follows Jesus "on the way" (10:46–52). In the oral performance of the gospel, these two stories evoke the reality of partial sight/knowledge and the difficulty and remarkable gift of complete sight.

The climactic episode in the drama of knowing/not knowing, saving and losing, opens the passion narrative. At Bethany, a woman breaks open a jar of costly ointment and pours it on Jesus's head while he sits at the table. Her prophetic action of anointing Jesus's head and Jesus's acknowledgment that she has "anointed my body beforehand for its burial" (14:8) reveal the paradoxical truth that the anointed one is also the one who will die. Rather than being wasteful, her pouring out all the ointment is the epitome of the way of life that Jesus teaches: losing life to save it. For this reason, her "good service" will be told wherever the gospel is proclaimed "in remembrance of her" (14:9).

The passion narrative recounts Jesus's betrayal and arrest, desertion by his followers, trial, torture, and execution by his enemies. Having exhibited extraordinary power in Galilee, Jesus becomes seemingly powerless and mostly silent, the one able to save others but unable to save himself (15:31). Jesus's cry from the cross, "My God, my God, why have you forsaken me?" expresses abandonment and despair, a realistic depiction of human loneliness and death.

Three critical moments of the naming of Jesus as Son punctuate the gospel. The first is at his baptism, when a voice from heaven says, "You are my Son, the Beloved; with you I am well pleased" (1:11). The second is at his transfiguration, when a voice from the cloud says, "This is my Son, the Beloved; listen to him!" (9:7). The third is after his death, when a centurion says, "Truly this man was God's Son!" (15:39). These three voices resonate within the hearers of the gospel, setting up an implicit but unexplained relationship between baptism, transfiguration, and crucifixion.

Mary Magdalene, Mary the mother of James, and Salome's arrival at the tomb culminates the theme of women following and serving Jesus (1:30–31; 15:40–41) and recalls the anointing at the table at Bethany (14:3–9). The young man announces "He has been raised" and commissions the women to tell the others that "he is going ahead of you to Galilee; there you will see him" (16:6–7). The ambiguous conclusion – that the women flee in silence and fear – has often been interpreted as failure and lack of faith. However, other heroes in the biblical tradition (Daniel, John, Ezekiel, Isaiah) are overcome by fear and struck dumb by extraordinary revelation. When they behold Jesus's resurrection, the faithful women fear, tremble, and are amazed. The gospel ends in the moments before their speech, anticipating reunion with Jesus in Galilee and ongoing ministry to restore the world.

Mark in Year B

The pattern of the Revised Common Lectionary, built around themes of the liturgical season, governs the placement of readings from Mark: in Advent, Jesus's apocalyptic speech (13:24–37) and the appearance of John baptizing (1:1–8); in the time after Epiphany, controversies and healings (Mark 1) and transfiguration (9:2–10); in Lent, Jesus's temptation and first passion prediction; and in the time after Pentecost, passages from Mark 3–13. The Markan passion narrative is assigned for the Sunday of the Passion, and the story of the sending out from the empty tomb, on Easter Sunday. Notable omissions from the RCL are the parable of the sower and teaching about parables (4:1–25), the exorcism of the Gerasene demoniac (5:1–20), and the two-stage healing of the blind man at Bethsaida (8:22–26). Readings from the Gospel of John in each season interrupt the connected narrative of Mark.

Within the liturgical year, the preacher can exploit the dramatic arc of Mark by drawing on the whole gospel when preaching on one episode. The paradox of seeing/not seeing, saving/losing, being served/serving, and power/weakness run throughout the gospel. Resurrection happens in Galilee when Peter's mother-in-law rises to serve and when Jesus tells the one who is paralyzed and the one whose hand is withered to rise (2:11; 3:3). The exorcism of Legion from the man in the tombs, the healing of the bleeding woman, and the raising of Jairus's daughter are all stories of resurrection that amplify the significance of Jesus's teaching and his death. Other key words such as *bread*, *serve*, *clothes*, and *save* set up resonances that reward spiritual and homiletical reflection.

The Gospel of John in Year B

The Gospel of John has its own narrative and symbolic integrity. Using a style and sensibility very different than Mark, John portrays Jesus as the preexistent Word who descends to "his own" and ascends at the time of his exaltation. The fourth gospel interprets the crucifixion as Jesus's being lifted up (John 3:14; 8:28; 12:32, 34). The motif of Jesus's "hour," summarizing the paschal mystery, runs through the entire gospel. Readings from John in year B are concentrated in Lent (3, 4, 5) and Easter (2, 4, 5, 6, 7). John's narration of events shapes the liturgies of Holy Week. Five Sundays in the time after Pentecost explore Jesus's bread of life discourse in John 6. Lenten readings from John use distinctive Johannine images: destroying and raising the temple, lifting up the Son of Man, dying and bearing much fruit to anticipate the resurrection. Readings in the Easter season recount the appearances to the disciples and Thomas, Jesus as good shepherd and true vine, and the prayer for the disciples from his farewell discourse. With John, as with Mark, effective preaching connects an individual passage in John with its role in the imaginative world of the whole gospel.

The Very Reverend Cynthia Briggs Kittredge
Dean and President, Seminary of the Southwest,
Austin, Texas

Advent

Preparing for Advent

The Climax of the Church Year

The First Sunday of Advent is not only the beginning of a new season, it is really the climax and conclusion of the Church Year. The apocalyptic readings leading up to the Christ the King propers on the Last Sunday after Pentecost reach their climax in the celebration of the Parousia on Advent Sunday, after which the theme rapidly modulates to the first Advent. Planning needs to take account of this continuity, so that eschatological themes are not suddenly introduced on a single Sunday and then trundled quickly off again. These eschatological readings give to the liturgy of the last few Sundays before Advent an aura of intense expectation, which should be reflected in other aspects of the liturgy.[1]

A reasonable procedure for overall planning would be to plan the month of November, from All Saints' Day to Christ the King, with the building Advent theme as a unit. The use of the lectionary in planning, the setting of seasonal themes for decoration of the church (such as late fall flowers), a uniform treatment of the psalm between the readings (singing or reciting it responsively as described on p. 582 of the prayer book, for example), and the use of an appropriate canticle such as 9 ("The First Song of Isaiah") or 19 ("The Song of the Redeemed") throughout the period in place of the Gloria in excelsis are possible ways to draw the period together. Thanksgiving Day will occur on the fourth Thursday of the month and can easily be included in the planning.

Advent as a Season

Advent itself should be planned as a distinct liturgical season. While Advent and Lent both share the characteristic of being seasons of preparation (and both can be used fruitfully for preparation for baptismal candidates), they have different tones and connotations in the Church today. Expectation, not penitence, is the major theme of preparation in Advent. It is the season of preparation for the coming of Jesus Christ, both his coming in history to Bethlehem, celebrated at Christmas, and his coming in glory at the end of time "to judge the living and the dead" to which Christians look forward. "The King shall come!" and "Rejoice!" are its watchwords. The great Advent figures who dominate the scripture readings are Isaiah, John the Baptist, and the Virgin Mary.

This preparation is also distinct from "getting ready for Christmas" in terms of planning and preparation for the ways that we celebrate that feast with family or friends (decorating our homes, buying and wrapping gifts, meal preparation). One priest would exhort her congregation each year with a countdown of "Shopping Days until Advent" during November, to encourage people to take care of as many of those mundane tasks of preparation as possible before Advent began, so that the focus during the Season of Advent could be on preparing one's heart for the renewed coming of Christ.[2]

Liturgical Color

Violet or deep blue,[3] as colors more appropriate to the season, are increasingly used for vestments and hangings in place of the red-purple introduced in the nineteenth century from the Roman sequence of liturgical colors but which many people feel tended to make the season more penitential.

In some places, rose vestments have been worn on the Third Sunday of Advent, also following a Roman tradition, related to penitence. This "lightening up" of a Sunday more than halfway through a long penitential season only makes

1 Because of the themes of the lectionary in November, some congregations have begun to experiment with an extended Advent, through the work of The Advent Project (www.theadventproject.org). See the section below for more information.

2 The Rt. Rev. Carlye J. Hughes, prior to becoming a bishop, when serving Trinity Episcopal Church, Fort Worth, TX, 2012–2018.

3 Some refer to this color as "Sarum Blue" implying that using this color was part of medieval practice at Salisbury Cathedral (Sarum) in England. That seems not to have been the case, though using blue is a perfectly fine choice for Advent. For more, see J. Barrington Bates, "Am I Blue? Some Historical Evidence for Liturgical Colors," *Studia Liturgica* (33:1, 2003), 75–88. A summary of that article can be found at https://www.praytellblog.com/index.php/2013/11/25/sarum-blue-the-great-untruth/, accessed March 20, 2023.

complete sense when Advent is observed as penitential.[4] This Sunday was known as Gaudete Sunday by Roman Catholics and Lutherans, because of the antiphon on its introit which begins with the word "Gaudete" ("Rejoice"). If the parish owns and wishes to use such vestments, that is perfectly fine. However, when Advent is observed as expectant, rather than penitential, this practice is somewhat out of place. There does not seem to be any good reason to introduce rose vestments where they have not been used. Likewise, without the penitential context, there is no particular reason that Advent wreaths should incorporate a rose-colored candle, though it is perfectly fine to do so.

Sunday Liturgies

The Sunday morning Advent liturgies should have a seasonal unity. The Gloria is not used, and either the Trisagion or the Kyrie is sung. The use of the same setting of one of these for the four Sundays will begin to give the services continuity. Canticle 16, The Song of Zechariah, is the traditional Advent canticle, and, unless it is being sung at Morning Prayer, the planners may wish to make a place for it at the eucharist. It could be sung, for example, as an entrance song or between the New Testament reading and the Gospel, either to a plainsong or Anglican chant setting from *The Hymnal 1982*, depending on the preference of the congregation.

Sermons for the four Sundays can be planned as a unity, not necessarily a series, covering the major themes of the season as highlighted in the readings for the particular Sunday. If the same person will not preach every week, it is especially important that the planning committee give attention to the total impact of the Advent preaching. The sermon themes and the readings will then form the basis for selecting hymns and anthems. At least this much of the planning will have to be done well in advance, so that the music can be selected and rehearsed.

Unless different forms of the Prayers of the People tied to the readings (such as locally written prayers or those found below in Content Resources for each Sunday) are used every week, a decision can be made to use the same form for the whole of Advent, further tying the services together. The Advent proper preface is used at all services, and Eucharistic Prayer B, with its strong emphasis on the incarnation, is a particularly appropriate choice for the period from Advent 1 through the Baptism of Christ.

The singing (or speaking) of one of the alternative fraction anthems (*confractoria*), such as "Be known to us, Lord Jesus" or "Blessed are those who are called" (S 171 or S 169 in *The Hymnal 1982*), in place of "Christ our Passover" during the breaking of the bread is another way to give seasonal unity to the services.

Two alternative seasonal blessings for Advent are in *The Book of Occasional Services 2022*[5]. The first contains four short paragraphs, to which all respond "Amen." The second is a simple introduction to the usual blessing. Either may be used, and a decision to use one or the other at every service during Advent is another seasonal possibility.

The Advent Wreath

The lighting of an Advent wreath is an appropriate seasonal symbol. Fundamentally, a devotion or liturgy that takes place in the home, many churches include an Advent wreath in their worship space and incorporate its use into the Sunday liturgy. The wreath is of evergreen with four candles, which may be white or the color of the Advent vestments. One candle is lit for each of the four weeks of Advent. This is done by people in their homes and may also be done at the beginning of the liturgy. Often a fifth candle in the middle of the wreath, the Christ candle, is lit on Christmas and throughout the twelve days. In the church, the wreath may be hung from the ceiling or placed on a stand or table in any convenient place where it can be seen by the people. *The Book of Occasional Services 2022* recommends that no particular ceremonial elaboration accompany its use but that at morning services it simply be lit before the services begin[6]. For services held in the evening, the candles may be lit after the Prayer for Light in the Order of Worship for the Evening in the BCP.

Evening Services

The use of the Order of Worship for Evening during Advent is particularly appropriate, since sunset will be early in the northern hemisphere, evenings long, and evening services easily begun in a darkened church. The order may replace the entrance rite of the Eucharist or be a separate evening service.

The order begins with a special greeting, "Light and peace, in Jesus Christ our Lord," and continues with a Prayer for Light. During Advent this is the collect for Advent 1. The appropriate number of candles on the Advent wreath are then lit and the lights in the church brought up. A proper Advent Lucernarium (Anthem at the Candle lighting) are provided, with musical settings if desired, in the Service Music Appendix of *The Hymnal 1982 Accompaniment Edition* (S 309). This may

4 Lent has an equivalent, Laetare Sunday, on the Fourth Sunday in Lent, where rose is used in some places.

5 *The Book of Occasional Services 2022* (New York, NY: Church Publishing, 2022), 10. Often referred to as BOS or BOS 2022 here.

6 BOS 2022, 20.

be spoken, sung by a cantor or other song leader while the candles are being lit, or this may be done in silence. Then either the hymn Phos Hilaron (as in Evening Prayer) "or some other hymn" is sung. Advent has a particularly suitable hymn for this purpose. "Creator of the stars at night" (Hymn 60). If the service is a Eucharist, it continues with the collect of the day. Otherwise, it continues with an evening psalm, a lesson, or a sermon, if desired; Canticle 15, The Song of Mary (Magnificat) or another canticle or hymn of praise; prayers; and a blessing. One of the forms for the eucharistic Prayers of the People or Suffrages B from Evening Prayer, concluding with the collect of the day and the Lord's Prayer, are good choices for the prayers. The blessing may be the proper seasonal blessing from the BOS.

One or more evening services, whether the Eucharist or Evensong, might be considered as special events for the Advent season. The BOS contains instructions for an Advent Festival of Lessons and Carols, which is another possibility for an evening service introduced by the lighting of the Advent wreath. This will provide an opportunity for the singing of more traditional Advent music than is convenient in four Sunday services and give the choir an opportunity to sing some things too difficult for congregational singing, as well as serving as a parish pre-Christmas party.

Advent Music

There is a wealth of Advent hymnody and anthems. In selecting appropriate music, remember that the Parousia (the second coming of Christ) theme of Advent I has shifted to the Annunciation or Visitation by Advent IV. The hymns about coming in glory are, therefore, best for the last Sundays after Pentecost in November and the First Sunday of Advent, so that by the Sunday before Christmas we can use hymns like *Rosa Mystica* (Hymn 81) or Annunciation/Visitation hymns.

Decorating the Church

A perennial cause of conflict between "purists" and "pragmatists" is the proper time to decorate the church for Christmas (*see also* The Advent Police). In reaction to the secular putting up of Christmas decorations in October, purists insist that nothing can be done until December 24, while the pragmatists plead that such a course of action is totally impractical and urge an earlier date. There is, of course, no reason why evergreens and wreaths cannot be used to decorate the church during Advent. Some churches put bows of Advent blue or purple (depending upon which color they use for the altar hangings and vestments) on their wreaths, changing them to red or white for Christmas. An alternative tradition is to "green" the church on December 17, so that the greens are in place for the festive liturgies of Advent 4. This may have the "practical" advantage of keeping the greens from drying out before Epiphany. December 17 is called "O Sapientia" because a special antiphon was sung before and after the Magnificat at evensong from that date until Christmas. These antiphons are preserved in the Hymnal (with the dates on which they were sung) as the verses of "O come, O come, Emmanuel" (Hymn 56).[7] The "greening" of the church and the use of this special music marked the increased sense of expectation as Christmas approached. A liturgy committee with imagination might find interesting ways to adapt and incorporate these medieval customs into their own preparation for Christmas.

7 These antiphons are also used thematically for the seven Sundays of an expanded Advent, for those churches following that practice.

An Expanded Advent[1]

William Petersen, one of the primary proponents of an expanded Advent through "The Advent Project," provides this simple introduction: "The proposal for an expanded Advent is rooted in a very simple idea: to make the Advent we celebrate congruent with the lectionary we already have. Everything else is commentary." One of the significant aims of this idea is that it is seeking to engage with the current lectionary and amplify its themes. This approach does not altering the lectionary, simply framing how this time of year might be identified and observed.

The Problem

Petersen and his colleagues in the Advent Project[2] identify two significant issues in the observance of Advent and Christmas that this approach is intending to address. The first is that Advent has been lost to "the Christmas Culture." Petersen writes "The Christmas decorations lurking in the back corners of supermarkets and home supply stores from late August, join with the surreptitiously expanding shelves of Christmas items in boutiques, pharmacies, and other retail establishments, just waiting for Hallowe'en to pass so that they can all explode into their full manifestation on November 1st." Effectively, the global culture of Christmas has eroded Advent, such that the themes, primarily the manifestation of God's reign, are largely unheard. Reclaiming Advent in the face of this barrage is one of the aims of an expanded Advent.

The second concern is how much the Church is already endorsing this rush to Christmas. Church leaders and planners are often under pressure to sing Christmas carols during Advent and often relent. Of course, many of those same carols are being heard in stores and on the radio already, in any case. Much of what passes for religious literature or popular religious practice also focuses on Advent solely as preparation for Christmas or as a countdown, including Advent Calendars (so-called, they are usually December countdown calendars, of course). Petersen notes that "Advent spirituality is reduced to pleas to take time out for reflection on these things amidst the bustle of the season. Thus, by the beginning of December we are well on our way to Bethlehem. The problem with this, of course, is that the primary focus of Advent is the full manifestation of the Reign of God." This primary focus is the theme of the lectionary readings from the Sunday after All Saints Day until the last week of Advent. The shift from eschatology to incarnation really is only seen in that last Sunday of Advent.

The Proposal

Those lectionary readings are a reminder that Advent was not always just the four Sundays prior to Christmas. That four-week pattern seems to emerge beginning in the seventh century, but wasn't common in the western church until the twelfth or thirteenth century. Prior to that change, Advent was nearly seven weeks, reflecting roughly the same time frame as its springtime counterpart, Lent. Nor was Advent always understood as the beginning of the liturgical year. However, by the time the Reformation came along in the western Church, in the sixteenth century, Advent had long stood as the four-week season that began the liturgical year. Until the twentieth century, Christians who observed Advent had no competition from the wider culture to rush to Christmas and the eschatological focus was in clear view. For much of the history of Advent, it was a season not as much about preparation for the incarnation, the celebration of Christmas, but a season that sets the context for the entire liturgical year as moving towards God's final end and purpose and keeps it, properly observed, from being merely a repetitive cycle.

An expanded Advent, then, seeks to restore this seven-week period that allows for greater consideration of these eschatological themes and see the season as much as the culmination of the year leading up to Advent as the beginning of a new consideration of the life and work of Christ as Christmas nears. The appointed readings support this interpretation in the current lectionary. The current lectionary in the Episcopal Church, the Revised

1 Adapted from William Petersen, "Rationale" found on The Advent Project website http://www.theadventproject.org/index.php/rationale/, accessed March 20, 2023.

2 The Advent Project originated and continues as a Seminar of the North American Academy of Liturgy.

Common Lectionary, was developed with a great deal of ecumenical consultation and is used by a large number of denominations. The lectionary reflects a change of atmosphere after the beginning of November, immediately calling to mind the eschatological themes of the Gospel. By expanding Advent, these themes are lifted up and are more clearly connected with the seasonal theme.

In practical terms, if Advent is expanded to include those additional Sundays and their readings, that changes the look and feel of worship. The Advent Project website has numerous resources available for worship and ideas about how to enact this in the life of the congregation.

Clearly no change to the lectionary or readings would be necessary. In an expanded Advent, the earliest date for the First Sunday of Advent would be November 5 and the latest date would be November 12. For those congregations accustomed to observing All Saints' Day on the Sunday after All Saints, that would mean a decision would occasionally have to be made about observing All Saints solely on its feast day rather than also on the Sunday following. The years affected would be when the Sunday after All Saints' Day fell on November 6, 7, or 8.

An additional traditional layer that can be added to these Sundays thematically are the "O Antiphons" which are preserved in the Advent hymn "O come, o come, Emmanuel." The verses are drawn from antiphons used for centuries with the Song of Mary (Magnificat), used by monastics during the final week of Advent at Evensong or Vespers. These seven antiphons can be overlaid on the seven Sundays of an expanded Advent:

Advent I	Nov. 5–12	*O Sapientia* Wisdom "wisdom from on high"
Advent II	Nov. 13–19	*O Adonai* Lord "Lord of might"
Advent III	Nov. 20–26	*O Rex gentium* Ruler of nations "desire of nations"
Advent IV	Nov. 27–Dec. 3	*O radix Jesse* Root of Jesse "branch of Jesse's tree"
Advent V	Dec. 4–10	*O clavis David* Key of David "key of David"
Advent VI	Dec. 11–17	*O Oriens* Morning Star "dayspring from on high"
Advent VII	Dec. 18–24	*O Emmanuel* God with us "Emmanuel"

In addition to emphasizing that the central focus of any Sunday is a focus on Christ, this plan has deep roots in the Advent tradition and would allow more exploration than simply the one or two Sundays when "O come, o come, Emmanuel" might be sung. Additionally, the Advent III theme of *Rex gentium* or Ruler of nations, is adjusted in sequence slightly so that it may line up with the current Last Sunday after Pentecost, commonly called Christ the King Sunday, which allows for that existing emphasis to be integrated into the expanded Advent. The alternative collects provided on the website as worship resources for these Sundays draw from this pattern of using the "O" antiphons as well.

Further information, including contact information for William Petersen, is available on The Advent Project website (www.theadventproject.org).

Advent – Major Feasts, Seasonal Rites, and Other Commemorations

The Advent Wreath[1]

The Advent Wreath is a visual symbol marking the progress of the season of Advent, originating as a domestic devotion and an opportunity for family prayer. It functions as a simple countdown-timer for the passage of Advent. Attaching symbolic meanings to particular candles is a more recent innovation. It is important to place the wreath in such a way so that it maintains the centrality of the essential symbols for the assembly: Font, Word, and Table.

When the Advent Wreath is used in the worshiping community at morning services, the appropriate number of candles on the wreath are lighted, without prayer or ceremony, with the other candles. In evening worship, the candle lighting in An Order of Worship for the Evening, described on page 143 of *The Book of Common Prayer*, is appropriate.

When used in private homes, the Advent Wreath provides a focus for devotions at the time of the evening meal. There are many resources for devotions produced to include the reading of Scriptures suitable for the Advent season. The short form for An Order Worship for the Evening (BCP, pages 109–112) is also recommended. In place of the Short Lesson of Scripture provided in the Order, one of the readings from the Daily Office Lectionary may be used, in whole or in part. (*The Book of Occasional Services 2022* provides weekly short lessons for this purpose on pages 20 and 21 and suggests substituting an Advent hymn for the Phos hilaron).

An Option for Advent Wreath Prayers at Home[2]

First Week in Advent

Leader: Almighty God, give us grace to cast away the works of darkness,

And put on the armor of light,

Leader: Now in the time of this mortal life in which your Son Jesus Christ came to visit us in great humility; that in the last day, when he shall come again in his glorious majesty to judge both the living and the dead, we may rise to the life immortal; through him who lives and reigns with you and the Holy Spirit, one God, now and for ever. ***Amen.***

Second Week in Advent

Leader: Merciful God, who sent your messengers the prophets to preach repentance,

And prepare the way for our salvation,

Leader: Give us grace to heed their warnings and forsake our sins, that we may greet with joy the coming of Jesus Christ our Redeemer: who lives and reigns with you and the Holy Spirit, one God, now and for ever. ***Amen.***

Third Week in Advent

Leader: Stir up your power, O Lord,

And with great might come among us;

Leader: And, because we are sorely hindered by our sins, let your bountiful grace and mercy speedily help and deliver us; through Jesus Christ our Lord, to whom with you and the Holy Spirit, be honor and glory, now and for ever. ***Amen.***

Fourth Week in Advent

Leader: Purify our conscience, Almighty God,

by your daily visitation,

Leader: That your Son Jesus Christ, at his coming, may find in us a mansion prepared for himself; who lives and reigns with you, in the unity of the Holy Spirit, one God, now and for ever. ***Amen.***

---

1 BOS 2022, 20–21.

2 Anne E. Kitch. *The Anglican Family Prayer Book* (Harrisburg, PA: Morehouse Publishing, 2004), 115–121.

Advent Blessing[3]

The following blessing may be used by a bishop or priest whenever a blessing is appropriate. It is a three-fold form, with an Amen at the end of each sentence, leading into a Trinitarian blessing.

May Almighty God, by whose providence our Savior Christ came among us in great humility, sanctify you with the light of his blessing and set you free from all sin. *Amen.*

May he whose second Coming in power and great glory we await, make you steadfast in faith, joyful in hope, and constant in love. *Amen.*

May you, who rejoice in the first Advent of our Redeemer, at his second Advent be rewarded with unending life. *Amen.*

And the blessing of God Almighty, the Father, the Son, and the Holy Spirit, be upon you and remain with you for ever. *Amen.*

or this

May the Sun of Righteousness shine upon you and scatter the darkness from before your path; and the blessing of God Almighty, the Father, the Son, and the Holy Spirit, be among you, and remain with you always.

Amen.

An Advent Litany of Darkness and Light[4]

May be used in place of the Prayers of the People or in conjunction with the Advent Wreath in the home. This litany is more in keeping with the themes early in Advent of darkness and light, helpfully reframing those themes.

Voice 1: We wait in the darkness, expectantly, longingly, anxiously, thoughtfully.

Voice 2: The darkness is our friend. In the darkness of the womb, we have all been nurtured and protected. In the darkness of the womb, the Christ-child was made ready for the journey into light.

You are with us, O God, in darkness and in light.

Voice 1: It is only in the darkness that we can see the splendor of the universe – blankets of stars, the solitary glowings of distant planets.

Voice 2: It was the darkness that allowed the magi to find the star that guided them to where the Christ-child lay.

You are with us, O God, in darkness and in light.

Voice 1: In the darkness of the night, desert people find relief from the cruel relentless heat of the sun.

Voice 2: In the blessed darkness, Mary and Joseph were able to flee with the infant Jesus to safety in Egypt.

You are with us, O God, in darkness and in light.

Voice 1: In the darkness of sleep, we are soothed and restored, healed and renewed.

Voice 2: In the darkness of sleep, dreams rise up. God spoke to Jacob and Joseph through dreams. God is speaking still.

You are with us, O God, in darkness and in light.

Voice 1: In the solitude of darkness, we sometimes remember those who need God's presence in a special way – the sick, the unemployed, the bereaved, the persecuted, the homeless; those who are demoralized and discouraged, those whose fear has turned to cynicism, those whose vulnerability has become bitterness.

Voice 2: Sometimes in the darkness, we remember those who are near to our hearts – colleagues, partners, parents, children, neighbors, friends. We thank God for their presence and ask God to bless and protect them in all that they do – at home, at school, as they travel, as they work, as they play.

You are with us, O God, in darkness and in light.

Voice 1: Sometimes, in the solitude of darkness, our fears and concerns, our hopes and our visions rise to the surface. We come face to face with ourselves and with the road that lies ahead of us. And in that same darkness, we find companionship for the journey.

Voice 2: In that same darkness, we sometimes allow ourselves to wonder and worry whether the human race is going to make it at all.

We know you are with us, O God, yet we still await your coming.

In the darkness that contains both our hopelessness and our expectancy, we watch for a sign of God's Hope. Amen.

Advent Festival of Lessons & Carols[5]

Because the primary act of worship on the Lord's Day and other Major Feasts is the Holy Eucharist, the Festival of Lessons and Carols will normally be an additional observance in most worshiping

3 BOS 2022, 10–11.

4 "An Advent Litany of Darkness and Light," in *The Wideness of God's Mercy: Litanies to Enlarge Our Prayers* Jeffrey W. Rowthorn, editor (New York: Church Publishing, 2007), 65–66.

5 BOS 2022, 22–26.

communities. If it is used as the liturgy of the Word in Holy Eucharist, a sermon is to be included.

If the festival takes place in the evening, it may be introduced by the Service of Light (Book of Common Prayer, page 109). After the Phos hilaron or the hymn sung in place of it, the service continues with the Bidding Prayer (page 22 or 24 of BOS 2022). Otherwise, the festival begins with a processional hymn, psalm or anthem, followed by the Bidding Prayer.

Nine lessons are customarily selected (but fewer may be used), interspersed with appropriate Advent hymns, canticles, and anthems. When possible, each Lesson should be read by a different lector, representative of the congregation and community. The Lesson from the third chapter of Genesis is never omitted.

Genesis 2:4b–9, 15–25
Genesis 3:1–22 or 3:1–15
Isaiah 40:1–11
Jeremiah 31:31–34
Isaiah 64:1–9a
Isaiah 6:1–11
Isaiah 35:1–10
Baruch 4:36 – 5:9
Isaiah 7:10–15
Micah 5:2–4
Isaiah 11:1–9
Zephaniah 3:14–18
Isaiah 65:17–25
If it is desired that the Lessons end with a reading from the Gospel, one of the following may be used:
Luke 1:5–25 or Luke 1:26–38 or Luke 1:26–56

December 12 – La Virgen de Guadalupe (Our Lady of Guadalupe)

While not on the Episcopal Church calendar as a feast day, this is a widely celebrated day. This commemorates of a vision of La Virgen (St. Mary the Virgin) to Juan Diego Cuauhtlatoatzin on December 9 and 12, 1531, on a hilltop in what is now part of Mexico City.

A complete rite to celebrate this feast, if desired, is provided on pages 29–34 of BOS 2022, including details about the procession with flowers, appointed collect and lessons, prayers of the people, a proper preface and postcommunion prayer, unique to this day, and hymn suggestions.

Collect of the Day

O God of power and mercy, you blessed your people at Tepeyac with the presence of *La Virgen de Guadalupe*: grant that her example of love to the poor and forsaken may stir our faith to recognize all people as members of one family. Teach us to follow in the way you have prepared for us, that we may honor one another in word and action, sharing with her your commonwealth of peace; through Jesus Christ our Lord, who lives and reigns with you and the Holy Spirit, one God, in glory everlasting. *Amen.*

The Lessons

Zechariah 2:10–13
or A selection from *The Nican Mopohua* (BOS 2022, 34)
Psalm 131 *or* 116
Revelation 11:19a; 12:1–6a
Luke 6:20–23

Proper Preface

Because in revealing *La Virgen de Guadalupe* at El Tepeyac, you have shown us your way of justice and peace, lifted up small and lowly, and assured us of your great love for the poor and weak.

December 16–24 – Las Posadas

BOS 2022 provides guidelines for the celebration of this extended outdoor procession on page 27. *Las Posadas* (Spanish for "the inn" or "lodgings") is a traditional Mexican festival of hospitality which recalls Mary and Joseph's journey to Bethlehem, searching for lodging for the birth of the Christ child. Beginning on December 16 and continuing for nine days leading up to Christmas Eve worship, a procession carries images of Joseph and Mary (or with two people dressed as Mary and Joseph, *los peregrinos* (the pilgrims)) to certain houses along the procession route. At each house, those inside sing to those outside, denying them entry. At the final stop, *los peregrinos* are recognized and invited into the home for closing devotions and refreshments or a meal.

November 30 – St. Andrew the Apostle

St. Andrew's feast day is a Major Feast on the Episcopal Church Calendar and the propers for the day are found in the Book of Common Prayer. *However, during Advent, it is not permissible to substitute Major Feasts for the Advent Sunday propers. The Collect for the Day is found on pages 185 or 237 of* the Book of Common Prayer.

The first-called of the Apostles, in most accounts, and identified as the brother of Simon Peter. Andrew is included in every naming of the disciples in the Gospels and features prominently in the narrative of the feeding of the multitudes. According to tradition, Andrew may have traveled to Scythia, Romania, Georgia, and the southern border of what is today Ukraine. He is the patron saint of Russia, Ukraine, and Scotland (where his relics where purported to have eventually landed). Tradition also narrates that he was crucified on a saltire or x-shaped cross.

December 21 – St. Thomas the Apostle

St. Thomas' feast day is a Major Feast on the Episcopal Church Calendar and the propers for the day are found in the Book of Common Prayer. *However, during Advent, it is not permissible to substitute Major Feasts for the Advent Sunday propers. The Collect for the Day is found on pages 185 or 237 of* the Book of Common Prayer.

John's Gospel narrates several incidents in Thomas's story. He was with Jesus when he went to Judea to visit friends at Bethany and was willing to travel with Jesus, even at risk to his own life. At the Last Supper, Thomas questioned our Lord: "Lord, we do not know where you are going; how can we know the way?" Thomas questioned Christ's resurrection until Jesus himself showed Thomas his wounds. Though often called "doubting Thomas," the resurrection appearance to Thomas is a testament to his belief, as Thomas responds "My Lord and my God!" According to tradition, Thomas evangelized the Persians and parts of India. The Syrian Christians of India cherish the tradition that he brought the Gospel to India. The Gospel of Thomas, an apocryphal writing, is attributed to Saint Thomas the Apostle.

The First Sunday of Advent

Sunday on or between November 27 and December 3

Keep Awake!

Anchor Points – The Propers and the Season

The fixed points for each service are the appointed or proper readings and collect as well as the themes of the day or season.

Readings and Psalm

Isaiah 64:1–9

Today's reading is included in a psalm of lamentations and intercession (63:7–64:11). When the exiles returned to their land, they found Israel still desolate and the temple still in ruins (64:10–12). Their conviction that God desired Israel's salvation wavered in the face of the immense task of restoration and their own continuing sense of sinfulness and alienation. The prophet recalls the parenthood of God in order to stress God's role as Israel's begetter, the One that gives life and identity to Israel – a reminder of the permanence of their relationship with God, in which rests all their hope.

Psalm 80:1–7,16–18

This lament of the nation for deliverance probably comes from the northern kingdom, whose tribes are enumerated. The "Shepherd of Israel" (the only occurrence of this phrase in the psalms) is pictured as enthroned over the ark between the wings of the cherubim. The psalm's refrain echoes the blessing given by Aaron in Numbers 6:24–26.

1 Corinthians 1:3–9

Paul adapts the customary introduction of ancient letters and combines the usual greetings, "grace" (Greek) and "peace" (Hebrew). More than good wishes, these words describe salvation as "grace," God's gift, and as "peace," the harmony of the kingdom of God. In the thanksgiving, Paul sets forth the themes of the letter and carefully places the Corinthians' present individualistic use of the gifts into a context of future revelation and shared responsibility in the community.

Mark 13:24–37

Jesus's terse parable about the deputized servants who await the master's return urges us to live in that balance between keen anticipation and faithful obedience. The former without the latter may lead to idleness and a neglect of service. An unwavering commitment to responsibilities without an eager hope may result in feelings of drudgery and despair or spiritual and moral lassitude. The final word to all is, "Keep awake!"

Collect

Almighty God, give us grace to cast away the works of darkness, and put on the armor of light, now in the time of this mortal life in which your Son Jesus Christ came to visit us in great humility; that in the last day, when he shall come again in his glorious majesty to judge both the living and the dead, we may rise to the life immortal; through him who lives and reigns with you and the Holy Spirit, one God, now and for ever. *Amen.*

Proper Preface

Advent – Because you sent your beloved Son to redeem us from sin and death, and to make us heirs in him of everlasting life; that when he shall come again in power and great triumph to judge the world, we may without shame or fear rejoice to behold his appearing. (Rite II, BCP 378; Rite I, BCP 345)

Seasonal Pairings

See the table below for choices appointed for this day. Preferences are put in **bold**. Not all choices are suitable for all congregations or community, though, so consider these preferences as a starting point before making a decision about your own congregation.

	Advent I	Rite I	Rite II	EOW1	BOS 2022
Color	Violet or Deep Blue				
Entrance Rite	Customary; some churches use the Great Litany (148); EOW1 has an **Advent opening acclamation**	148 *or* 323	148 *or* 355	**50**	
Song of Praise/Kyrie	***Glory to God (Gloria in excelsis) is not used in Advent (BCP 406).*** Kyrie or **Trisagion**; BCP Canticles 10, 11, 13, 18 *or* EOW1 Canticles 18, B, L	324	356; C10 – 86; C11 – 87; C13 – 90; C18 – 93	C18 – 28; B – 30; L – 36	
Collect		159–160	211–212		
Creed	Nicene Creed	326, 327	358	53	
Prayers of the People	**Locally written**; options below; BCP Forms (*especially* 2 *or* 3)	329	387–393	54–55	
Offertory Sentence	"Restore us, O God of hosts; show the light of your countenance, and we shall be saved." Psalm 80	343–344	376–377		
Eucharistic Prayer	**One that allows use of the Advent preface; EOW1 Prayer 3 uses Wisdom imagery, which works well in Advent**	**2–340**	**B – 367**	3–62	
Proper Preface	Advent	345	378		
Breaking of the Bread (Fraction)	***Alleluias are permitted in Advent, but may be omitted.*** Christ our Passover (BCP) *or* Be known to us (Hymn S 171) *or* Blessed are those who are called (Hymn S 172)	337	365	God of promise – 69	
Postcommunion Prayer		339	**Almighty and everliving God – 365**	Loving God – 70	
Blessing	**Seasonal in BOS**				**10**
Dismissal	**Let us go forth in the Name of Christ**	340	366		
Notes					

Content Resources

Reading Between the Lines

A appeal for divine intervention, ripping through and rending the heavens is a plea for demonstration of God's power and judgement on human iniquity to nations of the world. Alarmingly, God can break and remold Israel, just as a potter can break and remold a pot. Metaphors of a shepherd leading a flock in the Psalm seek to temper divine anger. Waiting for such an intervention is not passive: Paul commends to the Corinthians' expectant longing for divine revelation. Similarly, Jesus' urgent call to discernment: *Watch out!* is both preparation for divine intervention and discernment of false rumors. Opponents and even heavenly powers, including the sun, moon, and stars will shake at signs of divine presence described in Daniel as "the Son of Humanity coming in clouds." This figure is a term used by Jesus in the gospels to speak of himself, here as an impending figure of judgement sending out angels to gather the chosen as a sign of the end.

Central Themes

Each year, at the beginning of Lent, on Ash Wednesday, we receive the Church's most powerful and direct invitation into the life of faith (BCP, 264). Our collect today stands to serve in the same manner and is a clear reminder of what our work should be in the days and weeks ahead. "Dear People of God: The season of Advent provides a time in which we who, because of notorious distractions and fear of death have strayed, are called out of that bright chaos into a still night. I invite you, therefore, in the name of the Church, to the observance of a holy Advent: by self-examination, prayer, and worship, now in the time of this mortal life. May God give us grace to cast away the works of darkness, which blur and distort the mysteries of death and new life, and grant us the armor of light, that we may wait in service and devotion, making way to receive the Christ child again. *Amen.*"

North of the equator, Advent is a time of days growing shorter and nights growing longer. The collect for Advent 1 invites us to "cast away the works of darkness, and put on the armor of light." This is an appropriate start for Advent, which is a both/and season. We are both preparing for the second coming of Christ and also retelling the stories of the preparation for the birth of Jesus. This collect invites us to solemnly reflect on the desolation of the end times, while also inviting us into a time of hope about God's incarnation. Preach into the both/and of Advent.

Note: Be very cautious about equating darkness with evil and light with good. *Concerns about how that corresponds to implicit association of these themes with skin color or racial characteristics should be kept in mind. Exploring additional ideas such as chaos/meaning or scarcity/abundance (including thirst/refreshment, hunger/fulfillment) may be helpful to expand the imagery.*

Engaging All Ages

Walking into the church you are reminded that something special is afoot. Your senses awake with the fragrance of evergreen boughs circling a ring of candles. Only one candle burns – a tiny but determined flicker of light. You notice that the inside of the church is dressed differently. Purples and blues adorn the worship space. The music is ripe with expectancy and the clergy and worship ministers move down the aisle with palpable anticipation. It is the First Sunday of Advent. Our journey towards Christmas begins. It's time to begin to prepare the manger of your heart.
Jesus is coming.

Prayers of the People: Option 1

Creator of the stars in the sky, the sun, and the moon, You are the light by which we wake and work.

Illumine our darkness, and keep us alert.

Surround your church, her leaders, and people, with your armor of light. We pray especially for *N.*, our presiding bishop; *N.*, our bishop; and *N.*, our priest. Strengthen them as they reach out to you in prayer and hope. Open their hearts to your will.

Illumine our darkness, and keep us alert.

We pray for our leaders: especially *N.*, our president; *N.*, our governor; and the Congress and courts of this land. Savior of the nations, guide those who govern, and awaken those they lead, that we may all live in the spirit of cooperation and share so that all have enough: food, care, and peace.

Illumine our darkness, and keep us alert.

For people across the world whose spirits bend under the yoke of oppression and struggle, give the people of this community a sense of togetherness and support. Open our eyes to those who fall by the wayside and whose faces and needs remain invisible.

Illumine our darkness, and keep us alert.

Lover of our souls, you continue to mold us in your image and hold us in your hands. We ask your blessing on those who struggle with illness, anxiety, grief, or isolation. Today we pray for *N.*

Illumine our darkness, and keep us alert.

Father of us all, we pray for those who have recently returned to your embrace and those who are broken with grief.

Prayers of the People: Option 2

As the new year dawns, let us pray to prepare for the Day of the Lord, saying "Holy One, enlighten the eyes of our hearts."

For the holy church of God, for its members in all places and our mission of creating peace and concord in the nations of the world, we pray:

Holy One, enlighten the eyes of our hearts.

For our beloved country and for those chosen to lead, for *N.*, our President, *N.*, our Governor, for those who represent us, and those who serve in courts of law, we pray:

Holy One, enlighten the eyes of our hearts.

For our Presiding Bishop, *N.*, our Bishop *N.*, for our parish clergy; for the ministry of all the baptized and for all the holy people of God, we pray:

Holy One, enlighten the eyes of our hearts.

For the welfare of God's creation, all nations, tribes, and peoples, help us to stay awake in expectation, caring for this world and one another day by day, we pray:

Holy One, enlighten the eyes of our hearts.

For the concerns of this family of faith, that we may do your will in feeding the hungry, working toward peace, and using our resources wisely, we pray:

Holy One, enlighten the eyes of our hearts.

For those who suffer in body, mind, or spirit, we pray:

Holy One, enlighten the eyes of our hearts.

For all those whom we love but see no longer, we pray:

Holy One, enlighten the eyes of our hearts.

I invite your additional prayers, silently or aloud:

Silence.

Presider: O God, you promise a peace the world cannot give: overwhelm us with such an awareness of your peace and presence that we become your peacemakers; through Jesus Christ our Redeemer. *Amen.*

Hymn Selections

The Hymnal 1982

Blest be the King whose coming 74
Hark! a thrilling voice is sounding 59
The King shall come when morning dawns 73
Before the Lord's eternal throne 391
Immortal, invisible, God only wise 423
Judge eternal, throned in splendor 596
O day of God, draw nigh 600, 601
How firm a foundation 636, 637
O Jesus, I have promised 655
Strengthen for service, Lord, the hands 312
"Sleepers, wake!" A voice astounds us 61, 62
Lo! he comes, with clouds descending 57, 58

Lift Every Voice and Sing II

Have thine own way, Lord 145
Better be ready 4
My Lord, what a morning 13

Wonder, Love, and Praise

God the sculptor of the mountains 746, 747
Signs of endings all around us 721

The Second Sunday of Advent

Sunday on or between December 4 and December 10

Prepare the way!

Anchor Points – The Propers and the Season

The fixed points for each service are the appointed or proper readings and collect as well as the themes of the day or season.

Readings and Psalm

Isaiah 40:1–11

Unlike other instances of the highway image in Isaiah where the people journey on a path prepared by God, this highway is prepared for God's travel. Verses 3–4 reflect the practice of sending messengers ahead of visiting royalty. The prophet shows that the comfort due to God's people is inextricably linked to God's presence and the revelation of glory. Joy, fearlessness, and comfort result from the supreme good news: "Here is your God!" (v. 9). As sovereign ruler and tender shepherd, God comforts the people.

Psalm 85:1–2,8–13

This lament seems to have been composed for a particular situation of affliction (vv. 4–6), and then to have passed into general use. Thanksgiving is given for the return from exile (vv. 1–3), and the Lord's continued help is requested. The Lord's answer comes (vv. 8–13), perhaps as an oracle uttered by a prophet or priest. Verse 11 beautifully reassures the people of God's gracious care. These four qualities – steadfast love, faithfulness, righteousness, and peace – spring from God and unite to work for the good of God's people.

2 Peter 3:8–15a

Today's reading responds to the anxiety of many about the apparent delay of Christ's eagerly expected second coming (3:1–7). Peter explains that this delay is not divine procrastination but divine mercy. God's view of time is different from ours, and God's forbearance will bring about repentance and salvation. Peter emphasizes how Christians are to live now, even indicating that their repentance may hasten the Lord's coming. Peter exhorts them to increase in the grace and knowledge of Jesus so as not to be useless.

Mark 1:1–8

Verse 1 stands as the title of the new literary form that Mark created. The word gospel, (Greek *evangelion*), in secular usage meant "good news," often about an important event such as the birthday of the Emperor Augustus. Mark's good news of Jesus Christ includes both the message that Jesus proclaimed and the person and significance of Jesus himself. Thus, his "gospel" is not only a life of Jesus but also a proclamation of the foundational belief that Jesus is the promised Jewish messiah ("Christ") and "Son of God."

Collect

Merciful God, who sent your messengers the prophets to preach repentance and prepare the way for our salvation: Give us grace to heed their warnings and forsake our sins, that we may greet with joy the coming of Jesus Christ our Redeemer; who lives and reigns with you and the Holy Spirit, one God, now and for ever. *Amen.*

Proper Preface

Advent – Because you sent your beloved Son to redeem us from sin and death, and to make us heirs in him of everlasting life; that when he shall come again in power and great triumph to judge the world, we may without shame or fear rejoice to behold his appearing. (Rite II, BCP 378; Rite I, BCP 345)

Seasonal Pairings

See the table below for choices appointed for this day. Preferences are put in **bold**. Not all choices are suitable for all congregations or community, though, so consider these preferences as a starting point before making a decision about your own congregation.

	Advent II	Rite I	Rite II	EOW1	BOS 2022
Color	Violet or Deep Blue				
Entrance Rite	Customary; EOW1 has an **Advent opening acclamation**	323	355	**50**	
Song of Praise/Kyrie	***Glory to God (Gloria in excelsis) is not used in Advent (BCP 406).*** Kyrie or **Trisagion**; BCP Canticles 9, 10, 16, 18 or EOW1 Canticles 16, 18, D, E, G.	324	356; C9 – 86; C10 – 86; C16 – 92; C18 – 93	C16 – 27; C18 – 28; D – 32; E – 32; G – 34	
Collect		159–160	211–212		
Creed	Nicene Creed	326, 327	358	53	
Prayers of the People	**Locally written**; options below; BCP Forms (*especially* 2 *or* 3)	329	387–393	54–55	
Offertory Sentence	"The Lord God will feed his flock like a shepherd; he will gather the lambs in his arms, and carry them in his bosom, and gently lead the mother sheep." (Isaiah 40)	343–344	376–377		
Eucharistic Prayer	**One that allows use of the Advent preface; EOW1 Prayer 3 uses Wisdom imagery, which works well in Advent**	**2–340**	**B – 367**	3–62	
Proper Preface	Advent	345	378		
Breaking of the Bread (Fraction)	***Alleluias are permitted in Advent, but may be omitted.*** Christ our Passover (BCP) *or* Be known to us (Hymn S 171) *or* Blessed are those who are called (Hymn S 172); Agnus Dei ("Lamb of God") with its connection to John the Baptizer would be appropriate for today.	337	365; 407	God of promise – 69	
Postcommunion Prayer		339	**Almighty and everliving God – 365**	Loving God – 70	
Blessing	**Seasonal in BOS**				**10**
Dismissal	**Let us go forth in the Name of Christ**	340	366		
Notes					

Additional Note:

The Feast of Our Lady of Guadalupe (December 12) may fall during this week. See above for more information about ways to celebrate this, if desired.

Content Resources

Reading Between the Lines

Themes and images ameliorating divine wrath are in evidence: consolation, mercy, truth, grace and forgiveness. Prophets prepare a way in the wilderness to make possible return of exiles to Israel in the time of Isaiah and restoration of Zion and to offer water purification for forgiveness of sins in the Second Temple Period from John the Baptist preparing "the way of the Lord" in the desert. But this is no time to delay. Mark uses the connective *kai,* (and) more frequently than English translations indicate to convey pace and urgency. Most translations slow down Mark's momentum by dividing the narrative into sentences and paragraphs for scripture readers, although Mark's momentum is driven by urgency of the good news of Jesus, not the drama of our Advent. Similarly, the Epistle picks up notions of rapid change and even a collapse of time signaling need for moral preparation for the day of the Lord.

Central Themes

Listening. Waiting. Stillness. It's a common theme across our texts, which claim over and over that it is in waiting and rest that we are restored. Strengthened. Reset to our original powers and purpose. Modern-day truth tellers urge us to stop. Unplug. To look up. Look around. Listen. This is how we make way for God's life to permeate ours. Quaker theologian Dr. Howard Macy writes "Waiting builds strength, in part, by moving us away from deceptive self-reliance and toward dependence on God. In stillness we not only grant God freedom to act but we also confess that we must sing 'the Lord is the strength of my life' (Ps 27:1). Dependence comes quite easily in times of emergency, of course, as when the Israelites were backed up against the sea, with Egyptian chariotry bearing down on them. In that instance Moses told the terrified people, 'The Lord will fight for you, you need only to be still' (Ex 14:14). But when we are in less danger of being run over by enemy chariot wheels, many of us tend to rely on our own cunning and prowess to face everyday life, compounding the error of pride with a false estimate of our resources for living. Waiting wants to teach, in part, that God is more than an emergency kit to be broken open only after we have made a mess of our life on our own."[1] The prophets have spoken – what are you waiting for – or are you waiting at all?

This week's reading from 2 Peter addresses our impatience with the way things are, whether they be issues in our own lives, the life of our congregation, or the world around us. We cry out to God, "How long, O Lord?!" and the answer is "As long as it takes." Pick up the newspaper to see what God is waiting on now: gun violence, dishonest politics, greed. Look in your own community and your own heart to see the work you still have to do. God's patience is mighty. God is waiting. It is our work that needs to be done.

Engaging All Ages

John the Baptist is one of the Bible's most interesting characters. In today's gospel we meet him for the first time. What if John were to appear in your worship service today in real time? Could someone (perhaps dressed outrageously) suddenly enter and interrupt your sermon with calls to "Prepare the way of the Lord!" while sprinkling the congregation with water? What kind of dialogue might you have with them in real time to bring John's message of two thousand years ago applicable today? What does repentance mean now, in this year?

Prayers of the People: Option 1

Let us lift up our voices to God in strength, saying, "Be patient with us and prepare us, Lord."

Together as your Church, we long to see your face. Speak to us, Lord, as we walk through the wilderness listening for the sound of your voice. Give our leaders patience, wisdom, and a heart for your will: for *N.*, our presiding bishop; *N.*, our bishop; and *N.*, our priest.

In your mercy,

be patient with us and prepare us, Lord.

1 Howard R. Macy, *Rhythms of the Inner Life – Yearning for Closeness With God* (The Barclay Press: Newberg OR, 1988 1992): 52.

We pray for all who govern, especially *N.*, our president, and for the Congress and courts of this land. Guide the leaders of the nations as they work for the welfare of their people and the good of all.

In your mercy,

be patient with us and prepare us, Lord.

Awaken us to the suffering of people near us and those far from us. Call forth in us a spirit of generosity and kindness. Equip us to respond to their needs. Arouse in us a sense of urgency to demonstrate your Good News in our lives and voice it, that all may hear. Make us messengers of your love.

In your mercy,

be patient with us and prepare us, Lord.

We ask you to comfort those who have lost hope, who struggle with anxiety about the future, who live in fear. Bring healing to those for whom we now pray: *N.* We pray for those who have died, that their memories be blessings in our lives.

In your mercy,

be patient with us and prepare us, Lord.

The Celebrant adds a concluding Collect.

Prayers of the People: Option 2

As we heed the call to prepare the way of the Lord, let us prepare our hearts in prayer, saying, "Come, Lord Jesus."

Leader: We pray for those who work to prepare the way of the Lord, especially those in the Church. We pray for our Presiding Bishop, *N.*, for our Bishop(s), *N.*, for our parish clergy and lay leaders, and for all those who serve God's people. May your Church strive to be a vessel of peace, O God, and hear our prayer:

Come, Lord Jesus.

We pray for our President, *N.*, for the Congress and the Supreme Court, for our Governor *N.* and our Mayor *N.*; we pray for all those in positions of power, that they may seek to work for justice and peace in every place, leveling mountains of fear and raising valleys of hopelessness, that your will may be known on earth. May you guide and govern us, O God, and hear our prayer:

Come, Lord Jesus.

We pray for nations torn by war, strife, and violence. We pray for all those in harm's way. We pray for those who hunger and those who suffer for the sake of conscience. We pray for those who seek refuge far from home.

May they find consolation and strength in the face of your Son Jesus, O God, and hear our prayer:

Come, Lord Jesus.

We pray for all those who struggle and suffer. We pray for the poor, the sick, the oppressed and those in prison. We pray for all victims of violent crimes and their families. We pray for those who mourn and for those who have known bitterness. We pray all those with any need we name now, silently or aloud . . .

Silence

Shine the light of your Christ into our broken world, O God, and hear our prayer:

Come, Lord Jesus.

We pray for this community of faith, that, like John the Baptizer, we may bear witness that God is coming into the world in our own lives. Give us hope and strength, O God, and hear our prayer:

Come, Lord Jesus.

We praise you for the manifold gifts of our lives. We give thanks for all the blessings of our lives, including those that you would like to name now, silently or aloud . . .

Silence

We pray that you may fill us with your grace, that we may be truly thankful, O God, and hear our prayer:

Come, Lord Jesus.

We pray for those who have died. We pray that we may join with them, with [the blessed Virgin Mary, blessed John the Baptizer, and] all the saints in the fellowship of the Church Triumphant.

O God, hear our prayer:

Come, Lord Jesus.

The Celebrant offers a concluding collect.

Hymns for the Day

The Hymnal 1982

Blessed be the God of Israel 444
Redeemer of the nations, come 55
Savior of the nations, come 54
Comfort, comfort ye my people 67
O heavenly Word, eternal Light 6 3, 64
Once he came in blessing 53
Songs of praise the angels sang 426
The Lord will come and not be slow 462
O day of God, draw nigh 600, 601
Hark! a thrilling voice is sounding 59
Herald, sound the note of judgment 70
On Jordan's bank the Baptist's cry 76
Prepare the way, O Zion 65
There's a voice in the wilderness crying 75
What is the crying at Jordan? 69

Lift Every Voice and Sing II

Prepare ye the way of the Lord 11
Christ is coming 6

Wonder, Love, and Praise

Blessed be the God of Israel 889

The Third Sunday of Advent

Sunday on or between December 11 and December 17

The promised day of God is dawning. John is the herald of that day.

Anchor Points – The Propers and the Season

The fixed points for each service are the appointed or proper readings and collect as well as the themes of the day or season.

Readings and Psalm

Isaiah 61:1–4,8–11

The prophet speaks a message of hope to those returning from exile in Babylon. He describes an ultimate year of Jubilee – a time of full blessing brought by divine favor. The blessing is accompanied by a day of vindication that will bring full restitution for injustice. Thus, he looks back to the Mosaic law regarding the jubilee year and forward to the day of the Lord.

Psalm 126

In this psalm the people sing for joy over their deliverance from captivity. The psalmist recalls the Lord's restoration of Zion (vv. 1–3), pleads for continued restoration in the present (v. 4) and hopes for renewed joy to come out of sorrow (vv. 5–6).

Canticle 15 (Luke 1:46b–55)

This excerpt from Mary's song of praise, the Magnificat, echo many gospel themes stressed by Luke: the joy of salvation, the reversal of this world's values, God's option for the poor and lowly, and the fulfillment of the Old Testament promises. This song of God's lowly handmaid is a foreshadowing of the way in which the Kingdom of God will transform our world.

1 Thessalonians 5:16–24

The Thessalonian Christians are to welcome the charismatic gifts, but with discernment. In speaking of spirit, soul, and body, Paul does not intend to divide the human person into separate components. Rather, in Hebraic style, he describes to the human person in the threefold components of relation to God, of present vitality and of physical body. God both wills and works the sanctification of the total person.

John 1:6–8,19–28

All of the gospels portray John the Baptist as the forerunner of Jesus. The people of Jesus's time had a variety of expectations about the appearance of one or more figures who would bring the current age to an end. The most common hope centered on the coming of a political messiah who would be a member of the royal line of King David. Elijah was also expected as a herald. There was also a hope for the revival of prophecy by a prophet-like-Moses. When questioned, John the Baptist rejects all of these identifications. He is only "the voice of one crying out in the wilderness" (v. 23; Isaiah 40:3). Likewise, the baptism that he practices points away from himself. It is only a preparation for the One already present but as yet undisclosed.

Collect

Stir up your power, O Lord, and with great might come among us; and, because we are sorely hindered by our sins, let your bountiful grace and mercy speedily help and deliver us; through Jesus Christ our Lord, to whom, with you and the Holy Spirit, be honor and glory, now and forever. *Amen.*

Proper Preface

Advent – Because you sent your beloved Son to redeem us from sin and death, and to make us heirs in him of everlasting life; that when he shall come again in power and great triumph to judge the world, we may without shame or fear rejoice to behold his appearing. (Rite II, BCP 378; Rite I, BCP 345)

Seasonal Pairings

See the table below for choices appointed for this day. Preferences are put in **bold.** Not all choices are suitable for all congregations or community, though, so consider these preferences as a starting point before making a decision about your own congregation.

	Advent III	Rite I	Rite II	EOW1	BOS 2022
Color	Violet *or* Deep Blue *or* Rose				
Entrance Rite	Customary; EOW1 has an **Advent opening acclamation**	323	355	**50**	
Song of Praise/Kyrie	***Glory to God (Gloria in excelsis) is not used in Advent (BCP 406).*** Kyrie or **Trisagion**; BCP Canticles 11, 16, 18 or EOW1 Canticles 16, 18, E, G, H. (If Canticle 15 is used in the readings, rather than Psalm 126, it would **not** be a suitable choice to use for the Song of Praise.)	324	356; C11 – 87; C16 – 92; C18 – 94	C16 – 27; C18 – 28; E – 32; G – 34; H – 34	
Collect		159–160	211–212		
Creed	Nicene Creed	326, 327	358	53	
Prayers of the People	**Locally written**; options below; BCP Forms (*especially* 2 *or* 3)	329	387–393	54–55	
Offertory Sentence	"May the God of peace himself sanctify you entirely; and may your spirit and soul and body be kept sound and blameless at the coming of our Lord Jesus Christ." (I Thessalonians)	343–344	376–377		
Eucharistic Prayer	**One that allows use of the Advent preface; EOW1 Prayer 3 uses Wisdom imagery, which works well in Advent**	**2–340**	**B – 367**	3–62	
Proper Preface	Advent	345	378		
Breaking of the Bread (Fraction)	***Alleluias are permitted in Advent, but may be omitted.*** Christ our Passover (BCP) *or* Be known to us (Hymn S 171) *or* Blessed are those who are called (Hymn S 172); Agnus Dei ("Lamb of God"), with its connection to John the Baptizer would be appropriate for today.	337	365; 407	God of promise – 69	
Postcommunion Prayer		339	**Almighty and everliving God – 365**	Loving God – 70	
Blessing	**Seasonal in BOS**				**10**
Dismissal	**Let us go forth in the Name of Christ**	340	366		
Notes	In some places, the color rose is used on this Sunday, recalling a time when Advent was practiced as a more penitential season and needed a "lightening up" Sunday, traditionally called "Gaudete Sunday."				

Additional Note:

The Feast of Our Lady of Guadalupe (December 12) may fall during this week. See above for more information about ways to celebrate this, if desired. The Feast of St. Thomas the Apostle (December 21) falls during this week or next.

Content Resources

Reading Between the Lines

Themes of grace and comfort on this Gaudete Sunday combine with encouragement and joy even for exiles, "to provide for those who mourn in Zion – oil of gladness instead of mourning;" and for Mary, a teenager in a tiny

Galilean village, who sings, "My spirit rejoices in God my Savior." Paul encourages prayer practices that have become the fabric of monastic life, "Rejoice always; pray without ceasing." The poetic language and poignancy of Psalm 126, sung perhaps by captured Israelite prisoners in Babylon, begins by describing conditions of deprivation and exile, building upon them by giving voice to a dream of restoration. All Truth and Reconciliation work starts with truth. No reconciliation or hope is possible without acknowledging true accounts of the past.

The Magnificat allows us to recognize the prophetic voice of Mary before she gives birth to Jesus. In it, she describes God's strong arm acting on behalf of the humble and meek, and against the proud and powerful, and she will teach Jesus this theology of reversal. In fact, Advent is a Marian month. In it we observe the feast of the Immaculate Conception, the Annunciation, and stories of Jesus' birth. Syrian Christian Tradition celebrates in the Sundays before Christmas a series of annunciations: to Zechariah, to Mary, to Elizabeth (Mary's Visitation), and to Joseph with the nativity of John the Baptist.

In John's Gospel, John the Baptist is a voice of witness attesting frequently and emphatically to the primacy of Jesus, and to Jesus' designation as Lamb of God, the sacrificial Passover Lamb who takes away the sin of the world (1:29). In John's Gospel, Jesus dies on Passover.

Central Themes

There was a person sent from God whose name was You. You come as a witness to testify to the light, so that others might believe through you. You yourself are not the light, but you come to testify to the light.

That is our work as those who serve God in the church, to do as John does – point to Jesus. We are challenged by bishops and staff parish committees and strangers on airplanes or at parties – what, exactly, do you think you are doing, and what qualifies you to do it? Just as they demanded of John, "Who are you?, let us have an answer for those who sent us. What do you say about yourself?" You say, "I am the voice of one crying out in the wilderness, 'Make straight the way of the Lord.'" By virtue of our own baptisms we are commissioned and sent forth to baptize others into this new life. Being mindful and focused on that vocation has the power to transform planning for worship, Christian formation, outreach, and justice initiatives. Not to point to ourselves. Not to call attention to our clever marketing or evangelism programs. But to pull Jesus out from the crowds, fling your arm around his shoulder like you might your new best friend at a gathering, and say, "Here. Here is someone I really want you to meet." You are called to testify to that light.

As mentioned above, a traditional Advent feast in Mexico is the Feast of Our Lady of Guadalupe, December 12th. That feast falls either during the second or third week of Advent. One way to make that connection on Sunday morning is using the option for the Song of Mary, the Magnificat, in place of the psalm. In that canticle, we hear Mary's fulsome response to God's astounding action in her very body. The artist Ben Wildflower has a powerful woodcut of Mary not as meek and mild, but a woman of power and strength.[1] Mary can open up our preaching in myriad ways today as well as Advent IV.

Engaging All Ages

What are moments of peace or statements of hope that you can invite children to name during the liturgy? Are there youth who might write the prayers of the people for this Sunday that connect to the hope and light that we wait for this Advent season?

Prayers of the People: Option 1

Presider: Holy God, you have spoken through your prophets and called us to make straight the way of the Lord: Visit us with your grace to cause righteousness and praise to spring up before all the nations, as we pray: God has done great things for us, and we are glad indeed.

Litanist: O God of peace, you have called your people to rejoice always and to pray without ceasing, giving thanks in all circumstances: Sanctify your Church and her members that our spirit and soul and body may be kept sound and blameless at the coming of our Lord Jesus Christ.

God has done great things for us,

and we are glad indeed.

God of Justice and Mercy, you love justice and hate wrongdoing: Guide our leaders and all in authority, that they may bring good news to the oppressed, bind up the brokenhearted, proclaim liberty to the captives, repair the ruined cities and cause righteousness and praise to spring up before all the nations.

God has done great things for us,

and we are glad indeed.

God of Compassion, look upon the needs of the world: Proclaim the year of your favor, and clothe your

1 https://benwildflower.com/products/magnificat-t-shirt

children with the garments of salvation and the robe of righteousness.

God has done great things for us,

and we are glad indeed.

God of Grace, be among us in this community that we may be a people whom you have sanctified to testify to the light and to become oaks of righteousness.

God has done great things for us,

and we are glad indeed.

Receive our prayers for those for whom we pray in intercession, especially...

Hear our gratitude as we offer our thanksgivings, especially for...

Comfort all who mourn, giving them a garland instead of ashes, the oil of gladness instead of mourning, the mantle of praise instead of a faint spirit, as we remember before you those who have died, especially...

God has done great things for us,

and we are glad indeed.

Presider: Loving God, your Advent people look expectantly for the coming of Christ: As the earth brings forth its shoots, and as a garden causes what is sown in it to spring up, nurture our prayers and the thoughts of our hearts, that we may receive with joy the goodness of your strength and live in the power of the Holy Spirit, through Jesus Christ our Savior. *Amen.*

Prayers of the People: Option 2

As witnesses to your light and truth, we come to you in prayer, O Lord.

Infuse the heart of your church with your Spirit and focus it on your mission. Renew your people and their leaders as they serve your purpose. Remind us continually whose we are.

Silence

Turn the hearts and actions of all the world's leaders to justice and peace. We pray for N our President, N our Governor, the Congress and courts of this land.

Silence

Open our eyes to what is going on around us. Open our hearts to our brothers and sisters throughout the world. Move us to open our hands in love when they are in need and to stand up for them when they are oppressed. We pray for those suffering from natural disasters, from unjust economies, from hunger and want.

Silence

We know people around us who are suffering from anxiety, scarcity, illness, and loneliness. Some of them we know, and most are unknown to us. We ask that you assure them of your presence and sustain them with your grace. We pray for those we know by name:

Silence

Our hearts break when someone whom we love dies. Today we mourn for ____________ , recently departed. May we be a comfort as we walk with his/her grieving loved ones.

Hymns for the Day

The Hymnal 1982

Blessed be the God of Israel 444
Tell out, my soul, the greatness of the Lord 437, 438
Watchman, tell us of the night 640
Blest be the King whose coming 74
Hail to the Lord's Anointed 616
Hark! the glad sound! the Savior comes 71, 72
O day of God, draw nigh 600, 601
If thou but trust in God to guide thee 635
O heavenly Word, eternal Light 63, 64
Rejoice, the Lord is King! 481
Herald, sound the note of judgment 70
On Jordan's bank the Baptist's cry 76
Prepare the way, O Zion 65
There's a voice in the wilderness crying 75

Lift Every Voice and Sing II

Prepare ye the way of the Lord 11

Wonder, Love, and Praise

Gracious Spirit, give your servants 782
Blessed be the God of Israel 889

The Fourth Sunday of Advent

Sunday on or between December 18 and December 24

Mary said, "Here am I, the servant of the Lord;
let it be with me according to your word."

Anchor Points – The Propers and the Season

The fixed points for each service are the appointed or proper readings and collect as well as the themes of the day or season.

Readings and Psalm

2 Samuel 7:1–11,16

After the fall of Jerusalem and the overthrow of the monarchy (587 BCE) the Davidic covenant came to be understood as God's assurance of a future ideal king from David's line, and this hope became an essential part of the Jewish expectation of the Messiah.

Canticle 15 (Luke 1:46b–55)

Mary's joyous song of praise, the Magnificat, echoes many of Luke's gospel themes: the joy of salvation, the reversal of this world's values, God's option for the poor and lowly, and the fulfillment of the Old Testament promises. This song of God's lowly handmaid is a foreshadowing of the way in which the Kingdom of God will transform our world.

Psalm 89:1–4, 19–26

Psalm 89 is a royal psalm comprised of a hymn praising God's power and faithfulness (vv. 1–18), a recapitulation of the covenant between God and David's descendants (vv. 19–37), and a lament praying for deliverance from enemies (vv. 38–52).

Romans 16:25–27

Today's reading is an expression of praise or doxology closing Paul's letter to the Romans. The good news that Paul makes known, the proclamation about Jesus Christ, is the "revelation of the mystery" (v. 25) of God's plan of salvation hidden in the Hebrew Bible and now made known in Christ.

Luke 1:26–38

Luke's infancy narratives show that the meaning of Jesus's life, death, and resurrection was already implicit in the circumstances of his conception and birth. He emphasizes the theological significance of these events and so presents the gospel message through them.

Collect

Purify our conscience, Almighty God, by your daily visitation, that your Son Jesus Christ, at his coming, may find in us a mansion prepared for himself; who lives and reigns with you, in the unity of the Holy Spirit, one God, now and for ever. *Amen.*

Proper Preface

Advent – Because you sent your beloved Son to redeem us from sin and death, and to make us heirs in him of everlasting life; that when he shall come again in power and great triumph to judge the world, we may without shame or fear rejoice to behold his appearing. (Rite II, BCP 378; Rite I, BCP 345)

Seasonal Pairings

See the table below for choices appointed for this day. Preferences are put in **bold**. Not all choices are suitable for all congregations or community, though, so consider these preferences as a starting point before making a decision about your own congregation.

	Advent IV	Rite I	Rite II	EOW1	BOS 2022
Color	Violet *or* Deep Blue				
Entrance Rite	Customary; EOW1 has an **Advent opening acclamation**	323	355	**50**	
Song of Praise/Kyrie	***Glory to God (Gloria in excelsis) is not used in Advent (BCP 406).*** Kyrie or **Trisagion**; BCP Canticles 9, 11, 18 or EOW1 Canticles 18, C, E, J, R, S. (If Canticle 15 is used in the readings, rather than Psalm 89, it would **not** be a suitable choice to use for the Song of Praise.)	324	356; C9 – 86; C11 – 87; C18 – 93	C18 – 28; C – 31; E – 32; J – 35; R – 40; S – 40	
Collect		159–160	211–212		
Creed	Nicene Creed	326, 327	358	53	
Prayers of the People	**Locally written**; options below; BCP Forms (*especially* 2 *or* 3)	329	387–393	54–55	
Offertory Sentence	"Mary said, 'My soul proclaims the greatness of the Lord, my spirit rejoices in God my Savior;'" (Canticle 15)	343–344	376–377		
Eucharistic Prayer	**One that allows use of the Advent preface; EOW1 Prayer 3 uses Wisdom imagery, which works well in Advent**	**2–340**	**B – 367**	3–62	
Proper Preface	Advent	345	378		
Breaking of the Bread (Fraction)	***Alleluias are permitted in Advent, but may be omitted.*** Christ our Passover (BCP) *or* Be known to us (Hymn S 171) *or* Blessed are those who are called (Hymn S 172)	337	365; 407	God of promise – 69	
Postcommunion Prayer		339	**Almighty and everliving God – 365**	Loving God – 70	
Blessing	**Seasonal in BOS**				**10**
Dismissal	**Let us go forth in the Name of Christ**	340	366		
Notes					

Additional Note:

The Feast of St. Thomas the Apostle (December 21) may fall during this week.

Content Resources

Reading Between the Lines

Readings ask how to make space or room for God. Nathan the prophet conveys to David not God's acquiescence in David's building plans, but instead, God's promise to David to establish his throne and lineage. Luke records that in the sixth month of Elizabeth's pregnancy, the angel Gabriel announces to Mary the advent of her child. Surprised, she "thinks carefully" about Gabriel's words, questioning him in dialogue how this will take place. Her query is at least as important as her *fiat*. It elicits a description of conception by means of the Holy Spirit, details of the child to be born, and the verification of the promise through news of Elizabeth's pregnancy: "this is the sixth month for her who was said to be barren." Mary departs at once for the hill town and the house of her kinswoman Elizabeth, and her husband Zachariah, likely seeking verification. In the 14th C. Chora Church, now a museum in Istanbul, Theodore Metochites renders an icon of Mary as the container (or space, Greek: *chora*) of the uncontainable, and Christ the Savior, both the second person of the Trinity, and the church itself, as the container (or space, Greek: *chora*) of all the living.

Central Themes

If you've had the honor of exploring this story in a circle of children, you have benefited from the frankness of their doubt and the joy of their reckless belief, not unlike their engagement with the story of Santa. They believe that some of it is true and that some of it is not actually possible. But they want very much for it all to have happened, because it means presents for them, and that Jesus will be born. So they'll just go along with the parts about the flying sleigh and the egg being fertilized with no sperm. Children are surrounded by stories with "messages," stories as vehicles for moral teaching – picture books with not-very-well-hidden lessons about the consequences of their choices. Whether modern and factual biographies or ancient fairy tales and mythology, they are able to recognize what matters in a story and have finely tuned lie detectors to call out the inconsistencies. And they seem quite comfortable in that space in distilling what is essential in the story, but not being bothered by the number of bears or the color of the cape. This particular story finds them in deep discussion about strangers, about pregnancy, and about being chosen by God to do hard stuff. It is easy for the modern thinker to brush it off as a big story used to make sure we keep telling the story. Another miraculous tale in which a larger truth, probably more important than the miracle itself, is conveyed. What can we learn from children about what's lost, and what's found, when insisting on fact over truth?

The theme of homelessness is strong on Advent 4. Many congregations have begun their La Posadas as a reminder of Mary and Joseph repeatedly asking for a place to stay and finding no room at the inns. In our Old Testament reading, David is ready to make God a house, and God is ready to make God's people a home. Check out artist Kelly Latimer's "Holy Family of the Streets" icon. What local issues of housing or homelessness might you connect to the readings this week?

Engaging All Ages

A Jesse Tree is a depiction in art of the ancestors of Christ, including the House of David as noted in today's lections. To visually represent the stories of God's people that symbolize "A shoot shall come out from the stock of Jesse, and a branch shall grow out of his roots" (Isa. 11:1), invite the congregation to create a Jesse Tree. In advance, assign families a story (Creation, Adam and Eve, Noah, Abraham, Isaac, Jacob, Joseph, Moses, Ruth, David, Solomon, Mary and Joseph, and others) and ask them to create or bring an ornament to represent the story to place on a tree within your church. Alternatively, hold a Jesse Tree ornament-making event. Numerous sources for their creation can be found on the internet.

Prayers of the People: Option 1

You astounded Mary with her invitation to bear your Son. Surprise us with your delight in us, with your invitation to do your will, with the light of Christ growing with in us. Surprise us, Lord, again and again.

Silence

We are your children. Increase the faith in us, day by day, season by season. Empower us to seek and do your will. Cause us to surprise ourselves by opening up our hearts to find that you are always there.

Surprise us, Lord.

We pray that the leaders of all the nations demonstrate wisdom and a heart for the good of their people and peace between neighbors.

Surprise us, Lord.

We pray that the peoples of all the nations realize freedom and an end to hunger and poverty. Enable a spirit of generosity to flow throughout the world.

Surprise us, Lord.

We pray for our neighbors with whom we work and live. Surprise us with what can be accomplished when we work together for the common good. Open our eyes to see you in each person we meet. Open our hearts and hands to each need we encounter.

Surprise us, Lord.

We pray for healing for those with troubled spirits, who suffer from addiction, loneliness, and despair. We ask for healing for those who struggle with the consequences of illness or recovering from surgery. Reveal to us how to join in your saving and healing work through the power of your Spirit.

Surprise us, Lord.

We pray for those who have died and now rest in your eternal embrace. May the light of your love surround them and comfort those who grieve their deaths. Surprise them with the sure hope of the Resurrection.

Surprise us, Lord.

We are your people. Increase the faith in us day by day. Surprise us with your loving, liberating, and life-giving presence.

Surprise us, Lord, again and again.

Prayers of the People: Option 2

Deacon or Presider: Let us join with Mary in her song of joy, and proclaim the greatness of the Lord as we pray.

Intercessor: We rejoice in the community of faith and pray for [*N.* and] all those preparing for baptism; we pray for our Presiding Bishop, *N.*, for our Bishop(s), *N.*, for our parish lay leaders and clergy, and for all those who, like Mary, have said yes to God.

Come, O come, Emmanuel.

We pray for our President, *N.*, for our Governor *N.* and our Mayor *N.*; we pray for all those in positions of power, that they may seek to lift up the lowly.

Come, O come, Emmanuel.

We pray for nations torn by war, strife, and violence. We pray for all those in harm's way. We pray that the hungry may be filled with good things and that those with plenty may learn to become empty for those in need.

Come, O come, Emmanuel.

We pray for all those who struggle and suffer. We pray for the poor, the sick, the oppressed and those in prison. We pray for those who mourn. We pray for all those with any need we name now, silently or aloud . . .

Silence

Remember your promise of mercy, Holy One, and help your people.

Come, O come, Emmanuel.

We praise you for the manifold gifts of our lives. We rejoice and exult in you, O God, and we give thanks for all the blessings of our lives, including those that you would like to name now, silently or aloud . . .

Silence

We pray that you may fill us with your grace, that we, like Mary, may bear Christ into our lives.

Come, O come, Emmanuel.

We pray for those who have died. We pray that we may join with them, [with the blessed Virgin Mary,] and with all the saints in the fellowship of the Church Triumphant.

Come, O come, Emmanuel.

The Presider offers a concluding collect.

Hymns for the Day

The Hymnal 1982

God himself is with us 475
Tell out, my soul, the greatness of the Lord 437, 438
Blessed be the God of Israel 444
Sing we of the blessed Mother 278
The angel Gabriel from heaven came 265
The Word whom earth and sea and sky 263, 264
Virgin-born, we bow before thee 258
O come, O come, Emmanuel 56
Come, thou long-expected Jesus 66
To the Name of our salvation 248, 249
Creator of the stars of night 60
Gabriel's message does away 270
Nova, nova 266
Praise we the Lord this day 267
Ye who claim the faith of Jesus 268, 269

Lift Every Voice and Sing II

Salamu Maria / Hail Mary, O Mother 51

Wonder, Love, and Praise

Blessed be the God of Israel 889

Christmas

Preparing for Christmas

Theoretically, no season should present fewer difficulties for planning than Christmas. It is a principal feast, usually with one of the largest congregations of the year. It has some of the best and best-known music, a clear theme, immense popularity, and people expect everything at the Christmas services to be done to the best of everyone's ability. In practice, there are many problems. Christmas is a victim of its secular success. Christmas carols have been playing in shopping malls for months. Everyone is so busy getting ready for Christmas that it is hard to find time for liturgical planning, choir and acolyte rehearsals, or altar work. Often children are so excited about the coming of Santa Claus that it is difficult to get their attention to celebrate the coming of Christ.

Christmas celebrates the birth of our Lord and the incarnation of the Divine Word. Its principal Gospel reading is John 1:1–14, not the Lukan account of the birth in Bethlehem (Luke 2:1–14) traditionally read at the first eucharistic celebration (the "midnight mass"). *The Book of Common Prayer* gives three different sets of readings for the day, as well as readings for Evening Prayer on Christmas Eve and both Morning and Evening Prayer on Christmas Day. Few congregations will have occasion to use all of them.

A Service Involving Children

The scheduling of Christmas services should be one of the first concerns of the liturgy committee. A nighttime, although not necessarily midnight, Eucharist has become the principal Christmas service in most congregations. At least one service should be scheduled for Christmas Day. It is important that thought be given to including the children of the parish in the Christmas celebration, and many congregations plan an early evening service on Christmas Eve, often beginning with a procession to the crèche, especially for younger children and their families. They often find older parishioners also like to come at an earlier hour.

Either the first or second set of readings, including the Lukan nativity Gospel, is usually the best choice for this service. Familiar Christmas carols and hymns can be sung and the most familiar service music used. If there is a junior choir, they might well lead the singing. *The Book of Occasional Services* contains prayers to be used at a station (or stop) at the crèche during the entrance procession.[1] Children can bring the figures (or at least the figure of the Christ child) to the crèche at this time and the nativity scene be set in place.

There are really no good alternatives to Gloria in excelsis for Christmas, but if it is not feasible to sing it at this service, it is better to sing a hymn such as "Angels we have heard on high" (Hymn 96), with its refrain of "Gloria in excelsis Deo," than to recite the Gloria. People usually sing on festive occasions, and to recite the song the angels sang really seems to reduce the element of festivity.

The first of the three prayer book collects is most suitable for a Christmas Eve service. Eucharistic Prayer B, or Eucharistic Prayer II in Rite One, are appropriate choices. One of the fraction anthems including "Alleluia!" will add to the festive spirit, and the Christmas blessing from the BOS[2] concludes with the Christmas theme.

An alternative possibility for a more solemn beginning to the service is to use the Service of Light from the Order for Evening, lighting all five candles of the Advent wreath, now adorned with white candles and a Christmas bow, and substituting Gloria in excelsis or a Christmas hymn for *Phos hilaron*. This is also a possible beginning for the midnight eucharist.

A Christmas Vigil[3]

Expanding upon that use of the Service of Light as the solemn beginning for a Christmas Eve Service, one could do an opening vigil for the service. Previous editions of the BOS gave direction for such a vigil before the midnight Eucharist. It begins with the Service of Light[4], using the Collect for the First Sunday after Christmas Day as the Prayer for Light. The seasonal Lucernarium

1 BOS 2022, 35–36.
2 BOS 2022, 11.
3 *The Book of Occasional Services 2003* (New York, NY: Church Publishing, 2004), 33.
4 *Found in* "Order of Worship for the Evening," BCP, 109.

(Hymn S 310 in the Accompaniment Edition of the Hymnal) may be used or Psalm 113 during the candle lighting, which would include the Advent Wreath. The *Magnificat* or a suitable hymn, such as "Of the Father's love begotten" may substitute for the *Phos hilaron.* A series of readings from Scripture follows. The readings may be adapted from the Christmas Festival of Lessons and Carols, also found in the BOS. Interspersed among the readings may be anthems, canticles, hymns, carols, or instrumental music. After the last reading, the procession to the creche may take place, using the prayers for the blessing of a creche mentioned above. The procession would then move to the altar area and the service would begin in its usual way. The length of the vigil will vary depending upon how much is read and sung. Some congregations will find it a most fitting way to prepare for their Christmas Eucharist. If it is to be done, it needs to be planned well in advance, with the instrumental musicians and singers taking an active part in the planning.

"Midnight Mass"

The nighttime Christmas Eve Eucharist is, de facto, the chief Christmas service. Traditionally, the readings called "Christmas Day" are assigned to this service. Some congregations, recognizing that few people will attend the daytime service on Christmas Day and hear the prologue to John read, either use "Christmas Day III" at midnight or alternate the readings among the services over the three years of the lectionary, using John 1 every third year. The second collect, which refers to "this holy night," is obviously intended for this service. If the congregation uses both Rite One and Rite Two, the relative strengths and weaknesses of using both for the Christmas Eucharist need to be weighed.

Whatever ceremonial embellishments the congregation is accustomed to use on important occasions should be used for this service: incense, golden vestments, handbells, trumpets, processional torches, banners, etc. A processional hymn with a station at the crèche makes a good beginning. Certainly a festal setting of Gloria in excelsis is called for. It is possible to sing (chant) the opening acclamation before it and the collect for the day after it. If this sounds festive to the parish, it can be a good idea; otherwise, it may merely seem merely fussy. The appointed psalm can be sung (even if it is normally spoken) after the first lesson and a congregational hymn, instrumental music, or a choir anthem sung after the second reading, during the gospel procession. It is important that the congregation have opportunity to sing familiar Christmas hymns, so a comprehensive plan for singing congregational hymns and choir music is helpful. If a formal Gospel procession is not a part of your usual Sunday services, this may be an occasion to implement one.

Some congregations will feel that Christmas is an "occasion" to omit the confession of sin, to make the service more festal. Others will feel that it is important to use the confession, since there will be a number of people present who do not attend church regularly, and the confession is an important part of their preparation for Christmas communion. One possibility is to use a form of the Prayers of the People (1, 5, or 6) that contains a petition for the forgiveness of sins, but some people will still consider it inadequate. There is no "correct" choice, but the discussion of whether to use the confession or not should in itself be valuable to the liturgy committee.

The Christmas proper preface states clearly the theological meaning of the festival, and it is desirable to choose a eucharistic prayer that permits its use. Eucharistic Prayer B, as we have already said, is the best choice with Rite Two. As at the earlier service, a different fraction anthem from that used during Advent will emphasize the change in season, and the more solemn form of the Christmas blessing from the BOS forms a fitting conclusion to the service.

The Twelve Days

The liturgical celebration of Christmas lasts twelve days, until the Epiphany on January 6, and includes the feasts of St. Stephen the first martyr (December 26), John the Apostle (December 27), the Holy Innocents murdered by Herod in his search for the Christ child (December 28), and the Holy Name of Jesus (January 1). Only Holy Name and Epiphany are observed on Sunday if they fall on that day. If December 26, 27, or 28 falls on Sunday, the saints' days are transferred to the following weekdays. If more than one of them is transferred, they are transferred as a block, to maintain the possibility of celebrating all three of them. There may be one or two Sundays after Christmas. Their services should be planned to share in as much of the Christmas festivity as possible, including liberal use of Christmas hymns and carols. The BOS contains instructions for a Christmas Festival of Lessons and Carols similar in structure to the Advent version of the service, and this may be planned for some appropriate occasion during the twelve days.

The celebration of the twelve days is extraordinarily difficult in American culture. The "Christmas season" to most Americans begins on or before Thanksgiving and ends on December 25. Scheduling Christmas events after Christmas seems an almost blatantly countercultural act. Holy Innocents Day (December 28) is a traditional day for a children's party. The scheduling, planning, and explaining of festive events at the church during the twelve days is one way to give reality to the season.

New Year's Day

Probably little can be done to celebrate St. Stephen, St. John, and Holy Innocents beyond scheduling a celebration of the Eucharist on those days for those willing and able to attend. But a service can be planned for the New Year. January 1, now called the Holy Name of Jesus by Episcopalians and the Solemnity of Mary the Mother of God by Roman Catholics, but formerly known as the Circumcision of Christ, has probably always been observed because people felt it was good to begin the year with a church service.

The Service for New Year's Eve in the BOS is a vigil service in the classic model of lessons, psalms, and collects. If it is desired to hold such a service, it could be scheduled for 11:00 or 11:30 p.m., concluding at midnight with either the singing of the *Te Deum* or the Eucharist of the Holy Name. I know of at least one congregation that follows up a New Year's vigil and Eucharist with a party in the parish house. This is certainly not for every congregation, but it is a good example of imaginative planning.

Christmas – Major Feasts, Seasonal Rites, and Other Commemorations

The Christmas Crèche[1]

At their entry into the church for the celebration of the Holy Eucharist, the Presider (and other ministers) may make a station at the crèche. The figure of the Christ Child may be carried in the procession and placed in the crèche. Other figures may also be brought in if desired.

The following anthem or some other hymn may be sung or said by all:

O great mystery,

and wonderful sacrament,

that animals should see the new-born Lord, lying in a manger!

Blessed is the Virgin whose womb was worthy to bear

Christ the Lord. Alleluia!

V. The Word was made flesh

R. And dwelt among us.

The Presider continues

Almighty God, who in the Incarnation of your Son has revealed to us the holiness of creation, be pleased to bless and hallow this image of his sacred birth, so that those who gaze upon it may behold this mystery, whereby humanity shares in your very nature; through Christ our Lord. ***Amen.***

The crèche may then be censed. The procession continues and all go to their usual places.

1 BOS 2022, 35–36.

Christmas Blessing[2]

The following blessing may be used by a bishop or priest whenever a blessing is appropriate. It is a three-fold form, with an Amen at the end of each sentence, leading into a Trinitarian blessing.

May Almighty God, who sent his Son to take our nature upon him, bless you in this holy season, scatter the darkness of sin, and brighten your heart with the light of his holiness. *Amen.*

May God, who sent his angels to proclaim the glad news of the Savior's birth, fill you will joy, and make you heralds of the gospel. *Amen.*

May God, who in the Word made flesh joined heaven to earth and earth to heaven, give you his peace and favor. *Amen.*

And the blessing of God Almighty, the Father, the Son, and the Holy Spirit, be upon you and remain with you for ever. *Amen.*

or this

May Christ, who by his Incarnation gathered into one things earthly and heavenly, fill you with his joy and peace; and the blessing of God Almighty, the Father, the Son, and the Holy Spirit, be among you, and remain with you always. *Amen.*

Blessing of a Christmas Tree

The Christmas tree stems from an ancient tradition of bringing evergreens into the home during the winter months as a hopeful reminder that spring would come. It has now become a familiar symbol of the Christian holiday in homes and in many churches.

Most Holy and Blessed One, you sent your beloved Son into the world to show us the path to true life. May the green of this tree remind us of the everlasting life you offer. May the boughs of this tree remind us that we are the

2 BOS 2022, 11.

living branches of your love. May the life of this tree remind us of the cross on which your Son gave his life. May the lights of this tree remind us that Christ is the light of the world. As we gather round this tree, we gather in your name, and in your light, and in your love. *Amen.*[3]

Christmas Festival of Lessons and Carols[4]

Nine Lessons are customarily selected (but fewer may be used), interspersed with appropriate carols, hymns, canticles, and anthems during this service, which can take place within the twelve days of Christmas. When possible, each Lesson should be read by a different lector, preferably voices of male and female readers as well as a variety of ages. The Lesson from the third chapter of Genesis is never omitted.

Genesis 2:4b–9, 15–25
Genesis 3:1–23 *or* 3:1–5
Isaiah 40:1–11
Isaiah 35:1–10
Isaiah 7:10–15
Luke 1:5–25
Luke 1:26–58
Luke 1:39–46 *or* 1:39–56
Luke 1:57–80
Luke 2:1–20
Luke 2:21–36
Hebrews 1:1–12
John 1:1–18

A Children's Christmas Presentation

While not a traditional "pageant," this presentation invites children to create a simple tableau without much rehearsal. It can occur during the sermon or at the end of a service, or can stand alone as a gathering of families for the telling of the birth of Christ with community singing.

Children assemble and put on simple costumes. Mary, Joseph, a donkey, and cows are seated beside a manger. Angels are behind and "above" them.

There are many, many resources available elsewhere for Children's Christmas Pageants. If used during the liturgy, finding one that coordinates well with the readings for the day is encouraged.

Mary, Joseph, and the Animals:
This Christmas time we worship
As we gather here tonight
To welcome Baby Jesus
Who came to bring us light.

All sing: Away in a Manger (v. 1)

Shepherds enter with sheep and gather around the manger.

Shepherds and Sheep:
We worship as the shepherds
Who came from hills so far.
They brought the little lambs
To see the baby lying there.

All sing: Rise Up, Shepherd and Follow

Angels:
We worship as the angels
Who sang the first Noel.
God had sent His only Son –
Glad tidings did they tell!

All sing: Angels We Have Heard on High (v. 3)

The Community Gathered:
To Jesus, Lord and Savior,
We bring ourselves this night.
We worship and adore Him
Who brought us peace and light.

All sing: Joy to the World

Candles can be distributed and lit as lights are turned down.

All sing: Silent Night

December 26, Saint Stephen, Deacon and Martyr

This is a Major Feast but may not substitute for the First Sunday after Christmas Day, if it should fall on a Sunday. In that case, it would be postponed, along with the two following feast days, by one day. The Collect for the Day is found on pages 186 or 237 of the Book of Common Prayer.

Stephen became the first deacon by his appointment to assist the apostles. He was one of the "seven men of good

---

3 Anne E. Kitch. *The Anglican Family Prayer Book* (Harrisburg, PA: Morehouse Publishing, 2004), 125–126.
4 BOS 2022, 37–41.

repute, full of the Spirit and of wisdom," chosen by the apostles to help them serve at tables and care for widows. Stephen served beyond tables, for the Acts of the Apostles describes him preaching and performing miracles. These activities pushed him to confront Jews, who accused him of blasphemy and brought him before the Sanhedrin; his powerful sermon before the Council is recorded in Acts 7. Enraged, councilmen dragged him out of the city to stone him to death. In fear, the Christian community scattered and thus, spread the Word.

December 27, Saint John the Evangelist

This is a Major Feast but may not substitute for the First Sunday after Christmas Day, if it should fall on a Sunday. In that case, it would be postponed, along with the feast of the Holy Innocents, by one day. The Collect for the Day is found on pages 186 or 238 of the Book of Common Prayer.

John, the son of Zebedee, with his brother James, was called from being a fisherman to be a disciple and "fisher of men." With Peter and James, he became one of the inner group of three disciples whom Jesus chose to be with him at the raising of Jairus' daughter, at the Transfiguration, and in the garden of Gethsemane. If, as is commonly held, John is to be identified with the "disciple whom Jesus loved," then he clearly enjoyed a very special relationship with his Master, reclining close to Jesus at the Last Supper, receiving the care of his mother at the cross, and being the first to understand the truth of the empty tomb. According to tradition, John later went to Asia Minor and settled at Ephesus. Under the Emperor Domitian, he was exiled to the island of Patmos, where he experienced the visions recounted in the Revelation to John.

December 28, Feast of the Holy Innocents

This is a Major Feast but may not substitute for the First Sunday after Christmas Day, if it should fall on a Sunday. In that case, it would be postponed by one day. The Collect for the Day is found on pages 186 or 238 of the Book of Common Prayer.

The Holy Innocents were the baby boys ordered killed by Herod. Herod the Great, ruler of the Jews, was described by the historian Josephus as "a man of great barbarity towards everyone." Appointed by the Romans in 40 BCE, Herod kept peace in Palestine for thirty-seven years. Ruthless yet able, this Idumaean was married to the daughter of Hyrcanus, the last legal Hasmonean ruler, so Herod always feared losing his throne. According to the story, the magi report of the birth of a King of the Jews scared him: he ordered the slaughter of all male children under two in Bethlehem. Although not recorded in secular history, the massacre of the Innocents keeps to Herod's character. Of course, the story has significant symbolic content, creating a resonance with the story of Moses in Exodus as well.

December 31, Service for New Year's Eve[5]

During the evening of December 31, which is the eve of the Feast of the Holy Name and also the eve of the civil New Year, this service begins with the Service of Light (BCP, 109), using the Collect for the First Sunday after Christmas Day as the Prayer for Light, and continues after the Phos hilaron with two or more of the following readings, each followed with a Psalm, Canticle, or hymn and a prayer.

The Hebrew Year

Exodus 23:9–16, 20–21
Psalm 111 *or* Psalm 119:1–8

O God our Creator, you have divided our life into days and seasons, and called us to acknowledge your providence year after year: Accept your people who come to offer their praises, and, in your mercy, receive their prayers; through Jesus Christ our Lord. ***Amen.***

The Promised Land

Deuteronomy 11:8–12, 26–28
Psalm 36:5–10 *or* Psalm 89, Part I

Almighty God, the source of all life, giver of all blessing, and savior of all who turn to you: Have mercy upon this nation; deliver us from falsehood, malice, and disobedience; turn our feet into your paths; and grant that we may serve you in peace; through Jesus Christ our Lord. ***Amen.***

A Season for All Things

Ecclesiastes 3:1–15
Psalm 90

In your wisdom, O Lord our God, you have made all things, and have allotted to each of us the days of our life: Grant that we may live in your presence, be guided by your Holy Spirit, and offer all our works to your honor and glory; through Jesus Christ our Lord. ***Amen.***

---

5 BOS 2022, 42–44.

Remember your Creator
Ecclesiastes 12:1–8
Psalm 130

Immortal Lord God, you inhabit eternity, and have brought us your unworthy servants to the close of another year: Pardon, we entreat you, our transgressions of the past, and graciously abide with us all the days of our life; through Jesus Christ our Lord. ***Amen.***

Marking the Times, and Winter
Ecclesiasticus 43:1–22
Psalm 19 *or* Psalm 148 *or* Psalm 74:11–22

Almighty Father, you give the sun for a light by day, and the moon and the stars by night: Graciously receive us, this night and always, into your favor and protection, defending us from all harm and governing us with your Holy Spirit, that every shadow of ignorance, every failure of faith or weakness of heart, every evil or wrong desire may be removed far from us; so that we, being justified in our Lord Jesus Christ, may be sanctified by your Spirit, and glorified by your infinite mercies in the day of the glorious appearing of our Lord and Savior Jesus Christ. ***Amen.***

The Acceptable Time
2 Corinthians 5:17 – 6:2
Psalm 63:1–8 *or* Canticle 5 *or* Canticle 17

Most gracious and merciful God, you have reconciled us to yourself through Jesus Christ your Son, and called us to new life in him: Grant that we, who begin this year in his Name, may complete it to his honor and glory; who lives and reigns now and for ever. ***Amen.***

While it is Called Today
Hebrews 3:1–15 (16 – 4:13)
Psalm 95

O God, through your Son you have taught us to be watchful, and to await the sudden day of judgment: Strengthen us against Satan and his forces of wickedness, the evil powers of this world, and the sinful desires within us; and grant that, having served you all the days of our life, we may finally come to the dwelling place your Son has prepared for us; who lives and reigns for ever and ever. ***Amen.***

New Heavens and New Earth
Revelation 21:1–14, 22–24
Canticle 19

Almighty and merciful God, through your well beloved Son Jesus Christ, the King of kings and Lord of lords, you have willed to make all things new: Grant that we may be renewed by your Holy Spirit, and may come at last to that heavenly country where your people hunger and thirst no more, and the tears are wiped away from every eye; through Jesus Christ our Lord. ***Amen.***

A Reading from the New Testament is always the final reading. A homily sermon or instruction may follow the readings. An act of self-dedication may follow.

The service may conclude with one of the following: 1) the Great Litany or some other intercession; 2) the singing of Te Deum *or other hymn of praise, the Lord's Prayer, the Collect the Holy Name, and blessing/dismissal; 3) with the Eucharist, beginning with the* Gloria in excelsis *or other song of praise. The proper for Holy Name is used.*

January 1, The Holy Name of Our Lord Jesus Christ

This is one of three Feasts of our Lord that is designated as taking **precedence** *over the Sunday lessons and collect, and so replaces the First Sunday after Christmas Day, when this feast falls on a Sunday. The Collect for the Day is found on pages 162 and 213 and the Lessons are found on page 901 of* the Book of Common Prayer.

According to Jewish tradition, the eighth day after the birth of a male was set for his circumcision, an event celebrated as a festal day. Liturgical commemoration of Jesus's circumcision, of Gallican origin, began after the Council in Tours (567) set January 1 as a fast day to counteract pagan festivals at the start of a new year. According to Roman tradition, this octave day of Christmas was dedicated to the Virgin Mary. Early gospelers stressed the name of the Christ, meaning "Savior" in Hebrew, to show he was human, flesh and blood. The name of Jesus signifies the saving freedom granted to us through Jesus the Christ.

The Nativity of Our Lord Jesus Christ: Christmas Eve

December 24

Glory to God in the highest heaven, and on earth peace among those whom he favors!

Anchor Points – The Propers and the Feast

The fixed points for each service are the appointed or proper readings and collect as well as the themes of the day or season.

There are three complete sets of readings to use between Christmas Eve and Christmas Day. It is not required to use all of them. Different sets of readings can be chosen for different services or they may all be the same. In many places, it is customary to use the third set (with John's Prologue) on Christmas Day and/or at the late service on Christmas Eve. Material presented here include the first two sets of Christmas propers; Christmas Day, below, includes the third set of readings.

Readings and Psalm (1)

Isaiah 9:2–7

From the Hebrew Bible we hear a hymn of thanksgiving and hope offered at the birth of a new king in Jerusalem. The prophet hails the one born to be the ruler of his people. His reign will end oppression and bring justice, righteousness, and a lasting peace. Christians hear these words and are reminded of the promises given in Jesus.

Psalm 96

A song of praise to the Lord in which the whole heavens and earth are invited to join.

Titus 2:11–14

This New Testament reading speaks of the two comings of Christ: first in his sacrificial ministry for all people and then in glory. He has enabled his disciples to free themselves from ways of evil. Disciplined and eager to do good, they look forward to the fulfillment of the hope God has given to the world in Jesus.

Luke 2:1–14 (15–20)

The gospel presents **the story of the birth of Jesus.** He is born amid very humble human circumstances. A government registration program requires Joseph and Mary to go to Bethlehem, the city of David. Because there was no other place for them to stay, Mary lays her new son in a stable manger.

An angel then appears to shepherds and announces the joyful news of the Savior's birth.

Or, if the longer version is used, the last sentence may read:

An angel announces the joyful news of the Savior's birth to shepherds who come to Bethlehem and report the angelic vision.

Readings and Psalm (2)

Isaiah 62:6–12

Centuries before Christ's birth, Isaiah had foreseen the coming of the Messiah as the establishment of God's reign. This event would summon all people into God's kingdom and make of them "The Holy People, The Redeemed of the LORD."

Psalm 97

The Psalm declares the might and power of God, using imagery from creation, and promises God's continued protection for the faithful.

Titus 3:4–7

Paul, writing to Titus, tells us that in the water of Baptism we, too, have been made part of that Holy People of God and given eternal life.

Luke 2:(1–7), 8–20

The gospel presents **the story of the birth of Jesus.** He is born amid very humble human circumstances. A government registration program requires Joseph and Mary to go to Bethlehem, the city of David. Because there was no other place for them to stay, Mary lays her new son in a stable manger. An angel announces the joyful news of the Savior's birth to shepherds who come to Bethlehem and report the angelic vision.

Collect

O God, you have caused this holy night to shine with the brightness of the true Light: Grant that we, who have known the mystery of that Light on earth, may also enjoy him perfectly in heaven; where with you and the Holy Spirit he lives and reigns, one God, in glory everlasting. *Amen.*

Proper Preface

Incarnation – Because you gave Jesus Christ, your only Son, to be born for us; who, by the mighty power of the Holy Spirit, was made perfect Man of the flesh of the Virgin Mary his mother; so that we might be delivered from the bondage of sin, and receive power to become your children. (Rite II, BCP 378; Rite I BCP 345)

Feast Day Pairings

See the table below for choices appointed for this day. Preferences are put in **bold**. Not all choices are suitable for all congregations or community, though, so consider these preferences as a starting point before making a decision about your own congregation.

	Feast of the Nativity of Our Lord: Christmas Eve	Rite I	Rite II	EOW1	BOS 2022
Color	White/Gold/Festive				
Entrance Rite	Customary; May include prayer at creche.	323	355	50	
Song of Praise/Kyrie	**Glory to God (Gloria in excelsis)** *or* Hymn 96 *or* similar	324	356		
Collect		160–161	212–213		
Creed	Nicene Creed	326, 327	358	53	
Prayers of the People	**Locally written**; options below; BCP form	329	387–393	54–55	
Offertory Sentence	"Worship the Lord in the Beauty of holiness; let the whole earth tremble before him. (Psalm 96) *or* "I am bringing you good news of great joy for all the people: to you is born this day in the city of David a Savior, who is the Messiah, the Lord." (Luke)	343–344	376–377		
Eucharistic Prayer	**One that allows use of the Incarnation preface**	**2–340**	**B – 367**	1–57	
Proper Preface	Incarnation	345	378		
Breaking of the Bread (Fraction)	Christ our Passover (BCP) *or* Whoever eats this bread (Hymn S 170) *or* Blessed are those who are called (Hymn S 172)	337	365	69	
Postcommunion Prayer		339	**Eternal God – 365**	God of abundance – 69	
Blessing	**Seasonal in BOS**				**11**
Dismissal	**Let us go forth in the Name of Christ**	340	366		
Notes	**Children's involvement where possible**				

Additional Notes:

Fraction Anthem at the Breaking of the Bread – The option provided in Rite I and Rite II ("Christ our Passover") is suitable throughout the season and the Alleluias should be included, to make it more festive. Explore other texts that may be used from *The Hymnal 1982* from S 151 to S 172 (sung or said). The text at Hymn S 170 ("Whoever eats this bread") or S 172 ("Blessed are those who are called") would both be thematically appropriate for Christmastide. You may want to lean into more familiar material, however, since attendance at Christmas often includes folks who attend infrequently. Primarily, it would be helpful to be sure to use a different form in Christmastide than in Advent, to emphasize the shift in seasons.

Content Resources

Reading Between the Lines

Luke's language (NRSV "In those days") intentionally echoes language of Hebrew Scripture through the Greek translation of the Hebrew Bible, the Septuagint (LXX), familiar to all NT authors. The opening words of Luke 2:1 and Luke 2:6 are the same, and better rendered as, "Now it happened . . ." echoing the same temporal phrase in the LXX from Genesis on. This is Luke's way of alerting listeners and readers of a text lacking punctuation and chapter divisions to pay attention to particular events. In these and other ways, we see the author Luke indicating clearly that the narrative of Luke-Acts continues and furthers the narrative of Hebrew Scriptures. Jesus' humble birth and recognition by lowly, itinerant shepherds is also acclaimed by angels as Savior, a title familiar to Jews and Greeks alike. "Firstborn son" indicates special status. Angelic song praising God in the highest heaven makes clear the highest power.

Central Themes

The congregation that gathers on Christmas Eve is meaningfully different from our week-to-week congregations. There are more visitors, more out-of-town family, more sweeties brought home to meet the parents. You've got Education for Ministry mentors next to people who couldn't name the Holy Family. One message they can all hear: God did not enter our world at a convenient time or in a convenient place. Mary and Joseph were in a strange city, sorely unprepared when Jesus arrived. Help your wide-ranging congregation accept that they need not be ready for God in order for God to show up. God is comfortable in the messiness of our real lives.

It started like any other Christmas Eve "Family Service." People arrived early, saving seats, checking their phones, thinking of things left undone that needed tending to, or people to see immediately following the service. They squirmed in their pews with their coats (not stored on the racks, which would slow down the quick escape after communion), wearing ill-fitting suits, itchy holiday sweaters, and coping with their insistence that they cram into pews together as a family. The opening hymn sets the tone, and the anticipation of the sweetness, silliness, and sentimentality of the annual parade of children (aka the pageant) starts to take hold. The congregation is invited to be seated, and to accompany the building of the children's Nativity Gospel tableau by singing an old English carol, naming the characters, animals, and birds as they processed to the front of the church. Verse one began in earnest, but their singing gradually faded away, and by the time Mary, Joseph, and the infant arrived up front, had the organ not been playing, you could have heard a pin drop. Joseph, a confident muscular nine-year-old boy who helps on his family's farm, is proudly carrying the baby Jesus down the aisle, taking care to stay near Mary. Mary, a very small and twisted girl of five, wrapped in the traditional blue costume, who navigated the long trek with her tiny aluminum walker, with a stride that goes sideways as much as forward: Determined. Beautiful. It took all of their verse and part of the next to get into place. By the third verse, the congregation seemed at last able to catch their breath, find their voices again, and sing the rest of the cast forward, many in tears. This part of the Holy Family's journey has always been about hardship, about overcoming obstacles to make way for miracles, about arduous journeys, and one closed door after another. That year we saw the beauty, hope, and tenacity of Mary afresh, and by the time the last candle was extinguished and the hem of the last coat crossed the church threshold out into the winter night, the possibilities of "heavenly peace" about which we sang together, seemed limitless.

Engaging All Ages

If your Christmas Eve service is one geared to families with young children, instead of giving a children's homily, invite children to bring forward figures (Mary, Joseph, the Christ child, animals, angels, and shepherds) during the reading of Luke's gospel. In lieu of a pageant, this is a means to involve individuals of all ages to "reenact" the story of Jesus's birth while assembling your congregational crèche if it owns one. If your church does not have one, perhaps a member of the congregation can lend one of their own. The bigger the figures the better!

Prayers of the People; Option 1

Presider

Gracious and Loving God, in Jesus you have filled all humanity with your divine life: Hear our prayers of joy and thanksgiving as we offer our sup- plications to you, saying: Glory to God in the highest heaven, and peace to God's people on earth.

Litanist

You have entrusted the Church with good news of great joy for all people: Inspire our witness that we may spread the light of Jesus' love to all humanity.

Glory to God in the highest heaven,

and peace to God's people on earth.

Let your power and compassion guide those who exercise authority on earth, that they may be servants of peace, bringing comfort and security to all who are vulnerable.

Glory to God in the highest heaven,

and peace to God's people on earth.

Embrace with your eternal protection all who are poor: refugees and the displaced, those threatened by violence, and families with no place to call their home.

Glory to God in the highest heaven,

and peace to God's people on earth.

Fill this community with hospitality and generosity, that we may care for one another and celebrate the joy of your presence in our humanity.

Glory to God in the highest heaven,

and peace to God's people on earth.

We entrust to your divine grace all for whom we pray, especially . . .

We give thanks for shepherds and all the vigilant who work while others sleep. Hear our grateful thanksgiving for all the gifts and blessings in our lives, especially . . .

We entrust into your eternal arms those who have died, especially . . .

Presider

Loving God, the joyful message of the angels fills us with gladness as we celebrate the coming of the Christ child to live among us in vulnerable humility: Let your divine light so dwell within us, that we may treasure your words, ponder them in our hearts, and continue the work of Christ's incarnation in our day, through Jesus our Savior, to whom with you and the

Holy Spirit be honor and glory, now and for ever. ***Amen.***

Prayers of the People: Option 2

With angel song bursting through the heavens, shattering the stillness of this night, you have our attention, God! We praise your name, your gift of yourself, with a joyful noise.

With those who have lived before us and those who come after us, we praise you. As your Church, we are amazed at your goodness. Give your church a sense of awe and wonder as we open our hearts to receive the gift of your very self among us.

May our lives reflect
the joy of your good news.

We pray for our leaders, who pass laws and make decisions that impact lives around the world. May their decisions reflect wisdom and justice and peace.

May our relationships reflect
the peace of your good news.

With people around the world, we rejoice at your presence in our world. With people around the world, we weep with those who are oppressed, hungry, living in fear of violence.

May our hearts reflect
the generosity of your good news.

We pray for those who live and work in our neighborhoods, who rush to our sides when we are in crisis. For those who are crying this night from pain, from broken relationships, from loneliness; with those struggling to be born and with those who are dying, we ask your healing and wholeness.

May our prayers reflect
the healing power of your good news.

For those who have died and entered the larger presence of your love, we pray.

May our lives reflect
the hope and comfort of your good news.

Hymns for the Day

The Hymnal 1982

Hark! the herald angels sing 87
It came upon the midnight clear 89, 90
Sing, O sing, this blessed morn 88
The people who in darkness walked 125, 126
Unto us a boy is born! 98
Joy to the world! The Lord is come 100
A child is born in Bethlehem 103
A stable lamp is lighted 104
Angels we have heard on high 96
Away in a manger 101
Go, tell it on the mountain 21
From heaven above to earth I come 80
God rest you merry, gentlemen 105
In the bleak midwinter 112
It came upon the midnight clear 89
Lo, how a Rose e'er blooming 81
O come, all ye faithful 83
O little town of Bethlehem 78, 79
Once in royal David's city 102
Silent night, holy night 111
The first Nowell the angel did say 109
The snow lay on the ground 110

Lift Every Voice and Sing II

Away in a manger 27
Go, tell it on the mountain 21
Mary borned a baby 22
Silent night, holy night 26
That boy-child of Mary was born in a stable 25

Wonder, Love, and Praise

Shengye qing, shengye jing /
Holy night, blessed night 725

The Nativity of Our Lord Jesus Christ: Christmas Day

December 25

Glory to God in the highest heaven, and on earth peace among those whom he favors!

Anchor Points – The Propers and the Feast

The fixed points for each service are the appointed or proper readings and collect as well as the themes of the day or season.

There are three complete sets of readings to use between Christmas Eve and Christmas Day. It is not required to use all of them. Different sets of readings can be chosen for different services or they may all be the same. In many places, it is customary to use the third set (with John's Prologue) on Christmas Day and/or at the late service on Christmas Eve. Material presented here includes the third set of readings; the first two sets of readings are above, at Christmas Eve.

Readings and Psalm (3)

Isaiah 52:7–10

The Hebrew scripture lection heralds a time of great joy as the Lord saves the people and brings deliverance to Jerusalem. The long exile is at an end. The messenger proclaims the good news, "The Lord reigns." The watchmen of the city respond with shouts of triumph to see God's salvation.

Psalm 98

A song of thanksgiving and praise to the victorious Lord, who has made righteousness known and shown faithfulness to God's people.

Hebrews 1:1–4 (5–12)

In this lesson the Letter to the Hebrews begins with a declaration of Jesus's sonship. He is far above all angels at the right hand of God. Previously God had spoken through the prophets, but now the will of God is expressed in the Son, through whom the world was created and who bears the stamp of divine being. After making purification for sins, he has taken his seat of greatest honor.

If using Hebrews 1:1–12, this concluding sentence applies:

A series of quotations from the Hebrew Bible is used to show the Son's superiority to the angels, who are the highest order of created beings.

John 1:1–14

The gospel opens with a hymn to the expression of God's very being, God's Word, who has now become flesh and lived among us. Through the Word all things have their life. The Word is the light of all humankind, and was witnessed to by John the Baptist. Although the world made by the Word did not recognize the Word, those who believe in the Word have been given the right to become children of God.

Collect

Almighty God, you have given your only-begotten Son to take our nature upon him, and to be born this day of a pure virgin: Grant that we, who have been born again and made your children by adoption and grace, may daily be renewed by your Holy Spirit; through our Lord Jesus Christ, to whom with you and the same Spirit be honor and glory, now and forever. *Amen.*

Proper Preface

Incarnation – Because you gave Jesus Christ, your only Son, to be born for us; who, by the mighty power of the Holy Spirit, was made perfect Man of the flesh of the Virgin Mary his mother; so that we might be delivered from the bondage of sin, and receive power to become your children. (Rite II, BCP 378; Rite I BCP 345)

Feast Day Pairings

See the table below for choices appointed for this day. Preferences are put in **bold**. Not all choices are suitable for all congregations or community, though, so consider these preferences as a starting point before making a decision about your own congregation.

	Feast of the Nativity of Our Lord: Christmas Day	Rite I	Rite II	EOW1	BOS 2022
Color	White/Gold/Festive				
Entrance Rite	Customary; May include prayer at creche.	323	355	50	
Song of Praise/Kyrie	**Glory to God (Gloria in excelsis)** *or* Hymn 96 *or* similar	324	356		
Collect		160–161	212–213		
Creed	Nicene Creed	326, 327	358	53	
Prayers of the People	**Locally written**; options below; BCP form	329	387–393	54–55	
Offertory Sentence	"Worship the Lord in the Beauty of holiness; let the whole earth tremble before him. (Psalm 96) *or* "I am bringing you good news of great joy for all the people: to you is born this day in the city of David a Savior, who is the Messiah, the Lord." (Luke)	343–344	376–377		
Eucharistic Prayer	**One that allows use of the Incarnation preface**	**2–340**	**B – 367**	1–57	
Proper Preface	Incarnation	345	378		
Breaking of the Bread (Fraction)	Christ our Passover (BCP) *or* Whoever eats this bread (Hymn S 170) *or* Blessed are those who are called (Hymn S 172)	337	365	69	
Postcommunion Prayer		339	**Eternal God – 365**	God of abundance – 69	
Blessing	**Seasonal in BOS**				**11**
Dismissal	**Let us go forth in the Name of Christ**	340	366		
Notes					

Additional Notes:

Fraction Anthem at the Breaking of the Bread – The option provided in Rite I and Rite II ("Christ our Passover") is suitable throughout the season and the Alleluias should be included, to make it more festive. Explore other texts that may be used from *The Hymnal 1982* from S 151 to S 172 (sung or said). The text at Hymn S 170 ("Whoever eats this bread") or S 172 ("Blessed are those who are called") would both be thematically appropriate for Christmastide. You may want to lean into more familiar material, however, since attendance at Christmas often includes folks who attend infrequently. Primarily, it would be helpful to be sure to use a different form in Christmastide than in Advent, to emphasize the shift in seasons.

Content Resources

Reading Between the Lines

(For Luke 2:1-7, see the previous entry)

Jesus' birth is announced by angels to shepherds with flocks of sheep. Perhaps Luke is pointing here to the significance of Jesus' birth for non-elites, anticipating Jesus' proclamation of good news to the poor (4:18) as well as Jesus' own homelessness (9:58). Here in Luke, Jesus and his supporters embark on a long journey to Jerusalem, one that will form followers, crowds, and disciples into a community, much in the same way that Israelite slaves wandered through the desert with their leader Moses, as they began to be formed by God into a nation. Bethlehem is also the city of David, the Shepherd King. That the child is laid in a manger, or crib, perhaps a feeding trough for domestic animals, introduces the notion, expanded in Christian tradition, that Jesus is born surrounded by cows, oxen, and other animals.

Central Themes

For many people, Christmas Day is all about presents. Although this may be less true for those who come to worship on Christmas morning, the idea of gifts is still in the air. Our reading from Hebrews reminds us that Jesus is the reflection of God. We can extrapolate from this to imagine ourselves as reflections of Jesus. What better gift can we give the world when we walk out of the doors than to reflect Jesus to the world and help others see Jesus reflected in their own lives?

In the lectionary resource *Preaching Creation Throughout the Church Year* the Rev. Dr. Jennifer Philips points out that John's Gospel today adds another element to the original creation story: energy. While certainly present in the darkness of Genesis, out of which the light first burst through, she suggests that John's language about the Word that was present in the beginning is about energy and light. She goes on to describe the scientific evidence of a background echo – of a hum – still ringing through the universe since the initial big bang, or as astronomers have since postulated – multiple big bangs. She writes, "In the east, that sound is called Aum (or Om), the 'unstuck sound' also used as a name for God. It is the primal sound of the universe that we may equate with the speaking of that Word into the nothingness before creation. The Word is a hum, a song, God's son et lumière, and Christians know it as light. The light we call Christ."[1] On this day we are reminded that there are always new beginnings, new opportunities to make way for light to break through the darkness and illuminate creation afresh.

Engaging All Ages

The language of the Gospel of John is filled with metaphor that may be difficult for children. Unpack it for all ages to hear: Jesus, God's Son, was born as a baby who would grow up to be the Savior – the One sent by God to rescue God's people. The angel said to the shepherds, "I bring you Good News." What was the good news? The good news was that God had sent the messiah, the Savior, the rescuer that they had been waiting for and what the prophets had been talking about for so many years. That's what Christmas is all about. And that is good news.

Prayers of the People: Option 1

Welcome! Let your presence among us be reflected in our lives.

Amen. Welcome, Lord, welcome.

With the gift of angel song and joyful spirits, we rejoice at your coming among us. Sustain us, your people, with joy deep in our hearts. Give our bishops, priests, deacons, and all our faithful leaders a renewed sense of purpose and direction, that they may lead us in the way you would have us go.

Amen. Welcome, Lord, welcome.

Give the leaders of the nations an urgency for peace and brotherhood, that the world you entered be blessed by good tidings.

Amen. Welcome, Lord, welcome.

Shower people throughout the world with your blessings of beauty and purpose, freedom and plenty.

Amen. Welcome, Lord, welcome.

Open our hearts to the needs of those around us who are hungry or lonely, who struggle with the burdens of living, whose spirits are restless for you.

Amen. Welcome, Lord, welcome.

Make whole those who suffer today with illness, with anxiety, with despair. May we care about them and care for them as our brothers and sisters.

Amen. Welcome, Lord, welcome.

Gather to your heart those who have died, who are now welcomed into your eternal embrace and surrounded by your glory.

Amen. Welcome, Lord, welcome.

Prayers of the People: Option 2

Deacon or Presider

As we join the whole creation and celebrate with joy the Word made flesh, let us offer prayers to God who dwells among us to the end of time.

Intercessor

By the wedding of the human and divine natures in Christ Jesus.

Glory and praise to you, O living God.

For *N.*, our Presiding Bishop, for *N.*, our bishop, for the clergy of this parish; for all bishops, priests, and deacons, for all who minister in Christ, and for all the holy people of God.

Glory and praise to you, O living God.

For [__________ and] all those who are preparing for Baptism; for all believers who put their trust in the incarnate Son of God.

Glory and praise to you, O living God.

1 Jennifer Phillips, *Preaching Creation Throughout the Church Year* (Boston, MA: Cowley Publications, 2000), 93.

For *N.*, our President, for the leaders of the nations and all in authority, and for peace and justice.

Glory and praise to you, O living God.

For the witness of Christ's love, that all may have an experience of that self-giving love and come to know our blessed Lord and Savior Jesus Christ.

Glory and praise to you, O living God.

For travelers, for those who are sick and suffering, for those who are hungry and oppressed, for those in prison, and for those who are dying and those who have diad, we pray.

Glory and praise to you, O living God.

For our deliverance from all affliction, strife, and need.

Glory and praise to you, O living God.

Remembering our most glorious and blessed Virgin Mary and all the saints, let us offer ourselves and one another to the living God through Christ.

To you, O Lord our God.

Presider

Source of grace and truth, accept the prayers we offer on this joyful feast. May we come to see the true light who shines throughout the world and who is God for all eternity; through Jesus Christ our Lord. ***Amen.***

Hymns for the Day

The Hymnal 1982

Watchman, tell us of the night 640
Angels, from the realms of glory 93
Dost thou in a manger lie 97
Now yield we thanks and praise 108
Once in royal David's city 102
The first Nowell the angel did say 109
Where is this stupendous stranger? 491
Joy to the world! the Lord is come 100
Let all mortal flesh keep silence 324
Love came down at Christmas 84
O Savior of our fallen race 85, 86
Of the Father's love begotten 82
On this day earth shall ring 92
Sing, O sing, this blessed morn 88
What child is this, who, laid to rest 115

Wonder, Love, and Praise

Where is this stupendous stranger? 726
From the dawning of creation 748

The First Sunday after Christmas Day

Sunday on or between December 26 and January 1

In the beginning was the Word

Anchor Points – The Propers and the Season

The fixed points for each service are the appointed or proper readings and collect as well as the themes of the day or season.

Readings and Psalm

Isaiah 61:10–62:3

Today's reading consists of verses from two hymns celebrating the expected glorification of Israel after the restoration of Jerusalem. The prophet, speaking for Zion, first uses the imagery of a wedding feast to express the joy of its vindication, then declares that the outworking of God's purpose is as mysterious, yet as certain, as the processes of nature.

Psalm 147 or 147:13–21

Psalm 147 is divided into three stanzas: vv. 1–6, 7–11 and 12–20, each beginning with a call to worship and continuing with motives for praise. The themes of God's sovereignty over the natural order and over human society are mingled throughout the psalm.

Galatians 3:23–25; 4:4–7

The Galatians apparently believed that faith in Christ needed to be combined with an adherence to Mosaic law. So Paul claims that subjection to the law was only temporary and now is superseded by Christ's work. The law was like a "disciplinarian" (3:24), the slave assigned to keep watch over the children going to school.

What humanity is given in Christ is not a better instructor, but a redeemer who sets us free. The Son is sent by God and "born of a woman," indicating his participation in ordinary humanity. Those who believe in the Son are adopted as God's children, making possible not merely a new status but also a new relationship with God.

John 1:1–18

The prologue to John's gospel is in the form of a hymn in stanzas. John may have adapted an earlier Christian or even pre-Christian hymn. For Greeks (and Hellenistic Jews), the Word (Greek, *Logos*) was the rational principle of the universe, giving meaning to all existence. For Jews, the word of God expressed God's eternal purpose active in creation, in revelation and in redemption.

The repetition of the phrase grace and truth (vv. 14, 17) underscores both the nature and mission of Jesus: He came "full of grace and truth" (v. 14) – that is, as the source of grace and truth – and he came to impart that grace and truth to those who "believed in his name" (v. 12).

Jesus's nature and mission combine to proclaim him as the ultimate revelation of God (1:18), not an aloof appearance of a transcendent and impersonal deity, but an in-the-flesh person who "lived among us" and calls us to know God, receive God, and live in the light of God.

Collect

Almighty God, you have poured upon us the new light of your incarnate Word: Grant that this light, enkindled in our hearts, may shine forth in our lives; through Jesus Christ our Lord, who lives and reigns with you, in the unity of the Holy Spirit, one God, now and forever. *Amen.*

Proper Preface

Incarnation – Because you gave Jesus Christ, your only Son, to be born for us; who, by the mighty power of the Holy Spirit, was made perfect Man of the flesh of the Virgin Mary his mother; so that we might be delivered from the bondage of sin, and receive power to become your children. (Rite II, BCP 378; Rite I BCP 345)

Seasonal Pairings

See the table below for choices appointed for this day. Preferences are put in **bold.** Not all choices are suitable for all congregations or community, though, so consider these preferences as a starting point before making a decision about your own congregation.

	The First Sunday after Christmas Day	Rite I	Rite II	EOW1	BOS 2022
Color	White/Gold/Festive				
Entrance Rite	Customary	323	355	50	
Song of Praise/Kyrie	**Glory to God (Gloria in excelsis)** *or* Hymn 96 *or* similar	324	356		
Collect		161	213		
Creed	Nicene Creed	326, 327	358	53	
Prayers of the People	**Locally written**; options below; BCP form	329	387–393	54–55	
Offertory Sentence	"And the Word became flesh and lived among us, and we have seen his glory" (John)	343–344	376–377		
Eucharistic Prayer	**One that allows use of the Incarnation preface**	**2–340**	**B – 367**	1–57	
Proper Preface	Incarnation	345	378		
Breaking of the Bread (Fraction)	Christ our Passover (BCP) *or* Whoever eats this bread (Hymn S 170) *or* Blessed are those who are called (Hymn S 172)	337	365	69	
Postcommunion Prayer		339	**Eternal God – 365**	God of abundance – 69	
Blessing	**Seasonal in BOS**				**11**
Dismissal	**Let us go forth in the Name of Christ**	340	366		
Notes	May be Holy Name (Jan 1) which takes precedence over Sun.				

Additional Notes:

Fraction Anthem at the Breaking of the Bread – The option provided in Rite I and Rite II ("Christ our Passover") is suitable throughout the season and the Alleluias should be included, to make it more festive. Explore other texts that may be used from *The Hymnal 1982* from S 151 to S 172 (sung or said). The text at Hymn S 170 ("Whoever eats this bread") or S 172 ("Blessed are those who are called") would both be thematically appropriate for Christmastide. Primarily, it would be helpful to be sure to use a different form in Christmastide than in Advent, to emphasize the shift in seasons.

Content Resources

Reading Between the Lines

The opening of John's gospel introduces to hearers the Logos, that is Word, also Wisdom, Thought, and Reason, a pre-existent being with God "in the beginning," enabling creation, life, and light that overcomes darkness. This Logos becomes flesh and dwells impermanently ("pitched a tent") amid humanity as a manifestation of God's glory, full of grace and truth. Logos is a being that moves from the singularity of God to the plurality of created life. The Logos that is Jesus Christ, the Word of God, empowers believers to become children of God and also makes God known.

Central Themes

The Rev. Dr. Wil Gafney has important words for us about the light and dark in today's readings, "It is far too easy for us as Americans to hear those words through our history of race and racism."[1] Light and dark are both a part of life. Light and dark are both part of God. As our reading from Isaiah says today, "my whole being shall exult in my God" – not just the "good" or acceptable parts, but my *whole* being. God is also present in our pain. Through the incarnation, God embraces both/and not either/or.

The possibility that God might actually care about our smallest distractions and pain, and walk with us in the most extreme joy and sorrow life has to offer, seems far more believable when recalling Jesus's humanity. The Word became flesh. Meat. Carne de Dios. For many Christians the most compelling aspect of the story of Jesus is that

1 https://www.wilgafney.com/2015/12/

he was fully human, that he walked the earth, had dirt in his sandals, ate food, went hungry, bled, ran and walked, cried and suffered. Immanuel. God with us. The fact that God actually does know how these very human things feel: The fleshy temptations of power, of control, of the myth of invincibility; having parents, getting angry, feeling abandoned. These are all very human experiences. We've been exploring the Word, Creator-God, from the beginning, from; the first light. Now human, flesh, and dwelling among us. While certainly not the first religion to make the claim that a human leader was also a deity, there is something about the "regular-ness" of the life of Jesus that is different: his friends, carpentry, teaching and learning, rifts with local leaders. It was in that daily existence that we beheld the Glory of God. The possibility that God might be revealed in our daily, regular lives seems even more believable. That our lives of devotion, of trying and failing, of service and stillness, may also be full of grace and truth.

Engaging All Ages

St. Francis of Assisi is credited with staging the first nativity scene in 1223. The only historical account we have of Francis' nativity scene comes from *The Life of St. Francis of Assisi* by St. Bonaventure, a Franciscan monk who was born five years before Francis' death. Invite congregants of all ages to bring and display their crèches after worship. Provide an opportunity for all to share stories about their crèches, such as its history and the tradition that they observe in setting up their crèche. If your church has a traditional crèche with an interesting story, invite a long-standing member or leader to share the story of that crèche.

Prayers of the People: Option 1

Presider

In Christ God's Word has become flesh dwelling among us, full of grace and truth. Let us pray to the true light which enlightens the world, that from the fullness of God all creation may receive grace upon grace, saying: What has come into being in Christ was life, and the life was the light of all people.

Litanist

Clothe your Church with the garments of salvation and cover her with robes of righteousness, O Gracious One, that we may be your witnesses to testify to the light.

What has come into being in Christ was life,

and the life was the light of all people.

Inspire the leaders of our nation and all in authority in the ways of grace and truth, that we may no longer be a people enslaved under the law but may know ourselves to be heirs, adopted as God's children.

What has come into being in Christ was life,

and the life was the light of all people.

Be our light in the darkness for all the world, that the fullness of your heart may be made known for the healing of the earth.

What has come into being in Christ was life,

and the life was the light of all people.

Live among us, O Word made flesh, and reconcile this community to your light.

What has come into being in Christ was life,

and the life was the light of all people.

May your people be a crown of beauty and a royal diadem in your hand, as we pray in faith for . . .

Hear our gratitude for your glory manifest among us, especially for . . .

Receive those who have died as heirs of eternal life, especially . . .

What has come into being in Christ was life,

and the life was the light of all people.

Presider

Loving and gracious Creator, from the beginning you have brightened our darkness with the light of your life: Let your vindication shine out like the dawn, and your salvation like a burning torch, that your Word made flesh may bring grace upon grace to all the earth, in the power of your Holy Spirit, through Jesus Christ our Savior. Amen.

Prayers of the People: Option 2

Emmanuel, God-with-us, we are overwhelmed with your presence, humble yet divine.

Our hearts are filled with longing for the day when all people will see your glory, when none of your people will know hunger, loneliness, or fear; when each of us will know the peace of your presence.

Pray for all whom God has made.

Our hope is for peace for all nations, and leaders whose desire is for justice and equality.

Pray for the peace of the world.

Our yearning is for wholeness for those who ache, whose lives are shattered, whose hope is lost.

Pray for those who suffer and for the end of their suffering.

Our hope is for those who have died and entered that place where there is no pain or grief, but life eternal.

Pray for those who have died.

Our deepest prayer is that we may learn and grow in your love, and bear witness to the world that God is with us.

Pray that the One who has given us these desires, give us also the grace and power to work toward their fulfillment.

Hymns for the Day

The Hymnal 1982

Arise, shine, for your light has come S 223ff
How bright appears the Morning Star 496, 497
Father eternal, Ruler of creation 573
Let all mortal flesh keep silence 324
Of the Father's love begotten 82
Word of God, come down on earth 633

Wonder, Love, and Praise

Arise, shine, for your light has come 883
From the dawning of creation 748

The Holy Name of Our Lord Jesus Christ

January 1

After eight days had passed, it was time to circumcise the child; and he was called Jesus.

Anchor Points – The Propers and the Feast

The fixed points for each service are the appointed or proper readings and collect as well as the themes of the day or season.

Readings and Psalm

Numbers 6:22–27

In our opening lesson, Moses, by God's command, instructs those set aside for priestly ministry to bless Israel, putting God's own name upon them. These words have come to be known as the "Aaronic blessing," as they were first entrusted to Aaron and his sons. Because there is a threefold form to the blessing, Christians have often here perceived intimations of faith in the triune God.

Psalm 8

The psalmist glorifies the name of the Lord, sovereign of the earth and the magnificent heavens, who has made human life to have mastery over all other earthly creatures.

Galatians 4:4–7

In the fullness of time, God sent God's own Son, born under the law, to redeem those under the law and to give them a new status as adopted children. Christians are not to see themselves as God's slaves, but as children and heirs to whom the Spirit has come, enabling them to speak to God in intimate terms, crying "Abba! Father!"

or

Philippians 2:5–11

From one of the earliest Christian hymns we hear how Christ Jesus accepted the condition of a servant, was obedient even to the point of death, and was then given the name above every name. It is possible that this poem was adapted by Paul or another disciple from the hopes for a savior of a people who did not yet know Jesus. Jesus has fulfilled humanity's dream of one who will share fully in the mortal condition before his exaltation. To him every knee shall bow and every tongue confess the great name of the Lord now known in person, Jesus.

Luke 2:15–21

Our gospel tells how the shepherds, after the angelic vision which announced the Savior's birth, come to Bethlehem to see for themselves the child who is to be named Jesus. They share with Mary and Joseph the words of the angels. In this little infant, laid in a manger, the shepherds perceive the fulfillment of the song of the heavenly hosts. After eight days, in accordance with the law, the baby is then circumcised and given the promised name.

Collect

Eternal Father, you gave to your incarnate Son the holy name of Jesus to be the sign of our salvation: Plant in every heart, we pray, the love of him who is the Savior of the world, our Lord Jesus Christ; who lives and reigns with you and the Holy Spirit, one God, in glory everlasting. *Amen.*

Proper Preface

Incarnation - Because you gave Jesus Christ, your only Son, to be born for us; who, by the mighty power of the Holy Spirit, was made perfect Man of the flesh of the Virgin Mary his mother; so that we might be delivered from the bondage of sin, and receive power to become your children. (Rite II, BCP 378; Rite I BCP 345)

Feast Day Pairings

See the table below for choices appointed for this day. Preferences are put in **bold**. Not all choices are suitable for all congregations or community, though, so consider these preferences as a starting point before making a decision about your own congregation.

	The Holy Name of Our Lord Jesus Christ	Rite I	Rite II	EOW1	BOS 2022
Color	White/Gold/Festive				
Entrance Rite	Customary	323	355	50	
Song of Praise/Kyrie	**Glory to God (Gloria in excelsis)** *or* Hymn 96 *or* similar	324	356		
Collect		162	213		
Creed	Nicene Creed	326, 327	358	53	
Prayers of the People	**Locally written**; options below; BCP form	329	387–393	54–55	
Offertory Sentence	"At the name of Jesus every knee should bend, in heaven and on earth and under the earth, and every tongue should confess that Jesus Christ is Lord, to the glory of God the Father." (Philippians)	343–344	376–377		
Eucharistic Prayer	**One that allows use of the Incarnation preface**	**2–340**	**B – 367**	1–57	
Proper Preface	Incarnation	345	378		
Breaking of the Bread (Fraction)	Christ our Passover (BCP) *or* Whoever eats this bread (Hymn S 170) *or* Blessed are those who are called (Hymn S 172)	337	365	69	
Postcommunion Prayer		339	**Eternal God – 365**	God of abundance – 69	
Blessing	**Seasonal in BOS**				**11**
Dismissal	**Let us go forth in the Name of Christ**	340	366		
Notes	If Holy Name (Jan 1) falls on a Sunday, it takes precedence over Sunday propers				

Additional Notes:

Fraction Anthem at the Breaking of the Bread – The option provided in Rite I and Rite II ("Christ our Passover") is suitable throughout the season and the Alleluias should be included, to make it more festive. Explore other texts that may be used from *The Hymnal 1982* from S 151 to S 172 (sung or said). The text at Hymn S 170 ("Whoever eats this bread") or S 172 ("Blessed are those who are called") would both be thematically appropriate for Christmastide. Primarily, it would be helpful to be sure to use a different form in Christmastide than in Advent, to emphasize the shift in seasons.

Content Resources

Reading Between the Lines

"Abba" is an Aramaic word addressing God as Father. When it occurs in the New Testament, here in the reading from Galatians, it is usually accompanied by its Greek equivalent, Pater, "Father." It is here the cry of adopted, perhaps the newly baptized, as God's children. As James Barr said long ago, "Abba" isn't Daddy."

The Philippian text is set out as a pre-Pauline hymn describing the descent and re-ascent of Christ Jesus. Jesus is, according to the hymn, a being existing with God before descending voluntarily and obediently into the human realm to take on human likeness, and the identity of a slave, even to the extent of being crucified on a cross. Then follows the exaltation by God of Jesus as Lord (Kyrios). It is one of the earliest of several such hymns in the New Testament.

Central Themes

The Feast of the Holy Name is a wonderful opportunity to name something that needs to be named, perhaps in your own life or perhaps in the life of your congregation or community. One strategy for dealing with anxiety in children is to help them describe it in great detail and make the anxiety into a being outside of themselves which they name. Once it is described and named, it can have a life separate from the child. It can be related to and managed in a different way. What needs to be described and named now in your context?

It is no secret, but still not said enough, that Jesus, Mary, and Joseph were members of an extremely devout Jewish family. Today's lesson shows them observing the Torah meticulously through Jesus's circumcision and naming. Joseph making a public proclamation, formally accepting this child as his son, is also in accordance with the Torah, solidifying the bonds of this young family. This combination of circumcision and naming caused for special feast days to rise up in the church. The Episcopal Church's website[1] has a handy dictionary/glossary with concise definitions and explanations their entry under "The Holy Name of our Lord Jesus Christ" to explain that in greater detail: "The name 'Jesus' is from the Hebrew Joshua, or Yehoshuah, 'YHWH is salvation' or 'YHWH will save.'" Devotion to the Holy Name of Jesus is particularly derived from Phil. 2:9–11, which states that God highly exalted Jesus "and gave him the name that is above every name, so that at the name of Jesus every knee should bend, in heaven and on earth and under the earth." This scriptural devotion is paraphrased by the hymn "At the name of Jesus" (Hymn 435) in *The Hymnal 1982*. Other hymns that express devotion to the Holy Name of Jesus include "To the name of our salvation" (Hymns 248–249) and "Jesus! Name of wondrous love!" (Hymn 252)." Have you ever engaged in a devotion or practice around this observance?

Engaging All Ages

Mary's son is given the name "Jesus," which in Hebrew means "The Lord saves." His name was given him during the Jewish ceremony of circumcision. As Christians, we are named at our baptism, having our name (from birth) taking on a new significance as one who is adopted into the family of Christ. A fun activity to do with all ages is to learn the significance of their own name: What does it mean? Is it a family name? Why did parents choose that name? How does a name put forth expectations of what that child might become?

Prayers of the People: Option 1

Thank you, Christ Jesus, for coming among us, for gracing us with your love and teaching us who you are.

As your name echoes through the ages,

we lift up our hands in praise.

Bless the people who bear your name. Give the bishops, priest and deacons wisdom and courage to lead your people in your name.

As your name echoes through the ages,

we lift up our hands in praise.

Open the eyes and hearts of the leaders of the nations to the needs of their people, to their desire for peace and justice. Empower us to work with our leaders to see that each person whom you have created, whom you love, for whom you died, will be treated with dignity.

As your name echoes through the ages,

we lift up our hands in praise.

Powerful Healer, release from pain those who suffer, restore them to wholeness and strength. Move us who bear your name to respond to their need with compassion and mercy.

As your name echoes through the ages,

we lift up our hands in praise.

Risen Lord, receive into your arms those who have died and comfort those who grieve their loss. We rejoice that they now know the fullness of joy with you and all your saints.

Grant that we may always honor your presence and exalt your name with our lips and in our lives.

As we lift our hands in praise.

Prayers of the People: Option 2

Deacon or Presider

We offer our prayers this day, O Lord, in the Name of your Son, Jesus Christ

Intercessor

God, source of light and life, guide and encourage your steadfast church, its laity and clergy.

Abide with us, Lord Christ.

O Lord, be present here with us, your faithful people, granting courage to this congregation, to N., our Presiding Bishop, N., our bishop(s) and to our parish clergy. We pray for [__________________________, and] all those preparing for Baptism.

Abide with us, Lord Christ.

We give thanks for the year that has passed, with its moments of sorrow and its moments of wonder, for the gifts of time and shared lives. Watch over us as we bravely enter a new year, full of promise, glorifying your Name.

Abide with us, Lord Christ.

1 https://episcopalchurch.org/library/glossary/holy-name-our-lord-jesus-christ

Mercifully grant leaders everywhere the gift of wisdom and insight, especially for N. our President, N., our Governor and N., our Mayor. Shepherd our decision makers with clear purpose and openness to perceive truth and justice.

Abide with us, Lord Christ.

Defend in your mercy Lord, those who are downtrodden, forgotten and rejected, shown to us in the paths of our daily lives. Kindle in our hearts the warmth and kindness of Christ's love to help especially those in great need.

Abide with us, Lord Christ.

May angels keep watch with those who mourn for those who have died, offering them consolation in their grief. Grant your heavenly rest and eternal peace to all those departed this world for the next.

Abide with us, Lord Christ.

I invite us all at this time, either silently or aloud, to lift up our needs and thanksgivings in the Holy Name of Jesus, our Sovereign and Redeemer of the world.

Silence. The People may offer additional prayers.

The Presider adds a concluding collect.

Hymns for the Day

The Hymnal 1982

Jesus, the very thought of thee 642
How sweet the Name of Jesus sounds 644
Now greet the swiftly changing year 250
O for a thousand tongues to sing 493
To the Name of our salvation 248, 249
Sing praise to our Creator 295
A stable lamp is lighted 104
All hail the power of Jesus's Name! 450, 451
All praise to thee, for thou, O King divine 477
At the name of Jesus 435
From east to west, from shore to shore 77
Jesus! Name of wondrous love! 252

Lift Every Voice and Sing II

Blessed be the name 78
Glorious is the name of Jesus 63
There is a name I love to hear 95
There's something about that name 107
God be with you 234
The Lord bless you and keep you 231

Wonder, Love, and Praise

God be with you till we meet again 801
You're called by name, forever loved 766

The Second Sunday after Christmas

Sunday on or between January 2 and 5

As Jesus shared our humanity, we are invited to share in his divine life.

Anchor Points – The Propers and the Season

The fixed points for each service are the appointed or proper readings and collect as well as the themes of the day or season.

Readings and Psalm

Jeremiah 31:7–14

This passage uses legal terms for the ransom or redemption of someone who has sold themselves into slavery. The right of redemption lay with the kinspeople, a right that Jeremiah exercised with respect to his family's field (chap. 32) and that he saw the Lord exercising with respect to Israel, the child of God.

Psalm 84 or 84:1–8

This psalm combines elements of hymn (vv. 1, 10–11), lamentation, and intercession (vv. 8–9). Likely composed on the occasion of a pilgrimage to the temple, the psalm expresses the strength of the psalmist's longing for the temple and the trials and rewards of the journey.

Ephesians 1:3–6, 15–19a

After the initial greeting, the greeting is displaced by a blessing in the form of a hymn. The hymn centers on the revelation of God in Christ, through whom believers are chosen and destined for adoption and for participation in Christ's mission of redemption. In his thanksgiving, the author shows by example the importance of making requests of God in prayer, not to coerce God, but to allow believers to cooperate in the working out of God's will.

Note: There are three Gospel reading options for today. The first option includes the flight to Egypt; the second is the visit of Jesus to the Temple at age 12; and the third is the beginning of the Magi story, anticipating Epiphany.

Matthew 2:13–15, 19–23

Today's reading, full of allusions from the Hebrew Bible, points to Jesus as the fulfillment of messianic expectations. Joseph receives guidance through dreams and models the perfect obedience that the earlier Joseph, son of Jacob, showed in Genesis 37 and 39–45. Like his earlier counterpart, Joseph, with Mary and Jesus, escapes murderous threats caused by jealousy, taking refuge in Egypt. Jesus's infant experience also recalls the great story of Moses. Like Moses, Jesus's life was threatened along with those of other baby boys.

or

Luke 2:41–52

This Gospel contains the only account we have of Jesus' childhood. The twelve-year-old Jesus seems, to the teachers in the temple, a religiously precocious boy; to his parents, a straying child who, in Joseph's typical fatherly admonition, has caused his mother to worry; to us, a reminder of the God incarnate, hidden within a human being. It is through the eyes of faith opened by the events of Jesus' ministry and his death and resurrection that we see the irony of God visiting his own temple and amazing the experts on divine matters with his knowledge. By faith we are also confronted with the God who so condescends to human nature as to live subject to human parents.

or

Matthew 2:1–12

The Gospel reading anticipates the feast of the Epiphany later this week. It is the account of the coming of the Magi, or Wise Men, from the east to worship the newborn King. This manifestation of the Son of God to the Gentiles announces that the gift of redemption is for all people.

Collect

O God, who wonderfully created, and yet more wonderfully restored, the dignity of human nature: Grant that we may share the divine life of him who humbled himself to share our humanity, your Son Jesus Christ; who lives and reigns with you, in the unity of the Holy Spirit, one God, for ever and ever. *Amen.*

Proper Preface

Incarnation - Because you gave Jesus Christ, your only Son, to be born for us; who, by the mighty power of the Holy Spirit, was made perfect Man of the flesh of the Virgin Mary his mother; so that we might be delivered from the bondage of sin, and receive power to become your children. (Rite II, BCP 378; Rite I BCP 345)

Seasonal Pairings

See the table below for choices appointed for this day. Preferences are put in **bold**. Not all choices are suitable for all congregations or community, though, so consider these preferences as a starting point before making a decision about your own congregation.

	The Second Sunday after Christmas Day	Rite I	Rite II	EOW1	BOS 2022
Color	White/Gold/Festive				
Entrance Rite	Customary	323	355	50	
Song of Praise/Kyrie	**Glory to God (Gloria in excelsis)** *or* Hymn 96 *or* similar	324	356		
Collect		161	214		
Creed	Nicene Creed	326, 327	358	53	
Prayers of the People	**Locally written**; options below; BCP form	329	387–393	54–55	
Offertory Sentence	"How dear to me is your dwelling, O Lord of hosts! My soul has a desire and longing for the courts of the Lord; my heart and my flesh rejoice in the living God." (Psalm 84)	343–344	376–377		
Eucharistic Prayer	**One that allows use of the Incarnation preface**	**2–340**	**B – 367**	1–57	
Proper Preface	Incarnation	345	378		
Breaking of the Bread (Fraction)	Christ our Passover (BCP) *or* Whoever eats this bread (Hymn S 170) *or* Blessed are those who are called (Hymn S 172)	337	365	69	
Postcommunion Prayer		339	**Eternal God – 365**	God of abundance – 69	
Blessing	**Seasonal in BOS**				**11**
Dismissal	**Let us go forth in the Name of Christ**	340	366		
Notes	Does not occur in every year. Epiphany takes precedence, if on a Sunday.				

Additional Notes:

Fraction Anthem at the Breaking of the Bread – The option provided in Rite I and Rite II ("Christ our Passover") is suitable throughout the season and the Alleluias should be included, to make it more festive. Explore other texts that may be used from *The Hymnal 1982* from S 151 to S 172 (sung or said). The text at Hymn S 170 ("Whoever eats this bread") or S 172 ("Blessed are those who are called") would both be thematically appropriate for Christmastide. Primarily, it would be helpful to be sure to use a different form in Christmastide than in Advent, to emphasize the shift in seasons.

Content Resources

Reading Between the Lines

Psalm 84 describes the poetic longing of the Psalmist to be in God's house, much as the swallow has found a nest to lay eggs, as if her nest were adjacent to God's altar, and thereby in a safe place. On an unexpected visit to Hagia Eirene, the abandoned and rarely open but twin church of Hagia Sophia, (Aya Sofya) in Istanbul, I have felt sentiments of this Psalmist, looking at birds nesting in the dusty, decrepit rafters, under which we read an inscription of this psalm.

In the gospel reading, an angel warns Joseph that the life of the child and his mother is in danger. Joseph saves the life of the child and his mother by fleeing to Egypt to evade Herod's clutches. The presence of the Holy Family in Egypt and the journey they undertook there documents the origins of the Coptic Church.

Luke's unique account of Jesus' separation from his parents, their frantic search, and discovery of Jesus in the temple in dialogue with religious authorities there, identifies Jesus' growth in wisdom and learning.

Central Themes

We have three options for Gospel readings this Sunday. One thing they all have in common is a theme about travel; more specifically, they are all about the fear and danger of travel. The first option is to connect deeply with the plight of Central Americans making their way through foreign lands to flee death. Luke's story resonates with the caravans of people that move through Mexico to reach the United States every few years. Remembering that group can help us understand how a teen might get misplaced along the way. And the final gospel option reminds us that political leaders do not always have our best interests at heart.

The multitude of options for readings today make one grateful for the focus of the collect. It is there that the words and images of the last few weeks start taking a gradual turn. Christmas brought us the child promised in Advent. We have sought and found this Christ child and are in awe of the incarnation: the humanity of God. But now it is our turn, our opportunity to be the Word, the original energy and light of creation. The collect asks "that we may share the divine life of him who humbled himself to share our humanity." So, it seems, this is not a one-way enterprise. Jesus took on human flesh so that we might see how the divine life can be embodied in a human, not just in a human whose greatness was foretold and who was visited by magi, but in a human whose family was in trouble and who was a refugee. He was a human who was also a teenager, who had the same communication problems with his parents as we all do, a human who was, and is, just like us. How can we share his divine life in a way that is anything like how he shared our humanity?

Engaging All Ages

There are choices with today's gospel. Luke speaks of Jesus as a boy visiting the temple, the only story of his childhood that we have. Matthew tells of the Holy Family's flight to Egypt, which is the only account of them becoming refugees in Egypt as they run from Herod's wrath. No matter the choice you make, both of them could easily connect with all ages. When was your first visit to a holy site or your church? When have you had to flee from danger? Elicit your emotions and feelings and invite others to do the same.

Prayers of the People

The true light has come into the world, and we have seen his glory. We pray that this light will always shine through us as we make our way through the world you have made.

From his fullness,

we have all received, grace upon grace.

We pray that the true light will illumine your faithful people. We pray for all bishops, priests and deacons who guide and support your people in their ministries.

From his fullness,

we have all received, grace upon grace.

We pray that the true light will enlighten those in authority throughout the world; that the way to justice and peace will be clear, that the needs of people in every corner of the world will be met, and that violence and poverty will be no more.

From his fullness,

we have all received, grace upon grace.

We pray that the true light will highlight those who need your love and peace the most; those who suffer from illness and anxiety, those whose relationships are broken, those who live in fear and despair. We pray for healing for ____________ .

From his fullness,

we have all received, grace upon grace.

We pray that those who have died will be joyfully received into your eternal light, and find bliss in your everlasting glory. We pray for the recently departed: ____________ . Bring us all into your glorious light when our journey here is complete.

We pray this in the name of your Son, Jesus Christ, who has brought us out of darkness into the light. From his fullness,

we have all received, grace upon grace.

Hymns for the Day

The Hymnal 1982

Jesus, the very thought of thee 642
How sweet the Name of Jesus sounds 644
Now greet the swiftly changing year 250
O for a thousand tongues to sing 493
To the Name of our salvation 248, 249
Sing praise to our Creator 295
A stable lamp is lighted 104
All hail the power of Jesus's Name! 450, 451
All praise to thee, for thou, O King divine 477
At the name of Jesus 435
From east to west, from shore to shore 77
Jesus! Name of wondrous Love! 252

Lift Every Voice and Sing II

Blessed be the Name 78
Glorious is the Name of Jesus 63
There is a name I love to hear 95
There's something about that Name 107
God be with you 234
The Lord bless you and keep you 231

Wonder, Love, and Praise

God be with you till we meet again 801
You're called by name, forever loved 766

Epiphany

Preparing for Epiphany

Epiphany (January 6) is the final day of the Christmas season. It celebrates the manifestation of Christ. Its gospel is the visit of the "wise men," or Magi. The baptism of Christ was originally also an Epiphany theme, and in the Eastern churches it is the primary Epiphany theme. But the present calendar commemorates the baptism on the Sunday after Epiphany. The miracle of changing water to wine at the wedding feast at Cana, now read as the gospel on the Second Sunday after the Epiphany only in Year C, is also a traditional secondary theme. Epiphany is also known as the Feast of Lights, celebrating Christ as the light of the world (John 1:5, 9). Since it is not a secular holiday in the United States, the only reasonable way to plan its celebration in most places is to schedule an evening Eucharist. This can begin with the Service of Light from the Order of Worship for the Evening, giving candles to the congregation to be lit after the seasonal prayer for light. An Epiphany hymn with the theme of light can be substituted for the Phos hilaron. The Epiphany seasonal blessing concludes the service.

American Roman Catholics follow the practice of transferring this celebration to the first Sunday of the new year. While the prayer book still expects that the feast itself be observed on January 6, it does permit the use of the Epiphany gospel on the Second Sunday after Christmas, in years when there is one. While this is not the same as celebrating Epiphany, it does give an opportunity to the congregation to hear the story of the Magi.

Epiphany is the most obvious occasion for using incense in worship, since it is mentioned as a gift for the Christ child in the gospel. A simple way to use incense is to carry it before the gospel book during the gospel procession. If more extensive use is desired, the altar can be censed after the gifts have been prepared and placed upon it. Still more extensive use would be to carry incense in the entrance and exit processions and to cense the book at the announcement of the gospel and the congregation after the altar and gifts at the offertory. Another possibility is to burn incense in the sanctuary during the Great Thanksgiving, either instead of or in addition to carrying it in processions.

The Baptism of Christ

The baptismal theme originally associated with Epiphany has been moved by the present calendar to the Sunday following, thereby greatly clarifying the planning process for both days. The gospel in all three years of the lectionary is the baptism of Christ. The most obvious way to celebrate the day is by planning it as a baptismal festival for the whole congregation. The baptismal feasts on which *The Book of Common Prayer* suggests the celebration of baptism are the Easter Vigil, Pentecost, All Saints' Day, and the Baptism of our Lord. On all of the remaining baptismal feasts, baptism is an appropriate highlight of the principal parish Eucharist. Most of what is shared here is equally applicable to the other baptismal feasts in subsequent times during the church year.

The Baptism of Christ is the principal theme at the beginning of Epiphanytide, and the homilist may move from Christ's baptism directly to our participation in Christ through baptism. The prayer book suggests that sponsors might read the lessons, and this can be included in the planning of the service.

If the font is located in a place that makes it difficult for the congregation to participate, the entire first part of the service can be conducted from the chancel step with a procession to the font immediately before the Thanksgiving over the Water and (if necessary) a return to the front of the church between the baptism and consignation. Ideally, the celebrant should stand to face the congregation across the font, and the baptismal parties should be placed to include, rather than exclude, the congregation in the action. All of this needs to be worked out beforehand.

The Peace includes the welcome of the newly baptized. Not just the clergy, but members of the vestry and the liturgy committee should make it a point to greet the newly baptized, their parents, and sponsors. Other parishioners will follow their lead and welcome the new Christians.

After the exchange of the Peace, the service continues "with the Prayers of the People or the Offertory of the Eucharist." Continuing with the Prayers of the People often seems awkward, since the Peace has already been exchanged, though that is the clear first option. One way to address that is to keep the Prayers of the People brief and informal, after the Peace and prior to necessary announcements. Some have opted to move directly to the offertory and include necessary intercessions in Eucharistic Prayer D. The prayer book recommends that newly baptized adults, or the godparents of newly baptized infants, bring up the bread and wine at the offertory.

If There Are No Baptisms

Occasionally there will be a baptismal feast for which there are, in fact, no baptisms in a given congregation. Advance publicity and planning can reduce the likelihood of this happening, but it will sometimes happen. On all of the baptismal feasts, the congregation can renew their own baptismal vows in place of reciting the Nicene Creed (BCP, 312). The form included in the prayer book for the Easter Vigil (p. 292) is used. A brief introduction, comparable to that given for Easter, can be composed to introduce the renewal, or it can follow the sermon directly, the sermon itself serving as an introduction and explanation.

Whether or not there are baptisms, baptism is clearly the central theme for this service. The proper preface may be of the Epiphany or the Lord's Day. The preface for the Lord's Day 3.Of the Holy Spirit refers to our being made a new people in Jesus Christ "by water and the Holy Spirit" and appears to be the best choice. If Eucharistic Prayer D is used, there is no proper preface. The liturgical color for the day is white, gold, or festive, and the service music used during the Christmas season can be continued through this Sunday, although (if there are baptisms) the Gloria in excelsis is not needed, but may be used. The Epiphany seasonal blessing is also used on this Sunday.

Candlemas

Candlemas is the popular name for the Presentation of Our Lord Jesus Christ in the Temple, also called the Purification of St. Mary the Virgin. The day recalls a ritual of Jewish law related to firstborn sons that Joseph and Mary carried out (Luke 2:21-40). Luke's gospel tells how Simeon and Anna, devout Jews, honored the infant Jesus as the promised Messiah. The name derives from the custom of blessing candles on that day and carrying them in procession. This, in turn, is based on the line from the Song of Simeon that is a part of the gospel for the day: "A Light to enlighten the nations." A distinctive feature of this feast is an optional Candlemas procession that may begin the liturgy on that day.

The Season after the Epiphany

This season has a sort of thematic unity, in the series of epiphanies found in the gospels for the first few Sundays: the baptism, the healing miracles (in Year B), and the transfiguration on the final Sunday after the Epiphany. The idea of a seasonal theme, so well expressed in Christopher Wordsworth's great hymn "Songs of thankfulness and praise" (Hymn 135), which has been given a fourth stanza in *The Hymnal 1982* to celebrate the transfiguration, becomes increasingly difficult to sustain when the season is long.

The season after the Epiphany, just as the season after Pentecost, appears on liturgical calendars as vast expanses of green, the traditional liturgical color broken only by the occasional holy day. Roman Catholics call this "ordinary time." Sometimes Epiphany Season doesn't seem to be a season at all but simply "filler" taking up time until Lent. Although the prayer book does call this time of year Epiphany Season (BCP, 31) and Episcopalians call these Sundays "Sundays after the Epiphany," we have not really treated this period as a season in the same sense as others. Some churches have chosen, for example, to displace the Sunday propers with those of a saint or other festival more often than in other seasons. Strictly speaking, only The Presentation (February 2) and the dedication and patronal festivals of the local church may truly displace a "green" Sunday. The prayer book permits "the Collect, Preface, and one or more of the Lessons" for any Major Feast falling on a "green" Sunday to be substituted for those of the Sunday (BCP, 16). In practice, this may be desirable during these longer seasons.

The readings for Epiphany 6, 7, and 8 are the same as those for Propers 1, 2, and 3, though the collects appointed are different for each. Whether these lessons are used after Epiphany (or after Pentecost) in any given year will depend on whether Easter is early or late. This not only binds the two seasons of post-Epiphany and post-Pentecost together, it reinforces the idea that they have little seasonal integrity, as such. The principal focus of the Sundays is the Lord's Day itself, the weekly commemoration of the Resurrection. One of the three prefaces of the Lord's Day is used at the Eucharist. There is no proper preface for weekdays after Pentecost, while that of Epiphany may be used in the post-Epiphany season for both weekdays and Sundays, giving the "Epiphany Season" a slight emphasis as a seasonal unit.

The narratives of Jesus' baptism and transfiguration form a sort of frame for the season. They are both festivals of our Lord and may be kept as feasts with white vestments (though the Transfiguration as a Feast of our Lord is celebrated on its own day, August 6). The Epiphany preface is appointed for both. The Sundays in between are "green" and use either the Lord's Day preface or that of Epiphany. These are the Sundays on which your generically planned Sunday Eucharist will require little or no change. They should, nevertheless, be planned as a unit, assuring continuity of sermon themes, ceremonial and musical treatment.

Epiphany – Major Feasts, Seasonal Rites, and Other Commemorations

Epiphany Blessing[1]

The following blessing may be used by a bishop or priest whenever a blessing is appropriate. It is a three-fold form with an Amen at the end of each sentence, leading into a Trinitarian blessing. This may be used from the feast of the Epiphany through the following Sunday.

May Almighty God, who led the Wise Men by the shining of a star to find the Christ, the Light from Light, lead you also, in your pilgrimage, to find the Lord. *Amen.*

May God, who sent the Holy Spirit to rest upon the Only-begotten at his baptism in the Jordan River, pour out that Spirit on you who have come to the waters of new birth. *Amen.*

May God, by the power that turned water into wine at the wedding feast at Cana, transform your lives and make glad your hearts. *Amen.*

And the blessing of God Almighty, the Father, the Son, and the Holy Spirit, be upon you and remain with you for ever. *Amen.*

or this

May Christ, the Son of God, be manifest in you, that your lives may be a light to the world; and the blessing of God Almighty, the Father, the Son, and the Holy Spirit, be among you, and remain with you always. *Amen.*

Blessing for a Home

Twelfth Night (January 5), the Feast of the Epiphany (January 6), or another day during the week following, is an occasion for family and friends to gather for a blessing of their home for the coming year.

Following an eastern European tradition, a visual blessing may be inscribed with white chalk above the main door; for example, 20 + CMB + 24. The numbers change with each year, with this year being 2024. The three letters stand for either the ancient Latin blessing Christe mansionem benedicat, which means "Christ, bless this house," or the legendary names of the Magi (Caspar, Melchior, and Balthasar).

Celebrant Peace be to this house, and to all who dwell in it.

Visit, O blessed Lord, this home with the gladness of your presence, bless *all* who live here with the gifts of your love; and grant that *they* may manifest your love [to each other and] to all who lives *they* touch. May *they* grow in grace and in the knowledge and love of you; guide, comfort, and strengthen *them*; and preserve *them* in peace, O Jesus Christ, now and for ever. *Amen.*[2]

Feast of Lights: An Epiphany Pageant[3]

This service is one of darkness and light, showing how the message of Jesus spread throughout the world and throughout the ages to the present day. It can take the form of a simple liturgy of lighting candles in the sanctuary or can be one in which participants dress in costume to represent each of the persons in history who helped spread the Light of Christ. Traditionally, it is held on the Feast of the Epiphany, or on an evening at the beginning of this season.

Candles can be placed throughout the church, or on the altar. Characters can be seated in the congregation, come forth to stand in front and recite their lines, go light their candle,

1 "Seasonal Blessings," BOS 2022, 12.

2 Previously published in *The Book of Occasional Services 2003*, 49. Not included in more recent revisions.

3 Sharon Ely Pearson, "Feast of Lights: An Epiphany Pageant" part of Church Publishing Incorporated's *Skiturgies: Pageants, Plays, Rites & Rituals* collection.

then return to their seat. Have a candle lighter (taper) at a location so each participant to easily pick it up on their way to light "their" candle. Once the first candle is lit, subsequent candles can be lit from the flame of the previously lit candle.

There are many characters (41+/-), several without speaking roles. Ideally a different person represents each character; however, individuals can represent more than one person, especially if you are not dressing up as the person. This is an excellent pageant to be totally handed over to youth in its production and presentation as an offering to the congregation.

Costumes

Costumes that are used for Christmas pageants can be used – simple robes and headpieces for most of the characters that lived in the first century. Academic robes or period costumes can be used for later period characters.

Props

One candle (in a candlestick, holder, stand, etc.) per character located on the altar, chancel area, or around the sanctuary.

Candle lighter/taper

Candles (with paper followers to catch drips) per every member of the congregation or audience

Script

[NARRATOR]: We come to bear witness to the Light. In the fullness of time, God entered this world in the birth of Jesus, the Word of God, the Light of the world. Jesus grew to adulthood in Nazareth of Galilee. He came to the river Jordan to be baptized by John, and when he came up out of the water, the heavens opened and the Spirit of God descended upon Him, and God said, "You are my beloved Son."

[JESUS]: Let the Paschal candle be lit for Jesus Christ, the light of the world.

[NARRATOR]: Jesus chose twelve ordinary men to receive his light. He spoke to them saying: "While you have the light, believe in the light, that you may become children of light." Then he sent them as apostles to establish the Church, to spread his light to all people, in every race and in every nation on earth. Let a candle be lit for each of the Twelve Apostles . . .

[PETER]: Simon, called Peter. Jesus called me "the rock" on which he would build the Church.

[ANDREW]: Andrew, his brother. A fisherman.

[JAMES]: James, the son of Zebedee. Also a fisherman.

[JOHN]: John, his brother. A fisherman.

[PHILIP]: Philip.

[BARTHOLOMEW]: Bartholomew.

[MATTHEW]: Matthew, the tax collector.

[JAMES]: James, the son of Alphaeus.

[SIMON]: Simon, the Zealot.

[THOMAS]: Thomas. Following the resurrection, many felt I had doubts of Jesus' rising to new life.

[JUDE]: Jude

[JUDAS ISCARIOT]: Judas Iscariot. I was to betray Jesus with a kiss. Let my candle be extinguished for the light I was unable to carry to the end. *(Light candle, then extinguish by blowing out.)*

[MARY MAGDALENE]: I was the first witness to the resurrection of Jesus, and one who first bore that news to the Twelve. I had accompanied Jesus for much of His ministry, and my special and favored relationship with the Lord is shown in the fact that it was to me that Jesus first spoke after he had risen. From ancient tradition in the Church, I am accorded a status equal to an Apostle.

[MATTHIAS]: I am another who is ranked with the original Twelve. I was elected by the remaining eleven to take the place of Judas in their number.

[NARRATOR]: Let two candles be lit for Matthias and Mary Magdalene, who together show that the Apostolic Succession is proven not only by lineage but also by faithful presence and witness.

[NARRATOR]: Many women have served as disciples, witnesses, and apostles.

[MARY OF BETHANY]: *(Move forward with Martha of Bethany)* Mary of Bethany. I served Jesus many times at my home in Bethany. A week before his crucifixion, I took a jar of expensive perfume, poured it on his feet, wiping it with my hair. I loved to sit at Jesus' feet and listen to him.

[MARTHA OF BETHANY]: *(Move forward with Mary of Bethany)* Martha of Bethany. I was often focused on the details when Jesus came to visit us. But I knew Jesus was the source of eternal life, and believed God would give Jesus whatever he asked. I was right, my brother, Lazarus, was brought back to life.

[SAMARITAN WOMAN]: The Samaritan woman. I met Jesus at Jacob's well and was among the first to confess Jesus as the messiah.

[JOANNA and SUSANNA]: *(Say together.)* We traveled with Jesus through Galilee and financed his journeys.

[MARY]: I was the Mother of our Lord, and was present at the cross and among those gathered at Pentecost.

[PHOEBE and PRISCILLA]: *(Say together.)* We were deacons in the early church.

[JUNIA]: I was an apostle and contemporary of Paul.

[LOIS, EUNICE, and TABITHA: *(Say together.)* We were disciples during the early years of the Church.

[NARRATOR]: Let candles be lit for each of these faithful women of scripture and the early Church, who both led and served their communities of faith.

[NARRATOR]: These apostles went out into the world to spread the light of the gospel of Christ. There were many who opposed their witness and the Word.

[PAUL]: I was one of those who tried to put out the Light. I was known as Saul of Tarsus, a fanatical persecutor of all followers of Jesus until one day I was overcome by a vision of the Light of Christ. Taking the name of Paul, I carried that light throughout the Mediterranean world, establishing the Church far beyond the cities and people of the Jewish culture. From the seeds I planted and those who accompanied me, the light of Christ has spread from a small group in Jerusalem to two billion people in every nation on earth today. Today I am called, "the apostle to the Gentiles."

[NARRATOR]: The story of Jesus spread throughout the world.

[AUGUSTINE]: In the year 596, I, Augustine, was sent from Rome by Pope Gregory the Great to be a missionary to England. I became the first archbishop of Canterbury and reorganized the remnants of the old Celtic churches throughout Britain and Ireland, which had existed since the second century and had been built up by revered predecessors in the faith, such as Patrick of Ireland, Alban in England, David in Wales, and Ninian in Scotland.

[NARRATOR]: Let five candles be lit for these patriarchs of British Christianity.

(Patrick, Alban, David, and Ninian come forward to light candles)

[STEPHEN LANGON]: Reading and studying the Holy Scriptures was greatly facilitated by the system of dividing the Bible's texts into chapters and verses. I, Stephen Langon, introduced this relatively modern idea. I was an Englishman at the University of Paris and later, in 1207, became archbishop of Canterbury.

[THOMAS CRANMER]: I, Thomas Cranmer, became archbishop of Canterbury in 1533. I had been much influenced theologically by the Lutheran reformers in Germany, such as Martin Luther. When the English church rejected the authority of the papacy in 1534, I led the creation and adoption of a new liturgy for the Church, producing the first two versions of *The Book of Common Prayer*, which has been the lifeblood of Anglican worship throughout the world ever since. I am known as the father of Anglican liturgy.

[QUEEN ELIZABETH I]: It was I, a laywoman, whose genius, leadership, and personal faith truly established Anglicanism as a strong and distinct tradition. As Queen of England, I preserved and brought together into one church the ancient catholic order and the principles of the Reformation. My vision presented the possibilities of unity with diversity.

[SAMUEL SEABURY]: After the American colonies won independence, I was sent from Connecticut to Scotland in 1784 to be consecrated as the first American Anglican bishop. I, Samuel Seabury, thus secured the historic episcopate for the Episcopal Church.

[WILLIAM WHITE]: Three years later, the archbishop of Canterbury presided at the consecration of two others to be bishops for the Episcopal Church. I, William White, was one of these men from of Pennsylvania, and became the first presiding bishop of the Episcopal Church. I was the chief architect and wise overseer for the Church for almost fifty years. Every Episcopal bishop, past and present, can trace their ordinations back to my episcopacy.

[YOUR FIRST BISHOP]: ____________________was the first Episcopal bishop of______________, consecrated for this office in _________.

(Note any historical information).

[YOUR FIRST CLERGY PERSON/LAY LEADER]:

(Note the founding of your congregation and any leadership involved, including historical information about your church.)

[NARRATOR]: We, the people of_______________ *(name your congregation),* are now the recipients of the faith and faithfulness, which has been entrusted to us in _____________ *(your town or city)* as congregations in full communion with each other. With joy and gratitude, we ponder that the faith of Christ, announced by a miraculous star two thousand years ago, has been passed down through the centuries to our places of worship – by Magi, apostles, saints, bishops, local clergy and laypeople: men and women, extraordinary and ordinary. The light is passed from the Bethlehem manger to this place and to our homes. Our prayer is that we sustain and grow the Light that is Jesus Christ, and pass it on – to those now beside us, and around us, and to those who come after us. As an outward sign of this, everyone will please light each other's unlit candles.

May Almighty God, who led the wise men by the shining of a star to find the Christ, the Light from Light, lead you also, in your pilgrimage, to find the Lord. *Amen.*

By the shining of a star to find the Christ, the Light from Light, lead you also, in your pilgrimage, to find the Lord. *Amen.*

The Third Monday in January, Martin Luther King, Jr. Holiday

As a federal holiday, this day falls on the third Monday in January. The Episcopal Church observes his feast day as April 4th, the date of his assassination, but also gives permission is given to observe it on January 15, if desirable. While the Book of Common Prayer *does not permit substitution or transfer of this feast day for a Sunday, in terms of the lessons and collect appointed, the Sunday service near his January holiday can be designed to highlight his life and witness and explore ways to enact justice in our communities today. The federal holiday will fall on the Monday following the Second or Third Sunday after the Epiphany.*

Some schools celebrate the day by teaching their students about the work and ministry of Martin Luther King, Jr., and the struggle against racial segregation and racism. It has also become a day where Americans give some of their time on this day as volunteers in action in their communities. For congregations, this day can be a day of focused prayer, preaching, and education on the legacy Dr. King entrusted to us.

The Collect for MLK's feast day may be used during the service, from Lesser Feasts and Fasts:

Almighty God, by the hand of Moses your servant you led your people out of slavery, and made them free at last: Grant that your church, following the example of your prophet Martin Luther King, may resist oppression in the name of your love, and may strive to secure for all your children the blessed liberty of the Gospel of Jesus Christ; who lives and reigns with you and the Holy Spirit, one God, now and for ever. ***Amen.***[4]

Other resources are available, including this prayer:

Lord our God, see how oppression and violence are our sad inheritance, one generation to the next. We look for you where the lowly are raised up, where the mighty are brought down. We find you there in your servants and we give you thanks this day for your preacher and witness, Martin Luther King Jr. Fill us with your spirit: where our human community is divided by racism, torn by repression, saddened by fear and ignorance, may we give ourselves to your work of healing. Grant this through Christ our Lord. *Amen.*[5]

January 18, The Confession of Saint Peter the Apostle

This is a Major Feast and may substitute for the Sunday after the Epiphany when it falls on a Sunday. It falls on or during the week of the Second Sunday after the Epiphany. The Collect for the Day is found on pages 187 or 238 of the Book of Common Prayer.

Simon Bar-Jonah, a boisterous fisher, confessed to Jesus, "You are the Christ." Jesus renamed him Peter, the "rock," on which Jesus built his church. Peter and his brother Andrew were the first disciples; thus, Peter figures keenly in the gospels despite his ill manners. Peter tried to walk on water; Peter wished to build three tabernacles; Peter thrice denied knowing Christ. On the other hand, Peter courageously risked his life to be a disciple, openly declaring his belief in Jesus as the Christ, and he courageously headed the young church's missions. Peter transformed from ordinary Simon, overbearing and impetuous, to an extraordinary church leader, filled with the Holy Spirit.

January 18–25, Week of Prayer for Christian Unity

The Week of Prayer for Christian Unity is an international Christian ecumenical observance for eight days, held between the feasts of the Confession of St. Peter and the Conversion of St. Paul. The Sunday during the week will always be either the Third or Fourth Sunday after the Epiphany.

Collects in the Book of Common Prayer *that may wish to be used on this day include any of the following:*

Almighty Father, whose blessed Son before his passion prayed for his disciples that they might be

4 *Lesser Feasts and Fasts 2022* (New York, NY: Church Publishing, 2022), 175.

5 Christopher L. Webber, editor. *An American Prayer Book* (Harrisburg, PA: Morehouse Publishing, 2008), 124.

one, as you and he are one: Grant that your Church, being bound together in love and obedience to you, may be united in one body by the one Spirit, that the world may believe in him whom you have sent, your Son Jesus Christ our Lord; who lives and reigns with you, in the unity of the Holy Spirit, one God, now and for ever. ***Amen.***[6]

Lord Jesus Christ, you said to your apostles, "Peace I give to you; my own peace I leave with you:" Regard not our sins, but the faith of your Church, and give to us the peace and unity of that heavenly City, where with the Father and the Holy Spirit, you live and reign, now and for ever. ***Amen.***[7]

O God the Father of our Lord Jesus Christ, our only Savior, the Prince of Peace: Give us grace seriously to lay to heart the great dangers we are in by our unhappy divisions; take away all hatred and prejudice, and whatever else may hinder us from godly union and concord; that, as there is but one Body and one Spirit, one hope of our calling, one Lord, one Faith, one Baptism, one God and Father of us all, so we may be all of one heart and of one soul, united in one holy bond of truth and peace, of faith and charity, and may with one mind and one mouth glorify *thee*; through Jesus Christ our Lord. ***Amen.***[8]

Additional resources for study, prayer, music, and worship are offered in advance at http://www.oikoumene.org/en/resources/week-of-prayer, accessed May 22, 2020.

This litany for 'The Week of Prayer for Christian Unity" may be used as the Prayers of the People:

Litanist: We have come together in the presence of Almighty God to pray for the recovery of the unity of Christ's Church, and for the renewal of our common life in Jesus Christ, in whom we are all made one.

Silence

Let us give heed to the words of Holy Scripture which set forth God's will and purpose for the unity of his Church.

"Hear, O Israel, the Lord our God is one Lord; and you shall love the Lord your God with all your heart, and with all your soul, and with all your mind."

Lord, write your word in our hearts;

That we may know and do your will.

"There is one body, and one Spirit, as there is also one hope held out in God's call to you; one Lord, one faith, one baptism; one God and Father of all, who is over all and through all and in all."

Lord, write your word in our hearts:

That we may know and do your will.

"For Christ is like a single body with its many limbs and organs which, many as they are, together make up one body. For indeed we were all brought into one body by baptism, in the one Spirit, whether we are Jews or Greeks, whether slaves or free, and that one Holy Spirit was poured out for all of us to drink."

Lord, write your word in our hearts:

That we may know and do your will.

"But it is not for these alone that I pray, but for those also who through their words put their faith in me; may they all be one; as you, Father, are in me, and I in you, so also may they be in us, that the world may believe that you have sent me."

Lord, write your word in our hearts:

That we may know and do your will. Amen.[9]

January 25, The Conversion of Saint Paul the Apostle

This is a Major Feast and may substitute for the Sunday after the Epiphany when it falls on a Sunday. It falls on or during the week of the Third Sunday after the Epiphany. The Collect for the Day is found on pages 187 or 238 of the Book of Common Prayer.

Saul, an orthodox Jew, studied under the famous rabbi Gamaliel, but soon after Jesus died, Saul connected to the Christian movement. At first, he was determined to crush it as heresy. On his way to Damascus to persecute Christians, Saul converted dramatically, and dedicating himself to Jesus. He is better known to Christians as Paul, his name in the Greek-speaking world. He planted Christian congregations bordering the eastern Mediterranean. His letters manifest his alignment with the mind of Christ, thereby founding Christian theology. Although rather frail physically, he was strong spiritually: "I will all the more gladly boast of my weaknesses that the power of Christ may rest upon me." His martyrdom is believed to have occurred in 64 under Nero.

---

6 "Various Occasions 14. For the Unity of the Church," BCP, 255. See also p. 204 for the traditional language version.

7 "The Collect at the Prayers 6," BCP, 395.

8 "Prayers and Thanksgivings 14. For the Unity of the Church," BCP, 818.

9 "The Week of Prayer for Christian Unity," in *The Wideness of God's Mercy: Litanies to Enlarge Our Prayer* edited by Jeffrey W. Rowthorn (New York, NY: Church Publishing, 2007), 128–129.

The Third Sunday after the Epiphany, Religious Life Sunday,

The General Convention of the Episcopal Church has designated the Third Sunday after the Epiphany as Religious Life Sunday, as part of an effort to raise visibility and awareness of our religious orders. Resources may be found at https://www.religiouslifesunday.org/.

It may be desirable to include this collect at the conclusion of the Prayers of the People or some other suitable place in the service:

From Prayers and Thanksgivings 16. For Monastic Orders and Vocations

O Lord Jesus Christ, you became poor for our sake, that we might be made rich through your poverty: Guide and sanctify, we pray, those whom you call to follow you under the vows of poverty, chastity, and obedience, that by their prayer and service they may enrich your Church, and by their life and worship may glorify your Name; for you reign with the Father and the Holy Spirit, one God, now and forever. *Amen.*[10]

The Month of February, Black History Month

Black History Month may occur during the later portion of the Season after the Epiphany as well as the beginning of Lent. There are many ways to celebrate Black History Month within the Sunday liturgy. One immediate option is to highlight the stories of Black heroes and saints on the Episcopal Church calendar during this month. There are several that can be highlighted throughout the month. There are many more throughout the year that could be identified, of course.

More information and Collects on each of these may be found in Lesser Feasts and Fasts 2022.

February 4, Manche Masemola, Martyr, 1928

Born in Marishane, South Africa (1913?), into a non-Christian farm family, Masemola worshipped with the Anglican Community of the Resurrection as a girl, but her parents forbade her baptism, beating her as dissuasion. She prophesied that she would die at her parents' hand and be baptized in her own blood. On February 4, 1928, Masemola's parents indeed killed her. Although she had not been baptized, the church recognized her baptism by her desire for it. In 1935, a small band of pilgrims came to her grave; now hundreds visit every August. Her statue stands at Westminster Abbey, a twentieth-century martyr.

February 8, Bakhita (Josephine Margaret Bakhita), Monastic, 1947

Born in Sudan, Bakhita's enslavement at seven traumatized her so badly that she forgot her name. The slavers named her "Bakhita," "fortunate one." She remained a slave for twelve years. Finally in 1883, she was sold to the Italian consul in Khartoum, who gave her to his friend, with whom she traveled to Italy. As a nanny, Bakhita attended a Christian institute with her charge. There, she was baptized as Josephine. She became a Canossian Daughter of Charity in 1896. She said she found God in her heart without ever being evangelized. Bakhita stands as inspiration for all the victimized.

February 11, The Consecration of Barbara Harris

Barbara Clementine Harris was born in Philadelphia, Pennsylvania, on June 12, 1930. She was active in the civil rights struggles of the 1960s and continued as a powerful advocate for the civil enfranchisement of all people in the United States. Ordained as a priest in 1980, her ministry was in both the parish and the public square. She continued to address issues of civil injustice while also offering a prophetic critique of the Episcopal Church for its homophobia, racism, and sexism. Barbara Harris was the first woman elected as bishop when the Diocese of Massachusetts elected her bishop suffragan in 1988. Her election and subsequent consecration were not without controversy, including threats on her life by those opposed to the inclusion of women in the House of Bishops. Despite these threats, she was consecrated bishop on February 11, 1989.

February 13, Absalom Jones, Priest, 1818

Born a slave in 1746 in Delaware, Jones taught himself to read from the Old Testament. He bought his freedom in 1784, having previously purchased his wife's. He served

10 "Prayers and Thanksgivings 16. For Monastic Orders and Vocations," BCP, 819.

as a lay minister at St. George's Methodist Episcopal Church, evangelizing alongside his friend Richard Allen. The resulting numbers of blacks at St. George's caused the fearful vestry to segregate them into an upper gallery; the blacks indignantly left the building as one body. Jones and Allen were elected overseers of the Free African Society of black Christians in 1787. They worked ceaselessly for blacks to be included within the Episcopal Church, into which Jones was ordained a priest on September 21, 1802.

February 16, Janani Luwum, Archbishop and Martyr

Janani Luwum was born in 1922 to Acholi parents in Mucwini, Uganda, near the Sudanese border. He served as a teacher and lay reader, studied at St. Augustine's College in Canterbury and was ordained a priest in 1956, overseeing twenty-four congregations in Uganda. He returned to England to study at the London College of Divinity. In 1969, he was ordained Bishop of Northern Uganda and elected Archbishop of the Church of Uganda, Rwanda, Burundi, and Boga Zaire in 1974. This role brought him into direct confrontation with the Ugandan military dictator Idi Amin. Seeking to protect his people from the brutality of Amin's regime, Luwum and other religious leaders were summoned to Amin's palace accused of complicity in a plot to murder the President. Most of the clerics left that day, but Archbishop Luwum was ordered to remain and was not seen alive after that. His body was released to his family several weeks later. Luwum said, during this period of intense confrontation, "While the opportunity is there, I preach the gospel with all my might, and my conscience is clear before God."

February 20, Frederick Douglass, Social Reformer, 1895

Born a slave in 1818, Douglass broke the law by teaching himself to read. At fourteen, he converted to Christianity in the African Methodist Episcopal Church, which had music that bolstered his struggle for freedom. Douglass spoke on tours in the North sponsored by the American Anti-Slavery Society, but his renown as an orator magnified his fear of capture. When Douglass fled to England, his American friends bought his freedom so he could return to America, where he edited the *North Star*, a pro-abolition journal. Douglass championed the rights of African-Americans and of all women and children.

February 28, Anna Julia Haywood Cooper, Educator, 1964

Anna Julia Haywood Cooper was born on August 10, 1858, in Raleigh, North Carolina, to an enslaved Black woman, Hannah Stanley, and a white man, presumably her mother's owner. Two years after the Civil War ended, she attended St. Augustine Normal School and Collegiate Institute, founded by the Episcopal Church to educate African American teachers and clergy. Cooper later studied mathematics at Oberlin College, and moved to Washington, D.C., to teach at Washington Colored High School. Cooper emphasized the importance of equal education for African Americans. An advocate for African American women, Cooper assisted in organizing the Colored Women's League and the first Colored Settlement House in Washington, D.C. In 1892, her book *A View from the South* was published, in which she challenged the Episcopal Church to offer more direct support for the African American members of its church in their quest for advancement and improvement in a segregated society. She wrote, "religion (ought to be if it isn't) a great deal more than mere gratification of the instinct for worship linked with the straight-teaching of irreproachable credos. Religion must be life made true; and life is action, growth, development – begun now and ending never." In 1925, she completed her doctorate from the Sorbonne in Paris, the fourth African American woman to do so. She died on February 27, 1964, at the age of 105.

February 2, The Presentation of Our Lord Jesus Christ "Candlemas"

This is one of three Feasts of our Lord that is designated as taking ***precedence*** *over the Sunday lessons and collect, and so replaces the Sunday after the Epiphany, when this feast falls on a Sunday. This feast occurs on or after the Fourth Sunday after the Epiphany. The Collect for the Day is found on pages 187 and 239 and the Lessons are found on page 923 of* the Book of Common Prayer. *Note that the Feast could simply be celebrated with the Liturgy of Holy Eucharist, Morning Prayer, or Evening Prayer, without using the Candlemas procession material that follows. See additional information below to plan this feast, particularly when it falls on Sunday.*

The First Sunday in February, Theological Education Sunday

This date will fall either on the Fourth, Fifth, or Last Sunday after the Epiphany. Theological Education Sunday (TES) is officially recognized on the first Sunday in February. It is a day parishioners set aside to pray and give for all laity and clergy whose ministry is Christian education, wherever that ministry happens – in the home, preschool programs, parishes, colleges, universities, and seminaries. Established in 1999 by The Episcopal Church, this Sunday on the church calendar is an occasion for all parishioners to focus on education as a key aspect of mission. Guest preachers and seminarians sponsored by the congregation are often invited to preach.

Litanist: O God of truth, ever beckoning us to loftier understanding and deeper wisdom, we seek your will and implore your grace for all who share the life of divinity schools and seminaries in our day, knowing that, unless you build among us, we who teach and learn will labor but in vain.

Silence

For those who teach, that they may together bring fire and vision to a common task, knowing one field yet eager to relate it to all others; just in their academic demands, yet seeing each student as a child of God; fitted to teach not only by great learning but by great faith in humankind and in you, their God:

In them and in us, O God, kindle your saving truth.

Silence

For deans and presidents, trustees and development officers, and all others who point the way for theological education in our day, that their chief concern be not budgets and buildings and prestige, but men and women freed to know your whole will and roused to serve you in your Church:

In them and in us, O God, kindle your saving truth.

Silence

For janitors and maids, for cooks and keepers of the grounds, for those who prepare our food and wash our dishes, and for the host of other workers and suppliers whose faithfulness ministers to our common life:

In them and in us, O God, kindle your saving truth.

Silence

For parents and givers of scholarships, who support theological students, that they may not desire for them more income, or social acceptance, or glory of family or of donor, but look rather for new breadth of intelligence, the spirit made whole, and devoted Christian service in life:

In them and in us, O God, kindle your saving truth.

Silence

For the students themselves, that their confusion may be brief, their perspective constantly enlarged, and their minds and spirits alert to all that chapel and classroom, library and fieldwork assignment can mean in their lives.

In them and in us, O God, kindle your saving truth.

Silence

For every member of this community of learning and service, that with them we may be aware of your Holy Spirit leading us all into truth, and may grasp here your special intention for all our learning and striving:

In them and in us, O God, kindle your saving truth.

Silence

We know, O heavenly Father, that a seminary education is but the willing and planning of many people, each sought by your great love. Grant that we who would earnestly serve you may witness in the world to the reality of your gospel, as it is shown forth in Christ Jesus our Lord. ***Amen.***[11]

Early February, Super Bowl Sunday: Souper Bowl of Caring

Typically the first or second Sunday in February, which could be the Fourth, Fifth, Sixth or Last Sunday after the Epiphany. If it's the second Sundayin February, it could also be the First Sunday in Lent.

Souper Bowl of Caring is a national movement of young people working to fight hunger and poverty in their own communities around the time of the Super Bowl football game. In the weeks leading up to or on Super Bowl Sunday, young people take up a collection (many use a soup pot), asking for one dollar or one item of food for people in need. They give 100 percent of their donation directly to the local hunger-relief charity of their choice. Learn more at https://souperbowl.org, accessed May 22, 2020.

11 John Oliver Nelson, "For Theological Seminaries," in *The Wideness of God's Mercy: Litanies to Enlarge Our Prayer* edited by Jeffrey W. Rowthorn (New York, NY: Church Publishing, 2007), 165–166.

You may wish to incorporate a prayer focusing on these concerns in the liturgy that day or on the Sundays just prior to that day:

Almighty and most merciful God, we remember before you all poor and neglected persons whom it would be easy for us to forget: those who are homeless and destitute, those who are old and those who are sick, and all who have none to care for them. Help us to heal those who are broken in body or spirit, and to turn their sorrow into joy. Grant this, Father, for the love of your Son, who for our sake became poor, Jesus Christ our Lord. *Amen.*[12]

or this

We have seen your hand of mercy in the service of those who spread food, shelter, hope, and faith to suffering humankind. Plant more seeds in the bellies of the full, to burst forth in joy, to explode like the ripened grain with life-giving bread. Give us, we beseech you, in the bosoms of our souls, a passion for the powerless and a commitment to place all poverty in the past. *Amen.*[13]

February 24, Saint Matthias the Apostle

This is a Major Feast and may substitute for the Sunday after the Epiphany when it falls on a Sunday. It falls on or during the week of the Seventh Sunday after the Epiphany, when there is one. It may not substitute for the Last Sunday after the Epiphany or for a Sunday in Lent, if that's when it occurs. The Collect for the Day is found on pages 188 or 239 of the Book of Common Prayer.

Little is known of Matthias beyond his selection as a disciple. In the nine days between Jesus's ascension and the day of Pentecost, the disciples gathered in prayer. Peter reminded them that the defection and death of Judas had left the fellowship with a vacancy. The Acts of the Apostles records Peter's suggestion that one of the followers from the time of Jesus's baptism until his crucifixion "must become with us a witness to his Resurrection." After prayer, the disciples cast lots between nominees Barsabbas Justus and Matthias; the lot fell to Matthias. Tradition holds him as exemplary, a suitable witness to the Resurrection, but his service is unheralded by history and unsung by psalms.

---

12 "Prayers and Thanksgivings 35. For the Poor and the Neglected," BCP, 826.

13 Marcia King, "For an End to Poverty" in *Lifting Women's Voices: Prayers to Change the World* Margaret Rose, Jenny Te Paa, Jeanne Person, and Abagail Nelson, editors (Harrisburg, PA: Morehouse Pubiishing, 2009), 69.

End of Epiphany: Preparing for Lent

Epiphany Season can often be a short season. Begin to schedule meetings in January to plan for Lent, at the latest. Following are several practices that can occur near the very end of the Season after the Epiphany, just before Lent begins.

Burying the Alleluia

The Last Sunday after the Epiphany features the story of the Transfiguration in the gospel reading. This is also the last Sunday the word "Alleluia" will be used in liturgy, and preparations begin for the coming week's Ash Wednesday liturgy as well as the solemn season that follows.

As we keep the ancient practice of fasting from singing or speaking "alleluia" through the forty days of Lent, you may consider the practice of "burying" the alleluia at the end of the liturgy on the last Sunday before Ash Wednesday. This might mean simply singing an appropriate song at the end of the service or including the actual lowering of a visual alleluia banner (perhaps created by children) while singing. You could bury it in your churchyard or hide it away in a dark place (but remember where you put it!). Bring the alleluia back as part of the first alleluias at the Great Vigil of Easter or your Easter Festive Eucharist.

Leader: O God, make speed to save us, hallelujah, hallelujah.

O Lord, make haste to help us, alleluia, alleluia.

"Alleluia" is another way to say "Praise the Lord."

Our God is a loving God, worthy of praise.

The faithful people of God praise him for the great deeds he has done.

God created us out of dust, restored the land, took Israel out of exile, spoke through the prophets, and gives hope and forgiveness through his Son, Jesus Christ.

The Book of Psalms contains "Hallels" (Psalms 113–118) or special chants. These hymns of praise were sung on each step going up to the Temple during festive celebrations and pilgrimages.

Praise the Lord, all nations! Extol him, all peoples! For great is his steadfast love toward us; and the faithfulness of the Lord endures for ever. Praise the Lord. (Psalm 117)

Hallelujah! Praise God in his holy temple. (Psalm 150:1)

Let everything that has breath praise the Lord, Hallelujah. (Psalm 150:6)

We have much for which to be thankful. But there is not always joy in our lives. There is sadness and loneliness in the world. Sometimes we need time to think. Jesus spent forty days in the wilderness praying to God. Lent is our forty days of quiet time to prepare for the mystery of Easter. This is a time when we do not say "alleluia" in church. "Alleluia" is reserved for the great festive celebration of Easter.

How shall we sing the Lord's song in a foreign land? (Psalm 137:4)

(Silently bury the "Alleluia")

Leader: Almighty God, you bid your faithful people to rejoice in praise, but also to repent and reflect in silence. Give us grace and courage to devote our hearts to you and to love others as you would, through Jesus Christ our Lord, who lives and reigns with you and the Holy Spirit, on God, forever and ever. *Amen.*[14]

Shrove Tuesday

Pancakes or other festive foods

The day before Ash Wednesday was the day all households were to use up all milk, eggs, and fat to prepare for the strict fasting of Lent. These ingredients were made into pancakes, a meal which came to symbolize preparation for the discipline of Lent, from the English tradition. Other names for this day include Carnival (farewell to meat) and Mardi Gras (Fat Tuesday of the French tradition). Thus, many congregations have Shrove Tuesday pancake suppers or other celebrations.

O Lord, we as we prepare our hearts for our Lenten journey, bless these pancakes we are about to share. As they remind us of the rich ingredients from our kitchens that fill our bellies with satisfaction, may we also remember your time in the wilderness when you did not even have bread or water. Be present with us as we get ready to begin the holy season of Lent, strengthening us to be ready to serve you in the days and weeks to come. *Amen.*

14 Linda Nichols, "Farewell to Alleluia" as part of Church Publishing Incorporated's *Skiturgies* collection.

Making Pretzels

The pretzel has been used during Lent for over 1500 years. It is thought that originally pretzels were made by monks to resemble arms crossed in prayer. These breads were called "little arms." This can have deep spiritual meaning for us during Lent. Since basically only flour and water are used, pretzels can remind us of fasting.

Heavenly Father, we ask you to bless these little breads. Each time we eat them may we be reminded of the special season we are in and that through prayer we will become better people to each other. Let us not forget those who are in need of our prayers daily. Keep your loving arms around us, O Father, to protect us always. *Amen.*

Burning of Palms for Ashes

Ashes for Ash Wednesday are traditionally derived from burning the palm branches from the previous year's Palm Sunday service. This is especially engaging for children to understand where ashes come from. This may be done publicly on the Last Sunday after Epiphany or on Shrove Tuesday. You will want to invite members of the church to bring back their palm branches and collect them during Epiphany Season.

The primary concern here, rather than rite or ritual, is safety. Ensure that you are outdoors with ample ventilation and a clear area for the burning. Any fire-safe vessel large enough for the palm branches should be sufficient and a clear, safe surface that can handle heat (such as a grill) should be available to hold the vessel. Palm branches have oil and can burn with a lot of smoke. Care should be taken if it is windy, to avoid burning embers escaping. After the raw ashes have cooled, they will need to be ground and sifted to a fine powder. A little ashes go a long way on Ash Wednesday; it doesn't take many palm branches to provide for an entire congregation's ashes. Some advocate adding other ingredients to the ashes, but care should be taken to ensure that additions won't cause skin irritation for recipients on Wednesday. Naturally, one can also purchase ashes from a church supply company and a back up supply should be on hand. Just in case.

Reconciliation of a Penitent

"Shrove" comes from the verb "to shrive" (to confess and receive absolution) prior to the start of the Lenten season. Some churches may wish to offer availability of a priest to provide Reconciliation,

or private confession on this day. The services for this sacramental rite are found in the Book of Common Prayer *from pages 446–452. Reconciliation may also be made by appointment at any time with a priest.*

The old adage about private confession in the Episcopal Church is that "All can, some should, and none must" participate in this pastoral rite. For some, it is a practice of their Rule of Life, to make regular confession; for others it may be a way to address feelings of guilt or burdens about past actions that seem to linger. Hearing a discreet priest offer counsel and pronounce God's firm absolution may offer freedom and the ability to receive the forgiveness God promises.

The Epiphany

January 6

The significance of Jesus's birth is revealed to the world beyond Judea
The Manifestation of Christ to the Gentiles

Anchor Points – The Propers and the Feast

The fixed points for each service are the appointed or proper readings and collect as well as the themes of the day or season.

Readings and Psalm

Isaiah 60:1–6

In our Hebrew scripture lesson the prophet envisions the end of exile and the glorious restoration of Jerusalem. Although darkness covers the earth, the Lord will be a light making God's people shine. To this radiance shall come the nations. Rich treasures will be brought from afar to honor God.

Psalm 72:1–7, 10–14

The psalm asks that God endow the king with compassionate justice and righteousness, and that his reign may extend over all nations and throughout allgenerations.

Ephesians 3:1–12

Here is set forth the great theme of Paul's apostolic commission: the revealed mystery that Christ's salvation extends beyond Judaism to include all peoples. The apostle is near the end of his ministry and in prison at the time of the writing of this letter. Now it is recognized as God's eternal purpose that the Gentiles are to be members of the same body. The wisdom of God is made known through the church even in transcendental realms.

Matthew 2:1–12

Our gospel is the story of the wise men from the east, who, guided by a star, come to worship the child born to be king. Despite the wicked plotting of Herod, the Magi are able to bring their gifts to Jesus without betraying his exact location. Early Christians found in the rich symbolism and motifs of the story the fulfillment of both Hebrew scripture prophecy and the dreams of many peoples. The meaning of this birth, amid terrifyingly human circumstances, enlightens and transcends human history.

Collect

O God, by the leading of a star you manifested your only Son to the peoples of the earth: Lead us, who know you now by faith, to your presence, where we may see your glory face to face; through Jesus Christ our Lord, who lives and reigns with you and the Holy Spirit, one God, now and for ever. *Amen.*

Proper Preface

Epiphany – Because in the mystery of the Word made flesh, you have caused a new light to shine in our hearts, to give the knowledge of your glory in the face of your Son Jesus Christ our Lord. (Rite II, BCP 378; Rite I BCP 346)

Feast Day Pairings

See the table below for choices appointed for this day. Preferences are put in **bold**. Not all choices are suitable for all congregations or community, though, so consider these preferences as a starting point before making a decision about your own congregation.

	Feast of Epiphany	Rite I	Rite II	EOW1	BOS 2022
Color	White/Gold/Festive				
Entrance Rite	Customary	323	355	50	
Song of Praise/Kyrie	**Glory to God (Gloria in excelsis)**	324	356		
Collect		162	214		
Creed	Nicene Creed	326, 327	358	53	
Prayers of the People	**Locally written**; options below; BCP form	329	387–393	54–55	
Offertory Sentence	"They shall bring gold and frankincense and shall proclaim the praise of the Lord" (Isaiah)	343–344	376–377		
Eucharistic Prayer	**One that allows use of the Epiphany preface**	2–340	**B – 367** or D – 372	1–57	
Proper Preface	Epiphany	346	378		
Breaking of the Bread (Fraction)	Christ our Passover (BCP) or **Blessed are those who are called (Hymn S 172)**	337	365	69	
Postcommunion Prayer		339	**Eternal God – 365**	God of abundance – 69	
Blessing	**Seasonal in BOS**				**12**
Dismissal	**Let us go forth in the Name of Christ**	340	366		
Notes	Use incense, if available/permissible				

Additional Notes:

Fraction Anthem at the Breaking of the Bread – The option provided in Rite I and Rite II ("Christ our Passover") is suitable throughout the season and the Alleluias may be included. Explore other texts that may be used from *The Hymnal 1982* from S 151 to S 172 (sung or said). The text at Hymn S 172 ("Blessed are those who are called") is very appropriate for Epiphany as it emphasizes that all nations are called into Christ's life. Additionally, EOW1 has several options.

Content Resources

Reading Between the Lines

Epiphany signifies manifestation, light, and glory. The prophet Isaiah speaks God's promise to exiled and dispersed Israel, her radiance and restoration will be observed by nations, natural elements, and foreigners who will be drawn to that light. Matthew records a journey of star-discerning Magi travelling from the east; the homage they show discloses Jesus' identity. Revelation calls for wisdom: how do the Magi determine that following a star from their place of origin will lead them to a child born to be King? How does Herod assess the threat level of such a child? How do those in Herod's realm respond to the quest of the Magi? How does Joseph defend the child in his care against the threat Herod poses? Discernment is a question that haunts all who perceive light. Receivers discern divine revelation by means of a star, dreams, and prophecy. Each medium is particular to the recipient: for the foreign Magi astronomy, not scripture, provides authoritative revelation; Herod's advisors consult their scriptures, not the heavens; while Joseph, a righteous man and a devout Jew, is visited with dreams and angelic words. The stars, the scriptures, the dreams all speak joy, life and triumph for the child and his mother, to those who would receive that message. Herod, seeking his own security and power, receives from divine revelation only fear, deceit, stealth and murderous rage. Matthew asserts that the same God of Biblical revelation is also the source of astrological revelation to the Magi that brought them from a different culture and civilization across many miles with gifts of gold, frankincense and myrrh for the child born King of the Jews. We don't know what happens when they go home. We don't know how they deal with knowledge of the child. But we do know that God works through their lives and the lives of those with whom they come into contact.

Central Themes

Epiphany is here! The three kings arrive, bearing gifts for the baby Jesus. In both Isaiah and the psalm for today, the focus is on a God whose glory is revealed in defense of the poor, has pity on the weak and needy, and redeems their lives from oppression and violence. Consider how we might shift the focus away from crowns and expensive gifts to caring for the weak and oppressed. As God's hands and feet on earth we can honor God with gifts of service and love to others. Contact a local charity and find out what they most need right now. Encourage folks to learn about embedded racism by taking a class or hosting a discussion group. Use every way you know to lift others up.

In the lectionary resource *Brightest and Best*, Sam Portaro wonders how the story would change if the Magi were not actually kings or astrologers but itinerant entertainers and magicians, part of a class commonly accepted as fools. What if it was not their wise and strategic searching that brought them to Herod, but simple political ignorance? And maybe their dodgy relationships with various towns and villages would explain how they could so easily give Herod the slip. He goes on to suggest that it was not wisdom that they brought to the child, but that's certainly a gift with which they left. "Wisdom, then, is not the prerequisite to relationship with Jesus, but the product of knowing the Lord. Those who encounter God come away with more, and better, than what they bring. And is this not always the case in every relationship? If we ever come to know wisdom in our relationships, are we not always wiser on the way home?"

Engaging All Ages

Only Matthew tells us the story of the Magi, but does not describe their number or race or mode of travel. The biblical emphasis is on their travel from the east with three gifts, following a star that led them to Bethlehem, where they found the newly born child. The Magi brought expensive but very practical gifts: gold for a king, myrrh for burial preparation, and frankincense for praise to God. These gifts reveal the royal, divine, and sacrificial nature of the infant Jesus. Has anyone ever been on a quest like those of the Magi? What were you seeking? What gifts would you have brought to the Christ child, knowing what his life was going to be like when he grew up?

Prayers of the People: Option 1

Presider Gracious and loving Creator, in the manifestation of Christ you have revealed to all the earth the mystery of your love, spreading your illumination and your abundant promises to all humanity: Hear us now and visit us with that light, as we pray for the needs of all creation, saying: Arise, shine, for the light has come, and the glory of God has risen upon us.

Litanist Through the Church, the wisdom of God in its rich variety may now be made known: Help us, O Holy One, to manifest the boundless riches of Christ, becoming servants according to the gift of God's grace that was given us by the working of God's power.

Arise, shine; for the light has come,

and the glory of God has risen upon us.

Let nations come to your light and rulers to the bright-ness of your day, O God, that they may rule your people righteously and the poor with justice, to defend the needy among the people, that there may be abundance of peace till the moon shall be no more.

Arise, shine; for the light has come,

and the glory of God has risen upon us.

Thwart the schemes of the powerful against the weak throughout the world, that wisdom may serve justice and the wise may follow the child.

Arise, shine; for the light has come,

and the glory of God has risen upon us.

Manifest your Son to the peoples of our community and lead us to your presence, so all may see your glory face to face.

Arise, shine; for the light has come,

and the glory of God has risen upon us.

Deliver the poor who cries out in distress and the oppressed who has no helper, as we pray especially for . . .

We give grateful praise for Christ, in whom we have access to God in boldness and confidence through faith in him. Hear our prayers of thanksgiving, especially for . . .

We remember those who have entered into the mystery of your eternal life, especially . . .

Arise, shine; for the light has come,

and the glory of God has risen upon us.

Presider Gracious and loving God, we come before you with no gifts but ourselves: Accept and receive our lives that we may be manifestations of your presence; let the light of your Spirit shine within and among us, so we may share in the mystery of your purpose of blessing for all creation, through Jesus Christ our Savior. ***Amen.***

Prayers of the People: Option 2

We pray for all your faithful people, and those who are called to lead, that we may walk in your way of love and manifest your love to the world.

Shine your light on your Church, Lord.

We pray for all the nations of the world, that those in authority will work toward peace and equity for all their people.

Shine your light on the nations, Lord.

We pray for people everywhere, that their lives may be full, that their families may be secure, that their hearts be filled with your peace.

Shine your light on all your children, Lord.

We pray for the community in which we live, that neighbors care for neighbors creating a truly caring community for all.

Shine your light on this community, Lord.

We pray for those who are suffering in ways that are known or hidden to us. We pray for those who struggle mightily in this life for and those whose light is dimming. For those who are ill and those who care for them. For those who are born today and for those who will die. We pray especially for ___________; in Christ's name we pray.

Shine your light into the seasons and passages of our lives, Lord.

We pray for those who have been called into larger life with you, especially ___________. In thanksgiving for them, we pray.

Shine your perpetual light upon them, Lord.

Hymns for the Day

The Hymnal 1982

Hail to the Lord's Anointed 616
How bright appears the Morning Star 496, 497
Now the silence 333
Arise, shine, for your light has come S 223ff
O very God of very God 672
O Zion, tune thy voice 543
Now my tongue the mystery telling 329, 331
Our God to whom we turn 681
As with gladness men of old 119
Brightest and best of the stars of the morning 117, 118
Duérmete, Niño lindo/Oh, sleep now, holy baby 113
Earth has many a noble city 127
Father eternal, Ruler of creation 573
On this day earth shall ring 92
Songs of thankfulness and praise 135
Unto us a boy is born! 98
The first Nowell the angel did say 109
We three kings of Orient are 128
What star is this, with beams so bright 124
When Christ's appearing was made known 131, 132 (1, 2, 5)
Where is this stupendous stranger? 491

Lift Every Voice and Sing II

This little light of mine 160

Wonder, Love, and Praise

Arise, shine, for your light has come 883
Where is this stupendous stranger? 726

The First Sunday after the Epiphany: The Baptism of Our Lord Jesus Christ

Sunday on or between January 7 and 13

You are my Son, the Beloved; with you I am well pleased.

Anchor Points – The Propers and the Feast

The fixed points for each service are the appointed or proper readings and collect as well as the themes of the day or season.

Readings and Psalm

Genesis 1:1–5

Today's reading is the first of the two accounts of creation in Genesis. In solemn liturgical cadences, the writer shows how darkness and chaos give way to light and order as the waters part at God's command. In contrast to the dualistic interpretation of this worldview in other traditions, where chaos always threatens to overwhelm the world again, here God's sovereignty over creation is affirmed.

Psalm 29

Psalm 29 is a hymn to Yahweh as the God of storm that may have been written to counter the pagan worship of Baal as the thunder-god. The "glory" of the Lord gives God dominion over nature and over all gods. Thus, Yahweh alone is the source of strength and blessing for the people.

Acts 19:1–7

Just as God's Holy Spirit descended upon Jesus (Luke 3:22; 4:18; Acts 10:38) and upon the Pentecost community (Acts 2) to empower them for ministry, so now the Spirit falls on those prepared by John's baptism, creating a new community from twelve disciples and empowering them with gifts for ministry: tongues for praise and prophecy for witness.

Mark 1:4–11

In today's reading, Mark recounts the preaching of John the Baptist and the baptism of Jesus. For Mark, John's only message is to point toward the One to come. The title Son of God given to Jesus in 1:1 is confirmed by the voice from heaven. Mark's account implies that the vision and voice were perceived only by Jesus. The appearance of the Spirit in the form of a dove is probably an allusion to Genesis 1:2.

Jesus is revealed as both divine Son and as Spirit-filled servant. Yet his identity is hidden from his disciples and other contemporaries, only recognized at the end by the centurion (15:39). Jesus's baptism is a like a parable, at once revealing and concealing his identity and mission – a secret Mark shares with his Christian readers.

Collect

Father in heaven, who at the baptism of Jesus in the River Jordan proclaimed him your beloved Son and anointed him with the Holy Spirit: Grant that all who are baptized into his Name may keep the covenant they have made, and boldly confess him as Lord and Savior; who with you and the Holy Spirit lives and reigns, one God, in glory everlasting. *Amen.*

Proper Preface

Epiphany – Because in the mystery of the Word made flesh, you have caused a new light to shine in our hearts, to give the knowledge of your glory in the face of your Son Jesus Christ our Lord. (Rite II, BCP 378; Rite I BCP 346)

Feast Day Pairings

See the table below for choices appointed and suggested for this day. Preferences are put in **bold**. Not all choices are suitable for all congregations or community, though, so consider these preferences as a starting point before making a decision about your own congregation.

	Epiphany 1: The Baptism of Our Lord	Rite I	Rite II	EOW1	BOS 2022
Color	White/Gold/Festive				
Rite	Holy Baptism or Holy Eucharist?				
Entrance Rite	Customary	323	355	50	
Song of Praise/Kyrie	Eucharist: **Glory to God (Gloria in excelsis)**	324	356		
Collect		163	214		
Creed	Baptism: Baptismal Covenant Eucharist: Renewal of Baptismal Vows (292) strongly encouraged				
Prayers of the People	**Locally written**; options below; BCP form; see note below about Prayers of the People and Baptism	329	387–393	54–55	
Offertory Sentence	"Ascribe to the Lord the glory due his Name; worship the Lord in the beauty of holiness." (Psalm 29)	343–344	376–377		
Eucharistic Prayer	**One that allows use of the Epiphany preface**	2–340	**B – 367** or A – 361	1–57	
Proper Preface	Epiphany	346	378		
Breaking of the Bread (Fraction)	Christ our Passover (BCP) or Blessed are those who are called (Hymn S 172)	337	365	69	
Postcommunion Prayer		339	**Eternal God – 365**	God of abundance – 69	
Blessing	**Seasonal in BOS**				**12**
Dismissal	**Let us go forth in the Name of Christ**	340	366		
Notes	Light paschal candle for Baptism				

Additional Notes:
Fraction Anthem at the Breaking of the Bread – The option provided in Rite I and Rite II ("Christ our Passover") is suitable throughout the season and the Alleluias may be included. Explore other texts that may be used from *The Hymnal 1982* from S 151 to S 172 (sung or said). The text at Hymn S 172 ("Blessed are those who are called") is very appropriate for Epiphany as it emphasizes that all nations are called into Christ's life. Additionally, EOW1 has several options.

Content Resources

Reading Between the Lines

In the beginning, primeval water, over which God's Spirit blows in the darkness, is a source of God's creation of land and sky, day and night. God's speech brings light, and the resource of intelligibility into being. Commentators note that the syntax of Gen 1:4 is emphatic: God saw how good it was.

Baptism is an act of water purification and cleansing before worship or sacrifice. At John's purification ritual including repentance for forgiveness of sins, to which all people in Jerusalem go, Jesus comes up out of the water, sees a vision of the open heavens through which the Spirit descends on him, and hears God's words identifying him as "My beloved Son."

Central Themes

The Spirit of the Lord is deeply connected to water, commencing in Genesis and culminating in baptism. Think of opportunities to remind ourselves of baptism. Engage folks by asking them to tell a story they know of their own baptism or that of another. Consult parish records for baptism dates and include those names in the Prayers of the People for the nearest Sunday – and invite new members to include their own information in that list. Pray for godparents in upcoming baptisms. Children can make cut-out doves with their own names and baptism dates and turn them into a garland of doves or incorporate them into a banner.

Water was used by the Jewish people of Jesus's time as a symbol for a change in status or restoration; it is no surprise that John used the immersion in water for a ritual signifying repentance. It was a way of getting ready – preparing a way for the Lord. When Jesus was baptized by John, Mark's Gospel reports the heavens were torn apart, a spirit descended, and a voice from above made claims on his life. When we baptize in the church now, thousands of years later, we use words, hoping to open the heavens to receive the candidate, we claim them as our own, and as it is often reported, the infants who scream the loudest are the likeliest to have a sense of the sheer terror – the audacity – of it all, not to mention the temptations that lie ahead. The prayer book in the Church of New Zealand mentions the temptations in their collect for this Sunday, which reminds us that the Holy Spirit is in the calling and claiming of the sacrament and in the pushing and protection of what comes next, helping us "wrestle and reflect" that we might live into our vows.

Engaging All Ages

This is an important feast day of the Epiphany season. At his baptism, Jesus is revealed as the Son of God and sealed by God's Holy Spirit. It begins the time in the lectionary when Jesus enacts his baptismal ministry, revealing (being made manifest) himself as a preacher, teacher, and healer. Our own baptisms share in this manifestation or revelation. At baptism, each of us stood revealed as God's own child, sealed with the Holy Spirit, and called to ministry and mission. How are we followers of Jesus; how do we live out our baptismal promises at home and school, with friends and family?

Prayers of the People: Option 1

For use either with Baptism or the Renewal of Baptismal Vows

As we gather around the waters of baptism today, gather us to your heart. Increase our commitment to the vows we have made to follow you. Give our spiritual leaders wisdom, patience, and guidance.

Pray for God's people and their leaders.

As we survey the news of the nations, sharpen our attention to what is happening in the world around us. Compel us to pray for those in authority and for the people they govern, that there may be peace between nations and neighbors.

Pray for God's world and all her people.

As we build relationships with those with whom we live and work, open our eyes to your presence in their lives and the ways we can serve you by serving them.

Pray for your neighbors and friends.

As we see those who suffer in any way, increase our capacity to love and to pray.

Pray for those who are suffering with illness and the struggles of life.

As we say goodbye to those who have departed this life, comfort us in our grief, assuring us of your love.

Pray for those who have died.

Prayers of the People: Option 2

A simplified form, for use with Baptism, following the Peace and prior to the Offertory.

Presider

Let us bring our prayers and thanksgivings to God. Please offer any prayers you would like to add during the times of silence.

Intercessor

I invite your prayers for the Church, its members, and mission.

Silence

I invite your prayers for this nation and for all those who exercise its authority.

Silence

I invite your prayers for the broader community, for any needs across the world.

Silence

I invite your prayers for this community, for the needs that you know we face here in our community.

Silence

I invite your prayers for all those who suffer, for those in any trouble.

Silence

I invite your prayers of thanksgiving for *N.*, baptized today, and for any other thanksgivings.

Silence

I invite your prayers for those who have died.

Silence

Using the following or similar words, the Presider concludes the prayers.

Presider We lift up all these prayers, on our lips and on our hearts, to you, O Christ.

People ***Amen.***

Hymns for the Day

The Hymnal 1982

Songs of thankfulness and praise 135
All creatures of our God and King 400 (1–3, 7)
I sing the almighty power of God 398
Many and great, O God, are thy works 385
Most High, omnipotent, good Lord 406, 407 (1–4, 8)
Thou, whose almighty word 371
Thy strong word did cleave the darkness 381
Baptized in water 294
Christ, when for us you were baptized 121
From God Christ's deity came forth 443
"I come," the great Redeemer cries 116
O love, how deep, how broad, how high 448, 449 (1–3, 6)
The sinless one to Jordan came 120
When Christ's appearing was made known 131, 132 (1, 3, 5)
When Jesus went to Jordan's stream 139

Lift Every Voice and Sing II

Baptized in water 121
Spirit Song 118

Wonder, Love, and Praise

Baptized in water 767

The Second Sunday after the Epiphany

Sunday on or between January 14 and 20

Come and see.

Anchor Points – The Propers and the Season

The fixed points for each service are the appointed or proper readings and collect as well as the themes of the day or season.

Readings and Psalm

1 Samuel 3:1–10 (11–20)

Today's reading recounts the call of Samuel in the temple at Shiloh. Shiloh was at that time the resting place for the ark, the throne for the divine presence on earth. The setting in the temple and the time, probably just before dawn since the lamp was to burn all night, are traditional for divine revelation.

Psalm 139:1–6, 13–18

This is a prayer for deliverance. The psalmist puts his trust in the all-knowing and ever-present God who has known him thoroughly and intimately since his conception. The psalmist invites further examination and cleansing.

1 Corinthians 6:12–20

Paul calls the Corinthians to remember their spiritual status effected through baptism. They have been freed from guilt, united with the people of God, and placed into right relationship with God. Now their lives are to exemplify the moral effects of conversion. Paul knows that salvation embraces the whole person. Physically, the body incorporates the human personality and so is the instrument of relationship with God and with one another. Spiritually, the body is a temple that contains the Holy Spirit and so is sacred and must not be profaned by sinful behavior.

John 1:43–51

Nathanael's skepticism about Nazareth may rest on its obscurity, for it is never mentioned in Hebrew scriptures, in contemporary historical accounts, or in early rabbinical writing. Or he may distrust the whole region of Galilee, whose inhabitants were regarded by strict Jews as ethnically mixed and religiously impure. The "greater things," which Jesus promises that Nathanael will see, begin with the first sign in Cana (2:11) and culminate in Jesus's crucifixion, resurrection, and ascension. The sequence of titles in this chapter sets forth a process of understanding that the disciples did not complete until after the Resurrection.

Collect

Almighty God, whose Son our Savior Jesus Christ is the light of the world: Grant that your people, illumined by your Word and Sacraments, may shine with the radiance of Christ's glory, that he may be known, worshiped, and obeyed to the ends of the earth; through Jesus Christ our Lord, who with you and the Holy Spirit lives and reigns, one God, now and forever. *Amen.*

Proper Preface

Epiphany – Because in the mystery of the Word made flesh, you have caused a new light to shine in our hearts, to give the knowledge of your glory in the face of your Son Jesus Christ our Lord. (Rite II, BCP 378; Rite I BCP 346)

Seasonal Pairings

See the table below for choices appointed and suggested for this day. Preferences are put in **bold**. Not all choices are suitable for all congregations or community, though, so consider these preferences as a starting point before making a decision about your own congregation.

	Epiphany 2	Rite I	Rite II	EOW1	BOS 2022
Color	Green				
Entrance Rite	Customary	323	355	50	
Song of Praise/Kyrie	Gloria in excelsis or BCP Canticle 11, 19; EOW1 Canticle D, L	Gloria 324	Gloria 356; C11 – 87; C19 – 94	D – 32; L – 36	
Collect		163	215		
Creed	Nicene Creed	326, 327	358	53	
Prayers of the People	**Locally written**; options below; BCP forms	329	387–393	54–55	
Offertory Sentence	"Very truly, I tell you, you will see heaven opened and the angels of God ascending and descending upon the Son of Man." (John)	343–344	376–377		
Eucharistic Prayer	**One that allows use of the Epiphany preface *or, alternatively,* Prayer C**	2–340	**A – 361,** **B – 367** or C – 369	1–57	
Proper Preface	Epiphany *or* The Lord's Day 1, 2, or 3	344–346	377–378		
Breaking of the Bread (Fraction)	Christ our Passover (BCP) or Blessed are those who are called (Hymn S 172)	337	365	69	
Postcommunion Prayer		339	**Eternal God – 365**	God of abundance – 69	
Blessing	Customary *or* 2nd option in BOS				12
Dismissal	**Let us go forth in the Name of Christ**	340	366		
Notes	Sometimes during Week of Prayer for Christian Unity; possible feast substitution (Confession of St. Peter); possible MLK recognition				

Additional Notes:

Song of Praise/Canticle – Whatever is chosen – the Gloria, one of the Canticles from the BCP or EOW1, or some other option – it may be desirable to use it consistently through the season from Epiphany 2 through Last Epiphany.

Eucharistic Prayer C – While it does not allow for the inclusion of the seasonal proper preface, much of the language in the prayer is suitable for Epiphany, particularly the request "Open our eyes to see your hand at work in the world about us." Prayer C, however, also contains significant penitential language, so may be more suited for Lent. It shouldn't be used for both seasons consecutively, in any case.

Fraction Anthem at the Breaking of the Bread – The option provided in Rite I and Rite II ("Christ our Passover") is suitable throughout the season and the Alleluias may be included. Explore other texts that may be used from *The Hymnal 1982* from S 151 to S 172 (sung or said). The text at Hymn S 172 ("Blessed are those who are called") is very appropriate for Epiphany as it emphasizes that all nations are called into Christ's life. Additionally, EOW1 has several options.

Content Resources

Reading Between the Lines

Divine revelation calls for recognition and response. The prophet Eli's eyesight is fading, and with it, his ability to discern, but eventually he perceives that Samuel is hearing the voice of God, and instructs young Samuel to respond attentively and respectfully, "Speak, Lord, for your servant is listening."

In John 1, several differing responses to who Jesus, the Word made flesh, are portrayed as limited. Two disciples of John the Baptist encounter Jesus and as a result of a dialogue with him, they turn and follow him (John 1:36–7). Nathaniel's lower expectations are overcome by the invitation from Philip, and in his own encounter with Jesus he identifies Jesus first as Rabbi, Son of God, and King of Israel. But "greater things" are still to be discerned about Jesus and his relationship with God in addition to what can be seen as open heavens and angelic ascent and descent between divine and human realms.

Central Themes

Today we encounter a very personal God in deep relationship with us. Calling us by name and knowing us so well that God is in us, and our body is a temple of God. What if we loved ourselves as though God were inside of us? Would we shame ourselves? Or would we be a little more kind to ourselves? When considering some misstep or flaw in ourselves, why not listen to the voice that would speak to a loved one rather than shaming ourselves? God is in us, God knows us, and God loves us. Voices of doubt or shame are not the voice of God and love.

The Episcopal Church Resource *Invite, Welcome, Connect*[1] does a great job breaking down the basics of what you, as a parish, need to do to attract fellow travelers to connect them not only to the family of faith they find there, but to connect them to being an essential part of the hands and feet of Christ in the world, going forth from that place. The process is actually pretty straightforward. On some level it seems we want it to be more complicated. We secretly desire there to be some cosmic cultural, societal reason, or excuse why we can't seem to attract or retain new people. But the truth is much simpler. We have grown accustomed to our isolation, so reaching out and making connections becomes less natural to us; uncomfortable. And in the over accommodation of comfort, we lose sight of how essential connection is to being human. Many, if not most of us, have a moment they can point to, somewhere back at the very beginning, when that first connection to a life of faith occurred. It might have been in the afterglow of a church camp fire or a dazzling sermon or a song whose tune took just the right turn at just the right time to hook your longing right there in the car or the pew or the depths of yet another day. You heard your name, maybe in a loud shout accompanied by an enthusiastic embrace or in a barely audible whisper. But it was you, seen and named by God. And that was the moment that all of the other stories and songs and miracles actually began to matter. That's what happened to Nathanael in today's story. That's the grace of God, which we can give to others by stepping outside of our comfort zone to remember a name or admit we forgot one. We can speak to a stranger to offer a cup of coffee and an inquiring heart. It mattered to you. It matters to others.

1 *Invite. Welcome. Connect* (Mary Foster Parmer, Foreword Movement 2018). The entirety of the book, with additional resources, can be found at http://www.invitewelcomeconnect.com/.

Engaging All Ages

The ability to listen is an important skill. Whether it is noisy or quiet, if we are busy or still, alone or with lots of people, it is important to pay attention to what is happening around us. God is revealed to us in lots of ways, many of which are unexpected. If we are always alert, we may notice God speaking to us through our friends, family, teachers, and even those we don't know well. Benedict, a sixth-century monk, once said, "Listen, my child, . . . with the ear of your heart." How do we listen with our heart? What might God be calling you to do?

Prayers of the People: Option 1

Let us lift our hearts to the One who calls us, saying, We call to you, O Lord. And we are listening.

We pray for the Church, that the hearts of the leaders and those who are led be turned toward you. Call us to support your work in the world through the Church.

We pray for *N.* our Presiding Bishop, *N.* our Bishop, *N.* our priest.

We call to you, O Lord. And we are listening.

We pray for those who govern the nations of the world, that their leadership be wise and compassionate. Call us to informed and cooperative citizenship. We pray for *N.* our President, *N.* our Governor, the Congress and courts of the land.

We call to you, O Lord. And we are listening.

We pray for people in every corner of the world, especially for those who lack adequate food, shelter and hope. Call us to compassionate action. We pray for *N* [people] or *N* [places] that have suffered *N* [natural devastation, effects of war, or plague].

We call to you, O Lord. And we are listening.

We pray for those close to our hearts who suffer from illness, anxiety; who face challenges and transitions; who struggle with your will in their lives. We pray today for ____________.

We call to you, O Lord. And we are listening.

We pray for those who will be born this day, that they will be embraced by loving communities. We pray for those who are dying and those who now rest in your eternal embrace. Are there those you wish to name?

Loving God, we call to you. And we are listening.

Prayers of the People: Option 2

Deacon or Presider: Let us offer prayers and intercessions to the God who knows us completely and calls us to follow him, saying, "Christ have mercy".

Intercessor: We pray for this congregation, our clergy, our staff, our bishop(s) *N.* and *N.*, our Presiding Bishop.

Christ have mercy

For all public officials who dedicate their service to making our communities safe, tolerant and compassionate.

Christ have mercy

[If MLK Day is in the week following this Sunday, this petition may be added:

For the work of justice and racial reconciliation; for Martin Luther King, Jr. and all those who have given of themselves and who have sacrificed their lives on behalf of the marginalized and the oppressed.

Christ have mercy]

For all those in this world experiencing oppression, poverty, and isolation.

Christ have mercy

For the concerns of this congregation; for those needing care, employment, or healed relationships.

Christ have mercy

For those needing healing and all who are suffering in body, mind or spirit.

Christ have mercy

For those we love but see no longer and for all the departed. For those who mourn, that they may be consoled by your loving presence.

Christ have mercy

I invite any additional prayers, silently or aloud

Silence. The Presider adds a concluding Collect.

[*If MLK Day is in the week following this Sunday, the Collect for his feast day would be suitable:*

Almighty God, by the hand of Moses your servant you led your people out of slavery, and made them free at last: Grant that your Church, following the example of your prophet Martin Luther King, may resist oppression in the name of your love, and may secure for all your children the blessed liberty of the Gospel of Jesus Christ; who lives and reigns with you and the Holy Spirit, one God, now and for ever. ***Amen.***]

Hymns for the Day

The Hymnal 1982

Blessed Jesus, at thy word 440
Christ, whose glory fills the skies 6, 7
Christ is the world's true Light 542
How bright appears the Morning Star 496, 497
Lord, thou hast searched me and dost know 702
Thou, whose almighty word 371
God has spoken to his people 536
O Jesus, I have promised 655
Blest are the pure in heart 656
Lift up your heads, ye mighty gates 436
Sing praise to our Creator 295
Strengthen for service, Lord 312
Take my life, and let it be 707
All praise to thee, for thou, O King divine 477
In your mercy, Lord, you called me 706
The great Creator of the worlds 489
The people who in darkness walked 125, 126
What wondrous love is this 439
Ye servants of God, your Master proclaim 535

Lift Every Voice and Sing II

Lord, You have searched my heart 16
I have decided to follow Jesus 136

Wonder, Love, and Praise

I, the Lord of sea and sky 812
Will you come and follow me 757

The Third Sunday after the Epiphany

Sunday on or between January 21 and 27

The kingdom of God has come near

Anchor Points – The Propers and the Season

The fixed points for each service are the appointed or proper readings and collect as well as the themes of the day or season.

Readings and Psalm

Jonah 3:1–5, 10

Today's reading tells of Jonah's obedience to God's second call. As the capital city of Assyria, Nineveh not only posed a political danger, its "wickedness" (1:2) jeopardized Israel's spiritual welfare. The evil of the city and its inhabitants makes even more surprising the belief and repentance with which they respond to the message of this Israelite.

Psalm 62:6–14

This is a response to God's aid in time of trouble. In verses 9–12, the worshiping community is encouraged not to trust in status or wealth. In verses 11–12, the psalmist summarizes what he has learned: God's power and steadfast love (covenant loyalty) issue justice for all.

1 Corinthians 7:29–31

Today's reading falls within Paul's long response to the community's questions about marriage. Marriage, which for the ancients was primarily for the continuation of the family, has no more role in light of the "impending crisis" (v. 26), "distress in this life" (v. 28) and the "passing away" of "the present form of this world" (v. 31). The old world and its forms were no longer relevant because the new age had dawned with Jesus and would flower soon when Jesus returned. The absolute statements in these verses are not intended to be normative rules of life. They do, however, introduce a basis for a healthy perspective on establishing a value system for contemporary Christian life. Christians cannot approach their ordinary tasks with non-Christian motives.

Mark 1:14–20

Today's gospel recounts the beginning of Jesus's ministry. He proclaims "the good news of God" that the "kingdom of God has come near" (v. 14). God's promised rule over all that has been created and all God's past acts for salvation are now coming to fruition. The response to the presence of God's kingdom is conversion or repentance. In the Greek and Hebrew sense of the word, this is not a feeling of sorrow but the action of turning around, a total reorientation of self to God, not intellectual assent to a set of propositions nor an emotional reaction but a total response of oneself to the message.

Collect

Give us grace, O Lord, to answer readily the call of our Savior Jesus Christ and proclaim to all people the Good News of his salvation, that we and the whole world may perceive the glory of his marvelous works; who lives and reigns with you and the Holy Spirit, one God, for ever andever. *Amen.*

Proper Preface

Epiphany – Because in the mystery of the Word made flesh, you have caused a new light to shine in our hearts, to give the knowledge of your glory in the face of your Son Jesus Christ our Lord. (Rite II, BCP 378; Rite I BCP 346)

Seasonal Pairings

See the table below for choices appointed and suggested for this day. Preferences are put in **bold**. Not all choices are suitable for all congregations or community, though, so consider these preferences as a starting point before making a decision about your own congregation.

	Epiphany 3	Rite I	Rite II	EOW1	BOS 2022
Color	Green				
Entrance Rite	Customary	323	355	50	
Song of Praise/Kyrie	Gloria in excelsis or BCP Canticle 11, 19; EOW1 Canticle D, L	Gloria 324	Gloria 356; C11 – 87; C19 – 94	D – 32; L – 36	
Collect		163	215		
Creed	Nicene Creed	326, 327	358	53	
Prayers of the People	**Locally written**; options below; BCP forms	329	387–393	54–55	
Offertory Sentence	"Pour out your trust in God always, O people, pour out your hearts before him, for God is our refuge." (Psalm 62)	343–344	376–377		
Eucharistic Prayer	**One that allows use of the Epiphany preface *or, alternatively,* Prayer C**	2–340	**A – 361, B – 367** or C – 369	1–57	
Proper Preface	Epiphany *or* The Lord's Day 1, 2, or 3	344–346	377–378		
Breaking of the Bread (Fraction)	Christ our Passover (BCP) or Blessed are those who are called (Hymn S 172)	337	365	69	
Postcommunion Prayer		339	**Eternal God – 365**	God of abundance – 69	
Blessing	Customary *or* 2nd option in BOS				12
Dismissal	**Let us go forth in the Name of Christ**	340	366		
Notes	Religious Life Sunday; often the middle of the Week of Prayer for Christian Unity; possible feast substitution (Conversion of St. Paul); possible MLK recognition				

Additional Notes:

Song of Praise/Canticle – Whatever is chosen – the Gloria, one of the Canticles from the BCP or EOW1, or some other option – it may be desirable to use it consistently through the season from Epiphany 2 through Last Epiphany.

Eucharistic Prayer C – While it does not allow for the inclusion of the seasonal proper preface, much of the language in the prayer is suitable for Epiphany, particularly the request "Open our eyes to see your hand at work in the world about us." Prayer C, however, also contains significant penitential language, so may be more suited for Lent. It shouldn't be used for both seasons consecutively, in any case.

Fraction Anthem at the Breaking of the Bread – The option provided in Rite I and Rite II ("Christ our Passover") is suitable throughout the season and the Alleluias may be included. Explore other texts that may be used from *The Hymnal 1982* from S 151 to S 172 (sung or said). The text at Hymn S 172 ("Blessed are those who are called") is very appropriate for Epiphany as it emphasizes that all nations are called into Christ's life. Additionally, EOW1 has several options.

Content Resources

Reading Between the Lines

The readings and the Collect present and interpret the theme of calling and vocation. God changes God's mind about Nineveh when the people in that great city respond penitently with sackcloth and ashes as a result of Jonah's message of judgement. This is Jonah's second opportunity to respond to God's call. Yet repentance in response to divine revelation and judgment does not have the last word. We know from Jonah 4:10–11 that the pity of God for Ninevites and of Jonah for the death of the plant is of equal and perhaps greater importance to the survival of the city and its inhabitants.

Jesus' vocation and ministry in Galilee appears to be galvanized by the arrest of John the Baptist. Jesus' gospel or good news that the kingdom or realm of God is at hand is accompanied by a requirement for a complete transformation of heart and mind, namely repentance, and manifest in exorcisms, healings, and teachings, including metaphors and parables. There, the Jesus movement took shape around the calling of disciples, particularly two sets of fishing brothers, Simon Peter and Andrew, and James and John. Their acceptance of this vocation, to fish for people, is an extension of their former profession, and perhaps networks, and participates in Jesus' vocation and mission to bring about God's realm.

Central Themes

Simon, Andrew, James, and John heard Jesus's call and left their family business in the lurch to heed the call. They were fishermen, not learned men of God. Where is God's call in our lives? Would we listen if we hear it? What are the barriers that prevent us from listening, and what would it take for us to take a leap of faith and heed the call? Fear and insecurity can be powerful barriers to listening to a call. We don't need any special training; we just need to listen to what God is telling us and remember that God calls people to lay ministry more often than ordained ministry.

In 2017, the Most Reverend Michael B. Curry, Primate and Presiding Bishop of the Episcopal Church, initiated a national program, a rule of life for all persons, called "The Way of Love."[1] Through this program, individuals and congregations are encouraged to step into a wheel of moments that follow the path of our faith. We finally accepted that our faith does not neatly follow a series of steps or stages but is more like a labyrinth of beginnings and endings and depths and shallows in which we need to be less task-oriented and more faithful to being simply present at each turn. Today's reading names one of the stations – that of turning from what we are doing, hearing the call of Jesus to follow him, and taking (or not) that step. From the materials, "The Way of Love" says, "Like the disciples, we are called by Jesus to follow the Way of Love. With God's help, we can turn from the powers of sin, hatred, fear, injustice, and oppression toward the way of truth, love, hope, justice, and freedom. In turning, we reorient our lives to Jesus Christ, falling in love again, again, and again." What practices help you to turn again and again to Jesus Christ and the Way of Love?

» How will (or do) you incorporate these practices into your rhythm of life?

» Who will be your companion as you turn toward Jesus Christ?

The entire program, with an ever-expanding collection of downloadable resources for all ages and sizes of groups, can be found online.

Engaging All Ages

Today we have stories of turning our lives around – or at least following a different pathway or direction than we have gone before. The prophet Jonah, newly freed from the belly of a great fish, goes to Nineveh where the people have a "turn of heart" and repent of their bad ways. Jesus returns to Galilee preaching the nearness of God, inviting all to follow God's rule and have a change of heart. In what ways can we change our hearts and follow God?

Prayers of the People: Option 1

Merciful God, you continually call us into the deep, away from lives with no direction. Be present with us as we navigate the waters of faithfulness. Turn us in the direction of your voice and purpose.

Give us the courage to respond to your call and go where you lead us.

And the people say, "Amen."

We are abundantly blessed and praise you for your goodness and care of us.

For what are you grateful today?

We come to you with thankful hearts,
And the people say, "Amen."

Equip the leaders of your faithful people to lead with holy vision. We pray for wisdom and stamina for our bishops, priests, and deacons. Guide them as they guide your people.

And the people say, "Amen."

Strengthen our nation's relationships across boundaries and language. Put words of peace on the lips of every world leader. Open the eyes of people everywhere to the needs of their neighbors.

And the people say, "Amen."

We lift those who are hurting into your healing presence: for those facing the struggles of illness, uncertainty, broken relationships, and world weariness; for those who are dying, grant them a holy death.

For whom do you pray today?

We trust in your care, O Lord.
And the people say, "Amen."

1 *The Way of Love*, The Episcopal Church, USA. https://episcopalchurch.org/way-of-love.

Prayers of the People: Option 2

Deacon or Presider: The kingdom of God is near at hand. Let us earnestly call on God for the needs, concerns, and hopes of all peoples.

Intercessor: For the church of Jesus Christ in every place.

O Christ, hear us.

For *N.* our Presiding Bishop, for *N.* our bishop, for our parish clergy, *N.*, for all who minister in Christ.

O Christ, hear us.

For this holy gathering and for all who are hear God's deeper call.

O Christ, hear us.

For this congregation and all those whose lives we touch, for our Wardens, Vestry members, and Officers.

O Christ, hear us.

For this country, for all nations and their leaders, and for those who guard the peace.

O Christ, hear us.

For all those in danger and need: those who are sick and suffering, and for all who are prisoners, captives, and their families, for those who are hungry, unhoused, and oppressed.

O Christ, hear us.

For the dying and the dead, we pray.

O Christ, hear us.

For ourselves, our families, for those we love.

O Christ, hear us.

Remembering [the Blessed Virgin Mary, blessed *N.* and] all the saints, let us offer ourselves and one another to the living God through Christ.

To you, O Lord our God.

Presider: God of infinite mercy, hear the prayers of your people and stir up our souls with longing to embrace your gospel; through Jesus Christ our Lord. ***Amen.***

Hymns for the Day

The Hymnal 1982

Christ for the world we sing! 537
How wondrous and great thy works, God of praise! 532, 533
My God, thy table now is spread 321
Spread, O spread, thou mighty word 530
Give praise and glory unto God 375
God of mercy, God of grace 538
Sing praise to God who reigns above 408
There's a wideness in God's mercy 469, 470
Jesus calls us; o'er the tumult 549, 550
They cast their nets in Galilee 661

Lift Every Voice and Sing II

I'm just a poor wayfaring stranger 19
Soon and very soon 14
I have decided to follow Jesus 136

Wonder, Love, and Praise

As we gather at your Table 763
Put down your nets and follow me 807
Tú has venido a la orilla/
You have come down to the lakeshore 758
Will you come and follow me 757

The Presentation of Our Lord Jesus Christ *also called "Candlemas"*

February 2

Takes precedence over the Season after Epiphany, when it falls on Sunday

Jesus is the salvation that the world longs for.

Anchor Points – The Propers and the Feast

The fixed points for each service are the appointed or proper readings and collect as well as the themes of the day or season.

Readings and Psalm

Malachi 3:1–4

Nothing is known of this prophet except what can be deduced from his writings. Even the name Malachi, which means 'my messenger', may be a title rather than a personal name. This reading reflects the hope of the prophets for the coming of the Messiah and the inauguration of God's reign over all the earth. The "messenger" (or 'angel') to be sent may refer to the Jerusalem priesthood or may be a way of speaking of God's own appearance in human affairs. In the gospels this title is applied to John the Baptist, whose preaching uses the same images (Matthew 3:10–12).

Psalm 84

This psalm combines elements of hymn (vv. 1, 10–11), lamentation and intercession (vv. 8–9). It resembles the songs of Zion (found in Psalm 46, 48, 76 and 87) and the pilgrim Songs of Ascent (Psalms 120–124). Likely composed on the occasion of a pilgrimage to the temple, the psalm expresses the strength of the psalmist's longing for the temple and the trials and rewards of the journey.

or

Psalm 24:7–10

This psalm is part of a processional liturgy, perhaps to be used by a procession of people and priests carrying the Ark of the Covenant into the sanctuary for an annual celebration. It begins with a brief hymn (vv. 1–2) to God as creator. Then comes a teaching dialogue (vv. 3–6) on the conditions for entry into the sanctuary. The last section (vv. 7–10) then would be sung by a group outside the gates, likely carrying in procession the ark of the covenant, with which God's presence was associated.

Hebrews 2:14–18

The writer explains that Jesus' work as Savior is made possible because he is God incarnate, fully human and fully divine. God saved the human race not from the outside but by entering into the world and becoming human and, having taking humanity into the divine life, redeemed the human race.

Luke 2:22–40

The infancy narrative cycle concludes with this story of Mary's purification at the Temple and the presentation of Jesus to Anna and Simeon. This story meshes well with the Epiphany season themes of Jesus being made known to the world, "a light to enlighten the nations."

Collect

Almighty and everliving God, we humbly pray that, as your only-begotten Son was this day presented in the temple, so we may be presented to you with pure and clean hearts by Jesus Christ our Lord; who lives and reigns with you and the Holy Spirit, one God, now and for ever. *Amen.*

Proper Preface

Epiphany – Because in the mystery of the Word made flesh, you have caused a new light to shine in our hearts, to give the knowledge of your glory in the face of your Son Jesus Christ our Lord. (Rite II, BCP 378; Rite I BCP 346)

Feast Day Pairings

See the table below for choices appointed and suggested for this day. Preferences are put in **bold**. Not all choices are suitable for all congregations or community, though, so consider these preferences as a starting point before making a decision about your own congregation.

	Feast of the Presentation	Rite I	Rite II	EOW1	BOS 2022
Color	White/Gold/Festive				
Entrance Rite	**Candlemas Procession option** or Customary	323	355	50	**47–50**
Song of Praise/Kyrie	If the Candlemas procession is not used, either BCP **Canticle 5** or **17** or Gloria in excelsis should be used.	**C5 – 51;** Gloria 324	**C17 – 93;** Gloria 356		
Collect		187	239		
Creed	Nicene Creed	326, 327	358	53	
Prayers of the People	**Locally written**; option below; BCP forms	329	387–393	54–55	
Offertory Sentence	"Our eyes have seen the Savior, whom you have prepared for all the world to see: A Light to enlighten the nations, and the glory of your people Israel." (Luke – Canticle)	346	376–378		
Eucharistic Prayer	**Prayer B;** one that allows use of the proper preface	2–340	**B – 367;** A – 361	1–57	
Proper Preface	Epiphany	344–346	377–378		
Breaking of the Bread (Fraction)	**Blessed are those who are called (Hymn S 172)** or Christ our Passover (BCP) or	337	364	69	
Postcommunion Prayer		339	**Eternal God – 365**	God of abundance – 69	
Blessing	**2nd option in BOS** *or* Customary				**12**
Dismissal	**Let us go forth in the Name of Christ**	340	366		
Notes					

Additional Notes:

Candlemas Procession – See the material below for this option from BOS 2022.

Song of Praise/Canticle – If the Candlemas procession is chosen, no song of praise/Gloria is used. If the procession is not used, the Song of Simeon (Canticle 5 or 17) should be used, if possible. Music settings for this Canticle are found in *The Hymnal 1982* from S 253 to S 260.

Eucharistic Prayer – Eucharistic Prayer B is suitable for this day with its emphasis on the Incarnation, since this feast is closely tied with the birth narrative of Jesus and expresses incarnational theology in the Hebrews reading in particular. B also allows for the proper preface to be used, tying the themes of the Song of Simeon into the prayer.

Fraction Anthem at the Breaking of the Bread – S 172 (Blessed are those who are called) references the global scope of Christ's mission, which relates to the Song of Simeon in the Gospel reading.

Candlemas Procession

The Candlemas Procession is described and found in the BOS. The music is in the Appendix to the Accompaniment Edition of *The Hymnal 1982* (S 340–S 343). It works well before an evening Eucharist. It does require enough people to process and to sing, so advance planning and publicity are needed. The procession is completely optional. Some congregations may simply not wish to do it; others may not consider it practical for a weekday evening. Since The Presentation is one of the feasts that displaces the Sunday propers when it falls on that day, parishes that do not schedule the procession for a weekday evening may wish to hold one before the parish Eucharist in those years in which February 2 is a Sunday.

When circumstances permit, the congregation gathers at a place apart from the church so that all may go into the church in procession. If necessary, however, the procession takes place within the church., the Presider begins the rite standing just inside the door of the church, in this case. Candles for use in the church for the following year are present and candles to be carried in procession (or all those present may be provided with unlighted candles). These are lit during the opening canticle, the Song of Simeon, which is sung or said responsively. Hymn S 341 is available as a sung setting. The congregation then enters the church in procession carrying the lit candles, singing appropriate hymns. The procession makes a station, or stop, at some convenient point, and a collect is sung or said. Following that collect, Ps. 48:1–2, 10–13 may be sung (S 343) as the procession approaches the altar. The service continues with the collect of the day.

Liturgy from the Book of Occasional Services[1]

Presider Light and peace, in Jesus Christ our Lord.
People ***Thanks be to God.***

Dear people of God, forty days ago we celebrated the joyful feast of the incarnation of Jesus. Today we recall the day on which he was presented in the temple, fulfilling the law of Moses. Led by the Spirit, Simeon and Anna came to the temple, recognized the child as the Christ, and proclaimed him with joy. United by the same Spirit, we now enter the house of God, where we shall recognize Christ in the breaking of bread.

Let us pray.

O eternal God, who have created all things; on this day you fulfilled the petitions of the just Simeon: we humbly ask you to bless and sanctify these candles for our use. Graciously hear our prayers and be merciful to us, whom you have redeemed by your Son, who is the light of the world, and who lives and reigns with you and the Holy Spirit, one God for ever and ever. ***Amen.***

The following canticle is then sung or said, during which the candles are lighted, if the people are not already holding them.

A Light to enlighten the nations,
and the glory of your people Israel.

A Light to enlighten the nations,
and the glory of your people Israel.

Lord, you now have set your servant free
to go in peace as you have promised.

A Light to enlighten the nations,
and the glory of your people Israel.

For these eyes of mine have seen the Savior,
whom you have prepared for all the world to see.

A Light to enlighten the nations,
and the glory of your people Israel.

The Presider then says the following prayer

Let us pray.

O God, source of all light, today you revealed to the aged Simeon your light which enlightens the nations. Fill our hearts with the light of faith, that we who bear these candles may walk in the path of goodness, through Jesus Christ the Light of the World. ***Amen.***

The Procession

Deacon: Let us go forth in peace.

People ***In the name of Christ. Amen.***

During the procession, all carry lighted candles while appropriate hymns, psalms, or anthems are sung. In a suitable place, the procession may halt while the following or some other appropriate Collect is said.

O God, you have made this day holy by the presentation of your Son in the Temple, and by the purification of the Blessed Virgin Mary: Mercifully grant that we, who delight in her humble readiness to be the birth-giver of the Only-begotten, may rejoice for ever in our adoption as his sisters and brothers; through Jesus Christ our Lord. ***Amen.***

The following antiphon and psalm are appropriate as the procession approaches the Altar.

We have waited in silence on your loving-kindness, O Lord, in the midst of your temple. Your praise, like your Name, O God, reaches to the world's end; your right hand is full of justice.

In place of the long antiphon given above, this shorter form may be used with the appointed Psalm

We have waited on your loving kindness, O Lord, in the midst of your temple.

Psalm 48:1–2, 10–13

1 Great is the Lord, and highly to be praised; *
in the city of our God is his holy hill.

2 Beautiful and lofty, the joy of all the earth, is the hill of Zion *
the very center of the world and the city of the great King.

10 Let Mount Zion be glad and the cities of Judah rejoice, *
because of your judgments.

11 Make the circuit of Zion; walk round about her;
count the number of her towers.

12 Consider well her bulwarks; examine her stronghold; *
that you may tell those who come after.

13 This God is our God for ever and ever; *
he shall be our guide for evermore.

On arrival in the sanctuary, the Presider goes to the usual place, and the Eucharist continues with the Collect of the Day. After the Collect, all extinguish their candles.

1 "Candlemas Procession," BOS 2022, 47–50.

Content Resources

Reading Between the Lines

Faithfulness and expectations meet in this dramatic encounter in the Jerusalem temple. In accordance with the Law of Moses, Mary and Joseph bring their firstborn son to be presented to the Lord, offering a sacrifice of – "a pair of turtledoves or two young pigeons." Thus, Mary fulfills her obligation to be "purified," 40 days after the birth of her son.

Someone else, guided by the Spirit, goes to the Temple at the same time. It is Simeon, "righteous and devout, looking forward to the consolation of Israel, and the Holy Spirit rested on him." (Luke 2:25b). Already there in the Temple is Anna, an elderly prophet who "never left the temple but worshipped there with fasting and prayer night and day." (Luke 2:37b)

In their lives we hear the words of Psalm 84:
How lovely is your dwelling place, O Lord of hosts!

Simeon sees the child and breaks into his last song; Anna the prophet, already in the Temple, perhaps connected to it through her prophetic office (as we might infer from the case of Huldah, 2 Kings 22), now prophesies and will go on prophesying to all and sundry. Now that he has seen the Christ child, and received it into his arms, Simeon wants to die; Anna, in contrast, wants to live and proclaim the salvation and redemption of Jerusalem. She finds a new voice after 86 years. Simeon and Anna we see two different but complimentary examples of patience and faithfulness sustaining witness and service over many long years. These are people of hope – still living with a sense of expectation of a future moving towards them.

Central Themes

This feast day intersects many aspects of the church year all at once: the anticipation of Simeon is similar to Advent as well as the Malachi reading looking for the coming of the Day of the Lord; the Gospel narrative is part of the incarnational cycle of the birth of Jesus at Christmas; the feast is also a feast of revelation of Christ to the world, including the gentiles, an Epiphany theme; and the prophecy that a sword will pierce Mary's soul and that Jesus will be the occasion for the falling and rising of many, evokes the Passion narrative of Holy Week and Easter. Simeon's actions and prophecy are specifically part of the work of the Holy Spirit, tying Pentecost in as well. The Presentation contains a microcosm of the entire liturgical year – partly because the story is itself emblematic of the whole story of Christ. Fidelity to the law while also bringing something new is another theme in the readings on this day, which is a common theme throughout Jesus' ministry.

How many times in life do we have a completely integrative moment? Something we have been waiting to happen forever, which all kinds of expectations that may or may not be fulfilled, that can completely change our life? We see that happen in small ways, the accomplishment of completing a significant and difficult credential, like a degree or passing the bar or medical boards. We see it in achieving other life goals, whatever they may be, but all to a smaller degree than Simeon expresses. His encounter with Christ was everything he had been waiting for and preparing for during his entire life, so much so that he is at peace if this encounter is the last one he will ever have. Perhaps the birth of a child is the closest that many of us will get to a longed-for, anticipated moment that completely changes the rest of our life, though even that falls short of Simeon's experience. He is fulfilled. Completely.

Engaging All Ages

Though it takes preparation and communication ahead of time, the custom of blessing candles for the year can be a fun one for all ages. Consider inviting members to gather their candles they will use for the year – birthday candles, Advent candles, any other candles used in the home – and bringing them to be blessed. Or, if your church provides Advent candles to members, order them at the beginning of the year, to have them blessed on Candlemas to be handed out the Sunday before Advent I. The candles used in worship (or the oil, if your church uses oil filled candles) can be set purchased and set out ahead of time for this service as well. You can also make candles on the Sundays before February 2, especially with children and youth, so that they can have those candles blessed in the service.

Prayers of the People

Deacon or Presider: We long for the promise of God to be fulfilled, standing with Anna and Simeon, praying for the redemption of the world, saying "Let our eyes see your salvation."

Intercessor

For the Church and our call to work for reconciliation in Christ's name, we pray,

Let our eyes see your salvation.

For those in civil authority, that they may make decisions for the common good, we pray,

Let our eyes see your salvation.

For all those in places of strife, war and conflict; for those who suffer from systems of oppression and injustice; embolden us to respond with your love, justice, and mercy, we pray,

Let our eyes see your salvation.

For those who are without shelter, for those who hunger, for victims of inclement and violent weather; and for all those who are sick and suffering; open our hearts to respond in Christ's name, we pray,

Let our eyes see your salvation.

For all those who have died and know already the salvation that Christ promises; for all those who mourn, we pray,

Let our eyes see your salvation.

For the many blessings of our lives, for ourselves and all those we love, we pray,

Let our eyes see your salvation.

Presider

Almighty God, you have poured upon us the new light of your incarnate Word: Grant that this light, enkindled in our hearts, may shine forth in our lives; through Jesus Christ our Lord. ***Amen.***

Hymns for the Day

The Hymnal 1982

Angels from the realms of glory 93
How lovely is thy dwelling-place [P 84] 517
Love divine, all loves excelling 657
How bright appears the Morning Star 496, 497
Sing of Mary, pure and lowly 277
The great Creator of the worlds (1–4) 489
Blest are the pure in heart 656
Christ, whose glory fills the skies 6,7
Hail to the Lord who comes 257
Let all mortal flesh keep silence 324
Lord God, you now have set your servant free 499
Sing we of the blessed Mother 278
Virgin-born we bow before thee 258

Wonder, Love, and Praise

Lord, you have fulfilled your word 891

The Fourth Sunday after the Epiphany

Sunday on or between January 28 and February 3 (except February 2 – The Presentation)

Note: If Ash Wednesday falls during the week following this Sunday, move directly to the Last Sunday after the Epiphany instead

Jesus's authority is manifested in his deeds and words.

Anchor Points – The Propers and the Season

The fixed points for each service are the appointed or proper readings and collect as well as the themes of the day or season.

Readings and Psalm

Deuteronomy 18:15–20

This passage describes the role of the prophet to make known God's will, a role distinct from the fortune telling, communication with the dead, and divination practiced by pagans. Moses' teaching validates prophetic practice by telling of the establishment by Moses of a succession of prophets to mediate as he did between God and the people. A criterion is established to aid in distinguishing the true prophet from the false.

Psalm 111

Psalm 111 is a psalm of praise, celebrating God's presence in the history of God's covenant relationship with Israel. The psalmist recites a brief history of God's actions as clues to God's character.

1 Corinthians 8:1–13

In this reading, Paul discusses the guiding principle for resolving misunderstandings among Christians about participation in non-Christian culture. Most of the meat sold in the marketplace came from animals offered for sacrifice in pagan temples, and many social groups met for dinner in pagan shrines, though this did not necessarily involve recognition of the god. Christians in Corinth were divided on the issues of eating such meat or going to such dinners. Some felt that there was no harm in it. The "weak" (v. 9), however, avoided such meat and such occasions out of a fierce desire to follow the law. They were upset by the actions of their fellow-Christians. Paul claims that the "strong" were correct in their knowledge of the issue, but deficient in their love for fellow believers. For Paul the gospel means freedom from servitude to the law – a freedom exercised in love. Charity to one's fellow-Christians takes first place.

Mark 1:21–28

Jesus's teaching in the synagogue and freeing a person possessed by a demon in the synagogue illustrate the nature of Jesus's message. Mark emphasizes Jesus's activity as teacher, but in contrast to Matthew and Luke, he gives less of the content of Jesus's teaching. Rather, he stresses Jesus's effective, powerful authority. One manifestation of this authority is Jesus's exorcism of an unclean spirit. Mark does not tell miracle stories for the sake of arousing awe. He tells them to give witness to the meaning of Jesus's presence.

Collect

Almighty and everlasting God, you govern all things both in heaven and on earth: Mercifully hear the supplications of your people, and in our time grant us your peace; through Jesus Christ our Lord, who lives and reigns with you and the Holy Spirit, one God, for ever and ever. *Amen.*

Proper Preface

Epiphany – Because in the mystery of the Word made flesh, you have caused a new light to shine in our hearts, to give the knowledge of your glory in the face of your Son Jesus Christ our Lord. (Rite II, BCP 378; Rite I BCP 346)

Seasonal Pairings

See the table below for choices appointed and suggested for this day. Preferences are put in **bold**. Not all choices are suitable for all congregations or community, though, so consider these preferences as a starting point before making a decision about your own congregation.

	Epiphany 4	Rite I	Rite II	EOW1	BOS 2022
Color	Green				
Entrance Rite	Customary	323	355	50	
Song of Praise/Kyrie	Gloria in excelsis or BCP Canticle 11, 19; EOW1 Canticle D, L	Gloria 324	Gloria 356; C11 – 87; C19 – 94	D – 32; L – 36	
Collect		164	215		
Creed	Nicene Creed	326, 327	358	53	
Prayers of the People	**Locally written**; options below; BCP forms	329	387–393	54–55	
Offertory Sentence		343–344	376–377		
Eucharistic Prayer	**One that allows use of the Epiphany preface** *or, alternatively,* **Prayer C**	2–340	**A – 361,** **B – 367** or C – 369	1–57	
Proper Preface	Epiphany *or* The Lord's Day 1, 2, or 3	344–346	377–378		
Breaking of the Bread (Fraction)	Christ our Passover (BCP) or Blessed are those who are called (Hymn S 172)	337	365	69	
Postcommunion Prayer		339	**Eternal God – 365**	God of abundance – 69	
Blessing	Customary *or* 2nd option in BOS				12
Dismissal	**Let us go forth in the Name of Christ**	340	366		
Notes	Candlemas falls on or after this date; may be Theological Education Sunday; may be Souper Bowl of Caring				

Additional Notes:

Candlemas – If Candlemas (February 2) is on a Sunday, it replaces the Fourth Sunday after the Epiphany propers and the color is white/festive/gold. See planning pages for Candlemas above.

Song of Praise/Canticle – Whatever is chosen – the Gloria, one of the Canticles from the BCP or EOW1, or some other option – it may be desirable to use it consistently through the season from Epiphany 2 through Last Epiphany.

Eucharistic Prayer C – While it does not allow for the inclusion of the seasonal proper preface, much of the language in the prayer is suitable for Epiphany, particularly the request "Open our eyes to see your hand at work in the world about us." Prayer C, however, also contains significant penitential language, so may be more suited for Lent. It shouldn't be used for both seasons consecutively, in any case.

Fraction Anthem at the Breaking of the Bread – The option provided in Rite I and Rite II ("Christ our Passover") is suitable throughout the season and the Alleluias may be included. Explore other texts that may be used from *The Hymnal 1982* from S 151 to S 172 (sung or said). The text at Hymn S 172 ("Blessed are those who are called") is very appropriate for Epiphany as it emphasizes that all nations are called into Christ's life. Additionally, EOW1 has several options.

Content Resources

Reading Between the Lines

Jesus' proclamation of the gospel of God's realm in word and deed, and the calling of disciples, now shows readers and disciples the opposite of divine manifestation, namely, unclean spirits, or demons, during the course of synagogue worship on the Sabbath. Jesus' teaching with authority is greeted with astonishment by those present, and recognition by demonic forces. Their attempt to control Jesus involves shouting out his manifest identity, the Holy One of God. Indeed, as Holy One of God, Jesus' effective and powerful exorcism in the Synagogue at Capernaum expels the demonic spirit from the possessed person and from the holy place. Ideas of holiness and the holy connote here a separate realm of God, or a designated holy day, the Sabbath, accessible to worshippers through purification. So, next week, in Epiphany 5, Mark 1:32 shows that people knew to wait until Sabbath was over to bring sick and demon-possessed folk to Jesus, because of Jewish observance of the Sabbath.

Central Themes

The Baptismal Covenant asks whether we will persevere in resisting evil; the readings for today command we do so. The unclean spirit must be cast out. We do not generally encounter spirits the way people who lived in Jesus's time did, but we can find imagery in popular movies connected to the unclean spirit and vanquishing of evil. We tell these stories about resisting evil all the time. In sagas such as *Star Wars*, the rebellion stands up to evil at great risk and sacrifice; the Jedi set themselves apart as proud warriors willing to sacrifice their lives to fight those who abuse power. Frodo and his companions in *The Lord of the Rings* know how to stand up to the evil that they encounter. In many ways in our everyday lives, even without Jedi mind tricks or wizardry or rings of power, we can cast out unclean spirits by naming the evil we see and standing firmly against it.

The BOS does not provide a rite of exorcism, but it gives these guidelines: "someone in need of such a ministry, and anyone desiring to exercise it, makes the matter known to a presbyter, who in turn consults with the bishop. The bishop then determines whether exorcism is needed, who is to officiate at the rite, and what prayers or other formularies are to be used."[1] It goes on to say, "The rituals of exorcism, while weighty and never to be undertaken lightly, are not by nature esoteric. The Celebration of the Eucharist, especially in a place that has been disturbed, and the prayer of the Great Litany, for example, are ordinary practices."[2] So while the Presbyter has to clear it with the Bishop, it's a ritual, recommended to be done in community, which can be led by anyone deemed able. Another interesting thing about casting out demons: From ancient times, and still today in the Roman Catholic exorcism ritual, knowing the name of that which you are attempting to overwhelm is required. Are you casting out a fever, a particular spirit, or a known demon? Naming something or knowing its name means having power over that thing. In fact, God gives Adam the "power" to name things. Modern recovery programs prove that the very first step towards freedom is *naming* the problem. At the instant that the demon reveals his name, it shows that he has been weakened; if his name is unsaid, he is still strong. And even cooler, in this story the demon actually names Jesus. He attempts to turn the tables on who is casting out whom when he asks boldly, "What have you to do with us, Jesus of Nazareth? Have you come to destroy us? I know who you are, the Holy One of God." How does it feel when the demons you attempt to hold at bay turn on you, and say *your* name?

1 BOS 2022, 233.
2 BOS 2022, 233.

Engaging All Ages

"Jesus commands even the unclean spirits, and they obey him" (Mark 1:27). Unclean spirits can have a variety of interpretations, depending on one's age. Cleanliness is often associated with God and goodness, while unclean is connected to "evil" in scripture. Even a portion of the Lord's Prayer includes, "... and deliver us from evil." What is evil in today's world? In *The Scream*, Edward Munch's tormented screamer in the nightmarish landscape, we see how isolation and terror can overwhelm a person. How do we form community so that no one is treated like an outcast, "unclean" and alone?

Prayers of the People: Option 1

We gather in your name, Jesus, because we know who you are. You know our deepest needs and weaknesses, and we look to you in hope.

Hear our prayers, Holy One of God.

The world is hurting and restless for you, Lord. The earth is stressed and cries out for protection. Its peoples cry out in hunger and fear. We turn to you in need of deliverance.

Hear our prayers, Holy One of God.

We pray for your Church as it walks your Way of Life, your Way of Love. May your people and their leaders know deeply your loving, liberating life-giving presence.

Hear our prayers, Holy One of God.

We pray for those who govern all over the world, that they may pursue justice and practice peace. Equip them with the courage and resources to respond to the needs of their people.

Hear our prayers, Holy One of God.

For those who have lost their freedom to addiction, for those who wrestle with worry, for those who struggle with mobility, communication, and relationship. For those who are ill and facing surgery or treatments. For those who will soon give birth, and those who have lost a pregnancy. We look to you for care of all these to give them hope through your presence.

Hear our prayers, Holy One of God.

We commend to you the souls of those who have died and ask you to comfort those whose hearts ache with grief.

Hear our prayers, Holy One of God.

Prayers of the People: Option 2

Deacon or Presider: In the name of Jesus of Nazareth, let us pray for all who need the cleansing power of the Holy One of God.

Intercessor: For the church and all seek the truth of God. For *N.* our Presiding Bishop, for *N.* our bishop, for our parish clergy, *N.*, for priests, deacons, and all who minister in Christ.

God, hear our prayer.

For prophets in every land who rebuke the spirits of greed and violence, oppression and despair.

God, hear our prayer.

For those requiring ongoing care, for those burdened by anguish or illness, and for those who care for them with love and healing.

God, hear our prayer.

For all those seeking a deeper faith that they may experience the liberation of the spirit.

God, hear our prayer.

For those who have died and are in the presence of God's holy power.

God, hear our prayer.

For the many blessings of our lives, for ourselves and all those we love.

God, hear our prayer.

Remembering [the Blessed Virgin Mary, blessed *N.*] and all the saints, let us offer ourselves and one another to the living God through Christ.

To you, O Lord our God.

Presider: God our Teacher, speaking with holy authority, liberating us from the forces of evil, hear the prayers we offer this day and give us courage as we proclaim your truth; through Jesus Christ our Lord. ***Amen.***

Hymns for the Day

The Hymnal 1982

God the Omnipotent! King, who ordainest 569
God has spoken to his people 536
How wondrous and great thy works,
God of praise! 532, 533
God is love, and where true love is 576, 577
Lord, make us servants of your peace 593
Where charity and love prevail 581
Deck thyself, my soul, with gladness 339
From God Christ's deity came forth 443
O for a thousand tongues to sing 493
O love, how deep, how broad, how high 448, 449
Spread, O spread, thou mighty word 530
Thine arm, O Lord, in days of old 567
Thou, whose almighty word 371
Ye servants of God, your Master proclaim 535

Lift Every Voice and Sing II

Yield not to temptation 170

The Fifth Sunday after the Epiphany

Sunday on or between February 4 and 10

Note: If Ash Wednesday falls during the week following this Sunday, move directly to the Last Sunday after the Epiphany instead

Jesus's mission of "preaching" includes the whole of his ministry: teaching, healing, casting out spirits and finally his death and resurrection.

Anchor Points – The Propers and the Season

The fixed points for each service are the appointed or proper readings and collect as well as the themes of the day or season.

Readings and Psalm

Isaiah 40:21–31

Isaiah comforts the people with this mocking contrast between the power of God and the weakness of false gods. The outstanding characteristic of a god is power, and their God – in case they don't remember – is the ruler over all creation and all earthly rulers.

Psalm 147:1–12, 21c

Psalm 147 is divided into three stanzas: vv. 1–6, 7–11 and 12–20, each beginning with a call to worship and continuing with motives for praise. The themes of God's sovereignty over the natural order and over human society are mingled throughout the psalm.

1 Corinthians 9:16–23

In chapter 9, Paul defends his status as an apostle. His authority had apparently been questioned because he had waived two apostolic rights: being married and receiving support for preaching. The absolute claim of the gospel makes relative all cultural, ethnic, national, or legal values. The freedom that his decision gives him puts him in a position of servitude under "Christ's law" – the obligation of love. Paul's flexibility is neither cowardice nor compromise; rather, his freedom allows him to speak to and from the experience of others.

Mark 1:29–39

Today's reading continues the account of a day in Jesus's ministry. The healing of Peter's mother-in-law is presented without direct interpretation or theological comment. Then at sundown, when the sabbath was over, people are brought to Jesus for healing and the casting out of spirits. Silencing the spirits (v. 34) was apparently part of the common technique of exorcism. But Mark implies that Jesus does not wish his identity made known by evil spirits who have no credibility as witnesses.

Collect

Set us free, O God, from the bondage of our sins, and give us the liberty of that abundant life which you have made known to us in your Son our Savior Jesus Christ; who lives and reigns with you, in the unity of the Holy Spirit, one God, now and forever. *Amen.*

Proper Preface

Epiphany – Because in the mystery of the Word made flesh, you have caused a new light to shine in our hearts, to give the knowledge of your glory in the face of your Son Jesus Christ our Lord. (Rite II, BCP 378; Rite I BCP 346)

Seasonal Pairings

See the table below for choices appointed and suggested for this day. Preferences are put in **bold**. Not all choices are suitable for all congregations or community, though, so consider these preferences as a starting point before making a decision about your own congregation.

	Epiphany 5	Rite I	Rite II	EOW1	BOS 2022
Color	Green				
Entrance Rite	Customary	323	355	50	
Song of Praise/Kyrie	Gloria in excelsis or BCP Canticle 11, 19; EOW1 Canticle D, L	Gloria 324	Gloria 356; C11 – 87; C19 – 94	D – 32; L – 36	
Collect		164	216		
Creed	Nicene Creed	326, 327	358	53	
Prayers of the People	**Locally written**; options below; BCP forms	329	387–393	54–55	
Offertory Sentence	"Those who wait for the Lord shall renew their strength, they shall mount up with wings like eagles, they shall run and not be weary, they shall walk and not faint." (Isaiah)	343–344	376–377		
Eucharistic Prayer	**One that allows use of the Epiphany preface** ***or, alternatively,*** **Prayer C**	2–340	**A – 361,** **B – 367** or C – 369	1–57	
Proper Preface	Epiphany *or* The Lord's Day 1, 2, or 3	344–346	377–378		
Breaking of the Bread (Fraction)	Christ our Passover (BCP) or Blessed are those who are called (Hymn S 172)	337	365	69	
Postcommunion Prayer		339	**Eternal God – 365**	God of abundance – 69	
Blessing	Customary *or* 2nd option in BOS				12
Dismissal	**Let us go forth in the Name of Christ**	340	366		
Notes	May be Theological Education Sunday; May be Souper Bowl of Caring				

Additional Notes:

Song of Praise/Canticle – Whatever is chosen – the Gloria, one of the Canticles from the BCP or EOW1, or some other option – it may be desirable to use it consistently through the season from Epiphany 2 through Last Epiphany.

Eucharistic Prayer C – While it does not allow for the inclusion of the seasonal proper preface, much of the language in the prayer is suitable for Epiphany, particularly the request "Open our eyes to see your hand at work in the world about us." Prayer C, however, also contains significant penitential language, so may be more suited for Lent. It shouldn't be used for both seasons consecutively, in any case.

Fraction Anthem at the Breaking of the Bread – The option provided in Rite I and Rite II ("Christ our Passover") is suitable throughout the season and the Alleluias may be included. Explore other texts that may be used from *The Hymnal 1982* from S 151 to S 172 (sung or said). The text at Hymn S 172 ("Blessed are those who are called") is very appropriate for Epiphany as it emphasizes that all nations are called into Christ's life. Additionally, EOW1 has several options.

Content Resources

Reading Between the Lines

Abundant life that one exorcised person experienced and many saw is now brought home to the household of core disciples, Simon Peter and Andrew, and then expanded to include all ill or demon-possessed people. Healing is manifestly tangible. Jesus grasps or seizes Simon Peter's mother-in-law by the hand, raising her up from a bed of fever. Later on, Jesus extends his hand (either in anger or compassion, the text is not clear) and touches a leper who requests healing. Sometime later, a woman in a state of impurity lays a hand on his garment and is healed. In the same episode, Jesus touches a corpse and raises a young girl thought to have died. But the actions and force with which Jesus reaches out to heal are turned against him in the course of the gospel narrative. Those around Jesus – perhaps his family, perhaps his disciples – seek to restrain him early in his ministry, thinking him unbalanced. Jesus' healing ability is inhibited by the skepticism of those in his hometown. Crowds press against him. In the latter half of the gospel, opponents seize people Jesus knows: John the Baptist, the naked young man in the garden, and finally Jesus too. But restraint and arrest are not the last word for Jesus himself is raised by God to new life.

Central Themes

At the end of the passage from Mark, Jesus goes out to a "lonely place" by himself and prays, seemingly to recharge after a full day of healing and casting out demons. How often do we allow ourselves the grace to recharge? Lay or ordained, those of us engaged in the work we are called to do, get tired. If Jesus needs to recharge, shouldn't we allow ourselves the same? Take time to worship in a context where you are not the leader. Take time to find a quiet place that is removed from the noise of your daily work, and meditate and pray.

As noted last week, Jesus could not let the demons speak, because they knew him. They would speak his name and tell his story. Jesus still needed to buy time. To stretch the days, week, months he had remaining to proclaim the message of Good News, including casting out demons and curing the sick. Mark talks about the opportunity Jesus took advantage of – to go to neighboring villages to tell others. By the time the gospels of Luke and Matthew were written, it was not just to go into neighboring towns, but to go to the entire world. Restore this person not just to wellness, but to life. Free this village not from the demons, but from bondage, that they might live. The message of God is often initially about healing, but healing is rarely the point. Restoration of life is the point. You are healed so you can return to the meaning of your life. Return to the temple. Return to your family. Return to your status in the community whole and with respect. And like Peter's mother-in-law; to service. The gospel calls us not only to repent, but to return. In so many of the healing stories of Jesus the scene begins with the surprising inquiry "What do you want of me?" It would seem obvious: We wish to be well. But is wellness about the alleviation of a disease, the reduction of a fever, or is it about resurrection to new life?

Engaging All Ages

". . . but those who wait for God shall renew their strength, they shall mount up with wings like eagles . . ." (Isaiah 40:31). The eagle is associated with divine power in some religions. The hope people find in the eagle a source of healing and lifegiving rain. An eagle kachina doll (dance) is an expression of that hope. In addition to birds, wings are also associated with angels. A Hindu prayer states, "You are to me, O God, what wings are to the bird." Why are wings seen as powerful, healing, and hopeful? What would it be like to have wings? How do you express hope?

Prayers of the People: Option 1

Presider: To whom will we compare you, Holy One, the everlasting God, Creator of the ends of the earth, who stretches out the heavens like a curtain: Be near to us in our weakness and uphold us with your might, as we pray: Great is our God and mighty in power; there is no limit to God's wisdom.

Litanist: Holy One, who never faints or grows weary: Heal and empower your Church, entrusted with a commission to bear the Good News to all the earth, that we may be all things to all people, serving as slaves to all for the sake of the gospel.

Great is our God and mighty in power;

there is no limit to God's wisdom.

Holy One, who brings princes to naught and makes the rulers of the earth as nothing: Guide our nation and all who lead in the whole earth, that they may be servants of healing and may cast out all forms of oppression throughout your creation.

Great is our God and mighty in power;

there is no limit to God's wisdom.

Holy One, who gives power to the faint and strength to the powerless: Reach out your hand and lift up all who suffer from illness or fear, violence or threat, that those who wait upon the Lord shall renew their strength, mount up with wings like eagles, run and not be weary, walk and not faint.

Great is our God and mighty in power;

there is no limit to God's wisdom.

Holy One, who lifts up the lowly and makes grass to grow upon the mountains and green plants to serve humankind: Bless this community with compassion and grace, that we may serve one another with deference and respect.

Great is our God and mighty in power;

there is no limit to God's wisdom.

Holy One, whose understanding is unsearchable:

Touch with your healing compassion those for whom we pray, especially . . .

Hear our gratefulness for all the blessings of our lives, especially for . . .

Enfold into your eternal love those who have died, especially . . .
Great is our God and mighty in power;

there is no limit to God's wisdom.

Presider: We look toward your eternal glory, O Holy One, and raise our voices to you in prayer: Enter our homes and towns, our solitudes and cities; cast out all that oppresses and threatens your people, heal all who are weak and bring peace in our time, that your whole creation may sing out in praise to proclaim your message of love and hope, through Jesus Christ our Savior. ***Amen.***

Prayers of the People: Option 2

You have no equal, God. We come before you humbled, asking for your healing presence. Heal us and raise us so that we may serve you.

We are amazed at your creative genius – how you have stretched the heavens like curtains, and yet you bend to be with us.

We are amazed, God. We raise our hearts in awe.

Our world and our lives are in need of healing and direction. We ask you to guide your church and heal it where it is worn out and self-centered. Direct those who lead the church: bishops, priests, and deacons – all those in positions of leadership.

We ask for direction. Raise them up, God.

We ask you to heal the relationships between nations and neighbors. Give the leaders of the nations the courage to pursue justice and speak peace as an example for the world.

We ask for healing. Raise them up, God.

Many of us suffer from addiction, anxiety, and illness. Break the chains that bind them and heal them, God. Surround them with supportive people, the resources they need, and a tangible sense of your love.

We ask for healing. Raise them up, God.

We pray for those who have died, that they may know the fullness of your love in the life you have prepared for them. Comfort those who grieve their loss, and give them the confidence of your love that knows no limits of time or space.

We ask for assurance of your love.
Raise them up, God.

Hymns for the Day

The Hymnal 1982

Thy strong word did cleave the darkness 381
Immortal, invisible, God only wise 423
O bless the Lord, my soul! 411
The God of Abraham praise 401
In Christ there is no East or West 529
From thee all skill and science flow 566
Thine arm, O Lord, in days of old 567

Lift Every Voice and Sing II

In Christ there is no East or West 62

Wonder, Love, and Praise

The church of Christ in every age 779
From miles around the sick ones came 774
Heal me, hands of Jesus 773
O Christ, the healer, we have come 772

The Sixth Sunday after the Epiphany

Sunday on or between February 11 and 17

Note: If Ash Wednesday falls during the week following this Sunday, move directly to the Last Sunday after the Epiphany instead

Anchor Points – The Propers and the Season

The fixed points for each service are the appointed or proper readings and collect as well as the themes of the day or season.

Readings and Psalm

2 Kings 5:1–14

In the first reading, we have an outsider with leprosy, the commander of the army of the kingdom of Aram, enemies to the people of Israel. Naaman's reluctant obedience to follow God's direction, given by Elisha, brings him into new life, both physical and spiritual. Not only is Naaman healed but God's concern for all people, not just the people of Israel, is demonstrated. He becomes a visual testimony, both to wayward Israel and to the Gentile nations, that only submission and an attitude of trust can lead to wholeness and righteousness (a right relationship with God).

Psalm 30

This thanksgiving for healing was probably composed and sung in fulfillment of a vow. Both sickness and health are regarded as coming from the Lord – illness as a probable sign of sin while restoration to health would show innocence. Sickness brings the psalmist closer to the realm of Sheol, the grave, from which the Lord rescues him.

1 Corinthians 9:24–27

In today's reading, Paul concludes his argument about Christian liberty, rights and sacrifice for the sake of love with an illustration drawn from athletics. Like an athlete who sacrifices much in training and dedication, the follower of Jesus must also give up whatever impedes Christian love and service. Even good things, like liberties and fair expectations, must be relinquished so that the long course of serving the Lord can be finished triumphantly. Those who do so can anticipate a crown that will last forever.

Mark 1:40–45

Once again the Gospel reading is an account of a healing, this time of a leper, echoing the reading from 2 Kings. Leprosy in the time of the New Testament caused its sufferers to be excluded from human society and from the life of the religious community. Here Jesus reaches out and demonstrates that God excludes no one.

Collect

O God, the strength of all who put their trust in you: Mercifully accept our prayers; and because in our weakness we can do nothing good without you, give us the help of your grace, that in keeping your commandments we may please you both in will and deed; through Jesus Christ our Lord, who lives and reigns with you and the Holy Spirit, one God, for ever and ever. *Amen.*

Proper Preface

Epiphany – Because in the mystery of the Word made flesh, you have caused a new light to shine in our hearts, to give the knowledge of your glory in the face of your Son Jesus Christ our Lord. (Rite II, BCP 378; Rite I BCP 346)

Seasonal Pairings

See the table below for choices appointed and suggested for this day. Preferences are put in **bold**. Not all choices are suitable for all congregations or community, though, so consider these preferences as a starting point before making a decision about your own congregation.

	Epiphany 6	Rite I	Rite II	EOW1	BOS 2022
Color	Green				
Entrance Rite	Customary	323	355	50	
Song of Praise/Kyrie	Gloria in excelsis or BCP Canticle 11, 19; EOW1 Canticle D, L	Gloria 324	Gloria 356; C11 – 87; C19 – 94	D – 32; L – 36	
Collect		164	216		
Creed	Nicene Creed	326, 327	358	53	
Prayers of the People	**Locally written**; options below; BCP forms	329	387–393	54–55	
Offertory Sentence	"You have turned my wailing into dancing, O Lord; you have put off my sack-cloth and clothed me with joy." (Psalm 30)	343–344	376–377		
Eucharistic Prayer	**One that allows use of the Epiphany preface *or, alternatively,* Prayer C**	2–340	**A – 361,** **B – 367** or C – 369	1–57	
Proper Preface	Epiphany *or* The Lord's Day 1, 2, or 3	344–346	377–378		
Breaking of the Bread (Fraction)	Christ our Passover (BCP) or Blessed are those who are called (Hymn S 172)	337	365	69	
Postcommunion Prayer		339	**Eternal God – 365**	God of abundance – 69	
Blessing	Customary *or* 2nd option in BOS				12
Dismissal	**Let us go forth in the Name of Christ**	340	366		
Notes	May be Souper Bowl of Caring				

Additional Notes:

Song of Praise/Canticle – Whatever is chosen – the Gloria, one of the Canticles from the BCP or EOW1, or some other option – it may be desirable to use it consistently through the season from Epiphany 2 through Last Epiphany.

Eucharistic Prayer C – While it does not allow for the inclusion of the seasonal proper preface, much of the language in the prayer is suitable for Epiphany, particularly the request "Open our eyes to see your hand at work in the world about us." Prayer C, however, also contains significant penitential language, so may be more suited for Lent. It shouldn't be used for both seasons consecutively, in any case.

Fraction Anthem at the Breaking of the Bread – The option provided in Rite I and Rite II ("Christ our Passover") is suitable throughout the season and the Alleluias may be included. Explore other texts that may be used from *The Hymnal 1982* from S 151 to S 172 (sung or said). The text at Hymn S 172 ("Blessed are those who are called") is very appropriate for Epiphany as it emphasizes that all nations are called into Christ's life. Additionally, EOW1 has several options.

Content Resources

Reading Between the Lines

Mark's gospel is fascinated by the humanity and the body of Jesus, particularly human emotions. As we have seen, Mark's Jesus intentionally takes hold of sick people in order to heal them, but Jesus himself also becomes the object of human touch. He is actor, and he is also acted upon. Whilst Jesus clearly assents to the request for cleansing, Jesus' emotional response to a person with skin disease, perhaps leprosy, is enigmatic. Is it compassion (pity) or anger (indignation) at the condition of human frailty? Both are attested in textual traditions. The healing however is immediate. Jesus enjoins silence, except that the priest be told (thus acknowledging priestly laws of the day) and the sacrifice for a healed skin disease in Leviticus 14 be offered. Mark's gospel also describes the startling effect of Jesus' message in the cities of the Decapolis.

Central Themes

In the classic Cecil B. DeMille movie of *The Ten Commandments* there is a scene at the burning bush where Moses is being given various signs to use to convince the people of Israel and Pharoah that he is sent from God. One of the signs is being able to show his skin as leprous and then miraculously healed. As a child, this was always fascinating and somewhat troubling. It came across almost like a magic trick, rather than a sign of God's ultimate sovereignty. Stories of miraculous healings are always a little hard to know what to do with. They really aren't told to be a spectacle, but almost always are a sign of something deeper – of God's sovereignty over creation and the body, of God's ultimate care for God's people, that they would be healed.

The other primary theme today is the action of God to break through barriers of exclusion and invite all into the life and love of God. Those ideas of insider and outsider are never far from us. The church is constantly tempted to consider itself to be a society of those in God's favor and to regard those outside the church as living apart from God. We gather in Eucharist, however, as people who know ourselves to be agents of God's call to all people. As Jesus' own concern for all, especially those excluded by human society, manifested his oneness with God, so we are called to manifest God in our lives by being an inclusive community. We gather around a table spread for all people. Our lives and ministry are to reflect the inclusiveness of the Lord's table.

Engaging All Ages

It may be valuable to think about anyone that you may have experienced as being "cast out" – or to reflect on times when you have felt excluded or pushed aside. How did it feel? What was your response? If you saw it happen to someone else, could you think of anything that you could do to intervene or change the situation for the better? Structures of exclusion are very difficult to dismantle and take down. It requires keeping a clear vision on God's action and commitment to include all people.

Prayers of the People

Deacon or Presider

Let us pray for all people in the Church and the World who need mercy, justice, and peace, saying "Lord have mercy."

Intercessor

For the Church of God, [for ____________, our bishop(s),] and for all who witness to the glory of God.

Silence

Let us pray to the Lord,

Christ have mercy.

For this nation, this world and for the sharing of health and healing.

Silence

Let us pray to the Lord,

Christ have mercy.

For those stigmatized as unclean, and for those who touch and heal them.

Silence

Let us pray to the Lord,

Christ have mercy.

For all who practice the medical arts, and for physicians of the spirit.

Silence

Let us pray to the Lord,

Christ have mercy.

For all who are sick and in need of prayer. For those who are dying. For those we name now, silently or aloud.

Silence

Let us pray to the Lord,

Christ have mercy.

For the dead and for those who mourn. For those we name now, silently or aloud.

Silence

For the promise joy granted to [blessed ______________ and] all the saints. Let us pray to the Lord,

Christ have mercy.

Presider

O God, who bids us wash in healing waters, hear the prayers we offer you this day and enable us to proclaim your good news and spread the word of your salvation; through Jesus Christ our Lord. ***Amen.***

Hymns for the Day

The Hymnal 1982

If thou but trust in God to guide thee 635
New every morning is the love 10
Day by day 654
Awake, my soul, stretch every nerve 546
Fight the good fight with all thy might 552, 553
Lo! what a cloud of witnesses 545
Not far beyond the sea, nor high 422
Father, we praise thee, now the night is over 1, 2
O for a thousand tongues to sing 493
Thine arm, O Lord, in days of old 567

Lift Every Voice and Sing II
Wade in the water 143
He is King of kings 96

Wonder, Love, and Praise
Wade in the water 740
Guide my feet, Lord 819
When from bondage we are summoned 753 754
From miles around the sick ones came 774
Heal me, hands of Jesus 773
O Christ, the healer, we have come 772
You laid aside your rightful reputation 734

The Seventh Sunday after the Epiphany

Sunday on or between February 18 and 24

Note: If Ash Wednesday falls during the week following this Sunday, move directly to the Last Sunday after the Epiphany instead

Anchor Points – The Propers and the Season

The fixed points for each service are the appointed or proper readings and collect as well as the themes of the day or season.

Readings and Psalm

Isaiah 43:18–25

In chapter 43, God's people ready themselves for the long journey out of exile and into their homeland. God urges the people to let go of old victories so that God's greater plans may come to light. As the Israelites prepare to return to their homeland, they cling to the old stories of triumph, of their release from Egypt and their victorious march into the Promised Land. God bids them turn their eyes to the new work of God before them. Yet, in spite of God's faithfulness and the promise of restoration, the people do not turn to the Lord in hope. They neglect their calling as God's chosen ones. They have been "weary" of God and have "wearied" God with their rebellion. Nevertheless, God remains a God who blots out transgressions. God's plans for Israel are not even thwarted by their lack of cooperation.

Psalm 41

A Psalm that emphasizes the steadfastness of God standing with us, even when all else turn against us.

2 Corinthians 1:18–22

Paul's message to the Corinthians is that his ministry among them is sure and faithful, even though challenged by unexpected hardships. He comes in the name of Jesus Christ, the One who confirms the reliability of all God's promises through the ages. Paul does not minister according to his feelings or insights. He ministers according to God who works ceaselessly to "establish" (v. 21) both Paul and the Corinthians in Christ. God's Spirit, given now in our hearts, is the first installment of all that God has planned for those who are sealed, imprinted with the mark of divine ownership.

Mark 2:1–12

Today's Gospel gives us another manifestation of Jesus' role as Son of God and a way we manifest him today. The important message in the story is more than the healing of the paralyzed man; it is the announcement that Jesus exercises the divine authority to forgive sins. Only God can forgive sins and Jesus' demonstration of his ability to forgive is an announcement that in him God is dwelling among us.

Collect

O Lord, you have taught us that without love whatever we do is worth nothing: Send your Holy Spirit and pour into our hearts your greatest gift, which is love, the true bond of peace and of all virtue, without which whoever lives is accounted dead before you. Grant this for the sake of your only Son Jesus Christ, who lives and reigns with you and the Holy Spirit, one God, now and for ever. *Amen.*

Proper Preface

Epiphany – Because in the mystery of the Word made flesh, you have caused a new light to shine in our hearts, to give the knowledge of your glory in the face of your Son Jesus Christ our Lord. (Rite II, BCP 378; Rite I BCP 346)

Seasonal Pairings

See the table below for choices appointed and suggested for this day. Preferences are put in **bold**. Not all choices are suitable for all congregations or community, though, so consider these preferences as a starting point before making a decision about your own congregation.

	Epiphany 7	Rite I	Rite II	EOW1	BOS 2022
Color	Green				
Entrance Rite	Customary	323	355	50	
Song of Praise/Kyrie	Gloria in excelsis or BCP Canticle 11, 19; EOW1 Canticle D, L	Gloria 324	Gloria 356; C11 – 87; C19 – 94	D – 32; L – 36	
Collect		164	216		
Creed	Nicene Creed	326, 327	358	53	
Prayers of the People	**Locally written**; options below; BCP forms	329	387–393	54–55	
Offertory Sentence	"Happy are they who consider the poor and needy! The Lord will deliver them in the time of trouble." (Psalm 41)	343–344	376–377		
Eucharistic Prayer	**One that allows use of the Epiphany preface *or, alternatively,* Prayer C**	2–340	**A – 361, B – 367** or C – 369	1–57	
Proper Preface	Epiphany *or* The Lord's Day 1, 2, or 3	344–346	377–378		
Breaking of the Bread (Fraction)	Christ our Passover (BCP) or Blessed are those who are called (Hymn S 172)	337	365	69	
Postcommunion Prayer		339	**Eternal God – 365**	God of abundance – 69	
Blessing	Customary *or* 2nd option in BOS				12
Dismissal	**Let us go forth in the Name of Christ**	340	366		
Notes	The feast of St. Matthias the Apostle may fall on this Sunday.				

Additional Notes:
Song of Praise/Canticle – Whatever is chosen – the Gloria, one of the Canticles from the BCP or EOW1, or some other option – it may be desirable to use it consistently through the season from Epiphany 2 through Last Epiphany.

Eucharistic Prayer C – While it does not allow for the inclusion of the seasonal proper preface, much of the language in the prayer is suitable for Epiphany, particularly the request "Open our eyes to see your hand at work in the world about us." Prayer C, however, also contains significant penitential language, so may be more suited for Lent. It shouldn't be used for both seasons consecutively, in any case.

Fraction Anthem at the Breaking of the Bread – The option provided in Rite I and Rite II ("Christ our Passover") is suitable throughout the season and the Alleluias may be included. Explore other texts that may be used from *The Hymnal 1982* from S 151 to S 172 (sung or said). The text at Hymn S 172 ("Blessed are those who are called") is very appropriate for Epiphany as it emphasizes that all nations are called into Christ's life. Additionally, EOW1 has several options.

Content Resources

Reading Between the Lines

What does the translation "(Jesus) was at home" (Mark 2:1) convey to you? Jesus' home in Capernaum? Perhaps in a house he owns? William Tyndale translates simply, "he was in a house" which avoids connotations of a fixed family residence that the word "home" can imply. Jesus likely stayed in other people's houses in Capernaum and did not own one. But the NRSV modulates this idea, here, and in e.g., Mark 3:19 by translating, "Jesus went home…" and in 3:21 "his family…went out to restrain him…" Avoiding notions of home ownership, and residence in a private domain are important ways to separate the first century world from ours. A house in Capernaum likely indicates a small open domain inhabited by several generations of an extended family. Larger households would have included slaves.

The absolute use of "the word" connotes "the word of God" as in the Hebrew Bible, "the word of the Lord" cf. Mark 4:14, "the Sower sows the word..."; also, frequently in e.g., Luke 1:2, Acts 4:4, Gal 6:6 etc.

Jesus perceives the faith of those who "unroofed the roof" and let the paralyzed man down through it. This could include the faith of the paralyzed man. This is the first instance of the term faith, Pistis, in the gospel. Faith or trust appears in Mark throughout the gospel and more frequently than the key term, "the kingdom of God." This notion lies at the heart of Jesus message and while we found it throughout the New Testament Mark features it prominently. In Mark, Jesus commends people's faith or trust, and Jesus calls people to put faith into practice. It is intrinsic to Jesus's injunction to repent, to be obedient, and to wait for the coming of God's Kingdom and the Son of Man. As Teresa Morgan observes in her 2012 study, *Roman Faith and Christian Faith*, faith and trust language "captures much of what is central to Christian thinking in terms and concepts which were easily understood by all Greek and Latin speakers, Jewish and gentile, and this was an invaluable asset in its promulgation and evolution."

Central Themes

In addition to the overt themes of God's healing and the witness that action provides, an additional theme in today's Gospel and Epistle reading is the significance of the community of faith. Note in the Gospel reading that there is no mention of the sick man's faith. It was the faith of his friends, willing even to dig through the roof and lower the paralyzed man into Jesus' presence. Likewise, Paul holds up our role as affirming God's action by our own agreement, our "Yes," our "Amen." Even so, it is only through God that we can say "Yes." It is through God that we exercise the community's faith and thereby manifest God's love and forgiveness to the world.

We gather to celebrate the dying and rising of Jesus not primarily as a collection of individuals, each of whom has his or her own faith. We gather primarily as the community of faith, and our actions of thanksgiving and proclamation and prayer are shown to be God's acting in and through us as God brings healing and forgiveness and new life.

Engaging All Ages

There are all kinds of puzzles in this world. Some require us to look at things through a completely different lens or to think about a problem in a completely new way. Often puzzles can only be solved after we are willing to leave behind all our preconceived ideas and try something new. The man's friends in the Gospel were confronted with the puzzle of how to get their friend into the house where Jesus was, when it was completely full of people. They couldn't go in through the door or even the windows. Only when they thought about the problem in a completely new way did they realize that they could come in through the roof. Once they dug a hole in the roof.

God invites our creativity, our cleverness, but above all our commitment, in our life of faith. When we face challenges or problems/puzzles, God is with us nudging us forward to try another way. Our God is a God of second, third, and many more chances. God sticks with us when we keep faith, no matter what.

Prayers of the People: Option 1

Deacon or Presider

At this time and in this place, let us open our hearts to the Lord, and bring forth our needs and concerns saying, "O Lord, for your love's sake: Hear our prayer."

Intercessor

We pray for all people who profess faith in the one God. Strengthen our belief, increase our love, and deepen our commitment to your service. Draw us ever closer to you, and to one other.

Silence

O Lord, for your love's sake:

Hear our prayer.

We pray for *N.* our bishop and all bishops; we pray for our parish clergy and lay leaders and all those who seek to manifest the love of Christ in the world.

Silence

O Lord, for your love's sake:

Hear our prayer.

We pray for the welfare of the entire world. For those affected by violence, occupational hazards, and natural disasters; for those who are poor and those facing persecution, for refugees and prisoners. Bring peace to all the nations of the earth. Preserve and protect all who suffer, or are in any need or danger.

Silence

O Lord, for your love's sake:

Hear our prayer.

We pray for our nation. Temper our strength with sympathy, our might with justice, our riches with charity; and deliver us from all hardness of heart.

Silence

O Lord, for your love's sake:

Hear our prayer.

We pray for this congregation and for its mission and ministries; for our neighborhood and for this city. Make of us a people of purpose and a community of compassion.

Silence

O Lord, for your love's sake:

Hear our prayer.

We pray for the sick: for those who suffer from any mental or physical illness, and for those undergoing treatment for disease. For those we know who are sick, and for those we now name, either silently or aloud . . .

Silence

O Lord, for your love's sake:

Hear our prayer.

[With blessed ______________ and all the saints,]
We commend to your loving care all those who have died. For all those dear to us who have died, and for those we now name either silently or aloud . . .

Silence

O Lord, for your love's sake:

Hear our prayer.

Presider

Lord of Love, hear the pleas of your faithful people. In the bounty of your love and the multitude of your mercies, grant these and all our prayers and petitions as may be best for us, and in accordance with your will. ***Amen.***

Prayers of the People: Option 2

Presider or deacon

Let us offer prayers to our God, who gives us water in the desert and blots out our transgressions.

Intercessor

For the church of Jesus Christ following the way in the wilderness.

Lord, have mercy.

For a blossoming of peace among all nations and peoples.

Lord, have mercy.

For those burdened by their sins or wearied by the iniquity of others.

Lord, have mercy.

For those with are limited by infirmity and those who care for them.

Lord, have mercy.

For all who are sick or homebound, and for the dying and the dead.

Lord, have mercy.

For our parish community and for those who are alienated from the church.

Lord, have mercy.

Remembering the Blessed Virgin Mary, N, and all the saints, let us offer ourselves and one another to the living God through Christ.

To you, O Lord our God.

Presider

Loving God, ever faithful to your people, hear the prayers we offer you this day and forgive us our sins, that we may declare your praise; through Jesus Christ our Lord. ***Amen.***

Hymns for the Day

The Hymnal 1982

God is Love, let heaven adore him 379
Love divine, all loves excelling 657
Creator of the earth and skies 148
Baptized in water 294
Come, thou fount of every blessing 686
My God, accept my heart this day 697
To thee, O Comforter divine 514
Lead us, heavenly Father, lead us 559
Praise, my soul, the King of heaven 410
Now the silence 333
Songs of thankfulness and praise 135
Thine arm, O Lord, in days of old 567
There's a wideness in God's mercy 469, 470
Wilt thou forgive that sin, where I begun 140, 141

Lift Every Voice and Sing II

Baptized in water 121
Come, thou fount of every blessing 111

Wonder, Love, and Praise

The desert shall rejoice 722
Baptized in water 767
From miles around the sick ones came 774
Heal me, hands of Jesus 773
O Christ, the healer, we have come 772
Loving Spirit, loving Spirit 742
You're called by name, forever loved 766

The Eighth Sunday after the Epiphany

Sunday on or between February 25 and 29

Note: If Ash Wednesday falls during the week following this Sunday, move directly to the Last Sunday after the Epiphany instead

Anchor Points – The Propers and the Season

The fixed points for each service are the appointed or proper readings and collect as well as the themes of the day or season.

Readings and Psalm

Hosea 2:14–20

Many of the prophets foretold God's doing something radically new. In today's first reading, Hosea describes that new work of God as a totally new relationship between God and the people. Marriage is the image used. God plans, Hosea says, to unite the people with God as completely as marriage unites two people into one flesh.

Psalm 103:1–13,22

A song of praise, this psalm celebrates God's benefits in a comprehensive way, as signaled by the repetition of all throughout. God does whatever is needed to enhance life, as shown through God's steadfast love.

2 Corinthians 3:1–6

Paul, writing to the Corinthians, is appealing to the congregation which he founded to listen to him. He calls on them to remember the long and deep relationship they have with him in the Spirit of God.

Mark 2:13–22

Christ's work is not merely to show us how to carry on with our inherited spiritual life in better ways. He was sent into the world to bring a new way and a new life. So in response to those who asked him why he and his followers were not following the religious rules of their own time, he speaks of new ways breaking in. The new cannot be patched on to the old.

Collect

Most loving Father, whose will it is for us to give thanks for all things, to fear nothing but the loss of you, and to cast all our care on you who care for us: Preserve us from faithless fears and worldly anxieties, that no clouds of this mortal life may hide from us the light of that love which is immortal, and which you have manifested to us in your Son Jesus Christ our Lord; who lives and reigns with you, in the unity of the Holy Spirit, one God, now and for ever. *Amen.*

Proper Preface

Epiphany – Because in the mystery of the Word made flesh, you have caused a new light to shine in our hearts, to give the knowledge of your glory in the face of your Son Jesus Christ our Lord. (Rite II, BCP 378; Rite I BCP 346)

Seasonal Pairings

See the table below for choices appointed and suggested for this day. Preferences are put in **bold**. Not all choices are suitable for all congregations or community, though, so consider these preferences as a starting point before making a decision about your own congregation.

	Epiphany 8	Rite I	Rite II	EOW1	BOS 2022
Color	Green				
Entrance Rite	Customary	323	355	50	
Song of Praise/Kyrie	Gloria in excelsis or BCP Canticle 11, 19; EOW1 Canticle D, L	Gloria 324	Gloria 356; C11 – 87; C19 – 94	D – 32; L – 36	
Collect		165	216		
Creed	Nicene Creed	326, 327	358	53	
Prayers of the People	**Locally written**; options below; BCP forms	329	387–393	54–55	
Offertory Sentence	"Jesus said, 'Those who are well have no need of a physician, but those who are sick; I have come to call not the righteous but sinners.'" (Mark)	343–344	376–377		
Eucharistic Prayer	**One that allows use of the Epiphany preface *or, alternatively,* Prayer C**	2–340	**A – 361, B – 367** or C – 369	1–57	
Proper Preface	Epiphany *or* The Lord's Day 1, 2, or 3	344–346	377–378		
Breaking of the Bread (Fraction)	Christ our Passover (BCP) or Blessed are those who are called (Hymn S 172)	337	365	69	
Postcommunion Prayer		339	**Eternal God – 365**	God of abundance – 69	
Blessing	Customary *or* 2nd option in BOS				12
Dismissal	**Let us go forth in the Name of Christ**	340	366		
Notes					

Additional Notes:

Song of Praise/Canticle – Whatever is chosen – the Gloria, one of the Canticles from the BCP or EOW1, or some other option – it may be desirable to use it consistently through the season from Epiphany 2 through Last Epiphany.

Eucharistic Prayer C – While it does not allow for the inclusion of the seasonal proper preface, much of the language in the prayer is suitable for Epiphany, particularly the request "Open our eyes to see your hand at work in the world about us." Prayer C, however, also contains significant penitential language, so may be more suited for Lent. It shouldn't be used for both seasons consecutively, in any case.

Fraction Anthem at the Breaking of the Bread – The option provided in Rite I and Rite II ("Christ our Passover") is suitable throughout the season and the Alleluias may be included. Explore other texts that may be used from *The Hymnal 1982* from S 151 to S 172 (sung or said). The text at Hymn S 172 ("Blessed are those who are called") is very appropriate for Epiphany as it emphasizes that all nations are called into Christ's life. Additionally, EOW1 has several options.

Content Resources

Reading Between the Lines

The calling of Levi includes information that Jesus subsequently reclines at a meal in the house of Levi, which includes the company of "many tax collectors and sinners." Levi's presence amongst the disciples makes it clear that disciples have following and learning in common ("the Greek word "disciple" is connected to the Greek verb, "to learn"), but not socioeconomic status. Tax collectors and fisherfolk are from different economic backgrounds. Including Levi and his circle suggests that the Jesus movement now has access to wealthy people in Galilee and that "sinners" might indicate a group of people who resist using their wealth to alleviate poverty.

Central Themes

The church is often tempted to settle for convention and custom. But when we gather around the Lord's Word and the Lord's table, we find a vision of a new relationship with God and a new relationship with humanity. Our assumptions about ourselves, others, and God are turned upside down. All of human life is meant to look like the eucharistic feast, to which all people are called and accepted; this is what the scriptures call the marriage feast of the Lamb.

Engaging All Ages

A very common image for Christians is the butterfly. The process of transformation in the cocoon from caterpillar to butterfly reminds Christians of the promise of new life in Christ, especially around the Resurrection and Easter. However the image of the transformation of the butterfly is different than Resurrection. First of all, no one is surprised that a butterfly comes out of a cocoon. Everyone is surprised when someone who is dead comes out of their tomb. The butterfly is a natural process; resurrection is more than that.

But in the image of the butterfly we do have a symbol of transformation. The process that the caterpillar in the cocoon goes through before becoming a butterfly is intense. The caterpillar has to go through a complete rearrangement of its body into something else. It is the end of the caterpillar as much as the beginning of the butterfly. That sort of radically new transformation is something like what Jesus is teaching about in the readings. The life in God isn't a minor fix or a patch. It' a complete rearrangement of who we are and how we inhabit the world.

Prayers of the People

Presider or deacon

Let us offer prayers to the living God, whose Spirit gives life.

Intercessor

For the people of God in every place.

Lord, have mercy.

For all nations, their leaders and citizens,

Lord, have mercy.

For all who are oppressed, afflicted, or in need, and for those who work for a just distribution of food.

Lord, have mercy.

For married couples everywhere, and for all those in covenants of love.

Lord, have mercy.

For those who are sick and homebound in our community, and for those who visit and care for them.

Lord, have mercy.

For all of us gathered at the wedding banquet of the Lamb, and for those who have died.

Lord, have mercy.

Remembering the Blessed Virgin Mary, N, and all the saints, let us offer ourselves and one another to the living God through Christ.

To you, O Lord, our God.

Presider

God, our Lord and bridegroom, who gives us the new wine of an everlasting marriage feast, hear the prayers we offer you this day and take us to yourself in righteousness and justice; through Jesus Christ our Lord. ***Amen.***

Hymns for the Day

The Hymnal 1982

O bless the Lord, my soul! 411
Praise, my soul, the King of heaven 410
Praise to the Lord, the Almighty 390
God is working his purpose out 534
Sing praise to God who reigns above 408
Holy Spirit, ever living 511
O Spirit of Life, O Spirit of God 505
O Spirit of the living God 531
By all your saints still striving (St. Matthew) 231, 232
From God Christ's deity came forth 443
He sat to watch o'er customs paid 281
In your mercy, Lord, you called me 706

Lift Every Voice and Sing II

Bless the Lord, O my soul 65
Spirit of the Living God 115

Wonder, Love, and Praise

Bless the Lord, my soul 825
As we gather at your Table 763
You laid aside your rightful reputation 734

The Last Sunday after the Epiphany

Variable – The Sunday just prior to Ash Wednesday

This is my Son, the Beloved; listen to him!

Anchor Points – The Propers and the Season

The fixed points for each service are the appointed or proper readings and collect as well as the themes of the day or season.

Readings and Psalm

2 Kings 2:1–12

This story recounts the bodily ascension of Elijah and the commissioning of Elisha as his successor. "The company of prophets" (v. 3) come to meet Elisha. They are members of the prophetic guilds, often advisors to the king. When they come to the Jordan, Elijah parts the waters like Moses at the Red Sea and Joshua at the Jordan. Elisha asks Elijah for "a double share" (v. 9) – the portion of a firstborn son – of his spirit. The fire that separates the two men is associated with the power of God acting through Elijah.

Psalm 50:1–6

Psalm 50 focuses on the meaning of sacrifice. God's people have abandoned the covenant and forgotten the real significance of sacrifice. Their offerings do not feed a hungry God nor assure God's favor; they should rather be an expression of the people's reliance upon and thankfulness to God.

2 Corinthians 4:3–6

Paul defends his apostolic ministry against opponents in the Corinthian Church. To the charge of self-glorification, he replies that he preaches to make God known. He summarizes Christian belief in "Jesus Christ as Lord" (v. 5) and Christian ministry as service to others for Jesus's sake.

Mark 9:2–9

The account of Jesus's transfiguration echoes God's appearance to Moses on Mount Sinai (see Exodus 24:15–18 and 34:29–35). The voice from the cloud repeats the statement from Jesus's baptism (1:11) with the additional command "listen to him" (v. 7). As Moses represents the tradition of the law, so Elijah represents the prophetic tradition. Mark emphasizes Peter's confused responses. The dwellings he proposes building would be like those built in the vineyards at the time of the Jewish Feast of Booths.

Collect

O God, the strength of all who put their trust in you: Mercifully accept our prayers; and because in our weakness we can do nothing good without you, give us the help of your grace, that in keeping your commandments we may please you both in will and deed; through Jesus Christ our Lord, who lives and reigns with you and the Holy Spirit, one God, for ever and ever. *Amen.*

Proper Preface

Epiphany – Because in the mystery of the Word made flesh, you have caused a new light to shine in our hearts, to give the knowledge of your glory in the face of your Son Jesus Christ our Lord. (Rite II, BCP 378; Rite I BCP 346)

Seasonal Pairings

See the table below for choices appointed and suggested for this day. Preferences are put in **bold**. Not all choices are suitable for all congregations or community, though, so consider these preferences as a starting point before making a decision about your own congregation.

	Last Sunday after the Epiphany	Rite I	Rite II	EOW1	BOS 2022
Color	Green *or* White/Gold/Festive				
Entrance Rite	Customary	323	355	50	
Song of Praise/Kyrie	Gloria in excelsis or BCP Canticle 11, 19; EOW1 Canticle D, L	Gloria 324	Gloria 356; C11 – 87; C19 – 94	D – 32; L – 36	
Collect		165	217		
Creed	Nicene Creed	326, 327	358	53	
Prayers of the People	**Locally written**; options below; BCP forms	329	387–393	54–55	
Offertory Sentence	"Out of Zion, perfect in its beauty, God reveals himself in glory" (Psalm 50)	343–344	376–377		
Eucharistic Prayer	**One that allows use of the Epiphany preface or Prayer C**	2–340	**A – 361,** **B – 367** or C – 369	1–57	
Proper Preface	Epiphany	346	378		
Breaking of the Bread (Fraction)	Christ our Passover (BCP) or Blessed are those who are called (Hymn S 172)	337	365	69	
Postcommunion Prayer		339	**Eternal God – 365**	God of abundance – 69	
Blessing	Customary *or* **2nd Option in BOS**				**12**
Dismissal	**Let us go forth in the Name of Christ**	340	366		
Notes	**Incorporate "Alleluias" into the service where possible;** "burial" of the Alleluia option; may be Theological Education Sunday; may be Souper Bowl of Caring				

Additional Notes:

Song of Praise/Canticle – Whatever is chosen – the Gloria, one of the Canticles from the BCP or EOW1, or some other option – it may be desirable to use it consistently through the season from Epiphany 2 through Last Epiphany.

Eucharistic Prayer C – While it does not allow for the inclusion of the seasonal proper preface, much of the language in the prayer is suitable for Epiphany, particularly the request "Open our eyes to see your hand at work in the world about us." Prayer C, however, also contains significant penitential language, so may be more suited for Lent. It shouldn't be used for both seasons consecutively, in any case.

Fraction Anthem at the Breaking of the Bread – The option provided in Rite I and Rite II ("Christ our Passover") is suitable throughout the season and the Alleluias may be included. Explore other texts that may be used from *The Hymnal 1982* from S 151 to S 172 (sung or said). The text at Hymn S 172 ("Blessed are those who are called") is very appropriate for Epiphany as it emphasizes that all nations are called into Christ's life. Additionally, EOW1 has several options.

Content Resources

Reading Between the Lines

Jesus' transfiguration and the voice from Heaven declaring "This is my beloved Son" in Mark is the conclusion to Epiphany tide, and the transcendent manifestation of Jesus before the season of Lent begins. In the context it occurs, namely the central section of Mark's gospel (Mark 8–10) in which Jesus teaches the uncomprehending disciples of the necessity of the suffering and death of the Son of Man, both titles are reconfigured by their proximity to each other, and the event itself prefigures the coming of God's realm within one generation (9:1) and the interpretative shadow of the resurrection, in a gospel that ends with the empty tomb (16:8). The enigma and opacity of Mark is anticipated by the mysterious departure of Elijah in 2 Kings, and matched by Paul's notion of the veiling of the gospel to unbelievers who are thus unable to see the glory of Christ, the image of God.

Central Themes

The readings for today depict both heavy drama and Biblical glamour. Elijah is carried off to heaven in front of Elisha's eyes! Jesus is glistening and chatting with Elijah and Moses! But Jesus tells the disciples to tell no one and simply keeps teaching, preaching, and healing.

Reflect upon which path is Jesus's way: loud proclamations and "making booths" or quietly going down the mountain and continuing the messy work of helping the helpless? It's easy to jump on a bandwagon of winners and glory but much harder to lift up those of little means. Look for the losers and love them; treat them as Jesus would have done.

The early church uses the story of the Transfiguration to connect their movement to both Adam and to Elijah. And in doing so, it creates a lovely image of our humanity and our tendencies to both shield ourselves from, and embrace, theophanies, or appearances of God. At first, it's too bright! Then, the clouds come, we can look, and it turns out to be exactly what we wanted but feared: God. So, let's manage this.

In Session 10 of the Adult Guide to *These Are Our Bodies,*[1] the writers explore the nature of mystery. The number of places in scripture where we're told everything from "No one has ever seen God" (1 John 4:12) to the revelation of God being in *all* of creation, across species and gender, and most troubling, in all of us.

God's love is also not a mystery. It is said "Your task is not to seek for love, but merely to seek and find all the barriers within yourself that you have built against it."[2] The disciples long for understanding, for assurance, and for authority within the circle of Jesus. This moment gives them all they need on that front.

The desire to find clarity in this kind of alternate reality is not uncommon. Most cultures have stories of seeking and being sought by a higher power. Western societies are quick to domesticate these encounters; to explain them away, to contain them, even. Build dwellings? But being persons of faith, whose charge is to always join God in making all things new, we are best served by releasing our grip, setting down our plans, and being open to this mystery.

This kind of openness allows us to see God in relationships with one another, especially those in the context of a covenant. "Intimate couples who live in a sacred covenant find themselves swept up into a grand and risky endeavor: to see if they can find their life in God by giving it to another".[3] Grand. Risky. Revelatory. Seeing God on a mountain, in a troubled friend, in a lover. All require danger and being open to whatever new thing God might be trying to show you that you've probably known all along.

1 Heidi J. A. Carter, Marcus Halley, *These Are Our Bodies – Talking Faith & Sexuality at Church & Home*, (New York, NY: Church Publishing Inc, 2017): 137.

2 Often misattributed to Rumi: "Your task is not to seek for love, but merely to seek and find all the barriers within yourself that you have built against it." Helen Schucman in *Jesus's Course in Miracles* (2000) by Helen Schucman and William Thetford, Ch. 16, *The Forgiveness of Illusions*, p. 162. Or is it? See the discussion re attribution of this quote here: https://www.healthypages.com/community/threads/is-this-rumi-or-a-course-in-miracles.47135/.

3 *Enriching Our Worship 6: Rites for Blessing Relationships* (New York, NY: Church Publishing, 2019), 15.

Engaging All Ages

The Sundays after the Epiphany are framed by both the Feast of the Epiphany, with the star in the heavens, and Jesus's face shining like the sun at the Transfiguration. The light of God's revelation in Jesus becomes clearer as the disciples are called and the word is proclaimed throughout Epiphany. Prominently display in a group all the candles you use in worship during the church year: Advent wreath, Christ candle, baptism candles, altar candles, and small candles used in Advent/Christmas candle lighting services (especially effective if you had a Candlemas procession earlier in the season). As you light them, recall how they are used referring to the light they represent. In today's gospel reading Jesus shines brighter than any of them or all of them together, it's almost like God is saying to us, "This is my Son. Listen to him!"

Prayers of the People: Option 1

Let us hear your voice as we kneel in awe before you. May we not be the same, after recognizing your glory.

Merciful and gracious Lord, hear our prayer.

Speak to us of peace. Call us to work for justice and to care for the welfare of all your children: in our homes, in our workplaces, in our neighborhoods, in you Church, in the world. Shine your light in the dark places of our lives and in this world.

Merciful and gracious Lord, hear our prayer.

Call us to be a compassionate and prayerful presence for those whose hearts ache from grief, whose souls are weary or wounded. Overshadow us with your awesome presence. Walk down from the mountaintop with us, and walk before us into the places you would have us serve as witnesses to your healing and love.

Merciful and gracious Lord, hear our prayer.

Prayers of the People: Option 2

Deacon or Presider: My siblings in faith, through the light of Christ let us behold the needs of the world and offer our prayers, saying, Lord, reveal your glory through us.

Intercessor: For the Body of Christ, its many members and ministries; for this parish and diocese; for the Episcopal Church and *N.*, our Presiding Bishop; for the worldwide

Anglican Communion and *N.*, Archbishop of Canterbury; for all believers wherever they may be,

Let us pray to the Lord:

Lord, reveal your glory through us.

For this nation and for all nations; for nations and regions in conflict or facing catastrophe.

Let us pray to the Lord:

Lord, reveal your glory through us.

For *N.*, the President of the United States; *N.*, our governor; *N.*, our mayor; for those serving in harms' way; and for all those who serve in civil leadership.

Let us pray to the Lord:

Lord, reveal your glory through us.

For those who suffer from illnesses of any kind; for those who are infirm, lonely, destitute or homeless; for those who are hungry and needy; for those oppressed by racism, sexism, homophobia, and every other exclusion; and for those whose needs we do not know,

Let us pray to the Lord.

Lord, reveal your glory through us.

For those we lift up in prayer, silently or aloud, . . .

Let us pray to the Lord.

Lord, reveal your glory through us.

For those who have died, especially . . .

Let us pray to the Lord:

Lord, reveal your glory through us.

For those for whom we give thanks, especially those we name here . . .

Let us pray to the Lord:

Lord, reveal your glory through us.

Presider: Lord Jesus Christ, you set your face steadfastly to go to Jerusalem: Deliver us from the temptation to shrink from the hard paths of a dutiful life. Make us ready to meet all the counsels of your will, and to be obedient even to death; for with the Father and the Holy Spirit you live and reign for ever and ever. ***Amen.***

Hymns for the Day

The Hymnal 1982

Songs of thankfulness and praise 135
Alleluia, song of gladness 122, 123
God of the prophets, bless the prophets' heirs 359
Christ is the world's true Light 542
Christ, whose glory fills the skies 6, 7
From God Christ's deity came forth 443
Christ upon the mountain peak 129, 130
O light of Light, Love given birth 133, 134
O wondrous type! O vision fair 136, 137

Lift Every Voice and Sing II

Swing low, sweet chariot 18
Let the heav'n light shine on me 174

Lent

Preparing for Lent

Lent is the one season for which most parishes do plan. It needs to be planned in its totality. Before inviting guest preachers or working on individual special events, attention needs to be given to an overall seasonal plan, including the Sunday Eucharists, weekday services, Ash Wednesday, Holy Week, and any special services or programs to be added to the calendar.

The inner meaning of Lent is well described in the special liturgy for Ash Wednesday:

"[The] season of Lent provided a time in which converts to the faith were prepared for Holy Baptism. It was also a time when those who, because of notorious sins, had been separated from the body of the faithful were reconciled by penitence and forgiveness, and restored to the fellowship of the Church. Thereby, the whole congregation was put in mind of the message of pardon set forth in the Gospel of our Savior, and of the need which all Christians continually have to renew their repentance and faith."[1]

Preparation of candidates for baptism at the Great Vigil of Easter, then, is the primary purpose of Lent and, if there will be catechumens preparing for Easter baptism, this is the first consideration in Lenten planning. What is necessary for the formation of new members is generally also what is necessary for the renewal of those whose initial ardor has somewhat cooled. A program designed for catechumens will often be the same program needed for parish Lenten renewal.

Lent is also a season of repentance and renewal for the whole congregation. The same exhortation in the Ash Wednesday liturgy suggests self-examination and repentance; prayer, fasting, and self-denial; and reading and meditating on God's holy Word as the means to a holy Lent. Further suggestions are found in the second Lenten preface:

"You bid your faithful people cleanse their hearts, and prepare with joy for the Paschal feast; that, fervent in prayer and in works of mercy, and renewed by your Word and Sacraments, they may come to the fullness of grace which you have prepared for those who love you."[2]

1 BCP, 264f.
2 BCP, 379.

The prayer book has given us a master plan for our Lenten observances and a suggestion of the elements to be included. The mention of joy in the preface is most important. Joy and renewal by Word and sacrament are as important as prayer, fasting, and self-denial in the overall planning.

Planning Lenten Themes with the Propers

What then are the elements we need to consider for this Lent? Many of these are, of course, specific to your particular congregation, and no one, including a rector who has just arrived, can tell you what they are. The attempt to do global planning usually results in irrelevant programs and bored congregations. But there are a number of common elements and some questions we all need to ask.

The propers for the three years of the liturgical lectionary are quite different. It is important to plan for *this* year. In Year B they talk about the flood and the baptism of Christ, with only a passing reference to the temptation in the wilderness. It is appropriate to sing "Forty days and forty nights" on the first Sunday of Lent in Years A and C, but to sing it in Year B misses the major themes of the propers.

In Year B, Lent 2 gives us the binding of Isaac and the rebuke of Peter, with the call to deny yourself and take up the cross. Perhaps this is an opportunity to introduce the hymn "Lift high the Cross" (Hymn 475). Lent 3 features the decalogue and the cleansing of the Temple. Is this an occasion to use the Ten Commandments? The propers for Lent 4 include Ephesians 2 on salvation by grace through faith and the Johannine account of the feeding of the five thousand. This is the year in which Lent 4 retains its "Refreshment Sunday" theme. This year, but not in Years A and C, this can be a part of plans for the day. Lent 5 offers us the new covenant from Jeremiah, Psalm 51, Hebrews 5 on Christ the high priest, and John 12, concluding, "When I am lifted up from the earth, I will draw everyone to me." This is the theme of Hymn 603 in the 1982 Hymnal, "When Christ was lifted from the earth", which could be used. It is important that these powerful themes be treated as a group, leading naturally to the Markan Passion on the following Sunday of the Passion.

A Lenten "Look" for the Church Building

The use of a well-designed Lenten array can strikingly alter the interior appearance of the church and really mark Lent as a "different" season. The Sarum Lenten array, off-white or "unbleached linen" vestments and frontal with matching veils for crosses and statues, is increasingly being used in place of violet during Lent. There is no theological implication in using one or the other. It is a matter of taste and personal preference. A special Lenten processional cross may also be used – wood painted red with black edges is traditional, or the usual cross can be veiled. The use of red for Palm Sunday and the other days of Holy Week, incidentally, is both the old Sarum and new Roman custom and has much to commend it. Sarum Holy Week vestments tend toward the oxblood in color with black orphreys and have the advantage of not appearing to be festal. Whatever is actually done, planning for Lent should include ways to mark the season in the adornment of the church building as one more way to call the people's attention to the season.

A further note about veiling crosses and other objects: The practice that many churches follow of veiling crosses, mentioned above, and, in some places, covering statues or covering/closing icons is analogous to the practice of suppressing the Alleluia. A beautifully adorned cross, especially an empty cross, is a sign of Christ's victory. Churches will sometimes veil them as a way of suspending recognizing that victory until Easter. Similarly, images of the saints or of Christ, in statuary or icons, are symbols of the resurrection life in Christ and may be veiled or covered to suspend recognizing that truth until Easter, as well.

Selecting the Options for Liturgy

Many parishes appear to have made a policy decision that "during Lent we do Rite One." This may be a reasonable decision, but it should be rethought each Lent. It may, among other things, be grossly unfair to Rite One, which will become associated in the minds of the congregation with Lent and penitence. Eucharistic Prayers A and C of Rite Two are eminently suitable for Lenten use and can be considered as possibilities. *The Hymnal 1982* contains at least one excellent musical setting for Rite Two suitable for Lent because of its relative simplicity, David Hurd's "New Plainsong" (S 86, S 100, S 124, S 161).

Obvious choices for Lenten Sundays are the use of the Penitential Order at the beginning of the liturgy or the substitution of the Great Litany for all that precedes the collect. The Great Litany may be sung in procession to the music at S 67 in *The Hymnal 1982* or sung or recited from a litany desk at the front of the nave or sung "in the midst of the choir." It need not be led by a priest, and it is often desirable for a member of the choir to do so. Not only may this be musically preferable, it gives a lay member of the congregation another opportunity to take a prominent role in the leadership of the Sunday service. In any case, the celebrant says or sings "The Lord be with you" and the collect. If the Great Litany is used, the Prayers of the People are appropriately omitted. Gloria in excelsis, of course, is not used in Lent.

Another option worth considering is the use of Canticle 14, "A Song of Penitence" (Kyrie Pantokrator), in either a plainsong or Anglican chant setting. (S 237–S 241). The singing of the canticle may accompany the entrance procession, in place of the entrance hymn, possibly with the Penitential Order following. Using this penitential canticle at the beginning of the service sets a definite Lenten tone for the Eucharist. Alternatively, Canticle 14 can be used between the New Testament reading and the Gospel.

Simple musical settings for the psalms to be sung may be a good option during this season. The service music volume of the Accompaniment Edition of *The Hymnal 1982* has settings in Simplified Anglican Chant starting at S 408 and Plainsong settings may be found starting at S 446. A change in the method of treating the gradual psalm is another way to mark a distinct season.

Traditionally, Alleluia is not sung during Lent, and a Tract, psalm verses to be sung straight through without refrain or antiphon, may be used in place of an Alleluia verse between the New Testament lesson and gospel. The Tracts can easily be done by a cantor or small choir. These traditional selections may be used, or a hymn or canticle may be sung. One possibility is to use the same short congregational response, such as a single hymn or psalm verse, every Sunday as a mark of the season.

The Litany of Penitence from the Ash Wednesday liturgy (BCP, 267ff) can be used on one or more Sundays in place of the Confession of Sin. It "may be preceded by an appropriate invitation and a penitential psalm" (BCP, 269). If it is used on the First Sunday in Lent, the last paragraph of the Ash Wednesday invitation is appropriate (BCP, 265). For other Sundays, it can be easily adapted. To combine this option with the Great Litany at the beginning of the service, the recitation of the Decalogue, or the Penitential Order will almost certainly result in liturgical "overkill." Even in penitence, less is often more.

The Book of Occasional Services contains a collection of solemn Prayers over the People that provide a seasonal blessing during Lent. These prayers represent an early tradition of blessing and provide an example of a blessing without requiring a trinitarian reference. Six numbered prayers and one intended for use from Palm Sunday through

Maundy Thursday are included. The first may be used on Ash Wednesday and the next five on the Sundays in Lent. On the weekdays, the prayer from the previous Sunday may be used, or, if there is a daily celebration, a different one of the six prayers may be used every day. The deacon, or celebrant, introduces the prayer with "Bow down before the Lord." This is an invitation to the congregation to kneel or at least bow. The celebrant may extend both arms toward the congregation while saying (or singing) the prayer. Like the seasonal blessings, these prayers are completely optional. They are printed in BOS 2022 (pp. 12–13) in contemporary language. But, following the general rubric on page 14 of *The Book of Common Prayer*, "the contemporary idiom may be conformed to traditional language" for use in Rite One services.

Ash Wednesday

The first day of Lent has its own special liturgy. The Ash Wednesday liturgy is the first of the Proper liturgies for Special Days in *The Book of Common Prayer* (pp. 264–269). Since it is held only once a year, it requires not only planning but rehearsal if it is to be well done. The planning committee members can often help their successors by making notes about particular problems and, we hope, solutions for special liturgies such as this. This does not mean that the parish liturgy committee should simply look at the notes from last year's service and decide to do it again. Much of it may deserve repetition, some things can doubtless be improved, and other things the committee may simply choose to do differently.

Since Ash Wednesday is normally a working day for most people, the principal liturgy needs to be scheduled at an hour when most parishioners will be able to come. This usually means in the evening. At least one other service will be necessary in most congregations, and in many both an early morning and midday service will be helpful. The prayer book expects the principal service to be a Eucharist, and many parishes will celebrate the Eucharist at all services on this day. A public celebration of the office with a homily after the second reading is a good alternative for at least one service. Morning Prayer with a Lenten opening sentence, the Confession of Sin, Psalm 95 instead of the Venite, and Kyrie Pantokrator (Canticle 14) and Benedictus (Canticle 16) as the Canticles provide a bracing beginning for the day and the season.

The ceremony that gave its name to the day, the imposition of ashes, is an optional part of the proper Ash Wednesday liturgy. The form on page 265 of the Prayer Book could also be used to impose ashes on other occasions during the day, such as after the anthem at the daily office.

Ash Wednesday is a day of fasting and penitence, and its liturgy has an austere quality. It begins with "The Lord be with you" and the collect of the day, without any entrance rite. The singing of an entrance hymn is not actually forbidden, but neither is it offered as an option. Entering in silence is certainly an appropriate option. If it is desired to sing something during the entrance of the (choir and) ministers, the canticle Kyrie Pantokrator, suggested above for other occasions in Lent, is suitable.

The special ceremonies take place after the sermon. "[T]he Celebrant or Minister appointed invites the people to the observance of a holy Lent" (BCP, 264). The word *Minister* here and in other prayer book rubrics does not imply that the person is ordained. It is a technical term for the major assistants at liturgical functions. The celebrant, another priest or deacon, or a lay reader may issue the invitation, reading the form in the prayer book. It would be interesting to consider the effect of having this invitation read by a churchwarden or other lay leader of the congregation. Lay people are accustomed to hearing the clergy tell them to pray, fast, and deny themselves.

Following the invitation, the congregation kneels in the silence, and ashes may be imposed. It is not clear whether Psalm 51 (*Miserere*) is to be sung during the imposition or at its conclusion. If it is to be said, it must certainly follow the imposition, but, if the choir or a cantor would like to sing the psalm, either to a chant or an anthem setting during the imposition of ashes, it could be quite effective. All of these possibilities can be considered by the planning committee.

"Ashes to Go" has been a popular adaptation of Ash Wednesday, taking the central symbolic act of imposing ashes out into public spaces, such as train station platforms, street corners, or other areas with lots of foot traffic. While it is always valuable to think of creative ways to engage the broader community, especially with our deep liturgical life, some consideration should be given to what it means to separate this action of penitence and mourning from the rite, particularly from the Litany of Penitence. Some churches have provided a very brief card with prayers that could go with the person "on the go," allowing a deeper reflection on the meaning of the ashes throughout the day. That also provides an opportunity to let participants know when regular services are at your church, which gives them the option to follow up, if they wish. Another variation that some churches have adopted is to use the same location from "Ashes to Go" for distribution of palm branches on Palm Sunday and also as a station offering prayer at other times of the year. This more robust commitment to prayer and liturgy in the public square shifts "Ashes to Go" from something unusual to part of a strategy of engagement with the community.

Special Lenten Observances

Once the Ash Wednesday and Sunday liturgies are planned, then decisions about extra Lenten services, guest preachers, and all of the local Lenten concerns are in order. The total Lenten program may present a unified theme rooted in the liturgical readings for the Sundays, or there may be other themes in harmony or counterpoint to the main theme, as long as there are not discordant or competing themes.

Many parishes have a midweek evening service during Lent, either introducing an evening program or with a series of sermons. The Order of Worship for the Evening is almost ideally suited for such services of congregational common worship. There is a special Lenten prayer for light (BCP, 111). The Lenten *Lucernarium* or candle-lighting text is set to music in *The Hymnal 1982 Accompaniment Edition Volume I* (S 312). If the congregation's resources include a good cantor to lead the people in singing it, consider using it. But it is completely optional, and the candles may be lit in silence, and then either *Phos hilaron* or an appropriate Lenten hymn, such as "Kind maker of the world," the medieval office hymn (Hymn 152), sung. The intention of the service is that the music be congregational, not a cathedral-like performance by a choir, so singability and familiarity are important criteria for deciding what to use. The *Magnificat* may be sung to a plainsong or Anglican chant from the Hymnal or to a metrical setting. The excellent metrical setting to the Song of Simeon (*Nunc Dimittis*) by Rae E. Whitney, "Lord God, you now have set your servant free," is set in the Hymnal to Orlando Gibbons' *Song 1* (Hymn 499) and will be sung with joy by most congregations. It is not necessary to use the Evening Prayer psalm and lesson for the weekday on which the service happens to be held. The daily office lectionary was intended for course reading. An appropriate lesson from the previous Sunday or any day during the way can and should be chosen. The same choice is available for a psalm, or one of the evening psalms mentioned on page 143 of the Prayer Book may be used.

Sometimes nonliturgical services of various kinds are held or parish suppers and educational programs. **The Way of the Cross** is traditional on Fridays during Lent, excepting Good Friday, but may be used at other times. There are two forms of the Way of the Cross in the BOS, one of which is more widely used and includes stations that are added from tradition[3] and one which includes stations directly derived from Scripture.[4] The important thing is not so much the decisions that any particular parish makes in its Lenten planning but that there be planning and that *some* decisions that make sense in the worshiping life of that parish be made.

3 "The Way of the Cross," BOS 2022, 53–69.
4 "A Scriptural Way of the Cross," BOS 2022, 71–87

Preparing for Easter Baptism

The enrollment of candidates for Easter baptism traditionally takes place on the First Sunday in Lent. After the creed, the catechumens who are to be enrolled as candidates come forward with their sponsors. The sponsors are queried about the *bona fides* of the catechumens, and the congregation is asked if it approves of their being enrolled. The enrollment itself involves the candidates writing their names in a large book. This is followed by a litany led by the deacon (if there is one) and a blessing of the candidates by the celebrant. On the other Sundays in Lent, the candidates are prayed for by name, and special prayers may be said over the candidates on the Third, Fourth, and Fifth Sundays. These rites are for unbaptized candidates going through the catechumenate and are contained in *The Book of Occasional Services*.[5] All of this will require careful planning, especially if it has never been done before in the congregation.

In addition to these rites for catechumens, the BOS provides for the "Preparation of Parents and Sponsors of Infants and Young Children to be Baptized"[6] as well as "Preparation for Confirmation, Reception, or Other Reaffirmations of the Baptismal Covenant."[7] These programs are parallel to the catechumenate, for those who will be presenting infants or young children for Baptism and for those who are already baptized. Each of these involve a welcoming rite, usually before Lent, and an enrollment rite, usually the First Sunday in Lent, as above. These rites articulate the seriousness of sponsoring an infant or young child for Baptism and the significance for those seeking to reaffirm their baptismal faith. Lent is a period during which candidates for reaffirmation are "exploring the implications of their baptismal covenant and are preparing to reaffirm it at the coming Easter Vigil" and are recognized as "examples of conversion for the congregation in its journey toward Easter" and a Maundy Thursday rite of preparation for their reaffirmation of baptismal vows at the Paschal Vigil.

Obviously, if the catechumenate is in use in the parish, these programs need to form an important part of the observance of Lent. But even if there are no catechumens or adult candidates for reaffirmation, liturgical planning should include looking at all of this material, for these are the themes of Lent itself, and an understanding of them can be useful in planning a more general overall parish Lenten program.

5 BOS 2022, 154–169.
6 BOS 2022, 172–178.
7 BOS 2022, 191–196.

Lent – Major Feasts, Seasonal Rites, and Other Commemorations

Lenten Blessings[1]

In Lent, in place of a seasonal blessing, a solemn Prayer over the People is used, as follows:

The Deacon or, in the absence of a deacon, the Celebrant says:

Bow down before the Lord.

The people kneel and the Celebrant says one of the following prayers:

Ash Wednesday

Grant, most merciful Lord, to your faithful people pardon and peace, that they may be cleansed from all their sins, and serve you with a quiet mind; through Christ our Lord. ***Amen.***

Lent 1

Grant, Almighty God, that your people may recognize their weakness and put their whole trust in your strength, so that they may rejoice for ever in the protection of your loving providence; through Jesus Christ our Lord. ***Amen.***

Lent 2

Keep this your family, Lord, with your never-failing mercy, that relying solely on the help of your heavenly grace, they may be upheld by your divine protection; through Christ our Lord. ***Amen.***

Lent 3

Look mercifully on this your family, Almighty God, that by your great goodness they may be governed and preserved evermore; through Christ our Lord. ***Amen.***

1 BOS 2022, 12–15.

Lent 4

Look down in mercy, Lord, on your people who kneel before you; and grant that those whom you have nourished by your Word and Sacraments may bring forth fruit worthy of repentance; through Christ our Lord. ***Amen.***

Lent 5

Look with compassion, O Lord, upon this your people; that, rightly observing this holy season, they may learn to know you more fully, and to serve you with a more perfect will; through Christ our Lord. ***Amen.***

Catechumenate and Related Processes[2]

Full information is found in the BOS.

The sequence used for those preparing for baptism:

Pre-Lent – Inquiry and Admission of Catechumens
Lent I – Enrollment of Candidates for Baptism
Lent III–V – Special Prayers over Catechumens
Lent III – The Giving of the Creed
Lent V – The Giving of the Lord's Prayer

The sequence used for Parents/Sponsors or those already baptized:

Pre-Lent – Welcoming of Parents/Sponsors of Infants and Young Children
Lent I – Enrollment of Baptismal Candidates (Infants/Young Children)
Pre-Lent – Welcoming Candidates for Confirmation, Reception, or the Reaffirmation of Baptismal Vows
Lent I – Enrollment for Lenten Preparation

2 BOS 2022, 154–169, 172–178, 191–196.

Lenten Litany[3]

This litany can be used during a weekly Lenten study or at the end of a meal.

Create in us a clean heart, O God.

And renew a right spirit within us.

Create in me a clean heart, O God.

and renew a right spirit within me.

Have mercy on me, O God, according to your loving-kindness,

In your great compassion blot out my offenses.

Renew a right spirit within me.

Wash me through and through from my wickedness

And cleanse me from my sin.

Renew a right spirit within me.

For I know my transgressions

and my sin is ever before me.

Renew a right spirit within me.

Purge me from my sin, and I shall be pure;

Wash me, and I shall be cleaned indeed.

Renew a right spirit within me.

Give me the joy of your saving help again

And sustain me with your bountiful Spirit.

Renew a right spirit within me.

Glory to the Father, and to the Son, and to the Holy Spirit.

Create in me a clean heart, O God.

and renew a right spirit within me.

Souper Bowl of Caring

The first or second Sunday in February. If on the second Sunday in February, it could also be the First Sunday in Lent. See notes in the Season after the Epiphany section.

Black History Month

Black History Month may occur during the end of Epiphany or the beginning of Lent. See notes in the Season after the Epiphany.

3 Adapted from Psalm 51 by Anne E. Kitch. *The Anglican Family Prayer Book* (Harrisburg, PA: Morehouse Publishing, 2004), 134–136.

February 24, Saint Matthias the Apostle

This feast may fall during the end of Epiphany or in Lent. See notes in the Season after the Epiphany.

March 5, World Day of Prayer

Sponsored by Church Women United, a Christian group of women that strives to work for justice and peace, the origin of World Day of Prayer dates back to 1887, when Mary Ellen Fairchild James, a Methodist from Brooklyn, New York, called for a day of prayer for home missions. Each year, Church Women United selects a women's group from a different part of the world to write a prayer service for the day. Then, everyone, men and women alike, are encouraged to attend a prayer service using what the group wrote. Learn more at: www.worlddayofprayer.net

March 8, International Women's Day

Grant, O God, that all may recognize women as equal partners in creation and prophesy. By the grace of the Holy Spirit, empower women at home, at work, in government, and in the hierarchies of churches, temples, mosques, synagogues, and all other places of worship. Provide safety and protection, O Gracious Divinity, and inspire just laws against all forms of violence against women. We ask this through Christ our Savior, *Amen*.[4]

March 17, Patrick, Bishop and Missionary of Ireland, 461

While this is a Lesser Feast day, it is widely observed and is included in Lesser Feasts and Fasts 2022. Some churches do not observe Saints' days during Lent, as part of that practice of suppressing signs of Christ's victory during the Season of Lent. In any case, this feast day may not be observed on a Sunday, in lieu of the regular Lenten propers for that day.

Patrick was born in a Christian family on the northwest coast of Britain about 390. As a teen, Patrick was kidnapped to Ireland and forced to serve as a shepherd;

4 Christ Knight, "Equal Partners," in *Lifting Women's Voices: Prayers to Change the World,* Margaret Rose, Jenny Te Paa, Jeane Person, Abagail Nelson, editors (New York: Morehouse Publishing, 2009), 101–102.

as a young man, he escaped back to Britain, where he was educated as a Christian and took holy orders. A vision returned him to Ireland about 432. Patrick's missions of conversion throughout Ireland continued until his death. He adapted pagan traditions to Christian: he had Christian churches built on sites considered sacred, he had crosses carved on druidic pillars, and he reassigned sacred wells to Christian status. "St. Patrick's Breastplate," while attributed to him, is probably not his except as it expresses his zeal.

March 19, Saint Joseph

St. Joseph's feast day is a Major Feast on the Episcopal Church Calendar and the propers for the day are found in the Book of Common Prayer. *However, during Lent, it is not permissible to substitute Major Feasts for the Lenten Sunday propers. The Collect for the Day is found on pages 188 or 239 of* the Book of Common Prayer.

The Gospel according to Matthew honors Joseph as open to mysticism while also a man of compassion and devotion. Even so, he may have been perturbed when pressed to be Mary's protector and to be a father to Jesus. He accepted and provided nurturance; he protected Jesus and Mary by escorting them to Egypt to escape Herod's commanded slaughter of boy children. Joseph reared his son as a faithful Jew. Joseph himself, a descendant of David, was a pious Jew, a carpenter by trade. As such, he is enrolled as the patron saint of workers for not only working with his hands but also mentoring his son in this trade. Joseph exemplifies a loving husband and father, a man who trusted God.

March 22, World Water Day

Held annually as a means of focusing attention on the importance of freshwater and advocating for the sustainable management of freshwater resources. Learn more at: www.worldwaterday.org

We thank you, Almighty God, for the gift of water. Over it your Holy Spirit moved in the beginning of creation. Through it you led the children of Israel out of their bondage . . . In it your Son Jesus received the baptism of John and was anointed by the Holy Spirit as the Messiah, the Christ, to lead us, through his death and resurrection, from the bondage of sin into everlasting life.[5]

Thursday, March 25, The Annunciation of Our Lord Jesus Christ to the Blessed Virgin Mary

This day is a Major Feast and a Feast of our Lord. However, it is not permitted to replace the Sunday propers during Lent. If it falls during Holy Week or Easter Week, it is transferred to the first open day in the week following Easter II.

Mary's willingness to assent to God's call paved the path for God to accomplish the salvation of the world. March 25 is the day to commemorate the story of how God made known to a young Jew that she was to be the mother of his son. Her acceptance is the reason generations have called her "blessed." The Annunciation serves as a significant theme in the arts of the East and the West, a theme running through countless sermons and poems. The General Council of Ephesus in 451 affirmed the term, coined by Cyril of Jerusalem, for the Blessed Virgin: Theotokos ("the God-bearer"). Mary serves as God's human agent within the mystery of the Incarnation.

5 BCP, 306.

Ash Wednesday

God hates nothing he has made and forgives us when we are truly repentant.

Anchor Points – The Propers and the Day

The fixed points for each service are the appointed or proper readings and collect as well as the themes of the day or season.

Readings and Psalm

Joel 2:1–2, 12–17

In our Hebrew Bible reading the prophet pictures the day of the Lord as a time of judgment and darkness, but he holds out the hope of mercy if the people will repent. Some looked to the day of the Lord's coming as an event of great triumph and joy in Israel. But because of sin the sky will become black with swarms of locusts. The trumpet must be blown, calling for a solemn fast, a time for weeping, rending of hearts, and turning back to a compassionate Lord.

or

Isaiah 58:1–12

The lesson from the Hebrew Bible is a denunciation of the injustices of those who only act at their religion. There is a promise of the Lord's favor for those who genuinely repent and care for the needy. Fasts and many prayers are of no purpose and may be misused if they do not involve the liberation of the oppressed and help for the weak and afflicted. When there is justice and sharing, then the light of the Lord will rise out of the darkness and all the ruins will be rebuilt.

Psalm 103 or Psalm 103:8–14

A song of praise, this psalm celebrates God's benefits in a comprehensive way, as signaled by the repetition of all throughout. God does whatever is needed to enhance life, as shown through God's steadfast love. The source for the language at the imposition of ashes – Psalm 103:14.

2 Corinthians 5:20b – 6:10

In this lesson Paul urges the new disciples to be reconciled to God in this time of deliverance, and he reminds them of all the hardships he has patiently endured for their sake and for the gospel. The disciples' task is to respond to God's reconciling work in Christ who has taken upon himself their sinfulness so that they might have a right relationship with God. In order that he might offer his service without presenting any personal obstacles, Paul has accepted many of the paradoxes that were part of Jesus' own ministry. Although himself poor, he brings true riches to many.

Matthew 6:1–6, 16–21

In our gospel Jesus describes genuine charity, prayer, and fasting. For religious people the temptation is always strong to want to be recognized as full of piety more than to want honestly to be seeking God and the good of others. Praise and rewards for an outward show of religion all pass away. The real treasure is found in our relationship with God.

Collect

Note: The service on this day begins with the Salutation (BCP 264), which refers to the dialogue "The Lord be with you (*or* God be with you). ***And also with you.*** Let us pray" *before continuing with the Collect.*

Almighty and everlasting God, you hate nothing you have made and forgive the sins of all who are penitent: Create and make in us new and contrite hearts, that we, worthily lamenting our sins and acknowledging our wretchedness, may obtain of you, the God of all mercy, perfect remission and forgiveness; through Jesus Christ our Lord, who lives and reigns with you and the Holy Spirit, one God, for ever and ever. *Amen.*

Proper Preface

Lent – Through Jesus Christ our Lord; who was tempted in every way as we are, yet did not sin. By his grace we are able to triumph over every evil, and to live no longer for ourselves alone, but for him who died for us and rose again.

or this

You bid your faithful people cleanse their hearts, and prepare with joy for the Paschal feast; that, fervent in prayer and in works of mercy, and renewed by your Word and Sacraments, they may come to the fullness of grace which you have prepared for those who love you. (Rite II, BCP 379; Rite I BCP 346)

Pairings for this Day

See the table below for choices appointed and suggested for this day. Preferences are put in **bold.** Not all choices are suitable for all congregations or community, though, so consider these preferences as a starting point before making a decision about your own congregation.

	Ash Wednesday	Rite I	Rite II	EOW1	BOS 2022
Color	Violet *or* Lenten Array				
Entrance Rite	*None – begin with the Salutation "The Lord be with you." and the Collect of the Day*	264	264		
Song of Praise/Kyrie	*None at this service*				
Collect		166	217; 264		
Creed	*Not used at this service*				
Prayers of the People	*Not used at this service*				
Offertory Sentence	"For God says, 'At an acceptable time I have listened to you, and on a day of salvation I have helped you.' See, now is the acceptable time; see, now is the day of salvation!" (2 Cor.)	343–344	376–377		
Eucharistic Prayer	See notes below	1–333	**A – 361,** *or* C – 369	1–57 *or* 2–60	
Proper Preface	**Lent (Second Lenten Preface for Ash Wed. – echoes invitation to holy Lent)**	346	379		
Breaking of the Bread (Fraction)	Christ our Passover with Alleluias omitted *and/or* Agnus Dei	337	364; 407		
Postcommunion Prayer		339	**Almighty everliving God – 366**	Loving God – 70	
Blessing	**Solemn Prayer in BOS**				**13**
Dismissal	**Let us bless the Lord.**	340	366		
Notes					

Additional Notes:

Entrance Rite – There is no provision for a hymn or anything else prior to the Salutation. Typically, this means an entrance in silence or the vested ministers could already be in place prior to the beginning of the service.

Eucharistic Prayer – Prayer 1 in Rite I and Prayer A in Rite II each have language more focused on Christ's work on the cross, and both permit a seasonal proper preface. Eucharistic Prayer C in Rite II has significant penitential language, including the suffering servant imagery from Isaiah. EOW1 prayers 1 and 2 both incorporate language that could tie into Lenten themes.

Fraction Anthem at the Breaking of the Bread – The option provided in Rite I and Rite II ("Christ our Passover") is suitable throughout the season provided that the Alleluias are omitted. Another traditional text that may be used in place of the above or in addition to it, sung or said, is the Agnus Dei ("O Lamb of God").

Content Resources

Reading Between the Lines

Matthew's gospel presents Jesus' teachings in the Sermon on the Mount (Matthew 5–7) as words to be heard and put into practice. Here, Jesus warns listeners against doing righteous deeds required by God ostentatiously: almsgiving, prayer, and fasting, (for us, Lenten obligations) are all to be done unobtrusively and secretly, that is, without public recognition, acclaim, and honor. Only God, "your Father who sees in secret" knows of these acts. Access to the room through a door (Mt 6:6) means that it is a less public household space, perhaps more like an inner meeting place for private purposes, in a world where household spaces were used for public business.

Central Themes

We are called to remember a deep holy tension on Ash Wednesday. We are called to remember that we are finite creatures who are invited into eternal life by the infinite. We are called to remember that we are sinners and saints of God. We are called to remember that we are made of stardust and, yet, will return to the ground. This call to holy tension will not resolve itself quickly, and the Church remembers this from generation to generation, giving us an entire season every year – Lent – to contemplate its mysteries. Let this Ash Wednesday sit in the tension of being dust and being a beloved child of God. Both are true – and Ash Wednesday calls us to remember.

John O'Hara retells an ancient story in *Appointment in Samarra.* A servant at market bumps into Death, who appears to threateningly look at him. The servant obtains his master's horse and fearfully flees to the city of Samarra. The merchant goes to Death. Death says she was shocked as she was expecting to keep an appointment with the servant that night in Samarra. A story retold. A liturgy redone. Death is inescapable. Today marks this reality. Today also marks the start of a season of deeper reflection on Christ whose life, death, and resurrection forever altered that reality.

"Come back!" say the readings. "Be reconciled, and rejoice in God's love." And after a Mardi Gras of partying, the Church invites us to remember that we are finite creatures, formed of ashes and stardust. Increasingly, churches are offering "Ashes to Go" on street corners and train platforms and campus malls and office buildings, inviting all to remember, repent, and be reconciled. Engaging the conversation where people "live and move and have their being" begins to build bridges between church and community. To learn more about Ashes to Go, please see page 135 above or visit www.ashestogo.org.

Engaging All Ages

See also options for Ash Wednesday for Children.

On Ash Wednesday, we are reminded that we all came from dust, and at the end of our lives, we will return to being dust. Dust is not just the untidy substance that piles up when we forget to clean the bookcase. Dust may start as a giant boulder on a mountain, a fluff from a cottonwood tree, or coral from the reef, and each of these things played a role in God's creation. As you feel the ashes or dirt – the dust, traced on your forehead today – can you imagine the stories those particles could tell? And when the time comes, will your own ashes have stories aplenty from one who knows love as a child of God?

Prayers of the People

Note: There are not Prayers of the People at this service.

Hymns for the Day

Note: There is no Entrance Hymn at this service (see BCP, 264).

The Hymnal 1982

Eternal Lord of love, behold your Church 149
O bless the Lord, my soul! 411
The glory of these forty days 143
Before thy throne, O God, we kneel 574, 575
Kind Maker of the world, O hear 152
Lord Jesus, Sun of Righteousness 144
Creator of the earth and skies 148
Lord, whose love through humble service 610
Now quit your care 145
O day of God, draw nigh 600, 601
Lead us, heavenly Father, lead us 559
God himself is with us 475
Jesus, all my gladness 701

Lift Every Voice and Sing II

Bless the Lord, O my soul 65
Come, ye disconsolate 147
Thou my everlasting portion 122
Give me a clean heart 124

Wonder, Love, and Praise

Almighty Lord Most High draw near 888
Bless the Lord, my soul 825
Gracious Spirit, give your servants 782

Ash Wednesday for Children

Ash Wednesday Prayer

This collect is appropriate for a service with children, at home, at Morning Prayer, with grace, or at bedtime.

God of all mercy, you love all that you have made. You forgive the sins of all who are truly sorry. Create and make in us clean hearts, that we, humbly confessing our sins and knowing our brokenness, may receive forgiveness and blessing; through Jesus Christ our Lord, who lives with you and the Holy Spirit, one God, for ever and ever. *Amen.*[1]

1 Anne E. Kitch, *The Anglican Family Prayer Book* (Harrisburg, PA: Morehouse Publishing, 2004), 133.

Option 1: Ash Wednesday adapted for Children

This service follows the structure of the BCP Ash Wednesday service, simplifying and making it more interactive for increased engagement.

Gathering – Bring children and adults into the space comfortably so that all may see and hear easily. Consider ways that seating and cushions might be arranged to help with that. Open with prayer, adapting the Ash Wednesday collect (using the above form "Ash Wednesday Prayer" which is a children's adaptation of this collect, if desired). The Invitation to a Holy Lent may also be adapted to provide the background for the day.

Lessons – One or two lessons, as desired, read by children or young people if possible. Consider using a young reader's translation or a children's Bible to aid in easier understanding.

Sermon and Teaching on Ashes – This is the part that may not be for all settings. As part of the sermon, palm branches will be burned in the midst of the congregation gathered, to help explain where the ashes come from. (**Note**: the actual ashes administered need to be prepared **ahead of time.** Like on a cooking show, the final result needs to be ready to go before you start.) The children (and adults) need to be kept at a safe distance and fire extinguishers and containers of water need to be close by at hand. Ensure that the space is large enough or well-ventilated enough for this; palm branches can produce a lot of smoke. Be extra aware of vestments and keeping trailing edges of garments out of harm's way. You will need a fire safe vessel and a heat/fire safe table surface. Pass around the year-old dried palm branches so that the children and adults can feel and smell what they are like. When they return them, place them in the vessel on the table top (low enough for all to see). You can talk about the symbolism of the palms, how they were used at Palm Sunday last year. Set them on fire. As they burn, talk about what happens – that they actually change into something else. The branches burn and become smoke and ash. The smoke is carried away – invite them to watch the smoke go up. The ashes remain. As the fire dies down, prod the burnt material and help the children and adults to see the resulting ashes. Talk about how the ashes are a reminder of the palms, but the palms are gone. Let them know that these ashes are still too hot to use today and would need to be ground and sifted, but you have ashes that you already made in just the same way ready to go. Let them know that when we put ashes on our forehead, we are reminding each other that none of us will be here forever. That we need to use the time that we have to do what God would have us do. Ensure that the fire is completely extinguished and hand off all materials to a helper to set aside out of view.

Imposition of Ashes – Offer the prayer over the ashes in the *Book of Common Prayer*, if desired, and then impose ashes on all who wish to have them. Children may join in imposing ashes, either with the words or doing the imposition itself. Have plenty of wet wipes or other ways to clean hands and use them before you continue

Psalm 51 Song – There are simple tunes for "Create in me a clean heart, O God" from Psalm 51, which may be sung in place of the Psalm

Children's Litany of Penitence and the Peace – It may be useful to frame "sin" in terms of something getting in the way of a relationship, with God or one another. Or to speak in terms of how people sometimes can hurt each other with words or attitudes as much as with physical harm. This litany is invitational, framing a few ways to consider what people may need to ask forgiveness for, and then inviting the children to name those things. The congregation responds after each suggestion with a simple response such as "Lord have mercy" or "Christ have mercy" or "Forgive us God." An absolution (or declaration of forgiveness, if no priest is present) should be given at the conclusion, though simplified from the long form in the Ash Wednesday rite, followed by the invitation to share the Peace.

Make Eucharist – This may be done in a child-friendly simpler form, according to your parish practice, or using one of *the Book of Common Prayer* prayers, giving the children an opportunity to be up close to the Altar and to have the freedom of movement permitted in a child-friendly service. The service concludes with the Blessing and Dismissal.

Option 2: Let's Go! An Ash Wednesday Service for Children[2]

This interactive children's service for Ash Wednesday is suitable for children aged four through ten. The service consists of four interactive stations and a fifth station for the Imposition of Ashes and Eucharist. The fourth station includes the shrouding of an Alleluia Banner that can be created on the last Sunday of the Season after the Epiphany or at a Shrove Tuesday Pancake Supper. Ideally it should be cloth and large

2 This service was developed by Elizabeth Hammond and is part of the *Skiturgies: Pageants, Plays, Rites, and Rituals* collection from Church Publishing.

enough to hang from a banner or chart stand. Choose a location for each station; place the appropriate props at each station. Create a simple tune to go with the words of the chant to use as you process to the stations. Review and memorize a simple version of the two Bible stories. Prepare a take-home Lenten box for each child: small wooden boxes, each one with a small container of water, of oil, of ashes, and a votive candle. Tie a purple ribbon around each box.

Scenery/Props

Station One – Water: small table, container of water;

Station Two – Oil: small table, container of oil;

Station Three – Light: small table, candle, matches, or lighter. (A slightly darker location is best, if possible; lighting the candle should make a noticeable difference.);

Station Four – Alleluia Banner: Alleluia Banner, banner or chart stand, purple net;

Station Five – Ashes/Eucharist: container of ashes, small altar/table (a small child-height table placed in front of the main altar works well), purple cloth, cross, Bible, chalice and paten, Lenten boxes. bread, wine.

Gather/Introduction

Welcome the children and sit together in the area where you will conclude with the Eucharist. Say a short prayer. Using language personalized for your parish and children, explain that we are now in the season of Lent. Share what Lent is, how it is different from other seasons, why we have Lent, and some of your parish customs. Teach the words of the song and practice the first verse a few times.

Process to Station – Water . . . singing . . . Come into God's presence singing: "Alleluia, Alleluia, Alleluia."

Tell the story of Jesus' baptism. (Matthew 3:13–17, Mark 1:4–11, Luke 3:15–17, 21–22.) Invite the children to wonder about all the ways we use water.

Leader: Jesus wanted John to baptize him. Jesus went right under the water so he saw and felt and heard water everywhere! Jesus must have felt clean and refreshed! When we are baptized it is just the same for us. We are clean and refreshed. Jesus shows us how to get ready to follow him.

Invite the children to dip their fingers into the water. They might want to touch their foreheads with their wet fingers. Share a simple prayer of thanks.

Process to Station – Oil . . . singing . . . Come into God's presence singing: "Water that cleans, water that cleans, water that cleans."

Tell the story of the anointing at Bethany (John 12:1–8).

Leader: Jesus received a very special gift – Mary's gift of extravagant love. Jesus loved Mary. Mary may have felt tears because of so much love. Jesus shows us how to show love to the people around us.

Invite the children to dip a finger into the oil and, if they are comfortable, anoint one another on the backs of their hands. Share a simple prayer of thanks.

Process to Station – Light . . . singing . . . Come into God's presence singing: "Blessed by the oil, blessed by the oil, blessed by the oil."

Leader: Long, long ago, the people felt afraid and uncertain. They were very lonely. Jesus said to them, "I am the Light. I am always with you." When we light a candle, we know Jesus is close and we feel his love in our hearts. Jesus shows us how to shine in the world.

Invite the children to watch as you light the candle. (If you are feeling brave, have a votive for each child to light.) Share a simple prayer of thanks.

Process to Station – Alleluia Banner . . . singing . . . Come into God's presence singing: "Jesus the Light, Jesus the Light, Jesus the Light."

Leader: Alleluia is one of our special church words. It is a word of celebration. We don't say the word Alleluia during Lent, and we won't say it again until Easter.

Invite the children to help you hang/place/attach the banner to a stand or a wall. Shroud it with the purple net. Explain to the children that the net allows us to still see the word but not say it. (If appropriate for your congregation, allow the banner to stay in full view throughout Lent.)

Process to Station – Ashes/Eucharist . . . singing . . . Come into God's presence singing: "We are in Lent, we are in Lent, we are in Lent."

Show the container of ashes and talk about their significance and why we use ashes on this day. Invite the children to be anointed with ashes. The children may want to help say the words each time someone is anointed . . . "Remember that you are dust . . ."

Set the table together with a purple cloth, cross, Bible, chalice and paten. Continue with a Eucharist, a very simple retelling of the Last Supper. Invite the children to serve/share the bread to/with each other. Have an adult administer the chalice. End with a simple prayer of thanks.

Show the Lenten boxes. Remind the children of the stories we shared today. Invite them to find a special place at home for their box. Share a simple final prayer. Offer a blessing.

The First Sunday in Lent

He was in the wilderness forty days, tempted by Satan;
and he was with the wild beasts; and the angels waited on him.

Anchor Points – The Propers and the Season

The fixed points for each service are the appointed or proper readings and collect as well as the themes of the day or season

Readings and Psalm

Genesis 9:8–17

The story of the flood is itself an ancient one, shared by several Near Eastern cultures, but the biblical account has its own unique theological perspective. Through Noah, God makes the first covenant, a covenant with all humans and animals and every generation. The sign of the covenant, the rainbow, is a sign of peace, showing that God's wrath was over and the stability of the natural order was guaranteed. This first covenant demonstrates the trustworthiness of God who makes promises and keeps them.

Psalm 25:1–9

This is an acrostic psalm, each verse beginning with a successive letter of the alphabet. In verses 4–5, the psalmist asks God to teach him truth. He recognizes that his adversaries, both external (vv. 2, 19) and internal (vv. 7, 11, 17–18), are strong enough to triumph over him. His fear of the Lord compels him to acknowledge that God alone can make him into a person of true righteousness (v. 9), thus able to enjoy "the friendship of the Lord" (v. 14).

1 Peter 3:18–22

In today's reading, the author seems to have used parts of a hymn to frame statements about Jesus's authority and the meaning of baptism. Christ died "once," not only as a model to be followed but also to bring new access to God. The author draws parallels between the destructive, but cleansing, waters of the flood and the cleansing, saving waters of baptism. Verse 21b is translated more literally, "a pledge to God from (or of) a good conscience." Thus, the believer's baptism is effective not as a physical washing, but as a sign of one's new life in Christ.

Mark 1:9–15

Today's reading recounts Jesus's temptation in the wilderness. The event of empowerment by the Spirit at Jesus's baptism (vv. 9–11) immediately leads into a time of testing. The forty days recall the forty years of wandering in the wilderness (Deuteronomy 8:2), the forty days of Moses on the mountain (Exodus 24:18; 34:28) and the forty days of Elijah's journey (1 Kings 19:8). Exposure to temptation is a continuing theme of Jesus's ministry, in the desire of the crowds for a sign (8:11), in Peter's rebuke (8:32–33), and in the jeers of the crowds at his crucifixion (15:29–32).

Collect

Almighty God, whose blessed Son was led by the Spirit to be tempted by Satan: Come quickly to help us who are assaulted by many temptations; and, as you know the weaknesses of each of us, let each one find you mighty to save; through Jesus Christ your Son our Lord, who lives and reigns with you and the Holy Spirit, one God, now and for ever. *Amen.*

Proper Preface

Lent – Through Jesus Christ our Lord; who was tempted in every way as we are, yet did not sin. By his grace we are able to triumph over every evil, and to live no longer for ourselves alone, but for him who died for us and rose again.

or this

You bid your faithful people cleanse their hearts, and prepare with joy for the Paschal feast; that, fervent in prayer and in works of mercy, and renewed by your Word and Sacraments, they may come to the fullness of grace which you have prepared for those who love you. (Rite II, BCP 379; Rite I BCP 346)

Seasonal Pairings

See the table below for choices appointed and suggested for this day. Preferences are put in **bold**. Not all choices are suitable for all congregations or community, though, so consider these preferences as a starting point before making a decision about your own congregation.

	Lent I	Rite I	Rite II	EOW1	BOS 2022
Color	Violet *or* Lenten Array				
Entrance Rite	Customary *or* The Great Litany *or* A Penitential Order; use penitential acclamation	148, 319 *or* 323	148, 351, *or* 355	Litany – 46; penitential acclamation – 50	
Song of Praise/Kyrie	Kyrie *or* Trisagion; *or* BCP Canticle 14; *or* EOW1 Canticle G, H	324	356 C14 – 90	34	
Collect		166	218		
Creed	Nicene Creed	326, 327	358	53	
Prayers of the People	**Locally written**; options below; BCP forms (may be omitted if Great Litany used)	329	387–393	54–55	
Offertory Sentence	"Christ also suffered for sins once for all, the righteous for the unrighteous, in order to bring you to God" (1 Peter)	343–344	376–377		
Eucharistic Prayer	See notes below	1–333	**A – 361,** *or* C – 369	1–57 *or* 2–60	
Proper Preface	**Lent (First Lenten Preface for Lent I–III)**	346	379		
Breaking of the Bread (Fraction)	Christ our Passover with Alleluias omitted *and/or* Agnus Dei	337	364; 407		
Postcommunion Prayer		339	**Almighty everliving God – 366**	Loving God – 70	
Blessing	**Solemn Prayer in BOS**				**13**
Dismissal	**Let us bless the Lord**	340	366		
Notes	May be Souper Bowl of Caring; Enrollment of Candidates Baptism and/or Reaffirmation				161; 174; 195.

Additional Notes:

Entrance Rite – Some congregations begin the Lent I service with *The Great Litany*, sung or said, in place or in procession. The EOW1 form is in contemporary language and may be shortened. It may be sung to the traditional chant setting, if desired. Other options include using *A Penitential Order* to begin or beginning the service as usual (BCP 323/355), but with a penitential opening acclamation. EOW1 also provides a penitential acclamation. Some churches have used the Litany of Penitence from Ash Wednesday to begin each Sunday in Lent.

Song of Praise/Kyrie – The Gloria in excelsis is ***not*** used in Lent. Traditionally, a form of the Kyrie or Trisagion would be used. A few penitential canticles are mentioned above. If the Great Litany is used, it ends with the Kyrie and a Canticle would not be used.

Eucharistic Prayer – Prayer 1 in Rite I and Prayer A in Rite II each have language more focused on Christ's work on the cross, and both permit a seasonal proper preface. Eucharistic Prayer C in Rite II has significant penitential language, including the suffering servant imagery from Isaiah. EOW1 prayers 1 and 2 both incorporate language that could tie into Lenten themes.

Fraction Anthem at the Breaking of the Bread – The option provided in Rite I and Rite II ("Christ our Passover") is suitable throughout the season provided that the Alleluias are omitted. Another traditional text that may be used in place of the above or in addition to it, sung or said, is the Agnus Dei ("O Lamb of God).

Content Resources

Reading Between the Lines

The account of Jesus' baptism in Mark's gospel includes the detail that as Jesus comes up out of the water, the heavens are torn apart, and through them the Spirit descends as a dove. Noticing that the same verb describes the rending in two of the outer veil of the temple curtain that follows Jesus' last breath (15:37–38), scholars link these verbs, noting the significance of their placement at the beginning and end of Jesus' life. Furthermore, the Spirit's descent on Jesus at baptism can be linked to the verb "breathed his last" to describe Jesus' death (Greek: *pneuma* and *ekpneuo,* "expire.") These are cosmic bookends.

While most translations render Mark's present tense in 1:12, "the Spirit drives Jesus into the wilderness," by a past tense, "drove," Mark's vividness and dramatic description of the Spirit's agency could be noted. Perhaps testing follows baptism? In the wilderness, Jesus is aided by angels and wild beasts.

Central Themes

The Church has long used the image of Noah's Ark as an icon for Herself – the people of God sailing on the waters of this life into the saving love of God. In fact, many baptistries have an image of the ark surrounding the font to call to mind the life we are raised to from the waters of new birth. Today's readings tie the ark to Jesus's baptism in a way that reminds us of our own baptismal promise from God – that he will never again cause the storms of life to overwhelm the earth. And his bow in the sky will attest to his covenant with us – both with Noah and at our own baptism.

The classic story, *The Man in The Iron Mask*, by Alexandre Dumas, depicts twin brothers Louis XIV and Philippe. Philippe was sent away to the countryside to avoid a future dispute over the throne. Louis XIV discovers his twin and puts him in prison, placing on him an iron mask. Christ "was put to death in the flesh, but made alive in the spirit, in which also he went and made proclamation to the spirits in prison . . ." What parts of self do people lock up and hide away? Who needs to hear Christ's call to be one's whole self fully free?

Peter proclaims the connection between baptism and God's deliverance of Noah's family through water, reminding us that baptism also joins us to Christ's resurrection. The Thanksgiving over the Water of the baptismal rite draws a similar connection, from creation through the miraculously parted Red Sea to the Jordan and on to Golgotha and the empty tomb. Again and again, our God acts to bring deliverance. What liberations among your faith community might be part of this great overarching narrative of God at work, healing and saving?

Engaging All Ages

Each year, Lent encourages us to slow down and listen. It is also a season of patient waiting. Just as Noah waited and listened for God's teaching, as God waited and listened for Noah, and Jesus listened and waited for the right time to begin his ministry, Lent calls us to wait, watch, and listen for God's message. Rainbows are something everyone can watch for and experience if we slow down and look to the sky after the rain. Perhaps today you could draw a rainbow, writing in each band what you hope to find as you slow down, listen, and wait patiently this season?

Prayers of the People

Note: When the Great Litany is used for the Entrance Rite, the Prayers of the People may be omitted.

Option 1

In the beauty of our worship
In the silence of our hearts
In our committee meetings

Show us your ways, O Lord.
As we struggle to live together in peace
As we are tempted by inertia and complacency
When we forgot whose we are

Show us your ways, O Lord.
When many suffer while we eat well and sleep peacefully
When many beg to be noticed while we seek solitude
When many long for shelter from the storm

Show us your ways, O Lord.
Walk with us as welcome little ones into the world
Walk with us as we care for those who ache
Walk with us as we walk with those returning to you

Show us your ways, O Lord.

Option 2

Deacon or Presider

In this season of repentance and renewal, let us pray for the concerns of the Church and the world, saying "Lord, in your mercy, Renew us."

Intercessor

For the whole Church of God, and for all its members:

May the Church truly become the unified body of Christ, hearing and living out God's call in the world. We pray for all baptized Christians in their ministries, for *N.*, our

Presiding Bishop, for *N.*, our bishop and for all clergy and other ministers.

Lord, in your mercy,

Renew us

For our nation and every nation:

May all people learn to live together in peace, respecting one another's differences and autonomy. May all leaders be ever mindful of their responsibilities to their own people and to others in the world. We pray for our President, Congress, Courts, state and local officials, and for all leaders around the world.

Lord, in your mercy,

Renew us

For this community and all communities:

May we live together in love and harmony, striving for the building up of all members, for wholeness and justice, striving until none are left behind.

Lord, in your mercy,

Renew us

For the concerns of the whole world:

May those who face natural disaster find grace and relief; may those who face conflict and war find a loving spirit; and may all of us come to treat our neighbors as ourselves so that we and all this world may truly come to be God's new creation.

Lord, in your mercy,

Renew us

For all those who are in any pain or sorrow:

May they come to know your love and care and be brought to wholeness; for those who suffer in body, mind, or spirit; for the poor, the persecuted, and those in prison; for those who are lonely, homeless, or hungry; for all those we now remember . . .

Silence

Lord, in your mercy,

Renew us

For all the blessings of this life:

May we truly celebrate the life we have been given and our time with one another; for new beginnings, anniversaries, and birthdays, and for all the joys of this life; we thank you for all other thanksgivings we now offer, silently or aloud . . .

Silence

Lord, in your mercy,

Renew us

For all who have died:

May those who now live in the joy of God's presence [with blessed *N.* and all the saints] find their rest in God's peace, We pray for those we now name, silently or aloud . . .

Silence

Lord, in your mercy,

Renew us

Presider

O God, whose desire it is for all people to turn to you and be renewed in your love, grant these prayers in your mercy and according to your will; through Jesus Christ our Lord who lives and reigns with you and the Holy Spirit, One God, forever and ever. ***Amen.***

Hymns for the Day

Some congregations use the Great Litany as the Entrance Rite, which would replace the Entrance Hymn

The Hymnal 1982

Eternal Lord of love, behold your Church 149
Lead us, heavenly Father, lead us 559
Eternal Father, strong to save 608
Lord Jesus, think on me 641
O Love of God, how strong and true 455, 456
You, Lord, we praise in songs of celebration 319
Forty days and forty nights 150
From God Christ's deity came forth 443
Lord, who throughout these forty days 142
Now let us all with one accord 146, 147
O love, how deep, how broad, how high 448, 449
The glory of these forty days 143

Lift Every Voice and Sing II

We are often tossed and driv'n on the restless sea of time 207

Wonder, Love, and Praise

Lord Jesus, think on me 798

The Second Sunday in Lent

Jesus begins to teach the path of the cross and resurrection.

Anchor Points – The Propers and the Season

The fixed points for each service are the appointed or proper readings and collect as well as the themes of the day or season.

Readings and Psalm

Genesis 17:1–7, 15–16

This reading recounts God's surprising gift of an everlasting covenant to Abram. God also promises to bless Abram with numerous descendants even though he and his wife Sarai are in their nineties. Such an astounding promise challenges their trust in God to provide. Their new identity in relation to God is signified by receiving new names (Abraham and Sarah), much like newly baptized Christians as they become members of the new covenant community.

Psalm 22:22–30

Psalm 22 consists of a lament and a thanksgiving. The psalmist describes his suffering and his trust in God. The Lord has always been faithful to Israel and to him.

Romans 4:13–25

In chapter 4, Paul cites the examples of Abraham to prove that justification by faith is not contrary to the Old Testament. In Judaism at that time, Abraham was held up as a model of righteousness through works. Paul argues that Abraham's faith, his readiness to believe and act upon God's promise, put him in right relationship to God, apart from any works. This righteousness is open to all – Jew and Gentile – who trust in God, regardless of whether they keep the law.

Mark 8:31–38

Today's gospel begins with the first prediction of Jesus's passion, death, and resurrection. In Mark, the three predictions (8:31; 9:31; 10:33–34) are set into a common pattern: (1) prediction, (2) misunderstanding by the disciples, and (3) teaching on discipleship. Peter offers Jesus the title of Messiah, "the Christ" (8:29). In Mark, the general expectation of the Messiah seems to be a political leader. Jesus rejects this understanding. Mark reiterates throughout his gospel that Jesus's disciples cannot truly understand the meaning of Jesus as Messiah before, or apart from, the crucifixion.

Collect

O God, whose glory it is always to have mercy: Be gracious to all who have gone astray from your ways, and bring them again with penitent hearts and steadfast faith to embrace and hold fast the unchangeable truth of your Word, Jesus Christ your Son; who with you and the Holy Spirit lives and reigns, one God, for ever and ever. *Amen.*

Proper Preface

Lent – Through Jesus Christ our Lord; who was tempted in every way as we are, yet did not sin. By his grace we are able to triumph over every evil, and to live no longer for ourselves alone, but for him who died for us and rose again.

or this

You bid your faithful people cleanse their hearts, and prepare with joy for the Paschal feast; that, fervent in prayer and in works of mercy, and renewed by your Word and Sacraments, they may come to the fullness of grace which you have prepared for those who love you. (Rite II, BCP 379; Rite I BCP 346)

Seasonal Pairings

See the table below for choices appointed and suggested for this day. Preferences are put in **bold**. Not all choices are suitable for all congregations or community, though, so consider these preferences as a starting point before making a decision about your own congregation.

	Lent II	Rite I	Rite II	EOW1	BOS 2022
Color	Violet *or* Lenten Array				
Entrance Rite	Customary *or* A Penitential Order; **use penitential acclamation**	319 *or* 323	351 *or* 355	50	
Song of Praise/Kyrie	Kyrie *or* Trisagion; *or* BCP Canticle 14; *or* EOW1 Canticle G, H	324	356 C14 – 90	34	
Collect		166	218		
Creed	Nicene Creed	326, 327	358	53	
Prayers of the People	**Locally written**; options below; BCP forms	329	387–393	54–55	
Offertory Sentence	"If any want to become my followers, let them deny themselves and take up their cross and follow me." (Mark)	343–344	376–377		
Eucharistic Prayer	See notes below	1–333	**A – 361,** *or* C – 369	1–57 *or* 2–60	
Proper Preface	**Lent (First Lenten Preface for Lent I–III)**	346	379		
Breaking of the Bread (Fraction)	Christ our Passover with Alleluias omitted *and/or* Agnus Dei	337	364; 407		
Postcommunion Prayer		339	**Almighty everliving God – 366**	Loving God – 70	
Blessing	**Solemn Prayer in BOS**				**13**
Dismissal	**Let us bless the Lord.**	340	366		
Notes					

Additional Notes:

Entrance Rite – While the Litany is traditionally tied primarily to the First Sunday in Lent, there are several options for the beginning of the service throughout the season. Some congregations will use A Penitential Order to begin each Sunday in Lent. Others will begin as usual, but with a penitential opening acclamation. EOW1 also provides a penitential acclamation. Occasionally other variations have been observed, such as using the Litany of Penitence from Ash Wednesday for the beginning of each Sunday in Lent.

Song of Praise/Kyrie – The Gloria in excelsis is ***not*** used in Lent. Traditionally, a form of the Kyrie or Trisagion would be used. A few penitential canticles are mentioned above.

Eucharistic Prayer – Prayer 1 in Rite I and Prayer A in Rite II each have language more focused on Christ's work on the cross, a traditional Lenten emphasis, and both permit a seasonal proper preface. Eucharistic Prayer C in Rite II has significant penitential language, including the suffering servant imagery from Isaiah. EOW1 prayers 1 and 2 both incorporate language that could tie into Lenten themes.

Fraction Anthem at the Breaking of the Bread – The option provided in Rite I and Rite II ("Christ our Passover") is suitable throughout the season provided that the Alleluias are omitted. Another traditional text that may be used in place of the above or in addition to it, sung or said, is the Agnus Dei ("O Lamb of God).

Content Resources

Reading Between the Lines

In this the central section of Mark's gospel (Mark 8–10), Jesus speaks the word, three times to disciples, of the necessity of the suffering, death, and resurrection of the Son of Man. Formerly, Jesus spoke the word in parables to them and explained, "to you is given the secret of the kingdom of God," (4:11) and they heard as they were able (4:33). Now Jesus speaks openly and lucidly of "divine things" not "human things," including his death. Speaking openly in the Hellenistic and Roman world is the right of a democratic citizen. Biblical texts such as Wisdom of Solomon 5:1–2 speak of the righteous standing with great confidence confronting their fearful and uncomprehending oppressors, and this is what Jesus does to explain his own mission.

Central Themes

A good rule for hikers who find themselves lost in the wilderness is to return to the spot that you last knew as a point of reference. It's not a bad image for repentance, actually. Repentance (in Greek: *metanoia*) is not so much an act of self-flagellation as it is turning around and to face the direction you came from. Our Collect today asks God to "be gracious to all who have gone astray from your ways," and we are blessed to know that God will. So the question is, can we be gracious enough with ourselves to turn around when we are lost and return to God's goodness as our point of reference? Or will we stay "wandering far in the land that is lost," as it says in the words of the Reconciliation of a Penitent (BCP, 450)?

William Shakespeare wrote, "What's in a name? that which we call a rose / By any other name would smell as sweet / So Romeo would, were he not Romeo call'd / Retain that dear perfection he owes ..." A rose retains its core being, its very essence, no matter its name. But Romeo could be different. People choose to accept names given to them by others. People choose new names for themselves. Calling yourself or being called something new actually can change who you are. What is God calling you? What do you want to be called by God?

One scholarly interpretation of the Greek that is rendered "get behind me, Satan" is "walk in my footsteps." Abram's (Abraham's) willingness to walk God's way – by his faith – inspired God to bless him and his wife Sarai (Sarah) in seemingly impossible ways. How do our daily faithful choices – our faith expressed through our everyday actions – bring blessings we have not even imagined until they show up? Choices like those made by Eric Liddell, Fanny Crosby, George Herbert, and Polycarp are all celebrated this month. (See *Lesser Feasts and Fasts* for many more examples.)

Engaging All Ages

Who named you? In Lent, we hear many names ascribed to Jesus, such as Son of Man from today's Gospel lesson. We also hear stories of people getting new names from God, such as Abraham and Sarah. Naming someone is a very special job. In names, family ties are recognized, hope is instilled, and destiny is imagined. In this season of listening, how do you hear names of friends and family, as well as of Jesus, in new and different ways? Create a collage of the special names in your life or learn the meaning of your own name.

Prayers of the People: Option 1

We are in awe of you and your promises. Help us set our minds on you.

Your world is aching for healing. Make us good stewards of your creation, Lord. Grant our president and our leaders in the courts and Congress compassion and wisdom.

Have mercy upon us. Set our minds on you.

Your church is reaching for you. Help us to extend our reach to all whom you love.

Have mercy upon us. Set our minds on you.

Your people are being born, are ill, are both anxious and joyous. They are hungry and cold and don't know where to turn. They bend under the weight of their lives and rejoice in your life-giving love. Enable us to bring them your healing and fullness of life.

Have mercy upon us. Set our minds on you.

Prayers of the People: Option 2

Deacon or Presider

As we make on our Lenten journey, let us offer our prayers of intercession and thanksgiving.

Intercessor

We pray for the Church in all places, in all expressions, that we may be one.

O Christ, hear us.

We pray for *N.*, our Presiding Bishop, for *N.*, our bishop(s), and for our parish clergy. We pray for *N.* and all those preparing for Baptism.

O Christ, hear us.

We pray for our city, our state, and our country;
for legislatures and courts and for all elected officials;
[for upcoming primaries and elections].

O Christ, hear us.

We pray for those who suffer from violence and fear, especially all victims of gun violence; give us wisdom and courage in the face of suffering.

O Christ, hear us.

For all those who are injured, for those who are sick, for those needing ongoing care. For all those who seek healing.

O Christ, hear us.

For this community and this congregation; for our joys and for our challenges.

O Christ, hear us.

For those we love but see no longer; for all those who have died.

O Christ, hear us.

Let us pray for our own needs and those of others.

Silence. The People may add their own petitions.

Presider

Gracious God, who sees us through the eyes of love and compassion, give us your sight as we pray for your world and your people. Lead us into moments of your abundant goodness, that we may rejoice, but also draw us closer to you as we think on the sorrow of the Cross. Strengthen our repentance, when we, by our actions, increase that sorrow, and renew our hearts for the day to come; through Jesus our Redeemer. ***Amen.***

Hymns for the Day

The Hymnal 1982

I to the hills will lift mine eyes 668
Now let us all with one accord 146, 147
Praise our great and gracious Lord 393
The God of Abraham praise 401
How firm a foundation, ye saints of the Lord 636, 637
I call on thee, Lord Jesus Christ 634
My faith looks up to thee 691
Day by day 654
New every morning is the love 10
Praise the Lord through every nation 484, 485
Take up your cross, the Savior said 675

Lift Every Voice and Sing II

My faith looks up to thee 88
We've come this far by faith 208
I can hear my Savior calling 144
I have decided to follow Jesus 136
King of my life I crown thee now 31

Wonder, Love, and Praise

Will you come and follow me 757
You laid aside your rightful reputation 734

The Third Sunday in Lent

Jesus cleanses the Temple.

Anchor Points – The Propers and the Season

The fixed points for each service are the appointed or proper readings and collect as well as the themes of the day or season.

Readings and Psalm

Exodus 20:1–17

The Ten Commandments set forth the duties of the Israelites to God and to those within the community. The commandments are covenant demands founded on their special relationship to God that specify ways that right relationships are endangered or violated. The commandments concerning human interrelationships have parallels in other ancient cultures, but those concerning the people's relationship to God are unique to the Hebrew Bible.

Psalm 19

The psalmist celebrates God's revelation, expressed universally in creation and specially in the law. Pagan nations acclaimed the divinity of certain elements in nature (sun, moon, fire, etc.). Here the psalmist counters those claims by boasting that all of nature declares the glory of Israel's God, the Creator.

1 Corinthians 1:18–25

Paul sets forth the general principle that the wisdom of God appears to be folly to those wise in worldly terms, while to those in the process of salvation, it reveals the power of God. Human-centered wisdom, which is itself closely related to our efforts, will be overturned by God. Knowledge of God is possible through natural revelation, but the certainty sought for by submitting God to the world's criteria of proof, either pragmatically in "signs" (v. 22) of power or intellectually in "wisdom" (v. 22) is not possible. God's act of "foolishness" and "weakness" (v. 25) confounds both what the Jews expected of the Messiah and what Greeks believed about the immortal and impassible nature of divinity.

John 2:13–22

Today's gospel recounts the cleansing of the temple and the questioning of Jesus's authority. Jesus gives an enacted parable similar to the prophetic deeds of Jeremiah and Ezekiel. In the temple courtyard, unblemished animals were sold for sacrifice, and pagan coins were exchanged for Jewish coinage to pay the temple tax. Jesus attacks not only the dishonesty of the temple trade but also its very existence. The merchants had set up shop in the temple's outer courts, the only area open to Gentiles who came to pray and seek Israel's God.

Collect

Almighty God, you know that we have no power in ourselves to help ourselves: Keep us both outwardly in our bodies and inwardly in our souls, that we may be defended from all adversities which may happen to the body, and from all evil thoughts which may assault and hurt the soul; through Jesus Christ our Lord, who lives and reigns with you and the Holy Spirit, one God, for ever and ever. *Amen.*

Proper Preface

Lent – Through Jesus Christ our Lord; who was tempted in every way as we are, yet did not sin. By his grace we are able to triumph over every evil, and to live no longer for ourselves alone, but for him who died for us and rose again.

or this

You bid your faithful people cleanse their hearts, and prepare with joy for the Paschal feast; that, fervent in prayer and in works of mercy, and renewed by your Word and Sacraments, they may come to the fullness of grace which you have prepared for those who love you. (Rite II, BCP 379; Rite I BCP 346)

Seasonal Pairings

See the table below for choices appointed and suggested for this day. Preferences are put in **bold**. Not all choices are suitable for all congregations or community, though, so consider these preferences as a starting point before making a decision about your own congregation.

	Lent III	Rite I	Rite II	EOW1	BOS 2022
Color	Violet *or* Lenten Array				
Entrance Rite	Customary *or* A Penitential Order; **use penitential acclamation**	319 *or* 323	351 *or* 355	50	
Song of Praise/Kyrie	Kyrie *or* Trisagion; *or* BCP Canticle 14; *or* EOW1 Canticle G, H	324	356 C14 – 90	34	
Collect		167	218		
Creed	Nicene Creed	326, 327	358	53	
Prayers of the People	**Locally written**; options below; BCP forms	329	387–393	54–55	
Offertory Sentence	"The message about the cross is foolishness to those who are perishing, but to us who are being saved it is the power of God." (1 Cor)	343–344	376–377		
Eucharistic Prayer	See notes below	1–333	**A – 361,** *or* C – 369	1–57 *or* 2–60	
Proper Preface	**Lent (First Lenten Preface for Lent I–III)**	346	379		
Breaking of the Bread (Fraction)	Christ our Passover with Alleluias omitted *and/or* Agnus Dei	337	364; 407		
Postcommunion Prayer		339	**Almighty everliving God – 366**	Loving God – 70	
Blessing	**Solemn Prayer in BOS**				**13**
Dismissal	**Let us bless the Lord**	340	366		
Notes	Catechumenate – Giving of Creed				168

Additional Notes:

Entrance Rite – While the Litany is tied primarily to the First Sunday in Lent, there are several options for the beginning of the service throughout the season. Some congregations will use *A Penitential Order* to begin each Sunday in Lent. Others will begin as usual, but with a penitential opening acclamation. EOW1 also provides a penitential acclamation. Occasionally other variations have been observed, such as using the Litany of Penitence from Ash Wednesday for the beginning of each Sunday in Lent.

Song of Praise/Kyrie – The Gloria in excelsis is ***not*** used in Lent. Traditionally, a form of the Kyrie or Trisagion would be used. A few penitential canticles are mentioned above.

Eucharistic Prayer – Prayer 1 in Rite I and Prayer A in Rite II each have language more focused on Christ's work on the cross, a traditional Lenten emphasis, and both permit a seasonal proper preface. Eucharistic Prayer C in Rite II has significant penitential language, including the suffering servant imagery from Isaiah. EOW1 prayers 1 and 2 both incorporate language that could tie into Lenten themes.

Fraction Anthem at the Breaking of the Bread – The option provided in Rite I and Rite II ("Christ our Passover") is suitable throughout the season provided that the Alleluias are omitted. Another traditional text that may be used in place of the above or in addition to it, sung or said, is the Agnus Dei ("O Lamb of God).

Content Resources

Reading Between the Lines

The author of John's Gospel presents Jesus' action in the temple as incomprehensible to both "the Jews" and Jesus' disciples, for different reasons. "The Jews" in John's gospel hear and regularly misunderstand Jesus' sayings, whereas Jesus' disciples display temporal incomprehension until after Jesus' resurrection (2:22). While it is not clear how this rhetorical separation in the gospel corresponds to a parting of the ways between Jesus followers in John and "the Jews," a separation between these two groups in a gospel dated at the end of the first century is worth noting. Anti-Judaism in the fourth gospel reaches to the core of the message and is intrinsically oppressive rather than revelatory. However, scriptures themselves are not the only place or the end of divine revelation. The gospel cannot be reduced to its anti-Jewish elements. It projects an alternative world of all-inclusive love and life that can transcend its anti-Judaism, and this world of the text rather than the world of the author is a witness to divine revelation.

Central Themes

There is an excellent story as part of the Godly Play® curriculum that talks about the Ten Commandments as the "Ten Best Ways." What strikes me most about that phrasing is the reminder that God does not arbitrarily set forth a bunch of laws for us to follow because God is a stickler for rules. God gives us these "ways" as a guidepost for "keeping us both outwardly in our bodies and inwardly in our souls," as today's Collect says. They are the ways of living that will lead to a healthy life – both in this life and the life to come. They are for us, and we would do well to follow in God's ways.

"Give me your tired, your poor, / Your huddled masses yearning to breathe free": these words found at the Statue of Liberty present the United States as a place of peace and prosperity, of respite and rest, of Sabbath for those wearied by poverty, weighed down by oppression, or ravaged by war. For the refugee and resident alien, often this is truth. But especially for those who are considered illegal aliens, this country can be a place not of Sabbath but of struggle and strife. What ways does God call us to give Sabbath to such wearied people?

The Decalogue – the Ten Commandments – was once (from the time of Thomas Cranmer) the introduction to most celebrations of Holy Communion. With the adoption of the 1979 *Book of Common Prayer* and its emphasis on the Baptismal Covenant, the Decalogue came to be used largely as the introduction to the Penitential Rite, used by many congregations only during Lent and other penitential observances. Through our baptism, we become heirs of God's liberation. Just as Jesus liberated the temple from its misuse as a marketplace, God's deliverance of the Israelites from slavery freed them to follow the commands of God, not of their Egyptian masters or of their own sinfulness.

Engaging All Ages

The Ten Commandments listed in Exodus can seem old-fashioned and antiquated, such as telling people not to covet oxen or make idols. Even though they were given to Moses over 3,000 years ago, it does not mean they are irrelevant today. Have you ever noticed that the Ten Commandments can be broken into two parts? The first four commandments talk about how we are to relate to God. The second six commandments tell us how we are to relate to one another. In these ten lessons, God's beloved people are offered a glimpse of life in God's kingdom. What commandment(s) do you live into each day?

Prayers of the People: Option 1

We come before you in our own brokenness, in need of your grace and favor. We trust in the promise you have made to hear our prayers in the name of your Son, Jesus.

We pray for wisdom, courage, and strength for all of your followers, especially those in leadership of your church. Set their hearts on you alone.

Silence

We pray for the leaders of the nations, that they protect and provide for their people and work for peace and justice.

Silence

We pray for those who struggle with disappointments, with financial insecurities, with grief over lost loved ones, or lost dreams. We pray for relief of pain for those whose bodies and hearts ache. We ask for healing for all who suffer.

Silence

We pray for those who have died and now rest in your eternal embrace. Comfort the loved ones who mourn their loss.

Silence

All this we ask, O Lord, in Jesus's name, the one who lived and moved among us in our broken world, and who loves us still. ***Amen.***

Prayers of the People: Option 2

Deacon or Presider

Gentle people of God, as we renew our faith in this Lenten season, let us be truly fervent in prayer, saying: Lord, in your mercy, Hear our prayer.

Intercessor

Let us pray for the universal Church, its members and its mission that we may see Christ in each other and know that in Him we are all one. We pray for *N.*, our Presiding Bishop, for *N.*, our bishop(s), and for all Christians in their vocation.

Lord, in your mercy,

Hear our prayer.

Let us pray for this nation and all nations of the world that all strife and divisions may cease.

Lord, in your mercy,

Hear our prayer.

Let us pray for an end to armed conflict, an end to oppression of every kind, and an end to the violence that marks so many lives.

Lord, in your mercy,

Hear our prayer.

Let us pray for those who have been graced with abundance, that they will be mindful of those in our world who suffer from hunger, preventable disease and those who live in misery and poverty. Let us pray for all those in need.

Lord, in your mercy,

Hear our prayer.

Let us pray for this community gathered here today and for all those we love who are far from us that we may all sense God's healing touch in our individual lives and in our common life. We pray for all those we name now, either silently or aloud . . .

Silence

Lord, in your mercy,

Hear our prayer.

Let us pray for all those who have died in the hope of the resurrection, especially all those we name now, either silently or aloud . . .

Silence

Lord, in your mercy,

Hear our prayer.

Let us give thanks for the many blessings of this life, the gift of friendship, the gift of this time to study, pray and learn together. We pray to realize the gift of God's presence in all that we undertake. We give thanks for those gifts which we name now, either silently or aloud . . .

Silence

Lord, in your mercy,

Hear our prayer.

Presider

O Lord our God, accept the fervent prayers of your people; in the multitude of your mercies, look with compassion upon us and all who turn to you for help; for you are gracious, O lover of souls, and to you we give glory, Father, Son, and Holy Spirit, now and forever. ***Amen.***

Hymns for the Day

The Hymnal 1982
Kind Maker of the world, O hear 152
The spacious firmament on high 409
The stars declare his glory 431
Help us, O Lord, to learn 628
Praise the Lord! ye heavens adore him 373
Praise to the living God! 372
The glory of these forty days 143
Hail, thou once despised Jesus! 495
Nature with open volume stands 434
O Love of God, how strong and true 455, 456
Praise to the Holiest in the height 445, 446
There is a balm in Gilead 676 (1–2)
We sing the praise of him who died 471
You, Lord, we praise in songs of celebration 319
Christ is made the sure foundation 518
Lift up your heads, ye mighty gates 436
Only-begotten, Word of God eternal 360, 361
We the Lord's people, heart and voice uniting 51

Lift Every Voice and Sing II
There is a balm in Gilead 203 (1–2)

Wonder, Love, and Praise
God the sculptor of the mountains 746, 747

The Fourth Sunday in Lent

You must be born again.

Anchor Points – The Propers and the Season

The fixed points for each service are the appointed or proper readings and collect as well as the themes of the day or season.

Readings and Psalm

Numbers 21:4–9

This reading describes the incident that the evangelist John uses to understand the healing power of Christ's death on the cross. For their lack of faith in God's power to provide food for them on their wilderness journey, the people are punished by poisonous serpents. When the people admit their sinfulness and seek God's forgiveness through Moses' intercession, God provides an outward sign – the bronze serpent – that when looked upon unleashed God's life-giving power.

Psalm 107:1–3,17–22

This psalm encourages those whom God has rescued to give praise (vv. 1–3). Verses 17–22 recall God's healing in time of illness.

Ephesians 2:1–10

This letter was probably first circulated as an encyclical letter to a number of churches in Asia Minor. Chapter 1 centers upon the privileges of the believer's new life in Christ. Today's reading focuses on the process of restoration. God alone takes the initiative. In verses 8–10, there is a double aspect to salvation. It begins with "grace" (v. 5) and results in "good works" (v. 10). Faith is here a gift from God, not something we do. Works are required, but not as a prerequisite. The living out of the Christian life is not the cause of salvation, but its effect. Faith must always lead to good works.

John 3:14–21

Today's reading is taken from the first of John's lengthy expositions of Jesus's teachings. This discourse as a whole (3:1–21) moves from the work of the Spirit (3:3–8) to that of the Son (3:11–15) to that of the Father (3:16–21). Nicodemus comes to Jesus by night because of his interest in the signs Jesus has performed. Jesus seeks to draw him past these outward manifestations to a recognition of their inward significance. John3:16, one of the most familiar verses of scripture, succinctly describes God's goal – to offer eternal life, God's motivation – love for the world, and God's strategy – giving the Son. Jesus has become the watershed for life, both now and in the future.

Collect

Gracious Father, whose blessed Son Jesus Christ came down from heaven to be the true bread which gives life to the world: Evermore give us this bread, that he may live in us, and we in him; who lives and reigns with you and the Holy Spirit, one God, now and for ever. *Amen.*

Proper Preface

Lent – Through Jesus Christ our Lord; who was tempted in every way as we are, yet did not sin. By his grace we are able to triumph over every evil, and to live no longer for ourselves alone, but for him who died for us and rose again.

or this

You bid your faithful people cleanse their hearts, and prepare with joy for the Paschal feast; that, fervent in prayer and in works of mercy, and renewed by your Word and Sacraments, they may come to the fullness of grace which you have prepared for those who love you. (Rite II, BCP 379; Rite I BCP 346)

Seasonal Pairings

See the table below for choices appointed and suggested for this day. Preferences are put in **bold**. Not all choices are suitable for all congregations or community, though, so consider these preferences as a starting point before making a decision about your own congregation.

	Lent IV	Rite I	Rite II	EOW1	BOS 2022
Color	Violet *or* Lenten Array *or* Rose				
Entrance Rite	Customary *or* A Penitential Order; **use penitential acclamation**	319 *or* 323	351 *or* 355	50	
Song of Praise/Kyrie	Kyrie *or* Trisagion; *or* BCP Canticle 14; *or* EOW1 Canticle G, H	324	356 C14 – 90	34	
Collect		167	219		
Creed	Nicene Creed	326, 327	358	53	
Prayers of the People	**Locally written**; options below; BCP forms	329	387–393	54–55	
Offertory Sentence	"For God so loved the world that he gave his only Son, so that everyone who believes in him may not perish but may have eternal life." (John)	343–344	376–377		
Eucharistic Prayer	See notes below	1–333	**A – 361,** *or* C – 369	1–57 *or* 2–60	
Proper Preface	**Lent (Second Lenten Preface for Lent IV–V)**	346	379		
Breaking of the Bread (Fraction)	Christ our Passover with Alleluias omitted *and/or* Agnus Dei	337	364; 407		
Postcommunion Prayer		339	**Almighty everliving God – 366**	Loving God – 70	
Blessing	**Solemn Prayer in BOS**				**13**
Dismissal	**Let us bless the Lord**	340	366		
Notes					

Additional Notes:

Laetare/Refreshment Sunday – In some congregations, the fourth Sunday in Lent is observed as Laetare Sunday, from the Latin for "rejoice." Similar to Gaudete Sunday in Advent, it may use Rose as the color for the day. It is also known as "Mothering Sunday," from the sixteenth century tradition of attending the "Mother Church" on this day, or "Refreshment Sunday," as the midpoint of Lent when some of the disciplines of Lent were traditionally relaxed. Simnel cakes are traditionally baked in the United Kingdom for this day.

Entrance Rite – While the Litany is tied primarily to the First Sunday in Lent, there are several options for the beginning of the service throughout the season. Some congregations will use *A Penitential Order* to begin each Sunday in Lent. Others will begin as usual, but with a penitential opening acclamation. EOW1 also provides a penitential acclamation. Occasionally other variations have been observed, such as using the Litany of Penitence from Ash Wednesday for the beginning of each Sunday in Lent.

Song of Praise/Kyrie – The Gloria in excelsis is ***not*** used in Lent. Traditionally, a form of the Kyrie or Trisagion would be used. A few penitential canticles are mentioned above.

Eucharistic Prayer – Prayer 1 in Rite I and Prayer A in Rite II each have language more focused on Christ's work on the cross, a traditional Lenten emphasis, and both permit a seasonal proper preface. Eucharistic Prayer C in Rite II has significant penitential language, including the suffering servant imagery from Isaiah. EOW1 prayers 1 and 2 both incorporate language that could tie into Lenten themes.

Fraction Anthem at the Breaking of the Bread – The option provided in Rite I and Rite II ("Christ our Passover") is suitable throughout the season provided that the Alleluias are omitted. Another traditional text that may be used in place of the above or in addition to it, sung or said, is the Agnus Dei ("O Lamb of God).

Content Resources

Reading Between the Lines

John's central idea is "lifting up" as a reference both to the crucifixion of Jesus and the exaltation, an elevation also described as glorification. The death, ascent and resurrection of Jesus are the victory over Satan, "the ruler of this world." Using the language of irony, the cross is the means of Jesus' enthronement as victorious sovereign. It is also the place where Jesus' victory over Satan is made plain. In describing the cross as "glorification," the author of the Fourth Gospel uses a mythic pattern to make sense of the shock of Jesus' violent departure. John's notion of the cross as salvation includes Jesus' present, not deferred, vindication, judgment and exaltation.

Central Themes

After the Israelites were liberated and spent a little time in the harsh desert, they began complaining bitterly to Moses that they were better off in Egypt. In several similar passages to today's reading, we hear them asking to go back to back to the land of their slavery and misery. It seems that they were more accustomed to and comfortable with oppression than with freedom. The same can be said for us when we keep turning back to our sin and old ways of life. We are a free people no longer enslaved to sin. Don't go back to Egypt.

The Equal Justice Initiative (EJI) is a nonprofit focused on criminal justice reform, racial justice, and public education on these issues. They provide legal representation to prisoners who may have been wrongly convicted, poor prisoners without effective representation, and others possibly denied a fair trial. Like the crucifixion of Christ, organizations and activists such as EJI demand that we acknowledge the injustices of the world. Christ and those desiring justice and mercy do not condemn us but remind us as Martin Luther King Jr. said, "The arc of the moral universe is long, but bent towards justice."

Engaging All Ages

Often called "the football verse" because of the frequency with which people in stadiums hold signs that say "John 3:16," one of the best-known verses in the Bible can also be described as one of the most difficult. The proclamation that all who believe in God's Son, Jesus Christ, will be given eternal life, gives followers a clear message. As we pass the halfway point in Lent, may we find ways to be secure in our faith while also lifting up those around us who do not know God's gift of love and grace in Christ Jesus. What is one way in the coming week that you can share God's love and help people around you?

Prayers of the People: Option 1

When our faith is weak and our hopes seem empty, come to us, Spirit, and fill us again. You are rich in mercy, and our need is deep.

Lord, in your mercy, hear our prayer.

Lead us to let go of the burdens we carry: the guilt, the shame, the unrealistic expectations. Lead us to depend on you.

Lord, in your mercy, hear our prayer.

Guide each of us in the decision making of our common life: in our family relationships, our churches, and our communities.

Lord, in your mercy, hear our prayer.

Pull us closer to your compassionate heart. We pray for those in pain, for those who worry, for those whose livelihood is fragile, for those who grieve. We pray for ____________ .

Lord, in your mercy, hear our prayer.

Push us into the world to be the advocates for your expansive love among all the creatures you have created.

Lord, in your mercy, hear our prayer.

Receive those who have died into the arms of your abundant mercy.

Lord, in your mercy, hear our prayer.

Prayers of the People: Option 2

Deacon or Presider

In this holy season of Lent, let us offer our prayers to God, who leads us through the wilderness, saying "God of Love and Mercy, Hear our Prayer."

Intercessor

For the holy catholic church throughout the world, that in this season of repentance we may turn from our own shortcomings and be consumed by God's transforming grace. For *N.*, our Presiding Bishop, for *N.*, our bishop(s), for all who minister in the name of Christ, and for all the holy people of God,

God of Love and Mercy,

Hear our prayer.

For our nation and our leaders, that they may have the courage to guard the rights of those who are poor and powerless and that we all may recognize the common bonds of humanity.

God of Love and Mercy,

Hear our prayer.

For those who suffer, for the afflicted, and the oppressed, that they may be strengthened by the love of Christ as he shares their wounds.

God of Love and Mercy,

Hear our prayer.

For our congregation and for our common life together in this community, that we may continue, with discipline, to examine the difficult places in our community through the illumination of the light of Christ.

God of Love and Mercy,

Hear our prayer.

For our specific concerns and hopes that, in their naming, we may know and feel the Spirit of the living God among us and within us. For all those we name now, silently or aloud . . . *Silence*

For God's grace which fills us, that we may surrender our bread of anxiety and receive with grace the bread of life.

God of Love and Mercy,

Hear our prayer.

For all who have died, that they may rest completely and joyfully in God, even as they join [with *N.* and all the saints] this journey through the wilderness. For all those we name now, either silently or aloud . . .

Silence

God of Love and Mercy,

Hear our prayer.

Presider

O God, by your Word you marvelously carry out the work of reconciliation: Grant that in our Lenten fast we may be devoted to you with all our hearts, and united with one another in prayer and holy love; through Jesus Christ our Lord, who lives and reigns with you and the Holy Spirit, one God, for ever and ever. ***Amen.***

Hymns for the Day

The Hymnal 1982

Bread of heaven, on thee we feed 323
How wondrous and great thy works,
God of praise! 532, 533
Amazing grace! how sweet the sound 671
Come, thou fount of every blessing 686
In your mercy, Lord, you called me 706
O love, how deep, how broad, how high 448, 449
O Love of God, how strong and true 455, 456
Rock of Ages, cleft for me 685
Sing, my soul, his wondrous love 467
And now, O Father, mindful of the love 337
Lift high the cross 473
My faith looks up to thee 691
Spread, O spread, thou mighty word 530
The great Creator of the worlds 489
When Christ was lifted from the earth 603, 604

Lift Every Voice and Sing II

Amazing grace! how sweet the sound 181
Come, thou fount of every blessing 111
How to reach the masses, those of every birth 159
My faith looks up to thee 88

The Fifth Sunday in Lent

We wish to see Jesus.

Anchor Points – The Propers and the Season

The fixed points for each service are the appointed or proper readings and collect as well as the themes of the day or season.

Readings and Psalm

Jeremiah 31:31–34

Today's lesson comes from a section, chapters 30–31, called the "book of consolation." In it are gathered Jeremiah's oracles of hope for an eventual renewal and restoration for Israel. In today's passage, Jeremiah looks forward to a "new covenant" (v. 31). Unlike the old, this one will be written on the heart, which in Hebrew thought is the seat not of the emotions but of the will. This covenant is not new in content, for the Torah, the written law, is not replaced. It is new, however, in the means of its realization. The internalization of the covenant will enable people to keep it. The will of the individual shall become one with the will of God. There will be no need of teachers, for all will know the Lord, not just in intellectual terms but in the Hebrew sense of a close, intense and intimate personal relationship.

Psalm 51:1–13

This is one of the great penitential psalms. The hope and goal of the covenant was to live in right relationship with God and one another. Sin disordered relationships. The psalmist seeks not merely the removal of guilt, but the restoration of a right relationship to God.

or this

Psalm 119:9–16

This psalm is an acrostic psalm, in which the first line of each of its 22 eight-line stanzas begins with a successive letter of the Hebrew alphabet. It is the longest in the Bible. In this reading, the psalmist describes the virtue of young people who take delight in the commandments outlined in the Law found in the Torah. In doing so, they gain not only ritual purity, but draw close to God.

Hebrews 5:5–10

The epistle to the Hebrews is a tightly woven theological essay that stresses that Christianity has fulfilled the promises of Judaism. According to Jewish tradition, Jesus could not be a priest because he was from the tribe of Judah not Levi. But the author of Hebrews argues that in fact Jesus is the real High Priest because he, like Aaron and Melchizedek, was chosen by God for his priestly ministry on our behalf. The quotation from Psalm 2:7 affirms that Jesus was chosen by God, not self-appointed. His unique priesthood is modeled upon that of Melchizedek, whom the author later claims to be superior to Abraham and thus to Abraham's descendant Levi and the Levitical priests.

John 12:20–33

In this gospel passage, Jesus presents teaching concerning the meaning of his death. After his prayer to God, a voice from heaven is heard. Greeks wish to see Jesus, but he will not draw all others to himself until after he has died and has risen. Then, like a seed which falls into the earth, he will bear much fruit. Disciples must also learn to serve Jesus by following him in this way. Now is the hour for the Son of Man to be glorified – glorified both by his willingness to be lifted up on the cross to die for others, and afterward to be lifted up to heaven.

Collect

Almighty God, you alone can bring into order the unruly wills and affections of sinners: Grant your people grace to love what you command and desire what you promise; that, among the swift and varied changes of the world, our hearts may surely there be fixed where true joys are to be found; through Jesus Christ our Lord, who lives and reigns with you and the Holy Spirit, one God, now and for ever. *Amen.*

Proper Preface

Lent – Through Jesus Christ our Lord; who was tempted in every way as we are, yet did not sin. By his grace we are able to triumph over every evil, and to live no longer for ourselves alone, but for him who died for us and rose again.

or this

You bid your faithful people cleanse their hearts, and prepare with joy for the Paschal feast; that, fervent in prayer and in works of mercy, and renewed by your Word and Sacraments, they may come to the fullness of grace which you have prepared for those who love you. (Rite II, BCP 379; Rite I BCP 346)

Seasonal Pairings

See the table below for choices appointed and suggested for this day. Preferences are put in **bold**. Not all choices are suitable for all congregations or community, though, so consider these preferences as a starting point before making a decision about your own congregation.

	Lent V	Rite I	Rite II	EOW1	BOS 2022
Color	Violet *or* Lenten Array				
Entrance Rite	Customary *or* A Penitential Order; **use penitential acclamation**	319 *or* 323	351 *or* 355	50	
Song of Praise/Kyrie	Kyrie *or* Trisagion; *or* BCP Canticle 14; *or* EOW1 Canticle G, H	324	356 C14 – 90	34	
Collect		167	219		
Creed	Nicene Creed	326, 327	358	53	
Prayers of the People	**Locally written**; options below; BCP forms	329	387–393	54–55	
Offertory Sentence	"Jesus said, 'The hour has come for the Son of Man to be glorified. Very truly, I tell you, unless a grain of wheat falls into the earth and dies, it remains just a single grain; but if it dies, it bears much fruit.'" (John)	343–344	376–377		
Eucharistic Prayer	See notes below	1–333	**A – 361,** *or* C – 369	1–57 *or* 2–60	
Proper Preface	**Lent (Second Lenten Preface for Lent IV–V)**	346	379		
Breaking of the Bread (Fraction)	Christ our Passover with Alleluias omitted *and/or* Agnus Dei	337	364; 407		
Postcommunion Prayer		339	**Almighty everliving God – 366**	Loving God – 70	
Blessing	**Solemn Prayer in BOS**				**13**
Dismissal	**Let us bless the Lord.**	340	366		
Notes	Catechumenate – Giving of Lord's Prayer				169

Additional Notes:

Entrance Rite – While the Litany is tied primarily to the First Sunday in Lent, there are several options for the beginning of the service throughout the season. Some congregations will use *A Penitential Order* to begin each Sunday in Lent. Others will begin as usual, but with a penitential opening acclamation. EOW1 also provides a penitential acclamation. Occasionally other variations have been observed, such as using the Litany of Penitence from Ash Wednesday for the beginning of each Sunday in Lent.

Song of Praise/Kyrie – The Gloria in excelsis is ***not*** used in Lent. Traditionally, a form of the Kyrie or Trisagion would be used. A few penitential canticles are mentioned above.

Eucharistic Prayer – Prayer 1 in Rite I and Prayer A in Rite II each have language more focused on Christ's work on the cross, a traditional Lenten emphasis, and both permit a seasonal proper preface. Eucharistic Prayer C in Rite II has significant penitential language, including the suffering servant imagery from Isaiah. EOW1 prayers 1 and 2 both incorporate language that could tie into Lenten themes.

Fraction Anthem at the Breaking of the Bread – The option provided in Rite I and Rite II ("Christ our

Passover") is suitable throughout the season provided that the Alleluias are omitted. Another traditional text that may be used in place of the above or in addition to it, sung or said, is the Agnus Dei ("O Lamb of God).

Content Resources

Reading Between the Lines

Some Greeks present the disciples with a request to see Jesus. Jesus answers them "The hour has come for the Son of Man to be glorified." Since on earlier occasions in the gospel Jesus declares that his hour was not yet come (2:4; 7:6, 8; 7:30; 8:20), the realization of "the hour" here refers to the death and resurrection of Jesus. By offering it to Greeks, Jesus suggests its universal significance. It also anticipates 13:1.

The imagery of a grain of wheat that falls into the earth and dies (12:24), whereupon it bears much fruit, uses the language of harvest to interpret a beneficent death. There is no internal struggle in the face of his death, because Jesus recognizes the hour as the purpose of his mission. It is the final revelation of his relationship with God. Jesus' hour results in a glorification of God's name.

Central Themes

In our Gospel reading, we hear Jesus foreshadowing similar words that he will later pray in the Garden of Gethsemane – "Father, if it is your will, let this pass from me. But let not my will, but your will be done." These are powerful words for someone who is facing deep agony and uncertainty. We are reminded that his mother Mary said much the same words at the Annunciation to the angel's message (Luke 1:26–38). It is likely that Jesus learned this courage and faith from her. How can we pass on those same qualities with the Gospel we are preaching with our lives?

Hermann Rorschach developed a tool to evaluate people's psychology using inkblots. The process is an intriguing means by which to delve into the mind of an individual and to get a sense of how they perceive the world. Rorschach's test likely came from sources such as a late nineteenth century game that had people make inkblots and use them as prompts for creative writing. In Psalm 51, God blots out offenses. If God covers your offenses with the ink of Grace and is creatively rewriting your story, what story is God telling? What image of yourself do you see?

The pulpit in many Episcopal churches is engraved with the line from the Greeks in today's gospel reading: "We would see Jesus." Our preachers are taught to show us Jesus, not simply in the scriptures but in the lives and experiences of everyday people – "holding the Bible in one hand, and the newspaper in the other," as theologian Karl Barth urged. Just as Psalm 51 in our Daily Devotions for Families (BCP, 137) reminds us, it is God who "create[s] in us a clean heart," opening our eyes to "see [God's] hand at work in the world about us." (BCP, 372)

Engaging All Ages

Using the illustration of a grain of wheat falling to the ground, Jesus tells Peter that death is necessary for life and the bearing of fruit to occur. As we enter the final weeks of Lent, it can be important to reflect on who we are as children of God. Did we listen well through this season? Did we wait patiently? What do we need to do to better hear and act on God's love in the coming days and weeks? Just as a single grain of wheat can be bear much fruit, so can every person who bears God's love.

Prayers of the People: Option 1

We come before our loving and gracious God, asking that God's grace and love be kindled in our hearts and spoken on our lips.

Write your word on our hearts, O Lord;

that we may do your will as we praise your name. We pray for our spiritual leaders, that they may speak your truth and call your people into deeper discipleship.

Write your word on our hearts, O Lord;

that we may support the leadership of this nation in the pursuit of peace and justice for all people.

Write your word on our hearts, O Lord;

that with compassion we may respond to the needs of the world, neighbors near and far.

Write your word on our hearts, O Lord;

that we may speak comfort to those who suffer in any way and offer hope to those who grieve.

Write your word on our hearts, O Lord;

that we may live your truth in our lives as we confess your truth with our lips.

Prayers of the People: Option 2

Presider

Eternal and loving God, through the glorification of your Son Jesus you have taught us to follow him through death into eternal life: Glorify your name in us, as we bring before you the concerns of the world, saying: Create in us clean hearts, O God, and renew a right spirit within us.

Litanist

Blessed Father, your Son Jesus has taught your Church that when a grain of wheat falls into the earth and dies, it bears much fruit: Empower your people in our journey of sacrifice and compassion to follow Christ in such faithfulness that we may be glorified with him.

Create in us clean hearts, O God,

and renew a right spirit within us.

Almighty One, you have driven out the ruler of this world through the glorification of Jesus: Put your law of love within the hearts of all who hold authority among the nations, that they may hear of joy and gladness, so that the broken body of the world may rejoice.

Create in us clean hearts, O God,

and renew a right spirit within us.

Bring the joy of your saving help to all who suffer throughout the world, that they may hear of joy and gladness and be healed.

Create in us clean hearts, O God,

and renew a right spirit within us.

Gracious God, you have promised that all who serve your beloved will be honored in your sight: Have mercy upon this community, that all may know you, from the least to the greatest, and follow in the way that Christ has shown us.

Create in us clean hearts, O God,

and renew a right spirit within us.

Let our prayers ascend to Jesus, our eternal high priest, as we offer up our intercessions and supplications, especially for . . .

We thank you for the incarnation of your Son Jesus, who shares our sorrows and our joys. Hear our praise and thankfulness for all the blessings we enjoy, especially for . . .

We entrust into your life all of those who have surrendered their lives into your eternal keeping, especially . . .

Create in us clean hearts, O God,

and renew a right spirit within us.

Presider

Give us the joy of your saving help again, and sustain us with your bountiful Spirit, O God, as we follow Jesus in service to your world, that the salvation and glorification you have accomplished through his cross and resurrection may extend your eternal life throughout creation, now and forever. ***Amen.***

Hymns for the Day

The Hymnal 1982

Help us, O Lord, to learn 628
O God of Bethel, by whose hand 709
From God Christ's deity came forth 443
Hail, thou once despised Jesus! 495
O Love of God, how strong and true 455, 456
Lift high the cross 473
My faith looks up to thee 691
O love, how deep, how broad, how high 448, 449
What wondrous love is this 439
When Christ was lifted from the earth 603, 604
When I survey the wondrous cross 474

Lift Every Voice and Sing II

How to reach the masses, those of every birth 159
My faith looks up to thee 88

Wonder, Love, and Praise

O wheat whose crushing was for bread 760

Holy Week

Preparing for Holy Week

That Holy Week is the heart and center of the liturgical year is beyond dispute. Theologically and liturgically, if not in practice, the Great Vigil of Easter is the central service of the Church Year, and the principal liturgies of Maundy Thursday and Good Friday are closely related to it. They demand, and usually receive, our best efforts. Every parish plans its Holy Week observances, but many are disappointed in the results. Palm Sunday and Easter are high points, but often the rest of the week does not fulfill the hopes and expectations of the planners. Both planning and rehearsal of what has been planned are necessary. Before the first rehearsal is held, all the decisions about what is to be done should already have been made.

Technically, Holy Week planning could be considered a part of Lenten planning. But not only is Holy Week distinct from the rest of Lent, it is practical to have a different subcommittee or commission of your liturgical planning committee plan it. The broader the base of the planning, the better the possibility that the services will attract worshipers and be within the ability of the congregation to celebrate effectively. Also, the planners and liturgical participants will have an opportunity to learn about the meaning of the paschal mystery that the Holy Week liturgies celebrate and to become missionaries and advocates to their fellow parishioners, urging them to participate in the Holy Week liturgies.

Holy Week in the Small Church

One thing that discourages many small parishes is the memory many clergy and lay people have of how magnificently the Holy Week services were celebrated in large churches with extensive musical and clerical resources. "Our little church could never hope to duplicate the splendid worship of the Great Parish in the Big City!" This is true but largely irrelevant. Liturgy in small churches is different from that in large cathedrals, just as parish life is different, and the advantages are not all on one side.

A small parish can achieve a degree of participation in its liturgies that is impossible in a large congregation. The Holy Week services can be effectively celebrated by small groups using simple music and available resources, but they must be carefully planned to encourage congregational participation and to avoid attempting to do things beyond the skills of the participants.

The first step in planning is, as always, to assess the available resources. Just because something is in the Prayer Book or *The Book of Occasional Services* does not mean that it can or should be done. In most parishes it will not be realistic to plan Tenebrae for Wednesday night, a solemn Maundy Thursday Eucharist, the Good Friday liturgy, a Holy Saturday Word liturgy, the Great Vigil, and Easter morning as major services with "all the stops pulled out," with a Eucharist on Monday, Tuesday, and Wednesday, and the Stations of the Cross at some convenient time as additional offerings. The choir director, the altar guild, and the acolytes can help the parish to set a reasonable course. The special liturgies of Maundy Thursday, Good Friday, and the Great Vigil should be the primary foci.

Decide what services will be held. Start with the Liturgy of the Palms on Palm Sunday, the Maundy Thursday Eucharist, the Good Friday liturgy, and as solemn an Easter Eucharist as the traditions and resources of the parish permit. Then give serious thought to the Great Vigil.

Holy Week Services

Palm Sunday, Maundy Thursday, and Good Friday are the principal Holy Week services to which you should devote your primary resources. Then plan other services within the congregation's ability to participate. In planning for Holy Week, it is better to consider the needs of the congregation as a whole, and to plan corporate services for congregational participation than to provide a smorgasbord to meet the varying devotional needs of many individuals.

Additional services for Monday through Wednesday and for Holy Saturday may be scheduled and the daily offices may also be offered. However, tempting as it may be to schedule all of the above, it is important not to offer so many services that none is well attended and everyone feels guilty, exhausted, or both. Each congregation has its own pace and capacity for what should be scheduled during this week. Too many offerings may dilute the emphasis on the primary days to be observed.

Palm Sunday

Palm Sunday has a double title in *The Book of Common Prayer* that accurately expresses the nature of the day: "The Sunday of the Passion: Palm Sunday." The blessing of the palms and the triumphal procession modulate into a penitential Eucharist dominated by the gospel account of the crucifixion. The two themes are quite distinct and should not be mixed. Hymn choices related to the triumphant entry should all be placed prior to the Collect of the Day. From the collect forward, the liturgy focuses on the Passion Gospel narrative and the sacrifice of Christ at the cross. Some have advocated separating out these portions of the liturgy, to have a service solely focused on the triumphant entry and a separate service focused on the passion (or simply leave it until Good Friday). This suggestion is clearly not envisioned in the BCP and undermines the intention and integrity of the rite. The perceived triumph of the entry into Jerusalem is inextricably tied to the true triumph of Christ at the cross. Additional information on the liturgy is found in the Palm Sunday section below.

Monday through Wednesday in Holy Week

While full sets of lessons and Collects are appointed for these days, there is not a specific liturgy that is expected. Parishes that desire to observe these days could offer any of the regular liturgies of the Church: Morning Prayer, Evening Prayer, or Holy Eucharist, depending on the congregation's interest and desire. These may follow the congregation's usual customs for weekday services and be scheduled for any convenient hour. Suggestions for Holy Eucharist on these days are provided in the sections below.

Some churches incorporate Tenebrae into their offering for Wednesday in Holy Week.

Maundy Thursday

The Maundy Thursday liturgy is properly a Holy Week service, the only Eucharist celebrated between Wednesday and the Great Vigil. It is the first of the "Three Days," the *triduum*, which takes the congregation from Maundy Thursday and the Last Supper through Good Friday and crucifixion, through burial on Holy Saturday to the first word of Resurrection at the Great Vigil of Easter. Many parishes wish to emphasize this context, using Holy Week red vestments, and emphasizing the connections and continuity between the liturgies of these days. Some parishes celebrate it as a separate occasion, emphasizing the institution of the Eucharist, a sort of Corpus Christi. In that case churches often make more festal choices, such as using the color white and using of the Gloria in excelsis. One concern is whether bringing back using white during Holy Week would preempt the buildup toward Easter. Another concern would be that the Prayer Book does not include provision for this option, suspending the use of the Gloria, for example until Easter, but it is a custom in some places. Whichever emphasis is chosen, it needs to be fully implemented as one or the other. Vacillating between the two options provides an unclear direction for the liturgy. Additional comments on liturgical choices are found in the Maundy Thursday section.

Good Friday

The proper liturgy on this day should be the principal Good Friday service. The time of day it is held will depend on the convenience of the parish. The Good Friday liturgy as the solemn corporate commemoration of the great events of the day does not lend itself to being repeated. If it is necessary to have a second Good Friday service, one of the offices with a sermon or meditation or the Way of the Cross is often a good choice (though never as a replacement for the proper Good Friday liturgy).

The Good Friday liturgy is not a funeral for Jesus. Its theme is epitomized in the refrain to Anthem 1 for the veneration of the cross:

> We glory in your cross, O Lord,
> and praise and magnify your holy resurrection;
> for by virtue of your cross
> joy has come to the whole world. (BCP, 281)

Lent begins on Ash Wednesday with a close reflection on the congregation's own sinfulness and mortality, facing the limitations of being human. Lent comes to its culmination by placing the congregation in solidarity with the work of Christ upon the cross.[1] The extensive intercessions in the Solemn Collects prompt the congregation to join Christ in his salvific work for the world. Good Friday is not a spectator event, but a deep participation of every Christian in Christ's work of redemption and salvation for all. That is one reason why the Way of the Cross is unsatisfactory as the primary liturgy on Good Friday – it locates the congregation with the crowd in the narrative, with observers, rather than with Christ. Some have suggested asking the congregation to read the words of Christ in the Passion Gospel on Good Friday, rather than the crowd, as one way to emphasize this identity with Christ.

---

1 For more extensive reflection on this topic see James W. Farwell, *This is the Night: Suffering, Salvation, and the Liturgies of Holy Week* (London: Bloomsbury T&T Clark, 2005).

Holy Saturday

The Word liturgy for Holy Saturday is quite brief and is a convenient service for those about to prepare the church for Easter to celebrate together. Its use of an anthem from the burial rite and the focus of the lessons on the burial of Jesus provide a quiet, reflective service in the midst of the most dramatic services of the year.

Holy Week – Seasonal Rites, and Other Commemorations[1]

Holy Week Blessing[2]

The following prayer over the people may be used by a bishop or priest whenever a blessing is appropriate from Palm Sunday through Maundy Thursday.

Almighty God, we pray you graciously to behold this your family, for whom our Lord Jesus Christ was willing to be betrayed, and given into the hands of sinners, and to suffer death upon the cross; who lives and reigns for ever and ever. *Amen.*

Tenebrae[3]

The name Tenebrae (the Latin word for "darkness" or "shadows") has for centuries been applied to the ancient monastic night and early morning services (Matins and Lauds) of the last three days of Holy Week, which in medieval times came to be celebrated on the preceding evenings.

Apart from the chant of the Lamentations (in which each verse is introduced by a letter of the Hebrew alphabet), the most conspicuous feature of the service is the gradual extinguishing of candles and other lights in the church until only a single candle, considered a symbol of our Lord, remains. Toward the end of the service this candle is hidden, typifying the apparent victory of the forces of evil. At the very end, a loud noise is made, symbolizing the earthquake at the time of the resurrection (Matthew 28:2), the hidden candle is restored to its place, and by its light all depart in silence.

The BOS liturgy is designed primarily for use on Wednesday in Holy Week, so as not to displace the proper liturgies for Maundy Thursday or Good Friday.

1 This section heading omits "Major Feasts" because all Major Feasts in Holy Week are transferred to the first open weekday after Easter II, so that Holy Week and Easter Week observances are uninterrupted.

2 BOS 2022, 14.

3 BOS 2022, 88–106.

The Way of the Cross (Stations of the Cross)[4]

The Way (or Stations) of the Cross, is based on a medieval devotion said to have been brought back from the Crusades by St. Francis of Assisi. This service may be used throughout Lent, traditionally on Fridays, or at other times. There are two forms of the Way of the Cross in the BOS 2022, one which includes stations that are added from tradition and one which only includes stations directly derived from Scripture. The Way of the Cross may be a good alternative for an additional service on Good Friday, though not in place of the primary liturgy of the day. It can be adapted as a children's service or an outdoor service or both. The procession can also be omitted and the format used for a series of devotional addresses.

The Stations of the Cross for Children[5]

This is a script for a meditation for children, either gathered on the floor, or walking from station to station. Any of the following props may be used and passed around so that children can feel, smell, and taste the story.

Needed are: charoset (chopped apples, honey, and cinnamon) parsley, and salt water (Seder foods); a chalice and wine, flat bread, a bowl with oiled water; rough jute rope, rich purple fabric; a crown of thorns; a large bowl with water for Pilate; nails; Veronika's veil (gauzy fabric with a face vaguely chalked on it); a sponge with vinegar; cotton balls with fragrant oil; linen.

4 BOS 2022, 52–70; 71–87.

5 Susan K. Bock, *Liturgy for the Whole Church: Multigenerational Resources for Worship* (New York: Church Publishing, 2008), 93–94.

If you wanted to celebrate the beginning of our nation, where would you go to do it? (*Elicit answers: Boston, perhaps, or Philadelphia, or Washington DC.*)

And how would you celebrate? (*Probably with parades, fireworks, food for sure!*)

In Jesus's time, where do you think the Jewish people went to celebrate their liberation? (*To the city of Jerusalem*).

And do you know the name of the holiday that still marks their freedom? (*It is called Passover.*)

When Jesus lived, all the people would go up to Jerusalem for Passover. There they sang and danced and prayed and ate! At the Seder meal, they would tell their children the story of how God had saved them from slavery in Egypt.

> "Why is this night different from all other nights?" the children would ask.
> "On this night, God opened the Red Sea waters and the Jewish people passed through the sea on dry ground, but the Egyptians who chased them drowned in the sea!"
> "Why do we eat charoset?" the children would ask.
> "Because of the mortar for the bricks our mothers and fathers had to make in their hard labor in Egypt!"
> "Why do we eat parsley dipped in salt?" the children would ask.
> "Because of the bitterness and tears of our slavery!"
> "Why do we eat unleavened bread?" the children would ask.
> "Because there was no time to wait for the bread to rise the night we escaped from Egypt!"

Every spring, the Jewish people have gathered at Passover meals to tell that same story with the children. They say, "Next year, may we celebrate this meal in Israel, our home!"

They sing: **"Da da ye nu, da da ye nu, da da ye nu, dayenu, dayenu!"** (It would have been enough for us!)

> If God had split the sea for us, Dayenu!
> If God had sustained us in the wilderness for forty years, Dayenu!
> If God had brought us before Mount Sinai, Dayenu!
> If God had given us the Torah, Dayenu!
> If God had led us to the land of Israel, Dayenu!

Music for Dayenu *can be found online.*[6]

In Jesus's time, the people waited for a king to come and free them from the Romans who ruled over them in their own homeland. This king would come at Passover, entering the holy city riding on a colt. He would be like a god, able to heal blindness, and other miracles. So, when Jesus came onto Jerusalem on a colt, many thought he was the Messiah, and they made a huge parade, and shouted "Hosanna! Hosanna!" They made a path with their palms and their clothes. The children sang the loudest, and when people tried to quiet them, Jesus said, "If you silence them, the stones will start to sing!"

The people thought that Jesus would lead them into a great war, a war they could win, and that, after all these years they would be free at last! But there was no war, and the people became sad, scared, and angry. The same people who had welcomed him with such joy and love began to want to kill Jesus. Jesus knew what was happening. He knew the people wanted him dead. He was sad, scared, and angry, too, because he had thought things would surely turn out differently than this. But he trusted God, and listened to God every minute so that he would know what to do next.

Jesus gathered his friends in a small room and they shared their last meal together. As always, he blessed the bread and the wine, but this time he said something different. He said, "From now on, when you eat or drink like this, know I am with you. Remember how I loved you, and how I died on this night." After supper, Jesus got up from the table and washed his friends' feet, to show them how they ought to serve each other.

Here, the children may share bread and wine and pass the bowl of oiled water around to smell and feel. You may want to do a real foot-washing, while a simple song is sung.

One of Jesus's closest friends, Judas, was so angry that he left and told the police where to find Jesus so they could arrest him. The police paid Judas 30 pieces of silver for this information. Later, when Judas looked at his money and counted it, he realized that no amount of money is worth your love and loyalty. In the garden of Gethsemane, Jesus was praying, and Roman soldiers came to arrest him. They tied his hands together, like a criminal, though Jesus had never used his hands to hit or hurt anyone, but only to heal and soothe. The soldiers dressed him in a fancy purple robe, and a crown that they made of thorns.

These items may be passed around.

They blindfolded him, and spat at him, and beat him, and shouted, "Some king you are! If you're a prophet, then tell us who just hit you!" They took him to Pilate, who really wanted to know the truth about things. He said to Jesus, "Who are you?" Jesus was silent. Jesus knew that what was happening to him was not fair, and that, if he spoke, he might be able to save himself. But sometimes

6 www.chabad.org/multimedia/media_cdo/aid/255530/jewish/Dayenu.htm; accessed May 22, 2020.

we need to be silent, and he knew this was one of those times. Pilate washed his hands in a bowl of water in front of all the people as a sign that he would not be guilty for whatever might happen to Jesus.

Jesus was led to a hill. He was made to carry his own cross. He was so tired and hungry and sad that he had trouble carrying it. Many people gathered to watch the spectacle. Some made fun of him, some wept, and some helped him, like Veronika.

The legend of Veronika is that the image of Jesus's face remained on her veil when, breaking with tradition and safety, she ran to him, removed her veil, and wiped his face.

Simon helped him carry his cross.

They nailed him to a cross, and his life slipped slowly away from him. He wondered why this was happening to him, and where was his God now that he needed God more than ever. He became very thirsty, and some soldiers held up a vinegar-soaked sponge for him to suck on.

The sponge with vinegar may be passed around.

Just before he died, Jesus gathered up his last little bit of strength and shouted to God in the saddest, loudest cry anyone ever heard. And he died.

He was taken down from the cross and wrapped in white linen. Then he was put in a small cave for a tomb, and a huge stone was rolled in front of it. The next day, some women came with oil and spices to anoint Jesus's body.

The oil-soaked cotton and piece of linen may be passed around.

Only, when they got there, they found that the body was gone! They were angry and confused and ran to tell Peter and the others what they had discovered. This is a Holy Week story, whose end comes at Easter. I wonder how the story will turn out.

The Three Hours (Tre Ore)

This tradition is a nonliturgical service of preaching on the Passion, focused on the "Seven Last Words of Christ," generated by combining the distinct Gospel narratives together to identify those phrases, held from noon until 3 p.m. on Good Friday. The sermons or reflections are interspersed with hymns, prayers, and periods of silence. The service is of South American Jesuit origin, but became, nevertheless, the usual Good Friday service for both Catholics and Protestants until the liturgical reforms of the last half of the twentieth century. Today it is often an ecumenical service in a downtown church. Few congregations will wish to introduce such a service, but some may find it a well-established tradition. In your liturgical planning, avoid conflicting with it when scheduling the Good Friday liturgy, which should be the primary focus of the day.

The Sunday of the Passion: Palm Sunday

Variable – The Sunday Prior to Easter Day

The Triumphant Entry and the Passion

Anchor Points – The Propers and the Season

The fixed points for each service are the appointed or proper readings and collect as well as the themes of the day or season.

Readings and Psalm[1]

Isaiah 50:4–9a

Today's reading is the third of the four "servant songs" in Isaiah (the others are 42:1–4, 49:1–6 and 52:13–53:12). It is not certain whom the author intended the servant to represent; Christians have generally understood the suffering servant to be Jesus. The reading presents the servant as one who submits to God's purposes, whether in a personal response to God or in acceptance of suffering. The servant knows that he is called to be a misunderstood and ill-treated prophet to a sin-weary people. Nevertheless, he is confident that God will vindicate him. The servant songs helped Israel to interpret the suffering and humiliation of the exile. The early Church found in the songs a new significance: they helped the believers understand and proclaim the meaning of Jesus's suffering and resurrection.

Psalm 31:9–16

Psalm 31 is a lament by one surrounded by evil people. Trust in God encourages the psalmist to entrust himself to God's care. In anticipation of God's deliverance, the psalmist prays with thanksgiving and joy.

Philippians 2:5–11

Today's passage is generally considered to be a hymn to Christ that Paul has adopted to make his own point. The hymn contains an outline of Christ's saving work: divine preexistence (v. 6), incarnation (v. 7), death (v. 8), celestial exaltation (v. 9), heavenly adoration (v. 10), and Jesus's new title (v. 11). The first stanza (2:6–8) recounts Jesus's own action. His "equality with God" is not a prize to be "exploited" for his own advantage but is a treasure to lay down.

Mark 14:1–15:47

In his account of the passion story, Mark is constantly working to shape the story so that all the major themes of his gospel emerge. Jesus the powerful teacher and miracle worker – the Christ – must suffer. He will be misunderstood and completely abandoned by his disciples, as the hatred of those out to kill Jesus triumphs. But in Jesus's own weakness, the power of God was present to bring salvation. Mark's account is not an appeal to pity, sorrow, or even repentance. He is concerned about its message of salvation. It witnesses to the presence of God and to the evidence of God's purpose at work in the midst of the passion. The response called forth is faith. Mark stresses Jesus's utter loneliness, deserted by his disciples – even Peter. When formally confronted by the high priest, Jesus makes a clear proclamation of his status and destiny. Mark insists that Jesus's true identity can only be recognized by gazing on the crucified Christ and affirming with the centurion that "this man was God's Son!" (15:39).

Collect

Almighty and everliving God, in your tender love for the human race you sent your Son our Savior Jesus Christ to take upon him our nature, and to suffer death upon the cross, giving us the example of his great humility: Mercifully grant that we may walk in the way of his suffering, and also share in his resurrection; through Jesus Christ our Lord, who lives and reigns with you and the Holy Spirit, one God, for ever and ever. *Amen.*

1 This section covers the Eucharist readings rather than the Liturgy of the Palms.

Proper Preface

Holy Week – Through Jesus Christ our Lord. For our sins he was lifted high upon the cross, that he might draw the whole world to himself; and, by his suffering and death, he became the source of eternal salvation for all who put their trust in him. (Rite II, BCP 379; Rite I BCP 346)

Pairings for this Day

See the table below for choices appointed and suggested for this day. Preferences are put in **bold**. Not all choices are suitable for all congregations or community, though, so consider these preferences as a starting point before making a decision about your own congregation.

	Palm Sunday	Rite I	Rite II	EOW1	BOS 2022
Color	**Passiontide Red/Oxblood**				
Entrance Rite	**Liturgy of the Palms**	270	270		
Song of Praise/Kyrie	None when Liturgy of the Palms is used				
Collect		168	219, 270		
Creed	Nicene Creed (may be omitted)	326	358	53	
Prayers of the People	**Locally written**; options below; BCP forms	329	387–393	54–55	
Offertory Sentence	"Give thanks to the Lord, for he is good; his mercy endures for ever." (Psalm 118)	343–344	376–377		
Eucharistic Prayer		**1–333**	**A – 361**	1–57 *or* 2–60	
Proper Preface	Holy Week	346	379		
Breaking of the Bread (Fraction)	Christ our Passover with Alleluias omitted *and/or* Agnus Dei	337	364; 407		
Postcommunion Prayer		339	**Almighty everliving God – 366**	Loving God – 70	
Blessing	**Solemn Prayer in BOS**				**14**
Dismissal	**Let us bless the Lord**	340	366		
Notes					

Additional Notes:

Entrance Rite: The Liturgy of the Palms **–** The Liturgy of the Palms is the proper (appointed) rite for this service. Additional services on Palm Sunday may begin with this rite or an adaptation of it. The BCP, the Altar Book, and *The Hymnal 1982* provide the necessary texts and music. The music for the Liturgy of the Palms is at Hymn 153–157. Holy Week red is usually used today as the liturgical color. If copes are worn in the parish, the celebrant may wear one for the palm liturgy.

If palm branches are not available, any branches can be used, cut from the church yard or from parishioners' homes. The Liturgy of the Palms should begin apart from the church, outside if at all possible. Many churches make this procession an important part of their visible presence in their community. If remaining indoors, beginning in another part of the building is preferred. The palms can be set out in a convenient place where the congregation is gathering. If beginning the service away from the worship space is not possible, the palms may be placed at the church door and blessed there. If it is desired to simplify the ceremony and reduce the time, the palms may be distributed by the ushers as people arrive and then held up to be blessed at the appropriate time, rather than blessed in one location and distributed during the liturgy.

If a congregation is unable to process, they may hold their palms for the gospel and blessing, and then sing "All glory, laud, and honor" (Hymn 154) while the vested party processes to the altar. Alternatively, the congregation could gather in the parish house or even in the narthex. The opening anthem can be said, or the choir may lead its singing. The collect, gospel, and blessing of the palms may be said by the priest, and the Benedictus qui venit sung to any familiar tune. All enter the church, led by the crucifer, singing "All glory, laud, and honor" and concluding with the collect said before the altar.

The opening anthem may be sung or said as a versicle and response. A deacon, if there is one, reads the gospel at the Liturgy of the Palms. The reading may be accompanied by the ceremonial customary at the Sunday Eucharist. In the absence of a deacon, another priest may read the gospel, or it may be read as a lesson by a layperson without the gospel ceremonies. The blessing itself may be sung in the same way as the Eucharistic preface. The music for the responses is in the Hymnal and that for the celebrant's part in The Altar Book. No particular ceremonial actions are necessary, but a sign of the cross may be made over the branches at "Let these branches be for us . . . ," and they may be sprinkled with holy water or censed at the conclusion of the prayer. The clergy, acolytes, and ushers all assist in distributing the palms as expeditiously as possible, unless they were distributed prior to the service.

The palm procession need not involve thurifers, banners, torches, and many clergy, although they are all appropriate when they are available. Carrying the palm branches in procession into the church in celebration of Christ's triumphal entry into Jerusalem is the reason for blessing the palms, so the procession should be impressive and involve all of the congregation able to participate. The traditional music for the procession is the hymn "All glory, laud, and honor" (Hymn 154/155 – the text dates to the year 820). The verses may be sung by the choir, or groups within the choir, with the congregation joining in the refrain. If processing outdoors, it is often desirable to include musicians who can be heard clearly across the procession, such as brass instruments. Psalm 118:19–29 (Hymn 157) has an even longer association with the Palm Sunday procession, being quoted in the biblical account. An effective way to use both is to have the choir (or cantors) sing the verses of the psalm, with everyone joining in the antiphon, beginning the hymn when the procession enters the church. The psalm can be sung a capella or with handbells ringing the intervals, the organ accompanying the hymn.

The concluding collect of the procession (sometimes called a station collect) marks the distinct change in theme from "Palm Sunday" to "The Sunday of the Passion." Hymns or anthems with the triumphal entry as their theme belong at the palm liturgy, while music during the Eucharist reflects the passion theme. "Ride on! ride on in majesty!" (Hymn 156), for example, can be used as an additional hymn during the procession, while "O sacred head" (Hymn 169) is more appropriate at the offertory or the end of the service. Other "suitable anthems" may replace the opening anthem of the liturgy of the Palms from the Prayer Book or be sung during the distribution of palms. If the choir wishes to sing a Palm Sunday anthem, either of these places is suitable.

Passion Gospel – The Passion Gospel is the distinctive element of the Eucharist itself. It may be read responsively or sung. Many parishes enjoy reading the Passion dramatically, with the congregation taking the part of the crowd. Readers for the Passion can be recruited from the choir or congregation. When a deacon is available, they often serve as the narrator. The Passion Gospel may be read entirely by lay people.

Concluding the Rite – Selecting an appropriate hymn to lead into the rest of Holy Week is important. Some congregations will observe silence during the exit procession.

Content Resources

Reading Between the Lines

In ancient triumphal processions citizens acclaim a victor near the city gates and formally escort them through the city to the temple, accompanied with hymns. Mark follows this pattern except for the temple entry, which is likely delayed until after Jesus' death, and changed into the tearing of the temple veil (15:38–9). Two things are odd: the unridden colt, and the identity of the Lord in the saying, "the Lord needs it." Is it the Emperor, or Jesus, or the owner of the donkey? More broadly, could Jesus' words be meant to subvert and parody what might otherwise be a forcible surrender of the donkey to Roman soldiers? Could the Hosanna cries imitate those of imperial processions? If so, Jesus' action in the temple could be meant as a disruption of temple business in a city under Roman occupation. Since Mark sandwiches the event symbolically between two parts of a story in which Jesus looks for but does not find produce from a fig tree, and curses it, a temple supported by Rome, and Roman imperialism, seems doomed.

Central Themes

In the Holy Land, there is a church built over the spot where Jesus was tried and Peter denied him. Surrounding the altar are three large icons depicting a scene from that awful night and its ramifications. The first is of Jesus staring at Peter while he denies ever knowing his beloved teacher and friend. The second is of Peter alone with a look of utter grief on his face at his betrayal. And the third is when he is reunited with a post-resurrected Jesus who has forgiven him. All around the room are the words from the Apostles' Creed: "I believe in the forgiveness of sins." It's clear Peter came to believe this powerful gift, and so can we.

Nichole Nordeman sings a song, "Why?" A young girl recounts the day of Jesus's death. The girl asks, "Daddy, why are they screaming? / Why are the faces of some of them beaming?" Her father tries to keep her inside away from it all, but the young girl wonders about this man and wanders out to witness his final moments. The curiosity of this child makes the truth of the moment inescapable. Her innocence puts into stark relief the dark reality of the day. That shows us as Christians why the answer to our ultimate questions comes at such a great cost.

As the extended reading from Mark tells the story of Christ's Passion, Jesus goes to the cross with the nard of his anointing still perfuming his hair and his body. Jesus himself accepts the anointing as preparation for his burial. As we move from the triumph of the entry into Jerusalem to the grief of the crucifixion, we can forget that a real human being is at the center of the story – a human being who is also God incarnate. What are the anointings that prepare us for our own death and resurrection?

Engaging All Ages

On this day, people in churches all over the world will raise palms high, many singing and processing in honor of Jesus. This act is a reminder; though he was a threat to the powers and principalities of his time, Jesus gloriously enters Jerusalem with palms scattered in front of him. The palms were a symbol of victory, of goodness, of light in a dark world. At parades and events now, we see people lifting up signs and cheering when excited. As you celebrate Palm Sunday and the presence of love and light, you could make a picture or poster that shows the love and light in your life.

Prayers of the People: Option 1

Enter our hearts this day and every day, O Christ,

and lead us on this walk of love, O Lord.

Lead each member of your church in humility as we walk together. Guide our bishops and priests and deacons so that your glory may be revealed through them in your word and sacraments.

Lead us on this walk of love, O Lord.

Lead the authorities of every country in the way of justice for all of their citizens and peace between neighbors and nations.

Lead us on this walk of love, O Lord.

Lead each us to reach out our hands and hearts in love where there is suffering and anxiety, sickness and grief.

Lead us on this walk of love, O Lord.

Lead us to lead lives that please you as we walk this earth so that with those who have died we may join you in our eternal home.

Lead us on this walk of love, O Lord.

Prayers of the People: Option 2

Deacon or Priest

As we journey this week with Christ and celebrate the paschal mystery of his death and resurrection, let us earnestly pray to God for those following the way of the cross and for all peoples everywhere.

Intercessor

For (*N.* and) all who are to be baptized and for all those preparing for Baptism and their sponsors; for the Diocese of Jerusalem in the Anglican Province of Jerusalem and the Middle East; for the holy catholic church throughout the world, sharing the death and resurrection of Christ.

Christ, have mercy.

For *N.*, our Presiding Bishop, *N.*, our bishop(s), *N.* our parish clergy, and for all bishops, priests, and deacons; for all who minister in Christ and for all the holy people of God.

Christ, have mercy.

For *N.* our President, *N.* our Governor, *N.* our Mayor; for all nations, peoples, tribes, clans, and families.

Christ, have mercy.

For justice, mercy, and peace in all the world.

Christ, have mercy.

For all who are tempted, oppressed, afflicted, or in need.

Christ, have mercy.

For the dying and the dead, and for those who mourn.

Christ, have mercy.

For all refugees; for our families, friends, and companions, and for all those we love.

Christ, have mercy.

Remembering all those who have gone before us in faith, let us offer ourselves and one another to the living God through Christ.

To you, O Lord, our God.

Celebrant

Blessed are you, O Lord our God, whose Son humbled himself and became obedient to the point of death. Receive the prayers we offer this day for all those in need in everyplace; through Jesus Christ our Lord. ***Amen.***

Hymns for the Day

At the Liturgy of the Palms:

The Hymnal 1982

Opening Anthem, Blessing Over the Branches,
At the Procession: 153

Processional: The Hymnal 1982

All glory, laud, and honor 154, 155
Ride on! ride on in majesty! 156

Lift Every Voice and Sing
Ride on, King Jesus 97

Wonder, Love, and Praise
Mantos y palmas esparciendo /
Filled with excitement 728

At the Liturgy of the Word and Eucharist:

The Hymnal 1982
Alone thou goest forth, O Lord 164
Hail, thou once despised Jesus! 495 (1–2)
To mock your reign, O dearest Lord 170
At the Name of Jesus, every knee shall bow 435
Cross of Jesus, cross of sorrow 160
Morning glory, starlit sky 585 (4–6)
The flaming banners of our King 161
The royal banners forward go 162
What wondrous love is this 439
Ah, holy Jesus, how hast thou offended 158
And now, O Father, mindful of the love 337 (1–2)
Let thy Blood in mercy poured 313
My song is love unknown 458
Nature with open volume stands 434
O sacred head, sore wounded 168, 169
There is a green hill far away 167
When I survey the wondrous cross 474

Lift Every Voice and Sing II
O sacred head, sore wounded 36

Wonder, Love, and Praise
O sacred head, sore wounded 735

Monday in Holy Week

Variable – The Monday Prior to Easter Day

The way of the Cross is the way of life and peace.

Anchor Points – The Propers and the Season

The fixed points for each service are the appointed or proper readings and collect as well as the themes of the day or season.

Readings and Psalm

Isaiah 42:1–9

In our reading from the Hebrew scriptures, we hear of the mission of the Lord's servant, the one whom God has chosen to bring forth justice and salvation. This is the first of the "servant songs" that form a portion of the Book of Isaiah written at the time when the exile in Babylon was ending and the city of Jerusalem had begun to be restored. The servant is sometimes thought to be an historical individual, or is understood as an idealization of Israel. Christians see in the servant a prefigurement of the ministry of Jesus, who will become a light to the nations of the world.

Psalm 36:5–11

The psalmist celebrates the expansive love of God expressed in faithfulness and justice. God is a river of delight in whose light we see light.

Hebrews 9:11–15

Christ has inaugurated a new covenant, accomplishing all that was anticipated by the rites and rituals of the first covenant, that is, redemption from sin and transgression and the purification of conscience for the right worship of the living God.

John 12:1–11

Six days before the Passover, Jesus gathers with his friends in Bethany at the home of Lazarus, whom he had raised from the dead. Mary, the sister of Martha and Lazarus, anoints Jesus's feet with costly perfume, wiping his feet with her hair. This extravagant devotion is criticized by Judas Isacariot, but Jesus defends the action in ways that seem to prefigure his fast approaching death.

Collect

Almighty God, whose most dear Son went not up to joy but first he suffered pain, and entered not into glory before he was crucified: Mercifully grant that we, walking in the way of the cross, may find it none other that the way of life and peace; through Jesus Christ your Son our Lord, who lives and reigns with you and the Holy Spirit, one God, for ever and ever. *Amen.*

Proper Preface

Holy Week – Through Jesus Christ our Lord. For our sins he was lifted high upon the cross, that he might draw the whole world to himself; and, by his suffering and death, he became the source of eternal salvation for all who put their trust in him. (Rite II, BCP 379; Rite I BCP 346)

Seasonal Pairings

See the table below for choices appointed and suggested for this day. Preferences are put in **bold**. Not all choices are suitable for all congregations or community, though, so consider these preferences as a starting point before making a decision about your own congregation.

	Monday in Holy Week	Rite I	Rite II	EOW1	BOS 2022
Color	**Passiontide Red** *or* **Oxblood**				
Entrance Rite	Customary *or* **A Penitential Order; penitential acclamation**	319 *or* 323	351, *or* 355	50	
Song of Praise/Kyrie	Kyrie *or* Trisagion; *or* BCP Canticle 14; *or* EOW1 Canticle G, H	324	356 C14 – 90	34	
Collect		168	220		
Creed	Nicene Creed *optional*	326	358	53	
Prayers of the People	**Locally written**; BCP forms	329	387–393	54–55	
Offertory Sentence	"See, the former things have come to pass, and new things I now declare; before they spring forth, I tell you of them." (Isaiah)	343–344	376–377		
Eucharistic Prayer		**1–333**	**A – 361**	1–57 *or* 2–60	
Proper Preface	Holy Week	346	379		
Breaking of the Bread (Fraction)	Christ our Passover with Alleluias omitted *and/or* Agnus Dei	337	364; 407		
Postcommunion Prayer		339	**Almighty everliving God – 366**	Loving God – 70	
Blessing	**Solemn Prayer in BOS**				**14**
Dismissal	**Let us bless the Lord**	340	366		
Notes					

Content Resources

Reading Between the Lines

This passage is situated after the raising of Lazarus, which is why the narrative locates Bethany "where Lazarus was" (so Tyndale and KJV). Lazarus joins the meal, reclining at table. In this regard, Mary's action of anointing Jesus' feet and wiping them with her hair might well be motivated by gratitude. Because John situates the anointing just before Jesus' entrance into Jerusalem (12:12–19), where Jesus is hailed as "King of Israel," this passage is the anointing of a king – although kings were anointed on their heads, not their feet.

The NRSV translation, "the home of Lazarus," evokes erroneous associations of "home" as private and secluded. This is a public event at which Martha (probably), Mary, Lazarus, disciples and a "great crowd of the Jews" are present. The word for "wipe" (or "wipe dry") is also used by John in the upper room where Jesus washes feet and "wipes them dry" with a towel (13:5). We are told that the house was filled with the fragrance of the ointment, perhaps to contrast with the four-day stench of Lazarus' tomb (11:39). Key is John's presentation of Mary as the model disciple. She "follows" Jesus' example – albeit, prior to the example, doing what Jesus will do – washing and drying disciples' feet on the last occasion they are together.

Central Themes

The *Exercises* of Ignatian spirituality encourage the reader of scripture to imagine the fullness of a biblical story well beyond the page. What would it be like to imagine what happened next for Lazarus in this story from the gospel now that he has been raised from the dead by Jesus? His post-resurrected life was such a beacon of hope for those who would see the power of God in this world that the chief priests planned on having him killed. What happened to him following this story? And how might we be invited to live a life that makes others take notice of the Resurrection?

"Jesus came to Bethany, the home of Lazarus, who he had raised from the dead. There they gave a dinner for him. Martha served, and Lazarus was one of those at the table with him." Lazarus, one of Jesus's greatest miracles, is now just one of an unknown number at the table for dinner. What were Lazarus's thoughts and feelings? How does it feel to be dead and then alive again – not exactly resurrected like Christ but alive somehow? How does one live after dying? This Holy Week, what does dying to self and living again look like for you?

Isaiah proclaims that God has called each one of us "as a covenant to the people, a light to the nations, to open the eyes that are blind, to bring out the prisoners." We are chosen. Jesus eats dinner with Lazarus, the formerly dead man restored to life, and the people crowd the house to see both of them together – each one chosen as a witness to God's good news. How will we proclaim God's resurrection power in our own lives?

Engaging All Ages

Today's lessons include the story of Jesus visiting Mary, Martha, and Lazarus. Mary draws scorn from Judas Iscariot when she pours an entire pound of special perfume on the feet of her friend Jesus, but Jesus defends her actions. Think of a time when you had a special gift for someone, a gift that others may not have known about or understood. Was it hard to wait to share it? Were you worried that other people might not understand? Mary knows that Jesus is special and wants to offer him the very best. What is the very best part of you that you offer up?

Hymns for the Day

The Hymnal 1982

We sing the praise of him who died 471
Ancient of days, who sittest throned in glory 363
Jesus shall reign where'er the sun 544
Thy strong word did cleave the darkness 381
Weary of all trumpeting 572
Come, thou fount of every blessing 686
Cross of Jesus, cross of sorrow 160
Draw nigh and take the Body of the Lord 327, 328
Glory be to Jesus 479
Holy Father, great Creator 368
Let thy blood in mercy poured 313
God himself is with us 475
Just as I am, without one plea 693
Jesus, all my gladness 701
Jesus, the very thought of thee 642
There's a wideness in God's mercy 469, 470

Lift Every Voice and Sing II

Come, thou fount of every blessing 111
Just as I am, without one plea 137

Tuesday in Holy Week

Variable – The Tuesday Prior to Easter Day

The cross, an instrument of shameful death, has become the means of life for us.

Anchor Points – The Propers and the Season

The fixed points for each service are the appointed or proper readings and collect as well as the themes of the day or season.

Readings and Psalm

Isaiah 49:1–7

The servant of the Lord reflects movingly on his mission – its sorrows and frustrations – and God's high calling and promise to be with him. The servant is sometimes thought to be an historical individual, or is understood as an idealization of Israel. This song was probably composed as the exiles from Jerusalem were preparing to return to their devastated city. Despite appearances, the Lord will make this servant a light to the nations.

Psalm 71:1–14

The psalmist prays that God will continue to be his refuge and stronghold.

1 Corinthians 1:18–31

In this lesson Paul directs the attention of the Corinthians to God's way of using what is weak and lowly – even what the world regards as foolish – to accomplish the divine purposes. Paul emphasizes this understanding because a number of these new Christians had come to think of themselves as especially gifted, powerful, and wise. As the cross has shown, however, God's ideas about what is wise and noble are often quite different from ours. Our only boast can be in the Lord.

John 12:20–36

In this gospel passage Jesus presents teaching concerning the meaning of his death. After his prayer to God a voice from heaven is heard. Greeks wish to see Jesus, but he will not draw all others to himself until after he has died and risen. Then, like a seed which falls into the earth, he will bear much fruit. Now is the hour for the Son of Man to be glorified – glorified both by his willingness to be lifted up on the cross to die for others, and afterward to be lifted up to heaven. Disciples must learn to follow Jesus in his way – not walking in darkness but in the light.

Collect

O God, by the passion of your blessed Son you made an instrument of shameful death to be for us the means of life: Grant us so to glory in the cross of Christ, that we may gladly suffer shame and loss for the sake of your Son our Savior Jesus Christ; who lives and reigns with you and the Holy Spirit, one God, for ever and ever. *Amen.*

Proper Preface

Holy Week – Through Jesus Christ our Lord. For our sins he was lifted high upon the cross, that he might draw the whole world to himself; and, by his suffering and death, he became the source of eternal salvation for all who put their trust in him. (Rite II, BCP 379; Rite I BCP 346)

Seasonal Pairings

See the table below for choices appointed and suggested for this day. Preferences are put in **bold**. Not all choices are suitable for all congregations or community, though, so consider these preferences as a starting point before making a decision about your own congregation.

	Tuesday in Holy Week	Rite I	Rite II	EOW1	BOS 2022
Color	**Passiontide Red** *or* **Oxblood**				
Entrance Rite	Customary *or* **A Penitential Order; penitential acclamation**	319 *or* 323	351, *or* 355	50	
Song of Praise/Kyrie	Kyrie *or* Trisagion; *or* BCP Canticle 14; *or* EOW1 Canticle G, H	324	356 C14 – 90	34	
Collect		168	220		
Creed	Nicene Creed *optional*	326	358	53	
Prayers of the People	**Locally written**; BCP forms	329	387–393	54–55	
Offertory Sentence	"Very truly, I tell you, unless a grain of wheat falls into the earth and dies, it remains just a single grain; but if it dies, it bears much fruit. Those who love their life lose it, and those who hate their life in this world will keep it for eternal life." (John)	343–344	376–377		
Eucharistic Prayer		**1–333**	**A – 361**	1–57 *or* 2–60	
Proper Preface	Holy Week	346	379		
Breaking of the Bread (Fraction)	Christ our Passover with Alleluias omitted *and/or* Agnus Dei	337	364; 407		
Postcommunion Prayer		339	**Almighty everliving God – 366**	Loving God – 70	
Blessing	**Solemn Prayer in BOS**				**14**
Dismissal	**Let us bless the Lord**	340	366		
Notes					

Content Resources

Reading Between the Lines

John 12 is a turning point in the conflict between God and Satan. To "some Greeks" Jesus declares for the first time that the universal significance of the "hour" of death and resurrection of Jesus has come. Imagery of a grain of wheat that falls into the earth and dies (12:24), whereupon it bears much fruit, uses the language of harvest to interpret a beneficent death. Showing that the Son of Man (Humanity) must be lifted up as revealer and judge, John reverses the shame of the crucifixion by using imagery of death as a vindication and glorious enthronement.

"Whoever serves me must follow me" (12:26) encourages imitating Christ but also anticipates Jesus' action of washing the disciples' feet (13:3–20). "Now my soul is troubled" (12:27) describes Jesus' agony in the Johannine narrative alluding to Ps. 42:5, 11 (Ps. 41 LXX) ironically because Ps. 42 affirms, as John does, the psalmist's trust in God. Similarly, the absent Gethsemane is reframed: the first "prayer," ("And what should I say?"), is never prayed by Jesus and stands as a parody of Jesus' agony in the garden. The second prayer, "Father, glorify your name," in which Jesus lays down his life of his own free will (10:18), is the true prayer. Vv. 27–28 are an excellent example of the way John reshapes traditional material. Instead of anguish, Jesus recognizes the hour as the purpose of his mission and the final revelation of his relationship with God.

The words, "casting out," "judgment" and "ruler of this world" indicate a crucial point in the conflict between God and Satan, the "ruler of this world." Thus, the term world (*kosmos*) here is used in a negative sense to describe opposition to Jesus and his followers. The specific wording of judgment anticipates 14:30 where the betrayal, arrest and crucifixion of Jesus is prefaced by the phrase, "the ruler of the world is coming." Human actions leading to Jesus' death, driven by Satanic powers, are however undone by the glorification of the Father at crucifixion. In 12:31 forensic judgment is combined with warfare in which the "ruler of this world" is expelled. At the end of the passage, Jesus' teaching recalls and clarifies the enigmatic 3:14, "And just as Moses lifted up the serpent in the wilderness, so must the Son of Man be lifted up," which is now explained as the exaltation and glorification of the crucifixion. Followers are honorably numbered among the "children of light."

Central Themes

Many people wear a cross as a mark of their faith in a loving God who wants justice and peace on earth. But how many of us who wear them stop to consider that they used to be the ultimate symbol of pain and torture? They were used by the Romans as grim billboards warning people not to step out of line. If Jesus can turn even something as hate-filled and oppressive as a cross into the ultimate symbol of peace, how much more can he do with us? And how can we who wear his sign help transform this world in his name?

It has been said that "You may be the only Bible someone reads" and "You might be the only Jesus people see." In today's reading from the Gospel of John, some Greeks wish to see Jesus. Who are the Greeks in your life? Who are those who have yet to see Jesus in person? How can you truly and fully incarnate the life, death, and resurrection of Christ? When people encounter your life and living, will they have the opportunity to encounter the very real and present Jesus?

God commissions Isaiah to carry God's good news "to the end of the earth," and Charles Henry Brent (remembered on March 27 in *Lesser Feasts and Fasts*) responded to that call. As Missionary Bishop to the Philippines, Brent's determination to assure responsible and ethical treatment of non-Christian Filipinos in the Philippines distinguished him among missionaries. When his health failed, he returned to the US mainland, where he championed the ecumenical movement.

Engaging All Ages

Today's lessons speak of the wisdom that comes with faith. It allows those who believe in Jesus to have faith and wisdom in worshipping God. And that wisdom, that knowledge of God, allows Jesus to acknowledge that he is a little apprehensive about the end of his life but confident in God's purpose. When you pray, what is something you are scared to say, afraid to share because you are worried to tell God about it? This week, can you try to let it out, knowingthat through your faith God will always love you?

Hymns for the Day

The Hymnal 1982

My song is love unknown 458 (1–2, 7)
Christ, whose glory fills the skies 6, 7
God of mercy, God of grace 538
How wondrous and great thy works, God of praise! 532, 533
Beneath the cross of Jesus 498
Cross of Jesus, cross of sorrow 160
In the cross of Christ I glory 441, 442
Nature with open volume stands 434
We sing the praise of him who died 471
When I survey the wondrous cross 474
I heard the voice of Jesus say 692
I want to walk as a child of the Light 490
O Jesus, I have promised 655
The great Creator of the worlds 489
When Christ was lifted from the earth 603, 604

Lift Every Voice and Sing II

Jesus, keep me near the cross 28
On a hill far away stood an old rugged cross 38

Wednesday in Holy Week

Variable – The Wednesday Prior to Easter Day

The Son of Man is betrayed

Anchor Points – The Propers and the Season

The fixed points for each service are the appointed or proper readings and collect as well as the themes of the day or season.

Readings and Psalm

Isaiah 50:4–9a

Our first reading tells of the servant who speaks for the Lord and suffers persecution, but still trusts in God's help and vindication. This is the third of the "servant songs" that come from a period late in Israel's exile. The servant might be thought to be the faithful of Israel, the prophet himself, or another historical or idealized figure. The people are weary and tired of the Lord's calling, but the servant steadfastly continues. Christians have long perceived in these words a foretelling of Jesus's mission.

Psalm 70

A prayer for help and vindication.

Hebrews 12:1–3

The author of the Book of Hebrews exhorts hearers to persevere in the face of adversity, looking to the example of Jesus and encouraged by all those through the generations who have sought to be faithful to God in difficult circumstances.

John 13:21–32

At his final supper with his disciples Jesus is troubled by the knowledge of Judas's impending betrayal but tells his disciples that God is at work in the glorification of the Son of Man. Judas Iscariot departs into the night to do what he has determined to do.

Collect

Lord God, whose blessed Son our Savior gave his body to be whipped and his face to be spit upon: Give us grace to accept joyfully the sufferings of the present time, confident of the glory that shall be revealed; through Jesus Christ your Son our Lord, who lives and reigns with you and the Holy Spirit, one God, for ever and ever. *Amen.*

Proper Preface

Holy Week – Through Jesus Christ our Lord. For our sins he was lifted high upon the cross, that he might draw the whole world to himself; and, by his suffering and death, he became the source of eternal salvation for all who put their trust in him. (Rite II, BCP 379; Rite I BCP 346)

Seasonal Pairings

See the table below for choices appointed and suggested for this day. Preferences are put in **bold**. Not all choices are suitable for all congregations or community, though, so consider these preferences as a starting point before making a decision about your own congregation.

	Wednesday in Holy Week	Rite I	Rite II	EOW1	BOS 2022
Color	**Passiontide Red *or* Oxblood**				
Entrance Rite	Customary *or* **A Penitential Order; penitential acclamation**	319 *or* 323	351, *or* 355	50	
Song of Praise/Kyrie	Kyrie *or* Trisagion; *or* BCP Canticle 14; *or* EOW1 Canticle G, H	324	356 C14 – 90	34	
Collect		169	220		
Creed	Nicene Creed *optional*	326	358	53	
Prayers of the People	**Locally written**; BCP forms	329	387–393	54–55	
Offertory Sentence	"Come to us speedily, O God. You are our helper and our deliverer; O Lord, do not tarry." (Psalm 70)	343–344	376–377		
Eucharistic Prayer		**1–333**	**A – 361**	1–57 *or* 2–60	
Proper Preface	Holy Week	346	379		
Breaking of the Bread (Fraction)	Christ our Passover with Alleluias omitted *and/or* Agnus Dei	337	364; 407		
Postcommunion Prayer		339	**Almighty everliving God – 366**	Loving God – 70	
Blessing	**Solemn Prayer in BOS**				**14**
Dismissal	**Let us bless the Lord**	340	366		
Notes	Tenebrae is often used on this day (BOS 2022, 89–105)				

Content Resources

Reading Between the Lines

John reshapes the familiar story of Judas' betrayal to set in motion the decisive act in the cosmic conflict between God and evil. The story ends when Judas goes out into the night, aligned with the forces of darkness. In this account, perhaps the Beloved Disciple is a composite symbol for the Johannine community whose actions and discipleship mirror ways to follow Jesus.

At the outset, Jesus is "troubled in spirit" as an allusion not only to the pain of betrayal in the immediate context but also to 12:27, "Now is my soul troubled" (in the reading for Tuesday of Holy Week) when the Johannine equivalent of Gethsemane occurs. Normally fellowship and social bonds are cemented in a meal but here, betrayal takes place amongst friends. This reading acknowledges the agony of betrayal and locates it in Holy Week. Judas' betrayal is a means to glorify God.

At the meal Jesus inaugurates a series of "farewell discourses." See, for example, Moses (Deuteronomy 33); Paul (Acts 20:17–38); Stephen (Acts 7:2–60). John prepares the community for the death of Jesus through rereading earlier sayings. The Son of Man will be lifted up on the cross; but to the eyes of faith Jesus will be exalted into God's glory (12:32). Without diminishing its pain, John transforms the hour into an hour of celebration and victory (12:31–33).

John 13:31–32 is a typically dense Johannine statement. Perhaps it is best to take the 'now' in 13:31 as referring to the whole event which has arrived. 'And God is glorified in him' means that in this event God will be glorified because Jesus will be bringing his mission to completion. Later Jesus will pray: 'Father, the hour has come. Glorify your Son that the Son may glorify you' (17:2) and 'I have glorified you on earth…(17:4). On the cross he will declare: 'It is finished' (19:30).13:32 continues the same interwoven thought through mutuality: the Son glorifies the Father. The Father glorifies the Son. Again, the prayer in John 17 sheds further light on what is being said: 'And now, Father, glorify me with the glory I used to have with you before the world was' (17:5). The Father glorifies the Son 'with himself', that is, with the glory which is the divine presence.

The Son will seem to enter darkness, but this is the pathway through which God will surround him with God's glory. 13:31–32 affirms Jesus' knowledge of this. That is why John can also say that already in his life we saw God's glory (1:14). Jesus' suffering *is* his glory. Similarly, in 13:33 Jesus asserts, "Little children, I am with you only a little longer. You will look for me; and as I said to the Jews so now I say to you, 'Where I am going, you cannot come.'" This exact phrase occurs in 7:34 and 8:21 to describe people looking for and seeking an elusive Jesus, captured in the betrayal and arrest of the passion narrative (18:7–8).

Central Themes

Our gospel reading for today was a beloved one for the ancient Celtic Christians. They appropriated the figure of "the beloved disciple" from John's narrative to be a stand-in for each Christian follower of God. Thus, we are to be as close to Jesus as the beloved is in this scene – so close that he can hear his heartbeat. In contrast, Judas is walking away from the table, walking into the darkness of night. How can we stay close to our beloved Jesus and hear the very heartbeat of Christ?

A paceline is a strategy in the endurance sport of cycling. Riders get behind each other. The leader sets the pace cycling for a period of time until they peel off falling to last position. The second rider takes up lead position and the task of keeping pace. And this continues until riders decide to break away. This form of drafting can improve all riders' efficiency up to 30 percent. The effects of drag would significantly hold any single rider back. Perhaps the Cloud of Witnesses functions in this way by lessening the drag caused by the trials of this world.

The BOS offers a Tenebrae service that is often used on the Wednesday of Holy Week. The worship, which begins with the lighting of fifteen candles, includes psalms, readings, and responses. One by one, fourteen of the candles are extinguished, as the shadows (*tenebrae* in Latin) deepen. The last candle, symbolizing Christ, remains lit. Though hidden for a time during the ceremony, it is later restored, a reminder of Christ's triumph.

Engaging All Ages

Sometimes one of the hardest things to do is to forgive someone when that person has hurt us or our loved ones. When someone close betrays your trust or takes away hope, you can experience many different things: anger, sadness, distance, despair, uncertainty, exhaustion, and more. Is there someone who hurt you that you need to forgive today? Or is there someone you have hurt and to whom you need to offer a peace and love-filled apology? We are "surrounded by so great a cloud of witnesses" that in our faith we are able to "lay aside every weight" through Jesus (Hebrews 12:1). How can you lay aside the weight of hurt?

Hymns for the Day

The Hymnal 1982

Alone thou goest forth, O Lord 164
Bread of heaven, on thee we feed 323
Let thy blood in mercy poured 313
To mock your reign, O dearest Lord 170
Hail, thou once despised Jesus! 495
Lo! what a cloud of witnesses 545
The head that once was crowned with thorns 483
Ah, holy Jesus, how hast thou offended 158
Bread of the world, in mercy broken 301
O love, how deep, how broad, how high 448, 449

Maundy Thursday

Variable – The Thursday Prior to Easter Day

Just as I have loved you, you also should love one another.

Anchor Points – The Propers and the Day

The fixed points for each service are the appointed or proper readings and collect as well as the themes of the day or season.

Readings and Psalm

Exodus 12:1–4 (5–10), 11–14

In our first reading instructions are given, and the meaning of the Passover meal is told: it is a remembrance and reenactment of Israel's beginnings as a people when they were saved out of slavery in Egypt. The details indicate that several different traditions stand behind the Passover memorial. Perhaps it was the Israelites' attempts to keep ancient spring rites, derived from their shepherding and agricultural backgrounds, which caused the Egyptians to persecute them. With these traditions the story of God's judgment on Egypt and victory for God's people has become richly entwined.

Psalm 116:1–2, 12–19

An offering of thanksgiving and praise by one who has been rescued from death.

1 Corinthians 11:23–26

In this lection Paul recalls the tradition he received concerning the supper of the Lord on the night he was betrayed. The apostle reminds the Corinthians, who have shown an alarming tendency to divide up into factions, of the message he first delivered to them. This meal is a remembrance and reenactment of the Lord's offering of himself and forming of the new covenant. It proclaims the Lord's saving death and looks forward to his coming.

John 13:1–17, 31b–35

Our gospel tells how Jesus washes his disciples' feet during his last meal with them. This action symbolizes the love and humility of Christ in stooping down to wash those whom he loves from their sins. He has set for them an example, for he must soon depart. His disciples are to be characterized by servant love for one another.

Collect

Almighty Father, whose dear Son, on the night before he suffered, instituted the Sacrament of his Body and Blood: Mercifully grant that we may receive it thankfully in remembrance of Jesus Christ our Lord, who in these holy mysteries gives us a pledge of eternal life; and who now lives and reigns with you and the Holy Spirit, one God, for ever and ever. *Amen.*

Proper Preface

Holy Week – Through Jesus Christ our Lord. For our sins he was lifted high upon the cross, that he might draw the whole world to himself; and, by his suffering and death, he became the source of eternal salvation for all who put their trust in him. (Rite II, BCP 379; Rite I BCP 346)

Pairings for this Day

See the table below for choices appointed and suggested for this day. Preferences are put in **bold**. Not all choices are suitable for all congregations or community, though, so consider these preferences as a starting point before making a decision about your own congregation.

	Maundy Thursday	Rite I	Rite II	EOW1	BOS 2022
Color	**Passiontide Red** *or* **Oxblood** *or* White *see* Preparing for Holy Week, above				
Entrance Rite	Customary *or* A Penitential Order; **penitential acclamation**	319 *or* 323	351, *or* 355	50	
Song of Praise/Kyrie	**Kyrie** ***or*** **Trisagion;** *or* Glory to God (Gloria in excelsis) *see* Preparing for Holy Week, above	324	356	34	
Collect		169	274; 221		
Creed	None; optional footwashing after homily	274	274		107
Prayers of the People	**Locally written**; options below; BCP forms	329	387–393	54–55	
Offertory Sentence	"Jesus said, 'I give you a new commandment, that you love one another. Just as I have loved you, you also should love one another.'" (John)	343–344	376–377		
Eucharistic Prayer		**1–333**	**A – 361**	1–57 *or* 2–60	
Proper Preface	Holy Week	346	379		
Breaking of the Bread (Fraction)	**"My flesh is food indeed" S 168, S 169;** Christ our Passover with Alleluias omitted *and/or* Agnus Dei	337	364; 407		
Postcommunion Prayer		339	**Almighty everliving God – 366**	Loving God – 70	
Blessing	**Solemn Prayer in BOS**				**14**
Dismissal	**Let us bless the Lord**	340	366		
Notes	Optional reservation of the Sacrament for Good Friday; optional stripping of the altar; *see additional notes*				108

Additional Notes:

Vestments/Color – See the section Preparing for Holy Week, above, for more consideration on choosing Red or White, emphasizing the triduum or emphasizing the institution of the Eucharist.

Foot-washing[1] – The Prayer Book provides for the "maundy," or foot-washing. This requires a good deal of planning. How many people will have their feet washed? Will they be chosen representatives, or should all who wish to come forward be invited to do so? The BOS counsels that the whole assembly should be invited to take part. The presider and assistants wash the feet of the first persons to come forward, and then invite those whose feet have been washed to begin washing the feet of those who come after them, setting up a pattern rotating through those gathered.

People need advance instruction about what to wear so that they will be prepared and not be embarrassed. Lay members of the planning committee can be particularly helpful in setting this up. Hymn 576 ("God is love"), Hymn 606 ("Where charity and love dwell"), Taizé or similar simple chants, or settings of the anthems given on pages 274–275 in the Prayer Book (such as those at S 344-S 347 in the Appendix to the Accompaniment Edition of *The Hymnal 1982*) are appropriately sung during the washing.

Altar Guild and acolytes can be very helpful in removing and emptying water basins and keeping fresh water and towels ready for use.

The BOS provides an optional introduction for foot-washing which may be adapted:

"Fellow servants of our Lord Jesus Christ: on the night before his death, Jesus set an example for his disciples by washing their feet, an act of humble service. He taught that strength and growth in the life of the Kingdom of God come not by power, authority, or even miracle, but by such lowly service.

Therefore, I invite you who share in the royal priesthood of Christ, to come forward, that we may recall whose servant we are by following the example of my Master. Come remembering his admonition that what will be done for us is also to be done by us to others, for 'a servant is not greater than his master, nor is one who is sent greater than the one who sent him. If you know these things, blessed are you if you do them.'"[2]

Reserving the Sacrament – Reserving the sacrament for Good Friday communion is not contingent upon having an altar of repose and keeping a watch. A parish

1 BOS 2022, 107.

2 BOS 2022, 107.

that does not wish to introduce these customs may simply reserve the sacrament in both kinds in some convenient place, such as a chapel or the sacristy, from which it can be brought before communion in the Good Friday liturgy. The priest or deacon may simply take the sacrament to this place after communion without ceremony. Other parishes will wish to carry the sacrament solemnly to an altar of repose, with lights, incense, and to the accompaniment of music (Hymns 329–330 and 331, "Now, my tongue the mystery telling" is traditional). A "watch" may be kept here until the Good Friday liturgy. Matthew 26:40–41, "Could you not watch with me one hour? Watch and pray that you may not enter into temptation . . ." is usually given as the biblical warrant. In some places, a prayer vigil is kept instead from the end of the Good Friday liturgy to the beginning of the Easter Vigil, imitating the watch set before the tomb. Whether or not your congregation does either of these, it is certainly appropriate to encourage people to come to the church to pray during the period between Maundy Thursday and Easter. If the church is not usually left open, this can require a little planning to ensure the safety of people and property.

The Stripping of the Altar[3] – This optional action originated in the preparation for Good Friday, to create a bare, austere space for that liturgy. As far back as the middle ages, it became ritualized and made a public ceremony. It can be a powerful experience to engage the congregation in the careful removal of the hangings and liturgical vessels and objects.

"*If the custom of stripping the altar is observed as a public ceremony, it takes place after the Maundy Thursday liturgy. It may be done in silence; or it may be accompanied by the recitation of Psalm 22, which is said with Gloria Patri. The following antiphon may be said before and after the psalm:* 'They divide my garments among them; they cast lots for my clothing.'"

If Psalm 22 is used, it is suggested to assign it to a sole reader or cantor, so that the attention of the congregation is on witnessing the action of preparing the space for Good Friday.

Agapé Meal[4] – Another option is to incorporate a meal following the Maundy Thursday service. The BOS has guidelines for the order of the meal and the simple foods that would be appropriate, saying "The setting should be austere and the foods sparse and simple." There are suggested blessings for the wine, the bread, and other foods. It is important that this meal not be a festive meal, since the Lenten fast is not yet ended, nor should it attempt to replicate a seder meal.

3 BOS 2022, 108.
4 BOS 2022, 109–110.

Some congregations have further adapted the idea of including a meal in the Maundy Thursday service by setting the Liturgy of the Word The lessons, sermon, and foot-washing all take place in the setting of a simple congregational meal (with menu items not unlike the Agapé Meal), often in another space, such as the Parish Hall. At the Peace, the congregation moves to the church for Eucharist, Reservation of the Sacrament, and the Stripping of the Altar (if those latter two options are used).

Content Resources

Reading Between the Lines

Jesus, in full knowledge of his impending death and to prepare them for his departure, washes the reclining (13:12, 23) disciples' feet as a slave would during a shared meal to model hospitality, love, and service for their community. This action and interpretation serve to introduce the farewell discourses of John's gospel, and this action at the outset is intentionally paradigmatic. Washing disciples' feet in this manner not only enables the disciples' full recognition of who Jesus is, and of their obligations of servanthood to each other, but also, since it includes mention of Judas' evil act (13:2, 10), anticipates Jesus' betrayal and passion. Peter's objections recognize that Jesus' actions subvert hierarchal relations and replace them with more egalitarian notions of friendship. Thus, celebrating Passover together facilitates the disciples' growing awareness of changed relationships amongst themselves, foreshadowing of their ministries to subvert social domination patterns, and recognition of Jesus' death.

Jesus' explanation of his actions involves a different order of awareness underlying these discourses. After all, Jesus in John is the Word made flesh and the "one from heaven" (3.13). Jesus stresses understanding an inversion of titles and their implied power, using a beatitude to stress the importance of the action (v. 12–17). His foot washing of Judas includes anticipation of Judas' actions as evil and are part of Jesus' foresight and prophetic role (v. 20).

Central Themes

I recently saw a social media post that read, "What would you do if you knew your time here was limited? Jesus washed people's feet." I think that is a poignant message for those of us who know the heartbreaking end to his last night with his friends. His time was almost up, and he chose to give them an intimate action of love and service. We are left wondering, would I do the same?

What can a touch convey? A lover's kiss. A mother's and baby's cheeks caressing. A light pinch. A tight gripping of the wrist. In the past in France and England, it was believed that kings could heal the sick with a touch. Bishops lay hands on deacons, priests, and bishops, passing on the apostolic succession. Jesus touches feet and passes on power. Not from this titled person to the next titled person. Not power passed from old authority to newly ordained authority. Acts of service are the conduits by which God's power is passed from person to person.

Maundy Thursday worship often includes two poignant ceremonies: foot washing, recalling Christ's action at the Last Supper; and stripping of the altar, in preparation for the Good Friday liturgy. In many churches, both laity and clergy play a part. The increasingly frequent practice of each person both receiving and giving the foot washing embodies a mutuality of service that speaks volumes. Some congregations engage as many participants as possible in stripping the altar, demonstrating the community work of being the church.

Engaging All Ages

Today we celebrate with food. We read about the first Passover, a meal still celebrated in Judaism, and then hear the story of Jesus and his friends eating a final meal together. These were both special meals and special times for people to gather. They are two of the ways that we share love with one another. During dinner, Jesus got up and showed his friends how much he loved them by washing their feet. Find a special way to tell people how much you them today: washing feet, making a meal, drawing a picture, or more.

Prayers of the People: Option 1

Lord God, you are both host and servant at this meal and in our lives. Teach us, we pray, to follow your example of love, hospitality and service.

In your mercy, Lord,

hear our prayer.

We pray for your church, broken in many ways. We wait on your guidance and nourishment for our lives, for encouragement and strength for your mission.

In your mercy, Lord,

hear our prayer.

We pray for our leaders, responsible for shaping our common life, that they may lead us in ways of justice and peace.

In your mercy, Lord,

hear our prayer.

We pray for those who struggle to find food and shelter tonight, who hunger for peace, who ache for warmth and friendship. Heal broken hearts and spirits. Envelop the sick with your healing embrace. We pray for those who know the pain of betrayal, and for those who face death today.

In your mercy, Lord,

hear our prayer.

We leave this place singing hymns of love. Embed them in our lives that we may teach others to sing. We follow you into the garden, into the unknown, teach us to trust the lessons of this night.

In your mercy, Lord,

hear our prayer.

Prayers of the People: Option 2[5]

Deacon

Gracious God, in Jesus Christ you feed us and serve us with your very Life. Help us feed and serve the world in your name, by our prayers and by our witness, by the choices we make and by the actions we take. By your grace, we begin here and now, praying for all whom you love, asking you to hear our prayer.

Intercessor

For the Church, that we may remember the one whom we serve, and the cost of his service to us. Make us cleansing waters and healing balm to the prisoner, the captive, the poor, and all in need.

God, in your mercy, ***hear our prayer.***

For those given charge of the welfare of nations. May they remember that the leader is one who serves. We pray for own president and cabinet, for the congress, for the leaders of our city, and for all who govern.

God, in your mercy, ***hear our prayer.***

For those who must make hard moral choices, who hold the lives of others in their hands. For doctors and nurses and rescue workers; for ethicists and lawmakers.

God, in your mercy, ***hear our prayer.***

For those whose feet are dirty because they have no shoes, whose hearts are broken because they have no hope. For those who own only the clothes on their backs. For those without homes and for those who are alone.

God, in your mercy, ***hear our prayer.***

---

5 Adapted from prayers originally composed by the Rev. Dr. James W. Farwell for the Chapel of the Good Shepherd of The General Theological Seminary, New York, NY, c. 2006.

For those for whom life is hard. For those whose minds are not clear. For those in harm's way, especially soldiers and civilians in places of war and strife around the world. For all those in mortal danger.

God, in your mercy, ***hear our prayer.***

For those who are sick and all those in any other need. We pray for all those we now name. *Silence*

God, in your mercy, ***hear our prayer.***

For those who mourn and all whose lives have been taken by the hand of others. Grant us both the courage to seek justice, and the strength to forgive.

God, in your mercy, ***hear our prayer.***

For those who have died, for all those whose memory will live in the members of this community. For all others who have died, whom we now name. *Silence*

By the power of Christ who died our death, may they know the power of everlasting life.

God, in your mercy, ***hear our prayer.***

The prayers conclude with this collect.

Presider

God of Jesus Christ: Teach us to serve all people in your name. By your Spirit's power, make us light, to dispel the darkness of sorrow and sin. Break us and make us bread for the world. Sustain us through the night of suffering and speed the coming of your kingdom, when the servant will be known as the Lord of all and love will forever abound; through Jesus Christ our Lord. ***Amen.***

Hymns for the Day

The Hymnal 1982

Go to dark Gethsemane 171
What wondrous love is this 439
Now, my tongue, the mystery telling 329, 330, 331
When Jesus died to save us 322
Zion, praise thy Savior, singing 320
Thou, who at thy first Eucharist didst pray 315

Lift Every Voice and Sing II

In remembrance of me, eat this bread 149
This is my body given for you 155
Do this in remembrance of me 272

Wonder, Love, and Praise

O wheat whose crushing was for bread 760
As in that upper room you left your seat 729, 730
Three holy days enfold us now 731, 732, 733
You laid aside your rightful reputation 734

At the footwashing:

The Hymnal 1982

God is Love, and where true love is 576, 577
Where charity and love prevail 581
Where true charity and love dwell 606
Jesu, Jesu, fill us with your love 602

Lift Every Voice and Sing

Jesu, Jesu, fill us with your love 74

Wonder, Love, and Praise

Ubi caritas et amor 831

At the stripping of the altar:

Wonder, Love, and Praise

Stay with me 826

Good Friday

Variable – The Friday Prior to Easter Day

We adore you, O Christ, and we bless you,
because by your holy cross you have redeemed the world.

Anchor Points – The Propers and the Day

The fixed points for each service are the appointed or proper readings and collect as well as the themes of the day or season.

Readings and Psalm

Isaiah 52:13–53:12

Our opening lesson is the poem of the Lord's servant who suffers and bears the sins of many. The passage is the fourth and last of the "servant songs" that form a portion of the Book of Isaiah written when the exile was coming to an end. The servant is sometimes thought to be a historical individual or is understood as an idealization of the faithful of Israel. This "man of sorrows," who was "despised and rejected," "wounded for our transgressions," and one whom the Lord at last vindicates, is perceived by Christians to be a prefigurement of Jesus.

Psalm 22

A psalm of lamentation and a plea for deliverance by one who feels deserted and pressed in on every side, expressing final confidence in God and God's goodness.

Hebrews 10:16–25

In this reading we hear that God has established the promised new covenant through which our sins are forgiven and God's laws are written on our hearts. Given such confidence, we are to be unswerving in our hope and strong in our encouragement of one another.

or

Hebrews 4:14–16; 5:7–9

In our New Testament reading we are encouraged to have full confidence in drawing near to God because Jesus, our great high priest, knows our every weakness and temptation and makes intercession for us. Having learned obedience through suffering, he has become the source of salvation for all who obey him.

John 18:1–19:42

Our gospel is the story of Jesus's trials before the Jewish council and Pilate, followed by his final sufferings and death.

Collect

Almighty God, we pray you graciously to behold this your family, for whom our Lord Jesus Christ was willing to be betrayed, and given into the hands of sinners, and to suffer death upon the cross; who now lives and reigns with you and the Holy Spirit, one God, for ever and ever. *Amen.*

Proper Preface

There is no Eucharist celebrated on this day, so there is no proper preface appointed.

Pairings for this Day

See the table below for choices appointed and suggested for this day. Preferences are put in **bold.** Not all choices are suitable for all congregations or community, though, so consider these preferences as a starting point before making a decision about your own congregation.

	Good Friday	Rite I	Rite II	EOW1	BOS 2022
Color	**Passiontide Red** *or* **Oxblood** *or* None				
Entrance Rite	Enter in silence; kneel for silent prayer				
Song of Praise/Kyrie	None				
Collect	Optional opening dialogue prior to the collect	169	276; 221		
Creed	None; optional hymn after Sermon				
Prayers of the People	The Solemn Collects	277	277		
Conclusion A	Hymn after Solemn Collects, Lord's Prayer, Final Prayer	280, 282	280, 282		
Conclusion B	Veneration of the Cross, Lord's Prayer, and Final Prayer	281–282	281–282		
Conclusion C	[Optional Veneration of Cross,] Confession of Sin, Lord's Prayer, Communion from Reserved Sacrament, Final Prayer	281–282	281–282		
Notes	Stations of the Cross are ***not suited*** to take the place of the Good Friday liturgy				52

Additional Notes:

Concerns about anti-Semitism in the rite – Concerns about the impact of Good Friday on anti-Semitism have a long history. Traditional practices such as The Reproaches, a Good Friday devotional dialogue that includes in its history grossly anti-Semitic language and imagery, was considered for inclusion in the 1979 *Book of Common Prayer*, but was delated at the 1976 General Convention. There have been attempts at recovering this practice and revising it to avoid such language, such as in the Canadian *Book of Alternative Services,* but it is a practice that is difficult to divorce from its history.

Continuing concerns have been voiced regarding a few aspects in the 1979 BCP Good Friday liturgy, but most particularly about repeated references in John's Passion Gospel to "the Jews," and the historical impact of that gospel on Christian-Jewish relations. Important questions about alternative translations have resulted in an effort to revise the liturgy as well as provide an alternative form of the John passage for this service. General Convention 2022 considered material submitted, based primarily on the work of Dr. Daniel Joslyn-Siemiatkoski, a professor at the Seminary of the Southwest at that time. Some bishops have authorized the proposed material in their dioceses.[1] The material is not yet authorized generally, however.

Vestments/Color – The color of the day, typically, is Red, as is the rest of Holy Week, though some will opt for no color at all in a bare space. The celebrant may wear a cope, alb (or surplice), and stole, or eucharistic vestments. Assisting clergy and acolytes wear their usual vestments, albs or cassock, and surplice. Some use eucharistic vestments only if administering communion on this day and opt for office vestments (cassock, surplice), if communion is not distributed. These are matters for local custom, typically.

Some prefer to conduct the service only wearing a black cassock without surplice, creating an austere visual that suggests that the color is black. However, that choice is simply opting for no vestment and no color (since the cassock is originally equivalent to street dress). That custom on this day derives from the "Tre Ore" (The Three Hours) practice, which used cassocks because it was not a liturgical service, but an extended time of reflection, and so vestments were not worn. Therefore the clergy wearing only a cassock, their "street clothes," are not vested. This custom does not make sense when followed at the liturgy.

Entrance Rite – The service begins in silence. An optional opening dialogue may precede the Collect of the Day or the officiant may simply begin the collect, after silent prayer, kneeling.

Music Choices – There are several special options for hymns. A hymn may follow the Sermon; a hymn may follow the Solemn Collects (if concluding the service at that point); the hymn "Sing my tongue, the glorious battle" or a hymn extolling the glory of the cross may follow the Veneration of the Cross, if that option is used. There is no entrance hymn, nor closing hymn appointed.

Essential Elements – Only two primary elements of this rite are required: ***the Passion Gospel and the Solemn Collects***. The Veneration of the Cross is optional and not necessarily suited for every congregation; Communion from the Reserved Sacrament is optional and not necessarily suited for every congregation.

1 Information on the proposed material may be found at "Lenten Resources 2022" The Episcopal Diocese of Texas https://www.epicenter.org/article/lenten-resources-2022/, accessed March 29, 2023; also at "Good Friday Alternative Rite" The Episcopal Diocese of Central New York https://cnyepiscopal.org/wp-content/uploads/2021/03/good-friday-alternative-rite-d.-joslyn-siemiatkoski.zip, accessed March 29, 2023.

The Passion Gospel – The Passion from John's Gospel may be read dramatically or sung. It may be desirable to handle it differently from the synoptic Passion read on Palm Sunday. Whatever decision is made, both for today and Palm Sunday, the purpose is to proclaim Christ crucified, not to have a beautiful experience. The sermon follows the Passion immediately and is obviously a major proclamation of the day's theme.

The Solemn Collects – The Solemn Collects are an extended form of the Prayers of the People. Whether they are sung or said, the pattern is for a deacon or layperson to bid the prayers of the congregation, including any of the petitions provided or adapting others, depending on current prayer concerns. After a pause for prayer, the presider prays the collect. The ancient tradition was to have the bidder invite the people to kneel for each bidding and then, after silent prayer, invite them to stand for the collect. This really does involve a lot of getting up and down, which may be distracting. Many, probably most, congregations direct the people either to stand or to kneel throughout the Solemn Collects.

Optional Veneration of the Cross – A cross large enough to be easily visible should be used. The provided anthems may be sung or said (*The Hymnal 1982* Appendix, S 349-S 351). During this time, the congregation may remain in place, kneeling before the large wooden cross. In some places, individuals may come forward to venerate the cross, depending on congregational custom and culture. The suggested hymn, "Sing, my tongue the glorious battle," is found at Hymns 165 and 166 in *The Hymnal 1982* and at S 352 in the appendix. If Communion from the Reserved Sacrament is administered, it is usually retrieved from the Altar of Repose during the hymn.

Optional Communion from the Reserved Sacrament – This is also called the Liturgy of the Presanctified Gifts, in some places. If communion is to be administered, the sacrament is brought simply to the altar, the confession and Lord's Prayer said, and communion administered in the usual way, making use of the customary ministers of communion. It is customary that all reserved sacrament is consumed during this service, if this option is used, and the Sanctuary Light (Presence Lamp) is extinguished. It is left to the pastoral judgment of the priest whether a small remainder be kept in emergency reserve, away from the worship space, for extreme unction, should the need arise prior to the first Eucharist of Easter. The altar is stripped after communion, and, following the single, final prayer given in the Prayer Book, the altar party leaves in silence. There is no additional blessing or dismissal.

Content Resources

Reading Between the Lines

Some years ago, Fr. Raymond Brown described the narrative of Jesus' trial in John's gospel thus: Jesus is so eloquent and self-assured that we are left to conclude that it is Pilate who is put on trial to see whether he is of the truth. It's not Jesus who fears Pilate, it is Pilate who is afraid of Jesus the Son of God. The real question is not what will happen to Jesus who controls his own destiny, but whether Pilate will betray himself by acceding to the outcry of the very people he is supposed to be governing.

Social scientific commentary by Jerome Neyrey notes that crucifixion is shameful but Jesus' suffering in John's Gospel is seen as a way to elevate his status. For example, although capture and arrest normally denotes dishonor, John 18 shows Jesus demonstrating power and control; in John 18:4 Jesus steps forward to take charge of the situation to meet the advancing detachment of soldiers. In 18:6 Jesus responds to their inquiry, "I am he," at which point the soldiers draw back and fall to the ground leaving Jesus alone standing. Readers of John know that Jesus is declaring his divine identity, thus causing involuntary prostration (Craig S. Keener).

Honor is signaled by bodily posture: Jesus' control of the situation extends even to his command about the safe departure of his disciples, "Let these others go." (18:8). Weak people do not tell a cohort of Roman soldiers what to do. Jesus knows what will happen, he asks questions, he controls the events by giving commands and thus might well receive profound respect from his opponents. He is without doubt the most honorable person in the situation. Nevertheless, Jesus is crucified by means of collusion between Jewish leaders in Jerusalem (18:30,35) through Judas, and Pilate himself (19:16), although Jesus delivers his own life (19:30). In this Jesus demonstrates courage, an esteemed quality of the time. Finally, women at the cross, including Jesus' mother alongside the Beloved Disciple supplant the other disciples and Peter who have denied Jesus or fled. From the cross Jesus entrusts Mary to the Beloved Disciple (19:26–7), thus creating a new household.

Central Themes

Jesus was given an immensely costly burial. Joseph of Arimathea, who is called a "secret disciple," gives him a new grave hewn out of the rock. Not only would have this been extremely expensive, it also meant that he would never be able to use it for himself because the first person buried in a tomb would dictate whose family could be buried there. On top of that, Nicodemus, who was also not a public follower of Jesus, gave a "mixture of myrrh and aloes, weighing about a hundred pounds." This gift would have also been unbelievably expensive. But costly too was the act of giving Jesus such a burial for men who were effectively risking their lives to do so. How can we honor Jesus's death and life even if it is costly for us?

There is a video online, *Ted Neeley – Gethsemane* (New York 2006). Forty years after the film *Jesus Christ Superstar*, Neeley reprises his role. Jesus stands robed in white against a black backdrop. In the Garden of Gethsemane the reality of what is to come sets in. Jesus sings, "If there is a way / Take this cup away from me." The song rises in crescendo with agony, anguish, and confusion. Ultimately, falling in resignation, he sings, "God, thy will is hard." It is impassioned incarnation of the deeply human experience of Jesus that we are called to live into on Good Friday.

The Book of Occasional Services stresses that the Proper Liturgy for Good Friday must not be displaced by the service of the Way of the Cross (or Stations of the Cross). Particularly on Good Friday, some congregations, especially those in urban areas, make a point of taking the Way of the Cross into the streets around the church. Some mark the stations at places where violence has occurred. Making connections with the neighborhoods where churches are located can be a way of acknowledging a community's pain and building relationships for healing.

Engaging All Ages

Today is a sad and solemn day in the life of Jesus. On Good Friday, we read the story of Jesus's final hours. It can be hard to talk about or think about, but today, remember that Jesus died, offering himself as a sacrifice in an ultimate act of love for all of us. It can be confusing because many people are both very sad and very grateful. At dinner tonight, can you keep the lights low as we remember solemnly the death of Jesus, while at the same time you make space to offer prayers of love and thanks to Jesus?

Prayers of the People

The Solemn Collects are the appointed form for the intercessions on this day.

Hymns for the Day

Note: There is no Entrance Hymn on this day (see BCP, 276).

The Hymnal 1982

To mock your reign, O dearest Lord 170
Alone thou goest forth, O Lord 164
Cross of Jesus, cross of sorrow 160
From God Christ's deity came forth 443
There is a green hill far away 167

Lift Every Voice and Sing

He never said a mumbalin' word 33

Hymns Appropriate for Singing after the Sermon

The Hymnal 1982

Ah, holy Jesus, how hast thou offended 158
O sacred head, sore wounded 168, 169
At the cross her vigil keeping 159
Go to dark Gethsemane 171
Morning glory, starlit sky 585
Were you there when they crucified my Lord? 172

Lift Every Voice and Sing

O sacred head, sore wounded 36
Every time I think about Jesus 32
They crucified my Lord 33
Were you there when they crucified my Lord? 37 (1–3)

Wonder, Love, and Praise

O sacred head, sore wounded 735
When Jesus came to Golgotha 736

Hymns Appropriate for Singing before the Cross

The Hymnal 1982

In the cross of Christ I glory 441, 442
Sing, my tongue the glorious battle 165,166
When I survey the wondrous cross 474

Lift Every Voice and Sing

Jesus, keep me near the cross 29
On a hill far away stood an old rugged cross 38

Wonder, Love, and Praise

Faithful cross, above all other 737

Hymns Appropriate for Singing after the Solemn Collects

The Hymnal 1982

Lord Christ, when first thou cam'st to earth 598
O sacred head, sore wounded 168, 169
Sunset to sunrise changes now 163
Were you there when they crucified my Lord? 172

Lift Every Voice and Sing

King of my life I crown thee now 31
O how he loves you and me 35
There is a fountain filled with blood 39
Were you there when they crucified my Lord? 37 (1–3)
When on the cross of Calvary 34

Wonder, Love, and Praise

O sacred head, sore wounded 735

Holy Saturday

Variable – The Day Prior to Easter Day

In the garden there was a new tomb in which no one had ever been laid

Anchor Points – The Propers and the Day

The fixed points for each service are the appointed or proper readings and collect as well as the themes of the day or season.

Readings and Psalm

Job 14:1–14

Job reflects on the brevity of human life. Nature may renew itself but not mortals who have but an impossible hope that they might meet God after the grave.

or

Lamentations 3:1–9, 19–24

Our first reading is a poem of lamentation and complaint from one who feels besieged by God and circumstance, yet chooses to affirm the steadfast love of the Lord and a belief that confidence in God is ultimately well placed.

Psalm 31:1–4, 15–16

A song of trust by one who looks to the Lord for mercy and protection.

1 Peter 4:1–8

Believers are encouraged to live lives devoted to the will of God, steering clear of all forms of dissipation. Because Christ has suffered in the flesh, his followers must be willing to do likewise, disciplining themselves for the goal of life in the spirit. Of primary importance is the practice of love for one another.

Matthew 27:57–66

A man of privilege and a disciple, Joseph of Arimathea, wraps the body of Jesus in clean linen and places the corpse in his own newly hewn tomb. Other disciples of Jesus witness the burial. Jesus's religious opponents appeal to Pilate to place a guard at the tomb lest Jesus's disciples steal his body, and Pilate gives them permission to seal the tomb.

or

John 19:38–42

Nicodemus and Joseph of Arimathea prepare Jesus's body for burial according to custom, interring Jesus's corpse in a new tomb in a garden where nobody had previously been laid.

Collect

O God, Creator of heaven and earth: Grant that, as the crucified body of your dear Son was laid in the tomb and rested on this holy Sabbath, so we may await with him the coming of the third day, and rise with him to newness of life; who now lives and reigns with you and the Holy Spirit, one God, for ever and ever. *Amen.*

Proper Preface

There is no Eucharist celebrated on this day, so there is no proper preface appointed.

Pairings for this Day

See the table below for choices appointed and suggested for this day. Preferences are put in **bold**. Not all choices are suitable for all congregations or community, though, so consider these preferences as a starting point before making a decision about your own congregation.

	Holy Saturday	Rite I	Rite II	EOW1	BOS 2022
Color	**Passiontide Red** *or* **Oxblood** *or* None				
Entrance Rite	None; begins with Collect of the Day				
Song of Praise/Kyrie	None				
Collect		170	283; 221		
Creed	None				
Prayers of the People	"In the midst of life" is sung or said	484	492		
	There is no celebration of the Eucharist today, so no Offertory Sentence, Eucharistic Prayer, Proper Preface, Breaking of the Bread, Postcommunion Prayer				
Conclusion	Lord's Prayer and the Grace	283	283		
Notes					

Additional Notes:

Vestments/Colors – The traditional color continues to be Red, as part of Holy Week, though there are often few hangings or vestments visible to reflect that color. This is a very brief liturgy and vestments may or may not even be used. If vestments are worn, Office vestments are appropriate (cassock, surplice, and optional tippet), though often cassock, surplice, red stole or alb and red stole are worn.

Entrance/Exit Rite – No provision is given for an entrance or closing hymn. The liturgy simply begins with the Collect of the Day and concludes with the Grace.

Context – Some congregations will begin the rehearsal for the Easter Vigil and/or the work day to prepare for Easter with this liturgy, with those already gathered. Clearly identifying this service as a Holy Week liturgy and **not** an Easter liturgy is important, especially for congregations that celebrate the Great Vigil of Easter later that day, on Easter Eve.

Content Resources

Reading Between the Lines

In the Parecclesion of Chora Church, Istanbul, now Kariye Mosque, a 14 Century Anastasis fresco commissioned by Metochites, a wealthy Orthodox Byzantine aristocrat, depicts an eastern version of the Harrowing of Hell on Holy Saturday. A risen Christ conquers Satan pulling Adam and Eve by their hands upwards out of the realms of the dead. This tradition is mentioned in 1 Peter 4:6.

The tradition of Holy Saturday is that it is a day spent in silence and it is one of the few places in the Prayer Book where the homily is optional. It might be wise to receive the Scripture readings in silence.

Prayers of the People

The burial rite anthem "In the midst of life" is sung or said in place of the Prayers of the People on this day.

Hymns for the Day

The Hymnal 1982

My song is love unknown 458 (1–2, 7)
Christ, whose glory fills the skies 6, 7
God of mercy, God of grace 538
How wondrous and great thy works, God of praise! 532, 533
Beneath the cross of Jesus 498
Cross of Jesus, cross of sorrow 160
In the cross of Christ I glory 441, 442
Nature with open volume stands 434
We sing the praise of him who died 471
When I survey the wondrous cross 474
I heard the voice of Jesus say 692
I want to walk as a child of the Light 490
O Jesus, I have promised 655
The great Creator of the worlds 489
When Christ was lifted from the earth 603, 604

Lift Every Voice and Sing II

Jesus, keep me near the cross 28
On a hill far away stood an old rugged cross 38

Easter

Preparing for Easter

The Great Vigil of Easter celebrates our Lord's passage from death to life and our participation in that victory through the paschal mystery. The sacraments of baptism and eucharist are both the signs and the means of this participation, for in the Easter sacraments we go down into the grave with Christ and are raised with him to new and unending life with Christ in God. Lent and Holy Week are preparation for this passover. In the Vigil, we celebrate the Easter sacraments and as a people pass over with Christ from darkness to light, from penitence to rejoicing, from death to life. Throughout the Great Fifty Days, we celebrate Christ's passover and our own. The Vigil ushers in the Great Fifty Days. The service begins in Lent and ends in Easter. Easter itself is really both the eighth day of Holy Week, which cannot be planned or celebrated apart from it, and the first day of the Fifty Days we call the Easter season.

The Great Vigil of Easter

The Easter Vigil can be celebrated effectively with a small group of people, and if your parish has never done it before, you may wish to start small. But if it is planned as a second-class celebration, it will clearly not be seen as the principal liturgy of the year. Many parishes have decided to go "all out" to make the Vigil clearly something special. If your congregation does not celebrate the Easter Vigil, or if you are seeking to establish it, you may wish to send a team to experience it at a nearby church, before beginning your own planning.

What you need are musicians, readers, worshipers, preferably one or more candidates for baptism, and clergy. The Prayer Book says explicitly, "It is customary for all the ordained ministers present, together with lay readers, singers, and other persons, to take active parts in the service" (BCP, 284). Use not only the clergy but all of the liturgical resources available. Make it self-evidently the work of the worshiping congregation. It does not require great resources, but it does take all that you have.

Set a time between dark and sunrise. Congregations in areas where Easter sunrise services are typical may wish to begin the Vigil a half hour to an hour before sunrise, ending with the Eucharist in the clear light of Easter morning. This can be very effective, for congregations willing to rise early. Most places will choose an evening hour, especially if the candidates for baptism are infants. Decide how long you wish the service to last. This will be your primary consideration in choosing the number of readings. There are nine in the Prayer Book. At least two are required. The use of all nine, each followed by a homily, psalm, silence, and collect will produce an "all night" vigil. For a vigil of more moderate length, preach only one homily, after the Gospel (or any other reading), and reduce the number of readings. The reading from Exodus is always used, and a different selection of the others may be used each year. Four to six Old Testament readings are usual.

If at all possible, light the fire outdoors. Beginning the Vigil in a cloister or garden is both appropriate and effective. If there is a deacon, the deacon leads the congregation into the dark church carrying the Paschal Candle, the light of Christ scattering the darkness of night. If you have no deacon, then a priest does this. As the procession moves down the aisle, the entire congregation may be given candles lighted from the Easter fire and held during the Exsultet. If they are not needed for the worshipers to see, they may be put out during the readings and relit for the baptisms. The Exsultet deserves to be sung. If the deacon is not up to it, a choir member or cantor may sing it. Even if the deacon is not singing, they should still stand near the Paschal Candle.

The lessons may be read by individual lectors, read dramatically by groups, or presented in a number of ways that available talent and imagination may suggest. Use as many different lay people as possible. The psalm or canticle following the reading may be read or sung in any of the ways suggested for the psalm at the Eucharist. They need not all be done in the same manner. Some might be sung by the choir to more difficult or to anthem settings. If there are several priests participating in the Vigil, they share the reading of the collects among them.

The baptisms may take place either after the final Old Testament reading with its psalm and collect or in the usual place after the Gospel and sermon. Both choices have their advantages. If the baptistry is not at the front of the church, the Paschal Candle is taken from its stand

and carried at the head of the procession to the font. The Prayer for the Candidates (BCP, 305) may be sung as a processional litany. The Thanksgiving over the Water may also be sung. This is *the* appropriate occasion on which to sing it. Any priest and congregation that regularly, or occasionally, sings the sursum corda and eucharistic preface can sing the thanksgiving over the font. After the thanksgiving, the celebrant may sprinkle the congregation with the baptismal water as a sign of the renewal of their baptismal vows.

The Vigil is the most traditional time for adult baptisms. (The preparation of candidates during Lent was discussed previously on page 136). If you are unable to schedule any baptisms, at least bless the water to be a reminder of baptism and sprinkle the congregation with it after the renewal of vows.

If the font is not at the front of the church, additional flowers and Easter decorations may be brought into the sanctuary during the baptism so that they will be seen when the procession returns to the altar. Some parishes prefer to vest and decorate the altar during the Gloria in excelsis. Another possibility is to have the sanctuary decorated for Easter before the beginning of the Vigil but to keep it in darkness, except for the Paschal Candle, until the beginning of the Eucharist and then to turn on all of the lights at the Easter acclamation.

Make the Eucharist comparable to your festal Sunday services. Many parishes find it effective to introduce the organ only at the beginning of the Eucharist, using, for example, a guitar or a recorder to lead the music between the lessons during the first portion of the service. The Easter acclamation, "Alleluia. Christ is risen," followed by the singing of Gloria in excelsis or the Pascha nostrum, is the occasion for the pealing of the church bells, the sounding of the organ, and the breaking forth of Easter joy. Handbells, tambourines, and every conceivable instrument have been used to enhance the sense of entry into joy. The acclamation may be said from the baptistry, the procession returning to the sanctuary during the Gloria.

If the repeated alleluias and Psalm 114 are not sung between the epistle and Gospel, then an Easter hymn making ample use of "Alleluia" should be sung in its place. Have a Gospel procession, so that the Easter Gospel is seen and heard to be the climax of the many readings from Scripture. At least one parish uses a trumpet before the announcement of the Gospel to make this point. The sermon need not be long, but it must proclaim the good news of the Resurrection. Some follow a tradition of using St. John Chrysostom's Easter homily at the Great Vigil. If there are adult baptisms, the newly baptized may bring up the elements of bread and wine at the offertory. If there are infant baptisms, godparents of the newly baptized may do so.

It is important to include familiar Easter hymns in the Eucharist. At the offertory, during communion, after communion, and before the dismissal are obvious places. There are many places during the Vigil for the choir to "show its stuff," and singing a congregational hymn at the offertory instead of a choir anthem might reduce the strain on both choir and congregation. The service may conclude with the Easter seasonal blessing[1] and the dismissal with "Alleluia, alleluia" added to both the dismissal and the response.

A single priest, a song leader, two or three readers, and an enthusiastic congregation, no matter how small, can celebrate the Vigil with great effectiveness. It is better to plan something that you can do well than to try to do too much. But if you plan a celebration suitable for a congregation of fifty in a parish of five hundred communicants, people cannot be blamed for concluding that this is an optional extra for the pious and not the parish's *real* Easter celebration.

Most parishes will lack the resources to celebrate the Vigil "with all the stops pulled out" and then to attempt to do the same thing again on Easter morning. If this is the case, a policy decision is in order. Which service will get the greater share of our resources? Logically and theologically the Vigil should take precedence, but this may be practically and pastorally impossible, especially if the Great Vigil is not deeply embedded in parish tradition. Canonically, the decision is the rector's, but this is precisely the type of decision a parish worship committee is most useful in helping a priest to make. At the very least, they can share the heat for an unpopular decision, but at best they will be good judges of the parish climate and advocates of *good* liturgical change.

Easter Day

If we have avoided the danger of thinking too small in planning the Vigil, we must be wary of going too far in the opposite direction and making the services of Easter Day seem anticlimactic. There will be parishioners for whom the Eucharist on Easter Day is the occasion for an infrequent visit to the church. It is good evangelism to make them feel that something significant is going on in which they could be regular participants. There will also be regular churchgoers in whose background the Vigil has had no place and for whom the service on Easter morning is the significant religious event of the year. The Resurrection Gospel is, of course, the core of the Liturgy of the Word. The resurrection of Christ and the meaning of our participation in it is the obvious sermon topic. A reading from Acts may replace the Old

1 BOS 2022, 14–15.

Testament lesson today and does so throughout the Fifty Days. Singing familiar Easter hymns is an important way to involve the congregation. Exactly what hymns are used will, of course, vary from congregation to congregation. The parish worship committee may well be better able to identify them than either the rector or the organist. The service almost always will begin with a processional hymn. Incense, processional torches, banners, flags, or whatever says to that congregation, "This is an important occasion!" should be included. The celebrant may wear a cope if that is part of the parish tradition, and the procession may circle the church.

The Eucharist begins with the Easter acclamation. Two excellent alternatives to Gloria in excelsis for use on Easter morning are "This is the feast of victory for our God" (Hymn 417/418) or the Easter canticle "Christ our Passover" (S 16–20, Rite One; S 46–S 50, Rite Two). Alleluia is traditionally sung before the Gospel during Easter. An alleluia chant may be used in this place, or one of the many Easter hymns using alleluia as a refrain may be sung. One way to bind the season together is to use the same alleluia on all the Sundays of Easter. Have a Gospel procession, as described for the Vigil.

Some large parishes may have adult baptisms at the Vigil and infant baptism on Easter Day. The renewal of baptismal vows from the Vigil takes the place of the Nicene Creed. The *Lutheran Book of Worship* and the Methodist supplementary liturgical resource *From Ashes to Fire* recommend sprinkling the people with water from the baptismal font after they have renewed their vows. This is an appropriate ceremony to remind the congregation of their own baptisms, although it is not mentioned in the Prayer Book. A simple explanation of what the renewal of baptismal vows on Easter is all about as a part of the sermon can give people new insights not only into holy water but into the meaning of Easter and of baptism as well

Increasingly, parishes have felt that the general confession was inappropriate during the Easter festival and have omitted it throughout the Fifty Days, though the rubric permits omission only "on occasion."[2] If the entire congregation had participated in the liturgies of Lent and Holy Week, this would certainly be the proper choice. On the other hand, some congregations have felt it important to include the confession of sin in their Easter services to remind us all – especially those who did not participate in the Holy Week liturgies – that sharing in the Easter joy is not without cost. If the confession is omitted, it is helpful, at least on Easter Day, to use a form of the Prayers of the People that includes a petition for the forgiveness of our sins (such as form 1 or 5).

2 BCP, 330 and 359.

Any of the fraction anthems containing alleluia are suitable for Easter. "At the Lamb's high feast we sing" (Hymn 174) is an Easter eucharistic hymn suitable for use during or immediately following communion, although there are many other good choices.

The Fifty Days

The Great Fifty Days are the period of rejoicing in the Risen Lord between the Easter Vigil and Pentecost. During this season the Paschal Candle is lit at all services and "Alleluia" is sung on all possible occasions. The church is decorated festively. There is no fasting, and traditionally there was no kneeling (although that custom has fallen into disuse in most places). Traditionally, the liturgical color is white, except for the Day of Pentecost, although something can be said for the Sarum rule of using the "best" regardless of color. The church, like the congregation, should be dressed up.

A fixed feature of the Eastertide lectionary is that a lesson from Acts be included. During this season, it replaces the Old Testament reading, a distinctive Easter feature that focuses on the initial post-resurrection Christian community.

The parish worship committee may also consider other ways of marking the unity of the Fifty Days. The same fraction anthem, for example, may be sung every Sunday. The congregation can stand for the eucharistic prayer and to receive communion, if they regularly kneel, reviving the directive of the Council of Nicea forbidding kneeling during Eastertide. *Weekday Eucharistic Propers*[3] contains collects and readings for the weekdays of the Easter season. In many churches, images of the saints are veiled during Lent (and in some places, saints' days are not observed during Lent) because the saints are signs of Christ's triumph and resurrection. Conversely, during Eastertide, it is even more appropriate to celebrate and mark those saints' days and their stories (though they cannot be substituted for a Sunday during this season).

Rogation Days

Monday, Tuesday, and Wednesday before Ascension Day are the traditional Rogation Days, although the Prayer Book recognizes the possibility of celebrating them at another time. Their traditional themes are the planting of crops and prayer for their increase. *The Book of Common Prayer 1979* provides three sets of propers: for fruitful seasons, for commerce and industry, and for stewardship

3 *Weekday Eucharistic Propers* (New York, NY: Church Publishing, 2017).

of creation. The Rogation Days have no direct connection with the Fifty Days. It is simply that spring planting occurs at this time in northern Europe. A procession through the fields of the parish, blessing the fields, was the original English way of celebrating the Rogation. The BOS 2022 has directions for a Rogation procession (p. 113) that may be held on a weekday, concluding with the Eucharist, or on a Sunday afternoon as a separate service. In a rural parish in which the parishioners plant crops, this can be an important observance, but it should be scheduled according to the agricultural not the liturgical calendar. In more urban settings, some congregations have adapted this as a procession through their neighborhood, stopping at shops and businesses and asking if they can offer a prayer or a blessing for the business before continuing the procession.

Ascension Day

Ascension Day never falls earlier than April 30 nor later than June 3. Sunset is typically late and the weather is mild. It is a much-neglected opportunity and is almost tailor-made for an evening service. It can also be the occasion for a parish supper, which is one way to improve attendance on a weekday evening. In many parts of the country, the climate lends itself to the first outdoor service of the season and a picnic supper.

It is important to plan for Ascension Day as a principal feast. Planning small will almost inevitably produce commensurate results. The Ascension Day hymns – such as "See the Conqueror mounts in triumph" (Hymn 215), "Hail the day that sees him rise" (Hymn 214), or "Alleluia! sing to Jesus" (Hymn 460/461) – are among the most singable and popular of our hymns. People should be given an opportunity to sing them. That means planning a service with music. Often the simple expedient of proposing this well ahead of time to the choir, with the suggestion that the choir be the parish's guests at the supper and have their rehearsal afterward, will transform them into eager allies instead of reluctant participants.

The place to begin the actual planning for the service is, as always, with the lectionary. Liturgical planning for a specific service always begins with the appointed lessons. Then it enlarges its concerns to deciding among the various options provided by the Prayer Book and the specific concerns and requirements of the congregation and the occasion. Ascension Day is a part of the Great Fifty Days of Easter, and whatever seasonal planning has been done is a part of your context for the planning of the Ascension Day Eucharist.

The former custom of extinguishing the Paschal Candle after the Gospel on Ascension Day has been rethought and set aside in most places. The candle is a unitive symbol of the resurrection, which continues through the season, rather than a representational symbol of Christ's bodily presence. The candle is now indicated to burn during the entire Fifty Days of Easter[4] and is extinguished and moved to the baptistry only after the last service on the Day of Pentecost. It can then be lighted for baptisms and brought out for funerals throughout the year.

Even though you are planning a major service for Ascension Day, it is still a workday evening. Simplicity of music and congregational participation are high priorities. This does not mean that you should leave out marks of festivity in your congregation, whether they be incense and deacons in dalmatics or banners in the procession and academic hoods on the lay readers. But lengthy sermons and extended anthems will probably do better on another occasion.

Many large parishes find Ascension Day an opportunity to get people together who attended different Sunday services. Small congregations can use the occasion to have a joint celebration with a neighboring congregation, especially one that shares a priest with them.

The Day of Pentecost

The 50th day of the Great Fifty Days of Easter is the Day of Pentecost, which is itself a Principal Feast. The Season After Pentecost follows, of course, but the Day itself is part of Easter Season. The Christian feast of Pentecost is built upon a Jewish festival, explaining why the crowds from all over the known world were gathered in Jerusalem in the Acts account.

The Jewish feast, Shavuot, means "Weeks" (more fully, Hag Shavuot, meaning "Festival of Weeks"), referring to the fact that it is a "week of weeks" or fifty days after Passover. The Greek name for the festival is Pentecost, meaning "fiftieth." Shavuot was an agricultural festival, bringing in the winter barley harvest, but also celebrated the giving of Torah, to the Jewish people. The interplay between the giving of the Jewish Law and the outpouring of the Spirit in the Acts narrative is worth reflecting on, though these are not a pair of opposites (Law vs Spirit), when one recalls that Torah means not only "law" but "teaching" and refers to the first five books of the Bible.

The Paschal Candle burns through the Day of Pentecost and it is a baptismal feast in any case, which would indicate lighting the Paschal Candle. Baptisms, when possible, during this season should be scheduled for the Great Vigil of Easter or the Day of Pentecost, though any Sunday in Eastertide is suitable.

4 BCP, 287.

There is a provision for a Vigil for Pentecost, held the night before, which is analogous to the Great Vigil of Easter. Instructions are found in a paragraph just before the Collect for the Day of Pentecost, BCP, p. 175 or 227. This may be especially useful if you are preparing a group for Baptism or Confirmation during this season.

The Day of Pentecost is in the same calendar category as Easter Day, Christmas, and the other Principal Feasts and should be celebrated with great ceremony and emphasis. Congregations that use a kite, streamer, or flying banner in processions would want to be sure to include that on this day. Some congregations will incorporate reading some of the Lessons in other languages, to celebrate the Pentecost event of people hearing the disciples' proclamation in their own languages. The story in Acts is a reversal of the Tower of Babel, as the Spirit reconnects and unites people in the work God is calling them to. With that in mind, be cautious about a multilingual presentation, especially if the congregation is primarily monolingual. Many speakers saying aloud the same thing in different languages often results in no one being understood. One practice that has been effective is to take the Acts reading and begin with an amplified speaker in the congregation's dominant language and then to slowly add in other readers in other languages, starting at different verses throughout the reading. The additional readers would be situated around the Nave, without amplification. Those who have an ear for one of the languages being spoken would recognize it, without being distracted from the primary reader who would be heard above the rest. This practice also allows the reading to build until the final verse, with the full number of readers speaking at that point. It is also vital to have a print version of the reading available if a church attempts this practice, to ensure that the Lesson may be understood.

Other festivities can be created around the Day of Pentecost, including outdoor activities, since it is typically in late spring. Thematic events that churches have created include Pentecost kite-flying after the service as well as a "Tongues of Fire" potluck, inviting people to bring various kinds of spicy or spiced food that they enjoy. A chili cook-off could employ the same theme. Celebrations around Pentecost, unlike Christmas and Easter, have almost no visibility in the culture in the United States. This allows a freedom for creative thinking about ways to celebrate this important feast.

Easter – Major Feasts, Seasonal Rites, and Other Commemorations

Easter Season Blessing [1]

The following blessing may be used by a bishop or priest whenever a blessing is appropriate. It is a three-fold form, with an Amen at the end of each sentence, leading into a Trinitarian blessing.

May Almighty God, who has redeemed us and made us his children through the resurrection of his Son our Lord, bestow upon you the riches of his blessing. *Amen.*

May God, who through the water of baptism has raised us from sin into newness of life, make you holy and worthy to be united with Christ for ever. *Amen.*

May God, who has brought us out of bondage to sin into true lasting freedom in the Redeemer, bring you to your eternal inheritance. *Amen.*

And the blessing of God Almighty, the Father, the Son, and the Holy Spirit, be upon you and remain with you for ever. *Amen.*

or this

The God of peace, who brought again from the dead our Lord Jesus Christ, the great Shepherd of the sheep, through the blood of the everlasting covenant, make you perfect in every good work to do his will, working in you that which is well-pleasing in his sight; and the blessing of God Almighty, the Father, the Son, and the Holy Spirit, be among you, and remain with you always. *Amen.*

Blessings Over Food at Easter [2]

These blessings are appropriate for a parish meal following the Easter Vigil or over foods brought to the church for blessing.

Over Wine

Blessed are you, O Lord our God, creator of the fruit of the vine: Grant that we who share this wine, which gladdens our hearts, may share for ever the new life of the true Vine, your Son Jesus Christ our Lord. *Amen.*

Over Bread

Blessed are you, O Lord our God: you bring forth bread from the earth and make the risen Lord to be for us the Bread of Life: Grant that we who daily seek the bread which sustains our bodies may also hunger for the food of everlasting life, Jesus Christ our Lord. *Amen.*

Over Lamb

Stir up our memory, O Lord, as we eat this Easter lamb that, remembering Israel of old, who in obedience to your command ate the Pascal lamb and was delivered from the bondage of slavery, we, your new Israel, may rejoice in the resurrection of Jesus Christ, the true Lamb who has delivered us from the bondage of sin and death, and who lives and reigns for ever and ever. *Amen.*

Over Eggs

O Lord our God, in celebration of the Pascal feast, we have prepared these eggs from your creation: Grant that they may be to us a sign of the new life and immortality promised to those who follow your Son, Jesus Christ our Lord. *Amen.*

Over Other Foods

Blessed are you, O Lord our God; you have given us the risen Savior to be the Shepherd of your people: Lead us, by him, to springs of living waters, and feed us with the food that endures to eternal life; where with you, O Father, and with the Holy Spirit, he lives and reigns, one God, for ever and ever. *Amen.*

1 BOS 2022, 14.
2 BOS 2022, 111–112.

An Easter Pageant

He Is Lord: Good Friday Becomes Easter[3]

The intention of this play is to help participants get "inside" the Easter story and experience it the way people may have often done with the Christmas story. It may be been done effectively as the sermon on the Second Sunday of Easter. This timing enhances the celebration of The Great 50 Days of Easter, and if the local schools are on spring break during Holy Week and Easter weekend (and some families are therefore away) may enable people to be involved who may have missed those liturgies in their home church.

Scene 1: (The scene is just outside Jerusalem, late afternoon on Good Friday. The "house lights" are out except for dim lights at the altar. The congregation softly sings the first verse of "Where you there when they crucified my Lord?" Quietly, a group of men and women carry a man's body toward the altar.)

NARRATOR: It was the saddest day of their lives. Jesus of Nazareth, their Lord and Master, who had touched their lives more profoundly than anyone else, and who they had hoped would lead them to freedom and peace, was dead. He had died the cruel, painful death of crucifixion at the hands of the Roman Empire. (The group reaches the altar platform and gently slides the body, head first, behind the altar, and kneel there briefly.) Only the bravest of Jesus' followers have the courage to show up to help bury Jesus. Most of his followers – even Peter and James – are in hiding, afraid that the Romans might grab them next and execute them as well. (Spotlight shining on the altar goes on. The men and women stand up.)

JOSEPH OF ARIMATHEA: Well, it's the least I could do, giving him my tomb. I had hoped I would need it long before he would.

MARY, THE MOTHER OF JAMES AND JOSES: You're a good man, Joseph. My sons didn't even have the guts to show up today, when Jesus really needed to see who cared for him.

NICODEMUS: I brought some spices, but there isn't any time to anoint his body properly before burial, the way we Jews usually do. It's almost sundown, and the Sabbath will start soon.

MARY MAGDALENE: Don't worry, Nicodemus. We'll be back after the Sabbath, first thing Sunday morning, and do the right thing. At least I will. (The women only say "Me too.")

SALOME: John, you have a really important job. Jesus asked you to take care of his mother. (John stands silently with his arm protectively around Mary, Jesus' mother; they both nod.)

ANOTHER WOMAN FROM GALILEE Let's roll this big stone across the opening to his tomb. With all Jesus has had to go through already, the last thing we would want is to have some of the people who hate him come and steal his body and do more things to it.

(They all roll the stone across the opening of the tomb, say a silent prayer, and walk sadly offstage. The spotlight shining on the altar goes out. The dim lights at the altar then go out.)

Scene 2: (While the lights are out, the "body" is removed from behind the altar.)

NARRATOR: On the Sabbath, they all rested in accordance with the commandment. After the Sabbath was over, at sundown on Saturday, it was too dark to come to the garden where the tomb was. But very early on Sunday morning . . .

(THUNDERCLAP "special effect". Two angels appear from off stage to roll away the stone to reveal – the empty tomb. The lights over the congregation are still out. The dim lights over the altar come on.)

Mary Magdalene, Mary the mother of James and Joses, and Salome walk slowly toward the tomb.

(They all enter from offstage, at the opposite end of the church from the altar. One of them carries a jar of spices for anointing.)

MARY, THE MOTHER OF JAMES AND JOSES: Who will roll away the stone for us? There were lots more of us here on Friday and it was heavy enough then.

SALOME: Oops. Didn't think of that. I feel so stupid.

(Spotlight on the altar goes on.)

MARY MAGDALENE: Look! The stone is rolled away!

(They all run toward the tomb. Ignoring the angels, they stick their heads in and come back out, more upset than ever.)

This gets worse and worse! Somebody stole his body!

ANGEL: Why do you seek the living among the dead? He is not here; he is risen from the dead, and he is Lord! Tell his other followers that he will meet them in Galilee, just as he said he would.

SALOME: I am totally creeped out.

3 Francis A. Hubbard (New York: Church Publishing, 2011). This Easter pageant is part of the *Skiturgies: Pageants, Plays, Rites and Rituals* collection.

MARY, THE MOTHER OF JAMES AND JOSES: Let's get out of here. I can't handle this.

(Salome and Mary, the mother of James and Joses run away. Angels both exit. Mary Magdalene stays at the tomb, crying buckets of tears. Jesus, who has been out of sight behind the altar, stands and walks toward her.)

JESUS: Ma'am, why are you crying? Who are you looking for?

MARY MAGDALENE: (Still sobbing, her face in her hands.) Mr. Gardener, if you've moved his body someplace, please show me where, and I'll come and take care of him.

JESUS: Mary.

MARY MAGDALENE: (She stops crying and slowly lifts her head and opens her mouth wide while staring at him, then leaps up joyfully.) Rabbi! You ARE alive! (She hugs him.)

JESUS: Now you know it's true, Mary, and you've touched me, so you know I'm not just a vision or a ghost, but real. Now the important thing is for you to go and tell the others!

MARY MAGDALENE: Right! Got it!

(Jesus disappears behind the altar again. The house lights start to come up slowly. Mary Magdalene starts to run down the aisle away from the altar, and encounters three men who are walking very slowly from the back of the church.)

MAN #1: (To Mary Magdalene.) Why are YOU looking so happy today? I thought you loved Jesus! WE all did. This is the worst week of our lives!

MARY MAGDALENE: Guys! Guys! He's alive! Jesus is risen from the dead! He just told me to tell you!

MAN #2: (He looks at Man #3 while pointing at his own head and making circular motions with his finger.)

MAN #3: Yeah, she never was too tightly wrapped.

MAN #1: Cut her some slack, guys! She's stressed out, just like we are. People sometimes think weird things when they're stressed out. (He puts his hand condescendingly on Mary Magdalene's shoulder.) You'll be all right, Mary.

MARY MAGDALENE: (She stamps her foot.) I AM all right! Better than I've ever been, in fact. (Man #2 and Man #3 snicker.) It's true! Go to Galilee and you'll see him too!

MAN #1: Now you not only expect us to believe you, but to travel all the way up there on your say-so?

MAN #2: Women! The stories they tell! (All three men nod, then exit.)

MARY MAGDALENE: ARGH! (Peter and John enter, and start walking slowly from the back of the church.) Oh, wait – there's Peter and John – maybe THEY'LL believe me. I'll start slower. Take a deep breath, Mary, Get a grip. Peter, John! Come quick! The tomb is empty! (Peter and John look up from a distance and start running toward the tomb.) It's empty because . . . (they run past her) because, um, because he is risen from the dead. (Mary sits down, discouraged, while the men ignore her and look in the tomb.)

PETER: Well, it's true, the tomb is empty.

JOHN: I wonder what it means.

PETER: Beats me. And who could possibly tell us? (They shrug and walk right by Mary Magdalene.)

MARY MAGDALENE: I can! I can! Jesus is alive! (Mary Magdalene waves her arms at them, but Peter and John don't notice her and exit, scratching their heads. Mary Magdalene, very frustrated, exits also, to the opposite side of the stage.)

Scene 3: (Cleopas and his companion enter from the back of the church and walk very slowly up the aisle.)

NARRATOR: That same afternoon, two of Jesus' followers, Cleopas and another man, were walking slowly and sadly from Jerusalem to Emmaus.

JESUS (He slips in from off stage alongside them.) What's up, guys? Why the long faces?

COMPANION: Where have YOU been for the last three days?

CLEOPAS: Yeah, are you the ONLY visitor to Jerusalem who doesn't have a clue?

JESUS: A clue about what?

CLEOPAS: About Jesus, the great prophet from Nazareth. Our fellow Jews – the high priest and most of the Council – convinced Pontius Pilate that he was a political revolutionary, so the Romans put him to death. We had thought he would be The One to deliver Israel from them!

COMPANION: That's the sad part; now comes the really strange and confusing part. Some of the women who were really devoted followers of Jesus said they went to his tomb early this morning and couldn't find his body, and they also told people they saw a couple of angels there who told them he was alive.

CLEOPAS: Peter and John went to check it out. They found the tomb empty all right, but that's all they found.

JESUS: What is there about this you don't get? It says in the scriptures that the Messiah would suffer on behalf of the people. "He was wounded for our transgressions." You remember that part? (They nod.) And Jesus himself said he would die and rise again. Let me spell it all out for you. (The three walk together as Jesus pantomimes talking and the others listen.)

NARRATOR: So, beginning at the beginning, Jesus explained all the things in the Hebrew scriptures which had to do with him.

(The three stop just in front of the altar.)

JESUS: Well, here's the inn you said you were going to stay at tonight. Good to talk with you, I got to keep going.

COMPANION: It's almost dark. Won't you at least have dinner with us?

(Jesus hesitates, and then nods. They all sit down on chairs around the altar, Cleopas and his companion on either side, and Jesus behind the altar, facing the congregation. Jesus stands up, picks up a piece of pita bread from the plate on the altar, raises his eyes to heaven and his hand in blessing, breaks the bread, and gives them each a piece. The men receive the bread and then gasp.)

CLEOPAS AND HIS COMPANION: JESUS!

(Jesus disappears behind the altar. The other two men look at each other with surprise and great joy.)

CLEOPAS: Didn't it feel like our hearts were on fire when he was explaining the Bible to us?

COMPANION: I was getting goose bumps the whole time!

CLEOPAS: We have to run and tell the others!

COMPANION: Amen to that! I don't care if it is dark and it's uphill all the way back to Jerusalem! (They both exit, running and very excited.)

Scene 4: (All of Jesus' male followers except for Cleopas and his companion are gathered together in Jerusalem, seated in front of the altar.)

PETER: (He stands.) I have seen the Lord.

ANOTHER MALE APOSTLE: Well, if YOU say so, I'll believe it.

PETER: Let everyone always remember that the women were the first to see, and the first to believe. I didn't have the guts to show my face at the foot of the cross – I was afraid the Romans would string me up next. Besides, I felt so ashamed after I denied that I even knew him. But Jesus – Jesus forgave me for everything! He says that everyone who believes in him gets a fresh start. (All nod appreciatively.)

(Cleopas and his companion run in from off stage.)

CLEOPAS AND HIS COMPANION: It's true! It's true! We've seen him! We've broken bread with him! The women were right. He is risen from the dead, and he is Lord!

(All the women enter from off stage and are greeted joyfully and respectfully by the men. All except Thomas, who stands apart, looking skeptical, sing, "He is Lord.")

THOMAS: Sorry, I won't believe until I see him and get close enough to touch him myself with my own hands.

JESUS: (He appears suddenly from behind the altar and walks toward them.) Shalom. Peace to you. (They ooh and ah and are a little tentative and afraid of him.) Don't be afraid. I'm not a ghost, or a vision. I'm real. Look at my hands and my feet – you can still see the marks of the nails, but nothing hurts any more. Violence and hatred have no power over me. Even death has no power over me. (He looks at Thomas.) Thomas, come on over. Check out my wounds. I'm the same guy who died on Friday.

(Thomas walks to him, reaches out to touch his hand, and then falls on his knees.)

THOMAS. My Lord and my God.

JESUS: (He looks at Thomas.) Do you believe because you have seen me? (He looks out at the whole congregation.) Even more blessed are those who believe without seeing me. (He addresses all of the disciples, male and female.) All of you are to continue to be my followers, even and especially when you can't see me the way you can today. By my power, you can forgive sins and heal people. You do not need to be afraid of anything any more, because through me, you can have abundant life, both now on earth and forever in heaven. I will be with you, coaching you and giving you strength, whatever you have to deal with. So, don't just sit there! Spread this Good News and make disciples of all nations, baptizing them in the Name of the Father, and of the Son, and of the Holy Spirit, and teaching them to believe all that I have taught you. I will be with you always.

(All of the cast and congregation stand and sing the first verse of "Jesus Christ is risen today.")

March 25, The Annunciation of Our Lord Jesus Christ to the Blessed Virgin Mary

See information on the Annunciation in the Lent section on Major Feasts. If the Annunciation falls during Easter Week, it is moved to the first open day afterwards, the Monday after Easter II.

April 22, Earth Day

Though not on the church calendar, this day is an important day to focus on our care of creation. In addition to the litany below, one may wish to adapt Prayer 1. For Joy in God's Creation (BCP 814), Prayer 40. For Knowledge of God's Creation (BCP 827), or 41. For the Conservation of Natural Resources (BCP 827) on this day or a Sunday near it. Additional excellent prayers for creation can be found in "Liturgical Materials Honoring God in Creation" in BOS 2022, 283–302, which includes several options for Prayers of the People and other resources. The materials for Rogation Day, below, and "A Litany for All Creation" in the Blessing of the Animals for St. Francis' Day, also found in the BOS 2022, may be useful additional sources for adaptation.

Earth Day Litany[4]

We have forgotten who we are.

We have become separate from the movements of the earth.

We have turned our backs on the cycles of life.

We have forgotten who we are.

We have sought only our own security.

We have exploited simply for our own ends.

We have distorted our knowledge.

We have abused our power.

We have forgotten who we are.

Now the land is barren

And the waters are poisoned

And the air is polluted.

We have forgotten who we are.

Now the forests are dying

And the creatures are disappearing

And the humans are despairing.

We have forgotten who we are.

We ask forgiveness.

We ask for the gift of remembering.

We ask for the strength to change, all for the love of our Creator. *Amen.*

4 United Nations Environment Programme. "Only One Earth," a United Nations Environment Programme publication for Environmental Sabbath/Earth Rest Day, June 1990. UN Environment Programme, DC2–803, United Nations, New York, NY 10017. Used by permission.

April 25, Saint Mark the Evangelist

This is a Major Feast but may not substitute for a Sunday during Easter Season. If it falls during the week after Easter Day, it is moved to the next available day, the Monday after Easter II. The Collect for the Day is found on pages 188 or 240 of the BCP.

All New Testament references to a man named Mark may not be to the same man, but if they are, he was the son of a woman householder in Jerusalem – perhaps the house in which Jesus ate his Last Supper. Mark may have been the naked young man who fled when Jesus was arrested in the Garden of Gethsemane. Paul referred to Mark in a letter to the Colossians as the cousin of Barnabas, with whom he was imprisoned; Paul was not satisfied by the reasons Mark gave for not accompanying Paul and Barnabas, so Paul refused Mark's company on a second journey. Early tradition names Mark as the author the Gospel of Mark.

May 1, Saint Philip and Saint James, Apostles

This is a Major Feast, but may not substitute for a Sunday during Easter Season. The Collect for the Day is found on pages 189 or 240 of the BCP.

Philip and James are known but a little – and that through the gospels. James has been called "the Less" to distinguish him from James the son of Zebedee and from Jesus's brother James – or maybe he was young, or short. He was listed among the Twelve as James the son of Alpheus, and he may also be the person labeled in Mark's Gospel as "James the younger," who witnessed the crucifixion. In John's Gospel, Philip has a greater presence: Jesus called Philip as a disciple right after naming Andrew and Peter; in turn, Philip convinced his friend Nathaniel to see the Messiah. Philip, at the Last Supper, declared, "Lord, show us the Father, and we shall be satisfied."

Graduation Prayers

Prayers for recognizing graduating students can be found in the section Season after Pentecost (Summer) – Major Feasts, Seasonal Rites, and Other Commemorations, below.

Rogation Days: Rogation Procession[5]

The Rogation Days are traditionally observed on the Monday, Tuesday, and Wednesday before Ascension Day. They may, however, be observed on other days, depending on local conditions and the convenience of the congregation.

5 BOS 2022, 113–123.

In ancient times, the observance consisted of an outdoor procession which culminated in a special celebration of the Eucharist. In more recent centuries, the procession has frequently taken place on a Sunday afternoon, apart from the Eucharist, and may be adapted to urban and suburban settings.

Hymns, psalms, canticles, and anthems are sung during the procession. The following are appropriate:

Canticle 1 or 12 (Benedicite)
Psalm 103 (Refrain: "Bless the Lord, O my soul")
Psalm 104 (Refrain: "Hallelujah")

At suitable places, the procession may halt for appropriate Bible readings and prayers. Numerous stations for prayer are in the BOS 2022 liturgy, adaptable to the neighborhood or region around the church building.

In addition to the readings listed on page 931 of the BCP, any of the following passages are appropriate:

Genesis 8:13–23
Leviticus 26:1–13 (14–20)
Deuteronomy 8:1–19 (11–20)
Hosea 2:18–23
Ezekiel 34:25–31
James 4:7–11
Matthew 6:25–34
John 12:23–26

Suitable prayers include Prayers 1, 29, 34, 38, 40–44, and Thanksgivings 1, 8, 9 from the section "Prayers and Thanksgivings" in the BCP, as well as the following:

Almighty and everlasting God, Creator of all things and giver of all life, let your blessing be upon this (see, livestock, plough, forest, ____________) and grant that *it* may serve to your glory and the welfare of your people; through Jesus Christ our Lord. *Amen.*

A proper preface and postcommunion prayer are included in the BOS for use at a concluding Eucharist

Prayers for Rogation Days: A Rite for the Blessing of a Garden[6]

The Rogation Days are traditionally observed on the Monday, Tuesday, and Wednesday before Ascension Day. They may, however, be observed on other days, depending on local conditions and the convenience of the congregation.

An additional rite is offered for the Blessing of a Garden on Rogation Days, which would be especially helpful when establishing a local community garden.

6 BOS 2022, 124–125.

Ascension Day Blessing[7]

Ascension Day may fall on a Thursday on or between April 30 and June 3.

The following blessing may be used by a bishop or priest whenever a blessing is appropriate. It is a three-fold form, with an Amen at the end of each sentence, leading into a Trinitarian blessing.

God the Father, who has given to his Son the name above every name, strengthen you to proclaim Jesus the Christ, the Son of God. *Amen.*

God the Son, our great high priest, who has passed into the heavens, clothe you with power from on high. *Amen.*

God the Holy Spirit, who pours out abundant gifts upon the Church, make you faithful followers of the risen Christ. *Amen.*

And the blessing of God almighty, the Father, the Son, and the Holy Spirit, be among you and remain with you always. *Amen.*

or this

May the risen Christ
Who has passed into the heavens
Clothe you with power from on high
And the blessing of God almighty, the Father, the Son, and the Holy Spirit, be among you and remain with you always. *Amen.*

An Ascensiontide Litany[8]

Christ was baptized as one of us, but he destroyed sins as God.

He was tempted as a human, but he conquered as God.

He wants us to rejoice, for he has overcome the world.

He hungered, but he fed thousands. He is the living bread that comes down from heaven.

He thirsted, but he cried, "If anyone thirsts, let them come to me and drink."

He promised that fountains would flow from those who believe.

He was wearied, but he is the rest of those who are weary and heavy-laden.

The demons acknowledge him, but he drives them out.

He plunges into the sea the legions of foul spirits and sees the prince of demons falling like lightning.

7 BOS 2022, 15.

8 "The Mystery of Christ – An Ascenstiontide Litany" in *The Wideness of God's Mercy: Litanies to Enlarge Our Prayer,* ed. Jeffrey W. Rowthorn (New York: Church Publishing, 2007), 89–90.

He prays, but he hears prayers.

He weeps, but he makes tears to cease.

He asks where Lazarus was laid because he was human; but he raises Lazarus because he was God.

He is sold, and very cheap – for only thirty pieces of silver; but he redeems the world at a great price – the cost of his own blood.

As sheep he is led to the slaughter, but he is the Shepherd of Israel – and now of the whole world.

He is bruised and wounded,
but he heals every disease and infirmity.

He is lifted up and nailed to the tree, but he restores us by the tree of life.

He lays down his life,
but he has the power to take it up again.

He dies, but he gives life; and by his death he destroys death.

He is buried, but he rises again.

He descends into hell, but he raises souls from death.

He ascends to heaven, and he will come again
to judge the living and the dead. Amen.

Second Sunday in May, Mother's Day *(on or between May 8 and 14)*

This secular holiday is not on the church calendar, but originates in a pacifist movement. Mother's Day in the parish can be a complex day pastorally, depending on the nature of an individual's relationship with their mother as well as the response of women in the congregation around all sorts of experiences around motherhood, which may include significant loss or grief. One may wish to reference the day in the prayers of the people, but great sensitivity should be considered.

A Mother's Day Prayer[9]

On this Mother's Day, we give thanks to God for the divine gift of motherhood in all its diverse forms. Let us pray for all the mothers among us today; for our own mothers, those living and those who have passed away; for the mothers who loved us and for those who fell short of loving us fully; for all who hope to be mothers someday and for those whose hope to have children has been frustrated; for all the mothers who have lost children; for all women and men who have mothered others in any way – those who have been our substitute mothers and we who have done so for those in need; and for the earth that bore us and provides us with our sustenance. We pray this all in the name of God, our great and loving Mother. *Amen.*

The Last Monday in May, Memorial Day *(on or between May 25 and 31)*

This federal holiday is not on the church calendar and focuses on honoring those who have died in armed service to the United States. Primarily, on this day, one may wish to include prayers in the intercession for those who have given their life in defense of the nation. In addition to the prayer below, one could adapt Thanksgiving 6. For Heroic Service, BCP 839.

A Prayer for Memorial Day[10]

Lord God, in whom there is life and light: Accept our thanks for those who died for us, our prayers for those who mourn, our praise for the hope you have given us. Refresh our hearts with dedication to heroic ideas, with appreciation for the honesty of the just, with obedience to upright laws. Forgive us when our patriotism is hollow, when our nationalism is arrogant, when our allegiance is half-hearted. Stir within us thanksgiving for all we have inherited, vigilance for the freedoms of all people, willingness to sacrifice for fellow citizens. Comfort us with the joy that Christ died for all those who died for us, bringing life and immortality to light for all who believe in Him. *Amen.*

May 31, The Visitation of the Blessed Virgin Mary

This is a Major Feast and Feast of Our Lord which may not substitute for a Sunday in the Easter Season, but may substitute for a Sunday after Pentecost, excluding Trinity Sunday, when it falls on a Sunday. The Collect for the Day is found on pages 189 or 240 of the BCP.

This Feast commemorates the visit of the Mary to her cousin Elizabeth (Luke 1:39–56). The pregnant Elizabeth greeted Mary: "Blessed are you among women, and blessed is the fruit of your womb." Mary responded with a song of praise, a thanksgiving known as the "Magnificat": "My soul

9 Leslie Nipps, "For Mother's Day" in *Women's Uncommon Prayers* (Harrisburg, PA: Morehouse Publishing, 2000), 364.

10 "The Last Monday in May," in *An American Prayer Book,* edited by Christopher L. Webber (Harrisburg, PA: Morehouse Publishing, 2008), 141–142.

proclaims the greatness of the Lord." The dramatic scene places the unborn John the Baptist, who was to prepare the way of the Lord to all Israel, in proximity with that Lord Himself. The gospel weaves in the story that when Elizabeth heard her cousin's greeting, John leapt for joy in his mother's womb.

June 11, Saint Barnabas the Apostle

This is a Major Feast which may not substitute for a Sunday in the Easter Season, but may substitute for a Sunday after Pentecost, excluding Trinity Sunday, when it falls on a Sunday. The Collect for the Day is found on pages 189 or 240 of the BCP.

Barnabas, born Joseph, was called an apostle, along with the Twelve, for his missions. Like Paul, Barnabas was a Jew of the Dispersion; Barnabas presented Paul to the apostles with the story of Saul's conversion to Paul. Later, Barnabas, having settled in Antioch, sent for Paul to help lead the Christian Church there. The two men, sent by the disciples, carried food and relief to the church during a famine in Jerusalem. Afterward, the church sent out the pair, starting from Cyprus. Their friendship split over Mark, who had left the mission to return to Jerusalem. Barnabas and Mark traveled to Cyprus, where tradition honors Barnabas as the founder of the church and places his martyrdom.

Day of Pentecost Blessing[11]

The Day of Pentecost may fall on or between May 10 and June 13.

The following blessing may be used by a bishop or priest whenever a blessing is appropriate. It is a three-fold form, with an Amen at the end of each sentence, leading into a Trinitarian blessing.

May Almighty God, who enlightened the minds of the disciples by pouring out upon them the Holy Spirit, make you rich with his blessing, that you may abound more and more in that Spirit for ever. *Amen.*

May God, who sent the Holy Spirit as a flame of fire that rested upon the heads of the disciples, burn out all evil from your hearts, and make them shine with the pure light of his presence. *Amen.*

May God, who by the Holy Spirit caused those of many tongues to proclaim Jesus as Lord, strengthen your faith and send you out to bear witness to him in word and deed. *Amen.*

And the blessing of God Almighty, the Father, the Son, and the Holy Spirit, be upon you and remain with you for ever. *Amen.*

or this

May the Spirit of truth lead you into all truth, giving you grace to confess that Jesus Christ is Lord, and to proclaim the wonderful works of God; and the blessing of God Almighty, the Father, the Son, and the Holy Spirit, be among you, and remain with you always. *Amen.*

11 BOS 2022, 16.

The Great Vigil of Easter

Variable – Between March 21 and April 24

This is the night, when Christ broke the bonds of death and hell, and rose victorious from the grave.

Anchor Points – The Propers and the Season

The fixed points for each service are the appointed or proper readings and collect as well as the themes of the day or season.

Readings and Psalm

Note: The Revised Common Lectionary made changes to the Great Vigil Lessons, used below, which may not be reflected Prayer Books printed before 2012.

Genesis 1:1 – 2:4a

Our lesson is the story of creation. As this ancient narrative opens, the Spirit of the Lord hovers like a great mother bird over the shapeless world. God then forms the heaven and the earth and all its creatures in six days. The seventh day is set aside as a day of rest. God's ultimate creative act is human life, made in God's own image, to whom rulership and responsibility over all other life are given.

Psalm 136:1–9, 23–26

A psalm in praise of a good Creator, a God of enduring mercy.

Genesis 7:1–5, 11–18; 8:6–18; 9:8–13

Noah and his household are commanded by the Lord to enter the ark, together with pairs of all animals. Forty days and nights of rain and flood cover the earth in water. Finally the waters subside, and the Lord makes a covenant with Noah, promising never again to destroy the earth by flood. As a sign of this covenant, God hangs God's own warrior's bow in the clouds, the rainbow which stretches in the sky's vast expanse.

Psalm 46

The earth may be moved and kingdoms shaken, but God is our refuge.

Genesis 22:1–18

This reading is the story of Abraham's willingness in obedience to the Lord's command to sacrifice his only son, Isaac, and the Lord's blessing of him. The narrative illustrates Abraham's readiness to abandon all to serve the Lord. Originally it probably also was used as a model story encouraging the substitution of animal for human sacrifices. Ancient Israel was given a better understanding of God's will, and because of his obedience, Abraham received God's promise to him and his descendants.

Psalm 16

Contentment, refuge, and joy are found in the presence of the Lord, who does not abandon God's faithful servant at death.

Exodus 14:10–31; 15:20–21

This reading is the story of the deliverance of Israel from bondage in Egypt. The people are terrified when they see the pursuing army and complain that it would have been better to live in slavery than to die in the wilderness. Moses urges them to have courage, for they will see the salvation of the Lord, who has called them to freedom to serve the one true God. The Lord then brings them safely through the sea and destroys the army of the Egyptians.

Exodus 15:1b–13, 17–18 (Canticle 8: The Song of Moses)

A song of praise to God for deliverance from captivity in Egypt and from the peril of pursuing armies.

Isaiah 55:1–11

In this lesson we hear how the return from exile will be a time of prosperity and abundance when God's covenant will be renewed. The prophet pictures the great day: for a people who have been near death there will be food and drink without cost. God's covenant with David is to be extended to all Israel, and other nations will come to see her glory. The life-giving word of the Lord will not fail to produce its fruit and, together with Israel, the natural world will rejoice and reflect God's power.

Isaiah 12:2–6 (Canticle 9: The First Song of Isaiah)

A song of praise and thanksgiving to God, the Holy One of Israel.

Baruch 3:9–15, 3:32–4:4

The lesson is a poem of praise to Wisdom, God's companion in the process of creation and God's precious gift to humankind. All who find her will be blessed, and she is embodied most especially in the Torah, the book of God's commandments.

or

Proverbs 8:1–8, 19–21; 9:4b–6

In this lesson Wisdom calls to all who will hear, offering understanding, direction, and insight into the way of righteousness and justice. She is God's gift to the wise and simple alike, and those who learn her ways will prosper.

Psalm 19

A hymn which glorifies the Creator God, with special praise for God's law and a prayer for avoidance of sin.

Ezekiel 36:24–28

A time is coming when God will place a new heart and spirit within the people, who will cleave to God and walk in righteousness. Ezekiel prophesies the restoration of the dispersed and humiliated people of Israel.

Psalm 42

The psalmist laments his inability to come to the house of God and thirsts for the presence of the Lord.

and

Psalm 43

A plea to God by one who is persecuted and in distress, to be able to come and worship in the Lord's temple.

Ezekiel 37:1–14

The prophet has a vision of the bones of a dead and hopeless people being restored to new life in their homeland. The Lord calls upon Ezekiel as son of man to prophesy that the people who have experienced exile and many hardships will live again. The Spirit of the Lord restores their spirit and breath, and they rise from death. Although this passage can be understood to anticipate the hope of individual resurrection, Israel did not yet have this belief.

Psalm 143

The psalmist prays earnestly for the help of God's presence.

Zephaniah 3:14–20

In this lesson the prophet foretells a time when the judgment of Israel will be ended and the mighty Lord will bring victory and renewal to the people. The city of Jerusalem and its holy Mount Zion may rejoice and sing. All enemies will be defeated and the crippled healed. The fortunes of Israel will be restored, and the nation will be praised by all peoples.

Psalm 98

A song of thanksgiving and praise to the victorious Lord, who has made righteousness known and shown faithfulness to God's people.

Romans 6:3–11

In this reading we hear that, as Christian disciples have been joined with Christ in his death through baptism, so they are to know a resurrection life like his. In union with Christ we have died to our sinful selves and have begun to experience a new way of life. In one sense our freedom from death still awaits us in the future, but, in another sense, we already know what it means to be alive to God in Christ Jesus and to realize the true meaning of life.

Psalm 114

A song of praise to the Lord, who has brought the people safely out of Egypt and through the wilderness to the promised land.

Matthew 28:1–10

Our gospel tells of Jesus' resurrection. It is about daybreak as the women come to the grave. No human eye sees Jesus rise, but there is an earthquake and an angel of the Lord rolls away the stone covering the tomb. He tells the two Marys that Jesus is going before his disciples to Galilee. With both fear and joy in their hearts, they run to tell the disciples and, on the way, are met by their risen Lord.

Collect

Almighty God, who for our redemption gave your only-begotten Son to the death of the cross, and by his glorious resurrection delivered us from the power of the enemy: Grant us so to die daily to sin, that we may evermore live with him in the joy of his resurrection; through Jesus Christ your Son our Lord, who lives and reigns with you and the Holy Spirit, one God, now and for ever. *Amen.*

or

O God, who made this most holy night to shine with the glory of the Lord's resurrection: Stir up in your Church that Spirit of adoption which is given to us in Baptism, that we, being renewed both in body and mind, may worship you in sincerity and truth; through Jesus Christ our Lord, who lives and reigns with you, in the unity of the Holy Spirit, one God, now and for ever. *Amen.*

Proper Preface

Easter – But chiefly are we bound to praise you for the glorious resurrection of your Son Jesus Christ our Lord; for he is the true Paschal Lamb, who was sacrificed for us, and has taken away the sin of the world. By his death he has destroyed death, and by his rising to life again he has won for us everlasting life. (Rite II BCP 379; Rite I BCP 346)

Feast Day Pairings

See the table below for choices appointed and suggested for this day. Preferences are put in **bold.** Not all choices are suitable for all congregations or community, though, so consider these preferences as a starting point before making a decision about your own congregation.

	The Great Vigil of Easter	Rite I	Rite II	EOW1	BOS 2022
Color	White/Gold/Festive				
Entrance Rite	Service of Light	285	285		
Song of Praise	Gloria in excelsis or Te Deum or Pascha Nostrum	294	294		
Collect	*Only first 2 options on 170 or 222; see 295*	170; 295	222; 295		
Creed	Baptismal Covenant *or* Renewal of Baptismal Vows	304/292	304/292		
Prayers of the People	**Locally written**; options below; BCP forms	329	387–393	54–55	
Offertory Sentence	"Christ being raised from the dead will never die again; * death no longer has dominion over him." (Romans)	343–344	376–377		
Eucharistic Prayer	**One that allows use of the Easter preface** *or* **Prayer D**	2–340	**A – 361, B – 367** or **D – 372**	1–57	
Proper Preface	Easter	346	379		
Breaking of the Bread (Fraction)	Options using an alleluia: S 151, S 152, S 154, S 155, S 167, S 171	337	364		
Postcommunion Prayer		339	**Eternal God – 365**	God of abundance – 69	
Blessing	Customary *or* **BOS**	339	366	70–71	**14**
Dismissal	**Let us go forth in the Name of Christ. Alleluia, alleluia.**	340	366		
Notes					

Additional Notes:

Schedule – The service is scheduled from sundown on Easter Eve until sunrise on Easter Day. The service should begin in enough darkness that the lighting of the new fire and the lighting of the Paschal Candle are significant. The question of whether to hold the service the night before or as an early morning sunrise service can make a vast difference in the experience of the service.

Entrance Rite – The service begins, when possible, outdoors with the lighting of the new fire and a candlelit procession of the congregation into the darkened Nave, following the Paschal Candle.

Service of Lessons – The series of lessons always includes the Exodus reading and may range from 2 to 9 (though at least 4 are suggested to convey the sense of a vigil service). The collect recommended to follow the reading from Baruch/Proverbs is the first collect on page 290 (previously followed a reading from Isaiah 4, no longer in the Great Vigil lectionary)

Creed – There is no creed as such at this service. In its place is the Baptismal Covenant, if there are Baptisms, or the Renewal of Baptismal Vows, if there are no Baptisms.

Eucharistic Prayer – There is not a Eucharistic Prayer that has distinct Easter/Resurrection themes, so selecting a Eucharistic Prayer that uses the Easter proper preface is an important option. Eucharistic Prayer D, which does not use a proper preface, may be desirable, because of the language expressing God's glory.

Fraction Anthem at the Breaking of the Bread – Certainly using options that incorporate "Alleluia" would be the most desirable. Several options in addition to "Christ our Passover" are provided in the Service Music section of *The Hymnal 1982*.

Content Resources

Reading Between the Lines

John Chrysostom's Paschal homily[1].

(This can be read out loud or adapted by the preacher)

If any be devout and love God, let them enjoy this fair and radiant triumphal feast.

If any be a wise servant, let them rejoicing enter into the joy of our Lord.

If any have labored long in fasting, let them now receive their recompense.

If any have wrought from the first hour, let them today receive their just reward.

If any have come at the third hour, let them with thankfulness keep the feast.

If any have arrived at the sixth hour, let them have no misgivings; because they shall in nowise be deprived.

If any have delayed until the ninth hour, let them draw near, fearing nothing.

If any have tarried even until the eleventh hour, let them, also, be not alarmed at their tardiness; for our Lord, who is jealous of his honor, will accept the last even as the first; he gives rest unto those who come at the eleventh hour, even as unto those who have wrought from the first hour.

Our Lord shows mercy upon the last, and cares for the first; and to the one he gives, and upon the other he bestows gifts.

And he both accepts the deeds, and welcomes the intention, and honors the acts and praises the offering.

Wherefore, enter you all into the joy of your Lord; and receive your reward, both the first, and likewise the second.

You rich and poor together, hold high festival.

You sober and you heedless, honor the day.

Rejoice today, both you who have fasted, and you who have disregarded the fast.

The table is full-laden; feast ye all sumptuously.

The calf is fatted; let no one go hungry away.

Enjoy ye all the feast of faith: Receive ye all the riches of loving-kindness.

Let none bewail their spiritual poverty, for the universal kingdom has been revealed.

Let none weep for their iniquities, for pardon has shown forth from the grave.

Let no one fear death, for the Savior's death has set us free.

He that was held prisoner of it has annihilated it.

By descending into Hell, He made Hell captive.

He angered it when it tasted of His flesh.

And Isaiah, foretelling this, did cry:

Hell, said he, was angered, when it encountered Thee in the lower regions.

Hell was angered, for it was abolished.

Hell was angered, for it was mocked. It was angered, for it was slain.

Hell was angered, for it was overthrown.

Hell was angered, for it was fettered in chains.

Hell took a body, and met God face to face.

It took earth and encountered Heaven.

It took that which was seen and fell upon the unseen.

O Death, where is your sting? O Hell, where is your victory?

Christ is risen, and you are overthrown.

Christ is risen, and the demons are fallen.

Christ is risen, and the angels rejoice.

Christ is risen, and life reigns.

Christ is risen, and not one dead remains in the grave.

For Christ, being risen from the dead, is become the first fruits of those who have fallen asleep.

To Him be glory and dominion unto ages of ages. Amen.

Central Themes

The Easter Vigil is the closest we ever come to having a game show take over the worship experience. There are pyrotechnics, lights, waterworks, and even bells that are rung and surprising moments. And we all win the prize beyond all prizes – life eternal! For death has no sting on this night and the grave has no victory. When Jesus triumphs over death, we are all the winners of his love! And that's better than anything we could ever hope to gain on our own – even on the best of game shows.

The 1998 animated film *The Prince of Egypt* beautifully visualizes Moses parting the Red Sea. He raises his rod, slams it down, and splits the sea, creating mighty walls of water. The Israelites eyes' widen, and they step back in terror. But they do move forward on this new path, and, staring up at the walls of water, they are amazed. Not dissimilar to the experience of Mary, Mary Magdelene, and Salome at the empty tomb coming upon an angel proclaiming the risen Christ. Lent's terror is past. The amazement of Easter is here. What amazing thing is ahead of you?

The rite and ceremony for the Great Vigil of Easter offers a panoramic view of Christian faith, moving from the kindling of new fire and the lighting of the Paschal candle, through the great stories and prophecy of the Old Testament, to the baptismal rite, and the joyous first

1 https://orthodoxwiki.org/Paschal_Homily, accessed April 29, 2023.

celebration of Easter Eucharist. The dramatic reenactment of the great story of salvation is particularly moving when adults are baptized during the service. What a glorious opportunity for full-immersion liturgy.

Engaging All Ages

To sit vigil means to wait and watch, thinking about what brought you to this point. Today, we read lessons that take us on a journey through God's story on Earth. We start with fire, which represents the light and life of Jesus. As you sit vigil today, praying and reading about God's story, look for signs of new light and life. Plant an indoor herb garden, paint a butterfly emerging from a cocoon, turn a mess of yarn into a warm scarf, and know that you can help bring signs of new light and life to the world in the name of Jesus.

Prayers of the People: Option 1

Cherishing the reality of our salvation and rejoicing in the new life we have in the Risen Christ, we shout, Alleluia! Amen!

We lift our hands and our hearts to you this night, O God, and raise our voices in shouts of praise. May our joy overflow into the world you love, that all might know you and your mighty works.

We humbly praise you, Almighty God,
Alleluia! Amen!

We bring before you the members and leaders of your church, the Body of Christ. Expand in us your compassionate heart. Fix our gaze on your glory and focus us on you and your mission.

We humbly praise you, Almighty God,
Alleluia! Amen!

Let the whole world know of your goodness through the actions of the leaders of the world. May all peoples live together in peace with equity and justice. May we be a blessing to this earth and it's peoples by being examples of integrity and kindness, truth and justice.

We humbly praise you, Almighty God,
Alleluia! Amen!

Shower these people with your healing grace: ____________ , Bring them comfort and confidence in your presence. Bless the efforts of those who care for them. Receive into your presence those who will die today. Welcome them into your glorious, eternal light.

We humbly praise you, Almighty God,
Alleluia! Amen!

Created in your image and for your purpose; Saved from rising waters and raised to newness in the waters of life,

we humbly praise you, Almighty God.
Alleluia! Amen!

Prayers of the People: Option 2

Deacon or Priest

Filled with joy on this royal feast of feasts, let us offer prayers to God who has given us the promise of new life in the risen life of his Son, Jesus Christ our Lord.

Leader

For the holy churches of God, for [*N.* and] all those in all places baptized this night, for *N.* our Presiding Bishop, for our bishop(s) *N.*, for our parish clergy and lay leaders, for this gathering and for all the holy people of God.

Glory and praise to you, O living God.

For the world and all people, for our nation and our community and our leaders, for *N.* our President, for *N.* our Governor, and *N.* our Mayor, that they may be given to wise action for the common good.

Glory and praise to you, O living God.

For victims of gun violence, for those marginalized and suffering in systems of oppression, for the dismantling of white supremacy and patriarchy; that the new life of the Resurrection may unravel all the ways we have damaged one another.

Glory and praise to you, O living God.

For all those in need, the suffering and the oppressed, travelers and prisoners, the dying and the dead.

Glory and praise to you, O living God.

For all refugees, for ourselves, our families, and those we love.

Glory and praise to you, O living God.

That with Christ we may crush beneath our feet all the powers of evil.

Glory and praise to you, O living God.

That Christ may fill us with the joy and happiness of his holy resurrection.

Glory and praise to you, O living God.

That we may long for that heavenly feast of rich food and well-aged wines, with all those that we love but see no longer, as the shroud of death is destroyed

Glory and praise to you, O living God.

Remembering our most glorious and blessed Virgin Mary and all the saints, let us offer ourselves and one another to the living God through Christ.

To you, O Lord, our God.

Presider

Blessed are you, O Lord our God, for the victory over death of your Son Jesus Christ. Hear the prayers we offer this holy day, and grant that we who have received new life in baptism may live for ever in the joy of the resurrection; through Jesus Christ our Lord. ***Amen.***

Hymns for the Day

The Hymnal 1982

At the Lamb's high feast we sing 174
Christ is arisen (Christ ist erstanden) 713
Christ Jesus lay in death's strong bands 185, 186
Christ the Lord is risen again 184
Christians, to the Paschal victim 183
Come, ye faithful, raise the strain 199, 200
Jesus Christ is risen today 207
The Lamb's high banquet called to share 202
The strife is o'er, the battle done 208
All who believe and are baptized 298
Baptized in water 294
Through the Red Sea brought at last 187
We know that Christ is raised and dies no more 296
O sons and daughters, let us sing 203 (1–3, 5)
On earth has dawned this day of days 201
All who believe and are baptized 298
Over the chaos of the empty waters 176, 177
We know that Christ is raised and dies no more 296

Lift Every Voice and Sing II

Christ has arisen 41
God sent his Son, they called him Jesus 43
Baptized in water 121
Wade in the water 143
Take me to the water 134

Wonder, Love, and Praise

Camina, pueblo de Dios/Walk on, O people of God 739
Day of delight and beauty unbounded 738
Baptized in water 767
God's Paschal Lamb is sacrificed for us 880
Wade in the water 740

The Sunday of the Resurrection: Easter Day

Variable – Between March 22 and April 25

Alleluia! Christ is Risen!

Anchor Points – The Propers and the Season

The fixed points for each service are the appointed or proper readings and collect as well as the themes of the day or season.

Readings and Psalm

Acts 10:34–43

The Easter reading from Acts gives a selection from Peter's missionary speech to Cornelius, a Gentile centurion, and his household. The conversion of Cornelius marks an important turning point in the understanding of God as impartial and consequently the outreach of the Church to Gentiles. Peter's sermon summarizes the basic preaching of the early Church. God anointed Jesus as Messiah "with the Holy Spirit and power" for a ministry of "doing good and healing" (10:38). God's saving action in Jesus is supported by apostolic witness (10:39, 41) and scriptural proof (10:43), issuing in a call to conversion. Along with the apostles, all those who celebrate the eucharist on Easter Day are witnesses to Jesus's resurrection.

or

Isaiah 25:6–9

Chapter 25 begins with a psalm of thanksgiving for deliverance. Isaiah imagines the end time, "that day" (v. 9) when the Lord will come for final judgment and salvation. On Mount Zion (24:23) the Lord will prepare a feast of rich abundance for all peoples. For Jews, all meals had religious significance. Here a feast provided by God becomes an anticipated element of the last days. Mourning will end, and death will be destroyed. Those who were preserved through God's judgment, described in chapter 24, the remnant, will celebrate God's faithfulness.

Psalm 118:1–2, 14–24

This psalm is the final psalm of the "Egyptian Hallel" (Psalms 113–118), a cycle of psalms used during the Passover festival. Its original use before the exile was probably as a liturgy of thanksgiving said at the temple gates.

1 Corinthians 15:1–11

In preparation for the next topic of discussion, the resurrection of the dead (15:12), Paul reminds the Corinthians of their common ground of belief. By quoting a traditional formulation of the essential proclamation about Christ (15:3–5), he recalls the basic creedal statements he taught them. In general, the statement "in accordance with the scriptures" expresses the conviction that these events took place according to God's purpose. It was, however, the lived experience of the early Christians, not merely the evidence of the Hebrew Bible, that shaped their belief.

or Acts 10:34–43

John 20:1–18

Today's reading describes the experience of the discovery of the empty tomb and the different responses of the disciples and the appearance of the Risen Christ to Mary Magdalene. Her first instinct is to tell Peter and the others. The simple fact of the empty tomb does not produce faith for Mary or for Peter. The evangelist recognizes that they did not, as yet, understand the meaning of scripture about the resurrection of the dead (v. 9). Only the beloved disciple, who is the model Christian disciple for John and his community, "saw and believed" (v. 8). Mary, Peter and the other disciples had to depend on the appearance of Jesus or a report of his appearance to trigger and confirm their belief.

or

Mark 16:1–8

Our gospel tells how three women disciples first learn of Jesus' resurrection. Coming to the tomb early in the morning, they are astounded to find its huge stone covering rolled back. A young man, in appearance like an angel, announces to them that Jesus is risen and will go before his disciples to Galilee. The event is awesome, even terrifying. The women flee from the tomb and, for at least a time, report nothing to anyone because of their fear.

Collect

O God, who for our redemption gave your only-begotten Son to the death of the cross, and by his glorious resurrection delivered us from the power of our enemy: Grant us so to die daily to sin, that we may evermore live with him in the joy of his resurrection; through Jesus Christ your Son our Lord, who lives and reigns with you and the Holy Spirit, one God, now and for ever. *Amen.*

or

Almighty God, who through your only-begotten Son Jesus Christ overcame death and opened to us the gate of everlasting life: Grant that we, who celebrate with joy the day of the Lord's resurrection, may be raised from the death of sin by your life-giving Spirit; through Jesus Christ our Lord, who lives and reigns with you and the Holy Spirit, one God, now and for ever. *Amen.*

Proper Preface

Easter – But chiefly are we bound to praise you for the glorious resurrection of your Son Jesus Christ our Lord; for he is the true Paschal Lamb, who was sacrificed for us, and has taken away the sin of the world. By his death he has destroyed death, and by his rising to life again he has won for us everlasting life. (Rite II BCP 379; Rite I BCP 346)

Feast Day Pairings

See the table below for choices appointed and suggested for this day. Preferences are put in **bold**. Not all choices are suitable for all congregations or community, though, so consider these preferences as a starting point before making a decision about your own congregation.

	The Sunday of the Resurrection: Easter Day	Rite I	Rite II	EOW1	BOS 2022
Color	White/Gold/Festive				
Entrance Rite	Customary; **Easter Acclamation**	323	355	50	
Song of Praise	Gloria in excelsis or Te Deum or **Pascha Nostrum**	324, 52, or **46**	356, 95, or **83**		
Collect	*1st and 3rd options for the Collect*	170	222		
Creed	Nicene Creed *or* Renewal of Baptismal Vows	326, 292	358, 292		
Prayers of the People	**Locally written**; options below; BCP forms	329	387–393	54–55	
Offertory Sentence	"This is the Lord's doing, and it is marvelous in our eyes. On this day the Lord has acted; we will rejoice and be glad in it." (Psalm 118)	343–344	376–377		
Eucharistic Prayer	**One that allows use of the Easter preface** *or* **Prayer D**	2–340	**A – 361,** **B – 367** or **D – 372**	1–57	
Proper Preface	Easter	346	379		
Breaking of the Bread (Fraction)	Options using an alleluia: S 151, S 152, S 154, S 155, S 167, S 171	337	364		
Postcommunion Prayer		339	**Eternal God – 365**	God of abundance – 69	
Blessing	Customary *or* **BOS**	339	366	70–71	**14**
Dismissal	**Let us go forth in the Name of Christ. Alleluia, alleluia.**	340	366		
Notes					

<u>*Additional Notes:*</u>

Song of Praise – The ancient and unique Song of Praise for Eastertide is the Pascha nostrum, found in Morning Prayer. While it is often not as familiar to congregations as the frequently used Gloria in excelsis, it is worth exploring settings for it that would help it become more familiar. It may be used throughout the Easter Season.

Baptisms – While the Great Vigil is the baptismal feast *par excellence*, Easter Day is not specifically identified as a baptismal feast, though baptisms may be held on this day. If baptisms occurred at the Great Vigil, the names of the newly baptized should be included in the intercessions and announcement may be made to the congregation about their baptism, to celebrate with the whole congregation.

Eucharistic Prayer – There is not a Eucharistic Prayer that has distinct Easter/Resurrection themes, so selecting a Eucharistic Prayer that uses the Easter proper preface is an important option. Eucharistic Prayer D, which does not use a proper preface, may be desirable, because of the language expressing God's glory.

Fraction Anthem at the Breaking of the Bread – Certainly using options that incorporate "Alleluia" would be the most desirable. Several options in addition to "Christ our Passover" are provided in the Service Music section of *The Hymnal 1982.*

Content Resources

Reading Between the Lines

Three readings of the day, I Cor 15:1–11, Acts 10:34–43, and John 20:1–18 describe bodily resurrection. The reading from Mark 16:1–8 infers it. Emerging in a context of 2nd Century BCE Jewish apocalyptic, itself a response to exile and persecution, resurrection for righteous Jews described in Daniel 12:2 represents a victory over death. Preaching to the Corinthians, Paul "hands on" even older salvific traditions that Christ "was raised on the third day" (I Cor 15:4) and appeared to many. Similarly, Luke conveys in Acts one of many sermons, this one by Peter in Caesarea, that "God raised (Jesus) on the third day" (Acts 10:40) to appear to witnesses, as the basis of preaching. In Mark 16:6 a young man in the empty tomb proclaims to women who had come to anoint the body of Jesus, "He has been raised; He is not here." Three independent texts proclaim a central tenet of early belief, in a remarkably similar way, namely, Jesus' resurrection by the power of God.

Bodily resurrection in John 20 is comprehended not by sight but by sound, namely, speech. Mary recognizes Jesus by hearing a voice. In this way, resurrection is grasped through human perception. Reception history of John 20:17 in art and music indicates that the connection of Mary and Jesus is stronger than any readings of *Noli Me Tangere* as prohibition of touch.

Central Themes

It is worth noting that Mary Magdalene is clearly shown to be a disciple of Jesus. She calls him "Rabbouni," which shows that she is his student, and is then sent to be the first evangelist of the Resurrection. She was not believed, and the men in her group felt they should go and see it for themselves. Do we tend to believe the stories of God's transforming love in this world? Or does it have to come from the right "source" for us to believe it's not "fake news." Perhaps we need to start listening more to those we are unaccustomed to giving credence and listen for the stories of resurrection in their lives.

"Alleluia. Christ is risen. The Lord is risen indeed. Alleluia." Forty days ago we buried our Alleluias and held our bated breath for week after week as we bore witness to the Passion of Christ. That Passion has come, Christ was buried, now it is Easter, and Christ is alive. Our tension and anxieties of Lent are released, and we exhale with joy the word "Alleluia." With it comes the end of our fasting, and with it comes something new. What new thing lives in your Alleluia? How will your life proclaim Alleluia for the next fifty days of Easter?

The Great Fifty Days of Easter – ten days longer than Lent – are meant to be a glorious extended celebration of our deliverance. The "alleluia" returns in hymns and worship. The BCP allows for omitting the General Confession during Eastertide. The Paschal candle – lit at the Easter Vigil – remains burning through Pentecost, as well as during baptisms and funerals. Many congregations stand for all prayers during the season. How might your congregation's liturgy express Easter joy for all seven Sundays of the season?

Engaging All Ages

On Good Friday, Jesus was carried into the tomb. This morning, the tomb is empty! As Christians, we hear this with happy ears, knowing that an empty tomb means that Jesus has been resurrected. And while Jesus is still with us, it is in a new and different way. One way to understand this is by making empty tomb rolls. There are many recipes out there, but the basic idea is that dough is rolled out to cover/surround a marshmallow. When the filled roll is baked, the marshmallow seems to disappear, but the essence is there as it has transformed into a part of the roll, just as Jesus is still with us.

Prayers of the People: Option 1

God of love, we rejoice with angels, and all the host of heaven, as we celebrate the Resurrection of your Son. Bless today's joyful celebration and turn our hearts to you with new delight and commitment.

We praise you, Almighty God. Alleluia! Amen!

God of mercy, bring your church to new life. Awaken in us a faithfulness that manifest itself in joy, in dedication to work of reconciliation in the world, in care for your creation, in awe of your glory.

We praise you, Almighty God. Alleluia! Amen!

God of wholeness, bring those who suffer to new life. We pray for those who bear the burden of pain and anxiety, whose relationships are shattered, whose lives are full of despair. Lead us to find ways to present with them and reflect your love for them.

We praise you, Almighty God. Alleluia! Amen!

God of light, bring those in authority to new life in the ways they lead their nations. Show them the path of integrity and truth that their people may live in peace, that all may have plenty.

We praise you, Almighty God. Alleluia! Amen!

God of eternity, we give thanks for those who have gone before us and have entered into new and everlasting life in your presence.

We praise you, Almighty God. Alleluia! Amen!

Prayers of the People: Option 2

Deacon or Presider

We come with anticipation on this first day of the week to become witnesses, sharing in the resurrection life of Jesus, as we pray: Alleluia! Christ is risen. He is risen indeed. Alleluia!

Litanist

Almighty One, you have filled your Church with new life and empowered us through the conquering love of Jesus: Raise us with your Spirit that we may live in the power of Christ's resurrection to bring life and light to all the world.

Alleluia! Christ is risen.

He is risen indeed. Alleluia!

The right hand of the Most High has triumphed over evil and death, bringing new hope to all the world: Speak your living truth to everyone who leads and holds authority among the nations, that they may be agents of life and justice.

Alleluia! Christ is risen.

He is risen indeed. Alleluia!

The Apostle Peter has taught us, O God, that you show no partiality, but you accept all who live reverently and do right: Let your peace extend to every person, that the power of evil and injustice may be banished, and all people may live as beloved children of the divine.

Alleluia! Christ is risen.

He is risen indeed. Alleluia!

Be with us in this community that we may be glad witnesses of your goodness, O Holy One.

Alleluia! Christ is risen.

He is risen indeed. Alleluia!

Christ the wounded healer has overcome all that can threaten us.

Let his resurrection power bring healing and hope to those for whom we pray, especially _______. Give thanks to God who is good, whose mercy endures for ever.
We offer our grateful gladness this Easter Day, especially for ____________. Christ has died and is risen, bringing life and immortality to light. We remember those who have died, especially __________. May they live in him and share in the joy of Easter.

Alleluia! Christ is risen.

He is risen indeed. Alleluia!

Presider

You have anointed Jesus of Nazareth with the Holy Spirit and with power, O Eternal One, and raised him from death on the cross into resurrection life: Feed us with his life as we eat and drink with him in this Easter Eucharist, that we may be his witnesses, sharing in the Spirit's work of reconciliation and peace, through the Risen One, Jesus Christ our Savior. ***Amen.***

Hymns for the Day

The Hymnal 1982

At the Lamb's high feast we sing 174
Christ is arisen (Christ ist erstanden) 713
Christ Jesus lay in death's strong bands 185, 186
Come, ye faithful, raise the strain 199, 200
Good Christians all, rejoice and sing 205
Jesus Christ is risen today 207
Look there! the Christ our brother comes 196, 197
The day of resurrection 210
The Lamb's high banquet called to share 202
The strife is o'er, the battle done 208
Hail thee, festival day 175
In Christ there is no East or West 529
Sing, ye faithful, sing with gladness 492
"Welcome, happy morning!" age to age shall say 179
This is the feast of victory for our God 417, 418
This is the hour of banquet and of song 316, 317
Alleluia, alleluia! Hearts and voices heavenward raise 191
Love's redeeming work is done 188, 189
Now the green blade riseth 204
We know that Christ is raised and dies no more 296

Christ the Lord is risen again 184
Christians, to the Paschal Victim 183
Lift your voice rejoicing, Mary 190
O sons and daughters, let us sing (1–3, 5) 203
On earth has dawned this day of days 201

Lift Every Voice and Sing II

Christ has arisen 41
Amen 233
In Christ there is no East or West 62
I come to the garden alone 69
They crucified my Savior 40

Wonder, Love, and Praise

Christ is risen from the dead 816, 817
Day of delight and beauty unbounded 738
God's Paschal Lamb is sacrificed for us 880

The Second Sunday of Easter

Variable – Between March 29 and May 2

Blessed are those who have not seen and yet have come to believe.

Anchor Points – The Propers and the Season

The fixed points for each service are the appointed or proper readings and collect as well as the themes of the day or season.

Readings and Psalm

Acts 4:32–35

In today's passage, Luke summarizes the life of the early Church in Jerusalem. Two descriptions of the believers' common life are given: complete community of goods and distribution to the needy, fulfilling the promise of Deuteronomy 15:4. The sharing of goods practiced by the Jerusalem church does not seem to have been repeated elsewhere. Although the care of the needy was always a feature of Christian communities, the important issue was not a particular economic principle, but the expression of the community's unity in love. The believers had one source and center of life, and were one in outwardly visible lifestyle.

Psalm 133

The psalmist offers a blessing for the covenant people that is also appropriate for families trying to live in unity.

1 John 1:1–2:2

The purpose of the message here is the attainment of "fellowship," oneness with Christ and other believers, in the face of threatened division. One divisive question was that of post-baptismal sin. The writer states that Christian believers are still sinful by nature and in act. Nonetheless, Jesus is our advocate, the one who speaks for us.

John 20:19–31

John's account of the first appearance of the risen Lord shows that Jesus has returned, bringing peace and joy. He shows his wounds to establish that the crucified Jesus and the risen Christ are one and the same. As he had promised, he then gives the disciples a mission and breathes upon them the Holy Spirit. Thomas personifies the elements of doubt that arise regarding the Resurrection. He expresses his disbelief in exactly the way Jesus had decried. Yet, without touching the Lord, he can still be brought to penetrate the meaning behind the marvel and to make a full affirmation of Christian faith. He consummates the sequence of titles given to Jesus by giving him the ultimate one of God. Jesus's blessing in response to him answers the problem of believers ever since the eyewitnesses died.

Collect

Almighty and everlasting God, who in the Paschal mystery established the new covenant of reconciliation: Grant that all who have been reborn into the fellowship of Christ's Body may show forth in their lives what they profess by their faith; through Jesus Christ our Lord, who lives and reigns with you and the Holy Spirit, one God, forever and ever. *Amen.*

Proper Preface

Easter – But chiefly are we bound to praise you for the glorious resurrection of your Son Jesus Christ our Lord; for he is the true Paschal Lamb, who was sacrificed for us, and has taken away the sin of the world. By his death he has destroyed death, and by his rising to life again he has won for us everlasting life. (Rite II BCP 379; Rite I BCP 346)

Seasonal Pairings

See the table below for choices appointed and suggested for this day. Preferences are put in **bold**. Not all choices are suitable for all congregations or community, though, so consider these preferences as a starting point before making a decision about your own congregation.

	Easter II	Rite I	Rite II	EOW1	BOS 2022
Color	White/Gold/Festive				
Entrance Rite	Customary; **Easter Acclamation**	323	355	50	
Song of Praise	Gloria in excelsis or Te Deum or **Pascha Nostrum**	324, 52, or **46**	356, 95, or **83**		
Collect		172	224		
Creed	Nicene Creed	326, 292	358, 292		
Prayers of the People	**Locally written**; options below; BCP forms	329	387–393	54–55	
Offertory Sentence	"Jesus said, 'Do not doubt but believe.' Thomas answered him, 'My Lord and my God!'" (John)	343–344	376–377		
Eucharistic Prayer	**One that allows use of the Easter preface** *or* **Prayer D**	2–340	**A – 361,** **B – 367** or **D – 372**	1–57	
Proper Preface	Easter	346	379		
Breaking of the Bread (Fraction)	Options using an alleluia: S 151, S 152, S 154, S 155, S 167, S 171	337	364		
Postcommunion Prayer		339	**Eternal God – 365**	God of abundance – 69	
Blessing	Customary *or* BOS	339	366	70–71	14
Dismissal	**Let us go forth in the Name of Christ. Alleluia, alleluia.**	340	366		
Notes					

Additional Notes:

Song of Praise – The ancient and unique Song of Praise for Eastertide is the Pascha nostrum, found in Morning Prayer. While it is often not as familiar to congregations as the frequently used Gloria in excelsis, it is worth exploring settings for it that would help it become more familiar. It may be used throughout the Easter Season.

Baptisms – While the Great Vigil is the baptismal feast *par excellence*, the Easter Season generally is a fitting season for baptisms, if some cannot be scheduled for the Great Vigil.

Eucharistic Prayer – There is not a Eucharistic Prayer that has distinct Easter/Resurrection themes, so selecting a Eucharistic Prayer that uses the Easter proper preface is an important option. Eucharistic Prayer D, which does not use a proper preface, may be desirable, because of the language exp

Fraction Anthem at the Breaking of the Bread – Certainly using options that incorporate "Alleluia" would be the most desirable. Several options in addition to "Christ our Passover" are provided in the Service Music section of *The Hymnal 1982*.

Content Resources

Reading Between the Lines

Every functioning group of people needs at least one hard-nosed realist who is utterly committed. Thomas served that function for the disciples: in John 11:16, 'Thomas, who was called the Twin, said to his fellow disciples, "Let us also go, that we may die with him,"' and in John 14:5, 'Thomas said to him, "Lord, we do not know where you are going. How can we know the way?"' Thomas loved Jesus enough to be willing to die with him, didn't get to do that, and then wasn't present when Jesus first appeared to the disciples. Would we have done any better believing friends who told us a dead mentor had risen and appeared to them? Wouldn't we think grief had temporarily deranged our friends? Wouldn't hope be too painful to entertain? Can't you hear it? "We saw the wounds in his hands and his feet!" "You were seeing things; I'll believe it when I feel them."

There is no shame in requiring the witness of our senses. The writer of the first letter of John explicitly cites the experience of having heard, seen, touched the word of life as grounds for his witness to us. Now, because we believe, like the apostles, we will look for and see the Word of life in everyone we encounter and in the world around us. And it is that constant expectation of seeing the Risen Lord that drives the "great power" Acts ascribes to the witness of the apostles, and if we let it, will drive our witness too.

Central Themes

In today's passage from 1 John, we hear about all that we have. He writes about all that we have heard, and seen, and looked, and touched regarding the Word of life. There are times in our life when we may feel like we don't have enough – enough time, or talent, or influence, or money, or power, or anything else that might seem helpful. But this passage reminds us that in Jesus, we already have everything we need to have the fullness of joy.

There are over 290 Kibbutzim. Collective communities unique to Israel. A first, Degania, was located south of the Sea of Galilee. Initially, Kibbutzim were primarily agrarian. Members had roles in the collective be that actual farming or preparing meals or educating children or other work. Today, a vast majority of Kibbutzim are privatized. Money has a lot more significance as it is used to pay salaries to members or used by members to purchase goods and services such as a home in the community. What would it mean and look like for you if things were "held in common?"

"Peace be with you," says Jesus, as he appears to the terrified disciples, as Luke tells the story. In every resurrection appearance, Jesus proclaims *shalom*. Then they all break bread together. "Then he opened their minds to understand the scriptures," writes Luke. In each celebration of Holy eucharist, we exchange the Peace. And when the eucharistic bread is broken, we proclaim, "Christ our Passover is sacrificed for us." In the breaking of the bread and the exchange of the peace, Christ is revealed to us, and reminds us that we are all connected.

Engaging All Ages

Science classes often include experiments where the results are not known or understood right away. Sometimes we believe and understand what we are being told immediately, but sometimes we want more information before believing or deciding. Thomas, one of the disciples, was kind of like that. His friends told him about Jesus, but he could not believe it until he saw Jesus himself. What is something unbelievable your friends or family has told you, something so crazy that you had to see and experience it yourself to believe it? What kind of questions did you ask to learn more? What questions do you need to ask to better recognize Jesus?

Prayers of the People: Option 1

We join our hearts and voices in praying for ourselves, our neighbors, the church, the world.

My Lord, and my God. Amen. Alleluia.

Even as your people, living in your world, as we praise your name, we recognize a twinge of fear and doubt in our hearts, we ask you to manifest your presence in our lives in a tangible and glorious way. We pray to you,

My Lord, and my God. Amen. Alleluia.

We pray for your followers throughout the world, that they have an experience of your love for themselves, and a genuine experience of love with each other. We pray to you,

My Lord, and my God. Amen. Alleluia.

We pray for those in authority everywhere, that they are sensitive to the needs of those they serve, that they create environments in which integrity, truth, and justice flourish. We pray to you,

My Lord, and my God. Amen. Alleluia.

We bring before you those who are on our hearts this day, who are suffering from spiritual or physical pain, who are paralyzed with anxiety and despair. Come into their lives with powerful healing, and into their hearts with words of comfort and peace. Hold those dying today close to your heart and welcome them into your eternal light and life. We pray to you,

My Lord, and my God. Amen. Alleluia.

Prayers of the People: Option 2

Deacon or Priest

In his victory over death, Christ Jesus gives us the blessing of new life. Let us offer our prayers for new life for all the world, saying "Savior, in your mercy, Hear our prayer."

Leader

Gracious God: Guide our hearts, that our witness to your abundant love will bring reconciliation to the Church. Guide our feet to those places where the awareness of your loving presence is needed. Guide our hands to those who need your loving touch. Guide and sustain *N.* our Presiding Bishop, *N.* our bishops, our parish clergy, and all your ministers.

Savior, in your mercy

Hear our prayer.

God of Justice: Guide this nation toward a path of justice for all peoples and grant all those in authority the desire to seek the common good so that the barriers which divide us may disappear.

Savior, in your mercy

Hear our prayer.

God of Mercy: Open our eyes to the poor, the destitute and the homeless and to victims of racism, exploitation or violence in any form. Sustain us in our efforts to combat fear, prejudice and ignorance in ourselves and in others.

Savior, in your mercy

Hear our prayer.

Creator God: Open our eyes to the renewing work of your Spirit that we may see in the beauty of spring flowers your promise of new life. Fill us with such reverence and awe for the mysteries of our world that we will strive to be faithful stewards of our natural resources.

Savior, in your mercy

Hear our prayer.

Loving God: Open our hearts to your love each day as we live together in community that we may see your face in our neighbors. Deliver us from pride, pretense, or self-occupation so that our time and energy may be spent seeking your wisdom in the service of others. We pray for our parish retreat next weekend.

Savior, in your mercy

Hear our prayer.

God of healing: Guide us to those who suffer and send your healing touch on those who are broken in body or spirit, for those we name now, either silently or aloud . . .

Silence

Savior, in your mercy

Hear our prayer.

God of Light and Life: Receive all those who have died that they may live eternally with you in your Light. We pray for all those we name now, either silently or aloud . . .

Silence

Savior, in your mercy

Hear our prayer.

God of Glory: Accept our heartfelt thanksgivings for the many blessings you have bestowed on us by your grace. We give thanks for our time together in this place as we prepare to be faithful servants of your Word. We give thanks for the joy of spring and for those things for which we now give you praise, either silently or aloud . . . *Silence*

Savior, in your mercy

Hear our prayer.

Presider

Guide us and sustain us, Almighty God, and grant us knowledge of the power of your love that has turned death into life, so that we may die daily to ourselves and live eternally in your Light; through Jesus Christ our Lord. ***Amen.***

Hymns for the Day

The Hymnal 1982

Christ the Lord is risen again 184
Good Christians all, rejoice and sing 205
Jesus is Lord of all the earth 178
Jesus lives! thy terrors now 194, 195
Sing, ye faithful, sing with gladness 492
This joyful Eastertide 192
I want to walk as a child of the light 490
Just as I am, without one plea 693
Awake, arise, lift up your voice 212
By all your saints still striving 231, 232 (2: St. Thomas)
How oft, O Lord, thy face hath shone 242
O sons and daughters, let us sing 206
We walk by faith and not by sight 209

Lift Every Voice and Sing II

Just as I am, without one plea 137
We walk by faith and not by sight 206

Wonder, Love, and Praise

From the dawning of creation 748
We are marching in the light of God 787

The Third Sunday of Easter

Variable – Between April 5 and May 9

We know the risen Christ in sacramental life.

Anchor Points – The Propers and the Season

The fixed points for each service are the appointed or proper readings and collect as well as the themes of the day or season.

Readings and Psalm

Acts 3:12–19

The book of the Acts of the Apostles recounts the early growth of the Christian Church. One of the major features of Acts is Luke's use of speeches by principal figures to provide reflection upon and analysis of events. These speeches demonstrate the basic preaching pattern of the apostolic Church to different audiences as the Church moves from the Jewish to the Gentile world. Today's reading is taken from the second of these discourses, Peter's Temple sermon, which begins with the basic proclamation about Jesus's death, and resurrection. This kernel is then fleshed out in a longer section identifying Jesus with various figures from the Hebrew scriptures.

Psalm 4

From the depths of his troubles, the psalmist expresses his trust in God as helper (savior). He knows that God will always help and answer his pleas, and this awareness brings peace. Because God is his savior, he can rest securely and warn others to trust in God alone.

1 John 3:1–7

Today's reading takes up the theme of Christians and sin, in the context of their adoption as "children of God" (v. 1). This special relationship to God was formerly extended to Israel as a people and especially to the king as Israel's representative. In Hebrew idiom, "to be the child of" meant to exhibit the characteristics of one's father. Christians are truly God's children now, yet they are still in the process of growing into resemblance to God by imitating Christ in their behavior.

Luke 24:36b–48

By showing the marks of the crucifixion, the risen Christ identifies himself as the earthly Jesus. He shows himself to be "really real," not a vision or a ghost. The account displays the Hebrew understanding of the person as particular and embodied, in contrast to the Greek sense of the person as merely the "soul." As in the Emmaus story, the disciples recognize Jesus in the context of a meal and in the exposition of the scriptures.

Collect

O God, whose blessed Son made himself known to his disciples in the breaking of bread: Open the eyes of our faith, that we may behold him in all his redeeming work; who lives and reigns with you, in the unity of the Holy Spirit, one God, now and for ever. *Amen.*

Proper Preface

Easter – But chiefly are we bound to praise you for the glorious resurrection of your Son Jesus Christ our Lord; for he is the true Paschal Lamb, who was sacrificed for us, and has taken away the sin of the world. By his death he has destroyed death, and by his rising to life again he has won for us everlasting life. (Rite II BCP 379; Rite I BCP 346)

Seasonal Pairings

See the table below for choices appointed and suggested for this day. Preferences are put in **bold**. Not all choices are suitable for all congregations or community, though, so consider these preferences as a starting point before making a decision about your own congregation.

	Easter III	Rite I	Rite II	EOW1	BOS 2022
Color	White/Gold/Festive				
Entrance Rite	Customary; **Easter Acclamation**	323	355	50	
Song of Praise	Gloria in excelsis or Te Deum or **Pascha Nostrum**	324, 52, or **46**	356, 95, or **83**		
Collect		173	224		
Creed	Nicene Creed	326, 292	358, 292		
Prayers of the People	**Locally written**; options below; BCP forms	329	387–393	54–55	
Offertory Sentence	"Offer the appointed sacrifices and put your trust in the Lord." (Psalm 4) *or* "Beloved, we are God's children now; what we will be has not yet been revealed. What we do know is this: when he is revealed, we will be like him." (1 John)	343–344	376–377		
Eucharistic Prayer	**One that allows use of the Easter preface** *or* **Prayer D**	2–340	**A – 361,** **B – 367** or **D – 372**	1–57	
Proper Preface	Easter	346	379		
Breaking of the Bread (Fraction)	Options using an alleluia: S 151, S 152, S 154, S 155, S 167, S 171	337	364		
Postcommunion Prayer		339	**Eternal God – 365**	God of abundance – 69	
Blessing	Customary *or* BOS	339	366	70–71	14
Dismissal	**Let us go forth in the Name of Christ. Alleluia, alleluia.**	340	366		
Notes					

Additional Notes:

Song of Praise – The ancient and unique Song of Praise for Eastertide is the Pascha nostrum, found in Morning Prayer. While it is often not as familiar to congregations as the frequently used Gloria in excelsis, it is worth exploring settings for it that would help it become more familiar. It may be used throughout the Easter Season.

Baptisms – While the Great Vigil is the baptismal feast *par excellence*, the Easter Season generally is a fitting season for baptisms, if some cannot be scheduled for the Great Vigil.

Eucharistic Prayer – There is not a Eucharistic Prayer that has distinct Easter/Resurrection themes, so selecting a Eucharistic Prayer that uses the Easter proper preface is an important option. Eucharistic Prayer D, which does not use a proper preface, may be desirable, because of the language expressing God's glory.

Fraction Anthem at the Breaking of the Bread – Certainly using options that incorporate "Alleluia" would be the most desirable. Several options in addition to "Christ our Passover" are provided in the Service Music section of *The Hymnal 1982.*

Content Resources

Reading Between the Lines

Luke's second account of Jesus appearance to the disciples, this time in Jerusalem, conveys similar themes to the first one (Luke 24:13–35) wherein Jesus appeared as a stranger on the road to Emmaus, namely, identity, recognition, and Jesus' words interpreting scripture. Since Year B does not include the first account of Jesus' appearance to two disciples on the road, a reminder might be helpful. In today's gospel, this second appearance of Jesus occasions fear, doubt, and terror. When Jesus invites the eleven Jerusalem disciples to examine his hands and feet, their joyful recognition of his identity does not yet amount to faith (v. 41). Eating, together with repetition of scriptural exposition (v. 44 cf. v. 27), encourages recognition. New elements include Jesus' command to proclaim repentance and forgiveness of sins to all nations, beginning from Jerusalem, and the sending of the Holy Spirit (v. 49), an allusion to the beginning of Acts, namely, volume two of Luke's gospel.

Central Themes

Can you imagine what it was like for the disciples to have a post-resurrected Jesus show up in their midst? These were the same group that denied him and left him for dead. And now he has come back from the dead and can walk through walls? They were right to be terrified, because they would have reason to doubt that Jesus would be pleased with them. Yet, he doesn't come looking for revenge. Rather, the very first words out his mouth are "Peace be with you." It seems with Jesus, forgiveness comes even to those who are terrified they won't receive it.

In "Peace be with you," the word translated to "Peace" is *Eirene*. Like most Greek words it can have many nuanced meanings. It can mean harmony between two or more people. It can mean a balance in the relationship between a person and a thing. In Greek mythology, Eirene was the goddess of peace and wealth. She had two sisters: Dike, the goddess of moral justice, and Eunomia, the goddess of laws and legislation. Like the middle sister keeping balance between the two, Eirene's peace and wealth are the product when these two are in good and right relationship.

The collects for Easter petition the living power of Jesus to open up new life to all. Our prayers and action can reflect God's desire of reconciliation for all. The collect for this Third Sunday of Easter asks God to "open the eyes of our faith, that we may behold him in all his redeeming work." It reminds us that the actions of the church and of individual Christians must be judged as to whether they are redeeming or demeaning works. Also, the healing ministry of the church involves the healing of society as well as individuals.

Engaging All Ages

Jesus preaches and teaches the importance of loving one another. According to Jesus and his followers, everyone who has faith is worthy of love and capable of loving others. But it is not just about ability; it is about action. Jesus did not just sit around; he went to people and helped them. He went to different places to teach people, to heal people, and to show others the goodness of people. And in his resurrection, he called on all of us to carry on that message. Helping at a food pantry, weeding a community garden, and teaching someone to read are some of the ways to help people in need. How will you love people in need?

Prayers of the People: Option 1

You have no equal, God. We come before you humbled, asking for your healing presence. Heal us, raise us so that we may serve you.

We are amazed at your creative genius – how you have stretched the heavens like curtains, and yet you bend to be with us.

We are amazed, God. We raise our hearts in awe.

Our world and our lives are in need of healing and direction. We ask you to guide your church and heal it where it is worn out and self-centered. Direct those who lead the church: bishops, priests and deacons; all those in positions of leadership.

We ask for direction. Raise our hearts to you, God.

We ask you to heal the relationships between nations, and neighbors. Give the leaders of the nations the courage to pursue justice and speak peace as an example for the world.

We ask for healing. Raise our hearts to you, God.

Many of us suffer from addiction, anxiety, and illness. Break their chains which bind them and heal them, God. Surround them with supportive people, the resources they need, and a tangible sense of your love.

We ask for healing. Raise our hearts to you, God.

We pray for those who have died, that they may know the fullness of your love in the life you have prepared for them. Comfort those who grieve their loss and give them the confidence of your love which knows no limits of time or space.

We ask for assurance of your love. Raise our hearts to you, God.

Prayers of the People: Option 2

Deacon or Presider

In this season of Easter, let us offer our prayers with all our heart, mind, and body, saying "Lord, in your mercy, receive our prayer."

Intercessor

Gracious God, inspire all church members and leaders – lay and ordained – to know your saving power, and serve you with true humility. We pray for the Church throughout the world,

Lord, in your mercy,

Receive our prayer.

Give discerning hearts and minds to those who hold authority in the nations of the world, that they may move toward peace and reconciliation and away from violence. We pray for all countries torn apart by violence and war. For those who have died in all places of strife, for civilians, for members of the military, and for their families. Comfort them in their loss.

Lord, in your mercy,

Receive our prayer.

Show us, your human family, how to share and mobilize resources so that those in need and those with plenty may join together. Deepen our desire, sharpen our will and intention to respect the dignity of all. We pray for all those in our own city, country, and around the world who suffer from homelessness or poverty, or who cannot find work.

Lord, in your mercy,

Receive our prayer.

Inspire all in this community to learn and grow in our knowledge and love of you. Bless our relationships with one another that we may speak and act in love, truth, and humility. Be in our praying, thinking, and all that we do, especially as we seek to expand our reach, that we may choose your will.

Lord, in your mercy,

Receive our prayer.

We thank you, Lord, for the joy of resurrection, and all the blessings of this life. We give thanks for all we name now, silently or aloud . . . *Silence*

Lord, in your mercy,

Receive our prayer.

Break the bonds of illness, addiction, despair, and loneliness by your healing power. We bring in prayer those who are suffering in body, mind, or spirit. Deepen our faith, Lord, in your power to heal. We pray for those we name now, silently or aloud . . . *Silence*

Lord, in your mercy,

Receive our prayer.

Give rest, O Christ, to those who have died with [__________________ and all] your saints, where sorrow and pain are no more, neither sighing, but life everlasting. We pray for those we name now, silently or aloud . . . *Silence*

Lord, in your mercy,

Receive our prayer.

Presider

Almighty God, you raised up Jesus Christ, that the whole world may shine forth your presence. Open the eyes of our faith, and so infuse us with the power of your Holy Spirit, that we may bear witness to his Name in all the cares and occupations of our lives; through Jesus Christ our Lord. ***Amen.***

Hymns for the Day

The Hymnal 1982

Christ is alive! Let Christians sing 182
Come, let us with our Lord arise 49
Good Christians all, rejoice and sing 205 (1, 3–5)
Sing, ye faithful, sing with gladness 492
Baptized in water 294
Sing praise to our Creator 295
Awake, arise, lift up your voice 212
Blessed Jesus, at thy word 440
Come, risen Lord, and deign to be our guest 305, 306
Come, ye faithful, raise the strain 199, 200
Look, there! the Christ our brother comes 196, 197
O sons and daughters, let us sing 203
That Easter day with joy was bright 193

Lift Every Voice and Sing II

Christ has arisen 41
Baptized in water 121
Children of the heavenly Father 213

Wonder, Love, and Praise

Day of delight and beauty unbounded 738
Baptized in water 767
You're called by name, forever loved 766

The Fourth Sunday of Easter

Variable – Between April 12 and May 16

I am the Good Shepherd who lays down his life for the sheep.

Anchor Points – The Propers and the Season

The fixed points for each service are the appointed or proper readings and collect as well as the themes of the day or season.

Readings and Psalm

Acts 4:5–12

According to Luke, the arrest of Peter and John is instigated by the Sadducees. The Sadducees held only to the written law, rejected the oral tradition followed by the Pharisees and did not believe in the resurrection of the dead. The Pharisees taught a future general resurrection, but Peter and John proclaim resurrection as a present and life-giving reality in Jesus.

Psalm 23

This psalm is probably the most familiar and popular psalm of all. It celebrates God's loving care for us under the guise of a good shepherd who provides food, security, and protection from all dangers. God guides us on our journey through life so that we might "dwell in the house of the Lord."

1 John 3:16–24

These verses discuss the mark of a Christian's life – love. This love is the proof that Christians have passed from death to life. Refusal to love one another is tantamount to murder. True love for one another is manifested in action, modeled upon the experience of Jesus's love for us. It is shown as self-sacrifice at the heroic level and in the daily exercise of generosity. Deeds, not devout protestations or guilty feelings, will reveal our true standing before God, who knows us better than we know ourselves.

John 10:11–18

In Hebrew scripture, God is called the Shepherd of Israel, as is David or the Davidic Messiah. Today's gospel develops the figure of the shepherd of the sheep. Jesus is "the good shepherd" (v. 11). The word good might be better rendered as "model." Jesus is the model shepherd, both because of his willingness to lay down his life and because of his intimate knowledge of his flock. The intimacy between the shepherd and his flock parallels that between the Father and the Son. The purpose of this mutual knowledge is to bring Jesus's followers, both the flock of Israel and the Gentile flocks, into union with him and with one another.

Collect

O God, whose Son Jesus is the good shepherd of your people: Grant that when we hear his voice we may know him who calls us each by name, and follow where he leads; who, with you and the Holy Spirit, lives and reigns, one God, for ever and ever. *Amen.*

Proper Preface

Easter – But chiefly are we bound to praise you for the glorious resurrection of your Son Jesus Christ our Lord; for he is the true Paschal Lamb, who was sacrificed for us, and has taken away the sin of the world. By his death he has destroyed death, and by his rising to life again he has won for us everlasting life. (Rite II BCP 379; Rite I BCP 346)

Seasonal Pairings

See the table below for choices appointed and suggested for this day. Preferences are put in **bold**. Not all choices are suitable for all congregations or community, though, so consider these preferences as a starting point before making a decision about your own congregation.

	Easter IV	Rite I	Rite II	EOW1	BOS 2022
Color	White/Gold/Festive				
Entrance Rite	Customary; **Easter Acclamation**	323	355	50	
Song of Praise	Gloria in excelsis or Te Deum or **Pascha Nostrum**	324, 52, or **46**	356, 95, or **83**		
Collect		173	225		
Creed	Nicene Creed	326, 292	358, 292		
Prayers of the People	**Locally written**; options below; BCP forms	329	387–393	54–55	
Offertory Sentence	"Little children, let us love, not in word or speech, but in truth and action." (1 John)	343–344	376–377		
Eucharistic Prayer	**One that allows use of the Easter preface** *or* **Prayer D**	2–340	**A – 361,** **B – 367** or **D – 372**	1–57	
Proper Preface	Easter	346	379		
Breaking of the Bread (Fraction)	Options using an alleluia: S 151, S 152, S 154, S 155, S 167, S 171	337	364		
Postcommunion Prayer		339	**Eternal God – 365**	God of abundance – 69	
Blessing	Customary *or* BOS	339	366	70–71	14
Dismissal	**Let us go forth in the Name of Christ. Alleluia, alleluia.**	340	366		
Notes	Sometimes called "Good Shepherd" Sunday				

Additional Notes:

Song of Praise – The ancient and unique Song of Praise for Eastertide is the Pascha nostrum, found in Morning Prayer. While it is often not as familiar to congregations as the frequently used Gloria in excelsis, it is worth exploring settings for it that would help it become more familiar. It may be used throughout the Easter Season.

Baptisms – While the Great Vigil is the baptismal feast *par excellence*, the Easter Season generally is a fitting season for baptisms, if some cannot be scheduled for the Great Vigil.

Eucharistic Prayer – There is not a Eucharistic Prayer that has distinct Easter/Resurrection themes, so selecting a Eucharistic Prayer that uses the Easter proper preface is an important option. Eucharistic Prayer D, which does not use a proper preface, may be desirable, because of the language expressing God's glory.

Fraction Anthem at the Breaking of the Bread – Certainly using options that incorporate "Alleluia" would be the most desirable. Several options in addition to "Christ our Passover" are provided in the Service Music section of *The Hymnal 1982*.

Content Resources

Reading Between the Lines

When Jesus declares emphatically in John 10:11, "I am the Good Shepherd," the writer of the Fourth Gospel is using a metaphor to describe Jesus as the Good Shepherd who saves, addresses, calls, protects, feeds, and leads the sheep back home. The sheep in turn hear, follow, recognize, and benefit from the shepherd's voice since they find pasture and still water. The good shepherd gives his (or her: in 2013 at the Artemesion in Sardis, our tour group saw a woman shepherd with her flock) life for the sheep because leaders protect and assume responsibility for the sheep; sheep know and trust shepherds. The hired hand, in contrast, flees when danger threatens in the shape of a predatory wolf, leaving the sheep exposed, vulnerable, and likely to die, since his loyalty is not to the sheep.

By using an adjective, "good," John also invites readers or hearers of the gospel to view the shepherd metaphor through the lens of honor and shame, the two most important values in the world of Jesus' time. In John 10:11 and 14, the shepherd leader is called *kalos* in Greek. *Kalos* connotes someone or something good, honorable, or noble. Its opposite is "shameful," or "bad." Since the shepherd gives his life for the sheep, and knows them, the shepherd is good, or honorable. The mutual knowledge of sheep and shepherd is similar to the relationship between Jesus and the Father (John 10:15). Knowing in John's gospel is relationship: to know the Father is to be in relationship to the Father. So, the shepherd is both courageous and honorable since he protects the sheep whereas the hired hand acts shamefully because he thinks only of himself. The sheep do not matter to him. Jesus' behavior as the good, honorable shepherd is presented as a model of honorable even salvific behavior to be emulated by others; in John 15:13, Jesus exhorts the disciples, "Greater love than this has no one, than that one lay down one's life for one's friend."

John 10 belongs to a sequence in the gospel that begins with the story of Jesus and the disciples encountering a blind man (John 9:1–3) and ends with those across the Jordan who believe in Jesus (John 10:42). We cannot understand the Good Shepherd metaphor apart from this context. Hearers of this narrative are invited to identify Jesus through actions and metaphors as healer, door, gate, and shepherd, rather than with the judgments of John's Jews(Judeans)/Pharisees. The Jesus encountered in John 9–10 as healer, gate, door, and shepherd of the sheep is also the resurrected Jesus and the Word of John 1, existing with God in the beginning, and now incarnate flesh, pitching a tent amongst us. John's Pharisees/Jews on one side, and the man born blind on the other model disbelief and belief in their attempted dialogue in John 9; the former "did/do not believe" that the man had been blind, and had received his sight, in contrast to the healed man who hears Jesus' voice before he sees Jesus and who comes, through dialogue and gradually deepening insight, to worship him saying, "Lord, I believe" (9.38). For the blind man, for Lazarus whom Jesus also called (11:43–44), and for us, hearing is crucial.

Jesus' identity can only be secured through insight which the healed man has by the end of chapter 9. Although cast out from worship in the synagogue, *he is found by Jesus the shepherd seeking lost sheep* whom he comes to worship. Whilst disciples, Pharisees, and the man born blind hear Jesus' words in John 9 and 10, John's Pharisees and Jews (Judeans) are not able to see, that is, to recognize Jesus' origin, identity, and potential. Indeed, a failure to understand leads to further division and misperception: "he has a demon," (10:20–21) whilst the truth is the complete opposite as we see in Jesus' declaration: "The Father and I are one" (10:30).

So, if John 9–10 are indeed a narrative sequence, why does Jesus choose the imagery of the Gate and the Good Shepherd to interpret the healing of the man born blind, now one of Jesus' sheep? Prof Karoline Lewis suggests it is because in John 18, Jesus will be the gate of the sheepfold, standing between and going out from the disciples who are safely in the garden towards the threatening soldiers outside the garden who have come to arrest him. Embodying God's love is making a conscious decision not to act in power over or coercion but to act in sacrificial self-giving.

Behind the Good Shepherd metaphor lie texts like Psalm 23 declaring, "The Lord is my shepherd, I have all I need." This shepherd provides food, water and protection for each sheep, whose worth is not determined by a search for them. "He restores my soul" is literally, "He brings me back." At the Psalm's ending we are not followed but chased and pursued by goodness and loving kindness every day of our lives, and wherever we are, there God will be.

Central Themes

The rod and staff of a good shepherd are not just there to be good props for Christmas pageants. They are they to be used as defensive tools against those who would hurt the good shepherd's flock. Yet, they are only used in this psalm to comfort. Easter is a time when we watch God turn all we think we know about pain and death and transform them into peace and life. How can we turn the weapons of this world and of our hearts into tools of peace instead?

We have the familiar image of the Good Shepherd – perhaps too familiar. Often images that have long histories can lack some of the power they first held. Their resonance can be dampened with each use. The image would have been recognizable to many including Christians and people of other faiths or no faith. In fact, originally, it was an image of paganism. And Christians would have used it to preach to pagans. The church has been expert at using known images to speak in new ways about Christ and God. What might be Good Shepherd-like images in your life?

The Fourth Sunday of Easter is known as "Good Shepherd Sunday." The lectionary this year assures us that the Good Shepherd knows us by name, protects us from evil, and lays down his life for us sheep. The images of the Good Shepherd remind us that he seeks out the lost and restores them to their community. How can these words and images inspire us to imitate the Good Shepherd, offering our lives – our skills, our resources, our time, and our love – for others?

Engaging All Ages

The Bible is full of stories and songs written in prose or poem form. Many of the best-known poems come from the Book of Psalms. Today we read Psalm 23, a poem written by David about God. In this psalm, David tells about his faith and trust in God. He knows that God will always keep him safe and will guide him even in the hardest moments. As you think about the ways you trust and follow God, write a poem of your own that tells others how you feel about walking with God through life.

Prayers of the People: Option 1

Lead your church into the way of love. Teach us to hear and follow your voice and your vision for the world.

Tender Shepherd,

call us each by name and lead us home.

Guide those around the world who make decisions that impact the lives of individuals and nations.

Tender Shepherd,

precede us all in the ways of justice and peace.

Lighten the burden of those suffering loss, illness, and anxiety, those whom we know and love and those who are unknown to us.

Tender Shepherd,

comfort them and shower them with your healing grace.

We pray for those who have died. Carry those who have finished their earthly journey into the next life and gently place them in God's eternal embrace.

Tender Shepherd,

hold them close to your heart forever.

Prayers of the People: Option 2

Deacon or Priest

As one flock with one Shepherd, let us lift our voices in prayer for the Church and the world.

Leader

Let us love, not in word of speech

But in truth and action to allow us to reach

The Good Shepherd calls us to abide

With the grace of God as our guide.

Amen, Come Lord Jesus.

Help us to lay down our life, assured

To pick up our life through Christ our Lord

We pray for our common ministries, as in truth and action we abide

With the grace of God as our guide.

Amen, Come Lord Jesus.

For our bishop, *N.*, and all those preparing for Confirmation,

for our youth, and all those in formation

That in truth and action they may abide

With the grace of God as their guide.

Amen, Come Lord Jesus.

May wisdom guide every national, state, and local official

For their work to be beneficial

That in truth and action they may abide

With the grace of God as their guide.

Amen, Come Lord Jesus.

Bring healing to a broken world

Rescue us from that which we make us unfurled

That in truth and action we all can abide

With the grace of God as our guide.

Amen, Come Lord Jesus.

May the sick and broken hearted be healed

May the souls of the departed be sealed

Give all comfort that they may abide

With the grace of God as their guide.

Amen, Come Lord Jesus.

Presider

Grant, we pray, Almighty God, that we who celebrate with awe the Paschal feast may be found worthy to attain to everlasting joys; through Jesus Christ our Lord, who lives and reigns with you and the Holy Spirit, one God, now and for ever. ***Amen.***

Hymns for the Day

The Hymnal 1982

Christ the Lord is risen again 184
Good Christians all, rejoice and sing! 205 (vs 1, 3–5)
My Shepherd will supply my need 664
Sing, ye faithful, sing with gladness 492
The King of love my shepherd is 645, 646
The Lord my God my Shepherd is 663
The strife is o'er, the battle done 208
At the name of Jesus 435
Christ is made the sure foundation 518
How sweet the Name of Jesus sounds 644
The Church's one foundation 525
To the Name of our salvation 248, 249
God is Love, and where true love is 576, 577
I come with joy to meet my Lord 304
Lord, whose love through humble service 610

Where charity and love prevail 581
Where true charity and love dwell 606
You, Lord, we praise in songs of celebration 319
Jesus, our mighty Lord 478
Praise the Lord, rise up rejoicing 334
Savior, like a shepherd lead us 708
Shepherd of souls, refresh and bless 343

Lift Every Voice and Sing II
The Lord is my Shepherd 104

Wonder, Love, and Praise
Ubi caritas et amor 831

The Fifth Sunday of Easter

Variable – Between April 19 and May 23

God is love, and those who abide in love abide in God, and God abides in them.

Anchor Points – The Propers and the Season

The fixed points for each service are the appointed or proper readings and collect as well as the themes of the day or season.

Readings and Psalm

Acts 8:26–40

Philip has been presented as evangelist to the despised Samaritans. Now he has been sent to another outsider. Ethiopia in the first century referred to southern Egypt, now the Sudan. The eunuch may have been a Gentile proselyte or a "God-fearer," who accepted much but not all of the Jewish law. As a eunuch, he would have been barred from Jewish worship, although Isaiah prophesied the inclusion of eunuchs. The fourth servant song from Isaiah (Isaiah 52:13–53:12), which becomes the inspiration for the eunuch's inquiries, was central for the early Church's understanding of Jesus's death and resurrection as Christians searched the scriptures to find confirmation of what they had seen to be true.

Psalm 22:24–30

Psalm 22 consists of a lament and a thanksgiving in which the psalmist describes the distress he is suffering and his trust in God. These verses express unwavering confidence in God's saving deeds.

1 John 4:7–21

The author repeats his earlier theme: God's indwelling in the Christian is manifested in love for one another. In this reading, the theme is set in the context of the nature of God. Love is God's most characteristic activity. But the author's assertion that "God is love" (v. 8) cannot be inverted to include the maxim that "love is God." Much of what we experience as "love" is far from God's love. God's love is not an emotion but an event, made known to us in and through Christ's incarnation and our redemption. Because this love is so intricately tied to Christ, the Christian's mission of love is of necessity a mission of witness. We love one another as a manifestation of God's life in us.

John 15:1–8

Jesus, as Son, the representative of Israel, is "the true vine" (v. 1) who fulfills the calling of Israel. The Father is the vine grower who "prunes" (v. 2, "trims clean") the branches. Jesus reassures the disciples that they are already "pruned" (v. 3, translated "cleansed" in the NRSV) by his word. For John, Christian life is an active and committed life. There cannot be a living, unproductive branch. Those who do not remain, or abide, are taken away. Those who do abide through prayer bear fruit and show themselves as Jesus's disciples.

Collect

Almighty God, whom truly to know is everlasting life: Grant us so perfectly to know your Son Jesus Christ to be the way, the truth, and the life, that we may steadfastly follow his steps in the way that leads to eternal life; through Jesus Christ your Son our Lord, who lives and reigns with you, in the unity of the Holy Spirit, one God, forever and ever. *Amen.*

Proper Preface

Easter – But chiefly are we bound to praise you for the glorious resurrection of your Son Jesus Christ our Lord; for he is the true Paschal Lamb, who was sacrificed for us, and has taken away the sin of the world. By his death he has destroyed death, and by his rising to life again he has won for us everlasting life. (Rite II BCP 379; Rite I BCP 346)

Seasonal Pairings

See the table below for choices appointed and suggested for this day. Preferences are put in **bold**. Not all choices are suitable for all congregations or community, though, so consider these preferences as a starting point before making a decision about your own congregation.

	Easter V	Rite I	Rite II	EOW1	BOS 2022
Color	White/Gold/Festive				
Entrance Rite	Customary; **Easter Acclamation**	323	355	50	
Song of Praise	Gloria in excelsis or Te Deum or **Pascha Nostrum**	324, 52, or **46**	356, 95, or **83**		
Collect		173	225		
Creed	Nicene Creed	326, 292	358, 292		
Prayers of the People	**Locally written**; options below; BCP forms	329	387–393	54–55	
Offertory Sentence	"Jesus said, 'I am the vine, you are the branches. Those who abide in me and I in them bear much fruit'" (John)	343–344	376–377		
Eucharistic Prayer	**One that allows use of the Easter preface** *or* **Prayer D**	2–340	**A – 361, B – 367** or **D – 372**	1–57	
Proper Preface	Easter	346	379		
Breaking of the Bread (Fraction)	Options using an alleluia: S 151, S 152, S 154, S 155, S 167, S 171	337	364		
Postcommunion Prayer		339	**Eternal God – 365**	God of abundance – 69	
Blessing	Customary *or* BOS	339	366	70–71	14
Dismissal	**Let us go forth in the Name of Christ. Alleluia, alleluia.**	340	366		
Notes					

Additional Notes:

Song of Praise – The ancient and unique Song of Praise for Eastertide is the Pascha nostrum, found in Morning Prayer. While it is often not as familiar to congregations as the frequently used Gloria in excelsis, it is worth exploring settings for it that would help it become more familiar. It may be used throughout the Easter Season.

Baptisms – While the Great Vigil is the baptismal feast *par excellence*, the Easter Season generally is a fitting season for baptisms, if some cannot be scheduled for the Great Vigil.

Eucharistic Prayer – There is not a Eucharistic Prayer that has distinct Easter/Resurrection themes, so selecting a Eucharistic Prayer that uses the Easter proper preface is an important option. Eucharistic Prayer D, which does not use a proper preface, may be desirable, because of the language expressing God's glory.

Fraction Anthem at the Breaking of the Bread – Certainly using options that incorporate "Alleluia" would be the most desirable. Several options in addition to "Christ our Passover" are provided in the Service Music section of *The Hymnal 1982.*

Content Resources

Reading Between the Lines

Acts 8:26–40 displays Luke's journey theme wherein conversations amongst fellow travelers include holy actions and revelations. The apostle Philip is dispatched by the Holy Spirit to a desert road, and travelling along that road he hears a pilgrim reading the Greek text of the Hebrew Bible. This is a court official returning to Ethiopia from a religious festival in Jerusalem. Philip joins him and the Eunuch invites Philip up into his chariot to explain what he is reading. As they converse, the Eunuch sees water and requests baptism. While the Ethiopian Eunuch's confession of faith before baptism is relegated to a footnote (8:37), Irenaeus quotes it in the second century (*Against Heresies III, 12.8).* The story anticipates the gentile mission of Acts 1:8.

Jesus' farewell discourses in John include images, metaphors, and allegories of Jesus as the good shepherd (10) and true vine (15) to express a sense of mystical union amongst God, Jesus, and the disciples. The image used of Jesus as True Vine draws on the depiction of Israel as God's vine in Hebrew Scripture particularly in Psalm 80:8–11, "You brought a vine out of Egypt; you drove out the nation and planted it..." with the result that a thriving vineyard spread from the Mediterranean Sea to the river Euphrates. In John 15, the essentially relational connections of the vinedresser, God; the true vine, the Son; and the disciples, the branches, are explained in intuitive and mystical images. An allegory of vine and indistinguishable branches describes ways Jesus lives on in disciples and followers.

15:1 is Jesus' last declarative "I am" followed a predicate noun. In declaring "I am the true vine," Jesus claims to be distinct from Israel (and the branches) but also the embodiment and thus fulfillment of imagery used of the nation of Israel. Jesus then explains to disciples ("you" is plural) how the grapevine, branches, fruit, and actions of the vinedresser describe the relationship of the community to the Father and Jesus. Use of the verb "to abide" or "remain" characterizes discipleship as a dependent, reciprocal, and organic relationship of believers with Jesus, based on the indwelling of the Spirit and the Father. Without the vine grower the vine will not grow and flourish and in turn, the vine grower needs the vine to produce as it is meant to do. Jesus commands abiding with other believers (v. 4). Repetition and re-statement of mutual abiding functions on both a descriptive and a meditative level; it consoles and sustains on going life of a group about to be traumatized by Jesus' death. By it, disciples can understand that believers will sustain an intimate connection to God. Nevertheless, a discipline of production and pruning is part of a living relationship with God and Christ. For example, in John 13:2, Judas' actions indicate to John that the disciple Judas acted in concert with the devil to hand Jesus over, and in 13:27, Satan enters into Judas Iscariot.

In verse 4–5, disciples see that because they do not act by themselves but relying instead on the strength and sap from vine and the vine grower, perceive that greater works are possible. Disciples are encouraged to ask for anything, on the basis of their relationship of dependence and trust, and in circumstances where they will no longer see the true vine. Abiding motivates inclusion of others.

In 15:8 glory connotes radiance and splendor, particularly of God. John's gospel also depicts ways Jesus' followers witness to Jesus' manifestation of glory. Jesus' mother is present at the start of his ministry as a witness to Jesus' revelation of his glory (2:11) and at the end of his life, the last revelation of glory. She embodies abiding with Jesus through witnessing his life and death, and she is the catalyst for the sign. Jesus' mother embodies a presence of discipleship and a witness to glory: she trusts that Jesus will act and allows him to act in freedom without coercion.

Central Themes

The reading today from Acts has an almost entirely forgotten character in it – the angel who told Phillip to get up and go. That angel is always there but is almost never noticed since they only get a quick mention before the action of this fast-paced story takes place. How many of us fail to see the messengers and messages that God sends us every day? What would our lives be like if we stopped long enough to consider the angelic messages that are sending us on our way?

"To Make You Feel My Love" is a classic song written by Bob Dylan that countless singers have covered. It is not a hymn but feels like a song about and by God. It begins, "When the rain is blowing in your face / And the whole world is on your case / I could offer you a warm embrace / To make you feel my love." A reading today tells us, "God is love." In what ways do you experience the warm embrace of God's love? How and through whom can God's love be made known to you?

The new life Christ promises is lived in relationship with God, as intimate as the connection between vine and branches. The Holy Spirit flows through us because of our connection to Christ, and, apart from him, we can do nothing. In the Baptismal Covenant, we promise to nurture those connections – through the apostles' teaching and fellowship, the breaking of bread, and prayer.

Engaging All Ages

Jesus tells us the vine cannot bear fruit alone. It is dependent on others to grow and prosper. We are the same way. Just as the queen's treasurer asked Phillip for help in understanding a passage of scripture that he might learn and grow, so are we called to guide and be led by other people, for us and the branches and vines around us to grow. The people around us who help us see God more clearly are sources of strength. Draw a picture of a grape vine where each branch is someone who helps you grow, learn, and love.

Prayers of the People: Option 1

We give you thanks for those who offer their best as leaders of your people – for our bishops, priests, and deacons. Pray for those who carry out your mission under their leadership.

Pray for God's Church.

Silence

We offer our prayers for the leaders of our nation – for our president, our governor, Congress, and the courts of this land. Give them courage and wisdom and a heart for justice.

Pray for justice and peace.

Silence

We pray for mercy for those who suffer from hunger, in poverty, in the wake of violent storms, after earthquakes. Sustain them in their struggles and give them hope. We are thankful for compassionate people who answer their call for help.

Pray for those who suffer around the world.

Silence

We pray for those who are ill, for those who live in fear and whose spirits are restless. Give comfort for those who are dying and those who stand beside them as they find their way home.

Pray for new and unending life in this world and the next.

Silence

We pray for those who have died.

Our hearts are full this day, Lord, as we embrace new life in you. We give you thanks for the gift of song and joyful spirits.

Prayers of the People: Option 2

Deacon

Christ has gathered us as branches of the true vine. Let us offer prayers to God who does for us whatever we ask.

Leader

For the whole world and all the churches of God.

Glory and praise to you, O living God.

For this holy gathering, [for our baptismal candidates *N.*], and for our sacrifice of praise and thanksgiving.

Glory and praise to you, O living God.

For all the baptized whose faces shine with the light of Christ.

Glory and praise to you, O living God.

For *N.* our Presiding Bishop, *N.* our Bishop, for our priest, *N.*, for all who minister and all the holy people of God.

Glory and praise to you, O living God.

For all nations, peoples, tribes, clans, and families.

Glory and praise to you, O living God.

For those who suffer and those who mourn; stir up in us a spirit of grace and generosity, that we may give freely to those in need.

Glory and praise to you, O living God.

For all places in strife and unrest, that you may inspire all your people to seek a just peace and that we may hear the voices of those who are unheard.

Glory and praise to you, O living God.

For all those requiring ongoing care and for all those in danger and need: those who are sick or suffering, prisoners, captives, and their families, those who are hungry, homeless, or oppressed.

Glory and praise to you, O living God.

For the dying and the dead, we pray.

Glory and praise to you, O living God.

For ourselves, our families, and those we love.

Glory and praise to you, O living God.

Remembering our most glorious and Blessed Virgin Mary and all the saints, let us offer ourselves and one another to the living God through Christ.

To you, O Lord, our God.

Presider

Blessed are you, O Lord our God, who abides in all who love you. Hear the prayers we offer this day and give us your Spirit of peace to love our brothers and sisters; through Jesus Christ our Lord. ***Amen.***

Hymns for the Day

The Hymnal 1982

Christ is alive! Let Christians sing 182
Come away to the skies 213
Come, my Way, my Truth, my Life 487
Good Christians all, rejoice and sing! 205 (vs 1, 3–5)
He is the Way 463, 464
Sing, ye faithful, sing with gladness 492
Thou art the Way, to thee alone 457
Descend, O Spirit, purging flame 297
In Christ there is no East or West 529
We know that Christ is raised and dies no more 296
God is love, and where true love is 576, 577
God is Love, let heaven adore him 379
I come with joy to meet my Lord 304
Lord, whose love through humble service 610
Love divine, all loves excelling 657
The great Creator of the worlds 489
Where charity and love prevail 581
Where true charity and love dwell 606
You, Lord, we praise in songs of celebration 319
Bread of heaven, on thee we feed 323
Like the murmur of the dove's song 513
Thou hallowed chosen morn of praise 198

Lift Every Voice and Sing II

In Christ there is no East or West 62
The angel said to Philip 50

Wonder, Love, and Praise

Here, O Lord, your servants gather 793
Ubi caritas et amor 831
Muchos resplandores/Many are the light beams 794
O blessed spring, where Word and sign 765

The Sixth Sunday of Easter

Variable – Between April 26 and May 30

As the Father has loved me, so I have loved you; abide in my love.

Anchor Points – The Propers and the Season

The fixed points for each service are the appointed or proper readings and collect as well as the themes of the day or season.

Readings and Psalm

Acts 10:44–48

This missionary speech in today's reading marks an important turning point in the outreach of the early Church. Many Jewish Christians feared and resisted the possible inclusion of Gentiles, but Luke makes clear that Peter himself (even before Paul) began the mission to the Gentiles under the direction of the Holy Spirit. Cornelius was a "God-fearing" Roman, one who worshiped God but had not adopted all of the Jewish religious practices. Cornelius receives the sacrament of baptism, but not before he and his gathered household receive the gift of the Holy Spirit. This event marks a new Pentecost. The circle of Christian faith has now broadened to include the inhabitants of "the ends of the earth" (1:8). The Spirit first came to Jews (2:1–4), then to the despised Samaritans (8:14–17), and now to the Gentiles.

Psalm 98

This psalm is closely related to Psalm 96. Its original setting may have been the enthronement festival of Yahweh, celebrated each year at the New Year's feast of Tabernacles. In later times the psalm was interpreted to herald the Lord's final coming. It presents the Lord, in faithfulness to the covenant, acting in history for the salvation of God's people.

1 John 5:1–6

The writing of 1 John seems to have been occasioned by a schism in the community due to heresy, specifically the denial of Jesus's humanity. The central theme of 1 John is that "God is love" (4:8). The significance of this statement is explored through repeated meditation that interweaves theology and ethics. Those who make the early baptismal confession, "Jesus is the Christ," have assented to a pattern for their behavior. As God's children, Christians are to love God and one another and to obey the commandments. Through trust in Jesus, the Christian may overcome the world.

John 15:9–17

Today's gospel reading from the discourse on the vine and the branches deals with the disciples' relationships with one another. Jesus's relationship with the Father has now become the model for all believers. The Father and Son's relationship of mutual indwelling is now extended to Christians. The Father's love for the Son is the basis, both in origin and in quality, of the Son's love for the believer. Believers are to love one another with a love characterized by self-sacrifice. Thus, while Christians are still "servants" (v. 15, literally "slaves") of Christ in terms of ministry (see 12:26; 13:14–16), they are "friends" (v. 15) of Christ in terms of intimacy with God. In and through this relationship Christians are appointed to "bear fruit" (v. 16).

Collect

O God, you have prepared for those who love you such good things as surpass our understanding: Pour into our hearts such love toward you, that we, loving you in all things and above all things, may obtain your promises, which exceed all that we can desire; through Jesus Christ our Lord, who lives and reigns with you and the Holy Spirit, one God, forever and ever. *Amen.*

Proper Preface

Easter – But chiefly are we bound to praise you for the glorious resurrection of your Son Jesus Christ our Lord; for he is the true Paschal Lamb, who was sacrificed for us, and has taken away the sin of the world. By his death he has destroyed death, and by his rising to life again he has won for us everlasting life. (Rite II BCP 379; Rite I BCP 346)

Seasonal Pairings

See the table below for choices appointed and suggested for this day. Preferences are put in **bold**. Not all choices are suitable for all congregations or community, though, so consider these preferences as a starting point before making a decision about your own congregation.

	Easter VI	Rite I	Rite II	EOW1	BOS 2022
Color	White/Gold/Festive				
Entrance Rite	Customary; **Easter Acclamation**	323	355	50	
Song of Praise	Gloria in excelsis or Te Deum or **Pascha Nostrum**	324, 52, or **46**	356, 95, or **83**		
Collect		174	225		
Creed	Nicene Creed	326, 292	358, 292		
Prayers of the People	**Locally written**; options below; BCP forms	329	387–393	54–55	
Offertory Sentence	"Jesus said, 'This is my commandment, that you love one another as I have loved you.'" (John)	343–344	376–377		
Eucharistic Prayer	**One that allows use of the Easter preface** *or* **Prayer D**	2–340	**A – 361, B – 367** or **D – 372**	1–57	
Proper Preface	Easter	346	379		
Breaking of the Bread (Fraction)	Options using an alleluia: S 151, S 152, S 154, S 155, S 167, S 171	337	364		
Postcommunion Prayer		339	**Eternal God – 365**	God of abundance – 69	
Blessing	Customary *or* BOS	339	366	70–71	14
Dismissal	**Let us go forth in the Name of Christ. Alleluia, alleluia.**	340	366		
Notes	Rogation Days fall during this week; Easter VI sometimes called "Rogation Sunday"				

Additional Notes:

Song of Praise – The ancient and unique Song of Praise for Eastertide is the Pascha nostrum, found in Morning Prayer. While it is often not as familiar to congregations as the frequently used Gloria in excelsis, it is worth exploring settings for it that would help it become more familiar. It may be used throughout the Easter Season.

Baptisms – While the Great Vigil is the baptismal feast *par excellence*, the Easter Season generally is a fitting season for baptisms, if some cannot be scheduled for the Great Vigil.

Eucharistic Prayer – There is not a Eucharistic Prayer that has distinct Easter/Resurrection themes, so selecting a Eucharistic Prayer that uses the Easter proper preface is an important option. Eucharistic Prayer D, which does not use a proper preface, may be desirable, because of the language expressing God's glory.

Fraction Anthem at the Breaking of the Bread – Certainly using options that incorporate "Alleluia" would be the most desirable. Several options in addition to "Christ our Passover" are provided in the Service Music section of *The Hymnal 1982.*

Rogation Days – The Monday, Tuesday, Wednesday before Ascension Day are Rogation Days, originally associated with planting crops. Many churches today see it as an opportunity to be visible in their community and get to know local businesses. See the material above about celebrating these days.

Content Resources

Reading Between the Lines

The Acts reading for this Sunday is the stub of a story that never appears in the Lectionary, the story of the vision of Cornelius and the vision and subsequent conversion of Peter to the Gentile mission. This predicating story is pivotal for an understanding of how the Torah-observant community we witness, for example, in Matthew's gospel, is led into an expansive inclusiveness. This story is crucial for understanding how God reinscribes and lifts the commands for one age, codified in one period of scripture, to meet the call of a new time, a new age.

The stub loses most of its impact without the story that precedes it in Acts 10:1–43. And although we hear Peter's preaching in vv 33–43 every Easter, Years A, B & C, we never hear the narrative that gave rise to that preaching, in any year. We never hear this narrative that undergirds the church's understanding that nothing and no one God has created may be called unclean, or outcast. In Acts 10:28 Peter says, "…God has shown me that I should not call anyone profane or unclean."

Since the lectionary does not ever include this scripture narrative, it is imperative that we take this opportunity to tell the whole story, starting with Acts 10:1. The writer of first John speaks to a community where there is some unidentified conflict about who is the child of God, and he exhorts them to obey God's commandments and thus show love for each other. In John 15:9–17 Jesus says "…I call you friends…. You did not choose me, but I chose you." Jesus ends this passage with "…love one another." We don't get to pick the friends of Jesus. Peter learned that through a vision. The church needs to hear the story of Peter and Cornelius, to help us learn how to love one another.

Central Themes

Many of us hope that we will have a legacy that will last long beyond our lifetimes. The pyramids are a good example of such a hope. They stand as monuments built to honor an individual pharaoh and his power. But, we should indeed hope to have a legacy that is a testament to God's love and power. Fred Rogers, the Presbyterian minister who created *Mr. Roger's Neighborhood,* is a good example of that kind of testament. He devoted his whole life to helping children – those who often have no power in this world – feel loved. What kind of legacy are we building?

"Let the sea make noise and all that is in it." In water, sound travels up to four times faster than through air. Whales have adapted to this fact. Though no one fully understands all the reasons why, whales sing. Their songs give shape and description to the world they inhabit. Songs also help them to communicate. As whales with different singing styles encounter one another, they often learn and adapt their songs so that their singing ends up more in concert. How is the song of your life adapting to be more in concert with those around you?

"This is my commandment, that you love one another as I have loved you." Christ's commandment opens us to lives transformed by his love. Each time we renew our baptismal promises, we remind ourselves and one another that we will "seek and serve Christ in all persons, loving [our] neighbor as [ourselves] … strive for justice and peace among all people, and respect the dignity of every human being."

Engaging All Ages

The lesson from John's gospel today reminds us of the commandment to love one another as God loves us. This sounds really difficult! Jesus loved us so much that it can be hard to imagine how we can offer that same love. Thankfully, Jesus left us ideas through the stories of his life. He loved people who were different than him. He met people where they were comfortable, such as in their homes and places of work. He shared the story of God's love over and over again. Draw a picture or write a note to someone in your neighborhood, school, or place of work who needs to know that God's love is real.

Prayers of the People: Option 1

We pray for your faithful people and our leaders, that your love may be the foundation of their common lives and at the heart of their ministry.

Teach us to abide in your love.

We pray for your world filled with creatures and spectacular plant life and grandeur beyond words.

Teach us to care for it with love.

We pray for the peoples of the world and honor them as those you have made and cherish.

Teach us to reach out to them with respect and love.

We pray for healing for those among us who are ailing, aching, or anxious: ___________ .

Teach us to respond to their needs with love.

We pray for those who are at the end of their earthly lives, and for those who have recently entered eternal life, especially ___________ .

Teach us to remember them with love.

Uphold us by the riches of your grace, loving God. May your lessons of love continue to inspire and guide us as we move through this world and into the next.

Prayers of the People: Option 2

Presider

Gracious and loving God, your Son Jesus has laid down his life and called us his friends, and you have promised to give whatever we ask you in Christ's name: Hear our prayers for the whole human family and for the world, as we say: Sing to the Lord a new song, for he has done marvelous things.

Litanist

Your Church is the community of those who believe that Jesus is the Christ, and you have taught us that we have been born of God: Help us to show our love for you, O God, by loving your children and thus fulfilling Christ's command to us.

Sing to the Lord a new song;

for he has done marvelous things.

You have shown your righteousness openly in the sight of the nations, O Mighty One, and with your right hand and your holy arm have you won for yourself the victory: Extend your dominion over all the earth and imbue all in authority with your Spirit of love and compassion, that they may serve the world in peace and justice.

Sing to the Lord a new song;

for he has done marvelous things.

All creation witnesses to God's goodness; the sea and the lands, the rivers and hills ring out with joy before the Lord: Bless and protect this world and its fragile environment, and grant to all your children their necessities for daily life and peaceful freedom from all that may threaten.

Sing to the Lord a new song;

for he has done marvelous things.

You have taught us to keep your commandments by abiding in your love, O God: Bless this community with such faithfulness that your joy may be in us and that our joy may be complete.

Sing to the Lord a new song;

for he has done marvelous things.

Hear our prayers for our friends and for all who suffer, especially ____________________. Accept our grateful thanksgivings as we lift up our voice, rejoice and sing, especially for __________.

We entrust to your never-failing victory those who have died, especially ________________. Let our faith in you witness to the victory that conquers the world.

Sing to the Lord a new song;

for he has done marvelous things.

Presider

Blessed One, you have loved us, chosen us, and appointed us to go and bear fruit, fruit that will last: Honor the faithful prayers of your people, that all the earth may abide in your love and know the joy of your friendship, through Jesus Christ our Savior, who with you and Holy Spirit, lives and reigns one God, for ever and ever. ***Amen.***

Hymns for the Day

The Hymnal 1982

Alleluia, alleluia! Hearts and voices heavenward raise 191
As those of old their first fruits brought 705
Now the green blade riseth 204
O Jesus, crowned with all renown 292
Descend, O Spirit, purging flame 297
In Christ there is no East or West 529
O Love of God, how strong and true 455, 456
Sing, ye faithful, sing with gladness 492
Come, we that love the Lord 392
In your mercy, Lord, you called me 706
Lord, dismiss us with thy blessing 344
Lord, we have come at your own invitation 348
Lord, whose love through humble service 610

Lift Every Voice and Sing II

In Christ there is no East or West 62
One bread, one body 151

Wonder, Love, and Praise

Ubi caritas et amor 831

Ascension Day

Variable – 40 days after Easter Day
A Thursday on or between April 30 and June 3

The risen Jesus is lifted up into heaven and no longer seen by the disciples.

Anchor Points – The Propers and the Season

The fixed points for each service are the appointed or proper readings and collect as well as the themes of the day or season.

Readings and Psalm

Acts 1:1–11

In the opening passage of the Acts of the Apostles the author summarizes the last events and instructions of Jesus' earthly ministry before he is lifted up into heaven. The book is formally dedicated to Theophilus, who may have been an early convert to Christianity. Jesus tells his followers to wait for their baptism in the Holy Spirit, after which their missionary work will spread from Jerusalem out to all the world. Jesus will one day come again, but his disciples now have a message to bring to all peoples.

Psalm 47

A hymn of praise to the mighty king who is raised up and enthroned on high.

or

Psalm 93

God reigns, the Lord of all creation, and has established the earth and subdued the great waters.

Ephesians 1:15–23

In this lesson Paul gives thanks for the faith and love of the Ephesians and prays that they may see with their inward eyes the power of God, who has raised and enthroned Jesus far above all earthly and heavenly dominions. How vast is the treasure that God offers to those who trust in God! The Lord Christ now reigns as head of the church, which is his body and which experiences the fullness of his love.

Luke 24:44–53

In our gospel Jesus leaves his followers with the promise of the Holy Spirit and is carried up into heaven. The disciples are to await their empowerment from on high before beginning their mission to the world. Joyfully they return from Bethany, the town where Jesus had stayed before his passion. They enter the temple and praise God.

Collect

Almighty God, whose blessed Son our Savior Jesus Christ ascended far above all heavens that he might fill all things: Mercifully give us faith to perceive that, according to his promise, he abides with his Church on earth, even to the end of the ages; through Jesus Christ our Lord, who lives and reigns with you and the Holy Spirit, one God, in glory everlasting. *Amen.*

or this

Grant, we pray, Almighty God, that as we believe your only-begotten Son our Lord Jesus Christ to have ascended into heaven, so we may also in heart and mind there ascend, and with him continually dwell; who lives and reigns with you and the Holy Spirit, one God, forever and ever. *Amen.*

Proper Preface

Ascension – Through your dearly beloved Son Jesus Christ our Lord. After his glorious resurrection he openly appeared to his disciples, and in their sight ascended into heaven, to prepare a place for us; that where he is, there we might also be, and reign with him in glory. (Rite II BCP 379; Rite I BCP 347)

Feast Day Pairings

See the table below for choices appointed and suggested for this day. Preferences are put in **bold**. Not all choices are suitable for all congregations or community, though, so consider these preferences as a starting point before making a decision about your own congregation.

	Ascension Day	Rite I	Rite II	EOW1	BOS 2022
Color	White/Gold/Festive				
Entrance Rite	Customary; **Easter Acclamation**	323	355	50	
Song of Praise	Gloria in excelsis or Te Deum or **Pascha Nostrum**	324, 52, or **46**	356, 95, or **83**		
Collect		174	226		
Creed	Nicene Creed	326, 292	358, 292		
Prayers of the People	**Locally written**; options below; BCP forms	329	387–393	54–55	
Offertory Sentence	"God has gone up with a shout, the Lord with the sound of the ram's-horn." (Psalm 47)	343–344	376–377		
Eucharistic Prayer	**One that allows use of the Ascension preface** *or* **Prayer D**	2–340	**A – 361,** **B – 367** or **D – 372**	1–57	
Proper Preface	Ascension	347	379		
Breaking of the Bread (Fraction)	Options using an alleluia: S 151, S 152, S 154, S 155, S 167, S 171	337	364		
Postcommunion Prayer		339	**Eternal God – 365**	God of abundance – 69	
Blessing	Customary *or* **Ascension Day blessing in BOS**	339	366	70–71	**15**
Dismissal	**Let us go forth in the Name of Christ. Alleluia, alleluia.**	340	366		
Notes	The Paschal Candle is lighted through the Day of Pentecost.	287	287		

Additional Notes:

Song of Praise – The ancient and unique Song of Praise for Eastertide is the Pascha nostrum, found in Morning Prayer. While it is often not as familiar to congregations as the frequently used Gloria in excelsis, it is worth exploring settings for it that would help it become more familiar. It may be used throughout the Easter Season.

Eucharistic Prayer – Selecting a Eucharistic Prayer that uses the Ascension proper preface is a helpful way to emphasize the themes of the day. Eucharistic Prayer D, which does not use a proper preface, may be desirable, because of the language expressing God's glory.

Fraction Anthem at the Breaking of the Bread – Certainly using options that incorporate "Alleluia" would be the most desirable. Several options in addition to "Christ our Passover" are provided in the Service Music section of *The Hymnal 1982*.

Seasonal blessing – Note that there is a proper blessing for Ascension Day in the BOS.

Content Resources

Reading Between the Lines

Beginnings and endings play such important roles in narrative. In the beginning, Luke and Matthew each tell a particular story of a young family and the birth of a child, while John reflects theologically on the nature of the Logos. At the end of their gospels, Matthew shows a farewell gathering on a mountain while Luke graphically depicts a bodily Ascension. But for John, the Ascension takes place offstage between two resurrection appearances, after Mary Magdalene's encounter with the risen Jesus and before the appearance to the disciples. Whether we relate to feet disappearing into the clouds or connect to what happened when Jesus ascended "to my father and your father," two things can be said about the gospel writers' understanding of Ascension. First, Jesus at some point permanently disappeared, taking a resurrected body into heaven. Second, the Ascension of Jesus was necessary for the descent of the Holy Spirit. In John 20:19–23, read annually on Easter 2 and on Pentecost in Year A, Jesus breathes the Holy Spirit into the disciples, where Luke requires that Jesus be completely gone before the coming of the Spirit, but in both cases, Jesus has ascended to God first. The Feast of the Ascension has been observed 40 days after Easter, providing a tidy inclusio with Ash Wednesday 40 days before Easter, since the fourth century. For Luke the Ascension is an extension of Jesus' terrestrial sojourn in Luke Acts (Luke 9:51; Acts 1:10).

Central Themes

The Ascension is a classic image for use in glass windows over altars. In these, Jesus is often depicted surrounded by clouds rising in the lovely swirling colors of the sky. But we are told not to look there for Jesus anymore because he comes to us now in the work that we do in his name and in the fellowship we share at those altars. So how can we reconcile these two images? Perhaps we are invited to keep one eye looking heavenward with joy and anticipation and to keep one eye on the lookout for those who are in need of that joy in their lives so that we might share it.

In the 2009 animated film *Up*, two children, Carl and Ellie, share a dream of adventure but everyday life takes over. Eventually, Ellie dies. While Carl looks through a childhood scrapbook created by Ellie, he sees a page labeled, "Stuff I'm Going to Do." Following it are photos of things done by Carl and Ellie. Ellie writes, "Thanks for the adventure." Their hearts and minds had already adventured. Carl just needed the reminder. Is there a reminder that your heart and mind have already ascended with Jesus and that a part of heaven resides in you in the living world?

Catechesis of the Good Shepherd (a Montessori-based approach for children) teaches about the Ascension using the Paschal candle and imagery from the Eastern Church. With the children sitting in a circle around the lit candle, the catechist snuffs it out, and then they silently watch the wisps of smoke dispersing into the air. "I wonder where the smoke goes," she muses. "I wonder where Jesus goes." How might we increase awareness – among all believers – of Jesus's unseen presence all about us?

Engaging All Ages

After all the celebration of Easter and the joy of walking around with Jesus after his resurrection, today is the day when we finally have to say goodbye. On Ascension Day, we remember Jesus being carried up into heaven. But even though Jesus departed, God remains with us in the Holy Spirit. Light a candle. See the flame, the light of Christ. Now blow it out and notice the rising smoke that fills the air. Jesus may not be walking among us now, but our connection with him remains in the Holy Spirit that surrounds us.

Prayers of the People: Option 1

We stand amazed, O Lord, at your presence with us in our time and beyond time. We turn our gaze to you, and ask for your guidance and protection.

Fix the eyes of the church always on you, that we may see your glory and receive your blessing as we follow you in everything we do. Guide our leaders and give them hearts for you and your people.

Pray for the church.

Turn the hearts of the rulers of the nations toward the peace which you intend for all people, toward wise stewardship of the earth's resources, for the good of all people in every time and place.

Pray for the nations of the world.

Increase our efforts to become determined and compassionate carriers of your love and comfort to a broken world.

Pray for those in need of healing.

Receive those who have died into the heavenly kingdom where there is no pain or grief, where time is no more, where they sing with your glorious saints in light.

Pray for those who have died.

Fill us with your Holy Spirit, that we may be your faithful witnesses in every area of our lives, everywhere we go, to everyone we meet. We depend on your constant presence and power. In Jesus' name we pray. *Amen.*

Prayers of the People: Option 2

Presider

Christ has ascended high that he might fill all things: Listen to our prayers, O God, as we proclaim the riches of your glorious inheritance and the immeasurable greatness of your power for us who believe, saying, Clap your hands, all you peoples; shout to God with a cry of joy.

Litanist

O Gracious God of our Lord Jesus Christ, the Father of glory, give to your Church a spirit of wisdom and revelation as we come to know you, that we may be your witnesses to the ends of the earth.

Clap your hands, all you peoples;

shout to God with a cry of joy.

You reign over the nations, and the rulers of the earth belong to you: Put your power to work among those who hold authority throughout the world, that they may establish your peace and reconciliation among all people.

Clap your hands, all you peoples;

shout to God with a cry of joy.

Cover the earth with your grace, O Compassionate One, that all who suffer from any threat or oppression may know the power of your goodness.

Clap your hands, all you peoples;

shout to God with a cry of joy.

Fill our community with your blessing, O Loving One, that with the eyes of our hearts enlightened, we may know the hope to which you have called us.

Clap your hands, all you peoples;

shout to God with a cry of joy.

Receive our prayers, dear God, for all for whom we are called to pray, especially ____________________. Hear our song of praise and thanksgiving as we lift our gratefulness to you, especially for _________. You raised Christ from the dead and seated him at your right hand: Receive into your divine dwelling those who have died, especially ______________.

Clap your hands, all you peoples;

shout to God with a cry of joy.

Presider

Wonderful and Everliving God, your Christ reigns far above all rule and authority and power and dominion, and above every name that is named: Put all things under Christ's feet and fill the earth with the fullness of him who fills all in all, through the power of your Holy Spirit, One God, for ever and ever. ***Amen.***

Hymns for the Day

The Hymnal 1982

And have the bright immensities 459
Hail thee, festival day! 216
A hymn of glory let us sing 217, 218
Alleluia! sing to Jesus! 460, 461
Hail the day that sees him rise 214
See, the Conqueror mounts in triumph 215
The Lord ascendeth up on high 219
Crown him with many crowns 494
Hail, thou once despised Jesus! 495
It was poor little Jesus, yes, yes 468
Lord, enthroned in heavenly splendor 307
O Lord most high, eternal King 220, 221
Rejoice, the Lord is King 481
Rejoice, the Lord of life ascends 222
A hymn of glory let us sing 217, 218
Alleluia! sing to Jesus! 460, 461
Hail the day that sees him rise 214
See, the Conqueror mounts in triumph 215
The Lord ascendeth up on high 219

Lift Every Voice and Sing II

"Go preach my gospel," saith the Lord 161
He is king of kings, he is Lord of lords 96

The Seventh Sunday of Easter: The Sunday after Ascension Day

Variable – Between May 3 and June 6

The Church seeks the comfort of the Holy Spirit to strengthen them.

Anchor Points – The Propers and the Season

The fixed points for each service are the appointed or proper readings and collect as well as the themes of the day or season.

Readings and Psalm

Acts 1:15–17, 21–26

The choosing of twelve disciples as a special group seems to have been a sign of the coming age and of the new Israel. They are a distinct group whose numbers need to be restored after Judas's defection. In today's passage, the company of believers picks out two candidates who fulfill the criteria and then they cast lots to see who will replace Judas – a Hebrew custom to allow the operation of God's will (see Proverbs 16:33). Matthias was chosen and would share in ministry as the servant of the community and in apostleship as the missionary envoy of Christ.

Psalm 1

This psalm, with its call to a righteous life based on knowledge of the "law of the Lord," the Torah, serves as a fitting introduction to all the psalms. It springs from the wisdom tradition, which emphasized how to live in both material and spiritual prosperity. The righteous are those who have not taken the advice of the wicked, nor imitated their way of life, nor joined in their rejection of the law. They "meditate" (v. 2) upon it, literally, read it aloud in a low voice. The Lord is in intimate and personal relationship with the righteous.

1 John 5:9–13

Today's reading includes the end of the discussion on the witness to the Son of God, a statement of the point of the epistle and its purpose and the first part of an appendix. The testimony of God was manifested in two ways: first, through God's saving action in Jesus; second, through the result of that action – eternal life for the believer. Verse 12 encapsulates the call to decision, toward which the whole letter has been leading. Verse 13 summarizes the epistle in a way similar to John 20:31. The appendix speaks of prayer "according to his will" (v. 14) as John does of prayer "in his name" (John 14:13–14 and 16:23–24).

John 17:6–19

Chapter 17 is known as the "prayer of consecration" or "high priestly prayer" of Jesus. He offers himself to the Father and speaks as high priest in offering intercession for others. Jesus's ministry on earth is completed. He has revealed God to the disciples. For John, this prayer is the expression of Jesus's union and communion with the Father, spoken aloud before the disciples so that they may share that union. It is revelation as well as intercession. Jesus prays for himself (17:1), for the disciples (17:9) and for future believers (17:20). He prays that the disciples may be kept safe from the world by the power of the name God has given him. The disciples – and all Christians – are consecrated, set apart, as Jesus was by his incarnation. This is not merely for self-purification but for mission into the world. The mission of the disciples, continuing the presence of Jesus, brings the world to judgment.

Collect

O God, the King of glory, you have exalted your only Son Jesus Christ with great triumph to your kingdom in heaven: Do not leave us comfortless, but send us your Holy Spirit to strengthen us, and exalt us to that place where our Savior Christ has gone before; who lives and reigns with you and the Holy Spirit, one God, in glory everlasting. *Amen.*

Proper Preface

Ascension – Through your dearly beloved Son Jesus Christ our Lord. After his glorious resurrection he openly appeared to his disciples, and in their sight ascended into heaven, to prepare a place for us; that where he is, there we might also be, and reign with him in glory. (Rite II BCP 379; Rite I BCP 347)

Seasonal Pairings

See the table below for choices appointed and suggested for this day. Preferences are put in **bold.** Not all choices are suitable for all congregations or community, though, so consider these preferences as a starting point before making a decision about your own congregation.

	Easter VII: The Sunday after Ascension Day	Rite I	Rite II	EOW1	BOS 2022
Color	White/Gold/Festive				
Entrance Rite	Customary; **Easter Acclamation**	323	355	50	
Song of Praise	Gloria in excelsis or Te Deum or **Pascha Nostrum**	324, 52, or **46**	356, 95, or **83**		
Collect		175	226		
Creed	Nicene Creed	326, 292	358, 292		
Prayers of the People	**Locally written**; options below; BCP forms	329	387–393	54–55	
Offertory Sentence	"Happy are they who have not walked in the counsel of the wicked, nor lingered in the way of sinners, nor sat in the seats of the scornful!" (Psalm 1)	343–344	376–377		
Eucharistic Prayer	**One that allows use of the Ascension preface *or* Prayer D**	2–340	**A – 361, B – 367** or **D – 372**	1–57	
Proper Preface	Ascension	347	379		
Breaking of the Bread (Fraction)	Options using an alleluia: S 151, S 152, S 154, S 155, S 167, S 171	337	364		
Postcommunion Prayer		339	**Eternal God – 365**	God of abundance – 69	
Blessing	Customary *or* **Ascension Day Blessing in BOS**	339	366	70–71	**15**
Dismissal	**Let us go forth in the Name of Christ. Alleluia, alleluia.**	340	366		
Notes	The Paschal Candle is lighted through the Day of Pentecost.	287	287		

Additional Notes:

Ascensiontide – The ten days from Ascension until Pentecost function almost as a mini-season within a season, Ascensiontide, with its own proper preface and seasonal blessing.

Song of Praise – The ancient and unique Song of Praise for Eastertide is the Pascha nostrum, found in Morning Prayer. While it is often not as familiar to congregations as the frequently used Gloria in excelsis, it is worth exploring settings for it that would help it become more familiar. It may be used throughout the Easter Season.

Eucharistic Prayer – Selecting a Eucharistic Prayer that uses the Ascension proper preface is a helpful way to emphasize the themes of the day. Eucharistic Prayer D, which does not use a proper preface, may be desirable, because of the language expressing God's glory.

Fraction Anthem at the Breaking of the Bread – Certainly using options that incorporate "Alleluia" would be the most desirable. Several options in addition to "Christ our Passover" are provided in the Service Music section of *The Hymnal 1982.*

Content Resources

Reading Between the Lines

In John 17:6–19, the middle part of Jesus' Farewell Discourse, Jesus prays to the Father, in the presence of and for his disciples (the whole prayer is oddly divided in the Lectionary amongst Easter 7A, 7B, and 7C. The selection here in Year A focuses on the veracity of the words of the prayer conveyed by the Word. The prayer starts with a direct address, "Father," signifying an intertextual relationship to Lord's Prayer of Matthew, Luke, and the Didache. This protracted prayer includes three sections with three petitions: for himself (vv. 1, 5: "Glorify me"), for God to safeguard his disciples when they are sent as Jesus was sent (v. 11, 15, 17: "Keep them in your name; "Keep them from the evil one;" and, "Sanctify them in the truth; your word is truth"), and for those who have come to believe through his disciples to be united, (v. 20–21: "That they may be completely one," and "that the world might believe"; and v. 24: "that they may be with me where I am, to see my glory, which you have given me…"). In our selection, Jesus' prayer repeats, for the disciples, that the disciples are given to Jesus by God (vv. 6, 9, & 24), and that he has given them words he was given by God (v. 8, 14). The verb "to give" occurs more frequently here than anywhere else in the New Testament, conveying the unending reciprocal donation of God to the Son and then disciples to the world (v. 18) for the purpose of guarding, protecting and sanctifying the disciples who now engage the ongoing mission of Jesus (v. 17–18).

Central Themes

In the reading from Acts, we hear of the casting of lots to appoint Matthias to replace Judas as an apostle. He is one of two candidates for the job, the other being Joseph called Barsabbas. We never hear how either one of them felt about this outcome, but we can assume that they both lived out their lives fulfilling the duties that God called them to. We may not know if we will be called to notoriety or obscurity in our service to God. But to worry about that would be to miss the point. All service to God is made great, no matter the size of the role.

How did you get to this congregation? For some, it was internet searches of churches in the area. For some, your family persuaded or friends invited. For some, it may be a long and complicated story. In many cases, it may seem as if by random chance, circumstance after circumstance somehow leading to this moment and place. But God is not random. Like Matthias, where you are may be where God has called you to be.

In Christ's high priestly prayer in today's gospel, he asks God to protect us, guard our unity, and help us witness to the truth. Our baptismal promises to "persevere in resisting evil … repent and return to the Lord … and proclaim by word and example the Good News of God in Christ" are the way we live into Christ's prayer for us.

Engaging All Ages

Part of Disney's *Fantasia* movie was created when artists listened to classical compositions and drew or painted what they heard in the music. They were asked to let go of any plans and just listen to their hearts and souls as the music played. Sometimes it is difficult to let go of control and simply let God work through us, to paint what the music makes us feel in the moment. Yet, as we come to the end of the Easter season, we are called to do just that. God calls us through Jesus Christ to volunteer to serve God's people in God's name, however that may happen. In prayer tonight, ask God to reveal the music and art of your soul that God is calling on you to share.

Prayers of the People: Option 1

Open our eyes to the wonder of the life you have given us: the creatures with whom we share this planet, the endless horizons, the intricate working of our bodies, the tenderness and complexity of human relationships.

Amen, merciful God, amen.

Open our hearts to the ways that we have hurt each other, that we may turn toward each other in love and turn closer together to you.

Amen, merciful God, amen.

Open our ears to the cries of those who suffer in body, mind, or spirit. We pray for those whose lives include hunger, financial insecurity, violence; whose homes are threatened by natural disasters; whose bodies ache with pain and whose lives are in the balance; who live in war zones, poverty, or fear.

Amen, merciful God, amen.

Open our lives to the path of righteousness, and align our vision with your vision of the world – created by you, redeemed by you, enlivened by your Spirit, and reconciled to you at the last

Amen, merciful God, amen.

Prayers of the People: Option 2

Deacon or Priest

Let us pray for the Church and for the World saying,
O Savior, hear us.

Leader

Heavenly Father, we pray for your holy Catholic Church, that our mission in the world will accomplish your will. Grant that every member of the Church may truly and humbly serve you.

O Savior, hear us.

Holy God, we pray for *N.* our Presiding Bishop, for *N.*, our bishop, and for our parish clergy; that all your people may proclaim your word and guide this parish to your glory.

O Savior, hear us.

Blessed Redeemer, we pray for *N.* our President, *N.* our Governor, *N.* our Mayor, and for all who govern and seek to govern in our nation and the nations of the world, that they will seek your justice and your will in their service.

O Savior, hear us.

Heavenly Father, we pray for all mothers and give thanks for their ministry; we pray for your blessing on all individuals of this world who, mentor, shelter and most of all love children of any age past or present who have been given into their care.

O Savior, hear us.

Holy God, we pray for your grace on those who are graduating, including ________________. We ask for your protection and guidance as they embark on new journeys.

O Savior, hear us.

Blessed Redeemer, we ask for healing and peace for all those who are burdened by illness, hardships and brokenness.

O Savior, hear us.

Heavenly Father, we praise you for your saints who have entered eternal joy, and ask for your compassion on those who are mourning their loss.

O Savior, hear us.

We pray for our own needs and those of others, silently or aloud.

Silence. The People may add their own petitions.

Presider

O God of Light, surround us with your presence, enfold us in your protective love and empower us to proclaim your word. Teach us to rely on your strength, speaking your truth to our families, neighbors, and the entire world, so we may serve you faithfully and honor your holy Name; for yours is the kingdom, O Lord, and you are exalted as head above all. ***Amen.***

Hymns for the Day

The Hymnal 1982

All hail the power of Jesus' name, 450, 451
Alleluia! sing to Jesus! 460, 461
Hail, thou once despised Jesus! 495
Lord, enthroned in heavenly splendor 307
Rejoice the Lord is King 481
The head that once was crowned with thorns 483
By all your saints still striving 231, 232
All who believe and are baptized 298
Crown him with many crowns 494
Draw nigh and take the Body of the Lord 327, 328
Eternal light, shine in my heart 465, 466
Many and great, O God, are thy works 385
For the bread which you have broken 340, 341
Humbly I adore thee, Verity unseen 314
Praise the Lord through every nation 484, 485
Thou, who at thy first Eucharist didst pray 315
Word of God, come down on earth 633

Lift Every Voice and Sing II

"Go preach my gospel," saith the Lord 161

Wonder, Love, and Praise

Come now, O Prince of peace 795
Unidos, unidos / Together, together 796
We are all one in mission 778

The Day of Pentecost

Variable – 50 days after Easter Day, between May 10 and June 13

Come Holy Spirit, our souls inspire!

Anchor Points – The Propers and the Season

The fixed points for each service are the appointed or proper readings and collect as well as the themes of the day or season.

Readings and Psalm

Acts 2:1–21

Like John, Luke understands the gift of the Spirit as a reversal of this world's confusion and social breakdown brought about at Babel (Genesis 11:1–9) and the fulfillment of the promise of a new community with a new form of covenant (Jeremiah 31:33). The law, personified, will be possessed by all and will dwell in the heart of each individual The empowerment brought by the Spirit is not babbling but proclamation. Those who heard it, whether they were residents of Jerusalem or pilgrims in town for the feast, were astounded by the variety of languages in which "God's deeds of power" (v. 11) were communicated. The diversity of their geographical origins represents the spread of the gospel to all the nations of the world.

or

Ezekiel 37:1–14

In our opening reading, the prophet has a vision of the bones of a dead and hopeless people being restored to new life in their homeland. The Lord calls upon Ezekiel as son of man to prophesy that the people who have experienced exile and many hardships will live again. The Spirit of the Lord restores their spirit and breath, and they rise from death. Although this passage can be understood to anticipate the hope of individual resurrection, Israel did not yet have this belief.

Psalm 104:25–35,37

This hymn to God as Creator shares the imagery of many Near Eastern nature poems and myths but changes their emphasis. Leviathan, the primeval water monster of chaos, is God's plaything. The created world is under God's sway and owes God praise. Sin disrupts the harmony of creation, and the psalmist prays for a restoration of the original wholeness.

Romans 8:22–27

Paul looks to the future of humanity and of the entire material universe, to the destiny that awaits them in Christ. The fate of humanity and the cosmos are inextricably linked. Paul, like many in the Hellenistic culture, saw the world as enslaved by spiritual forces of evil, yet he saw the God's will was supreme. At the second coming, the creation itself will be liberated. The end-times images of the Hebrew Scripture point to the hope that Paul here develops. Not only humankind, but all the material universe will be redeemed, sharing in the glory of God. Until that time, nature and Christians are "in labor pains" (v. 22), which mingle pain, hope and expectation. Salvation is not merely for individual human beings. It is cosmic in dimension.

or Acts 2:1–21

John 15:26–27; 16:4b–15

In this passage from his Farewell Discourse, Jesus warns the disciples of his impending death and of persecution to come. Yet death is to him primarily a return to the Father, and thus he tells them that it is to their advantage, for only thus can he send the Spirit to them. When the "Spirit of truth" (v. 26) comes, the Spirit will lead the disciples into an ever-deeper understanding of Jesus's revelation. Through the inspiration of the Spirit, the mission of the disciples will be one with that of Jesus.

Collect

Almighty God, on this day you opened the way of eternal life to every race and nation by the promised gift of your Holy Spirit: Shed abroad this gift throughout the world by the preaching of the Gospel, that it may reach to the ends of the earth; through Jesus Christ our Lord, who lives and reigns with you, in the unity of the Holy Spirit, one God, forever and ever. *Amen.*

or this

O God, who on this day taught the hearts of your faithful people by sending to them the light of your Holy Spirit: Grant us by the same Spirit to have a right judgment in all things, and evermore to rejoice in his holy comfort; through Jesus Christ your Son our Lord, who lives and reigns with you, in the unity of the Holy Spirit, one God, forever and ever. *Amen.*

Proper Preface

Pentecost – Through Jesus Christ our Lord. In fulfillment of his true promise, the Holy Spirit came down on this day from heaven, lighting upon the disciples, to teach them and to lead them into all truth; uniting peoples of many tongues in the confession of one faith, and giving to your Church the power to serve you as a royal priesthood, and to preach the Gospel to all nations. (Rite II BCP 380; Rite I BCP 347)

Feast Day Pairings

See the table below for choices appointed and suggested for this day. Preferences are put in **bold**. Not all choices are suitable for all congregations or community, though, so consider these preferences as a starting point before making a decision about your own congregation.

	The Day of Pentecost	Rite I	Rite II	EOW1	BOS 2022
Color	Red				
Entrance Rite	Customary *or* Holy Baptism	285; 299	285; 299		
Song of Praise/Kyrie	Gloria in excelsis or Te Deum	324; 52	356; 95		
Collect		175	227		
Creed	Baptismal Covenant *or* Renewal of Baptismal Vows	304/292	304/292		
Prayers of the People	**Locally written**; options below; BCP forms	329	387–393	54–55	
Offertory Sentence	"The eyes of all wait upon you, O Lord: And you give them their food in due season. You open wide your hand, and they are filled with good things. (Psalm 104, adapted)	343–344	376–377		
Eucharistic Prayer	**One that allows use of the Pentecost preface** *or* **Prayer D**	2–340	**A – 361,** **B – 367** or **D – 372**	3–62	
Proper Preface	Pentecost	347	380		
Breaking of the Bread (Fraction)	Options using an alleluia: S 151, S 152, S 154, S 155, S 167, S 171	337	364		
Postcommunion Prayer		339	**Eternal God – 365**	God of abundance – 69	
Blessing	Customary *or* **Day of Pentecost Blessing in BOS**	339	366	70–71	**16**
Dismissal	**Let us go forth into the world rejoicing in the power of the Spirit. Alleluia, alleluia.**	340	366		
Notes	This is one of the Baptismal feasts noted in the BCP (312); the commemoration of the First Book of Common Prayer falls on a weekday this week (more information in the section on the Season after Pentecost (Summer) below)				

Additional Notes:

Optional Vigil – The Prayer Book does provide an option for a Vigil of Pentecost, with instructions on pages 175 and 227 of the BCP. It begins with the Service of Light from Order of Worship for the Evening (BCP 109) and continues with the Collect of the Day. A series of lessons provided in the Lectionary (BCP 906) are provided, requiring three lessons to be read before the Gospel, each followed by a Psalm, Canticle or hymn. Holy Baptism, Confirmation, or the Renewal of Baptismal Vows follows the sermon. This may be an effective service for those preparing for Baptism or Confirmation in particular.

Creed – If there are baptisms, the Baptismal Covenant takes the place of the Creed. If there are not baptisms, it is strongly encouraged to use the the Renewal of Baptismal Vows.

Eucharistic Prayer – Selecting a Eucharistic Prayer that uses the Pentecost proper preface is a helpful option to incorporate the themes of the day. Eucharistic Prayer D may also be desirable, with its soaring language expressing God's glory for this Principal Feast. Prayer 3 in *Enriching Our Worship 1* has some additional language at the epiclesis of the people that may be helpful when focusing on the work of the Spirit in the church today.

Fraction Anthem at the Breaking of the Bread – Certainly continuing to use options that incorporate "Alleluia" would be the most desirable. Several options in addition to "Christ our Passover" are provided in the Service Music section of *The Hymnal 1982*.

Seasonal blessing – Note that there is a proper blessing for the Day of Pentecost in the BOS.

Content Resources

Reading Between the Lines

This gospel properly begins in John 14:16, where, with John 14:26, Jesus begins to describe the **Paraclete**, (rendered Advocate in NRSV). Paraclete language appears in such a small body of texts (John 14:16, 26; 15:6, 16:7, and in 1 Jn 2:1) that every reference counts. A very specific avatar of the Holy Spirit, this Paraclete, according to John 14:16, 26, will teach the disciples everything and remind them of everything Jesus has said to them. In John 15:6, this Paraclete is characterized as the Spirit of Truth. This Paraclete is not the exciting, dramatic rush of wind and fire described in Acts that has become emblematic of the coming of the Spirit. While dramatizing the Pentecost narrative in Acts is great fun, a working understanding of the Paraclete, the Spirit of Truth, may be of far greater use in our time and for our faith community. Louw and Nida's Dictionary of Semantic Domains 12:19 and 35:16 define **Paraclete** as "one who helps, by consoling, encouraging, or mediating on behalf of – 'Helper, Encourager, Mediator.'" Louw and Nida point out the difficulty of translating Paraclete and suggest "Helper" as a most useful equivalent, citing "as in one language in Central Africa, 'the one who falls down beside us,' that is to say, an individual who upon finding a person collapsed along the road, kneels down beside the victim, cares for his needs, and carries him to safety." In depicting the Holy Spirit that comes with the departure of Jesus as our Helper, and the Spirit of Truth, John gives us a Spirit that meets us in our deepest needs today.

Central Themes

Teenagers are frustrated when parents tell them they are not ready to hear something important. When work supervisors tell us the same thing, it feels diminishing. Yet Jesus admonishes, "I still have many things to say to you, but you cannot bear them now." In the Gospels, we learn that Jesus is preparing the way for us to receive God fully. Just as a field must be prepared for planting, our spirits must be prepared to receive the Good News of God's saving grace. Part of that preparation is setting aside things like pride in our own wisdom.

The South African Truth and Reconciliation Commission (TRC) was established in 1995 to help the country deal with the pain and trauma of apartheid. With Desmond Tutu as its leader, it brought to light the historic injustices of apartheid within a spirit of truth-telling, mercy, and forgiveness. The TRC helped shepherd into being a society connected across lines of race that could not have been imagined in previous years. The TRC is an example to followers of Jesus of how the Holy Spirit moves us to cross lines of difference, so "that barriers which divide us may crumble, suspicions disappear, and hatreds cease" (BCP 823).

John's Jesus has been promising the gift of the Advocate, aka "Comforter," aka Spirit, for this whole long speech (John 13–17), but the scent of it has been in the air for the whole of this gospel. Jesus will breathe that spirit on the infant Church at the moment of his glorification at his death and breathe it again on the gathered disciples post-Resurrection. It is the same reviving Spirit that animated lifeless bones in Ezekiel's vision. And it is the same Sprit who abides in us – that is, the Church. It shows itself when we love one another, all the others, as he, and the heart of our baptism, bade us do.

Engaging All Ages

Pentecost provides a perfect opportunity for a festive procession. Invite people of various ages to be part of the procession. Children and youth not participating in other parts of the service can sit with family during the service. Invite members of the procession to carry existing banners or wave simple dowel rods with strips of yellow, orange, red, and white fabric attached. Consider mentioning in the sermon or bulletin the significance of these colors.

Prayers of the People: Option 1

Intoxicate us with visions and dreams that will align us with you. Jolt us from our inertia into action.

Come into our lives with power.

Come, Holy Spirit, and stay with us.

Transform our melancholy into joy, our worry into peace, our despair into hope. We pray for healing for those who suffer from any distress or illness.

Come into our lives with healing.

Come, Holy Spirit, and stay with us.

Shape our weary and wounded souls into souls on fire for God's mission.

Come, Holy Spirit, and stay with us.

Prayers of the People: Option 2

Presider

Pour out your Spirit upon all flesh and inspire us, O Holy One, that we may proclaim your prophesy of justice and speak your message of compassion and love, saying: I will sing to God as long as I live; I will praise my God while I have my being.

Litanist

Let your Spirit rest upon your Church like tongues of fire, O God, to inspire us to do your will.

I will sing to God as long as I live;

I will praise my God while I have my being.

God looks at the earth and it trembles; God touches the mountains and they smoke: Let your glory go forth into all the world to guide the leaders of the nations and all in authority, that they may obey your Spirit and bless your people.

I will sing to God as long as I live;

I will praise my God while I have my being.

O Holy One, how manifold are your works; in wisdom you have made them all. Let your glory go forth to comfort all who live under poverty, violence, or threat, that everyone who calls upon the name of the Lord shall be saved.

I will sing to God as long as I live;

I will praise my God while I have my being.

You open your hand and fill all with good things, O gracious One: Bless this community, that our children may see visions and our elders dream dreams.

I will sing to God as long as I live;

I will praise my God while I have my being.

Comfort with your life-giving Spirit those for whom we pray, especially ______.

We will rejoice in the Holy One, and praise God with words of thanksgiving, especially for ______.

The breath of the Spirit breathes new life into all creation: Raise into your resurrection life those who have died, especially ______.

I will sing to God as long as I live;

I will praise my God while I have my being.

Presider

Let the fire of your divine love descend upon us, O God, to inspire and heal, to renew and empower, that the earth may be filled with your glory, and all creation sing to you in praise, through Jesus Christ the Risen One, in the power of the Holy Spirit, one God, for ever and ever. ***Amen.***

Hymns for the Day

The Hymnal 1982

This day at thy creating word 52
We the Lord's people, heart and voice uniting 51
A mighty sound from heaven 230
Hail thee, festival day! 225
Hail this joyful day's return 223, 224
Spirit divine, attend our prayers 509
Breathe on me, Breath of God 508
Go forth for God; go to the world in peace 347
Put forth, O God, thy Spirit's might 521
Eternal Spirit of the living Christ 698
Like the murmur of the dove's song 513
Come, gracious Spirit, heavenly Dove 512
Holy Spirit, ever living 511
Spirit of mercy, truth, and love 229
To thee, O Comforter divine 514
All who believe and are baptized 298
Baptized in water 294
Descend, O Spirit, purging flame 297
Over the chaos of the empty waters 176, 177
Spirit of God, unleashed on earth 299

Lift Every Voice and Sing II

There's a sweet, sweet Spirit in this place 120
Let it breathe on me 116
Spirit of the living God 115
Baptized in water 121

Wonder, Love, and Praise

Veni Sancte Spiritus 832
Filled with the Spirit's power, with one accord 741
Baptized in water 767

Season After Pentecost Summer & Autumn

The Season after Pentecost General Notes

The Post-Pentecost Season

Whatever season of the Church Year it is, we, in fact, live in the time between the original Pentecost and the anticipated Parousia, or Second Coming. Whether in the cosmic calendar we are at Pentecost 2 or in the week before Advent is not yet known. Planning for the post-Pentecost season, then, is planning for *now*. The season itself, to the extent that it can be called a season, begins on the Monday after Pentecost and continues until the Saturday before Advent 1. It is framed by the celebration of Trinity Sunday on the First and Christ the King on the Last Sunday after Pentecost, marked by numbered propers for the Sundays and a number of major and minor holy days on the weekdays. It does not have a seasonal unity other than the consecutive reading of the Gospel: Mark with portions of John 6 on the Sundays in August, following the Markan account of the feeding of the five thousand, in Year B.

Numbered Propers and Numbered Sundays after Pentecost

To navigate the remainder of the year, it may be helpful to talk about how these Sundays are organized in the lectionary. The Sunday after Pentecost is always Trinity Sunday, a Principal Feast. The remainder of the Sundays after Pentecost are organized around date-specific propers. There are appointed readings and a collect for each week, organized by a range of dates, until the beginning of Advent in late November or early December. These are the numbered propers. There are 29 numbered propers, though they rarely are all used. The first two propers are for weekdays only, after Pentecost and Trinity Sunday, and the earliest Sunday proper used is Proper 3. Propers 1, 2, and 3 use the same lessons as the late Sundays after Epiphany (The Sixth Sunday after the Epiphany, The Seventh Sunday after the Epiphany and The Eighth Sunday after the Epiphany), though there are different collects appointed for Propers 1, 2, and 3. The Last Sunday after Pentecost is always Proper 29.

The name given to a Sunday after Pentecost is simply "The [number] Sunday after Pentecost." Trinity Sunday is "The First Sunday after Pentecost: Trinity Sunday" and then Sundays are sequentially numbered through the end of the season. The sequential Sunday numbering is unrelated to the Sunday Proper, which is date based.

The longest possible Season after Pentecost, including Trinity Sunday and the Last Sunday after Pentecost, is 28 Sundays, which would use Propers 3–29. The shortest possible Season after Pentecost, including Trinity and Last Pentecost, is 23 Sundays, which would use Propers 8–29.

Lectionary Tracks: Track One and Track Two

The Revised Common Lectionary presents two different ways of reading Scripture, beginning with Proper 4 and continuing for the remainder of the Season after Pentecost, through Proper 29 (the Last Sunday after Pentecost: Christ the King). The New Testament and the Gospel Reading are the same for each track, but there is an alternate reading from the Hebrew Scriptures and the Psalter for each Sunday.

Track One provides Hebrew Scripture readings in a generally continuous form across several books through the season and is sometimes called a "semi-continuous" track (abbreviated SC in hymn selections below and other resources). Track Two provides a reading from the Hebrew Scriptures that is intended to be thematically tied to the appointed Gospel Reading. This track is sometimes called the "gospel related" track (or GR in hymn selections below and other resources). Each track selects a different Psalm to accompany the readings.

The value of this approach is that, over the course of time, it provides for more material to be read on Sundays. Generally speaking, it is advisable to follow the same approach throughout the season, whether Track One or Track Two, rather than switching between the two during the season. The next time this lectionary year comes around, perhaps it would be valuable to try the other track.

Given these options, it is important that the preacher is aware and clear on which set of readings are being used in a given service.

Because of the length of the Season after Pentecost, this volume divides it into two sections: Summer and Autumn. The Seasonal Rites, Major Feasts and Other Commemorations are organized from Trinity Sunday through the approximate end of August for Summer and then from the approximate beginning of September through the end of the season for Autumn, beginning on page 345.

Preparing for the Season after Pentecost (Summer)

Summer Planning and Schedules

Most places will lack both the interest and the resources for planning extensively for the individual Sundays of the summer. Trinity Sunday often marks the end of the "regular schedule," and nothing much is planned until school reopens in the fall. This is not unreasonable, but some general plans need to be made, which can be applied to the entire sweep of summer Sunday services. Will the services be conducted in the church? If they are, will it be too hot for anyone to worship? Unless your parish borders the Arctic Circle or is air conditioned, the answer to the second question may well be yes, and serious thought needs to be given to dealing with the heat. Otherwise, parishioners will deal with it by staying home.

Summer as a Liturgical Opportunity

Summer can be a time of liturgical opportunity, rather than a low point in the year. It can be used as a time to explore other liturgical formats or other liturgical spaces. Many parishes use the summer for outdoor worship. Planning worship for the open air raises a number of questions beyond the choice of readings.

Most obviously, an alternative plan in case of rain needs to be in place and well known to those who might attend. Wind, insects, and birds need to be considered in choosing places and equipment. Probably some amplification system will be needed if the voices are to be heard outside. Unless prayer books and hymnals are to be taken out for each service, some decisions about common forms that can be printed on a leaflet is essential. An alternative source of music is necessary. It may be a guitar, a person with a strong true voice who will lead the singing, a field organ, or a band. All have been successfully. Will traditional music or paperless music be used? This decision will influence and be influenced by the available musicians. Finally, outdoor services need to be kept relatively short, unless there are adequate comfortable seats for a longer service. Many people will wish the service to be short anyway.

Don't simply have the service outdoors. Creatively use the space you have. Pray for the beauty of nature, for rain and sunshine and light and life and health. Many of the Gospel pericopes have settings in fields or at lakes and speak of farming and similar activities. These can be used in the planning If the services are to be in the church, it can be decorated with garden flowers. Use simple settings of the service music that the congregation knows. The services can be *planned,* rather than rushed through. Ideally, people should feel they have missed something worthwhile if they are absent; at least they should not be sorry they came. We are talking about at least one-quarter of the Sundays of the year. They are too important to be ignored in your parish's plans for worship.

Season after Pentecost (Summer) – Major Feasts, Seasonal Rites, and Other Commemorations

May/June, Commemoration of the First Book of Common Prayer

This feast day is a lesser feast and is celebrated on a convenient open day during the week after the Day of Pentecost. It may not substitute for a Sunday.

On the Day of Pentecost, in 1549, the first Book of Common Prayer began its service to Anglicans. Through subsequent editions and revisions, the BCP continues to serve the Anglican Communion. The book was prepared by a commission, comprising learned priests and bishops, but Thomas Cranmer, Archbishop of Canterbury (1533–1556), stamped the book in style, substance, and format. Bishops and priests compiled the book from, among other sources, medieval Latin service books, Greek liturgies, ancient Gallican rites, and vernacular German forms. The English "Great Bible," authorized by King Henry VII in 1539, supplied the Psalter, and the Litany came from the English form going back to 1544.

Feast Day Blessing[1]

The following blessings may be used by a bishop or priest whenever a blessing is appropriate for this feast.

Trinity Sunday

The Lord bless you and keep you. *Amen.*

The Lord make his face to shine upon you, and be gracious to you. *Amen.*

The Lord lift up his countenance upon you, and give you peace. *Amen.*

The Lord God Almighty, Father, Son, and Holy Spirit, the holy and undivided Trinity, guard you, save you, and bring you to that heavenly City, where he lives and reigns for ever and ever. *Amen.*

or this

May God the Holy Trinity make you strong in faith and love, defend you on every side, and guide you in truth and peace; and the blessing of God Almighty, the Father, the Son, and the Holy Spirit, be among you, and remain with you always. *Amen.*

The Nicene Creed: A Chancel Drama[2]

This chancel drama may be appropriate for Trinity Sunday, involving three readers and a narrator.

[NARRATOR]: We believe in one God, the Father, the Almighty, maker of heaven and earth, of all that is, seen and unseen.

[READER 1]: When I stop to think about God the creator, I stand in awe!

You must admit, whether you believe in creationism or evolution, it's all pretty astounding. God created out of nothing, out of chaos. When we make something new, it's with the gifts of creation at our disposal. We can only create from what is already here; all the raw materials God made. Reminds me of the joke when Man told God he was going to do a better job with Woman and God told him to get his own dirt . . .

1 BOS 2022, 16–17.

2 Linda W. Nichols, *The Nicene Creed: A Chancel Drama* (New York: Church Publishing, 2011). Part of the Skiturgies collection.

God created everything that is, from the vast expanse of interstellar space, to galaxies and suns, to the planets in their courses (ref. BCP, 370) and Mother earth, to humans and the smallest of atoms. Is there any detail God didn't consider when making all this? Think about how big God's love must be! It's enough to make you stop and pause.

[READER 2]: What does "We believe" mean? Are we affirming that we have love of neighbor and self? Really? Are we unified in Christ? And to take it further, are "we" those who are already with Christ, those living now and those believers yet to come? Hopefully, we really are the Body of Christ; one big happy family, past, present, and future.

[NARRATOR]: We believe in one Lord, Jesus Christ, the only Son of God, eternally begotten of the Father, God from God, Light from Light, true God from true God, begotten, not made, of one being with the Father. Through him all things were made.

[READER 3]: It reminds me of that passage: In the beginning was the Word, and the Word was with God. He was in the beginning with God; all things were made through him, and without him not anything was made . . . John 1:1–3

Let's face it; there's been debate around the identity of Jesus since the beginning of the Church. I believe Jesus is the Son of God. Why can't Jesus be human and divine? It's a paradox and a mystery of faith. Why can't Jesus be both?

If you think about it, it is hard to believe. But, if God created all that is, and God is God, why can't God create someone both human and divine? And as human beings, baptized into the Body of Christ with God's spirit dwelling within us, we can now believe we are truly sons and daughters of God. We somehow know we belong to God's family.

Doesn't this mean that God loves us a lot? God loved us enough to come face to face with us.

[NARRATOR]: For us and for our salvation he came down from heaven: by the power of the Holy Spirit he became incarnate from the Virgin Mary, and was made man.

[READER 2]: The age-old question is: what does it mean to be made man and be the Incarnate Son of God? Middle Eastern culture dictates that Mary was a virgin or she would have been stoned. Her age meant she was a mere child. So what does this mean for us today?

Does my belief in Jesus as Savior depend on a virgin birth? Well maybe this means more, and is expressing something deeper. Can't God use any individual to express the plan for our salvation? God does not need to show his face through miracles. But for me, God knew in our weakness that we need signs to give us hope. Believing in the Incarnation, come to think of it, makes it easier to believe in the Resurrection. Talk about God's amazing plan for us! God sent the Son, because the Virgin Mary said "yes"! This is the deeper meaning, even though it's hard for us to believe. After all, it's a matter of childlike faith, isn't it?

[NARRATOR]: For our sake he was crucified under Pontius Pilate; he suffered death and was buried. On the third day he rose again, in accordance with the Scriptures; he ascended into heaven and is seated at the right hand of the Father.

[READER 2]: See what I mean, this is the hard part for me. Think about the Resurrection. In one moment, sin and death no longer has power over us. Christians have spent centuries talking about forgiveness and love of our neighbors as well as ourselves. We are to forgive as we have been forgiven. How many times? Seven times seventy, and God wants us to forgive those who persecute us. That's hard.

God made life never ending with the Resurrection of Jesus. We will be resurrected too! God wants to be with us forever. God loves each of us that much. Eternity is a long time to love me! Now that's something worth believing.

[NARRATOR]: He will come again in glory to judge the living and the dead, and his kingdom will have no end.

[READER 3]: Where is God's Kingdom? Are we talking heaven here on earth or a heaven yet to come? Are we talking present or future? Sometimes kingdom language is confusing. The Parables say the Kingdom of God is like: a Mustard Seed, the Good Shepherd, the Found Sheep, the Lost Coin, Use of Talents, a Heavenly Banquet . . . I guess Jesus wasn't understood any better in back then. I suppose the best we can do is try to use our talents for the advancement of the Kingdom.

It seems like I've attended many funerals, and I find great comfort with fellow believers that there's a place with no more sorrow and pain. I'm still not sure about that whole Day of Judgment thing. Do we ever really talk about that subject? May your Kingdom come, your will be done.

[NARRATOR]: We believe in the Holy Spirit, the Lord, the giver of life, who proceeds from the Father and the Son. With the Father and the Son he is worshiped and glorified. He has spoken through the Prophets.

[READER 1]: Finally, we complete the Trinity. I know folks who think it's just about the Father and the Son.

I must admit, the Holy Spirit is ghostly, no pun intended. It's a mystery that God breathed over creation to start everything and keeps it going. In the medical profession, isn't it breath that pronounces us dead or alive? Sometimes it's easier to comprehend the living God with the Spirit as one rather than God and Jesus as one . . .

Then there's the whole Pentecost – the Spirit or breath of God moved to give us prophesies, dreams, and visions. It's about hope. The Spirit is our Counselor, companion, and guide to help us see ourselves in God's plan. It seems like it's only by the Spirit of God that we can begin to understand all the prophets spoke about, the life of Christ, and all that proceeds from the Giver of Life.

[NARRATOR]: We believe in one holy catholic and apostolic Church. We acknowledge one baptism for the forgiveness of sins.

[READER 2]: Here's where my friends get tripped up: the whole "one holy catholic Church" thing. Some say denominations don't matter and others are so sure they have all the answers that they think everyone else is wrong. This doesn't make any sense! Either we're all baptized as Christians or we're not . . . Why can't we focus on what Jesus taught in the Upper Room the night before he died, "That we all be one"? If we really thought we were One Body, we would get along better with others and be good neighbors to those who do not know Jesus yet. Actions do speak louder than words.

[NARRATOR]: We look for the resurrection of the dead, and the life of the world to come.

[READER 1]: "Parousia" is a word we're hearing more and more in children's formation. It refers to when God's creation comes together; the Alpha and the Omega; the Beginning and the End; when all of creation is complete; when the lion lies down with the lamb. I resonate with the thought of paradise restored! (Pair-a-see-a OR Pa-roo-ze-a – one pronunciation is Greek & one is Latin)

There's an acclamation in the Eucharistic Prayer when we say after the Consecration: Christ has died, Christ is risen, Christ will come again (BCP, 363). What do we mean by this faith response? Well, it sums up what God did for us and what that means for us as we are now living in the Kingdom, which will last to the world to come, to the Age of Ages!

[NARRATOR]: Amen.

So it is. May the love of God be so forever and ever. Amen.

Graduation Prayers

Either of the following may be used

Gracious and loving God, who gives us the days and the years of our lives, grant your grace and wisdom to these graduating students as they extend their vision to new horizons. Grant them insight in times of uncertainty, strength in times of challenge, and courage in the face of fears and anxieties. Offer support, strength, and patience to the families of these graduates also, O Lord, as they face their own transitions in the days ahead. Sustain us all, day by day, that we may rejoice with one another, weep in solidarity with one another, strive for justice for one another, that you may form us more fully to become the image of Christ in this world, that the world may know your love through these lives and through each of our lives; through Jesus Christ our Lord. *Amen.*

or this

Precious Father, *I* especially pray for our teenagers and young adults at this time of school graduations; where they are lost, find them; when they are afraid, bring them comfort and love; and where they are confused, show them your will. Protect them, Father, and be with parents as they ride the roller-coaster of these years with their children. May they have the courage, the strength, the wisdom through your Holy Spirit to help guide them and in many cases just to hold on, and to be there as their children take on adult responsibilities in a chaotic, sinful world. *I* now place them under your loving wings. *Amen.*[3]

Last Monday in May, Memorial Day

May fall near the end of Easter or early in the Season after Pentecost. See notes in the Easter season section.

May 31, The Visitation of the Blessed Virgin Mary

May fall near the end of Easter, when late, or during Proper 3 or 4 in the Season after Pentecost. As a Major Feast, when it falls on the Second Sunday after Pentecost or afterwards, it can be used in place of the Sunday propers. See notes in the Easter season section.

3 Stephanie Douglas, "Protect Them and Lead Them," in *Women's Uncommon Prayers,* edited by Elizabeth Rankin Geitz, Ann Smith, Marjorie A. Burke (Harrisburg, PA: Morehouse Publishing, 2000), 155.

June 11, Saint Barnabas the Apostle

May fall near at the very end of Easter or during Proper 5 in the Season after Pentecost. As a Major Feast, when it falls on the Second Sunday after Pentecost or afterwards, it can be used in place of the Sunday propers. See notes in the Easter season section.

The Third Sunday in June, Father's Day *(on or between June 21–27)*

This holiday is not on the church calendar, but is a secular holiday. Like Mother's Day, Father's Day can be complex pastorally. One may wish to reference the day in the prayers of the people, but great sensitivity should be considered.

A Father's Day Prayer[4]

Gracious God, you entrusted your Son Jesus, the child of Mary, to the care of Joseph, an earthly father. Bless all fathers as they care for their families. Give them strength and wisdom, tenderness and patience; support them in the work they have to do, protecting those who look to them, as we look to you for love and salvation, through Jesus Christ our rock and defender. ***Amen.***

June 24, The Nativity of Saint John the Baptist

This is a Major Feast and Feast of Our Lord and may substitute for the Sunday after Pentecost when it falls on a Sunday. It falls during Proper 6 or Proper 7. The Collect for the Day is found on pages 190 or 241 of the BCP.

John was born the son of Elizabeth and Zachariah, who were aged. His birth is celebrated six months before that of Jesus since Elizabeth, Mary's cousin, had become pregnant six months before Mary. John has a role in all four gospels. His father lost speech when he disbelieved a vision foretelling John's birth, but when his speech was restored, he sang a canticle of praise, the *Benedictus*, now part of the Daily Office. John lived in abstention in the desert, clothed with camel's hair and a belt; he ate locusts and honey. He preached repentance, importuning hearers to prepare for the Kingdom and the Messiah and baptized them to signify new life. He baptized Jesus in the Jordan.

June 29, Saint Peter and Saint Paul, Apostles

This is a Major Feast and may substitute for the Sunday after Pentecost when it falls on a Sunday. It falls during Proper 7 or Proper 8. The Collect for the Day is found on pages 190 or 241 of the BCP.

Peter and Paul, each with his own commemoration as a renowned Church leader, are also remembered together because, by tradition, they were martyred together in Rome under Nero in 64. Paul was a well-educated, urbane Jew of the Dispersion; Peter was an untutored fisherman from Galilee. The two disagreed on the issue of mission to the Gentiles in the early years of the Church, but they were committed to Christ and to proclaiming the gospel, which they bore to Rome. According to tradition, Paul was decapitated by sword swipe, as befitted a Roman citizen; Peter suffered death on the cross, it is said, with his head pointed downward.

July 4, Independence Day

This is one of two United States holidays on the church calendar, along with Thanksgiving Day. It is listed as a Major Feast and may substitute for the Sunday after Pentecost when it falls on a Sunday. It falls during Proper 8 or Proper 9. The Collect for the Day is found on pages 190 or 242 of the BCP, though many find it problematic. The Collect for Various Occasion 17. For the Nation (BCP 207 or 258) may be used instead.

Care should be taken to ensure that any parish observance of this day continues to focus on the centrality of Christ and the Gospel, rather than simply on patriotism.

Ten years after July 4, 1776, General Convention called for observance of Independence Day throughout "this Church, on the fourth of July, for ever." Proper Psalms, Lessons, and Prayers were appointed for the national recognition of this day; however, they were rescinded in 1789 by General Convention with the intervention of Bishop William White. Although he supported the American Revolution, White revolted against observing the day, given that the majority of the Church's clerics remained loyal to the British government. Not until 1928 was provision made again for the liturgical notice of the day.

4 Adapted from "15 A Service for Father's Day" in *New Patterns for Worship* (London: Church House Publishing, 2008); online version https://www.churchofengland.org/prayer-and-worship/worship-texts-and-resources/common-worship/common-material/new-patterns-0, accessed March 31, 2023.

Independence Day Service of Readings and Music

Some congregations have found it helpful to assemble a service of various important readings from American history, along with the prayers provided in the BCP and the National Hymns in *The Hymnal 1982*. It is important that the selections represent the breadth of the American experience in order for it to be a liturgy for all people. Some common reading selections include:[5]

A Reading from the Mayflower Compact of 1620

A Reading from Abigail Adams to John Adams, March 31 1776,

advocating protection for women

A Reading from the Preamble to the Constitution, 1789

A Reading from Chief Seattle's Response

to a Government Official's Offer to Purchase the Remaining Seattle Land, 1845

A Reading from A Letter from the Birmingham Jail,

Dr. Martin Luther King, Jr., April 16, 1963

A Reading from Lincoln's 2nd Inaugural Address, 1865

Hymns may be sung between each reading.

Either *Thanksgiving 5. For the Nation* (BCP 838) or *Prayer 22. For Sound Government* (BCP 821) from the "Prayers and Thanksgivings" section in the BCP are helpful additions to the service. The readings from history would be concluded with the appointed readings for the day. This service can be constructed as an evening office, using Order of Worship for the Evening, or as a Eucharist.

An Independence Day Litany[6]

This litany is designed for use on days of national celebration (like Independence Day), or in times of national crisis.

Mighty God: the earth is yours and nations are your people. Take away our pride and bring to mind your goodness, so that, living together in this land, we may enjoy your gifts and be thankful. ***Amen.***

For clouded mountains, fields, and woodland; for shoreline and running streams; for all that makes our nation good and lovely;

We thank you, God.

For farms and villages where food is gathered to feed our people;

We thank you, God.

For cities where people talk and work together in factories, shops, or schools to shape those things we need for living;

We thank you, God.

For explorers, planners, diplomats; for prophets who speak out, and for silent faithful people; for all who love our land and guard our freedom;

We thank you, God.

For vision to see your purpose hidden in our nation's history, and courage to seek it in human love exchanged;

We thank you, God.

O God, your justice is like a rock, and your mercy like pure flowing water. Judge and forgive us. If we have turned from you, return us to your way; for without you, we are lost people. From brassy patriotism and a blind trust in power;

Deliver us, O God.

From public deceptions that weaken trust; from self-seeking in high political places;

Deliver us, O God.

From divisions among us of class or race; from wealth that will not share, and poverty that feeds on food of bitterness;

Deliver us, O God.

From neglecting rights; from overlooking the hurt, the imprisoned, and the needy among us;

Deliver us, O God.

From a lack of concern for other lands and peoples; from narrowness of national purpose; from failure to welcome the peace you promise on earth;

Deliver us, O God.

Eternal God: before you nations rise and fall; they grow strong or wither by your design. Help us to repent our country's wrong, and to choose your right in reunion and renewal.

Amen.

---

5 The Rev. Elizabeth Kaeton has developed a form of this that many have found helpful, which includes the text of readings and hymn selections. It may be viewed at http://telling-secrets.blogspot.com/2011/07/lessons-and-hymns-for-independence-day.html, accessed March 31, 2023.

6 "Litany for the Nation," in *An American Prayer Book,* edited by Christopher L. Webber (Harrisburg, PA: Morehouse Publishing, 2008), 39–41.

Give us a glimpse of the Holy City you are bringing to earth, where death and pain and crying will be gone away; and nations gather in the light of your presence.

Great God, renew this nation.

Teach us peace, so that we may plow up battlefields and pound weapons into building tools, and learn to talk across old boundaries as brothers and sisters in your love.

Great God, renew this nation.

Talk sense to us, so that we may wisely end all prejudice, and may put a stop to cruelty, which divides or wounds the human family.

Great God, renew this nation.

Draw us together as one people who do your will, so that our land may be a light to the nations, leading the way to your promised kingdom, which is coming among us.

Great God, renew this nation.

Great God, eternal Lord: long years ago you gave our fathers this land as a home for the free. Show us there is no law or liberty apart from you; and let us serve you modestly, as devoted people; through Jesus Christ our Lord. ***Amen.***

July 22, Saint Mary Magdalene

This is a Major Feast and may substitute for the Sunday after Pentecost when it falls on a Sunday. It falls during Proper 11 or Proper 12. The Collect for the Day is found on pages 191 or 242 of the BCP.

Mary of Magdala, near Capernaum, followed Jesus and cared for Him-who-healed-her. She appears in all four gospels' stories of the crucifixion as witness to Christ's death. She exemplifies women's faithful ministry for Jesus, as she and her sisters-in-faith went to the tomb to mourn and attend Jesus' body. That Jesus revealed himself to her, calling her by name, makes her the first witness to the risen Lord. She told the disciples, "I have seen the Lord." According to the Gospel of Mary, Peter, for one, did not believe that Jesus would show himself first to a woman. Mary's reputation, although twisted for centuries, maintains that she was an apostle.

July 25, St. James the Apostle

This is a Major Feast and may substitute for the Sunday after Pentecost when it falls on a Sunday. It falls during Proper 11 or Proper 12. The Collect for the Day is found on pages 191 or 242 of the BCP.

James' familiar name, James the Greater, distinguishes the brother of John from the other apostle named James (commemorated with Philip on May 1) but also from the other James, "the brother of our Lord." This James was the son of Zebedee, a prosperous Galilean fisher; with his brother John, James left his home and business to follow Christ's call. He seems to have belonged among those chosen for the privilege of witnessing the Transfiguration, the raising of Jairus' daughter, and the agony in the garden. Jesus called the brothers "Sons of Thunder" because of their quick tempers.

August 6, The Transfiguration of Our Lord Jesus Christ

*This is a Major Feast and a Feast of Our Lord. When this feast falls on a Sunday it **must** take precedence over the Sunday lessons and collect (see planning page for Transfiguration, when on a Sunday). It falls during Proper 13. The Collect for the Day is found on pages 191 or 243 of the BCP.*

God authenticated Jesus as God's son in a series of surprising manifestations. The Transfiguration is one of that series and, therefore, not to be taken only as a spiritual experience for Jesus, witnessed by Peter, James, and John. The Transfiguration fits with angels appearing at Jesus's birth and resurrection and with the Spirit's descent at Jesus's baptism. In the Transfiguration, according to the book of Matthew, the veil is drawn aside, and, again, a few witness Jesus as the earthborn son of Mary and as the eternal Son of God. In Luke's account, a cloud, a sign of divine presence, envelops the disciples, and a heavenly voice proclaims Jesus to be the Son of God. The Transfiguration story is also always appointed for the Last Sunday after Epiphany, but August 6 is the actual feast day.

August 15, Saint Mary the Virgin, Mother of Our Lord Jesus Christ

This is a Major Feast and may substitute for the Sunday after Pentecost when it falls on a Sunday. It falls during Proper 14 or Proper 15. The Collect for the Day is found on pages 192 or 243 of the BCP.

Mary has been honored as the mother of Jesus Christ since the beginnings of the Church. Two Gospels tell the story of Christ's birth to a virgin; Luke's Gospel gives glimpses of Christ's childhood in Nazareth under the care of his mother and earthly father, Joseph. During Jesus's ministry in Galilee, Mary often traveled with the women who followed Jesus, ministering to him; at Calvary, she stood with the women who kept watch at the cross. After the Resurrection, she accompanied the Twelve in the upper room. She was the person closest to Jesus, having humbly accepted God's divine will. Later devotions lay many claims for Mary that cannot be proven by Holy Scripture.

Other traditions refer to this day as the Assumption of Mary or the Dormition of the Theotokos, referring to the belief that Mary's body was taken up into heaven, upon her death. That is not a direct teaching in the Episcopal Church, but implicit references to this idea may be found in the Collect of the Day as well as hymnody associated with Mary in The Hymnal 1982.

Blessing for Feasts of the Virgin Mary:[7]

God, the Father, who has loved the eternal Son from before the foundation of the world, shed that love upon you his children. *Amen.*

Christ who by his Incarnation gathered into one things earthly and heavenly, fill you with joy and peace. *Amen.*

The Holy Spirit, by whose presence Mary became the God-bearer, give you grace to carry the good news of Christ. *Amen.*

And the blessing of God Almighty, the Father, the Son, and the Holy Spirit, be among you and remain with you always. *Amen.*

or this

May the Holy Spirit, by whose presence Mary became the God-bearer, give you grace to carry the good news of Christ. And the blessing of God Almighty, the Father, the Son, and the Holy Spirit, be among you and remain with you always. *Amen.*

August 24, Saint Bartholomew the Apostle

This is a Major Feast and may substitute for the Sunday after Pentecost when it falls on a Sunday. It falls during Proper 15 or Proper 16. The Collect for the Day is found on pages 192 or 243 of the BCP.

Bartholomew, though one of the twelve apostles, is known only by having been listed among them in the Gospels of Matthew, Mark, and Luke. His name means "Son of Tolmai," and he is sometimes identified with Nathanael, the friend of Philip, the "Israelite without guile" in John's Gospel, to whom Jesus promised the vision of angels ascending from and descending on the Son of Man. Nothing more is recorded. Some sources credit Bartholomew with having written a gospel, now lost but once known to Jerome and Bede. By tradition, Bartholomew traveled to India; another tradition has him flayed alive at Albanopolis in Armenia.

7 BOS 2022, 18.

Back to School

In many communities in the United States, school resumes in August or early September. While this is not a liturgical event, it is an important threshold and an opportunity for a pastoral prayer or ritual.

Marking the Beginning of a School Year[8]

God of all wisdom, we praise you for wisely gifting us with children and students. Give to each one a clear sense of your love, that they may feel your presence supporting them throughout this school year. Guide their choices, direct their quest for knowledge, bless their relationships, and use their successes and failures as opportunities to grow in understanding of who you would have them be. Continue, we pray, to shape them as branches of the one true vine, that they may ever walk in the way of Christ, grow strong in your Spirit's love for all people, and know the complete joy of life in you. In the name of Christ, we pray. *Amen.*

The Blessing of Backpacks[9]

(Children are invited to gather in the chancel with their backpacks. Following the blessing, small wooden crosses may be given out for the children to place inside the backpacks or themed luggage tags with a Christian image or Scripture verse may be attached to the backpack.)

God of Wisdom, we give you thanks for schools and classrooms and for the teachers and students who fill them each day. We thank you for this new beginning, for new books and new ideas. We thank you for sharpened pencils, pointy crayons, and crisp blank pages waiting to be filled. We thank you for the gift of making mistakes and trying

8 Linda Witte Henke, "From the Vine," in *Marking Time: Christian Rituals for All Our Days* (Harrisburg, PA: Morehouse Publishing, 2001), 63.

9 Wendy Claire Barrie, in *Skiturgies: Pageants, Plays, Rites, and Rituals* (New York: Church Publishing, 2011).

again. Help us to remember that asking the right questions is often as important as giving the right answers. Today we give you thanks for these your children, and we ask you to bless them with curiosity, understanding, and respect. May their backpacks be a sign to them that they have everything they need to learn and grow this year in school and in Sunday School. May they be guided by your love. All this we ask this in the name of Jesus, who as a child in the temple showed his longing to learn about you, and as an adult taught by story and example your great love for us. *Amen.*

The First Sunday after Pentecost: Trinity Sunday

Variable: May 17 and June 20

One God in Three Persons reminds us that relationship and relationality are at the heart of who God is and who we are.

Anchor Points – The Propers and the Feast

The fixed points for each service are the appointed or proper readings and collect as well as the themes of the day or season.

Readings and Psalm

Isaiah 6:1–8

This reading recounts the call of the prophet Isaiah. He has a vision of the Lord enthroned amidst the divine council in the setting of the temple at Jerusalem. The throne is the ark of the covenant. Above the Lord are the seraphs, literally "burning ones." Here, like the cherubim in the first chapter of Ezekiel, they indicate the heavenly creatures who give God worship. The triple repetition of holy emphasizes the mysterious, unapproachable quality of the divine. Isaiah responds to the vision of God's holiness with a sense of profound sinfulness before God's perfection, not only for himself, but for all the people. He is granted cleansing through the coal from the altar so that he may proclaim God's word to the people.

Psalm 29

Psalm 29 is a hymn to Yahweh as the God of storm that may have been written as an objection to the pagan assertion of Baal as the thunder-god. The "glory" of the Lord gives God dominion over nature and over all gods. Thus, Yahweh alone is the source of strength and blessing for the people.

or

Canticle 13

This is from the song of the Daniel's three Jewish companions thrown into a fiery furnace by the Babylonian King Nebuchadnezzar because they refused to worship an idol. Although only preserved in the Greek version of this book, the song also survives in the Aramaic version between verses 3:23 and 24. The verses are a litany of praise in which the first line blesses God, to which all respond with the same refrain. This portion of the song has long been used as a canticle in the Daily (or Divine) Office of the Western Church. In keeping with the pattern of other canticles of the Office, Canticle 13 as it appears in the BCP ends with a Trinitarian doxology uniquely paralleling the form of verses found in the ancient song.

Romans 8:12–17

The presentation of the Trinity in the Scriptures is not a matter of formal definition but of the living experience of God revealed in creation, redemption, and sanctification. In Romans 8 Paul mentions, within the space of one chapter, the Spirit as being the Spirit of God (8:9), the Spirit of Christ (8:9) and the Spirit of life in Christ Jesus (8:2). Paul seems neither to intend nor to feel the need for any particular distinction among these phrases. He emphasizes that the source of the Spirit is God, that the Spirit's full manifestation is in Christ and that Christians experience the Spirit communally in the body of Christ, the Church. The Spirit gives to Christians "the spirit of adoption" (v. 15). Christians are "joint heirs with Christ" (v. 17), sharing in the redemptive act of Christ's passion and resurrection and looking forward to sharing in his glorification.

John 3:1–17

Nicodemus, a member of the Sanhedrin, explains his interest as being caused by the signs Jesus has performed. Jesus seeks to draw him past these outward manifestations to a recognition of the inward significance of his activity. The discussion begins on the meaning of being born, or "begotten," "from above" (v. 3). In Greek, this phrase has two meanings. The first is "anew, again" – temporally – which is what Nicodemus understands on the physical level; the second is "from above" – spatially – which is what Jesus seems to intend. Jesus contrasts the realm of the Spirit, which is eternal and heavenly, with the realm of flesh, which is earthly, weak and mortal (but not necessarily sinful). Both flesh and spirit constitute human existence, but the Spirit is life itself. The life that the Spirit gives is not under human control, not anthropocentric, but theocentric, as shown by the illustration of the wind blowing where it will. Both the Greek and the Hebrew words for wind also mean spirit and breath.

Collect

Almighty and everlasting God, you have given to us your servants grace, by the confession of a true faith, to acknowledge the glory of the eternal Trinity, and in the power of your divine Majesty to worship the Unity: Keep us steadfast in this faith and worship, and bring us at last to see you in your one and eternal glory, O Father; who with the Son and the Holy Spirit live and reign, one God, for ever and ever. *Amen.*

Proper Preface

Trinity Sunday – For with your co-eternal Son and Holy Spirit, you are one God, one Lord, in Trinity of Persons and in Unity of Being; and we celebrate the one and equal glory of you, O Father, and of the Son, and of the Holy Spirit. (Rite II, BCP 380; Rite I BCP 347)

Feast Day Pairings

See the table below for choices appointed and suggested for this day. Preferences are put in **bold**. Not all choices are suitable for all congregations or community, though, so consider these preferences as a starting point before making a decision about your own congregation.

	First Sunday after Pentecost: Trinity Sunday	Rite I	Rite II	EOW1	BOS 2022
Color	White/Gold/Festive				
Entrance Rite	Customary; opening acclamation "Blessed be God" or one of the first two in EOW1	323	355	50	
Song of Praise/Kyrie	Canticle 7 or 21 Te Deum, Gloria in excelsis or BCP Canticle 2 or 13; EOW1 Canticle 21, N	C7 – 52; Gloria 324; C2 – 49	C21 – 95; Gloria 356; C13 – 90	C21 – 29; N – 37	
Collect		164	216		
Creed	Nicene Creed	326	358	53	
Prayers of the People	**Locally written**; options below; BCP forms	329	387–393	54–55	
Offertory Sentence	"God did not send the Son into the world to condemn the world, but in order that the world might be saved through him." (John)	343–344	376–377		
Eucharistic Prayer	**One that allows use of the Trinity Sunday preface**	2–340	**A – 361, B – 367**	1–57	
Proper Preface	Trinity Sunday	347	380		
Breaking of the Bread (Fraction)	Christ our Passover (BCP) or Blessed are those who are called (Hymn S 172)	337	364	69	
Postcommunion Prayer		339	**Eternal God – 365**	**God of abundance – 69**	
Blessing	**Seasonal Blessing in BOS**				**16–17**
Dismissal	**Let us go forth into the world, rejoicing in the power of the Spirit.**	340	366		
Notes	Chancel Drama on the Nicene Creed (above) might be useful this day; recognize graduates?				

Additional Notes:

Song of Praise/Canticle – Canticle 21, the Te Deum, is a strong choice for Trinty Sunday, but its success depends greatly on the setting used. EOW1 Canticle N is a nice choice, if emphasizing the Augustinian image of the Trinity as a relationship of love.

Creed – While the Nicene Creed is appointed, since this is a Sunday and a Principal Feast, some congregations use the Athanasian Creed found in the "Historical Documents of the Church" section of the BCP (pages 864–865). While that can be interesting, it is more likely to be frustrating and distracting from worship. Using the Athanasian Creed as part of an Adult Education program, perhaps especially on Trinity Sunday, would be a better way to incorporate it.

Eucharistic Prayer – If the congregation chants the beginning of the Eucharistic Prayer, the priest needs to be sure to practice the Trinity Sunday Proper Preface a few times. It is not used often and the language is a little involved.

Fraction Anthem at the Breaking of the Bread – The option provided in Rite I and Rite II ("Christ our Passover") is suitable and the Alleluias may be included (Hymn S 151 – S 156). The text at Hymn S 172 ("Blessed are those who are called") is appropriate for today as well. Additionally, EOW1 has several options.

Dismissal – "Alleluias" are omitted from dismissal after Pentecost, until next Easter. What is intended as a special celebration is used almost year-round in some congregations. To give Easter as much celebratory emphasis as possible, it is encouraged to follow the rubrics and drop the "Alleluias" at the dismissal the rest of the year. "Alleluia" may still be used at the breaking of the bread, though optional.

Content Resources

Reading Between the Lines

Isaiah 6 describes Isaiah's response to his prophetic vocation for which God prepares and calls him. Isaiah's vision is also about the nature of God. Unclean as he was, Isaiah is caught up into the divine presence as a preparation for his vocation. God solves the issue of impurity because God has a task for Isaiah that involves a calling to go and speak to God's people.

The theologian Sarah Coakley sees Romans 8 as an access point for understanding the Trinity. In contemplative prayer, people speak of the prayer that happens internally. This experience is the work of the Spirit, the movement of the Trinity, and part of God's creating activity. The experience of "being prayed in" is what Paul is talking about: "...the Spirit helps us in our weakness; for we do not know how to pray as we ought, but that very Spirit intercedes with sighs too deep for words." When words fail, it is the Spirit who articulates and intercedes for us in a prayer beyond words to convey intercession (Paul uses the language of "birth pangs"). Thus, the Spirit serves as an intermediary between God and people, proceeding from God, as divine gift (Romans 8:5), and simultaneously dwelling within believers (8:9). It is the agent of resurrection that belongs to the heavenly realm (8:11) simultaneously helping believers put to death deeds of the body (8:13). With her intercessions, the Spirit participates in the earthly life of believers who still experience weakness in waiting for the promised salvation (8:26). Whereas Christ is seated at the right hand of the Father (8:34), the Spirit remains with believers, communicating between two worlds.

The gospel presents a dialog between Jesus and Nicodemus. Nicodemus, who has a great deal of academic training, misinterprets being born again literally, and when Jesus clarifies in their dialogue that being born of water and the Spirit is a description of being born from above, Nicodemus says, "How can these things be?" Today's gospel also includes the famous passage in John 3:16 telling Nicodemus and everyone else that God so loved the world that he gave his only Son so that no one believing in him would perish but have everlasting life. The connection between Nicodemus and John 3:16 may not seem immediately evident. But it is not so strange that a conversation about birth, to which there are eight references in six verses, should end in a statement about life. As for Nicodemus, his search to understand Jesus' words may be criticized, but Nicodemus will never be excluded.

Today's gospel echoes and expands the message of Isaiah, namely, that humans in their outsider status in relation to the holy, are drawn up by God not into their own agenda but into the mystery of God's divine activity and love for the world. God works with us and in the world in multiple ways of self-giving and mutual respect, empowering and working through others just as we also have myriad opportunities in our lives to align ourselves with God's intentions for creation and human relations.

Central Themes

Athletic coaches often tell talented recruits to forget everything they have ever been taught about their sport. Coaches find it easier to train a newbie the winning way to play than to convince experienced recruits to drop bad habits. When Jesus focuses on how children come into God's presence, he reminds us that we are most open to following God's commandment to love others when we aren't hampered by unhelpful beliefs we've acquired. The rite of baptism signifies our decision to accept the beginning of a new spiritual life centered in Christ while rejecting the false teachings of the world.

In today's gospel, Nicodemus asks several questions directly of Jesus. Nicodemus appears later in John 7 to ask a question of his fellow Pharisees, and then in John 19 he comes to anoint Jesus's dead body. The reader never knows if Nicodemus fully "gets" who Jesus is. Still, Nicodemus models holy curiosity and shows up when it's important.

On this Trinity Sunday, what questions do we want to ask of Jesus? When should we be curious leaders and learners rather than stand in our certainty? Where are we called to show up?

Curious Nicodemus comes by night seeking, but confused by Jesus, he withdraws. Our Nicodemus is plucky, doesn't give up, appears again mid-gospel to defend the Jesus he once sought [7.50]. Finally, in the full light of a new day, he shows up again, another follower in tow, and claims the body of the subject of his earlier seeking [19.39]. Discipleship, whether in the gospel or in the Church, is often like that. We seek, perhaps lose our way, but then rejoin the quest. Finally, we, like our Nicodemus, learn that we've been the ones who've been found by the true Seeker.

Engaging All Ages

The Trinity is one of our most difficult theological doctrines. We believe in one God in three persons. This is truly a mystery. In his wisdom, Jesus spoke of himself in concrete, everyday images such as light, bread, shepherd, and vine. What images might we connect with God the Father? Perhaps the water of creation, soil, the earth. What about the Holy Spirit? Maybe wind or a dove. Consider using Andrei Rublev's famous icon of the Trinity as a way to incorporate images into your discussion. Sometimes God is best experienced through beauty, art, image, and poetry rather than intellect.

Prayers of the People: Option 1

Intoxicate us with visions and dreams that will align us with you. Jolt us from our inertia into action. Come into our lives with power.

Come, Holy Spirit, and stay with us.

Transform our melancholy into joy, our worry into peace, our despair into hope. We pray for healing for those who suffer from any distress or illness. Come into our lives with healing.

Come, Holy Spirit, and stay with us.

Work your ways in this world, and direct the leaders of the nations to embrace peace and justice.

Come, Holy Spirit, and stay with us.

Shape our weary and wounded souls into souls on fire for God's mission.

Come, Holy Spirit, and stay with us.

Prayers of the People: Option 2

Deacon or Priest

As children of God, led by the Spirit, let us pray for the needs, hopes, and concerns of the world.

Intercessor

For peace from on high and for our salvation.

Glory and praise to you, O living God.

For the peace of the whole world, for the welfare of the holy churches of God, and for the unity of all.

Glory and praise to you, O living God.

For this holy gathering, for those preparing to be baptized, confirmed, and received, and for those who enter with faith, reverence, and fear of God.

Glory and praise to you, O living God.

For *N.* our Presiding Bishop, for *N.* our bishop, for *N.* our parish clergy, for all priests and deacons, for all who minister in Christ, and for all the holy people of God.

Glory and praise to you, O living God.

For this congregation on the feast day of the Blessed Trinity, that our work together may continue to glorify God's holy Name.

Glory and praise to you, O living God.

For the world and its leaders, our nation and its people.

Glory and praise to you, O living God.

For those seeking healing, for ______________________ _______ and for all those in need, those who are suffering and all who are oppressed; we pray for travelers, prisoners, the dying and the dead.

Glory and praise to you, O living God.

For ourselves, our families, and those we love.

Glory and praise to you, O living God.

Remembering our most glorious and blessed Virgin Mary and all the saints, let us offer ourselves and one another to the living God through Christ.

Glory and praise to you, O living God.

Presider

Blessed are you, O Lord our God, who so loved the world that you gave us your only Son. Hear the prayers we offer this day and lead us into your kingdom; through Jesus Christ our Lord. ***Amen.***

Hymns for the Day

The Hymnal 1982

Holy Father, great Creator 368
Holy God we praise thy Name 366
How wondrous great, how glorious bright 369
I bind unto myself today 370
O Trinity of blessed light 29, 30
Sing praise to our Creator 295
Holy, holy, holy! Lord God Almighty! 362
Let all mortal flesh keep silence 324
My God, how wonderful thou art 643
O day of radiant gladness 48
O God, we praise thee, and confess 364
Round the Lord in glory seated 367
The God of Abraham praise 401
Baptized in water 294
And now, O Father, mindful of the love 337
Lift high the cross 473
O love, how deep, how broad, how high 448, 449
The great Creator of the worlds 489
When Christ was lifted from the earth 603, 604

Lift Every Voice and Sing II

Oh Lord, how perfect is your name 57
Baptized in water 121
Children of the heavenly Father 213
Every time I feel the spirit 751, 114

Wonder, Love, and Praise

God, beyond all human praises 745
God the sculptor of the mountains 746, 747
O threefold God of tender unity 743
O Trinity of blessed light 744
I, the Lord of sea and sky 812
Santo, santo, santo 785
Thuma mina/Send me, Lord 808
Every time I feel the spirit 751
Baptized in water 767

Proper 1

This proper is appointed only for use on the weekdays following the Day of Pentecost and not for Sunday use.

Anchor Points – The Propers and the Season

The fixed points for each service are the appointed or proper readings and collect as well as the themes of the day or season.

NOTE: The Readings are identical to The Sixth Sunday after the Epiphany. Please refer to that page for information on the readings, the themes of the day, and any other planning suggestions. The Collect for Proper 1 is only used in this week and not for Epiphany 6.

Readings and Psalm

2 Kings 5:1–14

Ps. 30

1 Corinthians 9:24–27

Mark 1:40–45

Collect

Remember, O Lord, what you have wrought in us and not what we deserve; and, as you have called us to your service, make us worthy of our calling; through Jesus Christ our Lord, who lives and reigns with you and the Holy Spirit, one God, now and for ever. *Amen.*

No Proper Preface is provided for this proper since this is appointed only for weekdays.

Note: *The lesser feast for the Commemoration of the First Book of Common Prayer falls during this week. Information for that feast is above with other Feasts and Seasonal Rites.*

Content Resources

Reading Between the Lines

Jesus' healing ministry in Galilee, according to Mark, attracts the attention of people who are ill and who take the initiative to seek Jesus. A person with a skin disease comes to him and kneeling down, requests healing, assuming that Jesus will indeed want this. The healing, accompanied by emotion, either pity or anger, the latter perhaps occasioned by the skin disease, is achieved by touch and verbal assent to the request. The skin disease disappears, and the person made clean. He is thrown out and warned sternly by Jesus not to broadcast the event, but to go to the priest to offer a sacrifice for a skin disease healing, thereby signifying respect for the law and authority of the priests. Nevertheless, the healed man who had been inhibited by a disease, proclaims the healing widely to the extent that Jesus' own movements were inhibited. Several themes will re-emerge in the gospel narrative: the initiatives made to him by others and their effect on Jesus and Jesus' body; Jesus' emotions; the narrative drama (there is more momentum in the Greek through use of the connective "and" than English translations convey); Jesus' physical grasp or touch to effect healing for many; issues of purity, impurity, and cleansing; Jesus' adherence to the law; his injunctions to silence whether successful or not, the spreading of Jesus' fame and its inhibiting effect.

Proper 2

This proper is appointed only for use on the weekdays following the Trinity Sunday and not for Sunday use.

Anchor Points – The Propers and the Season

The fixed points for each service are the appointed or proper readings and collect as well as the themes of the day or season.

NOTE: The Readings are identical The Seventh Sunday after the Epiphany. Please refer to that page for information on the readings, the themes of the day, and any other planning suggestions. The Collect for Proper 2 is only used in this week and not for Epiphany 7.

Readings and Psalm

Isaiah 43:18–25

Ps. 41

2 Corinthians 1:18–22

Mark 2:1–12

Collect

Almighty and merciful God, in your goodness keep us, we pray, from all things that may hurt us, that we, being ready both in mind and body, may accomplish with free hearts those things which belong to your purpose; through Jesus Christ our Lord, who lives and reigns with you and the Holy Spirit, one God, now and for ever; *Amen.*

No Proper Preface is provided for this proper since this is appointed only for weekdays.

Content Resources

Reading Between the Lines

Mark 2:1–3:6 contains five controversy stories of which today's gospel is the first. They indicate how Jesus succeeds in addressing hostile questions: "Why does this fellow speak in this way? (2:7); "Why does he eat with tax collectors and sinners? (2:16); "Why do the disciples of John and the disciples of the Pharisees fast, but your disciples do not? (2:18); "Why are they doing what is not permissible on the Sabbath? (2:24). Answers build on each other by making a clearer and specific case for the features of Jesus' particular ministry: to forgive sins as Son of Man (or Child of Humanity: 2:10); to call sinners (2:17); to announce his departure (2:19–20); to balance religious laws with human needs (2:27–28); to ask about the purpose of Sabbath regulations (3:4). These build on prior opposition from demonic powers with which Jesus has been contending from the outset. The central one of the controversy stories alludes alarmingly to Jesus being taken away by unidentified forces (2:20).

In the first controversy story, Jesus is in a very crowded house the roof of which friends of a man with paralysis unroof. They believe and trust that Jesus can heal him, so they let him down through it to Jesus' feet. Jesus' declaration to him, "Child, your sins are forgiven" meaning, "God has forgiven your sins," provokes the response of 2:7 and a charge of blasphemy. It is rebutted by Jesus' declaration that authority to forgive sins on earth is the domain of the Son of Man, that is, in this case, a particular human being (Jesus) mediating not God's judgment but healing and restoration to humankind.

Proper 3

Sunday on or between May 22 and 28

Anchor Points – The Propers and the Season

The fixed points for each service are the appointed or proper readings and collect as well as the themes of the day or season.

> *NOTE: The Readings for Proper 3 are identical to The Eighth Sunday after the Epiphany. Please refer to that page for information on the readings, the themes of the day, prayers of the people, and any other planning suggestions. The Collect for Proper 3 is only used in this Sunday and not for Epiphany 8.*

Readings and Psalm

Hosea 2:14–20

Ps. 103:1–13,22

2 Corinthians 3:1–6

Mark 2:13–22

Collect

Grant, O Lord, that the course of this world may be peaceably governed by your providence; and that your Church may joyfully serve you in confidence and serenity; through Jesus Christ our Lord, who lives and reigns with you and the Holy Spirit, one God, for ever and ever. *Amen.* (Rite II, BCP 229; Rite I, BCP 177)

Proper Preface

1. Of God the Father

For you are the source of light and life; you made us in your image, and called us to new life in Jesus Christ our Lord.

or this

2. Of God the Son

Through Jesus Christ our Lord; who on the first day of the week overcame death and the grave, and by his glorious resurrection opened to us the way of everlasting life.

or the following

3. Of God the Holy Spirit

For by water and the Holy Spirit you have made us a new people in Jesus Christ our Lord, to show forth your glory in all the world.

(Rite II, BCP 377–378; Rite I, BCP 344–345)

Content Resources

Reading Between the Lines

In today's gospel, Jesus calls disciples. They are named and numbered in Mark 3. The choice of twelve likely corresponds to the scattered 12 tribes of Israel. So, the calling of twelve may suggest hope for the restoration of Israel. The first to be called is Levi: a tax collector and sinner, namely a collector of taxes and tolls on behalf of the Roman Empire, who was also free unlawfully to levy further taxes for profit. At a subsequent meal in Levi's house, Jesus and his disciples recline in the company of "many tax collectors and sinners," thus occasioning the criticism of 2:16. In the course of table fellowship, Jesus speaks intentionally of his mission to call sinners, not righteous people. And Levi, as James Crossley says, has access to a network of wealthy people. Levi, Jesus' new disciple, likely now embarks on a new career of furthering Jesus' mission by no longer taxing the poor but the rich. Jesus explains that his disciples do not fast, because he, the bridegroom, is with them, but he will not always be. When he is taken away, perhaps arrested for some unknown reason, then they will fast. A shadow – Jesus' death – falls across the gospel.

Hymns for the Day

The Hymnal 1982

O bless the Lord, my soul! 411
Praise, my soul, the King of heaven 410
Praise to the Lord, the Almighty 390
God is working his purpose out 534
Sing praise to God who reigns above 408

Holy Spirit, ever living 511
O Spirit of Life, O Spirit of God 505
O Spirit of the living God 531
By all your saints still striving 231, 232 [*Use St. Matthew for verse 2*]
From God Christ's deity came forth 443
He sat to watch o'er customs paid 281
In your mercy, Lord, you called me 706

Lift Every Voice and Sing II

Bless the Lord, O my soul 65
Spirit of the Living God 115

Wonder, Love, and Praise

Bless the Lord, my soul 825
As we gather at your Table 763
You laid aside your rightful reputation 734

Proper 4

Sunday on or between May 29 and June 4

God's mission comes first

Anchor Points – The Propers and the Season

The fixed points for each service are the appointed or proper readings and collect as well as the themes of the day or season.

Readings and Psalm

(SC) 1 Samuel 3:1–10(11–20)

In our Hebrew scripture reading, we hear how Samuel learns that the Lord is calling him to make him God's prophet. Three times the boy Samuel misunderstands and thinks that it is his mentor Eli summoning him during the night. Finally Eli realizes it must be the Lord, and tells Samuel to be ready. In the morning, Samuel informs Eli of the punishment that is about to come upon his house. As Samuel grows, all Israel recognizes that he has been chosen by God to prophesy to the people.

Ps. 139:1–5,12–17

With marvelous wisdom, God alone perceives the heights and depths of life.

or

(GR) Deuteronomy 5:12–15

In our Hebrew scripture lesson, we hear the commandment to keep the Sabbath day holy. Six days are sufficient for labor, but the Sabbath is to be kept free from work and set aside for the Lord, a remembrance of the former captivity in Egypt and of God's deliverance.

Ps. 81:1–10

A psalm of festival praise and an exhortation to worship the Lord alone.

2 Corinthians 4:5–12

In this lesson, Paul teaches that although human weakness is all too apparent in those who preach the gospel, what is proclaimed is the glorious light of the revelation of God in Jesus Christ. The same divine light which first shone at the creation has now been manifested in Jesus. Human frailty becomes the means for God to prove that God is the source of the power of the gospel. Paul's sufferings and mortality are a way of sharing in the weakness and death in which Jesus himself participated. Yet through perseverance, they point beyond themselves to the source of life greater than death.

Mark 2:23 – 3:6

In the gospel, Jesus proclaims in word and sign that the Son of Man is sovereign over the Sabbath law. The interpretation of the Torah prevailing during this period regarded both the plucking of grain and healing to be forms of work, and therefore activities forbidden on the Sabbath day. Jesus, however, teaches that human need and the doing of good must always take precedence over rigid interpretation, for "the Sabbath was made for humankind, and not humankind for the Sabbath." Many Jewish teachers of the time agreed that the Sabbath must always be seen as a blessing for human life and not as an arbitrary requirement. Jesus goes beyond this in announcing that he possesses an even greater authority for human behavior than the law.

Collect

O God, your never-failing providence sets in order all things both in heaven and earth: Put away from us, we entreat you, all hurtful things, and give us those things which are profitable for us; through Jesus Christ our Lord, who lives and reigns with you and the Holy Spirit, one God, for ever and ever. *Amen.*

Proper Preface

1. Of God the Father

For you are the source of light and life; you made us in your image, and called us to new life in Jesus Christ our Lord.

or this

2. Of God the Son

Through Jesus Christ our Lord; who on the first day of the week overcame death and the grave, and by his glorious resurrection opened to us the way of everlasting life.

or the following

3. Of God the Holy Spirit

For by water and the Holy Spirit you have made us a new people in Jesus Christ our Lord, to show forth your glory in all the world.

(Rite II, BCP 377–378; Rite I, BCP 344–345)

Seasonal Pairings

See the table below for choices appointed and suggested for this day. Preferences are put in **bold**. Not all choices are suitable for all congregations or community, though, so consider these preferences as a starting point before making a decision about your own congregation.

	Proper 4	Rite I	Rite II	EOW1	BOS 2022
Color	Green				
Entrance Rite	Customary; opening acclamation "Blessed be God" or one of the first two in EOW1	323	355	50	
Song of Praise/Kyrie	Gloria in excelsis or BCP Canticle 9, 10; EOW1 Canticle B, Q	Gloria 324	Gloria 356; C9 – 86; C10 – 86	B – 30; Q – 39	
Collect		177	229		
Creed	**Nicene Creed**	326, 327	358	53	
Prayers of the People	**Locally written**; option below; BCP forms	329	387–393	54–55	
Offertory Sentence		343–344	376–377		
Eucharistic Prayer	**Summer – Rite I, suggest Prayer 1; Rite II, suggest Prayer C, if not used in the year already, otherwise A; EOW1 suggest Prayer 2.**	**1–333**	**C – 369** *or* **A – 361**	**2–60**	
Proper Preface	**The Lord's Day 2 – Of God the Son**	344–345	377–378		
Breaking of the Bread (Fraction)	Christ our Passover (BCP) or options at S 167 – S 172 in *The Hymnal 1982*; EOW1 options	337	364	69	
Postcommunion Prayer		339	**Almighty and everliving God – 366**	**Loving God – 70**	
Blessing	Customary	339	366	70–71	
Dismissal	**Go in peace to love and serve the Lord.**	340	366		
Notes	Memorial Day or The Visitation may fall on or near this Sunday; recognize graduates?				

Additional Notes:

Song of Praise/Canticle – Summer is a good time to try additional canticles to see if there is a setting that the congregation would enjoy more often. Suggested here is a canticle for the summer from the BCP and an option from EOW1 (Canticle 9 and Canticle B) as well as one or two that reflects themes of the day. The Gloria, of course, is always appropriate in this season.

Eucharistic Prayer –Using a consistent option for the summer simplifies choices. In Rite II, if Prayer C hasn't been used in a prior season this year, summer is a good time to put it into use. Otherwise Prayer A with the Lord's Day proper preface is sufficient. EOW1 Prayer 2 has creation imagery that may be desirable during the summertime.

Fraction Anthem at the Breaking of the Bread – The option provided in Rite I and Rite II ("Christ our Passover") is suitable and the Alleluias may be included (Hymn S 151 – S 156). Additional options in *The Hymnal 1982* at S 167 – S 172 or in EOW1. If using a new text or setting for this, schedule it for several weeks in a row to develop familiarity.

Dismissal – "Alleluias" are omitted from dismissal after Pentecost, until next Easter. What is intended as a special celebration is used almost year-round in some congregations. To give Easter as much celebratory emphasis as possible, it is encouraged to follow the rubrics and drop the "Alleluias" at the dismissal the rest of the year. "Alleluia" may still be used at the breaking of the bread, though optional.

Content Resources

Reading Between the Lines

Mark's gospel is written from a post 70 CE perspective in which Pharisees played a significant role, and strained relationships between Jesus followers and synagogues existed. Mark's Pharisees came into contact with a Jewish Jesus movement in Galilee. Josephus supports the presence of Pharisees in Galilee, and also observes expansionist Pharisaic attempts to obtain influence in local Herodian politics (Ant. 13. 408–418). This might be a context for Mark 3:6. Observers and critics of Jesus' healings and sayings, Pharisees see and disapprove of his eating with tax collectors and sinners. Mark's Pharisees object to Jesus' conduct in the synagogue and eating patterns of his disciples. They dispute with Jesus over meaning and application of the law: Jesus argues that God welcomes repentant sinners, and unclean people. The Pharisees accuse Jesus of not observing Jewish law, or traditions of the elders. In 3:5, Jesus is angered at their "hardness of heart" in the synagogue on the Sabbath, and when he heals the man with the withered hand, he avoids touch and thus the charge of working on the Sabbath, asking only that he "stretch out his hand" to restore it.

Central Themes

Some smart phones and watches now remind us to breathe, to take a break from life's constant din. Jesus' take on Sabbath got him into trouble, but Jesus' didn't disregard Jewish teaching. Jesus valued the Sabbath so much that he invited others to consider: "why do you practice Sabbath?" Do we meditate just because our smart watches told us to? Can practicing Sabbath help us unplug from the busy-ness not simply to rest? Can Sabbath help us ask deeper "why" questions? Take a break and consider, "Why do I do the work I do? Why do I practice faith?"

Let us remember where we have come from and how far the Lord has brought us. Time to reflect on this reality is sacred. When our mind is quiet we can hear the Lord calling us to ministry. As Samuel heard the Lord's call, we too must be ready to hear what the Lord is saying. The Lord commands us to recall the time of our physical bondage in order that we not take our current freedom for granted. Too often, we don't create the sacred space and time to reflect on our journey. Lord, teach us to stop, slow down the pace of our lives, so that we might hear your call to us.

The twenty-nine Collects for the Sundays that follow Pentecost fall broadly under four themes. Each theme is a statement of a basic Christian truth, which applies to us at any age: We are God's children. We have a personal relationship with Jesus Christ and a ministry of love to other people. God calls us to be open to the reality of the presence and action of the Holy Spirit. We believe in the Church as the Body of Christ in the world and in the Church's mission

A smart seminary professor was known for being the spikiest of all High Church clergy – the highest of the very high. But when it came time for him to instruct students on how to celebrate the Eucharist, he refused to let them become entrapped in layers of tradition. "You shouldn't do anything unless you find it meaningful, unless it deepens your own connection to Christ," he told his students. No solemn bow, no swoop of the hands, no chanted note was useful unless it pointed to the greater reality of the Divine. As Episcopalians, we love our liturgy – and with good reason. But occasionally, we can become entranced by the liturgy itself, and all the trappings thereof. The liturgy's true gift is not its beauty, its age, or its commonality. Its true gift is the liturgy's ability to connect us to God in Christ, and remind us of the pattern our lives should take.

Engaging All Ages

God calls a child – imagine! In the story of Samuel woken by God's call and then seeking guidance from a wise adult in his life, we receive a model for welcoming the young and inexperienced in our community. And yet it is a meaningful and necessary exercise for all ages. How do we experience God's call? Who helps me discern what God is asking of me? These are intimate questions. As we consider how personally God approaches each of us, we do well to identify the mentors, the wise elders who will guide us as we ask and then listen.

Prayers of the People

Presider

In freedom you have created us and called us to work and rest in your generous love, hear our prayers on behalf of all your creation, and empower us to share in your healing and reconciling work, as we pray: You call to us and we answer. Speak, Lord, for your servant is listening.

Litanist

Search out and purify your Church, O Holy One, that we may proclaim Jesus Christ as Lord not only in our words but in our deeds, living with freedom and courage to do good and to save lives at all times and in all places. You call to us and we answer.

Speak, Lord, for your servant is listening.

Let your dominion guide all rulers and authorities that they may know that extraordinary power belongs to God and does not come from us, and that they may exercise their own power in wisdom, compassion, and love.
You call to us and we answer.

Speak, Lord, for your servant is listening.

May your compassionate power be present to heal all who suffer throughout the world, that though afflicted, they may not be crushed; if perplexed, not driven to despair; when persecuted, not forsaken; and when struck down, not destroyed, that the risen life of Jesus may be made visible in their lives. You call to us and we answer.

Speak, Lord, for your servant is listening.

Let your light shine in our community and in our hearts: the light of the knowledge of the glory of God in the face of Jesus Christ, and the light present in every person we encounter.

You call to us and we answer.

Speak, Lord, for your servant is listening.

We bring to your healing compassion all for whom we pray on this our Christian Sabbath day, especially________ ________. We raise voices of thanksgiving for all of your grace toward us and for our abundant blessings, especially for ____________. We return to your enfolding heart those who have died, especially ________________.

You call to us and we answer.

Speak, Lord, for your servant is listening.

Presider

Holy and Wondrous God, by your never-failing providence you set in order all creation: Put away from us all hurtful things and give us those things which are profitable for us, through Jesus Christ our Savior, who lives and reigns with you and the Holy Spirit, one God, for ever and ever. ***Amen.***

Hymns for the Day

The Hymnal 1982

God has spoken to his people 536 (Semi-Continuous)
Lord, thou has searched me and dost know 702 (SC)
O Jesus, I have promised 655 (SC)
Make a joyful noise unto the Lord 710 (Gospel Related)
O day of radiant gladness 48 (GR)
This is the day the Lord hath made (Watts) 50 (GR)
We the Lord's people, heart and voice uniting 51 (GR)
Blessed Jesus, at thy word 440
Christ, whose glory fills the skies 6,7
Eternal Light, shine in my heart 465,6
Lord of all being, throned afar 419
Spread, O spread, thou mighty word 530
Thy strong word did cleave the darkness 381
God of mercy, God of grace 538
I call on thee, Lord Jesus Christ 634
There is a balm in Gilead 676
Thine arm, O Lord, in days of old 567

Lift Every Voice and Sing II

Lord, You have searched my heart [Ps. 139] 16 (SC)
Jesus, we want to meet 81 (GR)
This is the day that the Lord hath made (Garrett) 219 (GR)
Nobody knows the trouble I've seen 175
There is a balm in Gilead 203

Wonder, Love, and Praise

I, the Lord of sea and sky 812 (SC)
No saint on earth lives life to self alone 776
Heal me, hands of Jesus 773
O Christ, the healer, we have come 772

Proper 5

Sunday on or between June 5 and 11

Doing the will of God.

Anchor Points – The Propers and the Season

The fixed points for each service are the appointed or proper readings and collect as well as the themes of the day or season.

Readings and Psalm

(SC) 1 Samuel 8:4–11, (12–15), 16–20, (11:14–15)

First and Second Samuel, originally one book, tell of the transition in Israel's leadership from a system of charismatically appointed judges who appeared in times of crisis to a monarchy that would imitate the governing systems of the neighboring nations. First Samuel focuses on the man who ushered Israel through the political transition from judges to kings. Samuel united in himself many of the roles of the tribal confederacy period of Israel's history. He was a Nazirite dedicated to the Lord, a judge, a prophet, a priest and the reluctant leader of the movement to place a king over Israel.

Psalm 138

This psalm of thanksgiving has many parallels with the later parts of Isaiah, and was probably written sometime after the return from exile. The "gods" of verse 1 may be the members of the heavenly council or the rulers and gods of other nations. Verses 1–4 give praise for the Lord's help, and verses 5–7 describe the effect of God's majesty and mercy upon the kings of the earth. The psalm concludes with an expression of the psalmist's trust that God will personally care for him. Although all creation is under God's care, the Lord's intimate love is available to each individual.

or

(GR) Genesis 3:8–15

Today's reading about the Fall is excerpted from the second (2:4b–3:24) of the two creation stories in Genesis where God has placed a prohibition upon the tree "of the knowledge of good and evil." This is the wisdom that comes, not intellectually, but by experience. It is partly moral in content (2 Samuel 14:17; Isaiah 7:15); but more broadly, it encompasses the power to make distinctions in the whole range of human experience (Numbers 24:13; 2 Samuel 19:35). This power of judgment is to be exercised by humankind in obedience to God and as God's representative. Chapter 3 recounts human rebellion against God's prohibition.

Psalm 130

This psalm is a lament, a plea for deliverance from unspecified trouble. It is one of the Songs of Ascent (Psalms 120–134), perhaps sung by pilgrims on the way up to Jerusalem. The psalmist makes an implicit confession of sin (vv. 1–3). He puts his trust in the Lord and exhorts the community to do likewise. This psalm is also called the *De profundis* (from the Latin translation of its opening words). It is one of the seven traditional penitential psalms and has often been set to music.

2 Corinthians 4:13–5:1

Paul's letter continues to explain the nature of his ministry. Despite his suffering, his faith will not let him keep silent, he must bear witness as he illustrated by quoting Psalm 116:10 (quoted according to the Septuagint, the Greek Old Testament). His preaching, his suffering, and his faith are all for the Corinthians' sake so that the gift of grace may call forth the response of gratitude.

Paul combines static images drawn from Hellenistic dualism – outer/inner, seen/unseen – with a dynamic Hebraic eschatological outlook – present/future, old/new, transient/eternal. God's work of salvation and the Christian experience of it are both 'now' and also 'not yet.' In verse 17, Paul plays with the sense of the Hebrew word for glory, which also means heavy. Literally, 'the present lightness of affliction' prepares believers for "an eternal weight of glory," not as a compensation for suffering but as a product, a fruit, of it (Rom. 8:17).

Mark 3:20–35

In response to the blindness of family and authorities, Jesus uses a parable to draw his listeners toward a decision. He refutes the charge of collusion with Satan and shows that instead, through him, Satan himself is bound by a stronger power (Isaiah 49:24–25; Revelation 20:2–3), the sign of the coming of the kingdom. He then turns the charge against the scribes – all sins and blasphemies will be forgiven, except setting one's self against the very source of forgiveness by believing that the Spirit active in Jesus is satanic. Doing the will of God, on the other hand, brings one into intimate familial relationship with Jesus (Matthew 25:40; John 15:14; Hebrews 2:11–13).

Collect

O God, from whom all good proceeds: Grant that by your inspiration we may think those things that are right, and by your merciful guiding may do them; through Jesus Christ our Lord, who lives and reigns with you and the Holy Spirit, one God, for ever and ever. *Amen.*

Proper Preface

1. Of God the Father

For you are the source of light and life; you made us in your image, and called us to new life in Jesus Christ our Lord.

or this

2. Of God the Son

Through Jesus Christ our Lord; who on the first day of the week overcame death and the grave, and by his glorious resurrection opened to us the way of everlasting life.

or the following

3. Of God the Holy Spirit

For by water and the Holy Spirit you have made us a new people in Jesus Christ our Lord, to show forth your glory in all the world.

(Rite II, BCP 377–378; Rite I, BCP 344–345)

Seasonal Pairings

See the table below for choices appointed and suggested for this day. Preferences are put in **bold**. Not all choices are suitable for all congregations or community, though, so consider these preferences as a starting point before making a decision about your own congregation.

	Proper 5	Rite I	Rite II	EOW1	BOS 2022
Color	Green				
Entrance Rite	Customary; opening acclamation "Blessed be God" or one of the first two in EOW1	323	355	50	
Song of Praise/Kyrie	Gloria in excelsis or BCP Canticle 9, 18; EOW1 Canticle B, S	Gloria 324	Gloria 356; C9 – 86; C18 – 93	B – 30; S – 40	
Collect		178	229		
Creed	Nicene Creed	326, 327	358	53	
Prayers of the People	**Locally written**; options below; BCP forms	329	387–393	54–55	
Offertory Sentence		343–344	376–377		
Eucharistic Prayer	**Summer – Rite I, suggest Prayer 1; Rite II, suggest Prayer C, if not used in the year already, otherwise A; EOW1 suggest Prayer 2.**	**1–333**	**C – 369** *or* **A – 361**	**2–60**	
Proper Preface	**The Lord's Day 3 – Of God the Holy Spirit**	344–345	377–378		
Breaking of the Bread (Fraction)	Christ our Passover (BCP) or options at S 167 – S 172 in *The Hymnal 1982*; EOW1 options	337	364	69	
Postcommunion Prayer		339	**Almighty and everliving God – 366**	**Loving God – 70**	
Blessing	Customary	339	366	70–71	
Dismissal	**Go in peace to love and serve the Lord.**	340	366		
Notes	St. Barnabas Day may fall on this Sunday				

Additional Notes:

Song of Praise/Canticle – Summer is a good time to try additional canticles to see if there is a setting that the congregation would enjoy more often. Suggested here is a canticle for the summer from the BCP and an option from EOW1 (Canticle 9 and Canticle B) as well as one or two that reflects themes of the day. The Gloria, of course, is always appropriate in this season.

Eucharistic Prayer – Using a consistent option for the summer simplifies choices. In Rite II, if Prayer C hasn't been used in a prior season this year, summer is a good time to put it into use. Otherwise, Prayer A with the Lord's Day proper preface is sufficient. EOW1 Prayer 2 has creation imagery that may be desirable during the summertime.

Fraction Anthem at the Breaking of the Bread – The option provided in Rite I and Rite II ("Christ our Passover") is suitable and the Alleluias may be included (Hymn S 151 – S 156). Additional options in *The Hymnal 1982* at S 167 – S 172 or in EOW1. If using a new text or setting for this, schedule it for several weeks in a row to develop familiarity.

Dismissal – "Alleluias" are omitted from dismissal after Pentecost, until next Easter. What is intended as a special celebration is used almost year-round in some congregations. To give Easter as much celebratory emphasis as possible, it is encouraged to follow the rubrics and drop the "Alleluias" at the dismissal the rest of the year. "Alleluia" may still be used at the breaking of the bread, though optional.

Content Resources

Reading Between the Lines

Our readings from Genesis, I Samuel, and Mark identify the presence of evil in the world, and its consequences. How can the good be identified and practiced? Do we surrender choice to exploitive monarchic rule? How do we perceive who Jesus really is? Psalm 130 calls for patient discernment.

3:19b is best rendered by adding, "he (Jesus) *and the disciples* went home." But the confident translation of the NRSV at 3:21, "when his family heard (of crowds surrounding Jesus)" is rendered by KJV and Tyndale, "and when his friends heard it…" indicating concerns about Jesus by "those around him," namely, disciples or friends. Tensions between Jesus and his family of origin are apparently well known and reported later (3:31; 6). Familiarity breeds contempt. 3:23 is the first time in Mark that Jesus speaks in parables to answer the accusation by scribes from Jerusalem that he has a pact with Satan: how can Satan cast out Satan? If that were true, it would mean the end of Satan. Jesus implies that Satan has already been bound, in 1:12–13. Thus, accusations like those of scribes from Jerusalem against Jesus (or other prophets) is completely beyond the pale – in fact, an eternal sin against the Holy Spirit. Tensions between those following God and their family of origin are addressed by 3:35, and the family around Jesus redefined to include anyone who seeks to do God's will.

Central Themes

Ohana is a Hawaiian word that refers to a family of choice that is marked by the supportiveness of its members for one another. Members are not necessarily connected by blood or tribal ties. Instead, they are connected by their shared love or similar beliefs and their choice to be present for each other. Joining a congregation or community group is likewise about making the decision to be present for one another through good times like community events and tough times like natural catastrophes. In Hawaii, aunties and uncles are all the adults in your life who care about you.

Social media and technology have created new ways to connect and disconnect. Families and friends can video chat across the oceans. Facebook has made one of the definitions of "friend" a verb. We can "follow" old friends whereas before we might have lost touch with them. We can share photos with people we have never met. Jesus is questioning lines of connection in his time and redrawing lines of kinship and connection by asking, "Who is your family?" How do our connections today reveal the kingdom of God and/or the brokenness of the world?

Anyone who does the things Jesus had been observed doing must have been crazy or possessed by some out-of-control power, or so say some of his contemporaries who witnessed his actions. In many ways, Jesus was neither the expected messiah nor a conventional hero. He acted in countercultural ways, upsetting the conventions of a status-crazed society. So are we called to do when we act in the ways we promise to act in our baptismal covenant: serving Christ in everyone. Everyone, even those with whom we don't agree or whom we dislike. "I will" we said, "with God's help." Crazy Christians, indeed.

Engaging All Ages

When we hear of "Satan" or "the devil" it might bring to mind a red creature with horns, a pointy tail, and a pitchfork, something you might see while trick-or-treating at Halloween. This idea of Satan probably seems absurd to most of us. What Jesus is really talking about are the powerful forces in this world that are actively engaged against the loving, liberating, life-giving will of God. Have you encountered forces that pull you away from God's love? What brings you back? How do you stay connected to God when these forces are at play?

Prayers of the People: Option 1

We praise you for who you are, holy, tender, powerful God.

We praise you, for who you are and what you are to us, your people, for continuing to create us, empower us, and reconcile us to you.

In the name of the Triune God,

who was and is and is to come.

We praise you for who you are: Creator, Lover, Forgiver. Give us hearts of understanding and empathy. Help us to forgive as we have been forgiven.

In the name of the Triune God,

who was and is and is to come.

We praise you for who you are: Redeemer, Teacher, Reconciler. We pray for your Church. Teach us to walk in your ways, pay attention to your word living inside us and through us.

In the name of the Triune God,

who was and is and is to come.

We praise you for who you are, Empowerer, Healer, Provocateur. We pray for those among us in need of healing or comfort, support and compassion ___________ .

Invite us into your life of love; a life of compassionate service.

In the name of the Triune God,

who was and is and is to come.

We praise you for who you are: our eternal home. At the end of our lives, gather us in your embrace, that we may behold you face to face, and sing your praises without limit or end.

In the name of the Triune God,

who was and is and is to come

Prayers of the People: Option 2

Deacon or Presider

Holy God, ruler of heaven and earth, you have raised us into your eternal life, and you have brought into Christ's family all who do your will: When we call you, answer us and increase our strength within us; hear us as we pray for the needs of your creation, saying: Make good your purpose for us; O God, your love endures for ever.

Litanist

You have filled the Church with your Spirit, O Holy One, and you renew us day by day: Empower our mission of witness and service, so that your grace, as it extends to more and more people, may increase thanksgiving, to the glory of God.

Make good your purpose for us;

O God, your love endures for ever.

You are on high, yet care for the lowly, and perceive the haughty from afar: Reveal your glory to all who exercise power and authority and halt their deeds of pride, greed, and violence, so that all the rulers of the earth will praise you.

Make good your purpose for us;

O God, your love endures for ever.

Do not abandon the works of your hands: Look upon those who walk in the midst of trouble to keep them safe.

Make good your purpose for us;

O God, your love endures for ever.

Visit this community with your compassion and your grace, that we may glorify your Name and your word above all things.

Make good your purpose for us;

O God, your love endures for ever.

We do not lose heart as we pray for those who need our intercession, especially ___________. We will give thanks to you, O God, with our whole heart, especially for ______________. We know that the one who raised the Lord Jesus will raise us also with Jesus, and will bring us into his presence. Hear our prayers for those who have died, especially ______________.

Make good your purpose for us;

O God, your love endures for ever.

Presider

We believe and so we pray, O God, that your glory may enter our lives and infuse the world with resurrection power, through Jesus Christ our Savior, who with you, and the Holy Spirit, lives and reigns, One God, for ever and ever. ***Amen.***

Hymns for the Day

The Hymnal 1982

Before the Lord's eternal throne 391 (Semi-Continuous)
God the Omnipotent! King, who ordainest 569 (SC)
How wondrous and great thy works, God of praise! 532, 533 (SC)
From deepest woe I cry to thee 151 (Gospel-Related)
Out of the depths I call 666 (GR)
We walk by faith, and not by sight 209
Creating God, your fingers trace 394, 395
God of grace and God of glory 594, 595
Jerusalem, my happy home 620
Jesus lives! thy terrors now 194, 195
Light's abode, celestial Salem 621, 622
O what their joy and their glory must be 623

Lift Every Voice and Sing II

Sing the wondrous love of Jesus 20
We walk by faith, and not by sight 206
When peace like a river attendeth my soul 188

Wonder, Love, and Praise

Hallelujah! We sing your praises!/
Haleluya! Pelo tso rona 784

Proper 6

Sunday on or between June 12 and 18

The kingdom of God arrives through God's grace, not by human striving for power.

Anchor Points – The Propers and the Season

The fixed points for each service are the appointed or proper readings and collect as well as the themes of the day or season.

Readings and Psalm

(SC) 1 Samuel 15:34–16:13

Prior to today's reading, God had already rejected Saul as king because of his disobedience and had indicated that another had been chosen. In grief and fear, Samuel refuses to see Saul again. Unlike Saul, Samuel waits for God's instructions and follows them precisely. These instructions seem to run contrary even to what Samuel might have expected. God teaches him that human wisdom does not penetrate the depths that God's wisdom does.

Psalm 20

This psalm is a prayer for the king in a time of war before a battle. The people ask for God's help (vv. 2–6) and are confident that this help will be given (vv. 7–10). Scholars surmise that when used in a liturgy there might have been some indication of God's assurance that was given between the two sections.

or

(GR) Ezekiel 17:22–24

More than any other prophet, Ezekiel was called to transmit God's messages through enacted symbolism. His visions are balanced by a firm reliance in God's sovereignty. In today's reading, we hear this note of hope. Chapter 17 begins with a "riddle" that describes Israel as a tall cedar that has been broken off by a great eagle (Nebuchadnezzar). Verses 22–24 redirect the people's vision to God's purposes for Israel. While the people hoped for political restoration and restored power, God explains that Israel's role in the world is one of spiritual blessing, not political influence. God alone will accomplish Israel's true destiny.

Psalm 92:1–4, 11–14

This thanksgiving for the righteous rule of God seems originally to have been composed for individual use but was adapted for communal use on the sabbath. The Lord is to be praised at times of sacrifice (v. 2), both morning and evening. In verses 12–13, the psalmist repeats the theme of Psalm 1: God watches over the righteous and makes them "flourish." The righteous will have a long and happy life, the Hebrew ideal (v. 14).

2 Corinthians 5:6–10, (11–13), 14–17

In a metaphor mixed between images of inhabiting a dwelling and putting on a garment, Paul develops his thoughts about the resurrected body from the teachings of 1 Corinthians 15:35–54. Paul suggests that the believer is not "unclothed, but . . . further clothed" in the spiritual body. Though they are now not yet "with the Lord" in the full sense, they are still always in Christ even when "away from the Lord." They "walk by faith, not by sight," that is, not yet on the basis of an objectively verifiable Lord. Paul then turns the Corinthians' attention to the conduct of their earthly life, urging them to make it their aim to please the Lord in the knowledge that their reward at the final judgment depends not upon faith alone, but also upon their deeds.

Mark 4:26–34

The two parables of the kingdom in today's gospel reading both concern God's presence in our world. Both emphasize the process of growth and the contrast between beginning and end. The interpretation of the parable of the seed growing secretly (found only in Mark) may center upon different elements within the parable. One is the contrast between the invisible germination of the seed with the great final harvest. The long and hidden preparation of God's work is now visible in Jesus and will lead to the harvest of the final judgment. The parable of the mustard seed contrasts the smallness of the seed, proverbially although not literally the smallest of all, with its ability, when grown, to provide shelter. The image of "the greatest of all shrubs" is drawn from the symbol of the world-tree of life

Collect

Keep, O Lord, your household the Church in your steadfast faith and love, that through your grace we may proclaim your truth with boldness, and minister your justice with compassion; for the sake of our Savior Jesus Christ, who lives and reigns with you and the Holy Spirit, one God, now and for ever. *Amen.*

Proper Preface

1. Of God the Father

For you are the source of light and life; you made us in your image, and called us to new life in Jesus Christ our Lord.

or this

2. Of God the Son

Through Jesus Christ our Lord; who on the first day of the week overcame death and the grave, and by his glorious resurrection opened to us the way of everlasting life.

or the following

3. Of God the Holy Spirit

For by water and the Holy Spirit you have made us a new people in Jesus Christ our Lord, to show forth your glory in all the world.

(Rite II, BCP 377–378; Rite I, BCP 344–345)

Seasonal Pairings

See the table below for choices appointed and suggested for this day. Preferences are put in **bold.** Not all choices are suitable for all congregations or community, though, so consider these preferences as a starting point before making a decision about your own congregation.

	Proper 6	Rite I	Rite II	EOW1	BOS 2022
Color	Green				
Entrance Rite	Customary; opening acclamation "Blessed be God" or one of the first two in EOW1	323	355	50	
Song of Praise/Kyrie	Gloria in excelsis or BCP Canticle 9, 10; EOW1 Canticle B	Gloria 324	Gloria 356; C9 – 86; C10 – 86	B – 30	
Collect		178	230		
Creed	Nicene Creed	326, 327	358	53	
Prayers of the People	**Locally written**; options below; BCP forms	329	387–393	54–55	
Offertory Sentence	"If anyone is in Christ, there is a new creation: everything old has passed away; see, everything has become new!" (2 Cor)	343–344	376–377		
Eucharistic Prayer	**Summer – Rite I, suggest Prayer 1; Rite II, suggest Prayer C, if not used in the year already, otherwise A; EOW1 suggest Prayer 2.**	**1–333**	**C – 369** *or* **A – 361**	**2–60**	
Proper Preface	**The Lord's Day 1 – Of God the Father**	344–345	377–378		
Breaking of the Bread (Fraction)	Christ our Passover (BCP) or options at S 167 – S 172 in *The Hymnal 1982*; EOW1 options	337	364	69	
Postcommunion Prayer		339	**Almighty and everliving God – 366**	**Loving God – 70**	
Blessing	Customary	339	366	70–71	
Dismissal	**Go in peace to love and serve the Lord.**	340	366		
Notes	St. Barnabas' Day may fall near this Sunday; Father's Day may fall on this or next Sunday				

Additional Notes:

Song of Praise/Canticle – Summer is a good time to try additional canticles to see if there is a setting that the congregation would enjoy more often. Suggested here is a canticle for the summer from the BCP and an option from EOW1 (Canticle 9 and Canticle B) as well as one or two that reflects themes of the day. The Gloria, of course, is always appropriate in this season.

Eucharistic Prayer – Using a consistent option for the summer simplifies choices. In Rite II, if Prayer C hasn't been used in a prior season this year, summer is a good time to put it into use. Otherwise, Prayer A with the

Lord's Day proper preface is sufficient. EOW1 Prayer 2 has creation imagery that may be desirable during the summertime.

Fraction Anthem at the Breaking of the Bread – The option provided in Rite I and Rite II ("Christ our Passover") is suitable and the Alleluias may be included (Hymn S 151 – S 156). Additional options in *The Hymnal 1982* at Hymn S 167 – S 172 or in EOW1. If using a new text or setting for this, schedule it for several weeks in a row to develop familiarity.

Dismissal – "Alleluias" are omitted from dismissal after Pentecost, until next Easter. What is intended as a special celebration is used almost year-round in some congregations. To give Easter as much celebratory emphasis as possible, it is encouraged to follow the rubrics and drop the "Alleluias" at the dismissal the rest of the year. "Alleluia" may still be used at the breaking of the bread, though optional.

Content Resources

Reading Between the Lines

In Mark, people are amazed at Jesus' new teaching with authority (1:27), using only parables (4:33–4), taught to crowds and explained to disciples. Our assigned gospel transmits two similitudes in which God's present kingdom resembles scattered, growing grain seed and a tiny mustard seed that develops into a great shrub. Why does Jesus speak in parables? Perhaps because they are persuasive, non-coercive comparisons or analogies speaking of God's realm. In the first, growth is of itself (v. 28), without human involvement. So perhaps the point is that natural growth characterizes God's realm, independent of and hidden from human effort. Similarly, the process whereby the surprising growth of the mustard seed becomes "the greatest of all shrubs" providing branches and shelter, is paltry at first, but prone to become very significant. Placed in Mark 4, such stories enhance the expectations of disciples and crowds, first in regard to Jesus' teaching, and later as encouragement for their own efforts. Here, Paul's reassurance of confidence and faith is apt.

Central Themes

Memes are popular in social media. Many people make memes by capturing a meaningful quote and setting it in a nice type font and background. Not that long ago, memes appeared as quotes in inspirational art posters found on office and kitchen walls. Today when short and quick are esteemed, memes are a contemporary version of longer stories like parables and fables that share a moral lesson worth remembering. Try linking your favorite memes to biblical stories that speak to the same moral values. You'll get better at it each time you do it!

In the picture book *The Curious Garden* by Peter Brown, a young boy happens upon a struggling urban garden. The boy decides to tend to it with watering, pruning, and singing. As time passes, lush plants begin to spread and pop up in the most unlikely of places, taking others in the city by surprise. Based on an abandoned elevated railway in Manhattan, the story invites the reader to wonder where new life can grow in the most unlikely places. With what in our lives and areas can we compare the kingdom of God, or what parable will we use for it?

Mark's Jesus does not tell many parables. When he does tell one, he economizes on words, so today we hear these small nuggets of stories, nearly as small as seeds. Seeds, planted deep in dark soil, together with the unmentioned but implied sun and rain, do what they do naturally, the way that the God who first created everything that is, intended for them to do. Seeds insist on growing. And bestow their bounty on any passer-by, on everyone without exception. That's how the realm of God works, how the Church should work, growing quietly so that its deep roots might nourish unexpected harvests.

Engaging All Ages

Offer an herb planting station today. Set out supplies such as soil, seeds, watering cans, and pots. If budget is tight, ask people to bring their own pots or provide cleaned tin cans and jars from your recycling. Discussion prompts for planting station or take-home card could include: Seeds are small things with big potential. What else can you think of that starts out small and has the potential to grow great? What kind of support do seeds need to reach their potential? What kind of support do you need to reach your potential? What kind of support does our church community need to reach its potential?

Prayers of the People: Option 1

Gracious God, open our ears to hear your word. Open our hearts to receive it and transform us. Make your Church the fertile ground in which your love can grow.

In your mercy, Lord, hear our prayer.

Give leaders everywhere a heart for their people and the commitment to the common good. Cultivate in each of us seeds of peace and justice.

In your mercy, Lord, hear our prayer.

We pray for healing for those who suffer from any ailment, or isolation, or want. We pray for a peaceful end for those who will die today. And comfort for those who mourn.

Those for whom we pray today: ____________ . Sow in all of us seeds of compassion.

In your mercy, Lord, hear our prayer.

Strengthen your image in our lives that we may reflect your goodness, your righteousness, your kingdom in all that we say or do.

In your mercy, Lord, hear our prayer.

Prayers of the People: Option 2

Deacon or Priest

As the kingdom of God spreads among us, let us offer prayers for the whole world and for every person in every need.

Intercessor

For this holy gathering and for all who enter with faith.

Lord, have mercy.

For all nations, peoples, kin, and families.

Lord, have mercy.

For mercy, justice, and peace throughout the world.

Lord, have mercy.

For this city and for every place.

Lord, have mercy.

For all those requiring ongoing care, for all those in danger and need: those who are sick or suffering, those who hunger and those who are oppressed, for travelers and those in prison, for the dying and the dead.

Lord, have mercy.

For the blessings of our lives, for ourselves, our families, and those we love.

Lord, have mercy.

Lifting our voices with all creation, with the Blessed Virgin Mary and all the saints, let us offer ourselves and one another to the living God through Christ.

To you, O Lord our God.

Presider

God who scatters the seed of faith, hear the prayers we offer this day and make everything new; through Jesus Christ our Lord. ***Amen.***

Hymns for the Day

The Hymnal 1982

Lord, whose love through humble service 610
God moves in a mysterious way 677 (SC)
Seek the Lord while he wills to be found S217ff (SC)
How wondrous and great thy works, God of praise! 532, 533 (GR)
All glory be to God on high 421
All who believe and are baptized 298
Come away to the skies 213
Lord Christ, when first thou cam'st to earth 598
Love divine, all loves excelling 657
Rejoice, the Lord is King! 481
The Church's one foundation 525
We know that Christ is raised and dies no more 296
We walk by faith, and not by sight 209
Almighty God, your word is cast 588, 589
Come, ye thankful people, come 290 (2–4)
Father, we thank thee who hast planted 302, 303
For the fruit of all creation 424

Lift Every Voice and Sing II

We walk by faith, and not by sight 206
Sing the wondrous love of Jesus 20

Wonder, Love, and Praise

Camina, pueblo del Dios/
Walk on, O people of God 739
When from bondage we are summoned 753, 754
God the sculptor of the mountains 746, 747

Proper 7

Sunday on or between June 19 and 25

God's power to still the storms of nature and evil are revealed in Jesus.

Anchor Points – The Propers and the Season

The fixed points for each service are the appointed or proper readings and collect as well as the themes of the day or season.

Readings and Psalm

(SC) 1 Samuel 17:(1a, 4–11, 19–23), 32–49 (Track One, option)

This reading is probably one of the most well-known passages form the Old Testament and needs little commentary. The familiar figures of the lowly shepherd boy David who confronts the giant Goliath with nothing but his faith and five smooth stones has been used to teach many, many lessons for both the personal and social-political spheres. This story is part of a larger section charting the emergence of David as the leader of Israel who will supplant Saul as king. David's inability to use Saul's armor hints on the one hand that David will be a more faithful king who relies on the Lord rather than humanly-made defenses.

Psalm 9:9–20

This psalm (which together with Psalm 10 was originally one long poem) is a song of thanksgiving for victory and a plea for justice. It is an acrostic, that is, each line begins with a successive letter of the Hebrew alphabet. The psalmist focuses on the rescue of the oppressed poor from all their enemies, God's judgment of the world and rule over the nations, and his own concern for rescue.

or

(SC) 1 Samuel 17:57–18:5, 10–16 (Track One, alternate option)

Regardless of our interpretation of the precise nature of their relationship, Jonathan and David's abiding love for one another and their mutual covenant in the face of political obstacles and even physical danger counts among the most beautiful stories of affectionate solidarity in all scripture. This reading is further colored by the favor God has shown David in all of his military conquests and the love he garners from the people. As David's star dramatically rises, Saul's sets.

Psalm 133

The psalmist offers a blessing for the covenant people that is also appropriate for families and communities endeavoring to live in unity.

or

(GR) Job 38:1–11 (Track Two)

In our first reading, God appears to Job out of the whirlwind and demands to know whether he is wise enough to question the Creator of the heavens and earth. The challenge seems almost brutal. Job, out of all his distress, had complained about the unfairness of life. He is now forced to recognize how little he understands the ways of the world and of God.

Psalm 107:1–3, 23–32

This psalm encourages those whom God has rescued to give praise. Today's selection describes the fourth in a series of descriptions of divine rescues. Verses 23–32 portray divine rescues from the catastrophes of sea travel. God's action prompts a response of thanksgiving by the rescued.

2 Corinthians 6:1–13

Paul continues his explanation of how God's reconciling action is made manifest in his own mission and activity. Paul appeals to the Corinthians to "work together with him" (v. 1) so that God's merciful gift of salvation will not be "in vain." Now is the moment when God's saving love becomes a reality in their lives. But Paul is realistic when he notes that participating in God's reconciling activity requires a cost for the disciple. In fact, in a curious reversal of the usual practice, Paul recommends himself as an authentic Christian missionary by boasting not in his successes but in his apparent failures and sufferings.

Mark 4:35–41

Today's story of the stilling of the storm comes at the end of Jesus's proclamation of the kingdom in parables (4:1–34) and serves as a transition as Jesus and the disciples cross the Sea of Galilee to inaugurate the kingdom ministry for the Gentiles with a massive exorcism of a "legion" of demons. In chapters 5–8 they will crisscross the lake performing similar signs and wonders on both the Jewish and Gentile sides of the sea. The great storm is a test of what the disciples have learned from Jesus's teaching (4:34). But as always in Mark's gospel, the disciples fail to demonstrate that they have understood. Jesus's demonstration of power over nature is another indication that Jesus's ministry participates in God's power.

Collect

O Lord, make us have perpetual love and reverence for your holy Name, for you never fail to help and govern those whom you have set upon the sure foundation of your loving-kindness; through Jesus Christ our Lord, who lives and reigns with you and the Holy Spirit, one God, for ever and ever. *Amen.*

Proper Preface

1. Of God the Father

For you are the source of light and life; you made us in your image, and called us to new life in Jesus Christ our Lord.

or this

2. Of God the Son

Through Jesus Christ our Lord; who on the first day of the week overcame death and the grave, and by his glorious resurrection opened to us the way of everlasting life.

or the following

3. Of God the Holy Spirit

For by water and the Holy Spirit you have made us a new people in Jesus Christ our Lord, to show forth your glory in all the world.

(Rite II, BCP 377–378; Rite I, BCP 344–345)

Seasonal Pairings

See the table below for choices appointed and suggested for this day. Preferences are put in **bold**. Not all choices are suitable for all congregations or community, though, so consider these preferences as a starting point before making a decision about your own congregation.

	Proper 7	Rite I	Rite II	EOW1	BOS 2022
Color	Green				
Entrance Rite	Customary; opening acclamation "Blessed be God" or one of the first two in EOW1	323	355	50	
Song of Praise/Kyrie	Gloria in excelsis or BCP Canticle 9, 8; EOW1 Canticle B, D	Gloria 324	Gloria 356; C9 – 86; C8 – 85	B – 30; D – 32	
Collect		178	230		
Creed	Nicene Creed	326, 327	358	53	
Prayers of the People	**Locally written**; options below; BCP forms	329	387–393	54–55	
Offertory Sentence	"At an acceptable time I have listened to you, and on a day of salvation I have helped you.' See, now is the acceptable time; see, now is the day of salvation!" (2 Cor)	343–344	376–377		
Eucharistic Prayer	**Summer – Rite I, suggest Prayer 1; Rite II, suggest Prayer C, if not used in the year already, otherwise A; EOW1 suggest Prayer 2.**	**1–333**	**C – 369** *or* **A – 361**	**2–60**	
Proper Preface	**The Lord's Day 3 – Of God the Holy Spirit**	344–345	377–378		
Breaking of the Bread (Fraction)	Christ our Passover (BCP) or options at S 167 – S 172 in *The Hymnal 1982*; EOW1 options	337	364	69	
Postcommunion Prayer		339	**Almighty and everliving God – 366**	**Loving God – 70**	
Blessing	Customary	339	366	70–71	
Dismissal	**Go in peace to love and serve the Lord.**	340	366		
Notes	Father's Day may fall on this or next Sunday; Nativity of St. John the Baptist Day may fall on or near this Sunday.				

Additional Notes:

Song of Praise/Canticle – Summer is a good time to try additional canticles to see if there is a setting that the congregation would enjoy more often. Suggested here is a canticle for the summer from the BCP and an option from EOW1 (Canticle 9 and Canticle B) as well as one or two that reflects themes of the day. The Gloria, of course, is always appropriate in this season.

Eucharistic Prayer – Using a consistent option for the summer simplifies choices. In Rite II, if Prayer C hasn't been used in a prior season this year, summer is a good time to put it into use. Otherwise, Prayer A with the Lord's Day proper preface is sufficient. EOW1 Prayer 2 has creation imagery that may be desirable during the summertime.

Fraction Anthem at the Breaking of the Bread – The option provided in Rite I and Rite II ("Christ our Passover") is suitable and the Alleluias may be included (Hymn S 151 – S 156). Additional options in *The Hymnal 1982* at Hymn S 167 – S 172 or in EOW1. If using a new text or setting for this, schedule it for several weeks in a row to develop familiarity.

Dismissal – "Alleluias" are omitted from dismissal after Pentecost, until next Easter. What is intended as a special celebration is used almost year-round in some congregations. To give Easter as much celebratory emphasis as possible, it is encouraged to follow the rubrics and drop the "Alleluias" at the dismissal the rest of the year. "Alleluia" may still be used at the breaking of the bread, though optional.

Content Resources

Reading Between the Lines

There is no separation between Jesus' telling of parables and the stilling of the storm, since it is the same day, as Mark 4:35 makes clear. Jesus' quieting of the storm for more than one boat is the first indication of abilities to subdue natural forces, and the second command in 4:39 is the same verb used to silence the unclean spirit in 1:25. Furthermore, the disciples astonished question, when the storm subsides, asking who Jesus is, "that even the wind and sea *obey* him?" echoes and expands Jesus' opening words of his first parable, "Listen!" To hear and obey is to listen to and heed instructions, and to cultivate trust (faith). Careful listening, acquiescing, and awe are responses to Jesus' "new teaching...with authority he commands even the unclean spirits, and they obey him" (Mark 1:27).

Central Themes

Have you opened a big box of crackers to be surprised at the relative size of the contents? Or opened a beautiful package to find something unworthy of its wrapping? Have you watched a vocal competition show to be amazed at the powerful voice of a tiny competitor? It's easy to get fooled by appearances and fall into the trap of judging a book by its cover. If we base our reactions on appearances, we are forgetting that God, who creates us in God's image, creates in each of us gifts that may appear hidden or be undiscovered.

"Where were you when . . . ?" This question can connect people who recall similar experiences around an important cultural event. Such a question might remind them of a time when a loved one showed up for an important moment. It can disconnect when someone in the community was not invited or not present like when a parent misses the birth of their child. Someone's presence or absence may be an indication of your values. God asks Job, "Where were you when . . . ?" What do God's question and our answer reveal about God and about us?

Going "across to the other side" is nearly always risky business, as the little band of disciples learned, first on the sea, and later as they leaned into the ministry of being the Christ-bearers Jesus had trusted they could be. When we venture beyond our own comfortable, predictable borders, we're in unknown territory, a bit unsure of the surroundings, even a bit unsure of ourselves. Baptized, rooted in Jesus, disciples on the way, we face the unknown, emboldened by our faith. Baptism is, after all, ordination into ministry, calling for all our gifts to be spent, sometimes in unexpected ways.

Engaging All Ages

Just like the disciples were tossed around by "a great windstorm," we know what it is like to be on a journey in a fragile vessel. We know what it is like to be afraid. Jesus does not tell the disciples "There is nothing to fear." Instead, he indicates by word and action that the things we are afraid of do not have the last word. Put an index card in each bulletin. Invite people to write down one fear and add it to the offering plate as a symbol of our common experience of fear and our faith in offering our fear to God. After worship, collect the index cards and have the staff or prayer group pray for each card.

Prayers of the People: Option 1

Throughout our days, throughout our lives, in all our wanderings, we come before you, seeking your favor and blessing. We hunger for your kingdom even as we sing songs of praise. At the beginning of each day's journey, give us grace to say yes to you, God.

Silence

Gathered as the Body of Christ, your faithful people stand before you with grateful hearts. Work your purpose in us and through us. Grant that your Holy Spirit focus us on your will and bring us together. Pray for the church.

Silence

The world you have made is aching for peace between nations and neighbors. We pray for those who work for justice and reconciliation. Turn the hearts of those who sew discord and wage war, who benefit while others suffer. Pray for the world.

Silence

In times of pain and uncertainty, give us the strength to carry on. We pray for those who are struggling physically and those paralyzed by fear and anxiety. Make us your agents of healing and comfort. For whom shall we pray?

Silence

We pray for those who are at the end of their lives, and for those who have ended their journey. Grant them the peace you have promised, an eternal home that you have fashioned for them. For whom shall we pray?

Silence

Prayers of the People: Option 2

Deacon or Priest

To God who commands even the wind and the sea let us offer prayers for all creation.

For our Presiding Bishop, *N.*, for our bishop, *N.*, for our parish clergy, *N.*, for this holy gathering and for the people of God in every place.

Lord, hear our prayer.

For all nations, peoples, pods, kindred, and families.

Lord, hear our prayer.

For mercy, justice, and peace throughout the world.

Lord, hear our prayer.

For this city and every place.

Lord, hear our prayer.

For all those in every danger and calamity: those afflicted and suffering hardship, including those seeking healing; for those beaten and imprisoned, and those who are sleepless and hungry.

Lord, hear our prayer.

For all victims of violence and hatred.

Lord, hear our prayer.

For all the dying and the dead, and all who mourn.

Lord, hear our prayer.

For ourselves, our families and companions, and those we love.

Lord, hear our prayer.

Lifting our voices with all creation, with the Blessed Virgin Mary and all the saints, let us offer ourselves and one another to the living God through Christ.

To you, O Lord our God.

Presider

God of our salvation, hear the prayers we offer this day for all who are tossed in the storms of life, and open wide our hearts to accept your grace; through Jesus Christ our Lord. ***Amen.***

Hymns for the Day

The Hymnal 1982

Praise to the living God! 372
He who would valiant be 564, 565 (SC)
God is Love, let heaven adore him 379 (GR)
Many and great, O God, are thy works 385 (GR)
Songs of praise the angels sang 426 (GR)
Lead us, heavenly Father, lead us 559
Ye servants of God, your Master proclaim 535
Almighty Father, strong to save 579
Eternal Father, strong to save 608
Jesus, Lover of my soul 699

Lift Every Voice and Sing II

Little David, play on your harp 211 (SC)
If when you give the best of your service 190
I've been 'buked and I've been scorned 195
Jesus, Lover of my soul 79
Jesus, Savior, pilot me 80
When the storms of life are raging 200
When the waves of affliction sweep over the soul 204

Wonder, Love, and Praise

As newborn stars were stirred to song 788 (GR)

Proper 8

Sunday on or between June 26 and July 2

God's power to heal and bring life even out of death is revealed in Jesus.

Anchor Points – The Propers and the Season

The fixed points for each service are the appointed or proper readings and collect as well as the themes of the day or season.

Readings and Psalm

(SC) 2 Samuel 1:1, 17–27

This reading contains an elegy (from the Greek word for a mournful poem) that laments the deaths of Saul and his eldest son (and David's best childhood friend – "my brother") Jonathan. David urges that the news of their deaths not be spread since such news would certainly make their enemies rejoice and reveal the vulnerability of the nation when great leaders die. But although David the new king will ensure that Israel remains strong and united, nevertheless courageous warriors like Saul and Jonathan will be sorely missed. Their example serves as an encouragement for the living, for though these mighty men have fallen and their bow and sword are now silenced, David hopes that others will come forward to take their place.

Psalm 130

This psalm is a lament, a plea for deliverance from unspecified trouble. The psalmist makes an implicit confession of sin (vv. 1–3), puts his trust in the Lord and exhorts the community to do likewise. This psalm is also called the "De profundis" (from the Latin translation of its opening words, out of the depths). It is one of the seven traditional penitential psalms and has often been set to music.

or

(GR) Wisdom of Solomon 1:13–15; 2:23–24

Today's verses explain God's nature in view of the presence of death in creation. Death does not please God. God's creation is meant to be "wholesome." Human beings, made in the likeness of God, were created for "incorruption," but sin "summoned death" (1:16). Immortality, once intended for all, is now reserved for those who continue in a right relationship with God, the source of life and well-being.

Lamentations 3:21–33 (as a Canticle, following the reading)

From the depths of their suffering, the author of the book of Lamentations gives vent to his feelings of anguish in five carefully constructed laments. The first four poems are acrostics, each verse beginning with successive letters of the Hebrew alphabet. As we might say, these verses chart the gamut of pain "from A to Z."

But a lament is not just an outpouring of pain. It moves from the pain to the belief that God is present even in the greatest suffering. This trust is always coupled with the hope that this pain will not last forever. The mercy and compassion ("steadfast love") that characterize God's covenant relationship will eventually be manifest.

or

Psalm 30

This thanksgiving for healing was probably composed and sung in fulfillment of a vow. Both sickness and health are regarded as coming from the Lord – illness as a probable sign of sin while restoration to health would show innocence. Sickness brings the psalmist closer to the realm of Sheol, the grave, from which the Lord rescues him.

2 Corinthians 8:7–15

At the meeting of the elders in Jerusalem that dealt with the relationship between the Jewish and Gentile churches of Christians, Paul had agreed to "remember the poor" (Galatians 2:10). The Jerusalem community, persecuted by the Jewish leaders and suffering from the effects of sustained food shortages in Judea (Acts 11:27–30), was itself in particular need of help. Paul was diligent in encouraging the communities he had founded to donate for its relief (1 Corinthians 16:1–4). This provided a way of maintaining fellowship with the Jewish branch of the Church, with which relations were sometimes strained. In Paul's eyes, the Gentile churches were already indebted to the Jewish church for the gift of the gospel (Romans 15:27). He cites the example of the Macedonian churches in order to incite the Corinthians to similar efforts.

Mark 5:21–43

The gospel reading this week is the story of the raising of Jairus's daughter, including the intervening story of the woman with the hemorrhage. The author of Mark interweaves the stories, as both speak of faith and restoration, in both parallel and contrasting ways.

Jairus, "one of the leaders of the synagogue," (v. 22) comes to entreat Jesus on behalf of his daughter. The terms used throughout the story may be understood on several levels: Jairus's plea that Jesus touch his daughter, "that she may be made well, and live" may be interpreted also that she may be saved and have (eternal) life. The faith Jesus asks of Jairus can mediate grace to his daughter. It represents the faith of the community on behalf of the individual. Jairus is challenged (v. 36) to respond where the disciples have failed (4:40) and in the bold way the unnamed woman who just touched Jesus has so vividly illustrated.

Collect

Almighty God, you have built your Church upon the foundation of the apostles and prophets, Jesus Christ himself being the chief cornerstone: Grant us so to be joined together in unity of spirit by their teaching, that we may be made a holy temple acceptable to you; through Jesus Christ our Lord, who lives and reigns with you and the Holy Spirit, one God, for ever and ever. *Amen.*

Proper Preface

1. Of God the Father

For you are the source of light and life; you made us in your image, and called us to new life in Jesus Christ our Lord.

or this

2. Of God the Son

Through Jesus Christ our Lord; who on the first day of the week overcame death and the grave, and by his glorious resurrection opened to us the way of everlasting life.

or the following

3. Of God the Holy Spirit

For by water and the Holy Spirit you have made us a new people in Jesus Christ our Lord, to show forth your glory in all the world.

(Rite II, BCP 377–378; Rite I, BCP 344–345)

Seasonal Pairings

See the table below for choices appointed and suggested for this day. Preferences are put in **bold**. Not all choices are suitable for all congregations or community, though, so consider these preferences as a starting point before making a decision about your own congregation.

	Proper 8	Rite I	Rite II	EOW1	BOS 2022
Color	Green				
Entrance Rite	Customary; opening acclamation "Blessed be God" or one of the first two in EOW1	323	355	50	
Song of Praise/Kyrie	Gloria in excelsis or BCP Canticle 9, 19; EOW1 Canticle B, E	Gloria 324	Gloria 356; C9 – 86; C19 – 94	B – 30; E – 32	
Collect		178	230		
Creed	Nicene Creed	326, 327	358	53	
Prayers of the People	**Locally written**; options below; BCP forms	329	387–393	54–55	
Offertory Sentence	"The steadfast love of the Lord never ceases, his mercies never come to an end; they are new every morning; great is your faithfulness." (Lam) *or* "My heart sings to you without ceasing; O Lord my God, I will give you thanks for ever." (Psalm 30) *or* "I wait for the Lord; my soul waits for him; in his word is my hope." (Psalm 130)	343–344	376–377		

	Proper 8	Rite I	Rite II	EOW1	BOS 2022
Eucharistic Prayer	**Summer – Rite I, suggest Prayer 1; Rite II, suggest Prayer C, if not used in the year already, otherwise A; EOW1 suggest Prayer 2.**	**1–333**	**C – 369** *or* **A – 361**	**2–60**	
Proper Preface	**The Lord's Day 2 – Of God the Son**	344–345	377–378		
Breaking of the Bread (Fraction)	Christ our Passover (BCP) or options at S 167 – S 172 in *The Hymnal 1982*; EOW1 options	337	364	69	
Postcommunion Prayer		339	**Almighty and everliving God – 366**	**Loving God – 70**	
Blessing	Customary	339	366	70–71	
Dismissal	**Go in peace to love and serve the Lord.**	340	366		
Notes	Father's Day may fall on this Sunday; St. Peter's and St. Paul's Day may fall on or near this Sunday				

Additional Notes:

Song of Praise/Canticle – Summer is a good time to try additional canticles to see if there is a setting that the congregation would enjoy more often. Suggested here is a canticle for the summer from the BCP and an option from EOW1 (Canticle 9 and Canticle B) as well as one or two that reflects themes of the day. The Gloria, of course, is always appropriate in this season.

Eucharistic Prayer – Using a consistent option for the summer simplifies choices. In Rite II, if Prayer C hasn't been used in a prior season this year, summer is a good time to put it into use. Otherwise, Prayer A with the Lord's Day proper preface is sufficient. EOW1 Prayer 2 has creation imagery that may be desirable during the summertime.

Fraction Anthem at the Breaking of the Bread – The option provided in Rite I and Rite II ("Christ our Passover") is suitable and the Alleluias may be included (Hymn S 151 – S 156). Additional options in *The Hymnal 1982* at Hymn S 167 – S 172 or in EOW1. If using a new text or setting for this, schedule it for several weeks in a row to develop familiarity.

Content Resources

Reading Between the Lines

Mark 5:21–43 juxtaposes two stories showing parallels and contrasts as they pivot around Jesus. Both stories feature women: the first is the 12-year-old daughter of a leader of the synagogue. She is on the point of death in the house of her father. Her condition is publicly known because her father confronts Jesus, surrounded by a great crowd, begging him to come and lay his hands on her and save her. The second woman is older and has been suffering from a hemorrhage for 12 years. Both women are ritually unclean: the first by death and the second by a bleeding disorder. The second woman's condition is not known publicly, and although hidden in the crowd, she takes the initiative. Determining that if she touches Jesus she will be made well, she does so, and immediately, "the fountain of her blood dried up, and she knew in her body that she was healed from her disease." Aware healing power had left him and gone to a woman, and ignoring the disciples' objection that the whole crowd is pressing in on him, Jesus looks all around "to see she who had done it" (5:32). She acknowledges what has happened and Jesus says, "your faith has made you well." And Jesus continues to the house of Jairus where he raises her daughter from death. To be sure, the stories indicate that Jesus is a healer whose diminished powers and touch are nevertheless enough to raise Jairus' daughter from death. Are Marcan crowds and disciples following Jesus encouraged to speak out and act on their faith and trust of Jesus?

Central Themes

Hearing of earthquakes, wildfires, and hurricanes, we say "enough" on behalf of the people in harm's way. "Enough," we say when we've experienced our share of troubles. Yet, how often do we say, "enough," when we've been blessed with more than we need? How often do we say, "enough," when others have been given more than we think they deserve? A quick historical scan will reveal how much "enough" has changed in modern societies, where expectations of "needs" now include multiple pairs of shoes and big-screen televisions, which for many are still "extravagances."

The Wisdom of Solomon speaks of death as a sign of forces other than God at work in the world, inviting us into a stark look at death. Caitlin Doughty wrote *Smoke Gets in Your Eyes & Other Stories from the Crematory* as a response to how she saw the American fear of death warping our reality. She argues for radical change in how American culture views death and the "death industry" and a return to or creation of rituals that engage deaths' realities. As followers of Jesus, how do we engage death?

Mark's Jesus is a mightily successful healer, but he doesn't require huzzahs and confetti for his acts of healing. Surrounded by crowds large or small, his laser-like focus is always on the ones, insignificant though they may seem, to whom he is attending. So when the adult woman has been restored to health, he takes the time to speak to her. When the child comes back to life, his concern is that she is given something to eat. Thus he shows us, in both small ways and large, how we are called to act as his agents in the world. In what small ways might we do our part to heal our corner of the world?

Engaging All Ages

Jesus seems to be multitasking in today's Gospel. He is urgently on his way to heal a twelve-year-old girl on the brink of death when he is touched by a woman who had been hemorrhaging for twelve years. Although he is in a hurry, Jesus stops to find out who has touched him. In our earthly relationships – parents, children, siblings, friends, and partners – it may seem like we never have enough time. Humans cannot multitask while being fully present, but God is not restrained by the same limitation. God is never too busy to be with us, to hear our prayers, and to respond, often in unexpected ways.

Prayers of the People: Option 1

Grant us courage and good companions, humor and humility. We are thankful for this gathering of faithful friends and ask your blessing on those with whom we work and live and worship.

Be present within us and our relationships, Lord.

We pray for your mission in our communities and throughout the world. Open our eyes to see you at work in people, policies, and places.

Be present beside us as we work for reconciliation and peace.

We pray for the institutions that serve us, the courts that pursue justice, and all leaders who work for the common good. Give them wisdom to know and the courage to do what is right.

Be present before us as we form and live in community.

Many among us are hurting in ways that are known and in ways that are unknown to us. We pray for all who suffer and for those who care for them with skill and compassion.

Be present among us, and make your presence known in the ways we help each other.

We pray for those who have died and are now in their eternal home with you and the hosts of heaven.

Be present among them in everlasting glory.

Prayers of the People: Option 2

Deacon or Presider

Through Christ, your healing touch reaches into our suffering and our fear, O God, raising us to new life and wholeness: Empower our hearts with your generosity, that we may reach out also in concern for others, as we pray: We wait for you, O God; for with you there is mercy.

Litanist

Bless your Church with your gracious Spirit, O Holy One, that your people may excel in everything – in faith, in speech, in knowledge, in utmost eagerness, and in love, but especially that we may excel in generosity.

We wait for you, O God;

for with you there is mercy.

Fill our nation and its leaders with the spirit of freedom, that we may live into the ideals of liberty and justice for all and may extend the benefits of self- determination and peace throughout the world.

We wait for you, O God;

for with you there is mercy.

Let your healing and protection be powerfully present with all who are vulnerable throughout the world, especially women and children, that they may have the love and security that all people deserve.

We wait for you, O God;

for with you there is mercy.

Extend prosperity and equity to all people, and open our hearts with your generosity: Let those who experience abundance share with those who experience need, so that the one who has much does not have too much, and the one who has little does not have too little.

We wait for you, O God;

for with you there is mercy.

Be near to those who suffer with chronic pain or illness and with women who wish to bear children: Let your healing presence raise up those for whom we pray, especially______________. Our hearts wait for you with thankful hope as we offer our words of gratitude and praise, especially for____________________. Out of the depths we call to you to comfort those who grieve and togive your resurrection life to all who have died, especially______________. We wait for you, O God;

for with you there is mercy.

Out of your eternal abundance, O God, you gave to us your Son Jesus Christ, who though he was rich, yet for our sakes became poor, that by his poverty we might become rich: Let all who draw near to you be healed and empowered to serve your generous intentions for all your creation, in the power of your Spirit that dwells among us, through Jesus Christ our Savior. ***Amen.***

Hymns for the Day

The Hymnal 1982

Christ is made the sure foundation 518
The Church's one foundation 525
From deepest woe I cry to thee 151 (SC)
Out of the depths I call 666 (SC)
Immortal, invisible, God only wise 423
Praise to the living God! 372
As those of old their first fruits brought 705
Father all loving, who rulest in majesty 568
God of grace and God of glory 594, 595
Lord, whose love through humble service 610
Not here for high and holy things 9
O Jesus, crowned with all renown 292
Take my life, and let it be 707
O bless the Lord, my soul! 411
O for a thousand tongues to sing 493
Thine arm, O Lord, in days of old 567

Lift Every Voice and Sing II

Great is thy faithfulness 189 (GR)

Wonder, Love, and Praise

Give thanks for life, the measure of our days 775 (GR)
The steadfast love of the Lord never ceases 755 (GR)
Heal me, hands of Jesus 773
O Christ, the healer, we have come 772

Proper 9

Sunday on or between July 3 and 9

Jesus's rejection by his own people, but God's grace overcomes all.

Anchor Points – The Propers and the Season

The fixed points for each service are the appointed or proper readings and collect as well as the themes of the day or season.

Readings and Psalm

(SC) 2 Samuel 5:1–5, 9–10

Samuel, the last and greatest judge, grudgingly anoints Saul as the first king. After a turbulent reign ending in civil war, Saul dies violently and the tribes of Israel unite in their support of David as their new king. The tribal representatives recognize David's history of leadership even during Saul's reign. More importantly, they acknowledge the divine choice that appointed David as "heir apparent." David is anointed king by "all the elders of Israel" (v. 3).

Psalm 48

This psalm is a hymn in praise of Zion, the holy hill in Jerusalem on which the temple was built. The temple was the only place on earth where God physically dwelt. Thus it was the most sacred place in the world. But it was not only a sacred place but an unconquerable stronghold whose very sight caused enemies to cower. This rather idealized belief was shattered when the Babylonians overran the stronghold and destroyed the temple in 587 BCE.

or

(GR) Ezekiel 2:1–5

In our Hebrew scripture lesson, Ezekiel receives his prophetic commission: he is to speak the words of the Lord fearlessly to the rebellious people of Israel. Throughout this book, God addresses Ezekiel as *son of man,* meaning human being. But while only a mortal, the Lord's Spirit is with him so that the people will know that a prophet is in their midst. He will pronounce stern judgment on a nation that has sinned and is being sent into exile.

Psalm 123

This psalm is a lament in which the psalmist expresses confidence in God by the analogy of an attentive servant watching a master and hoping for a favor to be given. The psalmist hopes for an end to the contempt and humiliating insults that the arrogant now heap on them.

2 Corinthians 12:2–10

In this epistle lesson, Paul tells of both exaltation and infirmity, and the discovery of a strength that comes through weakness. The Corinthians wanted to boast of their revelations and visions. Well, Paul knows a man (he means himself) who once had an ecstatic experience. God has, however, revealed something still more important to him: that the divine power comes to its full strength when acting through human frailty.

Mark 6:1–13

The account of Jesus's rejection by his relatives and townspeople comes near the end of the Galilean ministry, and signals an extension of his kingdom ministry beyond the narrow confines of Galilee. The story echoes the Markan pattern found earlier in Capernaum where Jesus's teaching first evokes astonishment (1:22) and ends on a note of hostility (3:6) because he does not conform to their limited stereotypes of who he is and what he can and ought to be. This pattern will later appear in Jerusalem and his rejection there will end in his death (chaps. 12–14).

Collect

O God, you have taught us to keep all your commandments by loving you and our neighbor: Grant us the grace of your Holy Spirit, that we may be devoted to you with our whole heart, and united to one another with pure affection; through Jesus Christ our Lord, who lives and reigns with you and the Holy Spirit, one God, for ever and ever. *Amen.*

Proper Preface

1. Of God the Father

For you are the source of light and life; you made us in your image, and called us to new life in Jesus Christ our Lord.

or this

2. Of God the Son

Through Jesus Christ our Lord; who on the first day of the week overcame death and the grave, and by his glorious resurrection opened to us the way of everlasting life.

or the following

3. Of God the Holy Spirit

For by water and the Holy Spirit you have made us a new people in Jesus Christ our Lord, to show forth your glory in all the world.

(Rite II, BCP 377–378; Rite I, BCP 344–345)

Seasonal Pairings

See the table below for choices appointed and suggested for this day. Preferences are put in **bold**. Not all choices are suitable for all congregations or community, though, so consider these preferences as a starting point before making a decision about your own congregation.

	Proper 9	Rite I	Rite II	EOW1	BOS 2022
Color	Green				
Entrance Rite	Customary; opening acclamation "Blessed be God" or one of the first two in EOW1	323	355	50	
Song of Praise/Kyrie	Gloria in excelsis or BCP Canticle 9, 18; EOW1 Canticle B, G	Gloria 324	Gloria 356; C9 – 86; C18 – 93	B – 30; G- 34	
Collect		179	230		
Creed	Nicene Creed	326, 327	358	53	
Prayers of the People	**Locally written**; options below; BCP forms	329	387–393	54–55	
Offertory Sentence		343–344	376–377		
Eucharistic Prayer	**Summer – Rite I, suggest Prayer 1; Rite II, suggest Prayer C, if not used in the year already, otherwise A; EOW1 suggest Prayer 2.**	**1–333**	**C – 369** *or* **A – 361**	**2–60**	
Proper Preface	**The Lord's Day 2 – Of God the Son**	344–345	377–378		
Breaking of the Bread (Fraction)	Christ our Passover (BCP) or options at S 167 – S 172 in *The Hymnal 1982*; EOW1 options	337	364	69	
Postcommunion Prayer		339	**Almighty and everliving God – 366**	**Loving God – 70**	
Blessing	Customary	339	366	70–71	
Dismissal	**Let us go forth in the name of Christ.**	339	366		
Notes	Independence Day may fall on or near this Sunday				

Additional Notes:

Song of Praise/Canticle – Summer is a good time to try additional canticles to see if there is a setting that the congregation would enjoy more often. Suggested here is a canticle for the summer from the BCP and an option from EOW1 (Canticle 9 and Canticle B) as well as one or two that reflects themes of the day. The Gloria, of course, is always appropriate in this season.

Eucharistic Prayer – Using a consistent option for the summer simplifies choices. In Rite II, if Prayer C hasn't been used in a prior season this year, summer is a good time to put it into use. Otherwise, Prayer A with the Lord's Day proper preface is sufficient. EOW1 Prayer 2 has creation imagery that may be desirable during the summertime.

Fraction Anthem at the Breaking of the Bread – The option provided in Rite I and Rite II ("Christ our Passover") is suitable and the Alleluias may be included (Hymn S 151 – S 156). Additional options in *The Hymnal 1982* at Hymn S 167 – S 172 or in EOW1. If using a new text or setting for this, schedule it for several weeks in a row to develop familiarity.

Content Resources

Reading Between the Lines

Today's readings prompt the question: Is vocation always a blessing? What is it about a vocation that's a real challenge?

What does it mean to be a prophet sent by God to speak to a people rebellious against God (Ezekiel)? Or to live with a mystical revelation? Under what conditions would you consider sharing it? Paul's revelation is a defense of his apostleship, even accompanied by a thorn in the flesh which God won't remove. However, God's grace changes the relationship of power and weakness (2 Cor 12:9), because human weakness showcases God's power and allows it full play, thus enabling Paul to confound detractors and boast in his weakness.

What do you do when your vocation is rejected by your family and people who know you? And when their disbelief diminishes your abilities? Jesus' community in Mark 6 expects that he will remain a manual laborer, likely a carpenter or a worker in stone, for his entire life. Luke's Jesus, on the other hand, reads from and interprets Scripture in his first sermon (Luke 4). Mark 6:1 shows that Jesus' disciples alongside Jesus himself hear rejection from their communities of origin (Mark 10:28). Jesus' abilities are not completely inhibited (6:5), though curing a few sick people doesn't seem to count for much. But Jesus does have authority (6:7), and such authority that he can distribute it to the disciples. Jesus transforms followers into leaders, a feat of real power. It might be worth pushing the text to its culmination in 6:13–14 to recognize the success of the disciples and note how even devastating opposition can confirm vocations, as we will see in the next passage. 6:11 can be viewed within this wider horizon.

Central Themes

An adage attributed to scouting and military life tells us, "Always be prepared." This adage is repeated in myriad articles directed at the well-prepared traveler. In the film *Romancing the Stone*, adventurer Jack Colton grabs writer Joan Wilder's suitcase and tosses it into the jungle, because it doesn't contain anything that Joan will need in her new circumstance of being stranded in the jungle with Jack. Her suitcase and its contents are excess baggage and a hindrance to moving through the jungle. How many ideas and things are excess baggage in your life?

The documentary *Maiden*[1] tells the story of the first all-female crew to enter the Whitbread Round the World Race, a grueling nine-month sailing competition. The twelve-woman crew received widespread criticism and skepticism from others in the male-dominated sport, including doubts that they would even finish. Crew members each felt a strong personal pull to sailing. Like the disciples in today's gospel, this pull motivated them to dust off the rejections they received and persevere in their purpose. They finished second in their class. Have you persevered in the face of smaller adversities?

The problem with prophets is that they will speak the truth – no gilding the proverbial lily for these agents of God. In Israel's long history, that's been the case, and it has landed prophets in trouble every time. Part of their calling directed them to hold a mirror to their contemporaries in order to show them who they were, as opposed to who they were called to be: God's people in the world. Jesus, who inherits the prophetic mantle, is no exception. He bids disciples, in both the first century and the twenty-first, to do the same. How can we, partnering Jesus, be truth-tellers?

Engaging All Ages

Jesus clearly calls his disciples to tell the story with words as well as actions. Many of us would not know where to start if someone asked us to share our faith, but this need not be the case. Find someone who is at least ten years older or younger than you are. Set a timer for ten minutes and tell them what you believe. When you are finished, allow them to do the same. If you need a prompt, think about the Nicene Creed. What do you believe about God? Jesus? The Holy Spirit? The church? Forgiveness? Resurrection?

Prayers of the People: Option 1

Blessed Creator, you have filled the world with beauty and our lives with precious freedom. Grant us a spirit of gratitude for all that we have in this nation. Keep us mindful of those whose lives are challenged and limited by oppression and poverty.

Lord, in your mercy, hear our prayer.

You have claimed us for yourself and brought us close to your heart. Let your people rise to sing your praise as they align themselves with your mission. Keep us mindful of those whose hearts yearn for you and for those who are persecuted around the world in your name.

Lord, in your mercy, hear our prayer.

We thank you for bodies and minds, for friendships that nurture and challenge us. Keep us mindful of those who live in pain or fear or isolation. Strengthen our resolve to bring your love into their lives, to surround them with compassion.

Lord, in your mercy, hear our prayer.

---

1 https://www.imdb.com/title/tt8879946/, accessed May 6, 2023.

We give thanks for those we have known and loved, and who now are in your eternal embrace. Keep us mindful of those who are dying and keep alive the lessons of love we have learned from them.

Lord, in your mercy, hear our prayer.

Prayers of the People: Option 2

Deacon or Presider

Ever present God, you come to us through the teaching of your Son Jesus Christ, risen and manifest in every place and time: Grant that our eyes and ears may be open to his wisdom and his healing, that we may be sent forth in his name to do the work that he calls us to, as we pray: To you we lift up our eyes, for your power is made perfect in our weakness.

Litanist

Gracious God, you have given authority to your Church over many things that threaten your creation: Grant us the grace of your Spirit, that we may teach with Christ's wisdom and perform his deeds of power for the healing of the world.

To you we lift up our eyes,

for your power is made perfect in our weakness.

Let our nation hear the words of your prophets to reveal our impudence and stubbornness and to change our hearts: Give us just and compassionate leaders and protect our bulwarks and strongholds, that we may be a people of hospitality, welcoming your work of reconciliation and obeying your right hand of justice.

To you we lift up our eyes,

for your power is made perfect in our weakness.

Let your compassionate spirit go forth throughout the world to comfort and uphold all who suffer any form of weaknesses, insults, hardships, persecutions, and calamities, that they may be upheld by your strength and justice.

To you we lift up our eyes,

for your power is made perfect in our weakness.

Enable this community to see and to hear heavenly things and to treasure the mystery of your revelation so dearly that we may recognize and accept the unexpected gifts offered to us by our neighbors, family, and friends.

To you we lift up our eyes,

for your power is made perfect in our weakness.

Strengthen us humbly to persevere through our tribulations, O God, and heal all who need your gift of mercy, especially ___________. We thank you for your goodness revealed in all the blessings of life, especially for ___________. Receive into Paradise all who have died, especially ___________.

To you we lift up our eyes,

for your power is made perfect in our weakness.

Presider

Let your infinite grace, O Father, free us from all attachment, cynicism, and fear, that we may participate in your universal mission of teaching and healing through the reconciling Spirit of your Son, Jesus Christ our Savior. ***Amen.***

Hymns for the Day

The Hymnal 1982

Christ is made the sure foundation 518
The Church's one foundation 525
From deepest woe I cry to thee 151 (SC)
Out of the depths I call 666 (SC)
Immortal, invisible, God only wise 423
Praise to the living God! 372
As those of old their first fruits brought 705
Father all loving, who rulest in majesty 568
God of grace and God of glory 594, 595
Lord, whose love through humble service 610
Not here for high and holy things 9
O Jesus, crowned with all renown 292
Take my life, and let it be 707
O bless the Lord, my soul! 411
O for a thousand tongues to sing 493
Thine arm, O Lord, in days of old 567

Lift Every Voice and Sing II

Great is thy faithfulness 189 (GR)

Wonder, Love, and Praise

Give thanks for life, the measure of our days 775 (GR)
The steadfast love of the Lord never ceases 755 (GR)
Heal me, hands of Jesus 773
O Christ, the healer, we have come 772

Proper 10

Sunday on or between July 10 and 16

New life following a time of death and mourning.

Anchor Points – The Propers and the Season

The fixed points for each service are the appointed or proper readings and collect as well as the themes of the day or season.

Readings and Psalm

(SC) 2 Samuel 6:1–5, 12b – 19

Today's reading describes the great excitement and rejoicing that accompanied the relocation of the ark. This was the final sign that power had been transferred from Saul to David, hence the bitterness with which Michal, Saul's daughter perceives the unseemly merriment.

Psalm 24

This psalm is part of a processional liturgy, perhaps to be used by a procession of people and priests carrying the Ark of the Covenant into the sanctuary for an annual celebration. It declares God to be the Creator of all things; that God is not just a local deity. It begins with a brief hymn (vv. 1–2) to God as creator. Then comes a teaching dialogue (vv. 3–6) on the conditions for entry into the sanctuary. These first two sections may have been sung by a choir inside the temple gates. The last section (vv. 7–10) then would be sung by a group outside the gates, likely carrying in procession the Ark of the Covenant, with which God's presence was associated.

or

(GR) Amos 7:7–15

Today's reading follows the third of Amos' five visions (7:1–9:6) of the Lord's judgment upon the people. In response to the first and second visions, Amos had interceded for the people and God had relented, but now the condition of the nation is made so evident Amos cannot plead for them. By the Lord's measure, they are irrevocably warped (2 Kings 21:13; Isaiah 34:11).

Psalm 85:8–13

This national lament gives thanks for the exiles' restoration and recounts the people's affliction and need for God's continued help (vv. 4–6). The Lord's answer comes (vv. 8–13), perhaps as an oracle uttered by a prophet or priest. Verses 10–11 beautifully reassure the people of God's gracious care. These four qualities – steadfast love, faithfulness, righteousness, and peace – spring from God and are the genuine foundation for relationships among God's people.

Ephesians 1:3–14

In Greek, verses 3–14 are one long sentence, linked by relative clauses and prepositional phrases. The hymn is Trinitarian in emphasis, framed by the repeated phrase "the praise of his glorious grace" (1:6, the Father; 1:12, the Son; 1:14, the Holy Spirit), and centered about the revelation of God in Christ. Just as Christ's mission of redemption was not a belated stop-gap measure on God's part but rather part of God's will for all time, so likewise the believer has been chosen to participate in that mission since "before the foundation of the world" (v. 4).

Mark 6:14–29

In this section of the gospel, Mark uses one of his familiar "sandwich" constructions to highlight the meaning of the mission of the disciples. In between their sending (vv. 7–13) and their return (v. 30), instead of narrating the details of their mission Mark recounts the death of John the Baptist. His message is clear: there is no privileged form of discipleship. Sharing in Jesus's mission will always cost.

Collect

O Lord, mercifully receive the prayers of your people who call upon you, and grant that they may know and understand what things they ought to do, and also may have grace and power faithfully to accomplish them;

through Jesus Christ our Lord, who lives and reigns with you and the Holy Spirit, one God, now and for ever. *Amen.*

Proper Preface

1. Of God the Father

For you are the source of light and life; you made us in your image, and called us to new life in Jesus Christ our Lord.

or this

2. Of God the Son

Through Jesus Christ our Lord; who on the first day of the week overcame death and the grave, and by his glorious resurrection opened to us the way of everlasting life.

or the following

3. Of God the Holy Spirit

For by water and the Holy Spirit you have made us a new people in Jesus Christ our Lord, to show forth your glory in all the world.

(Rite II, BCP 377–378; Rite I, BCP 344–345)

Seasonal Pairings

See the table below for choices appointed and suggested for this day. Preferences are put in **bold**. Not all choices are suitable for all congregations or community, though, so consider these preferences as a starting point before making a decision about your own congregation.

	Proper 10	Rite I	Rite II	EOW1	BOS 2022
Color	Green				
Entrance Rite	Customary; opening acclamation "Blessed be God" or one of the first two in EOW1	323	355	50	
Song of Praise/Kyrie	Gloria in excelsis or BCP Canticle 9, **16;** EOW1 Canticle B, H	Gloria 324	Gloria 356; C9 – 86; **C16 – 92**	B – 30: H – 34	
Collect		179	231		
Creed	Nicene Creed	326, 327	358	53	
Prayers of the People	**Locally written**; options below; BCP forms	329	387–393	54–55	
Offertory Sentence	"Lift up your heads, O gates; lift them high, O everlasting doors; and the King of glory shall come in." (Psalm 24) *or* "Mercy and truth have met together; righteousness and peace have kissed each other." (Psalm 85)	343–344	376–377		
Eucharistic Prayer	**Summer – Rite I, suggest Prayer 1; Rite II, suggest Prayer C, if not used in the year already, otherwise A; EOW1 suggest Prayer 2.**	**1–333**	**C – 369** *or* **A – 361**	**2–60**	
Proper Preface	**The Lord's Day 1 – Of God the Father**	344–345	377–378		
Breaking of the Bread (Fraction)	Christ our Passover (BCP) or options at S 167 – S 172 in *The Hymnal 1982*; EOW1 options	337	364	69	
Postcommunion Prayer		339	**Almighty and everliving God – 366**	**Loving God – 70**	
Blessing	Customary	339	366	70–71	
Dismissal	**Let us go forth in the name of Christ**	339	366		
Notes					

Additional Notes:

Song of Praise/Canticle – With the focus on the end of John the Baptizer's ministry, Canticle 16 would be an appropriate choice for the Song of Praise.

Summer is a good time to try additional canticles to see if there is a setting that the congregation would enjoy more often. Suggested here is a canticle for the summer from the BCP and an option from EOW1 (Canticle 9 and Canticle B) as well as one or two that reflects themes of the day. The Gloria, of course, is always appropriate in this season.

Eucharistic Prayer – Using a consistent option for the summer simplifies choices. In Rite II, if Prayer C hasn't been used in a prior season this year, summer is a good time to put it into use. Otherwise, Prayer A with the Lord's Day proper preface is sufficient. EOW1 Prayer 2 has creation imagery that may be desirable during the summertime.

Fraction Anthem at the Breaking of the Bread – The option provided in Rite I and Rite II ("Christ our Passover") is suitable and the Alleluias may be included (Hymn S 151 – S 156). Additional options in *The Hymnal 1982* at Hymn S 167 – S 172 or in EOW1. If using a new text or setting for this, schedule it for several weeks in a row to develop familiarity.

Content Resources

Reading Between the Lines

By situating the account of Herod's birthday between Jesus' commission of the twelve and their return, (Mark 6:7–13; 6:30), Mark situates successful apostolic activity within the context of the death and beheading of John the Baptist, which is also understood in Mark as a foreshadowing of Jesus's own death. In addition, the odious, exaggerated story of the death of John the Baptist casts a shadow over the disciples' own healing ministry, for the capricious, dishonorable, oath-breaking behavior of the powerful local ruler, Herod Antipas – whose protection of John lasts as long as the entrée in a nightmarish birthday banquet – is a warning of the ominous context for missionary activities. The elite did not look favorably upon John's apocalyptic message, nor would they have taken kindly to his admonition about Herod's morals. That John's severed head was displayed publicly on a platter served as a warning to all connected to John and John's ministry. The tiny, honorable act of John's disciples is a poignant commentary (6:29).

Central Themes

Each Sunday we bring offerings to the church altar as a blessing in God's name. As church attendees, we offer the hospitality of the church to welcome all who come before God to pray, repent, and receive God's blessing. But what about after the service is over? Do we continue to extend the hospitality of God and God's people to all the people who have needs that we might help meet? Do we offer them "a cake of bread, a portion of meat, and a cake of raisins"? Charitable outreach is an integral part of following Jesus.

John the Baptist's imprisonment and beheading brings to light the brokenness in the power structures of Jesus's time. The podcast "Ear Hustle"[1] tells stories of the daily realities of life inside San Quentin Prison by those living and working there as well as post-incarceration stories. Hosted by Nigel Poor and Earlonne Woods, the listener hears personal stories, interviews, and music. The podcast explores the United States prison system, including the brokenness, hope, injustice, and new life, where prisoners continue the cycle of imprisonment and where they find freedom post-incarceration.

John preaches truth, is arrested for that truth-telling, and is executed by a reluctant agent of the state. This sounds a lot like the one to whom he points, whom he heralds, whose sandal he insists he is not worthy of tying. Jesus and John lose their lives because two so-called leaders, Herod and Pilate, are too craven to defend truth despite the clamor of others. There are too many times in our lives when standing up for the truth, speaking up for the rights of another and for justice seems too risky. But the gospel imperative, the clear implications of our baptism, call us to do just that.

Engaging All Ages

This is not a pleasant story. It is violent and grotesque. It serves as a painful reminder that not all stories have a happy ending. Sometimes the movies we watch, the books we read, the news we hear, and the stories we live do not offer us fairy-tale endings either. It is important to sit with this reality. But it is also important to remember that often, the stories we encounter are incomplete. This story from Mark's fifth chapter, just like any isolated episode within our own lives, is set within the larger context of a loving, liberating, life-giving God. Sometimes we must look outside the frame to find the grace we seek.

Prayers of the People: Option 1

For your church, we pray that we may reflect your love, your power, and your will in their relationships with each other and the world. Kindle in us your vision for the world.

Hear us, Lord,

for your mercy is great.

For those in authority around the world, we pray that they may serve their people well, that they will put the welfare of their people before their own needs or desires. Give us the grace to be good citizens and neighbors.

Hear us, Lord,

for your mercy is great.

For those who are ill, anxious, or forgotten: for those who have asked for our prayers today and for those who have no one else to pray for them, we pray:

Hear us, Lord,

for your mercy is great.

---

1 https://www.earhustlesq.com/

For those who are being born into new life and for those who are passing into eternal life, we pray that your angels faithfully guard and guide them on their journey.

Hear us, Lord,

for your mercy is great.

Prayers of the People: Option 2

Deacon or Presider

Let us dance before the Lord with all our might and offer prayers for all peoples in every place.

Intercessor

For this holy gathering, for our Presiding Bishop, *N.*, for our bishop, *N.*, for our parish clergy, and for the people of God in every place.

Hear our prayer.

For all nations, peoples, kin, and families.

Hear our prayer.

For mercy, justice, and peace throughout the world.

Hear our prayer.

For farmers and a good harvest, for those on vacation, and for safety from violent storms.

Hear our prayer.

For all who thirst and hunger; for all who are sick and those who are dying, for those who are poor and all who are oppressed for all travelers and those in prison, and for their families.

Hear our prayer.

For those who rest in Christ and for all the dead, we pray.

Hear our prayer.

For ourselves, our families and companions, and those we love.

Hear our prayer.

Lifting our voices with all creation, with the Blessed Virgin Mary and all the saints, let us offer ourselves and one another to the living God through Christ.

To you, O Lord our God.

Presider

Blessed are you, God and Father of our Lord Jesus Christ. Hear the prayers we offer this day and grant us our inheritance as your own people; through Jesus Christ our Lord. ***Amen.***

Hymns for the Day

The Hymnal 1982

Lift up your heads, ye mighty gates 436 (SC)
O day of God, draw nigh 600, 601 (GR)
Praise to the living God 372 (GR)
Amazing grace! how sweet the sound 671, 181
Baptized in water 294
Come, thou fount of every blessing 686
Hail, thou once despised Jesus! 495
In your mercy, Lord, you called me 706
Sing praise to our Creator 295
Sing, ye faithful, sing with gladness 492
Awake, thou Spirit of the watchmen 540
By all your saints still striving 231, 232 [*Use Nativity of St. John the Baptist for verse 2*]
King of the martyrs' noble band 236
"Thy kingdom come!" on bended knee 615

Lift Every Voice and Sing II

Amazing grace! how sweet the sound 181
Baptized in water 121
Come, thou fount of every blessing 111

Wonder, Love, and Praise

Baptized in water 767
Loving Spirit, loving Spirit 742
You're called by name, forever loved 766

Proper 11

Sunday on or between July 17 and 23

God dwells with us through Jesus.

Anchor Points – The Propers and the Season

The fixed points for each service are the appointed or proper readings and collect as well as the themes of the day or season.

Readings and Psalm

(SC) 2 Samuel 7:1–14a

The books of 1 and 2 Samuel tell of David's reign. Chapter 7 explains why David, whose reign was considered the high point of Jewish history, did not build the temple, although he desired to do so. The chapter is divided into Nathan's prophecy (vv. 1–17) and David's prayer (vv. 18–29).

Psalm 89:20–37

Psalm 89 is a royal psalm comprised of a hymn praising God's power and faithfulness (vv. 1–18), a recapitulation of the covenant between God and David's descendants (vv. 19–37), and a lament praying for deliverance from enemies (vv. 38–52).

or

(GR) Jeremiah 23:1–6

Today's reading is preceded by oracles against the three immediately previous kings of Judah (22:11, 18, 24). But as Jeremiah comes to Zedekiah, the weak-willed reigning monarch whose treachery brought about the final downfall of Jerusalem (chaps. 37–39), he does not name him directly. Instead he gives the Lord's judgment on all the "shepherds," the leaders of Judah (Ezekiel 34). God will raise up for them a king who will fulfill all the promises of the covenant with David. Jeremiah makes a play on Zedekiah's name (which means "the Lord is righteous"). Instead of the unjust Zedekiah, one will come who will accomplish the Lord's righteousness.

Psalm 23

This psalm is probably the most familiar and popular psalm of all. It celebrates God's loving care for us under the guise of a good shepherd who provides food, security, and protection from all dangers. God guides us on our journey through life so that we might "dwell in the house of the Lord."

Ephesians 2:11–22

Today's reading explains the consequences of Christ's saving work. The division between Gentile and Jew is as now obsolete and the distinguishing characteristic of circumcision abolished. Verses 14–18 are a hymn to the peace of Christ, who has broken down the wall of the law that kept Jew and Gentile apart. In the temple at Jerusalem there was an actual stone wall, dividing the outer and the inner courts of the temple, beyond which Gentiles could not go. This is symbolic of the whole system of separation that divided peoples now united in Christ.

Mark 6:30–44, 53–56

Today's gospel covers the return of the disciples to Jesus and the impressive growth of the crowds as a consequence of their witness and Jesus's ongoing miracles. Mark here uses the term "apostle" for the only time. It is not the official title that it becomes in Luke and Acts, but a simple reference to those sent out on mission (6:7).

Collect

Almighty God, the fountain of all wisdom, you know our necessities before we ask and our ignorance in asking: Have compassion on our weakness, and mercifully give us those things which for our unworthiness we dare not, and for our blindness we cannot ask; through the worthiness of your Son Jesus Christ our Lord, who lives and reigns with you and the Holy Spirit, one God, now and for ever. *Amen.*

Proper Preface

1. Of God the Father

For you are the source of light and life; you made us in your image, and called us to new life in Jesus Christ our Lord.

or this

2. Of God the Son

Through Jesus Christ our Lord; who on the first day of the week overcame death and the grave, and by his glorious resurrection opened to us the way of everlasting life.

or the following

3. Of God the Holy Spirit

For by water and the Holy Spirit you have made us a new people in Jesus Christ our Lord, to show forth your glory in all the world.

(Rite II, BCP 377–378; Rite I, BCP 344–345)

Seasonal Pairings

See the table below for choices appointed and suggested for this day. Preferences are put in **bold**. Not all choices are suitable for all congregations or community, though, so consider these preferences as a starting point before making a decision about your own congregation.

	Proper 11	Rite I	Rite II	EOW1	BOS 2022
Color	Green				
Entrance Rite	Customary; opening acclamation "Blessed be God" or one of the first two in EOW1	323	355	50	
Song of Praise/Kyrie	Gloria in excelsis or BCP Canticle 9, 10; EOW1 Canticle B, E	Gloria 324	Gloria 356; C9 – 86; C10 – 86	B – 30; E – 32	
Collect		179	231		
Creed	Nicene Creed	326, 327	358	53	
Prayers of the People	**Locally written**; options below; BCP forms	329	387–393	54–55	
Offertory Sentence	"So then you are no longer strangers and aliens, but you are citizens with the saints and also members of the household of God" (Eph)	343–344	376–377		
Eucharistic Prayer	**Summer – Rite I, suggest Prayer 1; Rite II, suggest Prayer C, if not used in the year already, otherwise A; EOW1 suggest Prayer 2.**	**1–333**	**C – 369** *or* **A – 361**	**2–60**	
Proper Preface	**The Lord's Day 3 – Of God the Holy Spirit**	344–345	377–378		
Breaking of the Bread (Fraction)	Christ our Passover (BCP) or options at S 167 – S 172 in *The Hymnal 1982*; EOW1 options	337	364	69	
Postcommunion Prayer		339	**Eternal God – 365**	**God of abundance – 69**	
Blessing	Customary	339	366	70–71	
Dismissal	**Let us go forth in the name of Christ**	339	366		
Notes	St. Mary Magdalene's Day may fall on or near this Sunday.				

Additional Notes:

Song of Praise/Canticle – Summer is a good time to try additional canticles to see if there is a setting that the congregation would enjoy more often. Suggested here is a canticle for the summer from the BCP and an option from EOW1 (Canticle 9 and Canticle B) as well as one or two that reflects themes of the day. The Gloria, of course, is always appropriate in this season.

Eucharistic Prayer – Using a consistent option for the summer simplifies choices. In Rite II, if Prayer C hasn't been used in a prior season this year, summer is a good time to put it into use. Otherwise, Prayer A with the Lord's Day proper preface is sufficient. EOW1 Prayer 2 has creation imagery that may be desirable during the summertime.

Fraction Anthem at the Breaking of the Bread – The option provided in Rite I and Rite II ("Christ our Passover") is suitable and the Alleluias may be included (Hymn S 151 – S 156). Additional options in *The Hymnal 1982* at Hymn S 167 – S 172 or in EOW1. If using a new text or setting for this, schedule it for several weeks in a row to develop familiarity.

Content Resources

Reading Between the Lines

The 23rd Psalm reminds us that, because God is "my" shepherd, I lack nothing. The shepherd lets me lie down, provides water for me, conveys me from wrong to right paths, revitalizes my life, feeds me in the presence of my enemies, all for the sake of his esteem. Goodness and mercy will pursue me my whole life long and where I am there God is.

The Year B lectionary prefers the Johannine version of the feeding of the 5,000 in Proper 12B. The omission of the Marcan version here, together with Mark 6:52, "for they did not understand about the loaves, but their hearts were hardened," which specifically identifies the disciples' misunderstanding of the loaves in the feeding narrative is unfortunate. This may well refer to the association Mark makes between the words and distribution of bread to thousands, and the Marcan version of the Last Supper in the context of a meal (14:22–25): taking, giving thanks, (he) broke. Mark 8:6, the feeding of the four thousand, which reiterates this pattern, is also omitted from the lectionary. Palm Sunday B includes a reading of Mark 14:1–15:47, which includes Mark's version of the Last Supper.

Today's gospel speaks of Jesus' compassion for the disciples; the crowd's hunger (6:31) and aimlessness, like sheep without a shepherd (6:34) along with the teaching of Jesus, all of which is addressed by what follows: the disciples' orderly arrangement and groupings of the crowd and the feeding of five thousand with fives loaves and two fish, plus leftovers (6:39–42). The touching of Jesus, "even the tassels of his cloak" likely refers to tassels or fringes on cloaks observant Israelites wore on garment corners (Num 15:38).

Central Themes

When a work team reports the progress on their assigned project, how often does the supervisor invite the team to take R&R – rest and relaxation – like a day off or to a team-building activity like going bowling together? What happens in your family when everyone pitches in to complete a major project like spring cleaning and a yard sale? How do we acknowledge the faithful church volunteers after a big Easter worship effort? Jesus said to the hard-charging disciples, "Come away . . . and rest a while," because when we rest in the stillness of God's presence, we are renewed.

Kevin Henke's first picture book *All Alone* invites the reader to wonder about the importance of time alone. What do you see, hear, and feel when you're alone? Of what do you dream? In today's gospel, the disciples return to Jesus and tell him all they have done. They are so busy that they do not even have time to eat – so many are in need. Jesus invites them to retreat and rest. When and where is Jesus inviting you to be alone?

Last Sunday, others nudged Herod into a decision he was reluctant to make. This week, others, in the form of nameless crowds, have a precipitating function. In both cases, it is the decision of one individual and his response to the crowd's prodding that makes all the difference.
In the first part of today's story, Jesus and his disciples go off to rest. But Jesus, always moved by the plight of others, turns to do the Jesus thing: heal and feed and nurture and welcome. He responds, not out of pity, but out of compassion. More than emotion, it is a real connection, an involvement in the lives of others. It is the Way of Love writ large.

Engaging All Ages

If you have ever lived with other people – parents, children, siblings, or roommates – you are probably familiar with your plans being interrupted by the needs of others. Someone beats you to the one available shower when you're already running late. Or drinks the rest of the milk. Or borrows a piece of clothing you wanted to wear. You miss work to take someone to the doctor. When Jesus's intended rest is interrupted by a needy crowd, he responds with compassion. What does a compassionate response to interruption look like in your life? How do you balance self-care and the needy crowd? Where does God show up in this discernment?

Prayers of the People: Option 1

You have made us in your image. Open our eyes to see your image in those with whom we worship, work, and live. Increase our desire for you and your ways.

In your mercy, O God,

draw each of us closer to your heart.

We lift before you the Body of Christ, our bishops, priests, and deacons, that they may faithfully lead us in our calling to be a light to the world.

In your mercy, O God,

draw each of us closer to your heart.

We lift before you the leaders of our nation: the president, the Congress, courts, and local authorities as well as those who govern around the globe. May they always reflect your justice and strive for peace among nations and neighbors.

In your mercy, O God,

draw each of us closer to your heart.

We lift before you all who suffer in body, mind, or spirit, and those who struggle with themselves or with difficult situations. Infuse them with your healing power and move us to reach out to them with compassion.

In your mercy, O God,

draw each of us closer to your heart.

We lift before you those who are dying and those who mourn. Receive the dying into your eternal embrace, accompanied by choirs of angels and greeted by the host of heaven.

In your mercy, O God,

draw each of us closer to your heart.

Prayers of the People: Option 2

Deacon or Presider

Blessed be the God and Father of our Lord Jesus Christ; your wisdom and insight has made known to us the mystery of your will to gather up all things in Christ: Move with power and justice throughout the earth, to unite all people into your divine life, we pray: The earth is God's and all that is in it, the world and all that dwell therein.

Litanist

You chose your Church in Christ before the foundation of the world, O gracious One: Fill us with such gladness and love of you that we may sing and rejoice in your presence, and bless all people in your name.

The earth is God's and all that is in it,

the world and all that dwell therein.

Raise up and protect prophets as of old who will challenge the rulers of this age and inspire us to be holy and blameless before you in love: Protect us from political intrigue and from the abuse of power, so that our nation may be a people of clean hands and pure hearts.

The earth is God's and all that is in it,

the world and all that dwell therein.

In Christ, you have blessed us with every spiritual blessing in the heavenly places; let your holy presence, strong and mighty: Be with all who live in places of injustice or violence; strengthen all who suffer for the sake of conscience; protect whistleblowers and those who confront injustice with truth; visit the prisoners with your mercy and wisdom.

The earth is God's and all that is in it,

the world and all that dwell therein.

Give this community wisdom and insight to hear the word of truth and to live in the glorious grace that you freely bestow on us in the Beloved, that your glory may dwell in our land.

The earth is God's and all that is in it,

the world and all that dwell therein.

We have set our hope on Christ as we offer our prayers of intercession: We pray for those who are ill, or who live with any threat or trauma, especially ______________. Hear our glad words of thanksgiving, especially for ______________. Raise to your eternal presence all innocents who die because of the decisions of the powerful. Remember all who have died, that they may be marked with the seal of the promised Holy Spirit, the pledge of our inheritance, especially ______________.

The earth is God's and all that is in it,

the world and all that dwell therein.

Presider

Hear us as we call upon you, O God, and establish among us your rule of justice and truth, that we may be protected from all evil and live according to the riches of the grace that you have bestowed upon us through Jesus Christ, who lives and reigns with you and the Holy Spirit, One God, forever and ever. ***Amen.***

Hymns for the Day

The Hymnal 1982

Hosanna to the living Lord! 486 (SC)
Only-begotten, Word of God eternal 360, 361 (SC)
Savior, again to thy dear Name we raise 345 (SC)
We the Lord's people, heart and voice uniting 51 (SC)
Give praise and glory unto God 375 (GR)
Hail to the Lord's Anointed 616 (GR)
My shepherd will supply my need 664 (GR)
Savior, like a shepherd lead us 708 (GR)
The King of love my shepherd is 645, 646 (GR)
The Lord my God my Shepherd is 663 (GR)
Christ is made the sure foundation 518
Hail, thou once despised Jesus! 495
In Christ there is no East or West 529
Just as I am, without one plea 693
The Church's one foundation 525
Dear Lord and Father of mankind 652, 653
O for a thousand tongues to sing 493
Thine arm, O Lord, in days of old 567

Lift Every Voice and Sing II
The Lord is my shepherd 104 (GR)
In Christ there is no East or West 62
Gentile or Jew, servant or free 151
Just as I am, without one plea 693

Wonder, Love, and Praise
Come now, O Prince of Peace 795
Now let us rise and hymn the grace 781
From miles around the sick ones came 774
Heal me, hands of Jesus 773
O Christ, the healer, we have come 772

Proper 12

Sunday on or between July 24 and 30

Jesus's compassion for the people leads him to respond with food for mind and body. God's power is revealed in Jesus.

Anchor Points – The Propers and the Season

The fixed points for each service are the appointed or proper readings and collect as well as the themes of the day or season.

Readings and Psalm

(SC) 2 Samuel 11:1–15

In another familiar story in the David cycle, David's character begins to unravel. Enamored by the beauty of Bathsheba, the wife of one of his loyal field officers, David abuses his royal power and conceives a child with her. Then, to cover up his crime, he brings Uriah from the front lines in hopes that he will sleep with his wife so everyone will think Bathsheba's child is his. But Uriah, more loyal than David imagines, does not go to his house while on leave. So to cover up his sin, David gives orders that Uriah should fight in the front line of battle, and then the other fighters abandon him so that he will be killed, which is exactly what happens.

Psalm 14

This lament psalm divides the world in two categories: the foolish and the wise. Although the foolish and wicked now persecute the wise and good, the psalmist envisions a time when God's judgment will make the appropriate rewards and punishments.

or

(GR) 2 Kings 4:42–44

Today's verses come from the Elisha cycle of stories that describe his prophetic ministry to the northern kings. In this short account, a man honors God, represented by the prophet, by offering him the first fruits of the new harvest. Elisha reflects God's compassion for the people and insists that the food be distributed to the hungry. The small offering is miraculously multiplied "according to the word of the Lord."

Psalm 145:10–19

This is an acrostic psalm, each verse beginning with a successive letter of the Hebrew alphabet. It invites praise for God's greatness (vv. 2–3), love of the people (vv. 8–10), kingship (vv. 11–13), help for the needy (vv. 14–16), justice and presence (vv. 17–18).

Ephesians 3:14–21

Today's reading is Paul's prayerful response to this ministry of grace that he has been given. He invites God's blessing on his audience so that they will experience Christ's presence and begin to grasp the universal implications of God's plan for them. He ends with a final hymn of praise (a doxology).

John 6:1–21

The feeding of the 5,000 is the only miracle of Jesus's ministry recorded in all four gospels. John's account seems to come from a tradition independent of, but parallel to, the other accounts. As so often emphasized in John, Jesus takes the initiative, even before the people arrive (1:38, 4:7, 5:6, 6:5). John looks at the miracle from a three-dimensional perspective. He recalls the past by alluding to Moses and the feeding of the Israelites with manna in the wilderness (6:5, 12, 31; Exodus 16:4, 16) and, secondarily, to Elijah (1 Kings 17:8–16), and Elisha (2 Kings 4:42–44). He recalls the present by the mention of the celebration of the Passover (6:4).

Collect

O God, the protector of all who trust in you, without whom nothing is strong, nothing is holy: Increase and multiply upon us your mercy; that, with you as our ruler and guide, we may so pass through things temporal, that we lose not the things eternal; through Jesus Christ our

Lord, who lives and reigns with you and the Holy Spirit, one God, for ever and ever. *Amen.*

Proper Preface

1. Of God the Father

For you are the source of light and life; you made us in your image, and called us to new life in Jesus Christ our Lord.

or this

2. Of God the Son

Through Jesus Christ our Lord; who on the first day of the week overcame death and the grave, and by his glorious resurrection opened to us the way of everlasting life.

or the following

3. Of God the Holy Spirit

For by water and the Holy Spirit you have made us a new people in Jesus Christ our Lord, to show forth your glory in all the world.

(Rite II, BCP 377–378; Rite I, BCP 344–345)

Seasonal Pairings

See the table below for choices appointed and suggested for this day. Preferences are put in **bold**. Not all choices are suitable for all congregations or community, though, so consider these preferences as a starting point before making a decision about your own congregation.

	Proper 12	Rite I	Rite II	EOW1	BOS 2022
Color	Green				
Entrance Rite	Customary; opening acclamation "Blessed be God" or one of the first two in EOW1	323	355	50	
Song of Praise/Kyrie	Gloria in excelsis or BCP Canticle 9, 19; EOW1 Canticle B, R	Gloria 324	Gloria 356; C9 – 86; C19 – 94	B – 30: R – 40	
Collect		180	231		
Creed	Nicene Creed	326, 327	358	53	
Prayers of the People	**Locally written**; options below; BCP forms	329	387–393	54–55	
Offertory Sentence	"May Christ dwell in your hearts through faith, as you are being rooted and grounded in love." (Eph)	343–344	376–377		
Eucharistic Prayer	**Summer – Rite I, suggest Prayer 1; Rite II, suggest Prayer C, if not used in the year already, otherwise A; EOW1 suggest Prayer 2.**	**1–333**	**C – 369** *or* **A – 361**	**2–60**	
Proper Preface	**The Lord's Day 1 – Of God the Father**	344–345	377–378		
Breaking of the Bread (Fraction)	**S 168 – S 170;** S 167, S 171 in *The Hymnal 1982*; EOW1 options; Christ our Passover (BCP)	337	364	69	
Postcommunion Prayer		339	**Eternal God – 365**	**God of abundance – 69**	
Blessing	Customary	339	366	70–71	
Dismissal	**Go in peace to love and serve the Lord**	340	366		
Notes	St. James' Day may fall on or near this Sunday				

Additional Notes:

Song of Praise/Canticle – Summer is a good time to try additional canticles to see if there is a setting that the congregation would enjoy more often. Suggested here is a canticle for the summer from the BCP and an option from EOW1 (Canticle 9 and Canticle B) as well as one or two that reflects themes of the day. The Gloria, of course, is always appropriate in this season.

Eucharistic Prayer – Using a consistent option for the summer simplifies choices. In Rite II, if Prayer C hasn't been used in a prior season this year, summer is a good time to put it into use. Otherwise, Prayer A with the Lord's Day proper preface is sufficient. EOW1 Prayer 2 has creation imagery that may be desirable during the summertime.

Fraction Anthem at the Breaking of the Bread – In this "bread of life – bread of heaven" mini-season, there are some fraction anthems that may be very suitable, especially Hymn S 168, S 169, and S 170 (spoken or sung). You could also use S 167 or S 171, though they seem to have the Emmaus story as a primary reference. They could still be suitable, though. Two of the EOW1 options would be appropriate in these 'bread' weeks.

Content Resources

Reading Between the Lines

In John 6:1–21 a large crowd follows Jesus as disciples do. Passover is near; and grass is flourishing in the season. Five thousand people are given a young boy's five loaves, made of the cheapest flour, and dried fish distributed through Jesus' own hands. However, following Jesus and being fed is not enough. It must include discernment, as the question to Philip indicates (6:5–6; see also 6:66–71). Initial faith is not fully adequate if it is based exclusively on signs. Such followers never move beyond seeking what Jesus can do for them (6:14, 26, 30). They identify Jesus inadequately as Prophet and King, but his kingdom "is not of this world" (18:36). Jesus withdraws to the mountain. Faith amongst disciples however may develop. The disciples by themselves get into a boat. In the darkness of a rough sea and a strong wind they are terrified to see Jesus walking across the sea. All accounts of this episode concur that Jesus then says, "It is I; do not be afraid." Fear is reasonable, but faith grows with understanding.

Central Themes

Gratitude is a human characteristic that we gain and lose repeatedly over a lifetime. Little children express their gratitude with glee when presented with a juicy peach. Their laughter and glee trigger the parents to offer more tasty foods. When we express gratitude for the small gifts of help and courtesy from our family and friends, they feel encouraged to repeat those favors in the future. Somehow, things like help with the house or yard work are offered more often when gratitude for that sharing of responsibilities is expressed joyfully. We participate in the miracle of abundance through our gratitude.

Yeast is tiny and does not look alive. Yet we know from experience that it is alive. And when it is combined with the right ingredients under the right circumstances, it brings bread to life: the taste, the size, the smell! Jesus knows how he is going to feed the large crowds before he asks his disciples what to do. In asking them, he asks them to dream with him. How does our experience with Jesus's sacred stories point our holy imagination to what is possible with even the smallest of resources?

In this first segment, Jesus, who nearly always initiates events in this gospel, again gets things rolling by noticing a crowd and their need for food. So close to Passover, the whiff of liberation and the miraculous is in the air. Like Moses, who led a crowd on that far-off occasion, Jesus also ascends a mountain; like Moses, Jesus also feeds a multitude in a new wilderness. Unlike Moses' manna, which was depleted in a day, the food that Jesus provides in abundance is still available. We don't multiply bread, but we can feed others in countless, varied ways.

Engaging All Ages

We live in a world where many are in need. Just like the disciples in today's gospel, we often look at the data and conclude that there is not enough to go around. Can you think of one such example? Hunger? Clean water? Affordable health care? If this one "shortage" were miraculously to be remedied, what would it look like? Tap into your wild and wonderful imagination. Write about or draw such a modern-day miracle. God is still acting in surprising ways that transform our human assumptions of what's possible. What would it look like for you to contribute to that miracle you imagined?

Prayers of the People: Option 1

We yearn for the fullness of God, that Christ may dwell in us and we in him.

We thank you for the gift of life and for our connection with all that you have made.

May we delight in your creation and protect it.

Fill us with the fullness of God.

Amen, Lord. Hear our prayer.

We thank you for creative compassionate leaders throughout the world. May they devote themselves to justice, peace, and the common good.

Amen, Lord. Hear our prayer.

We thank you for the endless and beautiful diversity of humanity. May we recognize and celebrate your image in every person we meet.

Amen, Lord. Hear our prayer.

We thank you for the promise of your presence in our lives. May our concern for those among us who are hurting bring us to prayer and may our care for them be healing balm.

Amen, Lord. Hear our prayer.

We thank you for the gift of new life in this world and the hope of new and everlasting life in the world to come. May those who have gone before us overflow with the fullness of your never-ending love and light.

Amen, Lord. Hear our prayer.

Prayers of the People: Option 2

Deacon or Presider

As we prepare to eat the meal of Jesus, let us pray for all who are tossed in the storms of life.

Intercessor

For this holy gathering, for our Presiding Bishop, *N.*, for our bishop, *N.*, for our parish clergy and for the people of God in every place.

Hear our prayer.

For all nations, peoples, pods, kin, and families.

Hear our prayer.

For mercy, justice, and peace throughout the world.

Hear our prayer.

For farmers and a good harvest, for travelers and those on vacation, and for safety from violent storms.

Hear our prayer.

For all those desiring healing and for all who are in danger and need: those who are sick and those who are dying, for all who are poor and those oppressed, for prisoners and captives, and for their families.

Hear our prayer.

For all victims of hatred and violence, we pray.

Hear our prayer.

For those who rest in Christ and for all the dead, we pray.

Hear our prayer.

For ourselves, our families and companions, and those we love.

Hear our prayer.

Lifting our voices with all creation, with the Blessed Virgin Mary and all the saints, let us offer ourselves and one another to the living God through Christ.

To you, O Lord our God.

Presider

Father of glory, hear the prayers we offer you this day, strengthen us with your Spirit, and let your Son dwell in our hearts, through Jesus Christ our Lord. ***Amen.***

Hymns for the Day

The Hymnal 1982

If thou but trust in God to guide thee 635
Before thy throne, O God, we kneel 574, 575 (SC)
As those of old their first fruits brought 705 (GR)
God, my King, thy might confessing 414 (GR)
We will extol you, ever-blessed Lord 404 (GR)
Awake, O sleeper, rise from death 547
Just as I am, without one plea 693
Not far beyond the sea, nor high 422
O love, how deep, how broad, how high 448, 449
O Love of God, how strong and true 455, 456
Bread of the world, in mercy broken 301
Hope of the world, thou Christ of great compassion 472
I come with joy to meet my Lord 304
My God, thy table now is spread 321
O Food to pilgrims given 308, 309
We the Lord's people, heart and voice uniting 51

Lift Every Voice and Sing II

If I have wounded any soul today 176 (SC)
Just as I am, without one plea 137
Break thou the bread of life 146

Wonder, Love, and Praise

All who hunger, gather gladly 761
O wheat whose crushing was for bread 760

Proper 13

Sunday on or between July 31 and August 6

Jesus is the bread of heaven.

Anchor Points – The Propers and the Season

The fixed points for each service are the appointed or proper readings and collect as well as the themes of the day or season.

Readings and Psalm

(SC) 2 Samuel 11:26–12:13a

Today's reading comes from the conclusion of the story of David's adultery with Bathsheba and the murder of her husband Uriah. Nathan's parable illustrates the power of parables. To enter into the parable's world is to risk self-revelation. When he hears the story, King David, as the guarantor of justice, reacts with outrage to the injustice recounted. Yet it is he himself, in the arrogance of his power, who has tried to put himself above the law. He has betrayed his anointing by God. This episode reminds us that the working out of God's purpose is not dependent upon perfect people, but upon God alone, despite the sinfulness of even God's chosen servants.

Psalm 51:1–13

This is one of the great penitential psalms. The psalm's title, added later, ascribes this psalm to David during the time of his repentance for the seduction of Bathsheba and the murder of her husband, Uriah (2 Samuel 11:11–12:25).

or

(GR) Exodus 16:2–4, 9–15

Today's reading recounts one of the many instances of the people's murmuring during the time of the Exodus as the Israelites demand that God live up to the divine demands of covenant partnership. As their God, Yahweh must demonstrate that he can provide and protect them as a household leader or father was required to do.

Psalm 78:23–29

This psalm is a long recital of the story of Israel's relationship with God. After the introduction (vv. 1–11), the psalmist recounts the wilderness experience (vv. 12–39), and the journey from Egypt to the land. The pattern of history involves God's gracious action (vv. 12–16), the people's rebellion (vv. 17–20), God's punishment (21–31) and forgiveness (vv. 32–39). It encourages the audience to learn the lessons from their history and respond more appropriately to God's choice of them as covenant partners.

Ephesians 4:1–16

This reading continues the ethical exhortations from last week. It examines the basis for the new life of the Gentile converts, contrasting it with their former lives. Their new life is not a result of their own discoveries and efforts but originates from God. It is the new life God recreates, through Jesus, in the Christian.

John 6:24–35

Today's passage from John is the preface to the bread of life discourse. It illustrates John's favorite ways of shaping a dialogue. One is the use of misunderstanding; another is that a question asked on one level is answered on a higher level. Set in the synagogue at Capernaum (6:59), this discourse relies on concepts and structures common to rabbinic sermons at the time. Verse 35 is the first of the many "I am" statements in the Gospel of John. Jesus uses the "I am" statements (bread of life, 6:35; light of the world, 8:12; door, 10:7; good shepherd, 10:11; resurrection and life, 11:25; way, truth and life, 14:6; true vine, 15:1) to reveal the dimensions of his relationship to humankind.

Collect

Let your continual mercy, O Lord, cleanse and defend your Church; and, because it cannot continue in safety without your help, protect, and govern it always by your goodness; through Jesus Christ our Lord, who lives and reigns with you and the Holy Spirit, one God, for ever and ever. *Amen.*

Proper Preface

1. Of God the Father

For you are the source of light and life; you made us in your image, and called us to new life in Jesus Christ our Lord.

or this

2. Of God the Son

Through Jesus Christ our Lord; who on the first day of the week overcame death and the grave, and by his glorious resurrection opened to us the way of everlasting life.

or the following

3. Of God the Holy Spirit

For by water and the Holy Spirit you have made us a new people in Jesus Christ our Lord, to show forth your glory in all the world.

(Rite II, BCP 377–378; Rite I, BCP 344–345)

Seasonal Pairings

See the table below for choices appointed and suggested for this day. Preferences are put in **bold**. Not all choices are suitable for all congregations or community, though, so consider these preferences as a starting point before making a decision about your own congregation.

	Proper 13	Rite I	Rite II	EOW1	BOS 2022
Color	Green				
Entrance Rite	Customary; opening acclamation "Blessed be God" or one of the first two in EOW1	323	355	50	
Song of Praise/Kyrie	Gloria in excelsis or BCP Canticle 9, 12 (Inv, III, Dox); EOW1 Canticle B, G	Gloria 324	Gloria 356; C9 – 86; C12 – 88	B – 30: G – 34	
Collect		180	232		
Creed	Nicene Creed	326, 327	358	53	
Prayers of the People	**Locally written**; options below; BCP forms	329	387–393	54–55	
Offertory Sentence	"Jesus said to them, 'I am the bread of life. Whoever comes to me will never be hungry, and whoever believes in me will never be thirsty.'" (John)	343–344	376–377		
Eucharistic Prayer	**Summer – Rite I, suggest Prayer 1; Rite II, suggest Prayer C, if not used in the year already, otherwise A; EOW1 suggest Prayer 2.**	**1–333**	**C – 369** *or* **A – 361**	**2–60**	
Proper Preface	**The Lord's Day 3 – Of God the Holy Spirit**	344–345	377–378		
Breaking of the Bread (Fraction)	**S 168 – S 170;** S 167, S 171in *The Hymnal 1982*; EOW1 options; Christ our Passover (BCP)	337	364	69	
Postcommunion Prayer		339	**Eternal God – 365**	**God of abundance – 69**	
Blessing	Customary	339	366	70–71	
Dismissal	**Go in peace to love and serve the Lord**	340	366		
Notes	The Transfiguration may fall on this Sunday – see the Transfiguration entry if it is on Sunday				

Additional Notes:

Song of Praise/Canticle – Summer is a good time to try additional canticles to see if there is a setting that the congregation would enjoy more often. Suggested here is a canticle for the summer from the BCP and an option from EOW1 (Canticle 9 and Canticle B) as well as one or two that reflects themes of the day. The Gloria, of course, is always appropriate in this season.

Eucharistic Prayer – Using a consistent option for the summer simplifies choices. In Rite II, if Prayer C hasn't been used in a prior season this year, summer is a good time to put it into use. Otherwise, Prayer A with the Lord's Day proper preface is sufficient. EOW1 Prayer 2 has creation imagery that may be desirable during the summertime.

Fraction Anthem at the Breaking of the Bread – In this "bread of life – bread of heaven" mini-season, there are some fraction anthems that may be very suitable, especially Hymn S 168, S 169, and S 170 (spoken or sung). You could also use S 167 or S 171, though they seem to have the Emmaus story as a primary reference. They could still be suitable, though. Two of the EOW1 options would be appropriate in these 'bread' weeks.

Content Resources

Reading Between the Lines

John's gospel attests that Jesus effects signs through the power of God (10:21 publicly refutes any other source). In 6:24–35, the feeding of the 5,000 and the crowds' request for a sign (6:30) results in the discourse on the bread of life (6:35–58). Signs capture people's attention and can lead them to faith or trust. In today's gospel, readers follow the crowds' active search for Jesus; where he is not, where they might look, and where he is. The crowds look for Jesus (v. 24) but finding him is work for food that perishes. In 6:35, Jesus' "I am" statement, "I am the bread of life; whoever comes to me will never hunger and the one believing in me will never thirst" is linked to the verb to believe or trust, so as to encourage crowds to work for food that does not perish. Since Jesus is God's instrument, belief is a response both to Jesus' unity with God and his work as God's agent. The crowds need food for eternal life which the Son of Man as God's agent will give them. They want to be active (v. 28). Jesus tells them that faith is indeed work, "your work is to believe in him whom He has sent."

Central Themes

Romantic partners sometimes express love by saying, "My partner completes me." Parents say, "My children fulfill me," as they beam with pride. The love we bear for our beloved feeds us more than any holiday meal. That love feeds our need for purpose and meaning in our lives by being connected to people who love us. Jesus says, "I am the bread of life," inviting us to enter into the interconnectedness of all of creation. When we love as Jesus teaches us to love, we connect to everyone, for all are created in God's image.

To live we need to eat. In an ideal world, we eat when we are hungry, and we eat enough. Yet, for some, this ideal has been distorted by not having access to enough food or by having a distorted relationship with food such as eating too much or too little. Jesus is pointing to life in Christ, using the comparison of our daily bread to the "bread of life." What does being nourished in Christ look like? What daily spiritual meals do we need? How are those needs distorted?

In John's Gospel, each of the discrete seven signs, of which the feeding of the five thousand is one, is meant to give onlookers and participants the ability to perceive something more significant than the mighty act itself. And each teaches a more nuanced sense of who Jesus is. His disciples had only noticed scarcity; Jesus notices opportunity. The crowds had eaten bread that satisfied hunger, but they were so focused on being full that they missed what was really happening at that gratis lunch. Jesus uses the bread as an extended metaphor for who he is – someone capable of sustaining life. The Way of Love invites us to join Jesus by considering how we can invite others to full, fulfilling lives.

Engaging All Ages

Our world is filled with signs: road signs, protest signs, no smoking signs. These signs convey information. Have you ever looked for a sign from God? Throughout scripture, signs from God convey information, but they also inspire action. The Magi saw a bright star telling of the birth of a new king. They were compelled to visit. The Israelites received manna in the wilderness and were nourished for their continued journey. Jesus inspired the disciples to proclaim Good News throughout the world. What signs have you received? What action do they call you to?

Prayers of the People: Option 1

O God, your people are hungry for your presence. Teach us to put our trust in you. Let us not forget the wonders you have shown us.

You are the Bread of Life;

Give us this bread always.

Your church is hungry for your presence. Give our leaders hearts for your truth and wisdom as they guide us. Bless our Presiding Bishop *N.*, our Bishop *N.*, and our priests and deacons. Empower us all to live the covenant we have made with you.

You are the Bread of Life;

Give us this bread always.

Your world is hungry for peace. We pray for the leaders of all the nations, that their hearts are intent on the common good for all people. We pray for *N.*, our President, those who serve in local governments, and for the courts and Congress of our land.

You are the Bread of Life;

Give us this bread always.

Your world is hungry for relief from hardship. We pray for your people in all corners of the world who want for food and shelter; who suffer from oppression and war.

Sustain them with your presence and lead us to come to their aid.

You are the Bread of Life;

Give us this bread always.

Your world is hungry for healing and compassion. We pray for those we hold dear to our hearts who suffer from any illness of body, mind or spirit: *N.*, . . . We pray also for those who have no one to pray for them.

You are the Bread of Life;

Give us this bread always.

Your world is hungry for comfort and eager for new life. Enfold those who have died into your embrace. May they rest in your eternal presence. May we all come to know the life that is eternal.

You are the Bread of Life;

Give us this bread always.

Prayers of the People: Option 2

Deacon or Priest

Gathered as the body of Christ, rich in the gifts of God, let us offer prayers for all who hunger and thirst.

Intercessor

For this holy gathering, for our Presiding Bishop, *N.*, for our bishop, *N.*, for our parish clergy, and for the people of God in every place.

Hear our prayer.

For the leaders of the nations, and for mercy, justice, and peace throughout the world.

Hear our prayer.

For farmers and a good harvest, for travelers and those on vacation, and for safety from violent storms.

Hear our prayer.

For all those in danger and need: the sick and the suffering, prisoners, captives, and their families, the hungry, homeless and oppressed.

Hear our prayer.

For those who rest in Christ and for all the dead, we pray.

Hear our prayer.

those in need of ongoing care; for ourselves, our families and companions, and those we love.

Hear our prayer.

Lifting our voices with all creation, with the Blessed Virgin Mary and all the saints, let us offer ourselves and one another to the living God through Christ.

To you, O Lord our God.

Presider

God and Father of all, hear our prayers for all in need and fill your hungry people with bread from heaven, through Jesus Christ our Lord. *Amen.*

Hymns for the Day

The Hymnal 1982

Jesus, Lover of my soul 699 (SC)
Just as I am, without one plea 693 (SC)
Glorious things of thee are spoken 522, 523 (GR)
Guide me, O thou great Jehovah 690 (GR)
O Food to pilgrims given 308, 309 (GR)
O God of Bethel, by whose hand 709 (GR)
O God, unseen yet ever near 332 (GR)
Shepherd of souls, refresh and bless 343 (GR)
Awake, O sleeper, rise from death 547
Come, risen Lord, and deign to be our guest 305, 306
Eternal Ruler of the ceaseless round 617
Lord, you give the great commission 528
O Lord Most High, eternal King 220, 221
Put forth, O God, thy Spirit's might 521
Sing, ye faithful, sing with gladness 492
Singing songs of expectation 527
Bread of the world, in mercy broken 301
Deck thyself, my soul, with gladness 339
Father, we thank thee who hast planted 302, 303
I am the bread of life 335
Lord, enthroned in heavenly splendor 307
My God, thy table now is spread 321
O Food to pilgrims given 308, 309
We the Lord's people, heart and voice uniting 51

Lift Every Voice and Sing II

Jesus, Lover of my soul 79 (SC)
Just as I am, without one plea 137 (SC)
Break thou the bread of life 146
Come, ye disconsolate, where'er ye languish 147

Wonder, Love, and Praise

Lord, you give the great commission 780
We are all one in mission 778
All who hunger, gather gladly 761
I am the bread of life 762
O wheat whose crushing was for bread 760

The Transfiguration of Our Lord Jesus Christ

August 6: When this Feast Day falls on Sunday, it takes precedence of that Sunday.

Christ's glory is revealed on the holy mountain.

Anchor Points – The Propers and the Feast

The fixed points for each service are the appointed or proper readings and collect as well as the themes of the day or season.

Readings and Psalm

Exodus 34:29–35

Today's account explains the purpose of Moses' regular practice at the tent of meeting. Moses had asked to see God's glory (33:18–23); apparently his ongoing communion with the Lord imparted a continuing revelation of divine glory. That vision of glory so transfigured Moses' face that he had to wear a veil. Moses' experience became a type of the glory of the new covenant. Unlike Moses' radiance, which would fade, believers behold the Lord's glory and are being transformed into the Lord's likeness with a glory that always increases.

Psalm 99 or 99:5–9

Psalm 99 is a hymn celebrating God's kingship. It's three stanzas each close with a refrain about God's holiness.

2 Peter 1:13–21

The author writes in response to anxieties about different teachings in the community and about the delay of the second coming. He appeals to the tradition of apostolic testimony, particularly to his experience as a witness to the transfiguration. The transfiguration manifests Christ in his power, confirming the messianic prophecies of the Hebrew Bible and pointing toward his return in glory.

Luke 9:28–36

Luke's account of the transfiguration points back to the Hebrew Bible parallels and forward to Jesus' death, resurrection, and ascension. Moses and Elijah, who represent the law and the prophets – both fulfilled by Jesus – speak with Jesus "of his departure," literally his exodus, the new exodus he will lead through his death. The new exodus is accomplished through Jesus' death, resurrection, and ascension. Jesus' glory is his own (9:32), not a reflected glory as Moses' was. God's voice confirms what it proclaimed at Jesus' baptism: Jesus is the Son, the Chosen, fulfilling the roles of Moses, of the Davidic king and of the servant.

Collect

O God, who on the holy mount revealed to chosen witnesses your well-beloved Son, wonderfully transfigured, in raiment white and glistening: Mercifully grant that we, being delivered from the disquietude of this world, may by faith behold the King in his beauty; who with you, O Father, and you, O Holy Spirit, lives and reigns, one God, for ever and ever. *Amen.*

Proper Preface

Epiphany – Because in the mystery of the Word made flesh, you have caused a new light to shine in our hearts, to give the knowledge of your glory in the face of your Son Jesus Christ our Lord. (Rite II, BCP 378; Rite I BCP 346)

Feast Day Pairings

See the table below for choices appointed and suggested for this day. Preferences are put in **bold**. Not all choices are suitable for all congregations or community, though, so consider these preferences as a starting point before making a decision about your own congregation.

	The Transfiguration	Rite I	Rite II	EOW1	BOS 2022
Color	White/Gold/Festive				
Entrance Rite	Customary	323	355	50	
Song of Praise/Kyrie	Gloria in excelsis or Te Deum (Canticle 7, 21)	Gloria 324; C7 – 52	Gloria 356; C21 – 9		
Collect		191	243		
Creed	Nicene Creed	326, 327	358	53	
Prayers of the People	**Locally written**; option below; BCP forms	329	387–393	54–55	
Offertory Sentence	"Proclaim the greatness of the Lord our God and worship him upon his holy hill; for the Lord our God is the Holy One." (Psalm 99)	343–344	376–377		
Eucharistic Prayer	**One that allows use of the Epiphany preface or Prayer D**	2–340	**A – 361, B – 367** or **D – 372**	1–57	
Proper Preface	Epiphany	346	378		
Breaking of the Bread (Fraction)	Christ our Passover (BCP)	337	364		
Postcommunion Prayer		339	**Eternal God – 365**	**God of abundance – 69**	
Blessing	Customary				
Dismissal	**Let us go forth in the Name of Christ**	340	366		
Notes					

Additional Notes:

Song of Praise/Canticle – The Te Deum is a customary canticle for Feasts of Our Lord, but other choices could be made, including the Gloria.

Eucharistic Prayer – Using the proper preface (Epiphany) adds thematic language to the Eucharistic Prayer. Prayer D would be appropriate in Rite II because of its emphasis on the glory of God.

Content Resources[1]

Reading Between the Lines

Today's readings involve visions of glory, suffering, and justice. "We've got some difficult days ahead. But it doesn't matter with me now. Because I've been to the mountaintop. And I've looked over. And I've seen the promised land. I may not get there with you. But I want you to know tonight, that we, as a people will get to the promised land." Martin Luther King Jr said those visionary words on the night before he was assassinated. He envisions what a society committed to justice for the Memphis Sanitation Workers would look like, and he invites all to the task of realizing that vision of a just, promised land.

Moses descends the mountain with the tablets of the law, and his face shone. Perhaps it was to remind the people of God's presence as they received the Law, enacted justice, and became a nation. (Ex 24:39). God is holy, that is, other (Psalm 99:3, 5, 9), yet that otherness is not unconnected or abstract but experienced in a specific place, namely, the Jerusalem Temple, on the mountaintop, and amongst people. In the course of the Psalm, we see that God is invested in particular humans. Moreover, God loves justice on earth (99:4).

Luke's "transfiguration" account answers Herod's question about who Jesus was (Luke 9:9). God's command, "Listen to him!" (9:35) offers disciples an invitation to participate in Jesus' exodus in Jerusalem (9:31), that is, in glory alongside suffering, as they strive together for the kingdom which God promises them (12:31–2). "Exodus" is not just Jesus' own suffering and death; it is a reference to Moses, as well as to "the restoration to Israel" that starts from Jerusalem and is to be proclaimed to all nations (Acts 1:6).

Central Themes

The story of Jesus' Transfiguration is all about change. It is an event that calls us to change into people who live with a sense of expectation and hope, who can act powerfully for the sake of the good and face opposition in life and not be overcome. And it's scary.

The change they witness produces so much fear in the disciples that they literally fall on their faces. This is perfectly natural; when we become used to things being a certain way, and they go a different way, it disorients us.

1 For additional thematic material, see the Last Sunday after the Epiphany, pp. 135-138, which also focuses on the Transfiguration.

There may be comfort in avoiding change, sticking to received tradition instead. Just remember Peter in this story. He thinks that he can contain the change by boxing it in three little tents up on the mountain. When we slide into that sort of nostalgia, we're in trouble. We must respond to change; we can begin in fear, but remember that we are empowered for bravery.

Engaging All Ages

For some, these stories in the Bible can seem fantastic – mythical. And that's not a bad thing! One of the goals of scripture is to increase our religious imaginations, to see the world as God sees the world. And perhaps more importantly, to live in a way that believes and hopes in and for the miraculous. For some, this will cause a serious case of eyes rolling.

For others, it's the bedrock of their faith. Either way, spend this week encouraging families and other members of your community to engage your religious imagination. Have parishioners write a new version of this well-known story. How would Jesus glory be revealed in a new story? Who would appear with him? How do we bear witness to what we know about who Jesus is?

Prayers of the People

Friends, God our Savior is our refuge! So let us pray to God, saying, "Incline your ear to us; hear our words."

God our Savior, show us your face. Satisfy your Church in your presence. Reveal to us your ways so that we might walk in the light of your truth.

Silence

Incline your ear to us;

Hear our words.

O God, your eyes are fixed on justice. We pray for all victims of war and violence and famine. Give heed to the cries of those in need throughout the world.

Silence

Incline your ear to us;

Hear our words.

God of abundance, you have blessed the earth to bring forth plenty. May we recognize the abundance in our own lives, so that those with little may also have their fill.

Silence

Incline your ear to us;

Hear our words.

O God, have compassion on the people of our region. Show us your marvelous loving-kindness so that trust in your goodness might replace our fears.

Silence

Incline your ear to us;

Hear our words.

God of blessing, we call upon you, for you answer us in our need. We pray this day for all those desperate for your blessing. Moved by compassion, heal the sick and suffering ones we hold in our hearts this day.

Invite the congregation to add their petitions and thanksgivings, followed by silence

Incline your ear to us;

Hear our words.

God our vindicator, justify the dead through the mercy of your Messiah. We pray that in the fullness of time, they may awake, beholding your likeness.

Silence

Incline your ear to us;

Hear our words.

Hymns for the Day

The Hymnal 1982

O Zion, tune thy voice 543
We sing of God, the mighty source (1–2) 386, 387
Christ is the world's true Light 542
Christ, whose glory fills the skies 6,7
From God Christ's deity came forth 443
When morning gilds the skies 427
Christ upon the mountain peak 129,130
O Light of Light, Love given birth 133,134
O wondrous type, O vision fair 136,137

Lift Every Voice and Sing II

Let the heav'n light shine on me 174
Jesu, joy of our desiring 75
I love to tell the story 64

Proper 14

Sunday on or between August 7 and 13

Jesus is the Bread of Life.

Anchor Points – The Propers and the Season

The fixed points for each service are the appointed or proper readings and collect as well as the themes of the day or season.

Readings and Psalm

(SC) 2 Samuel 18:5–9, 15, 31–33

Today's reading describes the results foreshadowed by the prophet Nathan's words to David after his murder of Uriah and marriage to Bathsheba. Strife, indeed, plagued his household and his son Absalom participated in a bloody uprising against him. Despite David's orders to "deal gently" with Absalom and thus lessen the expected harsh consequences of a son who would take up arms against a father, Absalom dies anyway as the result of a freak accident in which he was caught up by the hair in the branches of a tree, and thus easily killed.

Psalm 130

This thanksgiving for healing was probably composed and sung in fulfillment of a vow. Both sickness and health are regarded as coming from the Lord – illness as a probable sign of sin while restoration to health would show innocence. Sickness brings the psalmist closer to the realm of Sheol, the grave, from which the Lord rescues him.

or

(GR) 1 Kings 19:4–8

Today's reading is from the Elijah cycle of stories. Elijah was a prophet to Israel, sent to call the unfaithful kings back to the covenant. Elijah confronts King Ahab's endorsement and even sponsorship of Baal worship. Baal was believed to be the god of fertility, particularly in the forces of rain and harvest. Elijah comes in judgment on this infidelity to the covenant and prophesies a drought, powerfully demonstrating God's sovereignty. The drought ends at God's command, as demonstrated through Elijah's defeat of the Baal priests. Ahab's wife, Jezebel, seeks vengeance on the prophet, who flees for his life in utter despair. Elijah's exhaustion and hunger drive him to the brink of collapse, at which point an angel feeds him, touches him, and encourages him on his journey to Horeb, the mountain of God. The story acknowledges the depression and despair that can come on the heels of great successes and points, in the end, to the presence of God as the only source of strength.

Psalm 34:1–8

This psalm of thanksgiving has a strong didactic element similar to the wisdom teachings. It is an acrostic, each verse beginning with a successive letter of the Hebrew alphabet. The psalmist first gives thanks for deliverance, then testifies to God's goodness, calling upon the other worshipers to share the fruits of his experience. Finally, the psalmist elaborates upon the meaning of "the fear of the Lord" and its consequences.

Ephesians 4:25–5:2

Today's reading continues the ethical exhortation of the previous two weeks. The new life of the baptized is to be lived out in specific ways. Old patterns of behavior must be replaced with new ones. All discourse and behavior should build up the life of the community. Thus, all Christians participate in the unifying work of the Spirit in the Church (4:3). They are to imitate God's work of forgiveness and love shown in Christ's self-offering (Colossians 3:12–13). The phrase, "a fragrant offering" (5:2) is used in the Greek version of the Old Testament to describe the burnt offering (Exodus 29:18; Leviticus 2:9; 3:5), and later applied to the people themselves (Ezekiel 20:41). This whole section is based on the belief that Christian living is an integral corollary of Christian doctrine.

John 6:35, 41–51

This section of the discourse on the bread of life combines the themes of bread as the revelation of God in word and wisdom and bread as the revelation of God in the Eucharist. Various Old Testament parallels would prepare the hearer for understanding bread as the symbol of God's word. Amos describes a famine not of bread but of hearing the Lord's words (Amos 8:11); the image of wisdom giving "the bread of understanding" (Proverbs 9:5); the word of the Lord giving sustenance like bread (Isaiah 55:10–11). For Jesus's hearers, this bread would have meant the Torah. Jesus is that revelation of God. He does the Father's will, not his own. Those who really see him will have eternal life in the present and participate in the resurrection "at the last day" (v. 40).

Collect

Grant to us, Lord, we pray, the spirit to think and do always those things that are right, that we, who cannot exist without you, may by you be enabled to live according to your will; through Jesus Christ our Lord, who lives and reigns with you and the Holy Spirit, one God, for ever and ever. *Amen.*

Proper Preface

1. Of God the Father

For you are the source of light and life; you made us in your image, and called us to new life in Jesus Christ our Lord.

or this

2. Of God the Son

Through Jesus Christ our Lord; who on the first day of the week overcame death and the grave, and by his glorious resurrection opened to us the way of everlasting life.

or the following

3. Of God the Holy Spirit

For by water and the Holy Spirit you have made us a new people in Jesus Christ our Lord, to show forth your glory in all the world.

(Rite II, BCP 377–378; Rite I, BCP 344–345)

Seasonal Pairings

See the table below for choices appointed and suggested for this day. Preferences are put in **bold.** Not all choices are suitable for all congregations or community, though, so consider these preferences as a starting point before making a decision about your own congregation.

	Proper 14	Rite I	Rite II	EOW1	BOS 2022
Color	Green				
Entrance Rite	Customary; opening acclamation "Blessed be God" or one of the first two in EOW1	323	355	50	
Song of Praise/Kyrie	Gloria in excelsis or BCP Canticle 9, 17; EOW1 Canticle B, G	Gloria 324	Gloria 356; C9 – 86; C17 – 93	B – 30; G – 34	
Collect		180	232		
Creed	Nicene Creed	326, 327	358	53	
Prayers of the People	**Locally written**; options below; BCP forms	329	387–393	54–55	
Offertory Sentence	Jesus said, "I am the living bread that came down from heaven. Whoever eats of this bread will live forever; and the bread that I will give for the life of the world is my flesh." (John)	343–344	376–377		
Eucharistic Prayer	**Summer – Rite I, suggest Prayer 1; Rite II, suggest Prayer C, if not used in the year already, otherwise A; EOW1 suggest Prayer 2.**	**1–333**	**C – 369** *or* **A – 361**	**2–60**	
Proper Preface	**The Lord's Day 2 – Of God the Son**	344–345	377–378		
Breaking of the Bread (Fraction)	**S 168 – S 170;** S 167, S 171 in *The Hymnal 1982*; EOW1 options; Christ our Passover (BCP)	337	364	69	
Postcommunion Prayer		339	**Eternal God – 365**	**God of abundance – 69**	
Blessing	Customary	339	366	70–71	
Dismissal	**Go in peace to love and serve the Lord**	340	366		
Notes	The Transfiguration may fall near this Sunday; back to school prayers?				

Additional Notes:

Song of Praise/Canticle – Summer is a good time to try additional canticles to see if there is a setting that the congregation would enjoy more often. Suggested here is a canticle for the summer from the BCP and an option from EOW1 (Canticle 9 and Canticle B) as well as one or two that reflects themes of the day. The Gloria, of course, is always appropriate in this season.

Eucharistic Prayer – Using a consistent option for the summer simplifies choices. In Rite II, if Prayer C hasn't been used in a prior season this year, summer is a good time to put it into use. Otherwise, Prayer A with the Lord's Day proper preface is sufficient. EOW1 Prayer 2 has creation imagery that may be desirable during the summertime.

Fraction Anthem at the Breaking of the Bread – In this "bread of life – bread of heaven" mini-season, there are some fraction anthems that may be very suitable, especially Hymn S 168, S 169, and S 170 (spoken or sung). You could also use S 167 or S 171, though they seem to have the Emmaus story as a primary reference. They could still be suitable, though. Two of the EOW1 options would be appropriate in these 'bread' weeks.

Content Resources

Reading Between the Lines

In John 6:35, 41–51, we see that whilst signs can open up confirmation and the possibility of deepening faith, they can also have the opposite effect, as John understands from the beginning (1:11). Galilean Jews complain because Jesus said, "I am the bread that came down from heaven" (6:38) arguing that we know Jesus and his father and mother. The fourth gospel's awareness of these traditions reflected in Mark 6:1–6 and Matthew 13:53–58 do not preclude rejection of knowledge about Jesus' ultimate origin. Both can be true, as 6:44 shows: those coming to Jesus are also drawn by the Father, on the basis of which, "all shall be taught by God" (6:45). Isaiah 54:13 promises God's teaching with the blessing of prosperity. Talk of bread evokes Exodus traditions (6:49), and John's Jesus declares that he is living bread from heaven, and that this bread is "my flesh." Even v. 55, and Jesus' teaching that flesh alone is useless (v. 63) nevertheless causes many disciples to turn back (v. 66).

Central Themes

As humans enjoy greater prosperity, some people have become hoarders who hang onto material things. Fear of not having enough is one component of hoarding, and greed associated with acquiring things is another. Paul says, **"Be anxious for nothing, but in everything by prayer and supplication**, with thanksgiving, let your requests be made know to God (Philippians 4:6). . ." Our feelings of fear about not having enough is the subject of therapy sessions, but we all are familiar with breaking unhelpful habits such as acquiring more things than we need. Millennials and post-millennials born after 1980 have indicated that they don't want to inherit past generations' things. Maybe it's time we stop acquiring more things.

Jesus states that he is the bread of life and from heaven. Listeners grumble that he is Mary and Joseph's child, not from heaven. Jesus encourages them to shift their thinking from what they think they see to something greater. In Dolly Parton's autobiographical song "Coat of Many Colors," she tells the story of her mother sewing her a beautiful coat made with scraps from a rag box. Parton imagined she was like Joseph in his multi-colored coat. Her classmates teased her because they saw a coat of rags and knew she had little money. Yet when she wore her coat of many colors, she knew she was rich in love.

In John's Gospel, there are those who think they know and those who know they don't know. The "knowers" are complacent; they have the history down and quote scripture: Bread from heaven? Manna in the wilderness. A little knowledge can be a dangerous thing. Because they know, they are closed to new ways of knowing, to revelation. Not only do they miss the import of Jesus's "I am the Bread," they dismiss him. They had made up their minds and did not want to be confronted with something different, with what Jesus tried to teach them. When we "continue in the apostles' teaching," we resist the temptation to be the know-it-alls of the past.

Engaging All Ages

Look at a loaf of bread. Pull it apart. Smell it. Taste it. What does "bread" mean to you? Comfort? Deliciousness? Nourishment? Satisfaction? Home? A loaf of fresh, beautifully baked bread is both a work of art and completely mundane. How is it that Jesus is like bread? What is the comfort Jesus gives? Or the satisfaction? The nourishment?

Prayers of the People: Option 1

One God who creates, redeems and sustains us: you brought us into being, and we cannot exist without you.

Give us the strength we need for today

And the hope we need for tomorrow.

We pray for Christ's body, your church, and for those who lead and for those who follow. Grant that we not grieve your Holy Spirit with our words or actions. Remind us that we are members of one another. Teach us to be imitators of you.

Give us the strength we need for today

And the hope we need for tomorrow.

We pray for those in authority across the globe. Infuse them with wisdom and speak peace into their hearts. Expand your vision for the world to every corner of the earth, to every part of your creation.

Give us the strength we need for today

And the hope we need for tomorrow.

We pray for those who carry burdens of illness, pain, anxiety, or grief. May they draw strength from your presence and comfort from those around who care for them. We pray for *N.*

Give us the strength we need for today

And the hope we need for tomorrow.

We pray for those who have died, who are now surrounded by your glory and the songs of angels. Comfort those who mourn with your promise of hope and the resurrected life.

Give us the strength we need for today

And the hope we need for tomorrow. Amen.

Prayers of the People: Option 2

Deacon or Presider

For all the hungry and thirsty of the world, let us pray to the Lord who gives us the bread of eternal life, saying "Lord, have mercy."

Intercessor

For this holy gathering, for our Presiding Bishop, *N.*, for our bishop, *N.*, for our parish clergy, and for the people of God in every place.

Lord, have mercy.

For all nations and their leaders, and for mercy, justice, and peace in the world.

Lord, have mercy.

For all who grow and harvest food, for all travelers and those on vacation, and for safety from violent storms.

Lord, have mercy.

For those whose needs are known to you alone, and for all who may be sick, for those who are dying; for all who are in want or oppressed; for those in prison, their families and for all victims of violence and abuse.

Lord, have mercy.

For those who rest in Christ and for all the dead, we pray.

Lord, have mercy.

For those serving in the armed forces, for our city and every community, and for our families, companions, and all we love.

Lord, have mercy.

Lifting our voices with all creation, with the Blessed Virgin Mary and all the saints, let us offer ourselves and one another to the living God through Christ.

To you, O Lord, our God

Presider

Holy One in heaven, giver of the bread of life, hear the prayers we offer this day for all those in danger and need and bring your beloved children to your eternal banquet; through Jesus Christ our Lord. ***Amen.***

Hymns for the Day

The Hymnal 1982

From deepest woe I cry to thee 151 (SC)
Out of the depths I call 666 (SC)
Awake, O sleeper, rise from death 547
Baptized in water 294
God is love, and where true love is 576, 577
To thee, O Comforter divine 514
Where charity and love prevail 581
Where true charity and love dwell 606
Bread of the world, in mercy broken 301
Completed, Lord, the Holy Mysteries 346
Deck thyself, my soul, with gladness 339
Draw nigh and take the Body of the Lord 327, 328
Father, we thank thee who hast planted 302, 303
For the bread which you have broken 340, 341
I am the bread of life 335
Lord, enthroned in heavenly splendor 307
My God, thy table now is spread 321
O Food to pilgrims given 308, 309
We the Lord's people, heart and voice uniting 51

Lift Every Voice and Sing II

I will bless the Lord at all times 154 (GR)
Baptized in water 121
Break thou the bread of life 146
I am the Bread that came down from heaven 150

Wonder, Love and Praise

All who hunger, gather gladly 761 (GR)
I will bless the Lord at all times 764 (GR)
Baptized in water 767
Ubi caritas et amor 831
All who hunger, gather gladly 761
I am the bread of life 762
O wheat whose crushing was for bread 760

Proper 15

Sunday on or between August 14 and 20

God's Word (Logos, Wisdom) brings the life-giving knowledge of God.
God's Word is the very bread of life.

Anchor Points – The Propers and the Season

The fixed points for each service are the appointed or proper readings and collect as well as the themes of the day or season.

Readings and Psalm

1 Kings 2:10–12; 3:3–14

Today's reading comes from the beginning of the narrative of Solomon's reign, based largely upon the book of the Acts of Solomon (11:41). After forty years as king, David dies and his son Solomon succeeds him as king over Israel. Solomon is described as a generally faithful king, but his willingness to offer sacrifices in "high places" – which refers to older shrines not dedicated to worship of Yahweh – reveals a serious character deficiency that caused continual problems.

Psalm 111

Psalm 111 is a psalm of praise, celebrating God's presence in the history of God's covenant relationship with Israel. The psalmist recites a brief history of God's actions as clues to God's character.

or

(GR) Proverbs 9:1–6

In today's reading, wisdom is pictured as the giver of a banquet. Wisdom's invitation is issued, not to the proud or the mighty, but to the simple and the righteous. Wisdom's banquet is in contrast to that of folly (9:13–18) who lures the simple to destruction. The bread and wine of wisdom bring life and insight. This concept of sustenance parallels, in the eschatological tradition, the banquet to the final times (Isaiah 25:6, 55:1–5).

Psalm 34:9–14

This psalm of thanksgiving has a strong didactic element similar to the wisdom teachings. It is an acrostic, each verse beginning with a different letter of the Hebrew alphabet. The psalmist first gives thanks for deliverance, then testifies to God's goodness, calling upon the other worshipers to share the fruits of his experience. Finally, the psalmist elaborates upon the meaning of "the fear of the Lord" and its consequences.

Ephesians 5:15–20

Today's reading concludes the author's exhortations on Church life. The first part contrasts the paths of wisdom and of folly, which theme, like the contrast between light and darkness (5:7–13), is taken from the Old Testament wisdom tradition. The wise are to make "the most of the time," (literally, "redeem the present opportunity," Colossians 4:5) offered by the contemporary world.

John 6:51–58

In the gospel lesson, Jesus speaks of the flesh and blood of the Son of Man as the bread from heaven which must be eaten in order to share in the life of the eternal age. Previously in this gospel, the bread of life had seemed to signify Jesus's teaching and his presence. Now it is given still more significance with the understanding that the believer may share deeply in the life of Jesus and his self-offering. This experience is enacted in the Holy Communion.

Collect

Almighty God, you have given your only Son to be for us a sacrifice for sin, and also an example of godly life: Give us grace to receive thankfully the fruits of his redeeming work, and to follow daily in the blessed steps of his most holy life; through Jesus Christ your Son our Lord, who lives and reigns with you and the Holy Spirit, one God, now and for ever. *Amen.*

Proper Preface

1. Of God the Father

For you are the source of light and life; you made us in your image, and called us to new life in Jesus Christ our Lord.

or this

2. Of God the Son

Through Jesus Christ our Lord; who on the first day of the week overcame death and the grave, and by his glorious resurrection opened to us the way of everlasting life.

or the following

3. Of God the Holy Spirit

For by water and the Holy Spirit you have made us a new people in Jesus Christ our Lord, to show forth your glory in all the world.

(Rite II, BCP 377–378; Rite I, BCP 344–345)

Seasonal Pairings

See the table below for choices appointed and suggested for this day. Preferences are put in **bold**. Not all choices are suitable for all congregations or community, though, so consider these preferences as a starting point before making a decision about your own congregation.

	Proper 15	Rite I	Rite II	EOW1	BOS 2022
Color	Green				
Entrance Rite	Customary; opening acclamation "Blessed be God" or one of the first two in EOW1	323	355	50	
Song of Praise/Kyrie	Gloria in excelsis or BCP Canticle 9, 18; EOW1 Canticle B, M	Gloria 324	Gloria 356; C9 – 86; C18 – 93	B – 30; M – 37	
Collect		180	232		
Creed	Nicene Creed	326, 327	358	53	
Prayers of the People	**Locally written**; options below; BCP forms	329	387–393	54–55	
Offertory Sentence	Jesus said, "Very truly, I tell you, Those who eat my flesh and drink my blood have eternal life, and I will raise them up on the last day" (John 6)	343–344	376–377		
Eucharistic Prayer	**Summer – Rite I, suggest Prayer 1; Rite II, suggest Prayer C, if not used in the year already, otherwise A; EOW1 suggest Prayer 2.**	**1–333**	**C – 369** *or* **A – 361**	**2–60**	
Proper Preface	**The Lord's Day 2 – Of God the Son**	344–345	377–378		
Breaking of the Bread (Fraction)	**S 168 – S 170;** S 167, S 171 in *The Hymnal 1982*; EOW1 options; Christ our Passover (BCP)	337	364	69	
Postcommunion Prayer		339	**Eternal God – 365**	**God of abundance – 69**	
Blessing	Customary	339	366	70–71	
Dismissal	**Let us go forth in the name of Christ**	339	366		
Notes	St. Mary the Virgin's Day may fall on or near this Sunday; back to school prayers?				

Additional Notes:

Song of Praise/Canticle – Summer is a good time to try additional canticles to see if there is a setting that the congregation would enjoy more often. Suggested here is a canticle for the summer from the BCP and an option from EOW1 (Canticle 9 and Canticle B) as well as one or two that reflects themes of the day. The Gloria, of course, is always appropriate in this season.

Eucharistic Prayer – Using a consistent option for the summer simplifies choices. In Rite II, if Prayer C hasn't been used in a prior season this year, summer is a good time to put it into use. Otherwise, Prayer A with the Lord's Day proper preface is sufficient. EOW1 Prayer 2 has creation imagery that may be desirable during the summertime.

Fraction Anthem at the Breaking of the Bread – In this "bread of life – bread of heaven" mini-season, there are some fraction anthems that may be very suitable, especially Hymn S 168, S 169, and S 170 (spoken or sung). You could also use S 167 or S 171, though they seem to have the Emmaus story as a primary reference. They could still be suitable, though. Two of the EOW1 options would be appropriate in these 'bread' weeks.

Blessing – If your church is celebrating St. Mary the Virgin on this Sunday or referring to it, you may want to use the blessing for Feasts of St. Mary (BOS 2022, 18).

Content Resources

Reading Between the Lines

In the gospel of John 6:51–58, John 6:52 presents some of those listening to Jesus arguing amongst themselves: some rejecting what Jesus says and others questioning without apparently rejecting his words. To the group asking a question but not rejecting Jesus outright: "how can this man give us his flesh to eat?" (6:52), further teaching is given in 6:53 "Unless you eat the flesh of the son of man and drink his blood you do not have life within you."

The notion of or abiding or remaining is the primary characteristic of discipleship in John's Gospel, indicating committed, ongoing, personal and reciprocal relationship between Christ and believers. John 6:56, where it also occurs, indicates mutual indwelling. Craig Keener, *Gospel of John 2*, p. 999–1002, notes that "continuing to dwell is to persevere in keeping Jesus' commandments, especially to love one another."

Central Themes

The lesson Paul gave to the Ephesians was the same lesson God gave to Solomon: they were admonished to seek wisdom, the ability to discern what is right. The final admonition from Paul is to give thanks to God. Appreciative Inquiry is an approach to organizational change that emphasizes focusing on strengths rather than fixing weaknesses. Gratitude for our collective strengths lays the groundwork for building bridges based on shared strengths. When we appreciate our shared gifts, we have identified shared understandings on which to build our collective future. Together we discern the right steps forward for our families and communities.

Culture, family traditions, availability, personal ethics, religion, allergies, and preferences all are reasons for why we eat what we eat. Food defines a community, and our food choices defines us as people. The bread and wine of Holy Eucharist tell the story of who we are as Christians. As individual followers of Jesus, we take the bread and wine for different reasons. In the picture book *We Gather at This Table* by Anna V. Ostenso Moore and Peter Krueger, the reader is invited to ask the questions, "Why do you gather at this table? Why do you receive the bread and wine?"

After all the conversation about manna and Jesus as the new and improved manna, Jesus promises that his living bread will be sustenance for all. He knows that food and conversation go together, that both nourish, that both are necessary, and that the taste for one quickens the taste for the other. Both require a certain intimacy, an intimacy into which he invites us. We have to be close to savor, which was scary stuff for some in that early crowd. This chapter is, in part, about the Eucharist. We have promised to "continue in the breaking of the bread," that mysterious union that invigorates and ennobles us for the work we have been sent to do.

Engaging All Ages

We know how to eat bread. We have sourdough French toast for breakfast, sandwich bread for lunch, and soft rolls for dinner. We have dipping bread like naan, filled bread, and bread that's really a vehicle for cheese and pepperoni. Jesus says if we desire to abide in him, to dwell with God, to experience eternal life, we must consume his flesh and blood. How do we "eat" Jesus, the bread of life?

Prayers of the People: Option 1

We come to you, trusting that our prayers will be heard. So, we pray,

O God of abundant mercy

Hear our prayer.

For your church in our neighborhoods and around the world, may we work toward unity and pray with one heart and one voice. We pray for wisdom for our leaders; for the president, the Congress, and the courts.

O God of abundant mercy

Hear our prayer.

We come to you with thankful hearts, thankful for friends, family, and food; thankful for work, play and peace. Let us never forget those who are alone, hungry, out of work, and living in violent situations.

O God of abundant mercy

Hear our prayer.

We come to you trusting in your care and claiming the promise of your presence. We pray for healing for those who are in special need today: ___________ .

O God of abundant mercy

Hear our prayer.

We come to you for forgiveness – for paying more attention to our own needs than the needs of others, for listening more to our own voice than we listen to yours, and for all the ways we put up barriers between your love and our lives.

O God of abundant mercy

Hear our prayer.

We come to you as disciples. May your love be known in the words we say and the lives we live.

O God of abundant mercy

Hear our prayer.

We come to you on behalf of all who are in need of healing and peace: *N.* We give thanks for those in our community who provide care and comfort through long days and nights of pain. Make your presence known to those who are broken, lost, or grieving, and bring them the peace they seek.

O God of abundant mercy

Hear our prayer.

We come to you for hope, bringing before you those we love and see no longer. We rejoice that they now are free from all pain and delight in the never-ending life that awaits us.

O God of abundant mercy

Hear our prayer.

Prayers of the People: Option 2

Deacon or Presider

Let us share in the true food and the true drink with all those in desperate need.

Intercessor

For this holy gathering, for lay and clergy leaders in our church, and for the people of God in every place.

Lord, have mercy.

For all nations and their leaders, and for mercy, justice, and peace in the world.

Lord, have mercy.

For students and teachers, and all those returning to their studies.

Lord, have mercy.

For travelers and those on vacation, and for safety from violent storms.

Lord, have mercy.

For the sick and the suffering, prisoners and their families, the hungry and the oppressed, and all in danger and need.

Lord, have mercy.

For those who rest in Christ and for all the dead, we pray.

Lord, have mercy.

For our city and those who live in it, and for our families, companions, and all we love.

Lord, have mercy.

Lifting our voices with all creation, with the Blessed Virgin Mary and all the saints, let us offer ourselves and one another to the living God through Christ.

To you, O Lord, our God.

Presider

God of eternal life, who built a house of faithful people, have mercy on all who gather in your name and grant our prayers for all the world; through Jesus Christ our Lord. ***Amen.***

Hymns for the Day

The Hymnal 1982

All my hope on God is founded 665 (SC)
Be thou my vision 488
Creator of the earth and skies 148
Eternal light, shine in my heart 465, 466
God be in my head, and in my understanding 694 (SC)
God of grace and God of glory 594, 595 (SC)
God, you have given us power to sound 584 (SC)
Open your ears, O faithful people 536 (SC)
God, you have given us power to sound 584 (GR)
Open your ears, O faithful people 536 (GR)
Come, O come, our voices raise 430
Let all the world in every corner sing 402, 403
New songs of celebration render 413
O praise ye the Lord! Praise him in the height 432
Sing, ye faithful, sing with gladness 492
Singing songs of expectation 527
Songs of praise the angels sang 426
When in our music God is glorified 420
Bread of the world, in mercy broken 301
Completed, Lord, the Holy Mysteries 346
Deck thyself, my soul, with gladness 339
Draw nigh and take the Body of the Lord 327, 328
Father, we thank thee who hast planted 302, 303
For the bread which you have broken 340, 341
I am the bread of life 335
Lord, enthroned in heavenly splendor 307
My God, thy table now is spread 321
O Food to pilgrims given 308, 309
We the Lord's people, heart and voice uniting 51

Lift Every Voice and Sing II

I will bless the Lord at all times 154 (GR)
I'm goin'-a sing when the Spirit says sing 117
Break thou the bread of life 146
I am the Bread that came down from heaven 150

Wonder, Love, and Praise

Even when young, I prayed for wisdom's grace 906
I will bless the Lord at all times 764 (GR)
Wisdom freed a holy people 905 (GR)
As newborn stars were stirred to song 788
All who hunger, gather gladly 761
I am the bread of life 762
O wheat whose crushing was for bread 760

Proper 16

Sunday on or between August 21 and 27

The disciples respond to Jesus's pronouncement that he is the "bread of life."

Anchor Points – The Propers and the Season

The fixed points for each service are the appointed or proper readings and collect as well as the themes of the day or season.

Readings and Psalm

1 Kings 8:(1,6,10–11), 22–30, 41–43

Today's readings describe the solemn ceremony of the dedication of the Jerusalem temple, in particular the transfer of the ark of the covenant that was the sacred dwelling place of God and the tangible sign of God's enduring presence with the people. Solomon's dedication prayer recalls the long relationship of the people with Yahweh and asks that God's promises be fulfilled and that God will continue to be faithful to the people. God's powerful presence will even answer the prayers of foreigners who come to pray in this temple.

Psalm 84

This psalm combines elements of hymn (vv. 1, 10–11), lamentation and intercession (vv. 8–9). It resembles the songs of Zion (found in Psalm 46, 48, 76 and 87) and the pilgrim Songs of Ascent (Psalms 120–124). Likely composed on the occasion of a pilgrimage to the temple, the psalm expresses the strength of the psalmist's longing for the temple and the trials and rewards of the journey.

or

(GR) Joshua 24:1–2a, 14–18

The ceremony reported here may have been an annual renewal of the covenant. It follows the form of ancient Hittite political treaties (covenants among nations) of that time. Elements of such treaties were: a preamble (24:2a), a summary of historical relationships (24:2–13), the stipulations (24:14, 25), the recording of the treaty in written form (24:26), and the invocation of witnesses (24:22, 27).

Psalm 34:15–22

This psalm of thanksgiving has a strong didactic element similar to the wisdom teachings. It is an acrostic, each verse beginning with a different letter of the Hebrew alphabet. The psalmist first gives thanks for deliverance, then testifies to God's goodness, calling upon the other worshipers to share the fruits of his experience. Finally, the psalmist elaborates upon the meaning of "the fear of the Lord" and its consequences.

Ephesians 6:10–20

Suddenly, after the quiet consideration of domestic matters (5:21–6:9), today's reading sounds a call to battle. Christians are to "be strong," not from their own resources but by the strength of the Lord that fills them from baptism. Christians are to put on "the whole armor of God" (v. 11) in order to battle the spiritual forces of evil. These are active both in the world and in the supernatural realm, although in Christ's victory the decisive battle is already won (1:20–22; Colossians 2:15). Paul had a strong sense of the world as being under the domination of evil powers. The struggle of Christian freedom is to overcome this evil domination and live under the domination or rule of God.

John 6:56–69

In the gospel, we hear of different responses to Jesus's claim that he is the heavenly bread that gives eternal life to those who eat it. His are words of spirit and life, but many can understand them only in a materialistic sense and are like the Israelites who did not trust God in the wilderness. Yet, if this saying is hard for them to believe, more difficult still will be Jesus's ascent into heaven as the Son of Man. As Jesus knew would happen, many disciples now turn away, but Peter confesses him to be God's holy one who has the words of eternal life.

Collect

Grant, O merciful God, that your Church, being gathered together in unity by your Holy Spirit, may show forth your power among all peoples, to the glory of your Name; through Jesus Christ our Lord, who lives and reigns with you and the Holy Spirit, one God, for ever and ever. *Amen.*

Proper Preface

Of the Lord's Day

1. Of God the Father

For you are the source of light and life; you made us in your image, and called us to new life in Jesus Christ our Lord.

or this

2. Of God the Son

Through Jesus Christ our Lord; who on the first day of the week overcame death and the grave, and by his glorious resurrection opened to us the way of everlasting life.

or the following

3. Of God the Holy Spirit

For by water and the Holy Spirit you have made us a new people in Jesus Christ our Lord, to show forth your glory in all the world.

(Rite II, BCP 377–378; Rite I, BCP 344–345)

Seasonal Pairings

See the table below for choices appointed and suggested for this day. Preferences are put in **bold**. Not all choices are suitable for all congregations or community, though, so consider these preferences as a starting point before making a decision about your own congregation.

	Proper 16	Rite I	Rite II	EOW1	BOS 2022
Color	Green				
Entrance Rite	Customary; opening acclamation "Blessed be God" or one of the first two in EOW1	323	355	50	
Song of Praise/Kyrie	Gloria in excelsis or BCP Canticle 9, 19; EOW1 Canticle B, M	Gloria 324	Gloria 356; C9 – 86; C19 – 94	B – 30; M – 37	
Collect		181	232		
Creed	Nicene Creed	326, 327	358	53	
Prayers of the People	**Locally written**; options below; BCP forms	329	387–393	54–55	
Offertory Sentence	"Those who go through the desolate valley [will find it a place of springs, for the early rains have covered it with pools of water. They] will climb from height to height, and the God of gods will reveal himself in Zion." (Psalm 84)	343–344	376–377		
Eucharistic Prayer	**Summer – Rite I, suggest Prayer 1; Rite II, suggest Prayer C, if not used in the year already, otherwise A; EOW1 suggest Prayer 2.**	**1–333**	**C – 369** *or* **A – 361**	**2–60**	
Proper Preface	**The Lord's Day 3 – Of God the Holy Spirit**	344–345	377–378		
Breaking of the Bread (Fraction)	**S 168 – S 170;** S 167, S 171 in *The Hymnal 1982*; EOW1 options; Christ our Passover (BCP)	337	364	69	
Postcommunion Prayer		339	**Eternal God – 365**	**God of abundance – 69**	
Blessing	Customary	339	366	70–71	
Dismissal	**Let us go forth in the name of Christ**	339	366		
Notes	St. Bartholomew's Day may fall on or near this Sunday; back to school prayers?				

<u>*Additional Notes:*</u>

Song of Praise/Canticle – Summer is a good time to try additional canticles to see if there is a setting that the congregation would enjoy more often. Suggested here is a canticle for the summer from the BCP and an option from EOW1 (Canticle 9 and Canticle B) as well as one or two that reflects themes of the day. The Gloria, of course, is always appropriate in this season.

Eucharistic Prayer – Using a consistent option for the summer simplifies choices. In Rite II, if Prayer C hasn't been used in a prior season this year, summer is a good time to put it into use. Otherwise, Prayer A with the Lord's Day proper preface is sufficient. EOW1 Prayer 2 has creation imagery that may be desirable during the summertime.

Fraction Anthem at the Breaking of the Bread – In this "bread of life – bread of heaven" mini-season, there are some fraction anthems that may be very suitable, especially Hymn S 168, S 169, and S 170 (spoken or sung). You could also use S 167 or S 171, though they seem to have the Emmaus story as a primary reference. They could still be suitable, though. Two of the EOW1 options would be appropriate in these 'bread' weeks.

Content Resources

Reading Between the Lines

In John 6:56–69, Jesus' teaching in the synagogue at Capernaum continues, and he becomes aware of disciples' complaints and their implications; indeed, many turn back. So, Jesus asks, "What if you were to see the Son of Man ascending to where he was before? ... The words I have spoken to you are spirit and life. But there are some of you who do not believe." Hearing the word is crucial for faith, but people cannot hear the word unless they believe. Querying whether Peter will also depart, Peter replies, "Lord, to whom can we go? You have the words of eternal life." Simon Peters question in 6:68 indicates that words, (although they are not always reliable), when they are Jesus' words, can lead to people putting their trust or belief in Jesus. Jesus' words are human words, not unequivocally self-revelatory; they do not bring everyone to faith. Even Jesus' followers regularly fail to understand Jesus words ("this saying is hard; Who can accept it?" 6:60) but each time they do so, Jesus offers further teaching. But in John, Jesus knows and empowers disciples' teaching. In 17:20, Jesus' farewell discourse, Jesus' prayer is not only for the disciples but for those believing in him through their words.

Central Themes

A notion found in Hollywood films says you can judge a person by their shoes. Handmade leather shoes reflect affluence, while work boots indicate heavy labor work. Paul tells the Ephesians to wear shoes that "will make you ready to proclaim the gospel of peace." Vegans wear non-leather shoes to signify their peaceful respect for all living creatures. Some women avoid high heels to respect their bodily health. In addition to shoes, Paul said to "put on the whole armor of God," declaring the ultimate importance of adopting the truth and righteousness of God in our hearts and minds.

Many of us are removed from the production of our own food, only eating that which someone else has grown or made. That separation has allowed for brokenness in the food production process, abuse of creation, and exploitation of some farmers and producers. Jesus talks about the intimate relationship of abiding in one another through sharing bread. Food movements like Community Supported Agriculture (CSA), fair trade, community gardens, and imperfect food all speak to a need to reconnect with God's creation and those who produce our food.

The whole of this chapter has been difficult for some of its hearers to accept. As the chapter comes to a close, we learn that it is not simply Jesus's enemies who are affronted; some of his own disciples depart because it was too difficult; his words baffled and even scandalized. The end of the story is about disbelief. But it is also about faith. Peter and the Twelve may not yet grasp the truth of what he has claimed, but they believe him. And somehow, that is enough. The relationship is all, and the audacity of a faith beyond understanding. What does "this new community of love in Christ's communion bread" mean to you?

Engaging All Ages

As Jesus talks about the bread of life – again – some of his followers say, "This teaching is difficult; who can accept it?" Have you ever felt that a part of scripture or a part of our tradition is too difficult to accept? When we feel this way, it can seem like there is only one thing to do: walk away. But there is another option. Like the Twelve, we can continue to follow if we have come to believe that Jesus is the Holy One of God. That does not mean we never doubt. It means we are willing to struggle to understand more fully while remaining part of the community.

Prayers of the People: Option 1

Bless our questions and the stirring of our hearts. Grant us wonder and delight in your mystery.

We come before you, O God, saying

Bless us and keep us close.

We pray for your church, that we may be alert to your stirring, and aware of your presence. Guide and strengthen those in leadership: our bishops, priests, and deacons. Empower all who worship and serve in your church, in your name.

We come before you, O God, saying

Bless us and keep us close.

Our hearts ache for people around the world who live in poverty, hunger, and oppression. Keep us mindful of their needs, and move us to make a difference in their lives.

We come before you, O God, saying

Bless us and keep us close.

We are surrounded by people who are in pain, physically and spiritually. We pray that they are upheld by our prayers and come to know healing in their lives.

We come before you, O God, saying

Bless us and keep us close.

Some among us are dying, and some have passed into eternal life. We pray for those who mourn and ask that all may be assured of your unending presence and your promise of life eternal with your saints in light. We come before you, O God, saying

Bless us and keep us close.

Prayers of the People: Option 2

Deacon or Presider

As we proclaim the gospel of faith, let us pray in the Spirit for the desperate needs of all peoples.

Intercessor

For this holy gathering, for all those who lead our faith community, and for the people of God in every place.

Lord, have mercy.

For all nations and their leaders, and for mercy, justice, and peace in the world.

Lord, have mercy.

For for all students, teachers, and school staff, for all those who homeschool, and all those returning to their studies.

Lord, have mercy.

For abundant fruits of the earth, and for safety from violent storms.

Lord, have mercy.

For the sick and the suffering, travelers and those on vacation, prisoners, captives, and their families, and all those in danger and need.

Lord, have mercy.

For our city and those who live in it, and for our families, companions, and all we love.

Lord, have mercy.

For those who rest in Christ and for all the dead, we pray.

Lord, have mercy.

Lifting our voices with all creation, with the Blessed Virgin Mary and all the saints, let us offer ourselves and one another to the living God through Christ.

To you, O Lord, our God.

Presider

Blessed are you, God of Israel, whose words are spirit and life. Hear the prayers we offer this day and feed us with the bread of heaven; through Jesus Christ our Lord. ***Amen.***

Hymns for the Day

The Hymnal 1982

I come with joy to meet my Lord 304
Our Father, by whose Name 587
Praise the Lord, rise up rejoicing 334
Put forth, O God, thy Spirit's might 521
Thou, who at thy first Eucharist didst pray 315
How lovely is thy dwelling-place [Psalm 84] 517
I love thy kingdom, Lord 524
Only-begotten, Word of God eternal 360, 361
Spirit divine, attend our prayers 509
Ancient of Days, who sittest throned in glory 363
Guide me, O thou great Jehovah 690
Praise our great and gracious Lord 393
Sing praise to God who reigns above 408
Eternal Ruler of the ceaseless round 617
Go forward, Christian soldier 563
Soldiers of Christ, arise 548
Stand up, stand up, for Jesus 561
Alleluia! sing to Jesus! 460, 461
Blessed Jesus, at thy word 440
Bread of the world, in mercy broken 301
Help us, O Lord, to learn 628
I am the bread of life 335
I call on thee, Lord Jesus Christ 634
Lord, be thy word my rule 626
Lord, enthroned in heavenly splendor 307
O Christ, the Word Incarnate 632
Spread, O spread, thou mighty word 530
Word of God, come down on earth 633

Lift Every Voice and Sing II

I am the bread that came down from heaven 150

Wonder, Love, and Praise

Come now, O Prince of peace 795
Unidos/Together 796
Wisdom freed a holy people 905
From the dawning of creation 748
I am the bread of life 762
O wheat whose crushing was for bread 760

Preparing for the Season after Pentecost (Autumn)

Autumn Planning and Schedules

With the reopening of school, the actual planning year of most parishes begins. Like planning for other parish programs, liturgical planning for the fall must be done over the summer so that it is in place by Labor Day. If you wish to make changes in the schedule of services, the opening of school is a convenient time to do so. A reasonable planning procedure would be to plan September and October as a unit, seeking ways to bind the celebrations together so that they do not become unconnected and unending stretches of "green." The use of the lectionary in planning, the setting of seasonal themes for decoration of the church (such as fall flowers), a uniform treatment of the psalm between the readings (singing or reciting it responsorially as described on p. 582 of the Prayer Book, for example), and the use of an appropriate canticle (such as 13, "A Song of Praise" or 19, "The Song of the Redeemed") throughout the period in place of the Gloria in excelsis are all possible ways to draw the season together.

The month of November, from All Saints' Day to Christ the King, with the building Advent theme, can be a second unit, for which different choices are made. Look back at the Advent portion of this book for more information on these themes and options such as an expanded Advent, beginning on page 18.

Michaelmas

St. Michael and All Angels, or Michaelmas, on September 29, is the traditional beginning of the fall or Michaelmas term in England. It has a number of good hymns associated with it and may be seized upon as an occasion to plan something special for early fall. Some parishes will choose to bend the prayer book rubrics and celebrate Michaelmas on the last Sunday in September to begin things "in style" in the fall. Others will be content to use the collect at the Prayers of the People and sing one or two of the hymns. Most places will simply observe it on the weekday, celebrating or commemorating it at the Sunday eucharist only if September 29 actually is a Sunday.

All Saints' Day

All Saints' Day calls for a major parish celebration. It may be observed on the Sunday following *in addition to* its observance on the fixed date. While most parishes will wish to make their major observance on Sunday, the possibility of an evening service on November 1, with the opportunity to sing more of the All Saints' Day hymns, should not be overlooked. A parish dinner and evening program might make for a significant evening of prayer and good fellowship in the congregation. Some churches will take a cue from Halloween (which, of course, is rooted in All Saints' in any case) and invite parishioners to dress in costume as a particular saint.

All Saints' Day is one of the baptismal feasts, and an effort should be made to schedule baptisms for the Sunday eucharist (or the weekday service if that works better in your congregation). Notices in parish newsletters in the late summer and at the start of the program year should mention the time and date, urging those seeking baptism or those with children to be baptized to come forward. Occasions for the preparation of parents and godparents and the formation of adult candidates should be included in the fall schedule. If this custom is maintained year after year, people will begin to think in terms of All Saints' Day as a day for baptisms and to plan to invite family and friends for the occasion.

At those celebrations at which there are no baptisms, the Renewal of Baptismal Vows from the Easter Vigil (BCP, 292) can be included. A simple introduction explaining the baptismal significance of All Saints' Day and the relationship of baptism to our membership in the Church and the communion of saints would be appropriate.

All Souls' Day

The commemoration of All Faithful Departed, often called All Souls' Day, is November 2. The late John Heus, former rector of St. Matthew's, Evanston, and Trinity, New York, described All Souls' Day as the feast of the Christian democracy. All Saints' Day honors the heroes of the Church throughout the ages, while All Souls' Day remembers *all* of our fellow Christians who have gone before us. This distinction is most useful and avoids overtones of "purgatory." The Sunday celebration will almost necessarily include some recognition of all the faithful departed in the eucharist, and this should be well thought out in the planning. If prayers are going to be offered with a long list of those who are departed, that should take place whenever possible at the service for All Faithful Departed, rather than on All Saints' Day or the Sunday after All Saints' Day. Some parishes have planned a special event, such as evensong or the singing of a Requiem by the choir, for November 2nd, and incorporated the reading of the names of the departed into that service. Multiple voices, taking turns, can help with the reading of a long list as well.

Season after Pentecost (Autumn) – Major Feasts, Seasonal Rites, and Other Commemorations

Autumn Pledge Campaign: Stewardship Prayers

A Collect for Stewardship

God of abundance, who has planted us in this congregation and sustains us day by day, grow us in your grace, that we may become more fully the people you have called us to be; that we may flourish by your faith in us; and that we may accomplish your will with the gifts you have given us; through Jesus Christ our Redeemer. ***Amen.***

A Stewardship Litany[1]

God of life and love: We are quick to accept bounteous gifts from you, but slow to give thanks and to express our gratitude.

We hold too tightly the things of this life,
giving them the allegiance we owe only to you.

Take my life and let it be
consecrated, Lord, to thee.

Take my moments and my days;
let them flow in ceaseless praise,
let them flow in ceaseless praise.

Gracious God, we admit that our lives are too often out of balance; we are more willing to receive than to share, more ready to take than to give.

Create in us grateful and generous hearts, we pray,
and restore to us the joy of our salvation.

Take my hands and let them move
at the impulse of thy love.

Take my feet, and let them be
swift and beautiful for thee,
swift and beautiful for thee.

Merciful God, from whom comes every good and perfect gift, we praise you for your mercies:

your goodness that has created us,
your grace that has sustained us,

Your discipline that has corrected us, your patience that has borne with us,

and your love that has redeemed us.

Take my will, and make it thine;
it shall be no longer mine.

Take my heart, it is thine own;
it shall be thy royal throne,
it shall be thy royal throne.

Help us to love you, and to be thankful for all your gifts by serving you and delighting to do you will.

Accept now, Gracious God, our offerings,
these our pledges of resources and talents
for your service, and the commitment of our lives,
through Jesus Christ, who gave his all for us.

Take my silver and my gold,
not a mite would I withhold;
take my intellect, and use
every power a sthou shalt choose,
every power as thou shalt choose.

Take my love; my Lord, I pour
at thy feet its treasure store,
Take myself, and I will be
ever, only, all for thee,
ever, only, all for thee. Amen.

1 W. Alfred Tisdale Jr, "A Stewardship Litany," in *The Wideness of God's Mercy: Litanies to Enlarge Our Prayer,* edited by Jeffery W. Rowthorn (New York: Church Publishing, 2007), 124–125. Hymn stanzas by Frances Ridley Havergal; a shorter version is found as Hymn 707 "Take my life, and let it be," *The Hymnal 1982.*

First Monday in September, Labor Day *(on or between September 1–7)*

While this is a civil holiday that is not on the Episcopal Church Calendar, how we honor people's labor is important. Additionally, the BCP does provide a full set of propers, with the Collect for Labor Day provided on 210 and 261 and the lessons on page 932. The collect could be incorporated into the Prayers of the People on the Sunday prior to Labor Day or a service could be held that was focused solely on Labor Day.

BCP Collect for Labor Day

Almighty God, you have so linked our lives one with another that all we do affects, for good or ill, all other lives: So guide us in the work we do, that we may do it not for self alone, but for the common good; and, as we seek a proper return for our own labor, make us mindful of the rightful aspirations of other workers, and arouse our concern for those who are out of work; through Jesus Christ our Lord, who lives and reigns with you and the Holy Spirit, one God, for ever and ever. *Amen.*

Additional Prayer for Labor Day[2]

Lord God, our Creator. We deserve to labor among thorns and thistles, to eat by the sweat of our brow, to work without reward. For we confess we have spoiled your creation by our sin, we have marred your work by our neglect, we have hurt your work by our rebellion. We pray you, bless our labor by him who was once a carpenter, by him who came to be our servant, by him who saved us to serve. For his sake, keep us and all who labor from false dealing and unfair practice, from excessive profit and unjust gain, from slovenly service and irrational demands. Help us to labor with love, to labor with joy, to labor with faithfulness. Teach us that the best labor we give you is loving service to others. In Christ's name we ask it. *Amen.*

September 11, Remembering 9/11[3]

A prayer to be used in observances of the anniversary of September 11, 2001.

God the compassionate one, whose loving care extends to all the world, we remember this day your children of many nations and many faiths whose lives were cut short by the fierce flames of anger and hatred. Console those who continue to suffer and grieve, and give them comfort and hope as they look to the future. Out of what we have endured, give us the grace to examine our relationships with those who perceive us as the enemy, and show our leaders the way to use our power to serve the good of all for the healing of the nations. This we ask through Jesus Christ our Lord, who, in reconciling love, was lifted up from the earth that he might draw all things to himself. *Amen.*

September 14, Holy Cross Day

This is a Major Feast and Feast of Our Lord and may substitute for the Sunday after Pentecost when it falls on a Sunday. It falls on or during the weeks of Proper 18 or 19. The Collect for the Day is found on pages 192 or 244 of the BCP.

Supervision over the work of erecting a building complex in Jerusalem to mark the site of Christ's resurrection was entrusted to the Empress Helena, mother of Emperor Constantine. Under Helena's direction, the excavation discovered a relic, believed to be of the "true cross." Calvary stood outside the city in Jesus's time; when *Aelia Capitolina* succeeded Jerusalem, the hill was buried. Constantine's magnificent shrine included two main buildings: a basilica and a round church known as "The Resurrection." The buildings were dedicated on September 14, 335, the seventh month of the Roman calendar; the date was suggested by the account in 2 Corinthians of the dedication of Solomon's temple hundreds of years before.

September 21, International Day of Peace

A Litany for the International Day of Peace[4]

Remember, O Lord, the peoples of the world, divided into many nations and tongues. Deliver us from every evil that gets in the way of your saving purpose; and fulfill the promise of peace to your people on earth, through Jesus Christ our Lord. ***Amen.***

From the curse of war and the human sin that causes war;

O Lord, deliver us.

2 "The First Monday in September," in *An American Prayer Book*, edited by Christopher L. Webber (Harrisburg, PA: Morehouse Publishing, 2008), 148–149.

3 Frank W. Griswold, "Remembering September 11, 2001," from *An American Prayer Book*, edited by Christopher L. Webber (Harrisburg, PA: Morehouse Publishing, 2008), 113.

4 "World Peace," from *There's a Wideness in God's Mercy: Litanies to Enlarge Our Prayer*, edited by Jeffrey W. Rowthorn (New York: Church Publishing, 2007), 334–335.

From pride that turns its back on you, and from unbelief that will not call you Lord;

O Lord, deliver us.

From national vanity that poses as patriotism; from loud-mouthed boasting and blind self-worship that admit no guilt;

O Lord, deliver us.

For the self-righteous who will not compromise, and from selfishness that gains by the oppression of others;

O Lord, deliver us.

From trusting in the weapons of war, and mistrusting the councils of peace;

O Lord, deliver us.

From hearing, believing, and speaking lies about other nations;

O Lord, deliver us.

From groundless suspicions and fears that stand in the way of reconciliation;

O Lord, deliver us.

From words and deeds that encourage discord, prejudice, and hatred; from everything that prevents the human family from fulfilling your promise of peace;

O Lord, deliver us.

O God our Father: we pray for all your children on earth, of every nation and of every race, that they may be strong to do your will.

Silence

We pray for the Church in the world;

O Lord, give peace in our time.

For the United Nations;

O Lord, give peace in our time.

For international federations of labor, industry, and commerce;

O Lord, give peace in our time.

For departments of state, ambassadors, diplomats, and states persons;

O Lord, give peace in our time.

For worldwide agencies of compassion, which bind wounds and feed the hungry;

O Lord, give peace in our time.

For common folk in every land who live in peace;

O Lord, give peace in our time.

Eternal God: use us, even our ignorance and weakness, to bring about your holy will. Hurry the day when all people shall live together in your love; for yours is the kingdom, the power, and the glory forever. ***Amen.***

September 21 Saint Matthew, Apostle and Evangelist

This is a Major Feast and may substitute for the Sunday after Pentecost when it falls on a Sunday. It falls on or during the weeks of Proper 20 or 21. The Collect for the Day is found on pages 192 or 244 of the BCP.

A disciple of Jesus the Christ, Matthew left everything to follow the Master at his call. Matthew was identified with Levi, a tax collector, when tax collectors were seen as collaborators with the Roman State and, thus, spurned as traitors. Matthew was hardly the sort of person a devout Jew would associate with, yet Jesus noticed Matthew rather than someone else, such as a pious, proud, prayerful Pharisee. The disciple himself probably did not write the gospel of his name, instead named as author in homage. Through this gospel and its parables, Jesus speaks of faith and eternal life; of duty to neighbors, family, and enemies. Matthew is venerated as a martyr although circumstances of his death are unknown.

September 29, Saint Michael and All Angels

This is a Major Feast and may substitute for the Sunday after Pentecost when it falls on a Sunday. It falls on or during the weeks of Proper 18 or 19. The Collect for the Day is found on pages 193 or 244 of the BCP.

Christians have always felt attended by spiritual messengers, that is, angels: visible or not, human or not. These helpful spirits, powerful and enlightening, appear in Christian art in human form, their wings signifying swiftness and spaciousness, their swords attesting to their power, their dazzling raiment announcing their ability to enlighten. Many angels are mentioned in the Bible, but only four are named: Michael, Gabriel, Uriel, and Raphael. The archangel Michael, a powerful agent of God, wards off evil from God's people and delivers God's peace. Michaelmas has been celebrated in many parts of the world. Michael is patron saint of many churches, including Mont-St.-Michel off Normandy and Coventry Cathedral in England.

October 4, Saint Francis of Assisi, Friar, 1226

Though a Lesser Feast and not a Major Feast (and so cannot replace the Sunday propers when it falls on a Sunday), nonetheless, St. Francis is a very well known and popular saint. Additional information, including collect and lessons can be found in Lesser Feasts and Fasts 2022 on pages 450–451.

After a misspent youth as well as encounters with beggars and lepers, Francis embraced a life devoid of material goods. In 1210, Pope Innocent III confirmed The Rule for the Order of Friars Minor, the name chosen by Francis to underscore the "least" of God's servants. The order grew so large and lax that, by 1221, Francis had lost control of it. He remained joyful in his last years despite grievous suffering in body and spirit. Near his death, Frances received the *stigmata*, marks of Jesus's wounds, in his own hands and feet and side. Pope Gregory IX canonized Francis in 1228. Francis is admired for his bond with animals, if not imitated for voluntary poverty.

St. Francis' Day Blessing of Animals

The Book of Occasional Services 2022, *pages 126–140, offers extensive material for developing a service for Blessing of Animals, including readings, a Litany of Creation, and a service with the blessing for animals. Additional resources are also provided, allowing for adaptation. This service also includes an alternative Lord's Prayer that is more contemporary and inclusive than what has been available previously in authorized materials in the Episcopal Church.*

This material and the Rogation Days material represent some of the more recently developed creation care liturgical language for the Church.

Selections of the service are provided here; please see BOS 2022 for full information for preparing the liturgy.

Readings[5]

One or more readings selected from the following: Genesis 1:20–22a, 24–26a, 28,31a; Psalm 104:10–25, or **Psalm 104:24–25**, 27–28, 30–31;Wisdom 11:24–12:1; Job 12:7–10a; Matthew 6:25–26; Matthew 11:25–30; **Luke 12:22–32**; Canticle 12 portion (those in bold are the primary options listed; full text for each provided in BOS 2022)

5 BOS 2022, 134–137.

Litany for All Creation[6]

Presider

Call out the names of those animals for whom we care.
Call out the names of those animals who are no longer with us.

Silence

The Prayers may be led by a Deacon or other Leader.

Deacon Holy God, Creator of heaven and earth,
People ***Have mercy upon us.***

Deacon Holy and Mighty, Redeemer of the world,
People ***Have mercy upon us.***

Deacon Holy Immortal One, Sanctifier of the faithful,
People ***Have mercy upon us.***

Deacon Grant that all your creatures may serve you with thanksgiving;
People ***Pour out your blessing on earth, O God.***
or ***We beseech you to hear us, good Lord.***

Deacon Grant favorable weather, temperate rain, and fruitful seasons, providing food and drink for all your creatures;
People ***Pour out your blessing on earth, O God.***
or ***We beseech you to hear us, good Lord.***

Deacon Open our eyes to the wonder of creation, that we may see you in all your works;
People ***Pour out your blessing on earth, O God.***
or ***We beseech you to hear us, good Lord.***

Deacon Stir in us the desire to care for your creation;
People ***Pour out your blessing on earth, O God.***
or ***We beseech you to hear us, good Lord.***

Deacon Make us wise and faithful stewards of creation, caring for the earth, the waters, the air, and all that live therein;
People ***Pour out your blessing on earth, O God.***
or ***We beseech you to hear us, good Lord.***

Deacon Forgive us who waste and pollute your creation and strengthen us to restore what we have disregarded;
People ***Pour out your blessing on earth, O God.***
or ***We beseech you to hear us, good Lord.***

Deacon Look with compassion on those that are abused and mistreated, show us their dignity in your creation;
People ***Pour out your blessing on earth, O God.***
or ***We beseech you to hear us, good Lord.***

6 BOS 2022, 129.

Deacon Remember those creatures that have died yet remain dear to us that, that they may rejoice in your new creation;

People ***Pour out your blessing on earth, O God.***
or ***We beseech you to hear us, good Lord.***

Presider

Holy Immortal One: No sparrow falls without your knowing it; nothing dies but is remembered by you; nothing comes into being that you do not see. Give us courage and resolve to build up the common good, holding fast to the hope of a new creation in which all shall dwell eternally, through Jesus Christ, our Risen Savior. ***Amen.***

Alternative Lord's Prayer[7]

Holy One, our only Home,

hallowed be your name.

May your day dawn,

your will be done,

here as in heaven.

Feed us today,

and forgive us as we forgive each other.

Do not forsake us at the test,

but deliver us from evil.

For the glory, the power,

and the mercy are yours,

now and forever. Amen.

A Play for the Feast of St. Francis – St. Francis and the Wolf[8]

(As the play begins, all the actors, except the WOLF, gather in the chancel or in front of the congregation, if performing outside)

NARRATOR ONE: St. Francis loved God, and he loved everything God had created: the sun, moon and stars, trees, flowers, people . . . and animals. Francis *loved* animals.

NARRATOR TWO: Once, he preached to a flock of birds – and they listened!

NARRATOR ONE: Everywhere Francis went, he spoke about God's love and helped others to see and feel that love in the world around them.

NARRATOR TWO: And then one day, Francis came to the town of Gubbio, where the people hid in their houses and lived in fear.

FRANCIS: *(approaching a VILLAGER)* What is making you so afraid?

VILLAGER: There's a ravenous wolf on the prowl.

VILLAGER: He makes his meals on our sheep.

VILLAGER: Even our cows aren't safe from his attacks.

VILLAGER: Even our children aren't safe from his attacks!

FRANCIS: I will go and find this wolf, for it is God's will that people and animals should live together peacefully.

(He strides off, the villagers chasing after him.)

VILLAGER: Don't be so foolish!

VILLAGER: You don't know what he will do to you!

NARRATOR ONE: The villagers protested. But Francis didn't listen. He walked to the edge of the woods and followed the wolf's tracks.

NARRATOR TWO: The tracks ended, and out jumped the snarling, beady-eyed wolf! *(The WOLF jumps out!)*

FRANCIS: *(making the sign of the cross before the WOLF)* Brother Wolf! Do you know what you have done? You have terrorized a village! Have you no shame?

NARRATOR ONE: After these words, the wolf stopped.

(The WOLF bows his head in sadness. FRANCIS pats his head, and rubs his ears.)

FRANCIS: I know you have acted out of hunger, my brother. Please promise never to harm any of God's creatures. I will tell the villagers to feed you as long as you never hurt them or their animals again.

NARRATOR TWO: The wolf followed Francis back to the town square.

(The VILLAGERS gather around FRANCIS and the WOLF. The WOLF places his paw in FRANCIS' hand)

VILLAGERS: *(cheering)* Hooray! Francis has tamed the hungry wolf!

(The VILLAGERS now surround the WOLF, patting him and playing with him)

NARRATOR ONE: After that, the wolf went from door to door in Gubbio, and the townspeople fed him well, breakfast and dinner every day.

NARRATOR TWO: When, after two years, the old wolf died, the villagers wept with sorrow.

7 Martha Blacklock, Mother Thunder Mission, BOS 2022, 133.
8 Wendy Claire Barrie, "St. Francis and the Wolf," (New York: Church Publishing, 2011) is part of *Skiturgies: Pageants, Plays, Rites, and Rituals.*

NARRATOR ONE: Gubbio was, for that brief time, like God's Peaceable Kingdom.

FRANCIS: As the prophet Isaiah foretold, the wolf shall live with the lamb,

NARRATOR TWO: the leopard shall lie down with the kid,

FRANCIS: the calf and the lion and the fatling together,

YOUNGEST VILLAGER: and a little child shall lead them.

VILLAGERS: The cow and the bear shall graze, their young shall lie down together; and the lion shall eat straw like the ox.

They will not hurt or destroy on all God's holy mountain;
for the earth will be full of the knowledge of the Lord
as the waters cover the sea.

FRANCIS: Amen, and amen!

Second Monday in October, Indigenous Peoples' Day, *(on or between October 8–14)*

A Native American Thanksgiving for the Americas and Their People[9]

For our ancestors, who built nations and cultures; who thrived and prospered long before the coming of strangers; for the forfeit of their lives, their homes, their lands, and their freedoms, sacrificed to the rise of new nations and new worlds.

We offer a song of honor and thanks.

For the wealth of our lands; for minerals in the earth; for the plants and waters and animals on the earth; for the birds, the clouds and rain, for the sun and moon in the sky and the gifts they gave to our people that enabled the rise of new world economics.

We offer a song of honor and thanks.

For the many foods coaxed from the heart of Mother Earth; for the skills we were given to develop foods that now belong to the world: potatoes, corn, beans, squash, peanuts, tomatoes, peppers, coffee, cocoa, sugar, and many, many more.

We offer a song of honor and thanks.

For the medicines first discovered by our ancestors and now known to the world: quinine, ipecac, iodine, curare, petroleum jelly, witch hazel, and others; for the healing skills of our people and those how now care for us.
For tobacco, sage, sweet grass, and cedar that give spiritual healing by the power of their meaning.

We offer a song of honor and thanks.

For oceans, streams, rivers, lakes, and other waters of our lands that provide bountifully for us; for clams, lobsters, salmon, trout, shrimp, and abalone; for the pathways the waters provide.

We offer a song of honor and thanks.

For the friendship that first welcomed all to our shores; for the courage of those who watched their worlds change and disappear and for those who led in the search for new lives; for our leaders today who fight with courage and great heart for us.

We offer a song of honor and praise.

For the friends who suffered with us and stand with us today to help bring the promise and the hope that the New World meant to their ancestors.

We offer a song of honor and thanks.

For the strength and beauty of our diverse Native cultures; for the traditions that give structure to our lives, that define who we are; for the skills of our artists and craftspeople and the gifts of their hands.

We offer a song of honor and thanks.

For the spiritualty and vision that gave our people the courage and faith to endure and that brought many to an understanding and acceptance of the love of Christ, our Brother and Savior.

We offer a song of honor and thanks.

Accept, O God, Creator, our honor song, and make our hearts thankful for what we have been given. Make us humble for what we have taken. Make us glad as we return some measure of what we have been given. Strengthen our faith and make us strong in the service of our people, in the name of our Brother and Savior, Jesus Christ, your Son, in the power of the Holy Spirit. ***Amen.***

9 "1492–1992: A Celebration of Native American Survival. Earth and All the Stars" in *There's a Wideness in God's Mercy: Litanies to Enlarge Our Prayer,* edited by Jeffrey W. Rowthorn (New York: Church Publishing, 2007), 298–299. This litany was prepared for use at a service commemorating the quincentenary of the landing of Christopher Columbus in 1492 with its fateful impact on the Native American peoples, who despite all have survived to the day. The service was held on October 12, 1992 in the National Cathedral in Washington, D.C.

October 18, Saint Luke the Evangelist

This is a Major Feast and may substitute for the Sunday after Pentecost when it falls on a Sunday. It falls on or during the weeks of Proper 23 or 24. The Collect for the Day is found on pages 193 or 244 of the BCP.

Luke's Gospel serves not as a biography but as a history of salvation. Luke did not know Jesus, but he was inspired by those who had. He wrote the book that honors the name of the disciple and its sequel, the Acts of the Apostles. Luke wrote in Greek, allowing Gentiles to read his stories. Only Luke presents the familiar stories of the annunciation to Mary, of her visit to Elizabeth, of the child in the manger, and the angelic host's appearing to shepherds. He cites six miracles and eighteen parables not recorded by the other evangelists. In Acts, Luke tells of the coming of the Holy Spirit and the challenges faced by the apostles and the early church.

Third Weekend in October, A Children's Sabbath[10]

Variable – could occur between October 15 and 21

A Litany for Children's Sabbath[11]

Tortured by hunger and thirst, ravaged by disease and pollution;

Save all your children, Lord.

Savaged by the brutalities of war, victimized by violence and abuse

Save all your children, Lord.

Broken by exploitative child labor, stunted by suffering;

Save your children, Lord.

Thwarted by prejudice, deprived of beauty, joy, and laughter;

Save your children, Lord.

Uprooted by famine, war, and disaster, burdened by the debts of preceding generations;

Protect all our children, Lord.

Aged before they could be young, denied freedom, justice, and peace;

Protect all our children, Lord.

Nurtured and guided with love and understanding, provided with food and clothing and shelter;

Care for all your children, Lord.

Enriched by a safe and clean environment, empowered by education and opportunity;

Care for all your children, Lord.

Welcome and honored in our midst, brought to know and to love you as their Savior;

Care for all your children, Lord. Amen.

October 23, Saint James of Jerusalem, Brother of Our Lord Jesus Christ, and Martyr,

This is a Major Feast and may substitute for the Sunday after Pentecost when it falls on a Sunday. It falls on or during the weeks of Proper 24 or 25. The Collect for the Day is found on pages 193 or 245 of the BCP.

Saint James of Jerusalem is called the Lord's brother in the Gospel According to Matthew and the Epistle to the Galatians. However, other writers, following Mark's path, thought James was Jesus's cousin; certain apocryphal writings name him as Joseph's son by his first wife. After Jesus's resurrection, James was converted and eventually became Bishop of Jerusalem. Paul's first letter to the Corinthians notes that James beheld a special appearance of the Lord before the ascension; later, James was cordial to Paul at Jerusalem. At the Council of Jerusalem, it was James who would impose "no irksome restrictions" (circumcision) on Gentiles turning to God. His success at converting many to Jesus perturbed factions in Jerusalem, so he was cudgeled to death.

October 28, Saint Simon and Saint Jude, Apostles

This is a Major Feast and may substitute for the Sunday after Pentecost when it falls on a Sunday. It falls on or during the weeks of Proper 24 or 25. The Collect for the Day is found on pages 194 or 245 of the BCP.

Little is known of either Simon or Jude. The Gospels name Simon as one of the disciples, the "Zealot," but that adjective

---

10 More information and resources on A Children's Sabbath found a https://www.childrensdefense.org/childrens-sabbath-celebration/, accessed March 31, 2023.

11 Mary Ford-Grabowsky,"For Children at Risk," in *The Wideness of God's Mercy: Litanies to Enlarge Our Prayers,* edited by Jeffrey W. Rowthorn (New York: Church Publishing, 2007), 356.

may refer to his enthusiasm as much as to his membership in the "Zelotes" faction. John mentions him as being at the Last Supper. The Epistle of Jude, which may have been written by the disciple Jude, is mentioned by John as brother to James the Greater. By tradition, the two are associated with Persia; some stories characterize them as martyrs. Jude may be confused with another Thaddeus because of Jude's surname; still, he is prayed to as the patron of Lost Causes. More questions than answers ensnare these two.

October 31, All Hallows' Eve

Service for All Hallows' Eve[12]

All Hallows' Eve, which later became known as Halloween, is celebrated the night before All Saints' Day, November 1. The service begins in partial darkness with the Service of Light (Order of Worship for the Evening, page 109 of the prayer book), as follows:

Light and peace, in Jesus Christ our Lord.

Thanks be to God.

If I say, "Surely the darkness will cover me, and the light around me turn to night," darkness is not dark to you, O Lord; the night is as bright as the day; darkness and light to you are both alike. (Psalm 139:10–11)

Let us pray. Lord Christ, your saints have been the lights of the world in every generation: Grant that we, who follow in their footsteps, may be made worthy to enter with them into that heavenly country where you live and reign for ever and ever. ***Amen.***

Candles are now lighted. Then the Phos hilaron is said or sung:

O gracious Light,
Pure brightness of the everliving Father in heaven,
O Jesus Christ, holy and blessed!
Now as we come to the setting of the sun,
And our eyes behold the vesper light,
We sing your praises, O God:
Father, Son, and Holy Spirit.
You are worthy at all times
to be praised by happy voices,
O Son of God, O Giver of life,
And to be glorified through all the worlds.

Glory to the Father, and to the Son, and to the Holy Spirit;
as it was in the beginning, is now,
and will be for ever. Amen.

12 BOS 2022, 141–143.

The service continues with two or more lessons, each followed by a Psalm, Canticle, or hymn and a Prayer.

The Witch of Endor (1 Samuel 28:3–25)

It is appropriate that this lesson be read by a narrator, and by other readers for Saul, the witch, and Samuel.

Psalm 130

Let us pray. *(Silence)*

Almighty and everliving God, you have made all things in your wisdom and established the boundaries of life and death: Grant that we may obey your voice in this world, and in the world to come may enjoy that rest and peace which you have appointed for your people; through Jesus Christ who is Resurrection and Life, and who lives and reigns for ever and ever. ***Amen.***

The Vision of Eliphaz the Temanite (Job 4:12–21)

Psalm 13, or Psalm 108:1–6

Let us pray. *(Silence)*

You, O Lord, have made us from the dust of the earth and to dust our bodies shall return; yet you have also breathed your Spirit upon us and called us to new life in you: Have mercy upon us, now and at the hour of our death; through Jesus Christ, our mediator and advocate. ***Amen.***

The Valley of Dry Bones (Ezekiel 37:1–14)

Psalm 143:1–11

Let us pray. *(Silence)*

O God, you have called your people to your service from age to age. Do not give us over to death, but raise us up to serve you, to praise you, and to glorify your holy Name; through Jesus Christ our Lord. ***Amen.***

The War in Heaven (Revelation 12:(1–6)7–12)

Psalm 103:17–22, or Canticle 1 (parts I & IV)
or Canticle 12 (Invocation, Part III, Doxology)

Let us pray. *(Silence)*

O most merciful and mighty God, your son Jesus Christ was born of the Blessed Virgin Mary to bring us salvation and to establish your kingdom on earth: Grant that Michael and all your angels may defend your people against Satan and every evil foe, and that at the last we may come to that heavenly country where your saints for ever sing your praise; through Jesus Christ our Lord. ***Amen.***

A homily, sermon, or instruction may follow the Readings.

The service then concludes with the singing of Te Deum laudamus or some other song of praise, the Lord's Prayer, the Collect of All Saints' Day, and a blessing or dismissal.

November 1 and 2, *El Dia de los Muertos*: Day of the Dead[13]

Christians in parts of Mexico and Central America keep All Saints' Day (November 1) and All Souls' Day, (November 2) with special devotions to honor the dead and pray for them. These devotions have spread beyond their geographical origins in Mexico into other languages and cultures. For those who are observing this tradition for the first time, adapt it to your own needs and consider engaging in conversation with communities or individuals that have experience with this tradition.

Communities who observe *El Dia de Muertos* should consider the following principles:

1. Practices for keeping the Day include adornment of an altar or a sacred space to offer reverence for the dead, which may be placed in a home, church, or cemetery. Photographs of those being remembered are traditionally displayed. A place for prayer may be provided nearby.
2. Devotions may include prayers and thanksgivings for the dead. Resources for prayer may be found in the burial rites or the propers for All Saints' Day and All Souls' Day.

Seasonal Blessings[14]

The following blessings may be used by a bishop or priest whenever a blessing is appropriate for the following season and noted Sundays.

All Saints' Day

May Almighty God, to whose glory we celebrate this festival of all the Saints, be now and evermore your guide and companion in the way. *Amen.*

May God, who has bound us together in the company of the elect, in this age and the age to come, attend to the prayers of his faithful servants on your behalf, as he hears your prayers for them. *Amen.*

May God, who has given us, in the lives of his saints, patterns of holy living and victorious dying, strengthen your faith and devotion, and enable you to bear witness to the truth against all adversity. *Amen.*

And the blessing of God Almighty, the Father, the Son, and the Holy Spirit, be upon you and remain with you for ever. *Amen.*

The preceding blessing may be adapted for use at a Patronal Festival.

or this

May God give you grace to follow his saints in faith and hope and love; and the blessing of God Almighty, the Father, the Son, and the Holy Spirit, be among you, and remain with you always. *Amen.*

November 2, Commemoration of All Faithful Departed

Though a Lesser Feast and not a Major Feast (and so cannot replace the Sunday propers when it falls on a Sunday), this is an important commemoration for many. Additional information, including collect and lessons can be found in Lesser Feasts and Fasts 2022 on pages 490–491.

The New Testament uses the word "saints" to describe all members of the Christian community; in the Collect for All Saints' Day, the word "elect" is used similarly. From very early times, however, the word "saint" was applied primarily to people of heroic sanctity, their deeds recalled gratefully by succeeding generations. Beginning in the tenth century, the custom began to set aside another day on which the Church recognized the whole body of the faithful, unknown to the wide fellowship of the Church, a day to remember family and friends who have died. During the Reformation, observance of this day was abolished, but Episcopalians, redefining its meaning, include it as optional observance on their calendar.

Tuesday after the first Monday in November, Election Day *(on or between November 2–8)*

For an Election[15]

Almighty God, to whom we must account for all our powers and privileges: Guide the people of the United States (*or* of this community) in the election of officials and representatives; that, by faithful administration and wise laws, the rights of all may be protected and our nation be enabled to fulfill your purposes; through Jesus Christ our Lord. *Amen.*

13 BOS 2022, 144.
14 BOS 2022, 17.
15 BCP, 822.

Before an Election[16]

Holy God, throughout the ages you have called men and women to serve you in various ways, giving them gifts for the task to which they were called and strengthening and guiding them in the fulfillment of their calling; in this free land, you share with us that great responsibility and enable us to choose those who will serve you in positions of leadership in various offices of government.

Help us in so choosing to seek those who have an understanding of your will for us, a commitment to justice, a concern for those in greatest need, a love of truth and a deep humility before you; Send your Spirit among us that we may be guided in the choices we make that your will may be done on earth as it is in heaven. *Amen.*

A Prayer for an Election[17]

Sovereign Lord, foolish we are, believing that we can rule ourselves by selecting this or that person to rule over us. We are at it again. Help us not to think it more significant than it is, but also give us and those we elect enough wisdom to acknowledge our follies. Help us laugh at ourselves, for without humor our politics cannot be humane. We desire to dominate and thus are dominated. Free us, dear Lord, for otherwise we perish. *Amen.*

Fourth Thursday in November, Thanksgiving Day,
(on or between November 22 and 28)

This is one of two United States holidays on the church calendar, along with Independence Day. It is listed as a Major Feast, but is always on Thursday, so will not ever substitute for a Sunday after Pentecost. It falls during Proper 28 or Proper 29. The Collect for the Day is found on pages 194 or 246 of the BCP.

Thanksgiving Day is an American national holiday that is appropriately observed by a service of thanksgiving in church. The Eucharist is the traditional Christian service of thanksgiving. *The Book of Common Prayer* includes propers for the Eucharist and the daily offices for this day. Since it will always occur in the two weeks before the First Sunday in Advent, it can be a regular part of your seasonal planning. The theme of thanksgiving can be blended with the seasonal themes, remembering that we give thanks "above all for [God's] immeasurable love in the redemption of the world by our Lord Jesus Christ" (BCP 125). A Litany of Thanksgiving (BCP 836) may be used in place of the Prayers of the People at the Eucharist. Decoration of the church with harvest fruits and fall flowers and the singing of familiar Thanksgiving Day hymns are important to most worshipers and should figure in the planning. Using home-baked bread and local wine, even if you do not usually do so, can help people make the connection between the Lord's Table and the Thanksgiving dinner table.

A Litany of Thanksgiving[18]

Let us give thanks to God our Father for all his gifts so freely bestowed upon us.

For the beauty and wonder of your creation, in earth and sky and sea,

We thank you, Lord.

For all that is gracious in the lives of men and women, revealing the image of Christ,

We thank you, Lord.

For our daily food and drink, our homes and families, and our friends,

We thank you, Lord.

For minds to think, and hearts to love, and hands to serve,

We thank you, Lord.

For health and strength to work, and leisure to rest and play,

We thank you, Lord.

For the brave and courageous, who are patient in suffering and faithful in adversity,

We thank you, Lord.

For all valiant seekers after truth, liberty, and justice,

We thank you, Lord.

For the communion of saints, in all times and places,

We thank you, Lord.

Above all, we give you thanks for the great mercies and promises given to us in Christ Jesus our Lord;

To him be praise and glory, with you, O Father, and the Holy Spirit, now and for ever. Amen.

---

16 Christopher L. Webber, "Before an Election," by Christopher L. Webber in *An American Prayer Book*, edited by Christopher L. Webber (Harrisburg, PA: Morehouse Publishing, 2008), 150.

17 Stanley Hauerwas, "A Prayer for an Election" quoted by Christopher L. Webber in *An American Prayer Book*, 150.

18 BCP, 836.

Thanksgiving Hymn Suggestions

The Hymnal 1982

All people that on earth do dwell 377, 378
As those of old their first fruits brought 705
Come, ye thankful people, come 290
For the beauty of the earth 416
From all that dwell below the skies 380
Glory, love, and praise, and honor 300
Now thank we all our God 396, 397
Praise to God, immortal praise 288
We gather together to ask the Lord's blessing 433
We plow the fields, and scatter 291
When all thy mercies, O my God 415
For the fruit of all creation 424
I sing the almighty power of God 398
Let us, with a gladsome mind 389
O all ye works of God, now come 428
Seek ye first the kingdom of God 711
Sometimes a light surprises 667
Holy Father, great Creator 368
To God with gladness sing 399
By gracious powers so wonderfully sheltered 695, 696
Commit thou all that grieves thee 669
Jesus, all my gladness 701
Joyful, joyful, we adore thee 376

Lift Every Voice and Sing II

Give thanks to the Lord for he is good 93
God is so good 214

Wonder, Love, and Praise

Let all creation bless the Lord 885
O all ye works of God, now come 884

November 30, St. Andrew the Apostle

St. Andrew's feast day is a Major Feast on the Episcopal Church Calendar and the propers for the day are found in the BCP. As it always falls after the Last Sunday after Pentecost or after Advent I, it is not permissible to substitute it for a Sunday even when it falls on a Sunday. The Collect for the Day is found on pages 185 or 237 of the BCP.

The first-called of the Apostles, in most accounts, and identified as the brother of Simon Peter. Andrew is included in every naming of the disciples in the Gospels and features prominently in the narrative of the feeding of the multitudes. According to tradition, Andrew may have traveled to Scythia, Romania, Georgia, and the southern border of what is today Ukraine. He is the patron saint of Russia, Ukraine, and Scotland (where his relics where purported to have eventually landed). Tradition also narrates that he was crucified on a saltire or x-shaped cross.

Proper 17

August 28 and September 3

Put the love of God and neighbor above empty practices.

Anchor Points – The Propers and the Season

The fixed points for each service are the appointed or proper readings and collect as well as the themes of the day or season.

Readings and Psalm

Song of Solomon 2:8–13

This love song, attributed to King Solomon, describes the passionate love of a man and a woman and their yearning for union. But since it is included in the Bible, the lyrical poetry of their relationship also describes God's passionate love for the people of the covenant and for us. In today's reading, amidst the vibrant springtime imagery, the woman anticipates the excitement of meeting with her beloved and pictures his approach until she can hear his voice inviting her to fly away with him.

Psalm 45:1–2, 7–10

A poem for a royal wedding celebrating the ruler's majesty.

or

Deuteronomy 4:1–2, 6–9

Chapters 1–4 of the book of Deuteronomy outline God's care for God's people in the wilderness as the basis for obedience to the legal code set forth. Adherence to the law gives security and prosperity in the promised land. Disobedience to God's law forfeits the blessing. God's word is not to be altered by addition or subtraction, a common warning in ancient legal codes, although the "statues and ordinances" (v. 1) were later codified into 613 specific commandments.

Psalm 15

This psalm presents a brief entrance rite for someone desiring to enter the temple for worship.

James 1:17–27

The author addresses those who have been given "birth by the word of truth" (v. 18) – a phrase that could be used equally of humankind as the first fruit of the creation and of Christians as the first fruits of redeemed humanity. This implanted word brings salvation, but one must do it as well as hear it.

Mark 7:1–8, 14–15, 21–23

In the gospel passage, Jesus denounces those who find ways to ignore the genuine commandments of God, and he calls people to the awareness that the only evil which can corrupt a person comes from within. His judgments are occasioned by an accusation against his disciples that they are not following the rules of ritual cleansing. On one level, Jesus's words warn against the human tendency to fashion traditions that become more important than the law itself. More significantly still, his teaching points to the dangers involved in making legalism the basis for one's life.

Collect

Lord of all power and might, the author and giver of all good things: Graft in our hearts the love of your Name; increase in us true religion; nourish us with all goodness; and bring forth in us the fruit of good works; through Jesus Christ our Lord, who lives and reigns with you and the Holy Spirit, one God for ever and ever. *Amen.*

Proper Preface

Of the Lord's Day

1. Of God the Father

For you are the source of light and life; you made us in your image, and called us to new life in Jesus Christ our Lord.

or this

2. Of God the Son

Through Jesus Christ our Lord; who on the first day of the week overcame death and the grave, and by his glorious resurrection opened to us the way of everlasting life.

or the following

3. Of God the Holy Spirit

For by water and the Holy Spirit you have made us a new people in Jesus Christ our Lord, to show forth your glory in all the world.

(Rite II, BCP 377–378; Rite I, BCP 344–345)

Seasonal Pairings

See the table below for choices appointed and suggested for this day. Preferences are put in **bold**. Not all choices are suitable for all congregations or community, though, so consider these preferences as a starting point before making a decision about your own congregation.

	Proper 17	Rite I	Rite II	EOW1	BOS 2022
Color	Green				
Entrance Rite	Customary; opening acclamation "Blessed be God" or one of the first two in EOW1	323	355	50	
Song of Praise/Kyrie	Gloria in excelsis or BCP Canticle 13; EOW1 Canticle A, G	Gloria 324	Gloria 356; C13– 90	A – 30; G – 34	
Collect		181	233		
Creed	Nicene Creed	326, 327	358	53	
Prayers of the People	**Locally written**; options below; BCP forms	329	387–393	54–55	
Offertory Sentence	"Be doers of the word, and not merely hearers who deceive themselves." (James)	343–344	376–377		
Eucharistic Prayer	**Sept-Oct – Rite I, suggest Prayer 2; Rite II, suggest Prayer B, if A was used in the summer; EOW1 suggest Prayer 3.**	**2–340**	**B – 367**	**3–62**	
Proper Preface	**The Lord's Day 3 – Of God the Holy Spirit**	344–345	377–378		
Breaking of the Bread (Fraction)	Christ our Passover (BCP); S 167 – S 172 in *The Hymnal 1982*; EOW1 options	337	364	69	
Postcommunion Prayer		339	**Almighty and everliving God – 366**	**Loving God – 70**	
Blessing	Customary	339	366	70–71	
Dismissal	**Go in peace to love and serve the Lord**	340	366		
Notes	Labor Day may fall after this Sunday; back to school prayers?				

Additional Notes:

Song of Praise/Canticle – Suggested here is a canticle for the autumn from the BCP and an option from EOW1 (Canticle 13 and Canticle A) as well as one or two that reflects themes of the day. The Gloria, of course, is always appropriate in this season.

Eucharistic Prayer – Using a consistent option for September and October will help tie these week together, especially since some will be returning to worship after a time away.

Content Resources

Reading Between the Lines

Song of Solomon 2:8–13; Mark 7

Rabbi Akiva, contemporary of Jesus; leading first century scholar and sage, founder of a significant school of Rabbinic interpretation, says of the Song of Solomon (or: Song of Songs):

"All the Scriptures are holy, but the *Song of Songs*, is the Holy of Holies." Rabbi Akiva uses the same word that describes the "Holy of Holies," the holiest place in the Temple. His point, here made after the destruction of the Temple, may be taken literally. He says, "Though the visible Temple be destroyed, through the medium of the *Song of Songs*, it is still possible for those who pray to enter the (Holy of Holies), namely, the presence of 'the King'."

Origen, almost a contemporary of Rabbi Akiva, and who was the most influential interpreter of the *Song of Songs* in Christian tradition, reads it as a mystical text.

Origen understands the words, "My beloved answers and says to me, 'Arise and come away, my love, my fair one, my dove; for lo! the winter is passed, the rain is over and gone'" to explain the new life that will flourish in the soul after the "Winter" of tribulation has been endured. In fact,

Origen wrote that explanation of our lectionary passage today to encourage early Christian martyrs to remain faithful to Christ as they faced martyrdom. When the heart, he says, has been wounded with love for Christ, it is willing - eager, even - to endure the wounds of martyrdom. Now what Origen has to say about *eros* and martyrdom wasn't just hypothetical. In his childhood, his father died a martyr, as did he. Origen wrote commentaries on the *Song of Songs* identifying the speaker or bridegroom in the text as the voice of the Savior. As we hear the text or voice of the Savior, he says, "the hearer knows themselves truly to be the Bride" (that is, the spouse of Christ, the Church, and the soul of the Bridegroom who is both Solomon and at the same time the Savior.)" (Christopher King, *Origen on the Song of Songs as the Spirit of Scripture*, 13–15).

Mark 7:1–8, 14–15, 21–23 has at its core Jesus' answer to the question of why his disciples ate with unwashed hands, thus violating Pharisaic teaching. It is not what goes into the body that defiles it, but rather what comes out of it. Jesus' argument joins a wider discourse about the nature of Torah observance. Pharisees passed on to the people oral traditions like handwashing handed down by previous generations and not recorded in the law of Moses. These traditions, the Pharisees believed, enabled them to keep the law correctly. Jesus argues instead that sources of defilement come from within a person, and this is what defiles.

Central Themes

A walk in the park. Walk the dog. Golf – a walk spoiled. Bucket list – walking the Camino de Santiago. There are as many memes about walking as there are types of walks for causes like 5Ks for disease cures and civil rights marches. Walking for causes gets us into the streets to advocate for victims, funding, and justice. "Walk the talk" are three words that summarize this week's New Testament lesson. James says, "Be doers of the word, and not merely hearers." Unless we take action on God's commandment to love one another, we are merely "hearers who deceive themselves."

One of the best-known songs from the musical *Rent* is "Seasons of Love." The singers wonder how we should measure time: in sunsets, cups of coffee, what we learn, or bridges we burn? As the song ends, the listeners are encouraged to measure time by the love that they shared. In the Song of Solomon, which sometimes feels out of place in the biblical canon, we find a celebration of love and attraction between two people. How does its celebration of love inspire our sense of the world around us?

The narrator must explain about washing of hands and objects used because some of Mark's audience did not know the customs, indicating that they were probably Gentiles. In fact, though some segments of the Jewish population of the time did adhere consistently with the strictures, others did not. Sometimes, we expect that visitors to our communities understand how we worship and conduct the other business of church, but they would not know unless we tell them. Mark is inviting us to practice hospitality here. Joining a new community can be daunting and regular members intimidating. How do we invite others, newcomers and occasional visitors, to join us in welcoming, nonjudgmental ways?

Engaging All Ages

We have family traditions, school traditions, and church traditions. What traditions do you hold dear? Maybe it's eating a special food on Christmas morning, running a yearly 5K, or the annual family beach trip. What happens when something interrupts tradition? A family member develops a food allergy, a friend breaks a leg, a work schedule prevents travel? Traditions matter, but Jesus reminds us that loving God and loving our neighbor is even more important than tradition. Our traditions must be flexible so that we do not "abandon the commandment of God" in order to uphold tradition.

Prayers of the People: Option 1

Open our eyes to see that all we are and all we have comes from you, O God. We ask you now to increase in us a spirit of generosity and holy imagination.

Open our lips with your praise as we gather as the body of Christ. Keep the leaders of our faith communities deeply connected to you that you may guide their course as we journey together. We pray for our bishops, our priests and deacons, and all who support the work you have given us to do.

Silence

Open the hearts of the leaders of the world. Give them courage to work for a better future for their people, which reflects justice, kindness, and connection with each other. Open the path to peace in the world.

Silence

Open the hands of your people to reach out in love to those around the world who are in fear for their lives, who face violent weather, whose daily lives are made difficult by their circumstances. May your love be made manifest through us.

Silence

Open a path to wholeness for those who live in fear of any kind, who have lost their way, whose spirits are restless, whose bodies are hurting. We pray for healing for *N.*

Silence

Open your arms to embrace those who have recently died, especially *N.* Grant them entrance to your eternal kingdom, where there is no pain or grief.

Prayers of the People: Option 2

Deacon or Presider

Let us pray for the Church and the world, saying "Lord, hear our prayer."

Intercessor

We thank you, O God, for your love for us and for your presence with us always. May your light shine through us and bring your love to all people.

Lord, hear our prayer.

We pray for the nations of the world torn apart by strife. Help us know how to be channels of peace in your kingdom on earth.

Lord, hear our prayer.

Lead us to be doers of your Word and not hearers only, that we may do your will, in large and small ways, especially within our own communities.

Lord, hear our prayer.

We give thanks for the gift of labor and pray for full and just employment for all. Give us compassionate hearts and a willingness to stand with those who suffer or are in any trouble.

Lord, hear our prayer.

Have mercy on those who are no longer with us. Grant that, following the example of all your saints, we may truly believe and share our relationship with you with others.

Lord, hear our prayer.

We pray for all those who follow Christ. We pray for *N.* our Presiding Bishop, for our own bishops and our parish clergy, for all the holy people of God. Make us humble and obedient servants like your Son Jesus Christ.

Lord, hear our prayer.

We pray for any other concerns or thanksgivings, silently or aloud. *Silence*

Presider

O God, who created all peoples in your image, we thank you for the wonderful diversity of races and cultures in this world. Enrich our lives by ever-widening circles of fellowship, and show us your presence in those who differ most from us, until our knowledge of your love is made perfect in our love for all your children; through Jesus Christ our Lord. ***Amen.***

Hymns for the Day

The Hymnal 1982

Lord, dismiss us with thy blessing 344
Come away to the skies 213 (SC)
God, my King, thy might confessing 414 (GR)
Help us, O Lord, to learn 628 (GR)
Lord, be thy word my rule 626 (GR)
Praise to the living God! 372 (GR)
Surely it is God who saves me 678, 679 (GR)
Immortal, invisible, God only wise 423
Lord, whose love through humble service 610
O Master, let me walk with thee 659, 660
We plow the fields, and scatter 291
Before thy throne, O God, we kneel 574, 575
Blest are the pure in heart 656
God be in my head, and in my understanding 694
Lift up your heads, ye mighty gates 436
Lord Jesus, think on me 641
Rejoice, ye pure in heart! 556, 557
Take my life, and let it be 707

Lift Every Voice and Sing II

Give me a clean heart so I may serve Thee 124
Lord, I want to be a Christian 138

Wonder, Love, and Praise

Gracious Spirit, give your servants 782
The church of Christ in every age 779
We are all one in mission 778
Lord Jesus, think on me 798

Proper 18

Sunday on or between September 4 and 10

Faith is shown by one's actions, especially in showing compassion.
Jesus is a sign of the dawning of God's reign in this way.

Anchor Points – The Propers and the Season

The fixed points for each service are the appointed or proper readings and collect as well as the themes of the day or season.

Readings and Psalm

Proverbs 22:1–2, 8–9, 22–23

In today's reading, the proverbs relate the social status and guide the social interactions of the haves – the rich – and the have-nots – the poor. Justice and generosity will be rewarded by God, who is especially attuned to their plight.

Psalm 125

This is a psalm of trust that dispels the anxieties that God will waver in faithfulness to the people.

or

Isaiah 35:4–7a

In chapter 35 Isaiah imagines a future day when talk of anger and suffering is over and God's people are restored. Then God will bring salvation and wholeness for all who are physically and spiritually disabled. The people will be restored like a watered desert.

Psalm 146

This psalm calls for an unwavering trust in the Lord's goodness, power, and sovereign reign in the midst of outwardly dark and painful conditions.

James 2:1–10, (11–13), 14–17

James here focuses on favoritism shown to the rich and on the relationship of faith and works. God regards all people as equal (Job 34:19) and so should we. This is consistent with God's special concern for the poor, a major theme in the Old and New Testaments. The early Church was composed mostly of the poor.

Mark 7:24–37

In our gospel reading, Jesus, traveling in Gentile territory, heals the daughter of a Gentile woman and then a Deaf man with a speech impediment. The back-and-forth between Jesus and the Syrophoenician woman may seem playful or even harsh. It may be that through such a conversation Jesus saw how his mission was to include all peoples, as his followers came later to understand. The healing of the Deaf man can be recognized as a fulfillment of prophecy as the new age of the kingdom draws near.

Collect

Grant us, O Lord, to trust in you with all our hearts; for, as you always resist the proud who confide in their own strength, so you never forsake those who make their boast of your mercy; through Jesus Christ our Lord, who lives and reigns with you and the Holy Spirit, one God, now and for ever. *Amen.*

Proper Preface

Of the Lord's Day

1. *Of God the Father*

For you are the source of light and life; you made us in your image, and called us to new life in Jesus Christ our Lord.

or this

2. *Of God the Son*

Through Jesus Christ our Lord; who on the first day of the week overcame death and the grave, and by his glorious resurrection opened to us the way of everlasting life.

or the following

3. *Of God the Holy Spirit*

For by water and the Holy Spirit you have made us a new people in Jesus Christ our Lord, to show forth your glory in all the world.

(Rite II, BCP 377–378; Rite I, BCP 344–345)

Seasonal Pairings

See the table below for choices appointed and suggested for this day. Preferences are put in **bold**. Not all choices are suitable for all congregations or community, though, so consider these preferences as a starting point before making a decision about your own congregation.

	Proper 18	Rite I	Rite II	EOW1	BOS 2022
Color	Green				
Entrance Rite	Customary; opening acclamation "Blessed be God" or one of the first two in EOW1	323	355	50	
Song of Praise/Kyrie	Gloria in excelsis or BCP Canticle 13, 16; EOW1 Canticle A, Q	Gloria 324	Gloria 356; C13– 90; C16 – 92	A – 30; Q– 39	
Collect		181	233		
Creed	Nicene Creed	326, 327	358	53	
Prayers of the People	**Locally written**; options below; BCP forms	329	387–393	54–55	
Offertory Sentence		343–344	376–377		
Eucharistic Prayer	**Sept-Oct – Rite I, suggest Prayer 2; Rite II, suggest Prayer B, if A was used in the summer; EOW1 suggest Prayer 3.**	**2–340**	**B – 367**	**3–62**	
Proper Preface	**The Lord's Day 1 – Of God the Father**	344–345	377–378		
Breaking of the Bread (Fraction)	Christ our Passover (BCP); S 167 – S 172 in *The Hymnal 1982*; EOW1 options	337	364	69	
Postcommunion Prayer		339	**Almighty and everliving God – 366**	**Loving God – 70**	
Blessing	Customary	339	366	70–71	
Dismissal	**Go in peace to love and serve the Lord**	340	366		
Notes	Labor Day may fall after this Sunday; September 11 may fall after this Sunday; back to school prayers?				

Additional Notes:

Song of Praise/Canticle – Suggested here is a canticle for the autumn from the BCP and an option from EOW1 (Canticle 13 and Canticle A) as well as one or two that reflects themes of the day. The Gloria, of course, is always appropriate in this season.

Eucharistic Prayer – Using a consistent option for September and October will help tie these week together, especially since some will be returning to worship after a time away.

Content Resources

Reading Between the Lines

In the region of Tyre, Mark 7:24–37 reports that Gentile woman of Syrophoenecian origin pleads with Jesus to cast a demon out of her daughter. She has faith, or she would not have made her request. At first, he refuses. But in response to his rejection of her request, "Let the children be fed first, for is not fair to take the children's food and throw it to the dogs," her reply uses a metaphor: "Sir, even the dogs under the table eat the children's crumbs." And in Mark's gospel, Jesus has been using metaphor from day one: "Follow me, and I will make you fishers of people," he says to the fisherman Simon and Andrew (1:16–18). Jesus' teachings favor the figurative over the literal: his first teaching is in similes and parables (Mark 4). From this point of view, Jesus invited disciples and others to press beyond or even reject a literal in favor of a figurative, transcendent world view, because parabolic discourse presents the world not so much as it is but how it might be from a heavenly perspective.

Central Themes

Jesus healed a Deaf man in private. He commanded, "Be opened," and to tell no one of his deed. Was this a lesson in humility for the disciples? Perhaps. Boasting, even if it's about Jesus's miracle, is unnecessary. God's healing deeds are meant to benefit humans, whom God calls God's beloved children. God doesn't require advertising or promotion. Parents also don't require praise for their goodness toward their children. It's the command to

"Be opened" that matters. Beloved children are admonished to open their hearts to those in need without any expectation of fame or reward for doing the right thing.

In 2004 Wangari Maathai, a renowned Kenyan social, political, and environmental activist, became the first African woman to receive the Nobel Peace Prize. When her country lost many trees for corporate farming, she mobilized the women of her country to plant trees one by one. A few trees spread into a million and spawned the Greenbelt Movement, whose impact was felt globally. At one point, Maathai was arrested because her work was so disruptive to corporate profits. Her time in jail inspired her to speak globally and spread the reach of her work. Like the bold Syrophoenician woman in today's gospel, she spoke truth to power and asked hard questions.[1]

In the first section of this gospel, Jesus is a border walker: not far from home, but in alien territory, among foreigners who would not have been particularly friendly to Jews, nor the Jews to them. Xenophobia was a way of life. Mark's Jesus, a Jew, has thus far been working, preaching, healing, and generally ministering to his own kind. Though rebuffed, the Syro-Phoenecian woman persists; she engages Jesus and challenges his assumptions. Eventually, her request is granted. The characters who push back, question and challenge, tend to move further into the mysteries of faith. Recall Job, Mary of Nazareth, Jacob at the Jabbok River, and others. How do we wrestle with the faith and deepen it in creative, helpful ways?

Engaging All Ages

The Christian formation curriculum Godly Play claims that Jesus's work was to come close to people, people that no one else wanted to come close to. He came so close that he touched them. And this touch, this closeness, changed people. People were healed. Their minds were opened. They were restored to community. Who are we afraid to come close to? What is it that we do not want to dirty our hands with? What healing might occur through our proximity? Healing goes both ways. How might we be changed by coming close to people others don't want to touch?

Prayers of the People: Option 1

We are humbled by the good you can do through us when we give ourselves over to you. Keep us close to you that we may be unafraid to speak your truth. Make your church quick to listen for your voice as we move forward as doers of the word. We pray for all bishops, priests, and deacons; for those who support your mission of mercy in the world; those who teach; and those who take your word into their hearts.

Pray for the Church.

Silence

We are living on a vast and diverse planet. Guide those who guide others, that they may genuinely be concerned about the welfare of their people. Open our ears to the cries of your people who suffer in dark corners of this world, and open our hands to reach out to them with generous spirits.

Pray for the world.

Silence

We are burdened by illnesses, anxieties, addictions, and broken relationships. Cover us with your grace and compassion. Drive far from us the fear which keeps us from trusting your goodness. We ask you to heal those who suffer: *N.*

Pray for those who are suffering.

Silence

We are grieved by the loss of those who have died, especially *N.*, recently departed. Give us confidence in your promise of endless life with you, surrounded by your glory and accompanied by your saints and angels.

Pray for those who have died.

Silence

We are astounded beyond measure by your creative powers, O God, and celebrate the mystery of all your creation. But most of all we celebrate the mystery of your love and care for us, for the gift of your Son, and the encouragement of your Holy Spirit.

Prayers of the People: Option 2

Deacon or Presider

Ever-present and compassionate God, you care for all persons with your unconditional divine love, and you extend your liberating grace to all peoples: Open our hearts to be strong and fearless in the pursuit of justice and relief, especially on behalf of the poor and the stranger, as we pray: You care for near and far alike; liberate your children from their oppression.

Litanist

Gracious and loving God, you have called your Church to follow the royal law to love our neighbors as ourselves: Empower our witness of reconciliation that we may speak

1 Jen Cullerton Johnson and Sonia Lynn Sadler (illustrator) *Seeds of Change* (Lee & Low Book, 2010).

gracefully to those whose ears cannot yet hear the Good News of God's love and may serve generously those whose mouths cannot yet proclaim your grace.

You care for near and far alike;

liberate your children from their oppression.

You guide the leaders of the nations to show mercy and to eschew partiality: Free from their bondage those whose lot is only the leftovers and crumbs, and empower those who struggle to live on what falls from their masters' tables.

You care for near and far alike;

liberate your children from their oppression.

You embrace with your compassion, O God, those whom some call dogs and others who are poor or dishonored: Heal and comfort all who are in weakness or in need throughout the world.

You care for near and far alike;

liberate your children from their oppression.

You have chosen the poor in the world to be rich in faith and heirs of the kingdom: Reconcile our community that we may be people of radical hospitality, welcoming native and foreigner, rich and poor, without distinction or partiality.

You care for near and far alike;

liberate your children from their oppression.

You withhold your healing presence from no one: Honor our prayers for all who are in need, especially______________. You call us to share in your work of reconciliation and freedom. We thank you for the many ministries of this congregation: our work of worship, outreach, education, service, and fellowship. Hear our joy as we give you thanks, especially for________________. You keep your promise for ever; hear our prayers for those who have died, especially____________________.

You care for near and far alike;

liberate your children from their oppression.

Presider

Gracious and living God, your loving care reaches to the ends of the earth, rescuing those who live in bondage and fear: Open our eyes and ears to your call of compassion, that we may joyfully share in your eternal life, and bring all humanity into the goodness of your Spirit, through Jesus Christ our Savior. ***Amen.***

Hymns for the Day

The Hymnal 1982

I'll praise my Maker while I've breath 429
Immortal, invisible, God only wise 423 (SC)
On this day, the first of days 47 (SC)
Thou, whose Almighty word 371 (GR)
O for a thousand tongues to sing 493 (GR)
Father all loving, who rulest in majesty 568
Help us, O Lord, to learn 628
Jesu, Jesu, fill us with your love 602
Lord, whose love through humble service 610
When Christ was lifted from the earth 603, 604
From thee all skill and science flow 566
Give praise and glory unto God 375
Thine arm, O Lord, in days of old 567
Word of God, come down on earth 633

Lift Every Voice and Sing II

Jesu, Jesu, fill us with your love 4

Wonder, Love, and Praise

The desert shall rejoice 722 (GR)
From miles around the sick ones came 774
Heal me, hands of Jesus 773
O Christ, the healer, we have come 772

Proper 19

Sunday on or between September 11 and 17

The cost of discipleship includes bearing the cross.

Anchor Points – The Propers and the Season

The fixed points for each service are the appointed or proper readings and collect as well as the themes of the day or season.

Readings and Psalm

Proverbs 1:20–33

Today's reading is the first speech put into the mouth of Wisdom, personified as a woman. Following upon the warnings to those who find reasons to neglect the pursuit of wisdom (1:8–19), she delivers warnings of her own about the punishment for being enticed by false wisdom.

Psalm 19

The psalmist celebrates God's revelation, expressed universally in creation and especially in the law.

or

Wisdom 7:26–8:1

This canticle is an ode to Wisdom with a vivid theological assertion: Wisdom reflects the life and workings of God, so closely that she is in herself an aspect of the divine.

or

Isaiah 50:4–9a

The song in today's reading describes the servant as a disciple of the Lord and as a misunderstood, ill-treated prophet to a weary people. Using the image of a court of law, the servant expresses confidence that God will vindicate him. The servant songs provided a way for Israel to understand the significance of the suffering and humiliation of the exile. The songs later helped the Church understand and proclaim Jesus's suffering and resurrection.

Psalm 116:1–8

This psalm of thanksgiving recounts the vindication of a righteous sufferer. Such a psalm was recited as a testimony to other worshipers.

James 3:1–12

Today's reading looks at the power of speech. The tongue can expose faithlessness and foolishness. Its tremendous power is deceptive. The person who gains control over his or her tongue is a person who knows how to exercise discipline over his or her entire life. Teachers are required to watch their speech even more carefully because of the greater significance attributed to their words.

Mark 8:27–38

In the gospel, Peter recognizes that Jesus is the Christ, and Jesus then describes the true nature of the ministry of the Son of Man and what it means to follow in his way. The passage reminds us that during Jesus's lifetime and afterward there was speculation about his role. Some saw him as a kind of re-embodiment of John the Baptist or another prophet. Peter is called "Satan" because his words are a temptation to turn away from the suffering and death which come before resurrection. Disciples must also learn that the true self and true life are found by those who will let themselves be lost for the sake of Jesus and the gospel.

Collect

O God, because without you we are not able to please you, mercifully grant that your Holy Spirit may in all things direct and rule our hearts; through Jesus Christ our Lord, who lives and reigns with you and the Holy Spirit, one God, now and for ever. *Amen.*

Proper Preface

Of the Lord's Day

1. Of God the Father

For you are the source of light and life; you made us in your image, and called us to new life in Jesus Christ our Lord.

or this

2. Of God the Son

Through Jesus Christ our Lord; who on the first day of the week overcame death and the grave, and by his glorious resurrection opened to us the way of everlasting life.

or the following

3. Of God the Holy Spirit

For by water and the Holy Spirit you have made us a new people in Jesus Christ our Lord, to show forth your glory in all the world.

(Rite II, BCP 377–378; Rite I, BCP 344–345)

Seasonal Pairings

See the table below for choices appointed and suggested for this day. Preferences are put in **bold**. Not all choices are suitable for all congregations or community, though, so consider these preferences as a starting point before making a decision about your own congregation.

	Proper 19	Rite I	Rite II	EOW1	BOS 2022
Color	Green				
Entrance Rite	Customary; opening acclamation "Blessed be God" or one of the first two in EOW1	323	355	50	
Song of Praise/Kyrie	Gloria in excelsis or BCP Canticle 13, 18; EOW1 Canticle A, M	Gloria 324	Gloria 356; C13– 90; C18 – 93	A – 30; M – 37	
Collect		182	233		
Creed	Nicene Creed	326, 327	358	53	
Prayers of the People	**Locally written**; options below; BCP forms	329	387–393	54–55	
Offertory Sentence	"Jesus said, 'If any want to become my followers, let them deny themselves and take up their cross and follow me. For those who want to save their life will lose it, and those who lose their life for my sake, and for the sake of the gospel, will save it.'" (Mark)	343–344	376–377		
Eucharistic Prayer	**Sept-Oct – Rite I, suggest Prayer 2; Rite II, suggest Prayer B, if A was used in the summer; EOW1 suggest Prayer 3.**	**2–340**	**B – 367**	**3–62**	
Proper Preface	**The Lord's Day 2 – Of God the Son**	344–345	377–378		
Breaking of the Bread (Fraction)	Christ our Passover (BCP); S 167 – S 172 in *The Hymnal 1982*; EOW1 options	337	364	69	
Postcommunion Prayer		339	**Almighty and everliving God – 366**	**Loving God – 70**	
Blessing	Customary	339	366	70–71	
Dismissal	**Go in peace to love and serve the Lord**	340	366		
Notes	September 11 may fall on or after this Sunday; Holy Cross Day may fall on or near this Sunday; Int'l Day of Peace may fall after this Sunday				

Additional Notes:

Song of Praise/Canticle – Suggested here is a canticle for the autumn from the BCP and an option from EOW1 (Canticle 13 and Canticle A) as well as one or two that reflects themes of the day. The Gloria, of course, is always appropriate in this season.

Eucharistic Prayer – Using a consistent option for September and October will help tie these week together, especially since some will be returning to worship after a time away.

Content Resources

Reading Between the Lines

In this section of Mark's gospel Jesus elicits from the disciples a confessional response articulated by Peter to the central question of 8:29, "But who do you say that I am?" Peter's answer, "You are the Messiah," prompts the implicit question, "what sort of Messiah?" Jesus teaches the disciples, "the Son of Man must undergo great suffering and be rejected by the elders, chief priests and scribes and be killed and after three days rise again." (8:31). Peter's unsurprising rejection of this idea causes Jesus to say, "Get behind me, Satan!" stressing three times, in Mark 8, 9 & 10, that those who wish to come after him must deny themselves, take up their cross and follow me. A rejected, betrayed, cross-bearing and suffering Son of Man is not what Peter or anyone else had in mind. But the only way to save your life is by losing it (8:35). To this passage, we can add the temporal perspective of 9:1.

Central Themes

"Don't shoot the messenger" is a meme that originated in Sophocles' *Antigone*: "No man loves the messenger of ill." Even when the messenger is sent by God, people don't like to hear messages that call them on their neglect of needy neighbors. Fictional Irish bartender Mr. Dooley said, "The job of the newspaper is to comfort the afflicted and afflict the comfortable." Preachers who uphold the New Commandment to love others as Jesus loves us also deliver Mr. Dooley's message to "comfort the afflicted and afflict the comfortable." Give comfort to the poor in spirit, and remind others to do likewise.

James points to the harmful false teaching of the childhood refrain: "Sticks and stones may break my bones, but words will never hurt me." James compares the tongue to fire, something small that can cause extensive destruction. Words do hurt and even destroy! In an era of fires that burn down cities and viral words on social media that can destroy the dignity of others, we know this truth. Encouraging words can build someone up. Healthy fire can also renew ecosystems and give light and heat. How does our speech become a spiritual practice of renewal and not destruction?

We are at about the midpoint of this gospel; Jesus steps back from the crowd to do something like a midterm evaluation. He asks two questions: the first about what the disciples are hearing about him; the second to ask them pointedly how they would identify him. Of all the questions in the Bible – and they are legion – the second question here may be the most important of all. Who do we say that Jesus is for our time in our little corner of the world? What does that say about us, especially since our baptism claims us as one of his own? What does it say about agency in and our witness to the world?

Engaging All Ages

Jesus never promises that a life of Christian discipleship will be easy. In fact, he foretells the opposite: "If any want to become my followers, let them . . . take up their cross." Jesus is alive and well when he makes this proclamation, but he knows that soon "taking up the cross" will becomes a symbol of suffering. Symbols often have more than one meaning. Sacrifice is part of the Christian life, but so is resurrection. A cross can symbolize both: the discomfort we encounter for the sake of the gospel and the new life it brings. Consider decorating a cross on both sides to represent the complexity of discipleship.

Prayers of the People: Option 1

Almighty God, you spoke, and your words brought endless worlds into existence.

Remind us that our words and our lives matter. May our words and actions partner with each other in your holy purpose.

Silence

Empower the body of Christ to speak your truth to the world. Let our words and our actions be both simple and powerful, kind, and gentle. Bless our leadership with language to encourage your people to deepen their relationship with you.

Silence

Speak peace to the hearts of the world's leaders. Let their words and actions be those of integrity. Bless the children of all ages and all nations with a future that reflects your justice and loving-kindness. Give your people the courage to speak up for those who have no voice in this world.

Silence

Whisper words of hope and healing to the hearts of those who are ill or anxious and struggle with themselves or with their families. We pray for wholeness for *N.*

Silence

We pray for those who have recently been called home and pray for those who mourn their loss. When words fall short, let our presence reflect your love for them in their grief.

Silence

May the words of our mouths and the meditations of our hearts always be acceptable to you O Lord, our strength and our redeemer. ***Amen.***

Prayers of the People: Option 2

Deacon or Presider

With our tongues we bless the Lord and Father and beg for mercy on all in need.

Intercessor

For *N.* our Presiding Bishop, *N.* our bishop, for our parish clergy and lay leaders, for this holy gathering, and for the people of God in every place.

Christ, have mercy.

For mercy, peace, and justice among all peoples.

Christ, have mercy.

For abundant fruits of the earth, and for safety from violent storms.

Christ, have mercy.

For those who are sick and suffering, for travelers by land, by water, and by air, for those in prison and their families, and all those in desperate need.

Christ, have mercy.

For our cities and communities and all those who live in them, and for our families, companions, and all those we love.

Christ, have mercy.

For those who rest in Christ and for all those we love but see no longer.

Christ, have mercy.

For all other prayers of intercession and thanksgiving, which may be offered now, silently or aloud.

Silence

The people may add their own prayers

Presider

God of infinite mercy, hear the prayers we offer this day and save our lives through the good news of your Messiah; through Jesus Christ our Lord. ***Amen.***

Hymns for the Day

The Hymnal 1982

The spacious firmament on high 409 (SC)
The stars declare his glory 431 (SC)
O sacred head, sore wounded 168, 169 (vs 1–3) (GR)
Before thy throne, O God, we kneel 574, 575
Strengthen for service, Lord, the hands 312
Day by day 654
From God Christ's deity came forth 443
Glorious things of thee are spoken 522, 523
New every morning is the love 10
Praise the Lord through every nation 484, 485
Take up your cross, the Savior said 675
The Church's one foundation 525
You are the Christ, O Lord 254

Lift Every Voice and Sing II

O sacred head, sore wounded 36 (vs 1–3) (GR)
He never said a mumbalin' word 33 (GR)
I can hear my Savior calling 144
I have decided to follow Jesus 136
King of my life I crown thee now 31

Wonder, Love, and Praise

Even when young, I prayed for wisdom's grace 906 (SC)
O sacred head, sore wounded 735 (vs 1–3) (GR)
Will you come and follow me 757
You laid aside your rightful reputation 734

Proper 20

Sunday on or between September 18 and 24

Jesus predicts his passion a second time and reminds his disciples that to be great in the kingdom of God is to be the servant of all.

Anchor Points – The Propers and the Season

The fixed points for each service are the appointed or proper readings and collect as well as the themes of the day or season.

Readings and Psalm

Proverbs 31:10–31

Like Wisdom, the ideal woman is of more value than any earthly treasure and is a constant blessing to her family. The description of the wise woman comes to a climax with the summary of verses 30–31. Her wise activities and attitudes spring from her relationship with God. Thus, the author describes for us the daily life of an individual who has perfectly mastered the counsel of the rest of the book and embodies it in the way she lives.

Psalm 1

The righteous are those who have not taken the advice of the wicked, nor imitated their way of life, nor joined in their rejection of the law.

or

Wisdom 1:16 – 2:1, 12–22

Today's reading presents the faulty thinking of the ungodly who have forsaken God's wisdom and ways.

or

Jeremiah 11:18–20

Today's reading introduces the first of Jeremiah's six personal laments. He reflects on the hatred directed toward him and puts his confidence in God's plan. In spite of threats and persecution, suffering and sorrow, Jeremiah believes that God is sovereign over all the circumstances both of his life and of the life of the nation.

Psalm 54

The psalmist prays earnestly for God's intervention and salvation and ends his prayer with trust by thanking God for God's faithfulness.

James 3:13 – 4:3, 7–8a

Today's reading contains parts of two sections – one on earthly versus heavenly wisdom (3:13–18) and the second on causes of strife and warfare (4:1–6). James first addresses the problem of factions and cliques within the Christian community. Then the author turns to the question of the basic source of human hostility and aggression. Those who resort to violence, rather than to prayer, to obtain what they desire are like adulterers who are unfaithful in their relationship to God.

Mark 9:30–37

Today's reading begins a period of private ministry as Jesus concentrates on teaching the disciples. It includes the second of the three predictions of the passion in Mark. As in the others, the prediction confuses the disciples, so Jesus teaches them about discipleship. The disciples are typically dull, and they proceed to argue about their relative status in the kingdom. Jesus responds with a paradox and an enacted parable. As he will achieve lordship only through the path of suffering, so his disciples must follow him in suffering and in service.

Collect

Grant us, Lord, not to be anxious about earthly things, but to love things heavenly; and even now, while we are placed among things that are passing away, to hold fast to those that shall endure; through Jesus Christ our Lord, who lives and reigns with you and the Holy Spirit, one God, for ever and ever. *Amen.*

Proper Preface

Of the Lord's Day

1. Of God the Father

For you are the source of light and life; you made us in your image, and called us to new life in Jesus Christ our Lord.

or this

2. Of God the Son

Through Jesus Christ our Lord; who on the first day of the week overcame death and the grave, and by his glorious resurrection opened to us the way of everlasting life.

or the following

3. Of God the Holy Spirit

For by water and the Holy Spirit you have made us a new people in Jesus Christ our Lord, to show forth your glory in all the world.

(Rite II, BCP 377–378; Rite I, BCP 344–345)

Seasonal Pairings

See the table below for choices appointed and suggested for this day. Preferences are put in **bold**. Not all choices are suitable for all congregations or community, though, so consider these preferences as a starting point before making a decision about your own congregation.

	Proper 20	Rite I	Rite II	EOW1	BOS 2022
Color	Green				
Entrance Rite	Customary; opening acclamation "Blessed be God" or one of the first two in EOW1	323	355	50	
Song of Praise/Kyrie	Gloria in excelsis or BCP Canticle 13, 10; EOW1 Canticle A, H	Gloria 324	Gloria 356; C13– 90; C10 – 86	A – 30; H – 34	
Collect		182	234		
Creed	Nicene Creed	326, 327	358	53	
Prayers of the People	**Locally written**; options below; BCP forms	329	387–393	54–55	
Offertory Sentence	"The wisdom from above is first pure, then peaceable, gentle, willing to yield, full of mercy and good fruits." (James)	343–344	376–377		
Eucharistic Prayer	**Sept-Oct – Rite I, suggest Prayer 2; Rite II, suggest Prayer B, if A was used in the summer; EOW1 suggest Prayer 3.**	**2–340**	**B – 367**	**3–62**	
Proper Preface	**The Lord's Day 2 – Of God the Son**	344–345	377–378		
Breaking of the Bread (Fraction)	Christ our Passover (BCP); S 167 – S 172 in *The Hymnal 1982*; EOW1 options	337	364	69	
Postcommunion Prayer		339	**Almighty and everliving God – 366**	**Loving God – 70**	
Blessing	Customary	339	366	70–71	
Dismissal	**Go in peace to love and serve the Lord**	340	366		
Notes	Int'l Day of Peace may fall on or after this Sunday; St. Matthew's Day may fall on or after this Sunday				

Additional Notes:

Song of Praise/Canticle – Suggested here is a canticle for the autumn from the BCP and an option from EOW1 (Canticle 13 and Canticle A) as well as one or two that reflects themes of the day. The Gloria, of course, is always appropriate in this season.

Eucharistic Prayer – Using a consistent option for September and October will help tie these week together, especially since some will be returning to worship after a time away.

Content Resources

Reading Between the Lines

Jesus teaches the disciples again that the Son of Man "is to be betrayed, or turned over to human **hands**, and that they will kill him, and three days after being killed, that he will be raised," and when Jesus perceives that the disciples who have been with him since the ministry began, and who have listened to parables like the seed growing secretly, seen exorcisms, witnessed miracles all in God's name, do not understand what Jesus is saying, he explains that whoever wants to be first must be last of all and slave of all. And to demonstrate what he means, Jesus takes a little child, puts her in the middle of all of them, and clasping her firmly in his arms, says, "If you welcome one such child in my name, you welcome me."

In Mark's gospel, Jesus is given over into the hands of people and they indeed whip, pierce, denigrate and crucify his body. But the torture that is done to Jesus' body by human hands is undone, **yes undone** by every compassionate act of Jesus When Jesus sees the fever that is burning Simon Peter's mother-in-law, he grasps her by the hand and lifts her up. And the fever leaves her body. When Jesus sees a leper, he is moved with such pity that he stretches out his hand to touch him. The leper is made clean and healed. When Jesus enters the synagogue, and a man was there who had a withered hand, Jesus says to the man who had the withered hand, "Come forward." And when he becomes angry that people in the synagogue are silent about saving life or killing on the Sabbath, Jesus says to the man, "Stretch out your hand." And his hand was restored. With people who are ill, deaf, blind, possessed, sick and dead, Jesus reaches out his hands to them. His hands cross boundaries of human fear, frailty and isolation to offer compassion and healing and community. Jesus' merciful hands are signs of God's presence that restores healing and wholeness. Furthermore, the hands of others can also reach out and touch Jesus to claim that healing and wholeness for themselves. Hands can torture, shame, maim, denigrate and unmake the world. But Jesus' hands and through them God's hands and through them your hands can remake the world and undo shame, pain, illness, torture, and isolation.

Central Themes

Children have held "less than" status in many cultures historically. For example, "children should be seen and not heard." Children are not little adults. Young children are dependent on parents and older siblings as they learn to feed and clean themselves. They must be taught to evaluate their surroundings and learn to make good choices, often through trial and error. The innocence or "blank slate" of children makes them open to being led and taught to love others, to share, and to find joy in daily experiences. What if we retain that openness to love, sharing, and joy as we become adults?

James's words on resisting the devil and submitting to God are reflected in the baptismal liturgy in *The Book of Common Prayer*. Candidates for baptism or their parents and godparents are asked to renounce Satan, spiritual forces of wickedness, evil powers, sinful desires – all of which separate them from the love of God. They are asked to affirm their faith in Jesus Christ. In this they proclaim that they are turning their focus from that which distorts God to God from whom all of their actions should grow.

One of the threads in Mark's Gospel highlights the disciples' lack of understanding. An Episcopal bishop, Mark MacDonald, sometimes referred to them as the "duh-sciples" so inept were they at getting with the Jesus's program, much less getting Jesus and his passion for God. This business of becoming servants, welcoming children with their sticky fingers and sippy cups would have been difficult. They'd been basking in his reflective glory, wanting more. Inner circle sorts, they were put off by talk of servanthood. This is not uncharted territory: He went first, leading the way. How do we enact leadership from below, "serving Christ in others" as our baptism demands?

Engaging All Ages

We live in a culture that constantly encourages us to be first, to be the best. We get rewards, literally, for top grades and best sales figures and for reading the most books in the class. Sometimes these rewards benefit everyone, like when our car insurance rate drops because we've been a great driver for five years. But sometimes these rewards compel us to succeed at the cost of others. Jesus's words about the first and last might sound simple, but they are profoundly countercultural and call for a radical reorganization of our lives as students, children, parents, employees, employers, and citizens. What would servanthood in some of the roles you inhabit look like?

Prayers of the People: Option 1

We look to you, O God, to teach us how to be whom you created us to be. Shine your light on the path ahead. Catch us when we take a wrong turn, and by your Spirit, move us in the right direction.

We are your children;

Teach us how to live, O God.

We yearn for peace but are constantly at war with ourselves, our neighbors, and the nations throughout the world.

We are your children;

Teach us how to make peace, O God.

We, your church, are easily distracted by things that don't matter. Turn our eyes to you; open our hearts to you; deepen our love of you. Bless our bishops, priests, and deacons. May we teach each other how to walk in love.

We are your children;

Teach us how to serve you, O God.

Our bodies ache, our spirits are restless, and our minds grow weary with constant worry. Lead us to a place of wholeness and make each of us agents of healing in this world. We pray for those who have asked our prayers today: *N.*

We are your children;

Teach us how to trust in your healing embrace.

When a dear one dies, we ask that you receive them into your eternal kingdom as promised. We pray today for the repose of the soul of *N.*, recently departed. Assure those who grieve that you will not leave them desolate in their sorrow but hold their loved one close to your heart.

We are your children;

Teach us the way home to you.

Prayers of the People: Option 2

Deacon or Presider

As we welcome the children of God in the name of Jesus, let us offer prayers for all in every danger and need.

Intercessor

For this holy gathering, for *N.*, our Presiding Bishop, for *N.*, our bishop, and for the people of God in every place.

O Christ, hear us.

For the ministries of this congregation and for our clergy and lay leaders.

O Christ, hear us.

For all peoples and their leaders, and for justice, mercy, and peace in the world.

O Christ, hear us.

For all who work for daily wages, and for their employers and managers.

O Christ, hear us.

For abundant fruits of the earth, and for safety from violent storms, for those recovering from inclement weather.

O Christ, hear us.

For those who are sick and suffering, for travelers and the victims of war, prisoners and refugees, and the dying and dead.

O Christ, hear us.

For our cities and towns and those who live in them, and for our families, companions, and all those we love.

O Christ, hear us.

For all other prayers and thanksgivings that you would name now, silently or aloud.

Silence. The people may add their own prayers

Presider

God of mercy, hear the prayers we offer this day and send on us your wisdom from above, that our lives may be full of gentleness and understanding; through Jesus Christ our Lord. ***Amen.***

Hymns for the Day

The Hymnal 1982

God moves in a mysterious way 677 (GR)
How firm a foundation 636, 637 (GR)
Praise to the Lord, the Almighty 390
Sing praise to God who reigns above 408
If thou but trust in God to guide thee 635 (GR)
Commit thou all that grieves thee 669
Before thy throne, O God, we kneel 574, 575
Eternal Spirit of the living Christ 698
Hope of the world, thou Christ of great compassion 472
Lord, for ever at thy side 670
All praise to thee, for thou, O King divine 477
God is Love, let heaven adore him 379
Lord of all hopefulness, Lord of all joy 482
O love, how deep, how broad, how high 448, 449
O Master, let me walk with thee 659, 660
Sing, ye faithful, sing with gladness 492
When Jesus left his Father's throne 480

Lift Every Voice and Sing II

I am weak and I need thy strength and power 194 (GR)
I've been 'buked an' I've been scorned 195 (GR)
In God we trust 55 (GR)
When we walk with the Lord 205 (GR)

Wonder, Love, and Praise

Peace among earth's peoples is like a star 789
These three are the treasures to strive for and prize 803

Proper 21

Sunday on or between September 25 and October 1

Jesus's power breaks out in spontaneous acts of healing that cannot be confined to the church.

Anchor Points – The Propers and the Season

The fixed points for each service are the appointed or proper readings and collect as well as the themes of the day or season.

Readings and Psalm

Esther 7:1–6, 9–10; 9:20–22

The book of Esther, named after the Jewish heroine who, together with her uncle Mordecai, saves her people by foiling the murderous plot of Haman, an official in the Persian Empire, which controlled the fate of Israel after the exile. Because the Jew Mordecai would not do homage to him, Haman plotted his death and the death of all the Jews in the Persian empire. Today's reading tells how Esther reveals Haman's plot to the Persian King and how the King orders Haman to be hanged on the same gallows that he had constructed to execute Mordecai.

Psalm 124

This is a psalm of thanksgiving that recalls that the existence of the people of Israel depends upon God who saved them from the various enemies that threatened them. Their response is thanks and a continued resolve to depend on God's help.

or

Numbers 11:4–6, 10–16, 24–29

This reading focuses on the Lord's aid to Moses with his heavy responsibilities. The company led out of Egypt on the exodus journey seems to have included both Israelites and also some others, perhaps Egyptians who feared Israel's God or assorted wanderers – a mixed crowd (Exodus 12:38) who start the grumbling. Moses' boldness in his protests to God are striking. He feels defeated by the people's unreasonable demands. He complains about God's unreasonable demands of him, and God honors Moses' feelings and shares the Spirit with seventy community leaders. Such a manifestation of God's Spirit cannot be confined or controlled by humans – thus, when two men, not of the seventy and not present at the tent, also prophesy, Moses acknowledges them.

Psalm 19:7–14

The psalmist celebrates God's revelation, expressed universally in creation and specifically in the law.

James 5:13–20

James concludes his book with a final instruction to pray. Every occasion of life is an opportunity for prayer. Prayer must be both private and communal. It builds on the individual's relationship with the Lord and it intensifies the individual's relationships with others. The author underscores the power of prayer to affect the will of God by reminding his readers about Elijah, who prayed according to God's instructions and controlled nature.

Mark 9:38–50

In the gospel, Jesus bids his disciples to accept all who seek to do good in his name and to deal ruthlessly with whatever part of themselves causes sin. Early Christians were doubtless faced with people outside their communities who said they were acting in Christ's name. The tolerant answer given here suggests that Jesus's followers must avoid arrogance and be open to God's divine actions. On the other hand, it is a serious matter to lead a believer astray. The counsel to destroy offending parts of the body is exaggerated to make clear the importance of avoiding various sins. The description of hell is drawn from the garbage dump outside Jerusalem.

Collect

O God, you declare your almighty power chiefly in showing mercy and pity: Grant us the fullness of your grace, that we, running to obtain your promises, may become partakers of your heavenly treasure; through Jesus Christ our Lord, who lives and reigns with you and the Holy Spirit, one God, for ever and ever. *Amen.*

Proper Preface

Of the Lord's Day

1. Of God the Father

For you are the source of light and life; you made us in your image, and called us to new life in Jesus Christ our Lord.

or this

2. Of God the Son

Through Jesus Christ our Lord; who on the first day of the week overcame death and the grave, and by his glorious resurrection opened to us the way of everlasting life.

or the following

3. Of God the Holy Spirit

For by water and the Holy Spirit you have made us a new people in Jesus Christ our Lord, to show forth your glory in all the world.

(Rite II, BCP 377–378; Rite I, BCP 344–345)

Seasonal Pairings

See the table below for choices appointed and suggested for this day. Preferences are put in **bold**. Not all choices are suitable for all congregations or community, though, so consider these preferences as a starting point before making a decision about your own congregation.

	Proper 21	Rite I	Rite II	EOW1	BOS 2022
Color	Green				
Entrance Rite	Customary; opening acclamation "Blessed be God" or one of the first two in EOW1	323	355	50	
Song of Praise/Kyrie	Gloria in excelsis or BCP Canticle 13, 18; EOW1 Canticle A	Gloria 324	Gloria 356; C13– 90; C18 – 93	A – 30;	
Collect		182	234		
Creed	Nicene Creed	326, 327	358	53	
Prayers of the People	**Locally written**; options below; BCP forms	329	387–393	54–55	
Offertory Sentence		343–344	376–377		
Eucharistic Prayer	**Sept-Oct – Rite I, suggest Prayer 2; Rite II, suggest Prayer B, if A was used in the summer; EOW1 suggest Prayer 3.**	**2–340**	**B – 367**	**3–62**	
Proper Preface	**The Lord's Day 3 – Of God the Holy Spirit**	344–345	377–378		
Breaking of the Bread (Fraction)	Christ our Passover (BCP); S 167 – S 172 in *The Hymnal 1982*; EOW1 options	337	364	69	
Postcommunion Prayer		339	**Almighty and everliving God – 366**	**Loving God – 70**	
Blessing	Customary	339	366	70–71	
Dismissal	**Go in peace to love and serve the Lord**	340	366		
Notes	St. Michael and All Angels Day may fall on or after this Sunday				

Additional Notes:

Song of Praise/Canticle – Suggested here is a canticle for the autumn from the BCP and an option from EOW1 (Canticle 13 and Canticle A) as well as one or two that reflects themes of the day. The Gloria, of course, is always appropriate in this season.

Eucharistic Prayer – Using a consistent option for September and October will help tie these week together, especially since some will be returning to worship after a time away.

Content Resources

Reading Between the Lines

Once every three years the lectionary gives us a few snippets of Esther. But what a story lies behind those snippets! Esther, a (secretly Jewish) woman has won favor with the king of Persia, who has crowned her queen. Her uncle Mordecai hangs around the palace to keep an eye on her, for her safety. He overhears an assassination plot, and reports it through Esther, saving the king's life. King Ahasueras, apparently not a great judge of character, appoints a proud and ruthless politician, Haman, as his prime minister, and commands that everyone should do obeisance to Haman. Mordecai fails to bow down to Haman. Learning that this is because Mordecai is a Jew and will worship only his God, Haman buys an edict from the king that all the Jews in his empire should be put to death on the 13th of Adar, eleven months in the future. After Esther and her community spend three days in fasting during Passover, customarily a time where deliverance from slavery is celebrated by ritual eating, she risks her own execution by appearing in court uninvited. The king receives her and promises her his favor. Esther reveals to the king, in a way that is strategic and preserves the king's honor, that a fate far worse than being sold into slavery threatens her and her people due to the machinations of Haman. The king orders Haman's execution. Since no edict of the king can be revoked, Esther receives a second royal edict proclaiming the right of the Jews to defend themselves against any attempts on their lives on the 13th Adar, and plunder the wealth of those they defeat. On the day itself, Esther secures the right to continue the defense for one more day, justifying the establishment of the two-day festival of Purim, but they do not plunder their persecutors on either day. Esther thus secures the safety and well-being of Jewish people in 127 provinces from India to Ethiopia.

The Talmud considers Esther one of the seven woman prophets, along with Sarah, Miriam, Deborah, Hannah, Abigail and Huldah, even though Esther is arguably the least overtly religious book in the Bible. Esther focuses on people of the diaspora living a faithful life in the diaspora and as a politically active force in that diaspora, with no concern for the Temple or return to Jerusalem.

The literal absence of God from a canonical book of scripture is notable. Jon D. Levenson, in *Esther: A Commentary*, p. 21, comments: "…we must be all the more careful to differentiate God as he appears in this narrative from the God of so much of biblical tradition, whose presence is visible, audible and dramatic. Esther's God is one who works behind the scenes, carefully arranging events so that a justice based on the principle of "measure for measure" will triumph… In Fox's eloquent words, 'the willingness to face history with an openness to the possibility of providence…is a stance of profound faith.' (Michael Fox, *Character and Ideology in the Book of Esther*, Columbia, S.C., 1991, 246). It is, I submit, a profounder and more realistic stance of faith than that of most biblical tradition."

Central Themes

Contemporary counseling advises people in toxic relationships to make changes to become healthier themselves and to avoid toxic people and situations. Sometimes we have to walk away from habits and people that drag us down, like substance addictions or people who can't control their tempers. We must find new habits like healthy eating and new friends who support us. If we are the ones behaving badly, we must amend our ways so that we don't drag others down. Finding new habits and friends is likely easier than admitting one's toxic behavior and making amends, but both are necessary to becoming whole.

Today is the one time Esther shows up in the Sunday lectionary. Funny, bawdy, violent, troubling, hopeful – like our world today – her whole story deserves preaching. She wrestles with her call and acts faithfully and bravely within the challenging realities of her life to the point of risking her life. In such a time as this, our faith communities need to hear the sacred stories of strong females of faith: Constance and her Companions, Harriet Tubman, Malala Yousafzai, Pandita Ramabai, and Esther, to name a few.

Hyperbole was a favored way of getting one's point across. But it is more than that. Biblical folks generally thought in concrete ways. Arms and feet were the doers of action, good and bad; eyes and ears were the first receptors that would eventually lead to such actions. So it is not the poor extremities that were in danger of being hacked; the point is that we take care, consider carefully before acting by being intentional. Thoughts, words, and judgments casually launched can lead eventually to harmful, intolerable deeds. The positive antidote to this foolishness and nastiness is the Way of Love, which Jesus taught and the Church, at its best, continues to model.

Engaging All Ages

In today's gospel reading, Jesus warns against putting a stumbling block in front of another believer. This may be another way of saying, do not make it harder for someone else to love God, love themselves, love creation, and love their neighbor. Have you ever experienced a stumbling block? Has anyone ever made it harder for you to follow Jesus in the way of love? Perhaps someone drew you into gossip, judging another's appearance, disobeying your parents, or encouraging you to lie. When have you made it harder for someone else to walk in love?

Prayers of the People: Option 1

Speak to our hearts that yearn for you. Teach us to dwell and delight in your presence.

Have mercy, O Lord.

Fill us with the fullness of your grace.

Speak to your church and our leaders. Energize us with new life and endless possibilities. Teach us to be partners with you in holiness and power.

Have mercy, O Lord.

Fill us with the fullness of your grace.

We pray for our president, our Congress, and our courts. May harmony in diversity begin with us. Speak peace to the leaders of the nations, that conflicts may cease and mutual respect across boundaries and languages may prevail.

Have mercy, O Lord.

Fill us with the fullness of your grace.

Bring the peoples of the world together so that all will be fed and warm, and none will be threatened, that the language of hope is spoken freely in all corners of the globe.

Have mercy, O Lord.

Fill us with the fullness of your grace.

We pray for all who cry out in pain and those who suffer in silence for those who await healing and for those who have lost hope. For those who have asked for our prayers and for those who have no one to pray for them, bring your healing power to those who need it most: *N.*

Have mercy, O Lord.

Fill us with the fullness of your grace.

We pray for those who have ended their earthly journey and now are surrounded by angels and archangels and their unending songs of praise.

Bring us also to that heavenly shore and the fullness of your eternal grace.

Prayers of the People: Option 2

Note that this option is tied to the Numbers reading.

Deacon or Presider

As Eldad and Medad were blessed by the Spirit to prophesy, may we all be empowered to offer our prayers this day, saying "Hear our prayer."

Intercessor

We pray for the good of all churches of God and for the people of all faiths to come together, to appreciate differences, to gain deeper understanding of traditions, and to respect the principles and values that bind us together.

Hear our prayer.

We pray for our presiding bishop *N.*, our bishop *N.*, and for our one, holy, catholic and apostolic church.

Hear our prayer.

We pray for the ministries of this congregation, for our clergy and lay leaders.

Hear our prayer.

We pray dear God for our nation and the world, with people committed to love and respect for each other, who are willing to dialogue and work towards a unified nation. We also pray for our leaders in our local communities, in our state and in the nation. We pray for the President, the members of Congress and the Supreme Court; for our Governor and our Mayor – and all who serve in positions of authority and public service. Give them wisdom, strength, courage and humility as they lead our city, state and nation, we pray:

Hear our prayer.

We pray dear God for peace among nations, for the wellbeing of those who suffer from events beyond their control. We also pray for all those deeply affected by war and conflict. For courage for those who are afraid, for safety for those who are in danger, and for peace for those who are anxious and in distress, we pray:

Hear our prayer.

We pray dear God for our community of __________ and the special needs of those who are poor or unhoused, for those who are refugees, and for all who are marginalized:

Hear our prayer.

We pray dear God for all who suffer illness of the body, mind or soul, and those whose needs are known to you alone.

Hear our prayer.

We pray dear God for the souls of the departed. And for those who mourn their loss, we pray:

Hear our prayer.

We pray dear God in gratitude for the blessings you have bestowed upon us. For the things we take for granted and for the challenges that test our faith. Continue to bless our relationships within our families and with our friends; within our schools and with our colleagues. Guide us to use our time, talents and treasure for the good of others. With thanksgiving and gratitude, we pray:

Hear our prayer.

For all other prayers and thanksgivings that you would name now, silently or aloud.

Silence. The people may add their own prayers

Presider

Hear our prayers O Lord our God, creator of all. Guide us to be live our lives with humility, compassion and grace. Inform our decisions and actions, heal our transgressions, and empower us to create lives that are filled with love and forgiveness. May the Holy Spirit be ever by our side as we strive to live in sync with our Savior. With gratitude for who we are and the hope of being in fullness with God. ***Amen.***

Hymns for the Day

The Hymnal 1982

Awake, my soul, stretch every nerve 546
Fight the good fight with all thy might 552, 553
Lo! what a cloud of witnesses 545
God moves in a mysterious way 677 (SC)
God of the prophets, bless the prophets' heirs 359 (GR)
O Food to pilgrims given 308, 309 (GR)
Shepherd of souls, refresh and bless 343 (GR)
The stars declare his glory 431 (GR)
Commit thou all that grieves thee 669
If thou but trust in God to guide thee 635
O God of Bethel, by whose hand 709
Spirit divine, attend our prayers 509
Before thy throne, O God, we kneel 574, 575
Go forth for God; go to the world in peace 347
Lord, dismiss us with thy blessing 344
Where cross the crowded ways of life 609

Lift Every Voice and Sing II

It's me, O Lord, standin' in the need of prayer 177
Sweet hour of prayer 178
If I have wounded any soul today 176

Wonder, Love, and Praise

Guide my feet, Lord, while I run this race 819
All who hunger, gather gladly 761 (GR)
It's me, O Lord, standin' in the need of prayer 797
Gracious Spirit, give your servants 782

Proper 22

Sunday on or between October 2 and 8

The sanctity of human relationships.

Anchor Points – The Propers and the Season

The fixed points for each service are the appointed or proper readings and collect as well as the themes of the day or season.

Readings and Psalm

Job 1:1, 2:1–10

Today's reading outlines the basic story found in the prose sections that begin and end the book (1:1–2:13, 42:7–17) of the righteous sufferer, the proverbial "patient Job" (Ezekiel 14:14, 20; James 5:11). The poetic sections that have been inserted into the prose story – the dialogues of Job and his three friends, who come to comfort him in his suffering by explaining about God's ways of justice, and the final response of the Lord to Job – are post-exilic and date from between 600–300 BCE.

Psalm 26

This psalm seeks God's protection upon entering into the temple. The psalmist reminds God that he is upright, but he knows that he must be purified to share in the joy of being with God.

or

Genesis 2:18–24

This account of the creation of woman is taken from the second (2:4–24) of the two stories in Genesis. Humankind is introduced as social by nature (2:18). The word used for "man," *adam,* is a collective, not individual, term and represents both maleness and femaleness. The phrase "a deep sleep" usually indicates a state in which God sends someone an unsought vision or message. Unlike the creation of all other beings, woman was not created from the ground but from the essence of man, showing equality and identity.

Psalm 8

This hymn expresses amazement at the God-given dignity of the human being. Human value is rooted in God's decision to impart "glory and honor" and to make humans the stewards of creation.

Hebrews 1:1–4, 2:5–12

Today's reading begins a seven-week series of readings from the letter to the Hebrews. The author begins his letter by introducing its theme: Jesus is unique, the supreme voice and Word of God, the beginning of the universe and its final purpose. In his being, he is the fullness of God, and in his work, he is the expression of God.

Mark 10:2–16

Jesus's teaching on marriage and divorce is given in the context of controversy. The Mosaic regulation assumes the practice of divorce (by the husband); the "certificate of dismissal" was intended to protect the wife by freeing her to remarry. Jesus's answer transforms the question from what is legal to what is right. He quotes from both creation stories to reestablish God's original intention for marriage. The words "Let no one separate" refer to the husband, who was the agent of divorce in Jewish law, and not to a judicial authority. The kingdom calls for a return to the kind of relationships created before the fall, for obedience to the Creator's will rather than the use of a law necessitated by sin.

Collect

Almighty and everlasting God, you are always more ready to hear than we to pray, and to give more than we either desire or deserve: Pour upon us the abundance of your mercy, forgiving us those things of which our conscience is afraid, and giving us those good things for which we are not worthy to ask, except through the merits and mediation of Jesus Christ our Savior; who lives and reigns with you and the Holy Spirit, one God, for ever and ever. *Amen.*

Proper Preface

Of the Lord's Day

1. Of God the Father

For you are the source of light and life; you made us in your image, and called us to new life in Jesus Christ our Lord.

or this

2. Of God the Son

Through Jesus Christ our Lord; who on the first day of the week overcame death and the grave, and by his glorious resurrection opened to us the way of everlasting life.

or the following

3. Of God the Holy Spirit

For by water and the Holy Spirit you have made us a new people in Jesus Christ our Lord, to show forth your glory in all the world.

(Rite II, BCP 377–378; Rite I, BCP 344–345)

Seasonal Pairings

See the table below for choices appointed and suggested for this day. Preferences are put in **bold**. Not all choices are suitable for all congregations or community, though, so consider these preferences as a starting point before making a decision about your own congregation.

	Proper 22	Rite I	Rite II	EOW1	BOS 2022
Color	Green				
Entrance Rite	Customary; opening acclamation "Blessed be God" or one of the first two in EOW1	323	355	50	
Song of Praise/Kyrie	Gloria in excelsis or BCP Canticle 13, 9; EOW1 Canticle A, N	Gloria 324	Gloria 356; C13– 90; C9 – 86	A – 30; N – 37	
Collect		182	234		
Creed	Nicene Creed	326, 327	358	53	
Prayers of the People	**Locally written**; options below; BCP forms	329	387–393	54–55	
Offertory Sentence	"I will wash my hands in innocence, O Lord, that I may go in procession round your altar, singing aloud a song of thanksgiving and recounting all your wonderful deeds." (Psalm 26)	343–344	376–377		
Eucharistic Prayer	**Sept-Oct – Rite I, suggest Prayer 2; Rite II, suggest Prayer B, if A was used in the summer; EOW1 suggest Prayer 3.**	**2–340**	**B – 367**	**3–62**	
Proper Preface	**The Lord's Day 1 – Of God the Father**	344–345	377–378		
Breaking of the Bread (Fraction)	Christ our Passover (BCP); S 167 – S 172 in *The Hymnal 1982*; EOW1 options	337	364	69	
Postcommunion Prayer		339	**Almighty and everliving God – 366**	**Loving God – 70**	
Blessing	Customary	339	366	70–71	
Dismissal	**Go in peace to love and serve the Lord**	340	366		
Notes	St. Francis Day may fall on or near this Sunday; indigenous People's Day may fall after this Sunday				

Additional Notes:

Song of Praise/Canticle – Suggested here is a canticle for the autumn from the BCP and an option from EOW1 (Canticle 13 and Canticle A) as well as one or two that reflects themes of the day. The Gloria, of course, is always appropriate in this season.

Eucharistic Prayer – Using a consistent option for September and October will help tie these week together, especially since some will be returning to worship after a time away.

Content Resources

Reading Between the Lines

Job 1:1, 2:1–10

The book of Job begins and ends with a prose story. The land of Uts is in the Transjordan. The book draws on a motif of a pious man who suffers, and a friend who visits him, urging him to avoid criticizing God and observe instead signs of Providence around him. Job belongs to wisdom material in the Bible including Proverbs, some narrative material, and prophecy. Alongside the wisdom book of Ecclesiastes (Qohelet), Job offers a challenge to traditional theology of just retribution. The prologue describes a man of integrity who "feared God (Elohim) and turned from evil." Chapter 2 contains the plot. In the heavenly realm divine beings, including Satan assemble around YHWH. Addressing Satan, Yahweh, on hearing that Satan has been roving the earth, asks whether he has noticed, "my servant Job." YHWH describes Job: he is unique; blameless and upright; and he holds fast to his integrity in spite of Satan's futile attempt to set me against him. "Skin for skin!" says Satan. Only if his life is threatened will he respond. Satan suggests that if YHWH threatens his life, Job's behavior will change, and he will curse YHWH. So, YHWH hands Job over to Satan with the provision that his life be spared. Job then experiences a skin disease, and he takes pottery to scratch himself with as he sits on the ash-heap. Job's wife observes his plight, and asks, "Are you still persisting in your integrity?" She recommends that he curse God and die. He refuses, arguing, "Shall we receive good at the hand of Elohim and not receive the bad also?"

Central Themes

Church budgets include fixed costs, like salaries and building maintenance, and variable costs, like outreach and children's programs. Fixed costs are viewed as sacrosanct, while outreach and children's programs get cut when money is tight. What if we treated the church budget as a missional document to fulfill our dreams for our community? In 1961 President John F. Kennedy proposed a goal that "before this decade is out, of landing a man on the Moon." The moon landing happened in 1969. What if the congregation shared a dream of awesome outreach and children's programs? Would you collaborate to fulfill that dream?

The Pharisees were not asking if everyone could get divorced, just men. In their culture, adultery was seen as a crime only women could commit against their husbands. Women depended on their husbands for their financial and social well-being. Divorce left women very vulnerable, without a home and income. We see the struggle with this double-standard issue in our society today in many ways as in Taylor Swift's song "The Man." In it she acknowledges how she and her actions would be perceived in a positive way if she were a man.

Community is important to us, and hospitality is its centerpiece. Status was of crucial importance in the Mediterranean world of the first century. Children had no status in that world. Jesus dismisses the overly protective disciples and declares that the children are icons of a sort: they represent those who understand intuitively what it takes to enter and be received into the kingdom. Juxtaposed with the saying about marriage, the introduction of the children means that we cannot be so enamored of and enmeshed in legalism and status that we forget how to be receptive. The kingdom is not to be gained by status or rigidly following rules; it is a gift to be received gratefully, graciously, as children receive good gifts from adults.

Engaging All Ages

Jesus welcomes and blesses children. He says we should all receive the kingdom of God as a little child. What is special about children? What is the unique way that they engage with God and the kingdom? Jesus does not say that adults cannot receive the kingdom but that people of all ages should encounter it as children do. Children have an orientation of curiosity, wonder, love, trust, generosity, reverence, awe, and delight. How do we hold on to these spiritual gifts as we grow up?

Prayers of the People: Option 1

Merciful and loving God, we come before you seeking your grace. Create in us lives that are gracious and loving. We raise our hearts and voices to you, responding,

In your mercy, Lord

Hear our prayer.

Reveal yourself to us in the world you have fashioned: in the wonder of your creation and in the faces of our brothers and sisters. Strengthen our commitment to being good stewards of all that we are and all that we have. Keep us mindful of the billions of your children we will never know, and the generations which will follow us.

In your mercy, Lord

Hear our prayer.

Train our hearts on you and teach us to listen to your voice and follow your lead. Equip us, we pray, with all we need to do the work you have given us to do: to reflect your goodness in the world, to open our hearts to all people, to partner with you in your mission of reconciliation.

In your mercy, Lord

Hear our prayer.

Flood this nation with a yearning for justice for all people in all things. Shine a light into those instances where we have been wrong or where we have claimed more than our share while the needs of others have been ignored. Ignite in us a passion for your purpose in this world you love so dearly.

In your mercy, Lord

Hear our prayer.

As you never tire of loving us, may we never tire of caring for your people who are suffering in body, mind, or spirit. We thank you for experiences of new life and insight. We rejoice with those households expanding with new children and life-giving relationships. Hold close to your heart those who are making their final journey home to you. Grant them a peaceful end and a joyous entry into the communion of all the saints in light. We pray for *N.*

In your mercy, Lord

Hear our prayer.

Prayers of the People: Option 2

Deacon or Presider

Let us offer up prayers to Christ Jesus, who took little children in his arms and blessed them.

Intercessor

We pray for all the holy people of God; we pray for our Presiding Bishop, *N.*; our Bishop *N.*; our parish clergy, and all members of the Church. Lord, in your mercy,

Hear our prayer.

We pray for the ministries of this congregation and for our lay leaders. Lord, in your mercy,

Hear our prayer.

We pray for all elected and appointed leaders. Guide them with wisdom, mercy, and most especially, compassion for the poor and downtrodden. Guide us to persist in integrity and build towards a better future together. Lord, in your mercy,

Hear our prayer.

We pray for the earth, and for the fragile resources we so often despoil. Help us become greater stewards of the earth. Fill us with higher love for your Creation and let us more readily read your lessons from the Great Book of Nature. Lord, in your mercy,

Hear our prayer.

We pray for all organizations and volunteers working to feed those who are hungry and provide clothes for those who have little. Lord, in your mercy,

Hear our prayer.

We pray for those who need healing and ongoing care. We pray for those whose needs are known to you alone. We pray for those who are travelling and for those serving in the Armed Forces. We pray for those who are homeless, those in prison, and all who are suffering. Lord, in your mercy,

Hear our prayer.

We pray for those who have died. We pray for all those who have lost their lives in the course of spreading Christ's Love. Lord, in your mercy,

Hear our prayer.

Let us pray for our own needs, or those of others.

Silence. The people may add their own prayers

Lord, in your mercy,

Hear our prayer.

Lifting our voices with all of your Creation, with the Blessed Virgin Mary, and all the saints, let us be crowned with glory and honor through your Son, Christ Jesus.

To you, O Lord, our God.

Presider

Lord Christ, you took the little children into your arms, blessed them, and said that the kingdom of God belongs to them. Take us into your arms; bless us; wash away our sins. Welcome us to your kingdom, and let us sit at the table with the Father and the Holy Ghost, who reign with you in Heaven, now and forever. ***Amen.***

Hymns for the Day

The Hymnal 1982

Eternal Spirit of the living Christ 698
Only-begotten, Word of God eternal 360, 361
Commit thou all that grieves thee 669 (SC)
If thou but trust in God to guide thee 635 (SC)
O worship the King, all glorious above 388 (SC)
Surely it is God who saves me 678, 679 (SC)
For the beauty of the earth 416 (GR)
Joyful, joyful, we adore thee 376 (GR)
Your love, O God, has called us here 353 (GR)
All hail the power of Jesus's Name 450, 451
From God Christ's deity came forth 443
Hail, thou once despised Jesus! 495
Lead us, heavenly Father, lead us 559
My song is love unknown 458 (1–2, 6–7)
O love, how deep, how broad, how high 448, 449
The head that once was crowned with thorns 483
Now thank we all our God 396, 397

O God of love, to thee we bow 350
O God, to those who here profess 352
When Jesus left his Father's throne 480

Lift Every Voice and Sing II

Oh Lord, how perfect is your name 57 (GR)
Children of the heavenly Father 213
Jesus loves me! this I know 218
There's not a friend like the lowly Jesus 90
Jesus loves the little children 222

Proper 23

Sunday on or between October 9 and 15

The desire for wealth can lead to injustice, lack of compassion, and the estrangement from God.

Anchor Points – The Propers and the Season

The fixed points for each service are the appointed or proper readings and collect as well as the themes of the day or season.

Readings and Psalm

Job 23:1–9, 16–17

Today's reading comes from Job's reply to the friends whose attempts to comfort him are summarized by their refusal to recognize his innocence and their advice that he recognize and admit his guilt even if it is not apparent. Sensing the futility of the friends' accusations and explanations because they are based on the commonly accepted view of God's justice, Job wants to bring his dispute with God, his real adversary, to a judgment. Though he knows that he would be outmatched in a direct struggle, he firmly believes that even God would come to see the justice of his cause and consequently the wrongfulness of his suffering.

Psalm 22:1–15

The psalmist describes the distress he is suffering and his trust in God. The Lord has always been faithful to Israel and to him. But now he is tormented by enemies, whom he likens to savage beasts.

or

Amos 5:6–7, 10–15

Justice is completed by the fulfillment of mutual responsibilities that arise from the particular relationships within the community, all founded on the basic bond between the covenant community and God. Injustice involves the use of power by the rich and the strong in disregard for the community. Still God offers life to the people if they will seek the Lord. They are to seek God, however, not by relying on God's presence at religious shrines. They are to seek God by ensuring justice for all.

Psalm 90:12–17

This psalm faces squarely the dark realities of the human condition within the context of faith. It laments the shortness of human life and seeks God's presence so the people may rejoice in all their days.

Hebrews 4:12–16

God's word probes the inmost part of our being to reveal our true nature. Yet, in case this warning discourages us, the author reminds us of the graciousness of Jesus, our high priest. Verses 14–16 emphasize Jesus's solidarity with humanity. Like the high priest who annually made atonement by entering the Holy of Holies (Leviticus 16:1–19), Jesus "has passed through the heavens" (v. 14) to intercede for us. Because Jesus has gone before us, we can approach God's throne without fear, confident of finding a merciful reception.

Mark 10:17–31

Mark's account of the rich man centers on the difficulties of responding to the call to discipleship. This event illustrates Mark's parable of the sower, in particular those who hear God's word "but the cares of the world, and the lure of wealth, and the desire for other things come in and choke the word, and it yields nothing" (Mark 4:18). The focus is on God first. Thus, Jesus rejects the word "good" for himself and redirects the man's attention to God, the source of absolute goodness. The man's question reveals that he knows of his need for something more than a basic obedience to the commandments. Jesus's response focuses on the root issue for the man's conversion – his attachment to things. Jesus does not condemn material possessions, but urges detachment, freedom from "things" that allows for a more radical attachment to God.

Collect

Almighty and everlasting God, in Christ you have revealed your glory among the nations: Preserve the works of your mercy, that your Church throughout the world may persevere with steadfast faith in the confession of your Name; through Jesus Christ our Lord, who lives and reigns with you and the Holy Spirit, one God, forever and ever. *Amen.*

Proper Preface

Of the Lord's Day

1. Of God the Father

For you are the source of light and life; you made us in your image, and called us to new life in Jesus Christ our Lord.

or this

2. Of God the Son

Through Jesus Christ our Lord; who on the first day of the week overcame death and the grave, and by his glorious resurrection opened to us the way of everlasting life.

or the following

3. Of God the Holy Spirit

For by water and the Holy Spirit you have made us a new people in Jesus Christ our Lord, to show forth your glory in all the world.

(Rite II, BCP 377–378; Rite I, BCP 344–345)

Seasonal Pairings

See the table below for choices appointed and suggested for this day. Preferences are put in **bold**. Not all choices are suitable for all congregations or community, though, so consider these preferences as a starting point before making a decision about your own congregation.

	Proper 23	Rite I	Rite II	EOW1	BOS 2022
Color	Green				
Entrance Rite	Customary; opening acclamation "Blessed be God" or one of the first two in EOW1	323	355	50	
Song of Praise/Kyrie	Gloria in excelsis or BCP Canticle 13, 16; EOW1 Canticle A, S	Gloria 324	Gloria 356; C13– 90; C16 – 92	A – 30; S – 40	
Collect		183	234		
Creed	Nicene Creed	326, 327	358	53	
Prayers of the People	**Locally written**; options below; BCP forms	329	387–393	54–55	
Offertory Sentence	"Let us approach the throne of grace with boldness, so that we may receive mercy and find grace to help in time of need." (Hebrews)	343–344	376–377		
Eucharistic Prayer	**Sept-Oct – Rite I, suggest Prayer 2; Rite II, suggest Prayer B, if A was used in the summer; EOW1 suggest Prayer 3.**	**2–340**	**B – 367**	**3–62**	
Proper Preface	**The Lord's Day 2 – Of God the Son**	344–345	377–378		
Breaking of the Bread (Fraction)	Christ our Passover (BCP); S 167 – S 172 in *The Hymnal 1982*; EOW1 options	337	364	69	
Postcommunion Prayer		339	**Almighty and everliving God – 366**	**Loving God – 70**	
Blessing	Customary	339	366	70–71	
Dismissal	**Go in peace to love and serve the Lord**	340	366		
Notes					

Additional Notes:

Song of Praise/Canticle – Suggested here is a canticle for the autumn from the BCP and an option from EOW1 (Canticle 13 and Canticle A) as well as one or two that reflects themes of the day. The Gloria, of course, is always appropriate in this season.

Eucharistic Prayer – Using a consistent option for September and October will help tie these week together, especially since some will be returning to worship after a time away.

Content Resources

Reading Between the Lines

Job 23:1–9; 16–17

The speeches of Job, addressed to one or other of three companions Eliphaz, are written in verse. They each offer different forms of conventional wisdom to Job, arguing at first that God would do nothing unjust. Job replies to each in turn. Later on, they become unsympathetic, persuaded that Job has become blasphemous. In the meantime, Job has launched a lawsuit against God as a means of determining reasons for his predicament. He is determined that God should respond to his charges. Before the end of a book a fourth companion, Elihu, is introduced.

Job 23 is his response to Eliphaz's third discourse. Job had been arguing that because God does not know or care, the wicked flourish. Eliphaz pokes fun at Job's insistence that God is punishing him for unknown crimes. What Job regards as the distance of God is really God perspective on just acts. Wicked people do in fact suffer. Job insists that his suffering is genuine. He exclaims that if he could find God, he would bring God his lawsuit, and arguing his case before him. Job envisions that God would listen to Job, and make a defense, in the way an honest person gets a hearing and a day in court. But God evades Job's search and has weakened Job's resolve. Job is down but not out.

Central Themes

When catastrophes like earthquakes, hurricanes, and wildfires occur, mandatory evacuations are called because it becomes unsafe for people to remain in their homes. First responders do their best to help people evacuate and to protect property, but the first priority is always life over property. First responders often risk their own safety to help. It is selfishness – caring more about your belongings than others' lives – that leads some people to refuse evacuation, making rescues necessary. The lesson we learn from refugees fleeing their countries to find safety for their families is that the priority is, indeed, always life over property.

Job invites us into the spiritual practice of lament, which is a foreign practice for many. In *Reconciling All Things*[1], Emmanuel Katongole and Chris Rice write that "lament calls us into a fundamental journey of transformation. If we are to follow the path this practice lays out for us, we have to unlearn three things: speed, distance, and innocence." The authors encourage followers of Jesus us to slow down and notice the brokenness of their neighborhood and world, to draw close to that pain and name where they and their faith community have perpetuated the injustice. In this practice, we allow the wounds of the world to be heard.

In one major stream of the Judeo-Christian tradition, wealth was understood to be a blessing from God. The rich man who goes away has forgotten – perhaps because he was preoccupied with all that wealth – are blessed, or in this case wealthy, are to bless others in return. "Pay it forward" is not a twenty-first century invention; "striving for justice and peace" is our way of blessing. "The poor, the widow, the orphan, and the stranger at the gate" from the earlier tradition must never be forgotten or neglected. The prophets had insisted that the God of Israel protects their interests and will not deal kindly with those who disregard them.

Engaging All Ages

One way to trap a monkey is to put a delicious banana inside a strong glass jar. The monkey reaches in to get the food, but grasping the banana in a fist, its hand is too big to remove from the jar. In this compromised position, the monkey can easily be caught with a net. The rich man in today's gospel is holding on to his wealth so tightly that he traps himself. He cannot reach the kingdom of God. Money is not the only thing we clutch to the detriment of our relationship with God. What do you have trouble letting go of?

Prayers of the People: Option 1

That we may continually seek you and find you. That we may know, deep in our hearts, that we are yours.

We lift our hearts and voices to you.

Hear us, good Lord.

That your grace may always precede and follow. That our lives may be signs of your kingdom, and witnesses to your goodness.

We lift our hearts and voices to you.

Hear us, good Lord.

That there be peace in our hearts, in our churches, between neighbors and nations. May the peace we seek begin with you and overflow beyond measure.

We lift our hearts and voices to you.

Hear us, good Lord.

We give thanks for your extravagant care of us; for your seeking after us, finding us, and keeping us close. We pray

1 *Reconciling All Things* (IVP Books, 2008), 79.

that we may follow your model of loving-kindness to those with whom we live and work and worship. That your love for us may overflow into extravagant love for all your children.

We lift our hearts and voices to you.

Hear us, good Lord.

We pray on behalf of those who are suffering with pain, who are paralyzed by fear, who are listless and restless and tired. Relieve their misery, be with them in their distress. Bring them to a new sense of hope and wholeness. We pray for:

We lift our hearts and voices to you.

Hear us, good Lord.

We rejoice with those who have entered the larger life, who now reside among the saints in light. We pray for those who mourn and who experience a deep loss.

Hear us, good Lord.

Prayers of the People: Option 2

Deacon or Presider

With thankful hearts we pray, saying, hear us, Lord God.

Intercessor

We thank you heavenly Father for all our blessings. Help us share your many gifts with others.

Hear us, Lord God.

We pray for all God's holy people. We pray for our Presiding Bishop, *N.*, our Bishop *N.*, our parish clergy, and all members of the Church.

Hear us, Lord God.

We pray for the ministries of this congregation and for our lay leaders.

Hear us, Lord God.

Renew in us your call to bring your Kingdom on earth.

Hear us, Lord God.

Forgive us for our errors, for putting material comforts and our own desires before the needs of our siblings.

Hear us, Lord God.

We pray for those who suffer in any way and those in trouble. Make us channels of your healing power and love.

Hear us, Lord God.

Give rest to all the departed. We pray for all those who mourn.

Hear us, Lord God.

Be with us as we strive to follow in the footsteps of your beloved Son.

Hear us, Lord God.

Let us pray for our own needs, or those of others.

Silence. The people may add their own prayers

Presider

God of abundance, who has planted us in this congregation and sustains us day by day, grow us in your grace, that we may become more fully the people you have called us to be; that we may flourish by your faith in us; and that we may accomplish your will with the gifts you have given us; through Jesus Christ our Redeemer. ***Amen.***

Hymns for the Day

The Hymnal 1982

From deepest woe I cry to thee 151 (SC)
Out of the depths I call 666 (SC)
Father all loving, who rulest in majesty 568 (GR)
Give praise and glory unto God 375 (GR)
O day of God, draw nigh 600, 601 (GR)
O God, our help in ages past 680 (GR)
"Thy kingdom come!" on bended knee 615 (GR)
Alleluia! sing to Jesus! 460, 461
Before thy throne, O God, we kneel 574, 575
From God Christ's deity came forth 443
Completed, Lord, the Holy Mysteries 346
God himself is with us 475
Hope of the world, thou Christ of great compassion 472
Jesus, all my gladness 701
O for a closer walk with God 683, 684
O Jesus, I have promised 655
Sing praise to God who reigns above 408
Take my life, and let it be 707

Lift Every Voice and Sing II

I have decided to follow Jesus 136
Thou my everlasting portion 122

Wonder, Love, and Praise

Gracious Spirit, give your servants 782

Proper 24

Sunday on or between October 16 and 22

God calls the Christian into servant ministry, which means sharing in the suffering of others in order to bring life and healing.

Anchor Points – The Propers and the Season

The fixed points for each service are the appointed or proper readings and collect as well as the themes of the day or season.

Readings and Psalm

Job 38:1–7, (34–41)

The dramatic climax of the book comes with the appearance of Yahweh, creator of heaven and earth, in response to Job's challenge. The divine voice from the whirlwind responds with language filled with images of word and combat. God has come to engage with the human revolutionary Job and with the forces of chaos. Thus, God will destabilize Job's proposal that humans should rule over creation by pointing out their impotence and reaffirm the constant divine struggle against chaotic forces that seek to upset the ordered creation that God has established.

Psalm 104:1–9, 25, 37b

This hymn to God as Creator shares the imagery of many Near Eastern nature poems and myths but changes their emphasis.

or

Isaiah 53:4–12

In today's passage, the servant's role as representative is made clear. What was ours (infirmities, diseases, transgressions, iniquities) was made his, though he was righteous. Disaster and affliction were thought to be evidence of God's judgment on an individual's wickedness. Yet the life and death of the servant was in God's hands, and his experiences were a part of God's plan. Ultimately the righteousness of the servant will be made clear.

Psalm 91:9–16

This psalm is a wisdom psalm; that is, a psalm of *torah*, of instruction. It is a meditation upon God as the protector of the faithful from both human and demonic foes.

Hebrews 5:1–10

In this New Testament lesson, we hear how through obedience and suffering Christ reached the perfection of his destiny and was designated by God to be the eternal high priest. The high priesthood of Jesus is the great theme of the Letter to the Hebrews. Like the high priests of the old covenant, Christ is chosen from among human beings and so has sympathy with human weakness. But he is the Son and has now been named high priest forever. He succeeds Melchizedek, a royal and priestly figure from antiquity, and has been made the source of salvation for all who trust in him.

Mark 10:35–45

Today's gospel reading consists of two parts: the story about who would be greatest in the kingdom and Jesus's teaching about greatness and power. Jesus uses the occasion to expand on his earlier teaching in which he reversed the natural order of hierarchy and power. Within the Church, however, the humblest slave was to be most highly regarded. Jesus's own example sanctified the lowly and humble role of discipleship. Like him, the truly great person in the kingdom is the one who pours out his or her life in the service of others.

Collect

Almighty and everlasting God, in Christ you have revealed your glory among the nations: Preserve the works of your mercy, that your Church throughout the world may persevere with steadfast faith in the confession of your Name; through Jesus Christ our Lord, who lives and reigns with you and the Holy Spirit, one God, for ever and ever. *Amen.*

Proper Preface

Of the Lord's Day

1. Of God the Father

For you are the source of light and life; you made us in your image, and called us to new life in Jesus Christ our Lord.

or this

2. Of God the Son

Through Jesus Christ our Lord; who on the first day of the week overcame death and the grave, and by his glorious resurrection opened to us the way of everlasting life.

or the following

3. Of God the Holy Spirit

For by water and the Holy Spirit you have made us a new people in Jesus Christ our Lord, to show forth your glory in all the world.

(Rite II, BCP 377–378; Rite I, BCP 344–345)

Seasonal Pairings

See the table below for choices appointed and suggested for this day. Preferences are put in **bold**. Not all choices are suitable for all congregations or community, though, so consider these preferences as a starting point before making a decision about your own congregation.

	Proper 24	Rite I	Rite II	EOW1	BOS 2022
Color	Green				
Entrance Rite	Customary; opening acclamation "Blessed be God" or one of the first two in EOW1	323	355	50	
Song of Praise/Kyrie	Gloria in excelsis or BCP Canticle 13, 15; EOW1 Canticle A, L	Gloria 324	Gloria 356; C13– 90; C15 – 91	A – 30; L – 36	
Collect		183	235		
Creed	Nicene Creed	326, 327	358	53	
Prayers of the People	**Locally written**; options below; BCP forms	329	387–393	54–55	
Offertory Sentence	"The Son of Man came not to be served but to serve, and to give his life a ransom for many." (Hebrews)	343–344	376–377		
Eucharistic Prayer	**Sept-Oct – Rite I, suggest Prayer 2; Rite II, suggest Prayer B, if A was used in the summer; EOW1 suggest Prayer 3.**	**2–340**	**B – 367**	**3–62**	
Proper Preface	**The Lord's Day 2 – Of God the Holy Spirit**	344–345	377–378		
Breaking of the Bread (Fraction)	Christ our Passover (BCP); S 167 – S 172 in *The Hymnal 1982*; EOW1 options	337	364	69	
Postcommunion Prayer		339	**Eternal God – 365**	**God of abundance – 69**	
Blessing	Customary	339	366	70–71	
Dismissal	**Go in peace to love and serve the Lord**	340	366		
Notes	St. Luke's Day may fall on or near this Sunday; A Children's Sabbath may fall on or near this Sunday				

Additional Notes:

Song of Praise/Canticle – Suggested here is a canticle for the autumn from the BCP and an option from EOW1 (Canticle 13 and Canticle A) as well as one or two that reflects themes of the day. The Gloria, of course, is always appropriate in this season.

Eucharistic Prayer – Using a consistent option for September and October will help tie these week together, especially since some will be returning to worship after a time away.

Content Resources

Reading Between the Lines

Job 38:1–7, 34–41

Job's strategy to file a lawsuit in order to get the Deity to appear has succeeded and God appears in the first of several speeches. "Speaking out of a whirlwind" indicates that God has taken on the persona of a storm god, using the elements of nature aggressively as elements of war.

The Deity asserts dominance and aggression, posing questions that eliminate Job, and arguing that Job has made groundless arguments on the basis of ignorance. Noting that interpreters of Job regard these arguments as legitimate statements of divine providence, and that Job has a healthy self-esteem, Prof Edward L. Greenstein argues that Job is here treated in a bullying fashion noting that "God barely touches on anything connected to justice or to the providential care of humanity." God causes rain where it reaches no human, and food is offered to lions and ravens, in an amoral world (*Job: A New Translation*, p.166). God occupies the farthest reaches of earth from the world of Job: foundations of the earth, doors of the sea, horizon of dawn, gates of death, storage places of hail. Job's world is the traditional space of an elder with his peers.

Central Themes

Job jealousy occurs when we are convinced that we deserve a position more than the person selected. Jesus's disciples grumble when he says that one must be called by God for the priesthood. Qualifications like education and experience end up being less significant than inner qualities that defy ordinary description. We understand how an actor or singer might be chosen over a more experienced performer because of qualities described as "sparkle" or "a good fit." It's harder to accept the choices made when lofty resumes are compared. Yet calling is something that plays a bigger role than credited in many settings.

Polarizing politics, beautiful people, disasters – the extremes consume much of the media's attention. Jesus's response to James's and John's argument about who gets to sit next to Jesus is an opportunity to share stories of servant leadership, the stories that do not grab much media attention. The teacher who tutors a struggling student for no pay, the person who delivers meals to the housebound, the child who befriends the new classmate – these are all stories of servant leadership and hope that we have within our community.

The purpose of Jesus's life, ministry, and death is enunciated most clearly in Mark in the final verse of this week's gospel: "not to be served but to serve and to give his life as a ransom for many." In a status culture, where honor is valued and shame is be avoided, such goals upend cultural norms. The Way of Love, the twenty-first century edition of the Jesus Movement, embraces these goals. We understand that we most clearly identify ourselves as Christian when we follow the path he walked and to which he pointed. Serving others and giving others priority is our identity.

Engaging All Ages

Have you ever fought with a sibling over who gets to ride in the front seat? Or over who gets the corner piece of cake? Or who gets to choose what movie to see? In today's gospel reading James and John jockey for a seat next to Jesus for all eternity. Jesus explains again and again that these fights miss the point. The point is not who gets the best seat or the most icing. The point is arriving safely, being together, or enjoying a homemade treat. The point following Jesus in the way of love, which means giving up a bit of what we want for something more important.

Prayers of the People: Option 1

O God, Creator, Redeemer, Spirit – the One who knows and loves us best – we thank you for the great gift of your presence among us. Hold us close when we struggle with the noise of life. Call us to a quiet place so that we can hear your voice and come to understand your will.

Lord, in your mercy

Hear our prayer.

Keep your church rooted in your Word and grounded in your love. Guide our leaders as they walk beside us, supporting us in our journey of faith. We pray for *N.* our Bishop, etc.

Lord, in your mercy

Hear our prayer.

Give those in authority an imagination and determination for peace between peoples, of plenty for all, of justice for everyone, even those who are forgotten.

Lord, in your mercy

Hear our prayer.

In places where famine and weather disasters have destroyed lives and drained people of hope, we pray for those who suffer loss as well as those who seek to relieve their distress.

Lord, in your mercy

Hear our prayer.

We pray for healing for those close to us whom we now name: ____________ . Assure them of your goodness that never ends, your grace that surrounds them on every side. We pray also for those who are voiceless, who have never known you, who are imprisoned by fear, that we witness to them your steadfast love.

Lord, in your mercy

Hear our prayer.

We pray for those who are born today as well as those who are being welcomed home to your eternal kingdom. May your will for each of those you love be fulfilled here on earth and in the life to come.

Lord, in your mercy

Hear our prayer.

Prayers of the People: Option 2

Deacon or Presider

Gracious God, you manifest your power primarily in the service of your compassion and love for all humanity, and you are clothed with majesty and splendor: Listen to us as we call upon you in prayer, saying: O God, how excellent is your greatness; the earth is full of your creatures. Alleluia!

Litanist

You have called your Church to be your humble community of service, having been baptized with the baptism of Jesus: Guide your people into such faithfulness, that we may serve the world in your name and make intercession on behalf of all.

O God, how excellent is your greatness;

the earth is full of your creatures. Alleluia!

In this fallen world, there are rulers who lord it over your children and great ones who are tyrants over others: Honor the sacrifice and sufferings of your lambs and take away these perversions of justice, so that the great among us will be servants, and those who wish to be first will become the slave of all.

O God, how excellent is your greatness;

the earth is full of your creatures. Alleluia!

Hear our prayers and supplications through our great high priest Jesus as we intercede for all who suffer throughout the world, especially those who live under the rule of tyrants or who face violence, oppression, or poverty.

O God, how excellent is your greatness;

the earth is full of your creatures. Alleluia!

You have bound us to you in love and called us to share in your ministry of service: Empower those in our community who give their lives as servants of others, that the will of the Lord may prosper.

O God, how excellent is your greatness;

the earth is full of your creatures. Alleluia!

We offer our prayers for those for whom we are called to pray, especially ___________. We offer our grateful thanks for your presence and deliverance, especially for ___________. Let those who have died sit with the triumphant Christ in glory, as we remember ___________.

O God, how excellent is your greatness;

the earth is full of your creatures. Alleluia!

Presider

Almighty God, through your servant Jesus Christ, the righteous one, you have made many righteous, raising him from suffering into glory: Let your resurrection power be present to all in need as you strengthen us for the leadership of service in your name, through Jesus Christ, who with you and the Holy Spirit, lives in unity and love, forever and ever. ***Amen.***

Hymns for the Day

The Hymnal 1982

God is Love, let heaven adore him 379 (SC)
Many and great, O God, are thy works 385 (SC)
Songs of praise the angels sang 426 (SC)
Ah, holy Jesus, how hast thou offended 158 (GR)
Hail, thou once despised Jesus! 495 (GR)
Jesus, our mighty Lord, our strength in sadness 478 (GR)
O sacred head, sore wounded 168, 169 (GR)
To mock your reign, O dearest Lord 170 (GR)
From God Christ's deity came forth 443
O Love of God, how strong and true 455, 456
All praise to thee, for thou, O King divine 477
By all your saints still striving 231, 232 [*Use either St. Luke or St. James of Jerusalem for verse 2, depending on proximity to Sunday or emphasis.*]
For thy blest saints, a noble throng 276
Go forth for God; go to the world in peace 347
Jesu, Jesu, fill us with your love 602
Lord, we have come at your own invitation 348
O holy city, seen of John 582, 583
O Master, let me walk with thee 659, 660
Sing, ye faithful, sing with gladness 492

Lift Every Voice and Sing II

He never said a mumbalin' word 33 (GR)
O sacred head, sore wounded 36 (GR)
Jesu, Jesu, fill us with your love 74

Wonder, Love, and Praise

As newborn stars were stirred to song 788 (SC)
O sacred head, sore wounded 735 (GR)
O wheat whose crushing was for bread 760 (GR)
Gracious Spirit, give your servants 782

Proper 25

Sunday on or between October 23 and 29

Jesus comes to proclaim God's new day where people who are physically and metaphorically blind to injustice will see clearly the way of God.

Anchor Points – The Propers and the Season

The fixed points for each service are the appointed or proper readings and collect as well as the themes of the day or season.

Readings and Psalm

Job 42:1–6, 10–17

After Yahweh speaks, Job's lament in dust and ashes ends and a new response of praise begins. Job ceases his dispute, acknowledges God's power and wisdom, recognizes his incompetence and praises the wisdom and justice of God's mysterious ways. Although God vindicates Job's innocence and denounces the dogmatism of his friends, God's ways are still not to be comprehended. God is truly free of all human restraints, even beyond the highest human standards of justice and mercy.

Psalm 34:1–8, (19–22)

The psalmist first gives thanks for deliverance, then testifies to God's goodness, calling upon the other worshipers to share the fruits of his experience. Finally, the psalmist elaborates upon the meaning of "the fear of the Lord" and its consequences.

or

Jeremiah 31:7–9

Today's reading comes from a section (chaps. 30–33) consisting of promises of restoration (30:1–4). In it are gathered Jeremiah's oracles of hope for an eventual renewal for Israel. Jeremiah envisions the restoration of Judah by imagining God's fashioning a new exodus.

Psalm 126

In this psalm the people sing for joy over their deliverance from captivity.

Hebrews 7:23–28

Today's reading points out that Jesus's priesthood is also superior because of its permanence – he will forever function as our high priest – and because of his character – he is holy, blameless, unstained, separated from sinners. Thus, Jesus's sacrifice of himself, "once and for all" (v. 27), as he fulfills the role of high priest and sacrifice, was all that was needed, now and forever, to redeem humanity.

Mark 10:46–52

The story of the healing of Bartimaeus is filled with vivid detail. Bartimaeus calls Jesus "Son of David," a messianic title, recognizing Jesus's true identity. Although blind, Bartimaeus can "see" Jesus more clearly than others because of his faith. No healing word or action of Jesus is recorded, just a response to Bartimaeus's faith. On one level, his faith, in the sense of confidence and persistence, is answered with healing. On another level, his recognition of Jesus is answered with salvation. The phrase "made you well" means both heal and save. Bartimaeus responds by becoming a disciple.

Collect

Almighty and everlasting God, increase in us the gifts of faith, hope, and charity; and, that we may obtain what you promise, make us love what you command; through Jesus Christ our Lord, who lives and reigns with you and the Holy Spirit, one God, for ever and ever. *Amen.*

Proper Preface

Of the Lord's Day

1. Of God the Father

For you are the source of light and life; you made us in your image, and called us to new life in Jesus Christ our Lord.

or this

2. Of God the Son

Through Jesus Christ our Lord; who on the first day of the week overcame death and the grave, and by his glorious resurrection opened to us the way of everlasting life.

or the following

3. Of God the Holy Spirit

For by water and the Holy Spirit you have made us a new people in Jesus Christ our Lord, to show forth your glory in all the world.

(Rite II, BCP 377–378; Rite I, BCP 344–345)

Seasonal Pairings

See the table below for choices appointed and suggested for this day. Preferences are put in **bold**. Not all choices are suitable for all congregations or community, though, so consider these preferences as a starting point before making a decision about your own congregation.

	Proper 25	Rite I	Rite II	EOW1	BOS 2022
Color	Green				
Entrance Rite	Customary; opening acclamation "Blessed be God" or one of the first two in EOW1	323	355	50	
Song of Praise/Kyrie	Gloria in excelsis or BCP Canticle 13, 17; EOW1 Canticle A, M	Gloria 324	Gloria 356; C13 – 90; C17 – 93	A – 30; M – 37	
Collect		183	235		
Creed	Nicene Creed	326, 327	358	53	
Prayers of the People	**Locally written**; options below; BCP forms	329	387–393	54–55	
Offertory Sentence	"Taste and see that the Lord is good; happy are they who trust in him!" (Psalm 34) *or* "The Lord has done great things for us, and we are glad indeed." (Psalm 126)	343–344	376–377		
Eucharistic Prayer	**Sept-Oct – Rite I, suggest Prayer 2; Rite II, suggest Prayer B, if A was used in the summer; EOW1 suggest Prayer 3.**	**2–340**	**B – 367**	**3–62**	
Proper Preface	**The Lord's Day 1 – Of God the Father**	344–345	377–378		
Breaking of the Bread (Fraction)	Christ our Passover (BCP); S 167 – S 172 in *The Hymnal 1982*; EOW1 options	337	364	69	
Postcommunion Prayer		339	**Eternal God – 365**	**God of abundance – 69**	
Blessing	Customary	339	366	70–71	
Dismissal	**Go in peace to love and serve the Lord**	340	366		
Notes	St. Simon's and St. Jude's Day may fall on or near this Sunday				

Additional Notes:

Song of Praise/Canticle – Suggested here is a canticle for the autumn from the BCP and an option from EOW1 (Canticle 13 and Canticle A) as well as one or two that reflects themes of the day. The Gloria, of course, is always appropriate in this season.

Eucharistic Prayer – Using a consistent option for September and October will help tie these week together, especially since some will be returning to worship after a time away.

Content Resources

Reading Between the Lines

Job 42:1–6, 10–17

Job's response to God's reply is the object of much recent study. 42:6 is typically translated, "Therefore I despise myself (or: recant) and repent in dust and ashes." Prof Greenstein notes that "Despise myself" has an analogy in Job 9:21: "I'm fed up with (despise) my life." This verb can occur intransitively in Job 7:16, "I'm fed up." However, he declares that "recant" is an "invention of the translator" assuming a non-existent implicit object like "words." The verb phrase "I repent," can mean "to take pity or have compassion" (Psalm 90:13). "Dust and ashes" is a characterization of Job's abasement in Job 30:19, describing pitiful humanity. Thus Job 42:6 communicates defiance rather than surrender, and is better rendered, "That is why I am fed up; I take pity on "dust and ashes" (humanity). (Greenstein, *Job*, p. 185)

Central Themes

On more than one occasion Jesus says that a person's faith has made them whole. Faith is hard to describe. However, each of those whose faith Jesus said made them whole did one thing in common: they each called out without shame to ask Jesus to heal them. Each of those persons had the humility to admit their need for healing publicly and to ask for healing from Jesus even when his disciples tried to turn them away. Humility and persistence are empowering human traits, while their opposites, pride and impatience, become impediments to receiving the help that one needs.

In Jeremiah, God encourages us to praise and sing together about how God acts and will act within our communities. Today it can be hard to find common music that we can sing with our neighbors. The Justice Choir is an organization created to encourage local singing for worldwide social justice. Chapters have access to a free songbook that can be used to mobilize singing within and around movements, vigils, marches, rallies, and other public events. The hope is to harness the power of singing together to paint a dream of a just world and create change.

Bartimaeus is loud and will not be quieted. His persistence and honesty are rewarded despite the shushing and apparent embarrassment of others at his outbursts. Several verses before we meet Bartimaeus, Jesus had asked the same question of others, "What do you want me to do?" The Zebedees want honor and prestige in the kingdom. Bartimaeus wants only to regain his sight, but he is already more insightful than those two disciples and more than the rich man earlier in this chapter who couldn't give up his possessions. Bartimaeus immediately "throws off" his cloak, showing his willingness to follow Jesus "along the way." I wonder what we're ready to do once we follow Jesus.

Engaging All Ages

In today's gospel, Bartimaeus, a blind man, calls out to Jesus, "Have mercy on me!" Make a list of all that are crying out for mercy right now. You list might include children living in foster care, folks struggling with addiction, or creation. Pray over your list: *God of healing, be present with all those who cry out for mercy. Give them faith, peace, and hope in their time of distress. Help us to notice those around us asking for mercy and to be agents of your healing through love.* ***Amen.***

Prayers of the People: Option 1

We humbly bring our prayers before you and ask you to make of us what you created us to be: faithful followers, vessels of your love.

We praise you, and we bless you.

O Lord, hear our prayer.

We offer our prayers of gratitude for all you are and all you have done for us. Work through us, O God, and increase in us faith, hope, and charity.

We praise you, and we bless you.

O Lord, hear our prayer.

We hear you calling us, your church, to get up and keep moving. Expand our vision of your mission in the world, and don't let fear of discomfort hold us back. We pray for all who follow you, for those who bear the joys and burdens of leadership, for those who are crying out for more of you.

We praise you, and we bless you.

O Lord, hear our prayer.

We thank you for the freedoms and abundance many of us enjoy in this land. May we not take them for granted and keep them to ourselves. Give us courage to participate in civic life and to speak up for those values you have instilled in us for the good of all people. We pray for wisdom our president, the Congress, and courts of this land. May they conduct themselves with integrity.

We praise you, and we bless you.

O Lord, hear our prayer.

We lift to your presence those who are in the throes of physical pain or anxiety, difficult relationships and the weight of financial insecurity. Be their hope and their strength. Make them whole. We pray today for ____________.

We praise you, and we bless you.

O Lord, hear our prayer.

We praise you for the lives of those who have gone before us and now have come to eternal joys and unending glory with you and the host of heaven. We pray for those who have died.

We praise you, and we bless you.

O Lord, hear our prayer.

Prayers of the People: Option 2

Deacon or Presider:

Almighty and everlasting God, we pray to you with grateful hearts saying, "Help us to love what you command."

Intercessor

God who calls us to be a people of hope, love, and life, guide all your ministers to seek your will; we pray for all the baptized, for deacons, priests and bishops.

Help us to love what you command.

God of history, give wisdom to all in authority and to us as citizens of this land.

Help us to love what you command.

Bountiful God, in this season of stewardship, increase in us the gifts of faith, hope and charity, that we may respond in love to the needs of this parish family and those beyond our walls.

Help us to love what you command.

Loving God, who makes all things new, send the blessings of healing to all those troubled in body, mind, or spirit, especially those on our prayer list:

Help us to love what you command.

God of comfort, give rest to the departed, and stretch out your loving arms of to all who mourn.

Help us to love what you command.

God of vision, let us, like Bartimaeus, regain our sight when our vision has faltered or failed.

Help us to love what you command.

Let us now offer our prayers for our own needs and for the needs of others.

Silence. The people may add their own prayers.

Presider:

God of abundance, who has planted us in this congregation and sustains us day by day, grow us in your grace, that we may become more fully the people you have called us to be; that we may flourish by your faith in us; and that we may accomplish your will with the gifts you have given us; through Jesus Christ our Redeemer. ***Amen.***

Hymns for the Day

The Hymnal 1982

God moves in a mysterious way 677 (SC)
New every morning is the love 10 (SC)
O bless the Lord, my soul! 411 (SC)
Praise, my soul, the King of heaven 410 (SC)
Father, we thank thee who hast planted 302, 303 (GR)
God is working his purpose out 534 (GR)
Lord, whose love through humble service 610 (GR)
O God of Bethel, by whose hand 709 (GR)
Sing, ye faithful, sing with gladness 492 (GR)
Surely it is God who saves me 678, 679 (GR)
The Lord will come and not be slow 462 (GR)
Ye servants of God, your Master proclaim 535 (GR)
Alleluia! sing to Jesus! 460, 461
From God Christ's deity came forth 443
Hail, thou once despised Jesus! 495
The Lord ascendeth up on high 219
Amazing grace! how sweet the sound 671
From thee all skill and science flow 566
Give praise and glory unto God 375
I'll praise my Maker while I've breath 429
Just as I am, without one plea 693
O for a thousand tongues to sing 493
Thine arm, O Lord, in days of old 567
Word of God, come down on earth 633

Lift Every Voice and Sing II

I will bless the Lord at all times 154 (SC)
We are often tossed and driv'n on the restless sea of time 207 (SC)
He's got the whole world in his hand 217 (GR)
Amazing grace! how sweet the sound 181

Wonder, Love, and Praise

I will bless the Lord at all times 764 (SC)
Through north and south and east and west 822 (GR)
Gracious Spirit, give your servants 782
Heal me, hands of Jesus 773
O Christ, the healer, we have come 772

Proper 26

Sunday on or between October 30 and November 5

Loving God and neighbor are the greatest commandments.

Anchor Points – The Propers and the Season

The fixed points for each service are the appointed or proper readings and collect as well as the themes of the day or season.

Readings and Psalm

Ruth 1:1–18

Ruth's poetic words to Naomi, known as the "Song of Ruth," typify love that is freely given and a devotion found only in the most solemn human commitments. Jewish and Christian traditions point to Ruth's love as an example of faithful devotion blessed by God. The author of Ruth also holds to this view: Ruth's faithful devotion will help lead both women to not only survive, but also give rise to the lineage of great kings.

Psalm 146

The psalmist expresses thanksgiving that Yahweh is a God who cares for all who are most neglected by society. As the Maker of all, God is committed to defending and lifting up the least members of the created order.

or

Deuteronomy 6:1–9

Today's reading warns that Israel's prosperity depends upon obedience. The great commandment (Mark 12:29–30) positively restates the first commandment of exclusive loyalty to God (5:7). The stress is primarily upon God's unique claim on the Israelites. God's people are to know God's name and to respond single-heartedly to God.

Psalm 119:1–8

In this reading, the psalmist describes those who are blessed because of their fidelity to God's commands and asks God to give wisdom and discernment for keeping them.

Hebrews 9:11–14

The author discusses the sacrificial rites for spiritual cleansing as types, or visual representations, of the true, eternal sacrifice offered by Jesus Christ. Until Jesus, high priests offered the blood of animals. They passed once a year into the temple room called the Holy of Holies to make atonement in God's presence (9:1–7). But there is a "perfect tent (. . . not of this creation)" (v. 11) that has awaited the perfect high priest and the perfect offering. Jesus needed to enter it only once, for he offered his blood. Now our flesh is purified, but even more, our inner being has been made alive once more, made free from evil and free to worship God.

Mark 12:28–34

In the gospel, Jesus answers a question concerning the chief command of the law by reciting the double commandment to love God and one's neighbor. Jesus was not unique in bringing together these two great teachings from Israel's heritage, but the New Testament gives them special emphasis. They are closely linked, for in responding to God's love, we learn that we are lovable, and so begin to be able to love others as ourselves. In loving our neighbors, we discover the mystery that we are also loving in them their Creator. The man who asked Jesus the question repeats the commandments in his own words. He is not far from the kingdom.

Collect

Almighty and merciful God, it is only by your gift that your faithful people offer you true and laudable service: Grant that we may run without stumbling to obtain your heavenly promises; through Jesus Christ our Lord, who lives and reigns with you and the Holy Spirit, one God, now and for ever. *Amen.*

Proper Preface

Of the Lord's Day

1. Of God the Father

For you are the source of light and life; you made us in your image, and called us to new life in Jesus Christ our Lord.

or this

2. Of God the Son

Through Jesus Christ our Lord; who on the first day of the week overcame death and the grave, and by his glorious resurrection opened to us the way of everlasting life.

or the following

3. Of God the Holy Spirit

For by water and the Holy Spirit you have made us a new people in Jesus Christ our Lord, to show forth your glory in all the world.

(Rite II, BCP 377–378; Rite I, BCP 344–345)

Seasonal Pairings

See the table below for choices appointed and suggested for this day. Preferences are put in **bold**. Not all choices are suitable for all congregations or community, though, so consider these preferences as a starting point before making a decision about your own congregation.

	Proper 26	Rite I	Rite II	EOW1	BOS 2022
Color	Green				
Entrance Rite	Customary; opening acclamation "Blessed be God" or one of the first two in EOW1	323	355	50	
Song of Praise/Kyrie	Gloria in excelsis or BCP Canticle 13, 18; EOW1 Canticle A, K	Gloria 324	Gloria 356; C13– 90; C18 – 93	A – 30; K – 36	
Collect		184	235		
Creed	Nicene Creed	326, 327	358	53	
Prayers of the People	**Locally written**; options below; BCP forms	329	387–393	54–55	
Offertory Sentence		343–344	376–377		
Eucharistic Prayer	**Nov – Rite I, suggest Prayer 1; Rite II, suggest Prayer A; EOW1 suggest Prayer .2**	**1–339**	**A – 361**	**2–60**	
Proper Preface	**The Lord's Day 3 – Of God the Holy Spirit**	344–345	377–378		
Breaking of the Bread (Fraction)	Christ our Passover (BCP); S 167 – S 172 in *The Hymnal 1982*; EOW1 options	337	364	69	
Postcommunion Prayer		339	**Eternal God – 365**	**God of abundance – 69**	
Blessing	Customary	339	366	70–71	
Dismissal	**Let us go forth in the name of Christ**	339	366		
Notes	All Hallows' Eve may fall on or near this Sunday; All Saints' Day may fall on or before this Sunday; All Souls' Day may fall on or near this Sunday; Election Day may fall near this Sunday.				

Additional Notes:

Song of Praise/Canticle – Suggested here is a canticle for the autumn from the BCP and an option from EOW1 (Canticle 13 and Canticle A) as well as one or two that reflects themes of the day. The Gloria, of course, is always appropriate in this season.

Eucharistic Prayer – Suggesting to switch to a Eucharistic Prayer for the month of November, to unify this particular phase of the Season and to ensure that a eucharistic prayer that is scheduled for Advent (such as Rite II, prayer B) is not being used in the weeks at precede that season.

Content Resources

Reading Between the Lines

Ruth 1:1–18

Virtues Abraham Joshua Heschel identified as the "spiritual audacity and moral grandeur" of the Hebrew prophets in national life, are situated in the book of Ruth in a quotidian sphere, wherein ordinary people with limited choices nevertheless show ethical excellence. Ruth herself nurtures qualities that can bring about personal and even national change. And Ruth is an ancestor of King David, as the ending of the book shows.

The book of Ruth begins with Elimelech, from Bethlehem, who is married to Naomi. They have two sons. A famine drives them to Moab, where the sons marry. Ruth is the Moabite wife of one of the sons. All three men die. After her husband's death in Moab, Naomi lacks a male heir. Her economic insecurity necessitates a return to Bethlehem, and she urges Ruth and Naomi, wives of her sons, to stay in Moab. To her daughters in law she says: "May the LORD *deal kindly* with you, as you have dealt with the dead and with me." However, Ruth, now a widow, opts to stay with her mother-in-law. The words "deal kindly" can be rendered literally as, "May the Lord do *hesed*..." indicating a benevolent act. This central idea appears at 1:8, 2:20, and 3:10. Signifying hope for a just universe, it describes actions of Ruth and of God. *Hesed*, or *lovingkindness* is enacted freely, and may be reciprocated. In the Hebrew Bible, the *mercy* of God reveals justice in the world alongside *benevolence*. In some cases, *benevolence* even suspends justice. In Ruth, *hesed* is kindness beyond the call of duty. It is contagious and transforms the entire narrative. Ruth embodies *hesed* when she stays with Naomi. Her behavior inspires Boaz's generosity to Ruth (2:8–12). Ruth encourages Boaz to adopt a role of redeemer, which brings *hesed* into the public domain (4:1–10). Boaz marries Ruth and their public union is embraced. Ordinary people serve God's purposes through the cultivation of *hesed.* (*Ruth: JPS Bible Commentary* by Tamara Cohn Eskenazi and Tikva Frymer-Kensky).

Central Themes

"Love God, and love your neighbor as yourself." That's it. However, it turned out we humans needed clarification, because some people find it difficult to love themselves and, consequently, to love others. We don't recognize that we are created in God's image, and we don't see how we can be used to love God's other beloved children. Before his death upon the cross, Jesus gave a New Commandment to his disciples: "Just as I have loved you, you also should love one another." The standard is clear: we are to follow Jesus's example of loving us by loving one another.

In the movie *Mean Girls*, a new girl in a high school quickly learns about the social norms of her school and how shallow peer relationships can be. She has to decide who to call her friends and what the repercussions of those decisions are. At the beginning of Ruth, all of the men who are the source of societal stability for their wives die. Although it would have been understandable for Ruth to leave her mother-in-law, Naomi, Ruth is determined to stay. "Where you go, I will go. Your God will be my God." What relationships reflect God's love like that?

A scribe, often maligned in the gospels as an enemy, and Jesus engage in cordial conversation agreeing that the most important dictum handed down through the tradition is a melding of a portion of Deuteronomy and Leviticus: loving God with everything in you and loving others as well as you love yourself. The theme of the General Convention in 2009 was *Ubuntu,* a Bantu word meaning "I am because we are," or "humanity towards others," but is often used more broadly to express "the belief in a universal bond of sharing that connects all humanity." It is, along with the love of God and the Way of Jesus, another expression of the Jesus Movement and at the heart of the Way of Love.

Engaging All Ages

In today's gospel, Jesus clearly articulates the two commandments that are most important. Do you find one easier than the other? Why? Sometimes we get very focused on loving our neighbor and forget there are other ways to love God. The reverse is also true. How can we actively keep both these commandments? What ongoing practices most help you to love God? What practices are most helpful in loving your neighbor? Consider putting a sticky note on your mirror or alarm clock that says, "Love God. Love neighbor." Read it aloud once a day for a week.

Prayers of the People: Option 1

You are the perfect teacher, O God. Teach us to walk in your ways.

Teach us to love you

with all we are and all we do.

You are worthy of our praise. Teach us to sing your praises and delight in your Word for our lives. Instruct us how to serve you.

Teach us to love you

with all we are and all we do.

You are the perfect leader. Teach us to be attentive citizens of the world and support the efforts of peace, mindful of our responsibilities to the poor and suffering among us. We pray for our leaders.

Teach us to love you

with all we are and all we do.

You are the perfect healer. Incline our hearts and hands toward compassionate service to those who ache from loneliness, those who hunger, those who suffer great pain.

Teach us to love you

with all we are and all we do.

You show us perfect love. Teach us to love our neighbors, especially those with whom we struggle. Help us to mend our relationships with ourselves and with each other. Forgive us when we fail, and teach us to forgive the failures of others.

Teach us to love you

with all we are and all we do.

We pray for those whose journey here has ended, and bring them into the joys of your kingdom and perfect union with you.

You are the perfect teacher, O God. Teach us to walk in your ways. Teach us to love you

with all we are and all we do.

Prayers of the People: Option 2

Presider

Loving and gracious God, you have taught us to love you with all our heart and soul and mind and strength, and to love our neighbor as ourselves: Hear us as we express our love through prayer and intercession, saying: Alleluia! Sing to God a new song; sing praise in the congregation of the faithful.

Litanist

Eternal and Majestic One, you have raised Christ our High Priest into the Holy Place, obtaining eternal redemption for your people: Guide the Church and purify our conscience from dead works to worship you, the living God.

Alleluia! Sing to God a new song;

sing praise in the congregation of the faithful.

Almighty Ruler of All, guide all in authority to exercise their power with a commitment to compassion and justice, for you take pleasure in the people, and you adorn the poor with victory.

Alleluia! Sing to God a new song;

sing praise in the congregation of the faithful.

Merciful and Compassionate One, look upon refugees and immigrants, widows and families who are poor and threatened, who leave their homes seeking hope and prosperity: Guide them into new places of security and hospitality.

Alleluia! Sing to God a new song;

sing praise in the congregation of the faithful.

Creator and Sustainer, be with us in this community that we may be people who follow your law of love.

Alleluia! Sing to God a new song;

sing praise in the congregation of the faithful.

Receive our prayers of intercession into your eternal heart of love, as we pray, especially for______________. Your faithful people rejoice in our Maker and Monarch, hear our prayers of thanksgiving, especially for _____________________. Christ the high priest of the good things that have come has entered into heaven; bring all who have died into your eternal presence, especially_____________________.

Alleluia! Sing to God a new song;

sing praise in the congregation of the faithful.

Presider

Holy and gracious One, your eternal and unqualified love exceeds all we can desire or imagine: Guide us in your way, that we may love you, our neighbors, and ourselves with such singleness of heart, that your kingdom may come quickly among us, through Jesus Christ our great High Priest, in union with the Holy Spirit, One God, for ever and ever. ***Amen.***

Hymns for the Day

The Hymnal 1982

Awake, my soul, stretch every nerve 546
Fight the good fight with all thy might 552, 553
Lo! what a cloud of witnesses 545
Help us, O Lord, to learn 628 (GR)
Open your ears, O faithful people 536 (GR)
Praise to the living God 372 (GR)
Alleluia! sing to Jesus! 460, 461
Draw nigh and take the Body of the Lord 327, 328
From God Christ's deity came forth 443
Glory be to Jesus 479
Hail, thou once despised Jesus! 495
Let thy Blood in mercy poured 313
The Lord ascendeth up on high 219
For the fruit of all creation 424
Jesu, Jesu, fill us with your love 602
King of glory, King of peace 382
Rise up, ye saints of God 551
Where charity and love prevail 581

Lift Every Voice and Sing II

There is a fountain filled with blood 39
Jesu, Jesu, fill us with your love 74

Wonder, Love, and Praise
Guide my feet, Lord, while I run this race 819
Sh'ma Yisrael, Adonai Eloheinu 818 (GR)
Gracious Spirit, give your servants 782
Jesus said: The first commandment is this 815

All Saints' Day

November 1

Sunday after All Saints' Day

All Saints' Day may also be observed on the Sunday following in addition to November 1 (November 2–8)

We remember the saints of God – all faithful believers;
we are surrounded by a great cloud of witnesses.

Anchor Points – The Propers and the Feast

The fixed points for each service are the appointed or proper readings and collect as well as the themes of the day or season.

Readings and Psalm

Wisdom of Solomon 3:1–9

The first reading reflects on the condition of those who have died. While the world thinks they are gone, they instead now live with God and with God rule the universe. God continues to care for all the elect.

or

Isaiah 25:6–9

In the first reading. the prophet foresees the time to come when God will gather all people into the great feast of God's kingdom. This gathering of all the saints will be forever free from death.

Psalm 24

This psalm was likely originally an entrance liturgy, to accompany a procession into the Temple. The psalm describes the attributes of God and humanity who are encountering each other in Temple worship.

Revelation 21:1–6a

The second reading is John's vision of the final establishment of God's kingdom as the heavenly city Jerusalem. God dwells there forever with all the holy people of God and death and sorrow are forever ended.

John 11:32–44

The Gospel reading is the story of the raising of Lazarus. All of us, the baptized saints of God, also hear Jesus call out our name and command us to come out of death and into life. Today's liturgy celebrates the two primary ways in which we become holy people. First, we receive God's Spirit in baptism. Second, we are renewed in God's Spirit each time we celebrate the Eucharist.

Collect

Almighty God, you have knit together your elect in one communion and fellowship in the mystical body of your Son Christ our Lord: Give us grace so to follow your blessed saints in all virtuous and godly living, that we may come to those ineffable joys that you have prepared for those who truly love you; through Jesus Christ our Lord, who with you and the Holy Spirit lives and reigns, one God, in glory everlasting. *Amen.*

Proper Preface

All Saints – For in the multitude of your saints, you have surrounded us with a great cloud of witnesses, that we might rejoice in their fellowship, and run with endurance the race that is set before us; and, together with them, receive the crown of glory that never fades away. (Rite II, BCP 380; Rite I, BCP 347)

Feast Day Pairings

See the table below for choices appointed and suggested for this day. Preferences are put in **bold**. Not all choices are suitable for all congregations or community, though, so consider these preferences as a starting point before making a decision about your own congregation.

	All Saints' Day Sunday after All Saints' Day	Rite I	Rite II	EOW1	BOS 2022
Color	White/Gold/Festive				
Entrance Rite	Customary; opening acclamation "Blessed be God" or one of the first two in EOW1; *or* Holy Baptism	323; Baptism 299	355; Baptism 299	50	
Song of Praise/Kyrie	Canticle 7 or 21 Te Deum, or Gloria in excelsis; EOW1 Canticle 21, P	C7 – 52; Gloria 324	C21 – 95; Gloria 356	C21 – 29; P – 38	
Collect		194	245		
Creed	Baptismal Covenant, when baptizing; Renewal of Baptismal Vows, if no baptisms	304, 292	304, 292		
Prayers of the People	**Locally written**; options below; BCP forms	329	387–393	54–55	
Offertory Sentence	"'Death will be no more; mourning and crying and pain will be no more, for the first things have passed away.' And the one who was seated on the throne said, 'See, I am making all things new.'" (Revelation)	343–344	376–377		
Eucharistic Prayer	**Rite I, suggest Prayer 2; Rite II, suggest Prayer B or D; EOW1 suggest Prayer 2.**	**2–340**	**B – 367; D – 372**	**2–60**	
Proper Preface	**All Saints**	347	380		
Breaking of the Bread (Fraction)	**S 172 (Blessed are those who are called)**;Christ our Passover (BCP); S 170 (Whoever eats this bread); EOW1 options;	337	364	69	
Postcommunion Prayer		339	**Eternal God – 365**	**God of abundance – 69**	
Blessing	**Seasonal Blessing in the BOS**				**17**
Dismissal	**Go in peace to love and serve the Lord.**	340	366		
Notes					

Additional Notes:

Baptisms – This is one of the appointed days particularly appropriate for Holy Baptism. If there are no baptisms, the Renewal of Baptismal Vows is recommended in place of the Creed. The Paschal Candle is appropriately lighted for baptism.

Song of Praise/Canticle – The traditional canticle for this day is the Te Deum though that may be less familiar to a congregation. An additional option would be Canticle P from EOW1 which is from the Book of Revelation. Whatever Canticle is used, the setting should be abundantly celebratory for this Feast of All Saints.

Necrology/Prayers for the Departed – As much as possible, it is suggested to reserve any long or thorough listing of the departed for All Souls' Day, November 2. Of course, not all congregations are able to observe these separately.

Content Resources

Reading Between the Lines

On All Saints' Day 2003, the hockey arena on the campus of the University of New Hampshire in Durham was transformed into a cathedral for the consecration of the Reverend Gene Robinson, newly elected bishop of New Hampshire. Amongst the six co-consecrating bishops were Bishop Barbara Harris, former presiding bishop Edmund Browning, Presiding Bishop Frank Griswold, and Bishop Emeritus of the Lutheran Church of Sweden, Krister Stendahl. At least Bishop Griswold and Gene Robinson wore bulletproof vests because of death threats. Krister Stendahl did not look well. I wept as I watched him leave, singing the last two verses of the final hymn, "For all the saints who from their labors rest":

6 The golden evening brightens in the west; soon, soon to faithful warriors cometh rest; sweet is the calm of paradise the blest. Alleluia! Alleluia!

7 But, lo! there breaks a yet more glorious day; the saints triumphant rise in bright array; the King of glory passes on his way. Alleluia! Alleluia!

Wisdom 3 describes our eternal life with God as peace from struggle and release for the righteous from torment by the wicked. This beautiful 1st Century BCE Greek text, especially 2:12–20, likely influenced composition of the gospel passion narratives. Revelation 21, a seer's vision of the heavenly Jerusalem descending to earth, situates God with humanity, "wiping every tear from their eyes." Death and everything associated with it: crying, mourning and pain, will be gone. John 11:19 describes many Jews consoling Mary and Martha for the death of their brother Lazarus. Jesus grasps their grief (11:33) and "deeply moved in his spirit," weeps at the tomb of Lazarus. And out of that deep grief, great disturbance, and profound love comes new life.

Central Themes

Science has brought us knowledge of the existence of a quantum universe that requires new vocabulary and paradigms to explain how the world works. Jesus said to Martha, sister of Lazarus, "Did I not tell you that if you believed, you would see the glory of God?" While scripture tells us that we cannot bear looking directly at God, Jesus tells us that our faith will enable us to see "the glory of God." Viewing the images from the Hubble Telescope or studying the mysteries of the atomic and subatomic world just might be this generation's seeing "the glory of God."

We are all a part of the communion of saints, the whole family of God. Both the song and picture book "We Are" *We Are One*, respectively, written by Ysaye M. Barnwell and illustrated by Brian Pinkney, invite listeners and readers to reflect on how we are connected to our ancestors through time. Barnwell's words describe relationships like, "We are our grandmothers' prayers . . . daughters of dust, sons of great vision . . . We are Seekers of truth, Keepers of faith." Pinkney's illustrations depict what that might look like to young children. What would you add to this list? What would you draw?

This is the third time in John's gospel that someone has been invited to "come and see" (1:39, 4:29, 11:34). It has always led to discipleship. On this occasion, mourners address the invitation to Jesus, but by the end of this story, several of the others who have come to mourn are led to see, resulting in new discipleship for some of Lazarus's mourners. When we live the Way of Love, when we go the extra mile, listen to those whom others dismiss or ignore, dare to imitate Jesus's hospitality and compassion publicly, others might be prompted to come and see and begin to follow the way themselves.

Engaging All Ages

All Saints' Day provides an opportunity to honor the faithfully departed. When names are collected ahead of time and read aloud, some members of the worshiping body might miss the opportunity to contribute names (children, youth, visitors, and busy folks who didn't read the e-news). How might your church's honoring of the departed take place in a way that allows the most people to participate? Perhaps people could be invited to write names on index cards before the service that are brought forward during the offertory. Perhaps people could light a candle or place a battery-operated tea light as they say the name of a loved one.

Prayers of the People: Option 1

For your holy Church: for those who have led the way,

we give thanks.

For those who will follow us,

we rejoice in hope

For those who sit beside us, those whom we will never meet, who hunger for the riches of your grace,

give them strength for today and for tomorrow.

For those who hold earthly power throughout the world, give them who are in need of courage to hold the space for justice and peace, we pray:

give them strength for today and for tomorrow.

For those whose faith is fragile, who are beset by doubt and wounded by memories of hurt among your church, we pray:

give them strength for today and for tomorrow.

For all who suffer physical pain and for those whose take skilled, tender care of them, we pray:

give them strength for today and hope for tomorrow.

For those who face death today, may they join the throng of those before your throne who praise you, adored by angels and the throng of faithful people called your saints.

May we, too, sing your praises in harmony with those throughout the ages who have looked to you in hope, and have seen your glory. Give us joy, we pray and,

give us strength for each day and each tomorrow.

Prayers of the People: Option 2

Deacon or Priest

As we recall the blessed ones who have gone before us, let us offer prayers to God who adorns the poor with victory.

With the angels and archangels and the spirits of the blessed.

Lord, have mercy.

With Mary, mother of Jesus and bearer of God.

Lord, have mercy.

With the holy patriarchs, prophets, apostles, and martyrs.

Lord, have mercy.

With all the saints, witnesses to the gospel.

Lord, have mercy.

For [those baptized today/preparing to be baptized] all those around the world being baptized today.

Lord, have mercy.

For *N.* our bishop and *N., N.,* our parish clergy, for this holy gathering, and for the people of God in every place.

Lord, have mercy.

For all nations, cohorts, peoples, and languages.

Lord, have mercy.

For all those who are sick and those who suffer, for any who are hungry or thirsty, for those who are poor, the me, and all who are persecuted.

Lord, have mercy.

For the dead and those who mourn, we pray.

Lord, have mercy.

For our city and those who live and work in it, and for our families, companions, and all those we love.

Lord, have mercy.

For our ancestors and all who have gone before us in faith.

Lord, have mercy.

Lifting our voices with all creation, with the Blessed Virgin Mary and all the saints, let us offer ourselves and one another to the living God through Christ.

To you, O Lord our God.

Presider

Blessed are you, O Lord our God, for the triumph of Christ in the lives of your saints. Receive the prayers we offer this day and help us to run our course with faith, that we may swiftly come to your eternal kingdom; through Jesus Christ our Lord. ***Amen.***

Hymns for the Day

The Hymnal 1982

By all your saints still striving 231, 232
Christ the Victorious, give to your servants 358
For all the saints, who from their labors rest 287
For the bread which you have broken 340, 341
For thy dear saints, O Lord 279
From glory to glory advancing, we praise thee, O Lord 326
Give rest, O Christ 355
Give us the wings of faith to rise 253
Hark! the sound of holy voices 275
Let saints on earth in concert sing 526
Lift up your heads, ye mighty gates 436
Who are these like stars appearing 286
Ye watchers and ye holy ones 618
O what their joy and their glory must be 623
Ye holy angels bright 625
This is the feast of victory for our God 417, 418
This is the hour of banquet and of song 316, 317
Blessed city, heavenly Salem 519, 520
Christ is made the sure foundation 518
Glorious things of thee are spoken 522, 523
Jerusalem, my happy home 620
Jerusalem the golden 624
Light's abode, celestial Salem 621, 622
O holy city, seen of John 582, 583
O for a thousand tongues to sing 493
Thine arm, O Lord, in days of old 567
Thou art the Way, to thee alone 457
When Jesus wept 715
All who believe and are baptized 298
Baptized in water 294
Come away to the skies 213

Lift Every Voice and Sing II

Come, we that love the Lord 12
I want to be ready 7
Oh! What a beautiful city 10
Rockin' Jerusalem 17
Soon and very soon we are goin' to see the King 14
Baptized in water 121

Wonder, Love, and Praise

Give thanks for life 775
No saint on earth lives life to self alone 776
Baptized in water 767
I believe in God Almighty 768, 769
You're called by name, forever loved 766

Proper 27

Sunday on or between November 6 and 12

The offering of several women is a witness to the true faith of God.

Anchor Points – The Propers and the Season

The fixed points for each service are the appointed or proper readings and collect as well as the themes of the day or season.

Readings and Psalm

Ruth 3:1–5; 4:13–17

In the first part of today's reading, Naomi responds to Ruth's fidelity by desiring to find a husband for her, specifically her kinsman Boaz. So she hatches a scheme that will bring Ruth and Boaz together. The second part of the reading describes the happy ending as Ruth and Boaz marry and conceive a son who is named Obed. The elders of the village offer their blessings and recognize Ruth's value to Naomi. The author ends by affirming her importance to the covenant people for her great-grandson will be King David.

Psalm 127

Human groups do not simply prosper by our human efforts, but require the gift of God for continued life and happiness.

or

1 Kings 17:8–16

Today's story continues this theme and demonstrates God's special care for the prophet. Through divine guidance, Elijah finds a woman of faith, as evidenced by her obedience to the prophet. Though she is not an Israelite, and therefore not a member of the covenant people, she receives the benefits of the covenant through her faith. She becomes a living rebuke to the faithless Israelites, and she receives the commendation of Jesus.

Psalm 146

The psalm calls for an unwavering trust in the Lord's goodness, power and sovereign reign in the midst of outwardly dark and painful conditions. As the psalmist in this reading exhorts himself, he exhorts his readers to praise God with their whole beings.

Hebrews 9:24–28

This reading stresses the superiority of Jesus's sacrificial work to that of the Jewish high priest's. Jesus's work excels the other work by where, when and how it takes place. It is presented in the presence of God, not in an earthly temple. It is not made repeatedly but "once for all at the end of the age" (v. 26). His offering is definitive and unique, as final as death. And his offering is himself, not the "blood of goats and calves" (9:12). His continuing work is not a continual self-offering but the continual representation of and intercession for humanity.

Mark 12:38–44

This reading ends the series of Jerusalem controversy stories that conclude Jesus's public teaching. Although Jesus related positively to some scribes or scripture scholars, today's sayings indicate his inevitable breach with their general approach. This reaction was especially significant in the light of the clash of the early Church with a Judaism grown defensive after the fall of the temple. Hypocrisy and oppression among the scribes will "receive the greater condemnation" (v. 40) since they should know better.

Collect

O God, whose blessed Son came into the world that he might destroy the works of the devil and make us children of God and heirs of eternal life: Grant that, having this hope, we may purify ourselves as he is pure; that, when he comes again with power and great glory, we may be made like him in his eternal and glorious kingdom; where he lives and reigns with you and the Holy Spirit, one God, for ever and ever. *Amen.*

Proper Preface

Of the Lord's Day

1. Of God the Father

For you are the source of light and life; you made us in your image, and called us to new life in Jesus Christ our Lord.

or this

2. Of God the Son

Through Jesus Christ our Lord; who on the first day of the week overcame death and the grave, and by his glorious resurrection opened to us the way of everlasting life.

or the following

3. Of God the Holy Spirit

For by water and the Holy Spirit you have made us a new people in Jesus Christ our Lord, to show forth your glory in all the world.

(Rite II, BCP 377–378; Rite I, BCP 344–345)

Seasonal Pairings

See the table below for choices appointed and suggested for this day. Preferences are put in **bold**. Not all choices are suitable for all congregations or community, though, so consider these preferences as a starting point before making a decision about your own congregation.

	Proper 27	Rite I	Rite II	EOW1	BOS 2022
Color	Green				
Entrance Rite	Customary; opening acclamation "Blessed be God" or one of the first two in EOW1	323	355	50	
Song of Praise/Kyrie	Gloria in excelsis or BCP Canticle 13, 19; EOW1 Canticle A, P	Gloria 324	Gloria 356; C13– 90; C19 – 94	A – 30; P – 38	
Collect		184	236		
Creed	Nicene Creed	326, 327	358	53	
Prayers of the People	**Locally written**; options below; BCP forms	329	387–393	54–55	
Offertory Sentence	"The Lord sets the prisoners free; the Lord opens the eyes of the blind; the Lord lifts up those who are bowed down . . . The Lord shall reign for ever, your God, O Zion, throughout all generations. Hallelujah!" (Psalm 146)	343–344	376–377		
Eucharistic Prayer	**Nov – Rite I, suggest Prayer 1; Rite II, suggest Prayer A; EOW1 suggest Prayer 2**	**1–339**	**A – 361**	**2–60**	
Proper Preface	**The Lord's Day 2 – Of God the Son**	344–345	377–378		
Breaking of the Bread (Fraction)	Christ our Passover (BCP); EOW1 options	337	364	69	
Postcommunion Prayer		339	**Eternal God – 365**	**God of abundance – 69**	
Blessing	Customary	339	366	70–71	
Dismissal	**Let us go forth in the name of Christ**	339	366		
Notes	All Saints' Day may fall before this Sunday; Election Day may fall near this Sunday.				

Additional Notes:

Song of Praise/Canticle – Suggested here is a canticle for the autumn from the BCP and an option from EOW1 (Canticle 13 and Canticle A) as well as one or two that reflects themes of the day. The Gloria, of course, is always appropriate in this season.

Extended Advent – This would be the first Sunday of an extended Advent season. See the section on planning Advent for more information.

Content Resources

Reading Between the Lines

Widows are mentioned in three of today's readings (1 Kings 17:8–16; Mark 12:44; Ruth) for their generosity, courageous unconventional behavior, and exemplary *hesed* (loving kindness and loyalty). A second selection from Ruth in the lectionary readings follows Proper 26, highlighting Naomi's plan to improve their chances of survival beyond gleaning, and the successful execution of that plan by Ruth. Missing from our lectionary are the details of the plan's execution. Naomi instructs Ruth to bathe herself and approach Boaz at night after he has eaten, observing where he sleeps. Ruth follows Naomi's advice except that she does not wait for Boaz to speak; when he wakes up in the night to find her at his feet and inquires who she is, she replies, "I am your handmaid, Ruth. Spread your robe over your handmaid, for you are a redeeming kinsman." We do know that lying down at Boaz' feet (3:7), is risky, unconventional, even reckless behavior. But we don't know exactly what transpired or how to read the text by interpreting "feet," or "robe" (reading "robe" as "wings") in Ruth 3:9. The term "feet" here however is not the word that can connote genitalia, so the omitted lectionary text is deliberately ambiguous. But Naomi's plan worked. Boaz' fulsome response to Ruth includes praise, blessings for Ruth's "deed of loyalty," explanation, and promise. Ruth's "deed of loyalty" continues the theme of *hesed* in the book. Professor Frymer-Kensky proposes understanding that Boaz knows Ruth has come to him, "because as Naomi's kinsman, he can aid Naomi by aligning himself with Ruth. She shows loyalty to Naomi, and he blesses her for this." The story ends with Naomi becoming foster mother to the child of Ruth and Boaz, and women neighbors name the child Obed, at the end of the book. Obed is the ancestor of David.

Central Themes

"Don't judge people by their appearance" is a contemporary version of the meme "Don't judge a book by its cover." Stereotypes are judgments about people based on insufficient knowledge. It takes effort to get to know people and learn their stories. Former librarian Robert Morin lived frugally, eating TV dinners, and died at seventy-seven in 2015, leaving $4 million to the University of New Hampshire. Like the widow who gave two mites, all she had, Morin saved his money to support his alma mater. No one suspected his wealthy status in his final fifteen months in an assisted living center.

Popular DNA tests promise to reveal the story of who you are through your genetic history. The mail-in tests claim that you can trace where your ancestors originated, chart a family tree, discover living biological relatives, and even learn about your health risks. DNA tests are also available for your dog! Ruth's story ends with a quick family tree. What is unique is that Ruth, a foreigner, immigrant, and woman, is included in a family tree. Ruth is the great-grandmother of King David. What does that reveal about who we are as followers of Jesus?

Without explicitly stressing it, the gospels often juxtapose two types of people, those who live a life of self-aggrandizement, often at the expense of others, and those who live lives of righteousness, putting others before themselves. It is the living out of the choice Moses once gave to ancient Israel: "The word is very near you, in your heart and in your mind . . . choose then: life and good or death and evil" (Deuteronomy 30: 14–15). Near the end of the celebration of the Eucharist, we go out into the world, committing ourselves to the kind of service explicitly expected of us by Jesus (BCP, 365, 366).

Engaging All Ages

The temple of Jesus's day, like our modern-day churches, depended on financial gifts of others. In today's reading, Jesus points out two kinds of givers, the rich who give from their abundance, and the widow who gives from her poverty. Jesus does not make a clear statement about which is "better," but he does note that the widow has given more – everything she had. What compelled her to give so much? Can you think of any other Bible story in which someone gives everything they have? Is there anything so important to you that you would give your last two coins?

Prayers of the People: Option 1

Do the impossible in us, again and again, O God. Empty us of the fears we grasp so tightly. Fill us instead with trust in your goodness. Do the impossible through us.

We come before you, O God:

Fill us again with your presence.

When we quiet ourselves and take in the beauty of the wonders around us, we are full of awe at what you can do. We fill the air with song and praise as we come before you.

We come before you, O God:

Fill us again with your presence.

This world is broken, aching, and often empty of joy. Fill the lonely spaces with people who care. Fill the hungry places with enough to satisfy all. Fill those who have plenty with the commitment to share with those who are in need. Fill those who are world-weary with your peace.

We come before you, O God:

Fill us again with your presence.

We hold before you those who are ill, facing surgery or recovering from it; those who are overwhelmed with sadness and the cares of this world; those who are anxious about what lies ahead and stuck in regretting the past.

We ask you to shower all these people for whom we pray with your healing balm: *N.*

We come before you, O God:

Fill us again with your presence.

We pray for those who have died, that your will for them has been fulfilled, and they are now full of joy in your kingdom. We pray also for those they have left behind who love them. When their hearts are full of sorrow and the long days of grief seem endless, fill them with your presence and assurance of unending life in your presence.

We come before you, O God:

Fill us again with your presence.

Prayers of the People: Option 2

Deacon or Presider

As we await the coming of the Lord let us offer prayers to God who bears the sins of many.

For this holy gathering, for *N.*, our Presiding Bishop, *N.*, our bishop, for our parish clergy, and for the people of God in every place.

Lord, have mercy.

For mercy, justice, and peace among all peoples.

Lord, have mercy.

For good weather, abundant fruits of the earth, and peaceful times.

Lord, have mercy.

For our city and those who live in it and for all those we love.

Lord, have mercy.

For those needing ongoing care, for all widows and those who are poor, those who are sick or suffering, for prisoners, captives, and their families, for all those who hunger, are unsheltered or have been oppressed.

Lord, have mercy.

For those who rest in Christ and for all the dead, we pray.

Lord, have mercy.

For our deliverance from all affliction, strife, and need.

Lord, have mercy.

Lifting our voices with all creation, with the Blessed Virgin Mary and all the saints, let us offer ourselves and one another to the living God through Christ.

To you, O Lord our God.

Presider

God of our ancestors, hear the prayers we offer this day and bring the riches of salvation to all who await you in poverty; through Jesus Christ our Lord. ***Amen.***

Hymns for the Day

The Hymnal 1982

O heavenly Word, eternal Light 63, 64
God moves in a mysterious way 677 (SC)
Praise, my soul, the King of heaven 410 (SC)
I'll praise my Maker while I've breath 429 (GR)
Sometimes a light surprises 667 (GR)
Come, thou fount of every blessing 686
Cross of Jesus, cross of sorrow 160
Jesus came, adored by angels 454
Lo! he comes with clouds descending 57, 58
Lord, enthroned in heavenly splendor 307
Once he came in blessing 53
As those of old their first fruits brought 705
Blest are the pure in heart 656
God of grace and God of glory 594, 595
Lord, make us servants of your peace 593
Not here for high and holy things 9
Take my life, and let it be 707

Lift Every Voice and Sing II

Come, thou fount of every blessing 111

Proper 28

Sunday on or between November 13 and 19

The coming day of glory and judgment is ushered in by a time of frightening upheaval and persecution.

Anchor Points – The Propers and the Season

The fixed points for each service are the appointed or proper readings and collect as well as the themes of the day or season.

Readings and Psalm

1 Samuel 1:4–20

Today's reading tells the story of Samuel's birth. Like Sarah before her (see Genesis 16), Samuel's mother Hannah is barren and childless. Her barrenness was not only the source of private grief, but also brought public taunting from her husband's other wife, who was fertile. In her desperation, she promises that if God will give her the gift of a son, she in turn will give her son as a gift to God.

1 Samuel 2:1–10

These verses are Hannah's song of exultation, expressing her joy at being the recipient of the Lord's gift of a child.

or

Daniel 12:1–3

In our Hebrew scripture lesson, Daniel is given a vision of the end of human history: after a period of great distress, some will be brought to their salvation and others to eternal disgrace. This was a time of persecution for Israel which took place two centuries before the life of Christ. This oracle of hope makes use of imagery common to apocalyptic visions. Evil will mount up in a last desperate effort before Michael, Israel's patron angel, intervenes to bring justice. The names of all who will be saved are written in the book of life, which must for now remain sealed. In what is a new idea for Judaism, even the faithful dead will be raised to receive their reward.

Psalm 16

Though the psalm is one of supplication, the petition itself takes only one half of verse one. The remainder of the prayer is a meditation on the reasons the psalmist can turn to God in this time of need.

Hebrews 10:11–14, (15–18), 19–25

The author of Hebrews compares the work of the Levitical priest to the superior work of Jesus. The priest from Levi's line had to offer sacrifices on a daily basis. These sacrifices, though symbolic of forgiveness through the shedding of blood, could not accomplish true purity. Jesus offered a different kind of sacrifice. The greatness of this one sacrifice attained perfection, not just outward cleansing, and assured eternal consecration. No further offering for sin is required. In verses 19–25, the author draws out the implications of Jesus's complete work. As to our relationship with God, nothing remains to obstruct our full communion. As to our spiritual lives, we hope for the approaching day of final judgment and full revelation. As to our relationships with others, we live to encourage and support one another.

Mark 13:1–8

Chapter 13 of Mark is known as the "little apocalypse." It is full of ominous signs and strong counsel. Mark has combined various sayings of Jesus related to events in the near and far future. Some have already come true, but because prophecy often has many applications, they may someday be fulfilled again in a deeper way. Jesus's disciples comment on the temple's magnificence, which embodied for the Jews their religious hopes and identity. Yet this temple, finally finished in AD 64, was a pile of rubble after Titus's invasion and devastation in AD 70. Jesus bids his disciples to turn from the apparent permanence and grandeur of the temple in order to place their trust in God's sovereignty.

Collect

Blessed Lord, who caused all holy Scriptures to be written for our learning: Grant us so to hear them, read, mark, learn, and inwardly digest them, that we may embrace and ever hold fast the blessed hope of everlasting life, which you have given us in our Savior Jesus Christ; who lives and reigns with you and the Holy Spirit, one God, for ever and ever. *Amen.*

Proper Preface

Of the Lord's Day

1. Of God the Father

For you are the source of light and life; you made us in your image, and called us to new life in Jesus Christ our Lord.

or this

2. Of God the Son

Through Jesus Christ our Lord; who on the first day of the week overcame death and the grave, and by his glorious resurrection opened to us the way of everlasting life.

or the following

3. Of God the Holy Spirit

For by water and the Holy Spirit you have made us a new people in Jesus Christ our Lord, to show forth your glory in all the world.

(Rite II, BCP 377–378; Rite I, BCP 344–345)

Seasonal Pairings

See the table below for choices appointed and suggested for this day. Preferences are put in **bold**. Not all choices are suitable for all congregations or community, though, so consider these preferences as a starting point before making a decision about your own congregation.

	Proper 28	Rite I	Rite II	EOW1	BOS 2022
Color	Green				
Entrance Rite	Customary; opening acclamation "Blessed be God" or one of the first two in EOW1	323	355	50	
Song of Praise/Kyrie	Gloria in excelsis or BCP Canticle 13, 19; EOW1 Canticle A, P	Gloria 324	Gloria 356; C13– 90; C19 – 94	A – 30; P – 38	
Collect		184	236		
Creed	Nicene Creed	326, 327	358	53	
Prayers of the People	**Locally written**; options below; BCP forms	329	387–393	54–55	
Offertory Sentence	"Let us approach [the sanctuary] with a true heart in full assurance of faith, with our hearts sprinkled clean from an evil conscience and our bodies washed with pure water. Let us hold fast to the confession of our hope without wavering, for he who has promised is faithful." (Hebrews)	343–344	376–377		
Eucharistic Prayer	**Nov – Rite I, suggest Prayer 1; Rite II, suggest Prayer A; EOW1 suggest Prayer 2**	**1–339**	**A – 361**	**2–60**	
Proper Preface	**The Lord's Day 2 – Of God the Son**	344–345	377–378		
Breaking of the Bread (Fraction)	Christ our Passover (BCP); EOW1 options	337	364	69	
Postcommunion Prayer		339	**Eternal God – 365**	**God of abundance – 69**	
Blessing	Customary	339	366	70–71	
Dismissal	**Go in peace to love and serve the Lord.**	340	366		
Notes	Thanksgiving Day may fall after this Sunday				

Additional Notes:

Song of Praise/Canticle – Suggested here is a canticle for the autumn from the BCP and an option from EOW1 (Canticle 13 and Canticle A) as well as one or two that reflects themes of the day. The Gloria, of course, is always appropriate in this season.

Extended Advent – This would be the second Sunday of an extended Advent season. See the section on planning Advent for more information.

Content Resources

Reading Between the Lines

Wars, rumors of wars, earthquakes, famines. Not to mention floods, droughts, hurricanes (something Jesus never experienced), once-in-a-century weather events every year. Being in the end times has become ordinary.

But Hannah is extraordinary. Once every three years comes the opportunity to talk about Hannah. Hannah isn't just a story about an unlikely conception; we have lots of those. Only part of one wall of Herod's Temple, the temple Jesus knew, remains to this day. But to this day the prayer of Hannah in the temple at Shiloh reverberates in the lives of Jews and Christians, albeit in different ways, throughout the world.

The pattern of Hannah's prayer was codified as normative for Jews by Gamaliel II after the fall of Jerusalem in the first century CE. To this day the *Amidah*, the thrice daily prayer of observant Jews, is prayed the way Hannah prayed: standing as Hannah stood, with great intent like Hannah's, with the lips, but so quietly as to only be heard by God, as Hannah was praying when Elkanah mistook her for drunk.

For Christians, the Song of Hannah is the prototype for the Song of Mary, the Magnificat, said daily at the evening prayer in religious institutions throughout the world.

The prayer of one desperate, childless woman becomes the pattern of prayer for a whole faith community. The thanksgiving hymn of praise she sings when that prayer is answered becomes the source of another canticle for a different faith community. The Story of Hannah cries out to be told. One place to learn about Jewish traditions concerning Hannah is the *Shalvi/Hyman Jewish Encyclopedia of Women*, online.[1]

Central Themes

Scripture contains many stories that recount the impatience of humans, who have no notion of the expansiveness of eternal God's sense of time. God is the Alpha and the Omega. As human generations increase, so do our stories of war, earthquakes, and famine and our interpretations of their meaning. Meanwhile, we fret, and we fear. Jesus says to his disciples, "Beware that no one leads you astray." Jesus warns of the total destruction of society beginning with the temple and surrounding buildings, but he also promises a new Jerusalem where God's promises are kept. Having faith is about trusting in God's promises.

Downsizing elders' homes has become an increasing issue in the United States. There are the practical concerns of who wants which items – sometimes no one does – and the emotional challenges of divesting yourself of that which often symbolized your identity and family: your home and possessions. Who are you as a family without your gathering space/home? Who will remember you if they don't want your stuff? Jesus says the most impressive building in Jerusalem, the temple, will be destroyed, the building that pointed to who God is. Who is God without the temple? Who are Jesus's followers?

Jesus offers an interpretation and some hope to a people faced with the destruction of the most important structure to their lives of faith. It is not, he insists, and never was the building. The life of faith is not totted up in building blocks of stone, but in the relationship between God and people, between people and people. When the dismayed disciples ask Jesus when this ruin will occur, he doesn't answer them directly. Instead, he sets out for them yet again a way of life, the kind of way they've been learning at his side, doing what he's doing, speaking as he speaks. It is the Way of Love, and it takes time, commitment, and practice.

Engaging All Ages

Sometimes the structures we hold dear, structures that seem invincible like basilicas, friendships, or governments, crumble. It is jarring when something so durable tumbles. Natural disasters, war, and broken relationships cause us to ask, is anything everlasting? Is anything unchanging? Dependable? Creation may be finite, but the Creator is not. God is where we can rest our hope, our desire for everlasting, unchanging dependability. What structures, systems, and people do you depend on? How do you practice depending on God?

Prayers of the People: Option 1

Walk before and beside us into your future, loving and gracious God. Make us agents of healing, teachers of love, bearers of good news. Make us a blessing to those around us in your name.

Lord of love,

Hear our prayer.

We praise you for the examples of faithfulness throughout history and for surrounding us on every side with encouragement. Make us an example of faithfulness to those around us in your name.

Lord of love,

Hear our prayer.

1 https://jwa.org/encyclopedia/article/hannah-midrash-and-aggadah#pid-13233, accessed May 6, 2023.

We ask that your church be infused with a renewed send of your mission, with a greater devotion to you and affection for each other. Send us into the world where we are most needed, with the good news for which your world is desperate. Keep us from distraction, and spare us, O Lord, from numbing inertia.

Lord of love,

Hear our prayer.

We ask that those in governing positions around the globe be honest and seek the best for those they govern. We pray for legislators and judges, for the electorate. We pray for encouragement for those who are intent on doing the right thing in the face of difficult odds. We pray for our president.

Lord of love,

Hear our prayer.

We give thanks for medical personnel and those providing background support of medical teams. Bless those who give comfort to the sick and dying. We lift before you those who are ill and hopeful for your healing. We pray for ____________. We pray for those who have died, that they may be welcomed into the new life you have prepared for them in eternity.

Lord of love,

Hear our prayer.

Prayers of the People: Option 2

Deacon or Presider

Let us offer prayers for the Church and the world, saying "We pray to you, O Lord."

Intercessor

We pray for the good of all churches of God and for the people of all faiths to come together, to appreciate differences, to gain deeper understanding of one another, and to respect the principles and values that bind us together. Hear our prayer:

We pray to you, O Lord.

We pray for our Presiding Bishop *N.*, our own bishop *N.*, for our parish clergy, and our one, holy, catholic and apostolic church. Hear our prayer.

We pray to you, O Lord.

We pray for all ministries of this parish and for our lay leaders. Hear our prayer.

We pray to you, O Lord.

We pray for our nation and the world: For our President, members of Congress and the Supreme Court, our Mayor – and all who serve in positions of authority and public service. Give all leaders wisdom, strength, courage and humility. Hear our prayer:

We pray to you, O Lord.

We pray for peace among and within nations: For the wellbeing of those who suffer from violent events beyond their control. Heal the physical and emotional wounds of those affected by recent mass shootings. Hear our prayer:

We pray to you, O Lord.

We pray for our cities and communities and the needs of those who are poor, homeless, refugees, illiterate, and those who are marginalized. Bless all those who seek to offer support in our city and county government, our non-profit organizations, our schools, our colleges and universities, and in our faith communities. Hear our prayer:

We pray to you, O Lord.

We pray for all who suffer illness of the body, mind or spirit, and those with special needs. Hear our prayer:

We pray to you, O Lord.

We pray for the souls of the departed and for those all those who mourn. Hear our prayer.

We pray to you, O Lord.

As we gather this week to give thanks, we pray in gratitude for the blessings you have bestowed upon us. We are grateful for all that you give – from the modest things that make our lives comfortable to the great joys and even for the tribulations that make our lives challenging. Hear our prayer:

We pray to you, O Lord.

We pray for any other concerns or thanksgivings, silently or aloud. *Silence*

Presider

God of abundance, who has planted us in this congregation and sustains us day by day, grow us in your grace, that we may become more fully the people you have called us to be; that we may flourish by your faith in us; and that we may accomplish your will with the gifts you have given us; through Jesus Christ our Redeemer. ***Amen.***

Hymns for the Day

The Hymnal 1982

Help us, O Lord, to learn 628
Lord, be thy word my rule 626
O Christ, the Word Incarnate 632
Word of God, come down on earth 633
Christ, the fair glory of the holy angels 282, 283 (GR)
Judge eternal, throned in splendor 596 (GR)
O day of God, draw nigh 600, 601
The Lord will come and not be slow 462 (GR)
Come, thou fount of every blessing 686
Help us, O Lord, to learn 628
Lord, enthroned in heavenly splendor 307
O day of radiant gladness 48
We the Lord's people, heart and voice uniting 51
All my hope on God is founded 665
All who love and serve your city 570, 571
Lord Christ, when first thou cam'st to earth 598
O God of every nation 607
Thy kingdom come, O God! 613

Lift Every Voice and Sing II

My Lord, what a morning 13 (GR)
Steal away 103 (GR)
Come, thou fount of every blessing 111
Jesus, we want to meet 81
We have come into His house 245

Wonder, Love, and Praise

Signs of endings all around us 721 (GR)

The Last Sunday after Pentecost: Christ the King Proper 29

Sunday on or between November 20 and 26

This day is often referred to as the Sunday of Christ the King or Reign of Christ. "Jesus is Lord" (the earliest Christian creed) means that Jesus stands above all other earthly power and authority.

Anchor Points – The Propers and the Season

The fixed points for each service are the appointed or proper readings and collect as well as the themes of the day or season.

Readings and Psalm

2 Samuel 23:1–7

Today's reading recounts David's last words and affirms that God has spoken though David's words and deeds. God will ensure that David's dynasty will prosper and grow.

Psalm 132:1–13, (14–19)

This psalm is basically a processional hymn, probably used in the temple as part of the celebration of the king's enthronement.

or

Daniel 7:9–10, 13–14

Today's reading comes from the vision of the four beasts (7:1–14), which makes more explicit the history of the four kingdoms first introduced in 2:31–45. The divine judgment on the beasts determines the course of history on earth. To the Lord comes one like a human being. Here the comparison stresses the human form of the one who represents the universal, everlasting dominion given by God to the people. In Daniel, he probably stands for God's people (7:18, 27) who will receive the kingdom.

Psalm 93

This is one of the kingship psalms probably used for the great autumn festival at the turn of the year called Tabernacles or Booths.

Revelation 1:4b – 8

In this lesson, the revelation made known to a disciple named John begins with a greeting from the everlasting God, from the seven spirits which worship God, and from Jesus Christ, the firstborn from the dead. Jesus, who continues to love his disciples, is praised as the faithful witness whose sacrifice has formed a royal household, a new priestly people to serve God. Soon he will come, like the one foreseen by the prophet Daniel, on the clouds of heaven. He now rules over all earthly kings, and God, the Alpha and Omega, the first and the last, is sovereign over all.

John 18:33–37

The conversation of Jesus with Pilate, in contrast to his silence as recorded in the other gospels, may stem from John's interest in showing Pilate's concern to ascertain whether Jesus was a revolutionary. Jesus's counter-question seeks to determine whether Pilate is thinking of kingship in political (Roman) or religious (Jewish) terms. He then goes on to say that his kingdom is not "from this world" (v. 36) – it is not determined by, derived from or grounded in this world. Jesus witnesses to the truth of the reality of God, a revelation that has the effect of judgment (7:7). Jesus, not Pilate, is really the judge in this situation. Those who are grounded in the truth listen to Jesus with understanding and acceptance. Pilate tries to avoid making a decision between the world and truth.

Collect

Almighty and everlasting God, whose will it is to restore all things in your well-beloved Son, the King of kings and Lord of lords: Mercifully grant that the peoples of the earth, divided and enslaved by sin, may be freed and brought together under his most gracious rule; who lives and reigns with you and the Holy Spirit, one God, now and for ever. *Amen.*

Proper Preface

Of the Lord's Day

or

Baptism – Because in Jesus Christ our Lord you have received us as your sons and daughters, made us citizens of your kingdom, and given us the Holy Spirit to guide us into all truth.

(Rite II, BCP 381; Rite I, BCP 348)

Seasonal Pairings

See the table below for choices appointed and suggested for this day. Preferences are put in **bold**. Not all choices are suitable for all congregations or community, though, so consider these preferences as a starting point before making a decision about your own congregation.

	Last Pentecost: Christ the King Proper 29	Rite I	Rite II	EOW1	BOS 2022
Color	Green *or* White/Gold/Festive				
Entrance Rite	Customary; opening acclamation "Blessed be God" or one of the first two in EOW1	323	355	50	
Song of Praise/Kyrie	Gloria in excelsis or BCP Canticle 13, 18; EOW1 Canticle A, O	Gloria 324	Gloria 356; C13– 90; **C18 – 93**	A – 30; O – 38	
Collect		185	236		
Creed	Nicene Creed	326, 327	358	53	
Prayers of the People	**Locally written**; options below; BCP forms	329	387–393	54–55	
Offertory Sentence	"Look! He is coming with the clouds; every eye will see him" (Revelation)	343–344	376–377		
Eucharistic Prayer	**Rite I, suggest Prayer 1; Rite II, suggest Prayer A or D; EOW1 suggest Prayer 2.**	**1–333**	**C – 369** *or* **A – 361**	**2–60**	
Proper Preface	**Baptism** *or* The Lord's Day 2 – Of God the Son	**348;** 344–345	**381;** 377–378		
Breaking of the Bread (Fraction)	**Christ our Passover (BCP);** S 172 "Blessed are those called to the Supper of the Lamb" in *The Hymnal 1982*; EOW1 options	337	364	69	
Postcommunion Prayer		339	**Eternal God – 365**	**God of abundance – 69**	
Blessing	Customary	339	366	70–71	
Dismissal	**Let us go forth in the name of Christ**	339	366		
Notes	Thanksgiving Day may fall after this Sunday; St. Andrew's Day may fall near this Sunday.				

Additional Notes:

"Christ the King" – This name is not part of the Episcopal Church Calendar, at present, which simply calls this day "The Last Sunday after Pentecost." The title "Christ the King," however, is referenced in the Revised Common Lectionary in the back of the BCP and the collect and lessons are clearly following that theme. This feast dates back to 1925, when Pius XI added it to the Roman Catholic calendar. Many prefer to use the title "Reign of Christ" or similar to model more inclusive language.

Song of Praise/Canticle – Suggested here is a canticle for the autumn from the BCP and an option from EOW1 (Canticle 13 and Canticle A) as well as one or two that reflects themes of the day. The Gloria, of course, is always appropriate in this season.

Eucharistic Prayer – It is helpful to use either a prayer form that permits a proper preface, with Baptism being the preference on proper preface, or Prayer D. If Prayer B is about to be used for Advent through Epiphany, it is wise to avoid it in the 4–6 weeks prior to Advent.

Fraction Anthem at the Breaking of the Bread – The BCP "Christ our Passover" ties in well with the Gospel reading being from the Passion narrative. Another option, emphasizing eschatological imagery is S 172 "Blessed are those who are called to the Supper of the Lamb.

Extended Advent – This would be the third Sunday of an extended Advent season. See the section on planning Advent for more information.

Content Resources

Reading Between the Lines

"Everything will be all right in the end. If it's not all right, it is not yet the end." Patel, Hotel Manager, *The Best Exotic Marigold Hotel*, 2011. The liturgical year closes with a flourish of final trumpets and royal pageantry, heaven opening and Christ reigning. But the Gospel is drawn from the Passion narrative of John, with Jesus and Pilate parrying, briefly, about kingship and truth. Pilate probes to see what kind of king Jesus believes himself to be. Jesus' reign, in this world, is from the tree. The classic Christus Rex crucifix depicts a supremely composed Christ fully clothed in chasuble and stole, superimposed upon but not nailed to a cross, often crowned with a traditional king's crown. This symbol has evolved from depictions of Christ Pantocrator, Ruler over all, at least as early as Constantine. What Jesus does not tell Pilate is what Revelation asserts, Christ's lordship over all the nations and peoples of the earth. In the end, every eye will behold Jesus Christ coming.

How do we preach this in a post-colonial, multi-cultural world? How do we believe this?

In John's view, the reign of Christ is the triumph of truth. Jesus' reign is not of this world. Everyone who holds to truth hears his voice. Pilate's question immediately following today's gospel, Jn 18:38, is less cynical than apt: "What is truth?" Jesus does not claim that everyone who acknowledges him gets access to truth. Rather, everyone "who belongs to the truth," or more literally in the Greek, "who is of the truth," listens to Jesus.

And with this we are catapulted back to Jn 1:7, "this is the true light, which enlightens every human…"

No one in the New Testament recognizes the resurrected Jesus by sight. Can we be sure that we who claim to profess Jesus truly see him and belong to the truth? Can we be sure that those who profess a different faith, and who cleave to the light they see, and who belong to the truth they know, are not seeing Jesus in resurrected form? In the end, every eye will behold the Ruler over all, and every tongue confess.

Central Themes

It isn't simple to follow the lead of God, for as many times as Jesus talks about the kingdom of God, it is still beyond our comprehension, in the same way as God's self is beyond our understanding. Quantum physics and the wave-particle dichotomy provide a glimpse into the difficulty of trying to see what cannot be seen with the human eye or grasped by the human mind. God is the ultimate unity of apparently contradictory ideas: powerful, yet loving and merciful, and immanent, yet transcendent and heavenly. A central mystery is how Eternal-Infinite God can be both the Alpha and the Omega, a contradiction in human terms.

An estimated 1.9 billion people watched Meghan Markle and Prince Harry's wedding in 2019.[1] Even though the British royalty no longer "rule" the United Kingdom, curiosity about them is still widespread, evident in the intense interest in the subsequent tension between this couple and the royal family, as well as the close attention given to the death and funeral of Elizabeth II and the coronation of King Charles III from around the world. The royals exercise their power in setting trends and pointing public attention to ideas and causes. Many dream about what life would be like if they, too, were royalty. Pilate and Jesus have an enigmatic conversation about Jesus's kingdom and if he is a king. Through this conversation Jesus directs followers to imagine a God's kingdom on earth. How do we dream about God's kingdom?

Israel longed for a messiah, many of them for a ruler who would overthrow the Romans and restore peace. Nobody expected a Jesus who was born a homeless child of an unwed mother. He was just the sort of ruler that a Pilate of the gospel couldn't understand. This messiah king was just the sort of sovereign who so upset other rulers of his day that they killed him for it, for telling the truth and being so transparently God's own, acting as God would act in the world. He wasn't what they expected. What kind of ruler would we expect? What sort do we desire?

Engaging All Ages

Today is both the feast of Christ the King and the last Sunday of the liturgical year. It is kind of like the New Year's Eve of the church year. This week we celebrate the ascended Jesus as Lord of Lords, and next week we will begin the story again, preparing to welcome the Christ Child. Take this opportunity to reflect on your faith journey over the past year. How did you grow? What was hard? Did you have a favorite part? Consider thanking those who traveled with you over the last year, and set an intention for the coming year.

---

1 https://economictimes.indiatimes.com/magazines/panache/1-9-billion-people-watched-royal-wedding-report/articleshow/64243728.cms, viewed December 9, 2019.

Prayers of the People: Option 1

As the people of your hand and the people of your church, we approach you in deep humility and deep gratitude. May we reflect your image in all that we are and all that we do. We are awe of your glory and majesty.

Amen. Glory to you, Lord God.

As people of many nations, we ask you to instill in our leaders, our courts, and fellow citizens wisdom and integrity, that we may reflect your image in all that we are and all that we do. We are in awe of your righteousness.

Amen. Glory to you, Lord God.

As people who are flawed and frail, we ask you for healing for each of us and those we love, for those who face surgery, those who are consumed with endless worry and needless guilt, and those who turn their backs on their brothers and sisters.

We pray for ____________. We are in awe of your compassionate care and loving-kindness. Forgive us and heal us.

Amen. Glory to you, Lord God.

As people whose time is limited, we ask you to carry us at the end of our lives into your eternal habitation, where we will behold your glory forever. We pray for those who have recently died, *N.*:

We are in awe of your promise of eternal glory with the saints in light and in your presence forever.

Amen. Glory to you, Lord God.

Prayers of the People: Option 2

Deacon or Priest

We pray to Jesus Christ, who is our faithful witness, and freed us from sin by his blood.

Intercessor

We pray for all Christians, that we may all join together in unity and look forwards to the New Jerusalem together. We pray for *N.*, our Presiding Bishop; for our Bishop, *N.*, and for all the clergy of this parish. We pray to you,

God be with us.

We pray for all those baptized recently, for the ministries of this congregation, and for our lay leaders. We pray to you,

God be with us.

We pray for our nation and our elected and appointed leaders. We pray that they will be compassionate, just, and wise. Let them hear those who have come to speak truth to power. We pray to you,

God be with us.

We pray for our Earth, the pale blue dot that is the Eden that you have given us. We pray that you strengthen our stewardship of your Creation. We pray to you,

God be with us.

We pray for this city (____________), and all our cities and communities. We pray for the staff and residents of our night shelters, and for those who are homeless who cannot find shelter. We pray to you,

God be with us.

We pray for those who are sick and all who need nursing care. We pray for those who are traveling or serving in the armed forces. We pray for those whose needs are known to you alone. We pray to you,

God be with us.

We pray for our beloved ones who have gone to join you in your heavenly mansions, for all those who have died and for those who mourn. We pray to you,

God be with us.

For any additional prayers or thanksgivings you would offer, either silently or aloud

Silence. The people may add their own prayers.

Presider

Loving God, who is the beginning and the end of all things, hear our prayers. Guide us by your laws and by your love, that we may build the Earth as a temple to you. ***Amen.***

Hymns for the Day

The Hymnal 1982

Alleluia! sing to Jesus! 460, 461 (vs 1, 3–5)
All praise to thee, for thou, O King divine 477
Christ is the King! O friends upraise 614
Jesus shall reign where'er the sun 544
King of glory, King of peace 382
Lead on, O King eternal 555
Ye servants of God, your Master proclaim 535
All hail the power of Jesus's Name 450, 451 (SC)
Hail to the Lord's Anointed 616 (SC)
O God of Bethel, by whose hand 709 (SC)
Ancient of Days, who sittest throned in glory 363 (GR)
Come, thou almighty King 365 (GR)
Immortal, invisible, God only wise 423 (GR)
Jesus came, adored by angels 454 (GR)
Lo! he comes with clouds descending 57, 58 (GR)
The God of Abraham praise 401 (GR)
At the Name of Jesus 435
Crown him with many crowns 494
Draw nigh and take the Body of the Lord 327, 328
Jesus came, adored by angels 454
Let all mortal flesh keep silence 324
Lo! he comes with clouds descending 57, 58
Lord, enthroned in heavenly splendor 307
Rejoice, the Lord is King! 481
The head that once was crowned with thorns 483
Hail, thou once despised Jesus! 495
Lord Christ, when first thou cam'st to earth 5 98
My song is love unknown 458

Lift Every Voice and Sing II

He is King of kings, he is Lord of lords 96
Ride on, King Jesus 97

Appendix 1: Planning Morning Prayer for Sunday Worship

Morning Prayer is an integral part of our worship experience and history as Anglicans. Every day, people all over the world are praying Daily Morning Prayer, whether in churches, schools, monasteries, convents, or just as individuals. Online Morning Prayer (and the other daily offices) saw a significant increase during the COVID-19 pandemic in recent years.

On Sunday, Holy Eucharist is the principal act of worship for Episcopal Church congregations.[1] This identifies the Eucharist as the norm, but there are times when Sunday Morning Prayer is used as the primary worship service for a congregation instead. In some cases, that is a result of not having a priest available and a deacon or lay worship leader offers Morning Prayer. Some churches intentionally schedule Morning Prayer as part of their schedule, sometimes quarterly or monthly, to maintain connection with this part of our tradition and some of its features, such as the Canticles. This appendix is concerned specifically with planning for Sunday Morning Prayer as a primary congregational service, distinct from Daily Morning Prayer.

Just as with planning the Eucharist, we begin with the anchor points of the lesson and collect appointed for the day. While routine Daily Morning Prayer uses its own lectionary, separate from the schedule of readings used for the Eucharist, Morning Prayer as a primary service on Sundays uses the Eucharistic lectionary and the collect appointed for that Sunday or feast day. There is not a Proper Preface for Morning Prayer, since that is a feature of the eucharistic prayer. So, we begin with themes from the scheduled readings for the day. The material for each Sunday in this volume regarding the themes for the day, the interpretation of the readings, and hymn selection all should be referenced when planning Morning Prayer, just as for the Eucharist. The structure of the service and some of the liturgical choices are different, however. The service largely is built around two sections: The Lessons and The Prayers, with a few different options for the introduction to the rite. Rite One begins on page 37 and Rite Two begins on 75. Other specific page references are in the chart below.

1 BCP, 13.

Opening Rite Options

Many congregations will begin with an Entrance Hymn, though Morning Prayer does not specifically indicate that as an option. The opening portion of the rite offers several choices. The liturgy may begin with a sentence of scripture, seasonally appointed, or with a sentence of scripture followed by the confession of sin and absolution (prayer for forgiveness), or may begin directly with the opening dialogue (also called the Preces) "Lord open my lips" and proceed to the Invitatory and the psalm for the day.

If a confession of sin is desired in this service, it occurs at the beginning of the rite and is followed by an absolution, if a priest or bishop is present; a lay person or deacon alters the pronouns to turn it into a prayer for forgiveness, shifting declarative 2nd person pronouns ("you") into 1st person pronouns ("us"). If the confession is used, it *must* be preceded by a sentence of scripture; Morning Prayer cannot begin directly with the confession.

Invitatory and the Psalter

This portion is the formal beginning of the rite, beginning with the preces "Lord open our lips. And our mouth shall proclaim your praise." and the Gloria patri (with an "Alleluia," except in Lent). *The Book of Common Prayer* offers two invitatory options for most days, the Venite or Jubilate, and the Pascha Nostrum for Eastertide. *Enriching Our Worship 1* offers a few more options, drawn from the psalms, as well. There are seasonal proper antiphons that can be added to the invitatory, usually added to the beginning and end of the Venite or Jubilate. Additionally, there are musical settings in *The Hymnal 1982* for the invitatory.

The psalm used is the appointed psalm for that Sunday or feast day in the Revised Common Lectionary, just as would have been used at Eucharist. In Morning Prayer, it precedes the readings as part of the opening of the service, rather than as a response to the Hebrew scripture reading. The psalm concludes with the Gloria patri. The psalm may be spoken, using any of the options on page 582 of the prayer book, or may be chanted to multiple settings.

The Lessons

The appointed lessons for the Sunday or feast day are read here, with a canticle following the first and second reading. Any of the canticles in the prayer book may be used, though traditionally the canticle is from the same portion of scripture as the reading (so a reading from the Hebrew scriptures would be followed by a canticle from the same; likewise a New Testament reading would be followed by a canticle from that portion of scripture. Canticle selections tied to the season or feast day are found in this volume in each Sunday's entry. If the congregation is accustomed to saying/singing the Gloria in excelsis (Canticle 20), you may wish to include that as one of these canticles.

After the third reading, from the Gospel, the sermon may be given (or it may be offered at two other points mentioned below). If the sermon is not given here, the service may continue with the Apostles' Creed or a third canticle could be used. Many preachers will prefer to preach directly following the readings, which also would be more familiar to a congregation accustomed to Holy Eucharist.

The creed used in Morning Prayer is the Apostles' Creed. It would be included on any Sunday or feast day. There is not a provision in Morning Prayer to substitute the Renewal of Baptismal Vows in place of the Apostles' Creed. However, the Baptismal Covenant includes the Apostles' Creed, in any case, so a creative adaptation may be possible, even if not specifically indicated by the rubrics. The Creed concludes the portion of the service focused on the lessons.

The Prayers

The Prayers begin, appropriately, with the Lord's Prayer. Choosing which form of the Lord's Prayer is being used and making that clear to the congregation is important to identify. Following the Lord's Prayer are a set of suffrages, which mean intercessory petitions in this context. The marking of "V" and "R" indicate that these are read responsively between the officiant and the congregation, the officiant reading the "versicle" and the congregation reading the "response" (or responsory). The prayer book provides two options, Suffrages A and Suffrages B and *Enriching Our Worship 1* offers an additional set of suffrages that may be used instead.

The Collect of the Day, which is the appointed proper collect for that Sunday or feast day is offered and may be accompanied by additional collects, such as the Collect for Sundays. After the collect or collects, a prayer for mission is added from the three options in Morning Prayer unless a general form of intercession is planned to follow the hymn, below.

Following the prayer for mission, the sermon may be preached, if it was not preached directly after the readings, and a hymn or anthem may be sung. This is the most likely place for the offering to be gathered and the traditional spot for that action. The rubrics for the service simply indicate that an offering may be taken up during the service and this hymn is probably the most sensible place for the offering.

After the hymn or anthem, there is an option for "authorized intercessions and thanksgivings." One could choose to use the prayer for mission after the collects and simply invite the congregation to name additional prayers or thanksgivings here. Another option would be to offer a "general form of intercession" such as one of the Prayers of the People forms in the prayer book, or one of the options provided for a given Sunday in this volume, which would allow omitting the prayer for mission.

There are several options to conclude the service. The last required element in Morning Prayer is the prayer for mission (or intercessions), but usually at least one of the following is used: The General Thanksgiving, the Prayer of St. Chrysostom, closing dialogue, concluding sentence of scripture. One, some or all of these options may be used. Note that The General Thanksgiving is said by all, but the Prayer of St. Chrysostom is said by the officiant alone. Though not specified by the prayer book, many congregations may wish to add a Closing Hymn to the rite.

The third option for the sermon location is to be preached after the conclusion of the service.

	Sunday Congregational Morning Prayer – any proper	Rite I	Rite II	EOW1
Color	As appointed for the day			
Opening Rite	Passage of Scripture; Confession of Sin and Absolution/Prayer for Forgiveness	37–42	75–80	18–20
Invitatory and Psalter				
Opening Versicle and Gloria Patri		42	80	20

	Sunday Congregational Morning Prayer – any proper	Rite I	Rite II	EOW1
Invitatory	Usually Venite or Jubilate (Pascha Nostrum in Eastertide; EOW1 has additional options); seasonal antiphons optional	43–46	80–83	20–24
Psalm and Gloria patri	Using Sunday or feast day propers	46	83	
The Lessons				
Reading	Using Sunday or feast day propers			25
Canticle after First Reading	See Song of Praise options for the day; Canticle 20 Gloria in excelsis may be chosen except in Advent and Lent	47–52; 85–96	47–52; 85–96	25–41
Reading	Using Sunday or feast day propers			25
Canticle after Second Reading	See Song of Praise options for the day; Canticle 20 Gloria in excelsis may be chosen except in Advent and Lent	47–52; 85–96	47–52; 85–96	25–41
Gospel Reading	Using Sunday/feast day propers; may be followed by canticle and/or sermon			25
Creed	Apostles' Creed	53	96	41
The Prayers				
Lord's Prayer	Traditional or Contemporary?	54	97	42
Suffrages	A, B, or EOW1	55	97–98	42
Collect	Collect of the Day; may add Collect for Sunday or others	56–57	98–100	
Prayer for Mission	Three choices; may be followed by sermon.	57–58	100–101	
Office Hymn	Offertory usually gathered during this hymn	58	101	
Intercessions	Full Prayers of the People?	58; 383–392	101; 383–392	
The General Thanksgiving	Optional	58	101	
Prayer of St. John Chrysostom	Optional	59	102	
Concluding Versicle/ Response	Optional "Let us bless the Lord." (adding Alleluias from Easter Day through the Day of Pentecost)	59	102	
Concluding Scripture	Optional; may be followed by sermon	59–60	102	42

Morning Prayer as the Liturgy of the Word at Eucharist

Morning Prayer may also be used in conjunction with the Eucharist, taking the place of the Word of God or the Liturgy of the Word in the Eucharist.

From the Opening Sentence of Scripture (or Preces) through the Gospel Reading, the service of Morning Prayer would be followed. And in this case, a reading from the Gospel must be included. After the Gospel and sermon, the following pattern would be followed:

Nicene Creed (replacing Apostles' Creed)

Salutation ("The Lord be with you")

Collect of the Day (omitting the Lord's Prayer and Suffrages)

Full set of intercessions/Prayers of the People

The Peace

Offertory

The Holy Communion (Eucharistic Prayer, the Lord's Prayer, Breaking of the Bread, Communion)

Postcommunion Prayer

Blessing

Dismissal

Additional information on this option is found on page 142 of *The Book of Common Prayer.*

Appendix 2: Planning Ante-Communion (Liturgy of the Word) for Sunday Worship

On Sunday, Holy Eucharist is the principal act of worship for Episcopal Church congregations.[1] This identifies the Eucharist as the norm, but there are times when that is not possible, often as a result of not having a priest available. One option is Ante-Communion, a modified form of the first half of Holy Eucharist, the Word of God (sometimes called the Liturgy of the Word).

During the early days of the COVID-19 pandemic, when many congregations were not able to meet in person at all, this option was put into use more frequently than many congregations had seen in recent years. The other classic option for congregational worship, when Holy Eucharist is not available, is Morning Prayer, which is discussed in Appendix 1.

A congregation could choose either of these options. If a change is necessary at the last minute, such as a priest having to call in sick, Ante-Communion may be a simpler change to make, since it largely follows the same structure as Holy Eucharist. Familiarity for the congregation may also be a factor in choosing this rite. This appendix is concerned specifically with planning for Ante-Communion or the Liturgy of the Word as a primary congregational service on a Sunday or feas day.

Just as with planning a full service of Eucharist, we begin with the anchor points of the lesson and collect appointed for the day. Of course, this service follows the Eucharistic lectionary and the collect used is the one appointed for the Sunday or feast day. There is not a Proper Preface used with this service, since there is not a eucharistic prayer.

We begin with the themes from the scheduled readings for the day. The material for each Sunday in this volume regarding the themes for the day, the interpretation of the readings, and hymn selection all should be referenced when planning Ante-Communion, just as for a full Eucharist. There are a few specific differences at the beginning and end of the rite. The particular instructions for this rite are in *The Book of Common Prayer 1979* at the Additional Directions for the Eucharist:

> If there is no Communion, all that is appointed through the Prayers of the People may be said. (If it is desired to include a Confession of Sin, the service begins with the Penitential Order.) A hymn or anthem may then be sung, and the offerings of the people received. The service may then conclude with the Lord's Prayer; and with either the Grace or a blessing, or with the exchange of the Peace.
> In the absence of a priest, all that is described above, except for the blessing, may be said by a deacon, or, if there is no deacon, by a lay reader.[2]

Confession of Sin Option

Note that if Confession of Sin is intended to be used, it moves to the beginning of the service, in the form of the Penitential Order (Rite One 319, Rite Two 351). The absolution that follows the confession would be modified into a prayer for forgiveness, if clergy are not present, adapting the pronouns as described at the end of the Penitential Order.

The service then continues with the Gloria in excelsis, Kyrie, or Trisagion through the Prayers of the People, as in a conventional Eucharist.

Concluding the Rite

After the Prayers of the People, the service continues with a hymn or anthem (optional) and the offertory. The Lord's Prayer is then said and either the Grace is offered[3] or the Peace is exchanged.[4]

1 BCP, 13.

2 BCP, 406–407.

3 From 2 Corinthians 13:14, "The grace of our Lord Jesus Christ, and the love of God, and the fellowship of the Holy Spirit, be with us all evermore. *Amen.*" It may be used also at the conclusion of Evening Prayer, after the Great Litany, or at the end of the Penitential Order, if used as a standalone rite.

4 If a priest is leading the service, a third option is to pronounce the blessing.

	Ante-Communion – any proper	Rite I	Rite II	EOW1
Color	As appointed for the day			
Entrance Rite	Customary; opening acclamation "Blessed be God" or one of the first two in EOW1; Penitential Order if Confession is intended.	323; 319	355; 351	50
Song of Praise/Kyrie	Gloria in excelsis, Kyrie, Trisagion, or suggested canticle for the day	324; 47–52	356; 85–96	25–41
Collect	As appointed for the day			
Creed	Nicene Creed	326, 327	358	53
Prayers of the People	**Locally written**; options in this volum; BCP forms	329	387–393	54–55
Hymn/Offertory				
Lord's Prayer	Traditional or contemporary?	336	364	
Conclusion	The Grace (2 Cor 13:14) or the Peace (or the blessing, if a priest is present).			

Note on Communion from the Reserved Sacrament

The prayer book does provide for an option for a deacon, in the absence of a priest, to administer Holy Communion from the reserved Sacrament. This option is not automatically available, but requires the authorization of the local bishop and is entirely at their discretion. Some bishops provide for this option; some do not; others specify the circumstances where they will authorize it. Note also that this option is only relevant for deacons. There is no provision for a lay minister to distribute Holy Communion at a public worship service. Lay ministers, of course, can be licensed by the bishop to assist in distributing Communion alongside clergy at a service of Holy Eucharist as a Eucharistic Minister and can also be licensed to deliver Communion to those who are sick or homebound as a Eucharistic Visitor. Those licenses do not extend to administering Communion at a public service, however, in the absence of a priest or deacon.

See the instructions on page 408 of the BCP for a deacon to administer Communion, if authorized to do so.

Index of Seasonal Rites

Index of Major and Lesser Feast Days